MILITARISM IN A GLOBAL AGE

A volume in the series

The United States in the World

Edited by Mark Philip Bradley, David C. Engerman, and Paul A. Kramer

A list of titles in this series is available at www.cornellpress.cornell.edu.

MILITARISM IN A GLOBAL AGE

Naval Ambitions in Germany and the United States before World War I

Dirk Bönker

Cornell University Press
Ithaca and London

Copyright © 2012 by Cornell University

All rights reserved. Except for brief quotations in a review, this book, or parts thereof, must not be reproduced in any form without permission in writing from the publisher. For information, address Cornell University Press, Sage House, 512 East State Street, Ithaca, New York 14850.

First published 2012 by Cornell University Press
Printed in the United States of America

Library of Congress Cataloging-in-Publication Data
Bönker, Dirk.
  Militarism in a global age : naval ambitions in Germany and the United States before World War I / Dirk Bönker.
    p. cm. — (The United States in the world)
  Includes bibliographical references and index.
  ISBN 978-0-8014-5040-2 (cloth : alk. paper)
  1. Sea-power—Germany—History—19th century. 2. Sea-power—Germany—History—20th century. 3. Sea-power—United States—History—19th century. 4. Sea-power—United States—History—20th century. 5. Militarism—Germany—History—19th century. 6. Militarism—Germany—History—20th century. 7. Militarism—United States—History—19th century. 8. Militarism—United States—History—20th century. 9. Germany—History, Naval—19th century. 10. Germany—History, Naval—20th century. 11. United States—History, Naval—19th century. 12. United States—History, Naval—20th century. I. Title. II. Series: The United States in the world.
  VA513.B63 2012
  359'.03094309034—dc23   2011034818

Cornell University Press strives to use environmentally responsible suppliers and materials to the fullest extent possible in the publishing of its books. Such materials include vegetable-based, low-VOC inks and acid-free papers that are recycled, totally chlorine-free, or partly composed of nonwood fibers. For further information, visit our website at www.cornellpress.cornell.edu.

Cloth printing   10 9 8 7 6 5 4 3 2 1

Contents

Acknowledgments vii
List of Abbreviations ix

Introduction: Maritime Militarism
in Two Modern Nation-States 1

Part I. Military Force, National Industry, and Global Politics: Naval Strategies of World Power
1. World Power in a Global Age 23
2. Big-Power Confrontations over Empire 47
3. Maritime Force, Threat, and War 73

Part II. The Cult of the Battle: Approaches to Maritime Warfare
4. War of Battle Fleets 101
5. Planning for Victory 125
6. Commerce, Law, and the Limitation of War 149

Part III. The Quest for Power: The Navy, Governance, and the Nation

   7. Naval Elites and the State   175
   8. Manufacturing Consent   200
   9. A Politics of Social Imperialism   224

Part IV. A Militarism of Experts: Naval Professionalism and the Making of Navalism

   10. Of Sciences, Sea Power, and Strategy   251
   11. Between Leadership and Intraservice Conflict   275

Conclusion: Navalism and Its Trajectories   301

Notes   311
Bibliography   377
Index   413

Acknowledgments

I have accrued a great many debts during the writing of this book. Its completion offers a welcome opportunity to express my gratitude to those who have provided assistance throughout the process.

I thank first and foremost the Department of History at Johns Hopkins University, where I began my research for this book; the Center for European Studies at Harvard University, where I spent a valuable year as a James Bryant Conant post-doctoral fellow; and the History Department at Duke University, where I have been fortunate to teach in the past few years. I am also grateful to the Institute of European History in Mainz, the Fazit-Stiftung, and the German-American Academic Council for providing me with fellowships and grants. My research has been immensely facilitated by the superb assistance offered by the staff of the archives I have visited in Germany and the United States.

I deeply appreciate the many opportunities I have had to present my work at conferences and seminars. Among them were annual conferences of the American Historical Association, the German Studies Association, the Organization of American Historians, the Society for Historians of American Foreign Relations, and the Society of Military History; colloquia at Johns Hopkins, Harvard, Duke, and Boston Universities, the University of Iowa, the

Universität Bielefeld, the Freie Universität Berlin, and the Institute of European History in Mainz; various other conferences in Annapolis, Baltimore, Washington, D.C., Cambridge, Mass., Berlin, Cologne, and Hamburg; and a number of North Carolina Triangle–area venues, including the New Faces conference and speaker series of the Triangle Institute for Security Studies, the Triangle German Studies Workshop Series, and the Triangle Intellectual History Seminar. I thank the cofounders and fellow members of the Triangle Research Seminar in the History of the Military, War, and Society, which has been an important site of intellectual exchange for me.

Over the years, I have profited enormously from professional interactions and personal conversations with numerous individuals. Principal among them are Volker R. Berghahn, Frank Biess, David Blackbourn, Florian Buch, Andreas Daum, Kathleen Duval, Andreas Etges, Michael Geyer, Malachi Hacohen, Karen Hagemann, Bruce Hall, Andreas Helle, Rolf Hobson, Christine Johnson, Peter Karsten, Anna Krylova, Christian Lentz, Adriane Lentz-Smith, Gela Lingelbach, Lars Maischak, Nancy Mitchell, Sven Oliver Müller, Bradley Naranch, Jolie Olcott, Alex Roland, Peter Sigal, Philip Stelzel, Phil Stern, Cornelius Torp, Martin Vogt, Hans-Ulrich Wehler, and Thomas Welskopp. Michael Epkenhans has generously provided me with research materials.

The following historians read the entire manuscript and I am grateful for their time, support of my work, and incisive comments: Claudia Koonz, Paul Kramer, and Katharine D. Moran, as well as Geoff Eley and Michael Sherry. I am indebted to Vernon Lidtke for his guidance and intellectual engagement during the early stages of this project.

Publishing with Cornell University Press has been a rewarding experience, especially working with Michael McGandy and Susan Specter. I am grateful to the series editors for including my book in their list. I am delighted to thank the Duke History Department and its chair, Bill Reddy, for a generous subvention from the Military History Endowment, which has aided in the publication of this book.

I also offer special thanks to a select few: Paul Kramer has been invaluable, as an intellectual interlocutor, expert critic, and good friend. I like to think that his influence is written all over this book. Nikolas Matthes has given me his extraordinary friendship for so many years. My parents, Elke and Gerhard Bönker, put me in a position to further my education and to write this book, and they have provided key support along the way. And finally, Kate Moran has endured my working on this book and has always been there for me in more ways than I can enumerate.

Abbreviations

BA	Bundesarchiv
BA-MA	Bundesarchiv-Militärarchiv
CR	Committee Report
GB	General Board
GP	*Die Große Politik der Europäischen Kabinette, 1871–1914,* 40 volumes, ed. Johannes Lepsius et al. (Berlin, 1922–27)
GSAPK	Geheimes Staatsarchiv Preußischer Kulturbesitz
HSA	Hauptstaatsarchiv
JB	Joint Army and Navy Board
LC	Library of Congress
MD	Manuscript Division
N	Nachlass
NA	National Archives
NAR	*North American Review*
NWB	Naval War Board
NWC	Naval War College
NWCA	Naval War College Archives
ONI	Office of Naval Intelligence
PUSNI	*Proceedings of the U.S. Naval Institute*
Q	Question

QGA	Questions of General Application
RC	Report of Conference
RG	Record Group
RM	Reichsmarine
RMA	Reichsmarineamt
RRC	Report of Reconciling Committee
SF	Subject File
SN	Secretary of the Navy
WP	War Portfolio

Introduction

Maritime Militarism in Two Modern Nation-States

"Navalism, or naval militarism, is the twin brother of militarism on land and bears its repulsive and virulent traits. It is at present, to a still higher degree than the militarism on land, not only the consequence but also the cause of international dangers of a world war." Thus wrote the German socialist Karl Liebknecht in his famous indictment of militarism, *Militarismus und Antimilitarismus,* first published in 1907.[1] In *The Three Men behind the Gun,* a pamphlet published seven years later, the Reverend Charles E. Jefferson, a prominent U.S. pacifist, castigated the "militaristic movement" that had spread across the Western world and had led to the "phenomenal expansion of the military and naval establishments" in the past thirty years. "Militarism," Jefferson wrote, "blights like a pestilent wind the higher life of nations and eats like gangrene into the vitals of civilization." Among its symptoms were the elevation of the battleship to a "symbol of national glory" and the worship of "the fetish of Sea Power."[2]

As these two dissident voices illustrate, images of a new naval "militarism"— as defined by big navies, high levels of naval armaments, and an escalating maritime arms race—became a central part of the discourse on militarization before the outbreak of World War I in 1914. Sometimes involving the use of a newly coined term, "navalism" in English or *"Marinismus"* in German, this discourse drew upon a broad range of political preoccupations and languages; for better or worse, it has conditioned the understanding of "militarism," and particularly its German variant, until the present day.³ The incorporation of "naval militarism" into the analysis and critique of "militarism," a term that had first entered European political vocabularies in the 1860s and 1870s, was hardly surprising: this inclusion was a creative response to the rise of what diplomatic historian William L. Langer called the "new navalism" in his classic exploration of the global politics of imperialism, first published in 1930.⁴

By the turn of the twentieth century, this new militarist formation had become a multifaceted regime of power and knowledge. Its most visible manifestations were powerful battle fleets, and the global naval arms race that emerged as a major international phenomenon with many competitors and shifting centers of gravity. The dramatic international growth of navies, which contrasted sharply with the slow pace of naval armament increases in previous decades, created new, highly dynamic global equations of maritime force. The worldwide diffusion of sea power, which reached its prewar peak in 1914, marked the end of the naval mastery that the British Royal Navy had enjoyed for most of the nineteenth century.⁵

The magnitude of the arms buildup was most visible in sheer numbers, for, as historian Michael Geyer writes, the "hyper-reality of arms races...can only be appreciated metaphorically in the 'purest' of all representations."⁶ In 1880 the aggregate warship tonnage of the six major powers was 1,393,000 tons; ten years later it was 1,649,000 tons. The numbers for 1900, 1910, and 1914 were, respectively, 2,752,000 tons, 5,584,000 tons, and 7,283,000 tons. In short, the tonnage more than quadrupled in the twenty-five years before the outbreak of the Great War.⁷ Not coincidentally, the same period saw the flourishing of comparative statistics of naval strength, with its tabular expressions of maritime force and the "progress" of the world's navies, eagerly compiled by navy departments and surrounded by exhortations directed at policymaking communities to not fall behind in the maritime arms competition.

The massive naval arms buildups marked an important juncture in the militarization of the globe in the "long" twentieth century that emerged out of the transformation of states, empires, and warfare between the 1840s and 1870s.⁸ The national pursuit of sea power lent shape to a new global geopolitics of war and empire. The entire planet had become a single field of imperial action and site of geopolitical competition, underwritten by global networks of capital, commerce, communications, and transport.

Maritime force and its geopolitical use moved to center stage in a new diplomacy of global empire. This diplomacy filled established European notions of a bellicose *Realpolitik* with new military and imperial meanings while moving within an interlocking, multipolar global system of states and empires organized around various centers of gravity, distinct configurations of regional power, and ever-shifting lines of interimperial conflicts, alignments, and collaborations.[9]

At the same time, naval arms buildups redirected the domestic militarization of the participating countries. Contributing to the increasing institutional domination of society and the fabrication of the "iron cage" of bureaucratic machines (public and private), the rise of big navies enlarged existing military establishments and tightened the military grip on societal resources.[10] The shift toward material-intensive naval armaments drew the corporate sphere of industrial production into the orbit of militarization; it created a new political economy of warfare built around a coalescing institutional nexus between private industry and the military.[11]

Naval arms buildups cast their long shadow on the domestic politics of all countries, as political centers promoted policies of naval expansion and naval officers jockeyed for power and influence in systems of governance. Galvanizing national publics and interest groups, the pursuit of maritime force became a focal point of political mobilization, public debate, and nationalist identity politics.[12] Naval expansion also gave rise to broader popular cults and folkloric appropriations of the navy. Mediated by fast-developing mass media, the pursuit of maritime force entered the world of popular entertainment and consumption in the shape of spectacle and theater. Sea power became a focal point of mass longings and personal desires.[13]

Navalism, Germany, and the United States

This book is a study of navalism in two countries that were prime movers in the process of global maritime militarization before the First World War: Imperial Germany and the United States. During the nationalizing wars of the 1860s, Prussia/Germany and the United States had redefined the parameters of great-power status and warfare by charting new forms of wartime mobilizations of people, ideologies, and industries within the framework of an integral nation state.[14] Some thirty years later, the two powers became key participants in the naval arms race, even if they did not initiate or provide the sole impetus for the process of maritime arming (as is often claimed for the German naval buildup by historians who are mesmerized by the Anglo-German naval arms race and exceptionalize German navalism[15]). Remaking themselves as premier naval powers through rapid maritime buildups, the United States and Germany amassed the world's second and third most formidable navies in the fifteen years before the outbreak of World War I, behind only Great Britain, which remained the strongest naval power throughout the entire period (and beyond).[16]

I focus on the pursuit of maritime force by two dynamic industrial nation-states that moved along strikingly similar, and parallel, national trajectories in the new global age. As historians Charles Bright and Michael Geyer have convincingly argued, these trajectories involved the territorializing projects of two nation-states, one recently made and one reforged, which broke away from older configurations of empire and power in the Americas and the Eurasian rim and sought to avoid integration in a British-dominated world order. These intensely nationalistic projects aimed first at domestic development and industrial transformation within a protected national space and then at the outward projection of productive power and military force. The goal became national mobilization and international competition in the face of coalescing global networks of capital, markets, knowledge, force, and empire, which, by the late nineteenth century, had turned the exterior space of the "world" into the interior space of the "globe."[17]

Proceeding along these paths, which ultimately collided in the two world wars, Germany and the United States emerged, by 1900, as the two rapidly developing, forward-looking, and exemplary modern nation-states of the North Atlantic world. Elites and national intelligentsias in both nations staked claims to dominance in the twentieth century: economically, professionally, culturally, politically, and militarily. Looming large in each other's collective imagination as both rivals and models, the United States and Germany were engaged, by the 1890s, in what historians Christof Mauch and Kiran Klaus Patel have described as a "competition over modernity," a *Wettlauf um die Moderne*. This competition, in turn, drew on a wide array of relations of exchange, imitation, and mutual observation and involved economic, political, professional, academic, and cultural realms.[18]

Well before the First World War, Germany and the United States also directly confronted one another as adversaries in shared spaces of global competition as they pursued mutually entangled strategies of maritime arming, empire-building, and global projection. By the turn of the century, confrontations over empire in Latin America and East Asia marked the relations between the two countries, as did conflict over tariffs and the terms of bilateral trade. The crisis over Venezuela in 1902–03 was but one example of a flourishing German-American antagonism. Although its intensity varied during the entire prewar period (and has become the subject of considerable controversy among scholars), the antagonism also expressed itself in images of German-American enmity, whether in the present or future, that surrounded the accumulation of maritime force in each country. To a remarkable degree, an American-German arms race developed by the turn of the twentieth century, however overshadowed it was by the German obsession with British naval power and the Anglo-German naval arms race after 1906 in particular.[19]

A Professional Militarism

I explore the histories of German and U.S. navalism by focusing on naval elites, particularly their thought and practice. These officers fashioned this militarist formation and positioned themselves as its primary promoters in the national political arenas of both countries. Taking a front seat in national pursuits of maritime force and thus in the process of navalist militarization at large, German and American naval officers acted as key elite groups that lent meaning to, and acted on, the expansionist pursuits and global entanglements of the German and U.S. nation-states while also shaping their order and politics at home.

The two naval elites were firmly entrenched in their respective nation-states and deeply nationalist in outlook, yet they were also enmeshed in the world of transnational military politics: the web of exchanges, mutual observations, and influences among national militaries. As makers of navalism, German and U.S. naval thinkers participated in an ongoing debate regarding matters of maritime strategy and global empire among military thinkers across the Western world. The significance of such participation should not be underestimated: far from being of limited importance, or just an interesting vignette, this participation helped shape the formation of this group's ideas and agendas in important ways.

It is my central contention that a common militarism existed among German and U.S. naval elites. These elites belonged to a larger transatlantic discursive community that engaged in a common militarist project, underwritten by both German-American exchanges and competition, and taking on distinct shapes in each country as a product of particular national configurations of power and knowledge.

In Germany and the United States, naval officers created a militarism that fused the causes of the industrial nation, global power, elite rule, and the navy. Several characteristics marked this brand of militarism. Its protagonists placed the pursuit of maritime force at the center of each national quest for global power, industrial primacy, and self-determination. They stressed the military's mastery of big-power war, promising victory through battle-fleet warfare and decisive combat in temporally confined wars. They strove to make the military independent from politics and undue civilian interference. They aimed at forging a cohesive nation in the crucible of global power. Finally, they cast themselves as members of a technocratic elite that served its nation with expert knowledge of global politics and maritime warfare.

This militarist formation represented the desires and definitions of willful military elites positioning themselves as a socially exclusive, corporate body of professionals, who were committed to the cause of expertise and managerial proficiency in an industrial world while addressing themselves to the destiny of their fast-developing nations with global aspirations. Socially interwoven with the professional, commercial, and manufacturing elites of their countries, naval officers in Germany and the United States championed both elite rule and technocratic politics while embracing the professional organization of military violence. Presenting themselves as the expert custodians of the geopolitical interests of their nations and taking a broad outlook on the challenges of international competition and national mobilization that their countries faced, they partook in the discursive languages, imaginings, and knowledge of their national intelligentsia, of which they were a part.[20]

The navalism of the two elites claimed a perfect harmony between institutional expertise, national industry, and maritime superiority in a world of globalized politics and economy. These linkages go a long way toward explaining the broad political appeal of navalism in both Germany and the United States at the beginning of the twentieth century. These same linkages also help explain navalism's remarkable durability.[21] Feeding on an unwavering commitment by the two navies, this militarist formation managed to survive the confrontation with new realities during World War I and continually remade itself in the face of dramatic changes in maritime warfare, global affairs, and national politics. Navalism belonged to political and military modernities that have shaped the course of the past century.

Narratives of Militarism

In examining elite naval militarism in Germany and the United States, I reclaim the sense of commonality and mutual entanglement that had united many contemporaneous European and U.S. observers of the advance of militarism before 1914.[22] This common awareness of militarization was ultimately marginalized by the ideological polarities that first coalesced during World War I and were subsequently reinforced by the Second World War. The contrast between "authoritarian German militarism" and Western democracy became a central trope in dominant constructions of national difference in Europe and North America during the period of the world wars.[23] This binary imagery has suffused national historical narratives as well, including the classic accounts of German and U.S. histories, which are constructed around the notions of American exceptionalism and the German *Sonderweg,* or special path.[24] It has also cut off from the present the militarist past of Western societies before 1914 by associating militarism with the German military state and its peculiar preindustrial heritage, which is then believed to have come to an end after 1945.[25]

This book contributes to the writing of new histories of militarism and militarization in Germany and the United States beyond notions of national uniqueness. It intervenes in scholarly debates pertaining to both German and U.S. history and challenges its readers to rethink commonly accepted narratives that command the aura of common sense in each national historiography.

Thus, I move beyond classic accounts of German militarism, which have cast their long shadow on academic narratives of German history and Western militarization before World War I. Casting navalism as a professional militarism of experts and viewing it as one militarist formation among others, both elite and popular, my analysis refrains from exceptionalizing the German Imperial militarist experience, linking it to the Second Empire's compromised political modernity, and analyzing it as part of the German *Sonderweg,* spanning the nineteenth and twentieth centuries. Here, then, is one response to oft-heard calls to explore German militarism in tandem with militarist formations elsewhere, calls that have surrounded the debates over German militarism yet have yielded limited results, despite several impressive studies.[26]

The notion of a distinct authoritarian Prusso-German militarism set against political modernity and civil society has been, and still is, central to the "common sense of German historiography," as Geoff Eley, a leading scholar of modern Germany, once observed.[27] To be sure, scholarship has called into question the validity of this narrative. In his groundbreaking work on the Prusso-German military, Michael Geyer has insisted on the centrality of the professional organization of military violence and the industrialization of warfare for the understanding of military politics.[28] Historians such as Jakob Vogel, Frank Becker, or Jan Rüger have explored the complex intersections of bourgeois society, nationalist politics, popular culture, and militarism in Imperial Germany in new ways while stressing the pervasiveness of social and cultural militarization across Europe.[29] Historians of the European land arms race before 1914 have highlighted the multiple centers of military geopolitics and outlined a sequential narrative of a broader European politics of militarization and drift toward war, of which German pursuits were an integral but not exceptional, let alone all-propelling, part.[30]

Still, the idea of German militarism has proven remarkably resilient among historians of Imperial Germany. "Especially in regards to the German Empire," two historians have recently noted with barely concealed frustration, this narrative has been, "until today, mostly resistant to any convincing empirical attempts to demonstrate lines of differentiation," either in relation to social characteristics or national peculiarities.[31] Few scholars of Imperial Germany would disagree with the late historian Thomas Nipperdey, otherwise a sharp critic of the notion of a German *Sonderweg*, when he wrote that the "special position of the military" was a "dominant feature, politically and socially" in the Second German Empire and marked the limits of the empire's (bourgeois) modernity, thus setting it apart from other countries.[32] An emphasis on a special German militarism within the state, politics, and society has become one of the remaining explicit bastions of the old *Sonderweg* argument, which had stressed the failure of liberalism, the limits of civil society, and the dominance of preindustrial elites in Imperial Germany.[33]

Notions of a peculiar German militarism also continue to captivate historians of Imperial Germany even when scholars expressly seek to move beyond, or position themselves outside, the classical *Sonderweg* narrative. Most important, new work on the German army and its way of war has breathed new life into exceptionalist understandings of Prusso-German militarism.[34] The Imperial German military's extraconstitutional position and its (alleged) predilection for excessive violence have come to play an important role in current arguments about the deep continuities of German histories, culminating in the Nazi pursuit of war, mass murder, and racial empire.[35]

The notion of a distinctive Prusso-German militarism, then, has been firmly enshrined in the remarkably rich literature on Wilhelmine navalism and Volker R. Berghahn's foundational study of German naval policy in the era of Alfred von Tirpitz, the secretary of the navy from 1897 to 1916.[36] Berghahn has made Imperial German naval policy a defining element in the critical narratives of the Second German Empire and the *Sonderweg* of the 1960s and 1970s. Berghahn's work has served as the ground for all subsequent scholarship on the Wilhelmine navy and its navalism.[37]

Berghahn presented Imperial Germany and its navalism as the "special case" among the major imperial powers.[38] German naval expansion had aimed at revolutionizing the entire international system and instituting a Pax Germanica in lieu of the Pax Britannica; and it had initiated the sequence of events that eventually led to Germany's war-inducing policy of brinkmanship in 1914. At the same time, Berghahn rooted the navy's geopolitical expansionism in the domestic pathologies of Imperial Germany. In doing so, he followed the lead taken by radical historian Eckart Kehr's pathbreaking work on Wilhelmine battle-fleet building, first published during the Weimar Republic. Shaping part of his interpretation on Hans-Ulrich Wehler's work on social imperialism, Berghahn maintained that the pursuit of maritime force had been driven by domestic considerations and traditional Prussian elites' desires for "stabilization of the Prusso-German political system." With the help of the navy, Wilhelm II and his advisers had "wanted to overthrow the *status quo* internationally in order to preserve it at home."[39]

By casting the navy's policy makers as mere agents of a larger politics that originated from outside the military realm itself, Berghahn displaced the professional military and its technological reasoning from an historical understanding of Imperial Germany's naval militarism. This displacement was emblematic of the critical analysis of the Prusso-German military offered by *Sonderweg* scholars who tended to link this military to societal relations of domination and subordination in simple instrumental terms.[40] It has also informed all those studies of the Wilhelmine officer corps that have supplemented Berghahn's work by portraying the navy, in analogy to the army, as a predominantly preindustrial and monarchical institution in its political orientation, social mentality, and militarist disposition.[41]

I offer a new account of the Wilhelmine navy's militarism beyond Berghahn's *Sonderweg* interpretation. In so doing, I do not expand on the unproductive confrontation that has dominated the debate over Berghahn's work. His insistence on the overriding importance of social imperialism and antiparliamentarism for understanding Tirpitz's naval policy sparked a heated and at times acrimonious debate. Conservative historians, including specialists in German diplomatic history, advanced a competing interpretation of Wilhelmine imperial and naval policy that has stressed the logic of power politics and left little room for any domestic political origins.[42] Such an interpretation comes perilously close to an "apologia" for German (naval) militarism, as historian Charles Maier has observed.[43] It offers an explanation for Imperial Germany's expansionism, which resonates only too well with the justification of official German policy provided by its protagonists before 1918. Fittingly, most historians who adhere to this view are also willing to view the political authoritarianism and militarism of Imperial Germany as a natural result of the alleged "security dilemma" of the empire in the middle of Europe.

By contrast, the more general debate over the validity of the critical narratives of the Second German Empire and the *Sonderweg* and the vast amount of research they sparked have focused on other issues, such as the middle classes, radical nationalism, and popular politics. These debates have not produced a full-length reconsideration of the politics of the naval buildup and the outlook of the Wilhelmine navy.[44] By the same token, the fast-developing scholarship invested in addressing the "dark side" of Wilhelmine Germany's full-throttled modernity has not provided an entry point to a reconsideration of the navy's professional militarism either.[45]

Only relatively recently, historian Rolf Hobson has engaged in a long overdue effort to chart new directions beyond Berghahn's *Sonderweg* interpretations. Hobson has placed the making of German navalism within the context of mutual processes of convergence and differentiation among national schools of naval thought. Relating the navy's pursuit of sea power to a desire for institutional aggrandizement, and not to any social imperialist design, he suggested that Tirpitz had conceived the navy as a tool of a strictly defensive strategy of maritime deterrence that had posed no radical threat to British global power. If there had been anything "special" about German navalism, it had been the fact that Germany's system of governance had allowed Tirpitz to stay in office for long enough to mastermind continuous naval expansion according to a long-term program.[46]

This book builds on Hobson's intervention, which has remained limited by its primary focus on naval strategy. His general interpretation is also marred by his portrayal of German navalism (and its U.S. counterpart) as an irrational imperial ideology of sea power, as opposed to a truly professional strategy of national security. Such an interpretive strategy draws on classic definitions of imperialism and militarism by Joseph Schumpeter and Alfred Vagts. It is thus caught up in a set of artificial, and highly ideological, distinctions offered by contemporaneous liberal and democratic critics of the German military state and fits well with readings of Imperial German militarism in the *Sonderweg* mold.[47]

Rethinking U.S. Militarization

While offering a new interpretation of Wilhelmine navalism, my argument brings into sharp focus the advance of militarism in the United States during the Gilded Age and Progressive Era. To expand on the sense of commonality and mutual entanglement among contemporary observers of arms buildups and military geopolitics before World War I is to emphasize the active involvement of the United States in processes of militarization well before its emergence as a superpower at mid twentieth century. Contributing to the writing of new narratives of militarism and militarization in modern America, I move navalism to center stage as both a defining part of the convoluted history of militarized structures in the United States and as an important aspect of the development of American modernity. This, then, is an analysis that casts the military as what historian Richard John has called a key "agent of change" and thus engages with recent calls to examine the significance of the military for narratives of nineteenth- and early twentieth-century American histories.[48]

By now, the militarization of the United States has become the focus of a remarkably rich and ever-expanding scholarship.[49] Although scholars such as Michael Sherry have succeeded in positioning militarization as a pivotal theme of American modernity, their work has been shaped by the problematic assumption that the foundational moment of U.S. militarization came in the 1930s and 1940s and that civilian elites, and not the military itself, were militarization's progenitors and its primary protagonists on the national political level. Before midcentury, the argument goes, the militarization of the United States remained both limited and temporary, and linked primarily to episodic expressions of militant nationalism and particular moments of war mobilization. According to this view, World War I was a major albeit fleeting moment in the U.S. relationship to war and militarization that saw the beginnings of the national security state, the forging of a new relationship among government, business, and organized science, and the contested recalibration of civil society and identity politics in the crucible of the pursuit of "preparedness" and war.⁵⁰

Central to the common sense among historians of Gilded Age and Progressive Era America is the notion that in the United States nothing approximating European-style militarization occurred. The United States had lacked a large standing military establishment and a strong military as an autonomous center of power beyond civilian control. And its civil society had not been permeated by military values and martial notions of national militancy, and that despite the memorial politics surrounding the Civil War, or the cultures of patriotism and martial manhood of the 1890s and beyond (which in themselves have attracted considerable scholarly scrutiny).⁵¹ Few historians would disagree with historian Peter Karsten's claim that although the United States experienced some "increase in 'militarization'" between the Civil War and World War I, as expressed in the expansion of the armed forces and the flourishing of a "spirit of militarism" in public realms, it nonetheless managed to "avoid the militarization that gripped Europe for decades before 1914" and remained a dominantly nonmilitaristic country.⁵²

In line with such thinking most scholars describe the dramatic remaking of the U.S. Army and the U.S. Navy in the Progressive Era in ways that diminish its significance. This remaking is cast as an innocuous process of mere "modernization" and "professionalization" of armed forces that had experienced a period of demobilization and relative decline after the Civil War, a period an older nationalist historiography had referred to as the "dark ages" of American military history.⁵³ When relating the transformation of the American military, and especially the emergence of the U.S. Navy as a first-rate navy, to the rise of the United States as a world power, scholars usually insist on the limitation of American military power at the beginning of the twentieth century: they emphasize the disjuncture between the nation's modest military capabilities and its superior productive powers and stress the country's overall distance from the interlocking structures of European military geopolitics.

The emphasis on the limits, if not the absence, of militarization in the United States during the Gilded Age and the Progressive Era has also long been enshrined in the literature on American state formation and corporate transformation.⁵⁴ Trumpeting the peculiarities of American history, this body of literature has stressed the political subordination and institutional weakness of the armed forces and the absence of a strong bureaucratic state. It has also made an argument about the entirely civilian foundation of America's organizational modernity, which had originated from within big business and civil society, not the state or the military. This view has only recently been subjected to criticism. In his study of U.S. military procurement during the Civil War, Mark Wilson, for example, has foregrounded the "bureaucratic autonomy" of the professional military beyond immediate civilian governmental control, and he suggests that the military served as an important "incubator of bureaucratic administration in both government and business" after the Civil War.[55]

Although historians have offered a restrictive reading of the militarization of the United States in the Gilded Age and the Progressive Era, the making of modern American navalism between the 1880s and 1910s has nonetheless attracted considerable scholarly attention.[56] Emphasizing the pivotal role of civilian elite figures, interests, and politics in the process of navalist militarization, this literature has also brought into focus the distinct agency of naval elites as key makers and promoters of navalism who were bent on finding civilian allies and institutionalizing their ideas.[57]

In this book I advance a comprehensive interpretation of the professional militarism of the American naval elite that engages with several strands of existing scholarship on the U.S. Navy. To emphasize the ways in which these elites fused together the causes of the navy, elite rule, the industrial nation, and global power is to acknowledge the importance of historian Peter Karsten's influential interpretation, published in the early 1970s, of the emergence of American navalism in his magisterial collective biography of the U.S. naval officer corps between the 1840s and 1920s.[58] With broad strokes, Karsten analyzed the corps as a socially exclusive and self-centered "naval aristocracy" whose members owed their primary allegiance to their own military service and acted as the "elite servants of the ruling upper class."[59] A prominent protagonist of the emerging "new military history," Karsten offered a materialist account of the rise of the "new" American navalism at the close of the nineteenth century. He suggested that it had emerged as the navy's new collective ideology to further the institutional cause of the navy and the collective interests of its officer members. Offering "military policies attractive to the statesmen planning America's international role in the 20th century," naval professionals had created a "body of propaganda and rationalizations" to serve as an "ideological weapon in the appropriations battles of the fin de siècle."[60]

Karsten's interpretation linked up to the work of historians such as William A. Williams and Walter LaFeber, who had emphasized the central importance of the search for markets and social-imperialist calculations to explain the behavior of U.S. policy makers and their conduct of diplomacy in the nineteenth and twentieth centuries.[61] Since the 1960s, their scholarship has been central to the debate over the driving forces behind the U.S. pursuit of empire and rise to world power.[62] This debate, in turn, cast a long shadow on interpretations of fleet expansion, maritime strategy, and naval diplomacy offered by those historians who have studied American naval policy and strategy in the context of the rise of American overseas imperialism in the late nineteenth century and U.S. participation in imperial rivalries after 1898.[63] By contrast, the new wave of culturalist and gender interpretations of American empire and the U.S. engagement with the world has not yet entailed a major reconsideration of the politics of the U.S. Navy and its navalism.[64]

Whereas, in the context of scholarship on the geopolitical and military roles of the navy, the service and its navalism become folded into general accounts of U.S. empire and diplomacy, many historians of the U.S. Navy have stressed the distinct agency of the navy by charting directions that differ from Karsten's materialist analysis of the "naval aristocracy." Scholars such as Ronald Spector and James Abrahamson have made strides toward analyzing the U.S. naval officer corps of the late Gilded Age and the Progressive Era as a developing profession and viewing its politics from that particular angle.[65]

Although this body of work has used highly normative notions of professionalism and naturalized the meanings of its manifestations in the navy, its general emphasis provides an important point of reference for my own interpretation. Significantly, the same emphasis also has already lent itself to a limited recognition of the transnational dynamic of professional military thought and practice. The international reception of Mahan's work has been a staple among historians, even if they too often ask whether thinkers elsewhere offered the "right" readings of the "true" insights.[66] By the same token, historians of the U.S. Navy have made strides toward analyzing the history of naval intelligence and the system of military observation geared toward learning from other militaries.[67] All in all, the literature is sprinkled with references to the importance of European, and specifically German, examples for the U.S. Navy's approaches to its professional practices and institution-building, even as it elides the complexities of "perception, misperception, translation, transformation, co-optation, preemption, and contestation" that shaped the exchange and circulation of ideas and practice, as identified by Daniel Rodgers, a preeminent historian of cultural transfer in the Progressive Era.[68]

A Formational Analysis

In this book, I explore the central features of the militarism fashioned by German and U.S. naval elites before World War I. The book casts navalism as a distinct formation that cohered around a particular set of ideas and practices and shaped the military culture of the two navies; and it focuses on officers, the institutions through which they operated inside the realm of legally constituted politics, and their knowledge production within the context of official policy proposals, military planning, and public writings.[69] This, then, is not a sequential analysis of naval policymaking or a narrative of the evolving arms race and the coming of World War I. Neither is it a study of the actual appropriation of allocated resources and men by military institutions and their transformation into military means and soldiers, nor, for that matter, an examination of the civilian imaginings and politics that sustained or contested navalist militarization in both countries.

This book combines cross-national comparative history with the thematic concerns of transnational history. I make the case for the fundamental commonality of the two navies' navalism in the United States and Germany. But I also identify navalism's distinct shapes and emphases in each country as a product of national configurations of power and knowledge, and I pay attention to the mutual influences and the uneven movement and transfer of ideas and practices across the Atlantic that underwrote navalism's making. My analysis thus moves back and forth between Germany and the United States, and, when appropriate, covers the space in between; and it identifies national patterns as part of a broader transnational movement of politics and ideas. Cross-national comparative analysis and transnational perspectives are not necessarily opposites; in fact, it is their combination that promises to yield the most rewarding results, as long as this approach itself is grounded in history.[70]

My exploration of the making of navalism in two countries navigates two distinctive naval landscapes of key players and top institutions. In Germany, a single officer, Alfred von Tirpitz, emerged as an overarching figure to provide pivotal leadership over a long period of time. More than any other officer, Tirpitz was responsible for the formation of navalism as a set of ideas and practices during the 1890s when he established himself as the navy's foremost authority and bearer of its future. It was Tirpitz who authored, in 1894, the foundational text for the navy's entire navalist enterprise, known as *Service Memorandum IX*. As secretary of the navy from 1897 to 1916, he became the navy's foremost policy maker, wielding unparalleled power within the service and directing the entire pursuit of maritime force in a determined manner.[71]

The Imperial Naval Office, which was in official charge of the administration of the navy and its representation in the legislative process, emerged as a dominant center within an institutionally fragmented navy. Although small in size, the Naval Cabinet was another important locus of power. It oversaw personnel policy, served as a secretariat for the emperor, and regulated his dealings with his officers. Its two successive chiefs, Admiral Gustav von Senden-Bibrach and Admiral Georg Alexander von Müller, acted as power brokers within the service, controlling access to the Kaiser and mediating relations among high-ranking officers. Throughout the 1890s, the Naval High Command rivaled in importance the Imperial Naval Office as the agency in charge of naval operations and matters of strategy and tactics. After its dissolution in 1899, the Admiralty Staff became the new operational planning agency and its heads took on the role of the chief strategic advisers of the emperor. The leadership of the fleet emerged as a key authority and center of professional expertise as soon as the battle fleet reached a certain size and attained a separate command position.

In the United States, the General Board provided the navy with an organizing center of power and knowledge. Founded in 1900 to help prepare the navy for war, the Board established itself as a dominant voice in matters of strategy, policy, and building programs. Yet its authority remained limited. It did not possess any command authority over the fleet and its units, whose leading officers wielded considerable influence. It also lacked any directing power over the so-called bureaus, the primary organizational units of the Navy Department, which mostly concerned themselves with matters of administration, construction, and personnel. Its chiefs acted as independent power brokers who interacted directly with the secretary of the navy (and Congress, for that matter). The General Board worked in tandem with the Office of Naval Intelligence and the Naval War College, which had been created in the 1880s. Among the two, the College occupied a position of special prominence. It served as a hothouse for the development of navalist expertise, and it acted as a planning agency involved in the making of war plans and considerations of matters of strategy, policy, and technology.

It was within the institutional framework that individual officers provided important leadership. Serving as the navy's senior officer from 1898 to 1916, Admiral George Dewey enjoyed a degree of prominence, authority, and longevity in high office not matched by any other officer. Holding the lifetime rank of Admiral of the Navy, Dewey presided over the General Board. But he lacked the powers and talents of a Tirpitz. Beginning in 1890, Alfred Thayer Mahan exerted his enormous influence in his capacity as the navy's key ideologue. But his immediate involvement in decision making remained limited. Other officers such as Rear-Admirals Henry C. Taylor and Bradley A. Fiske acted as the navy's most important strategists, policymakers, and institution builders as they occupied key positions at particular moments in time.[72]

Structure of the Book

The arguments in this book fall into four thematic parts. Parts 1, 2 and 3 focus, in sequential order, on navalist approaches to global power, maritime warfare, and national politics. Part 4 probes the underlying premises and sinews of naval professionalism and the intraservice politics that molded the making of navalism in each country. The book as a whole brings together various larger narratives: of empire and military geopolitics, of warfare and military imaginaries, of state formation and national governance, and of expert knowledge and professional pursuits. Taking center stage in different parts of the book, each of them has its own concerns and analytics.

Part 1 is devoted to an investigation of German and U.S. navalist strategies of world power and their matrix of global empire, national industry, and maritime force, as they first came into clear focus by the beginning of the twentieth century and then evolved until the mid-1910s. These strategies, I argue, aimed at the remaking of the U.S. and German nation-states as autonomous nation-centered world powers in control of their own destinies, and they fused the same set of assumptions about geopolitics, economics, and sea power with particular notions of national destiny, empire, and the world (chapter 1). Claiming to live in a dangerous world, officers prepared for direct conflict between big powers over empire whose policies and interests they cast in similar ways (chapter 2). Their pursuit of superiority at sea aimed at the creation of a first-rate navy second only to the British, if second at all, while establishing a close nexus between assessments of comparative military strength and attitudes toward the desirability of great-power war in the present or near future (chapter 3).

Part 2 offers an analysis of the naval elites' military-operational imagination, the second axis of analysis. German and U.S. strategists, I demonstrate, conceived of the use of military force in common ways, marked first and foremost by shared investments in the concept of battle fleet warfare as a paradigm of warfare. Modeled on the example of terrestrial military-professional warfare, this paradigm congealed in the 1890s and then laid the groundwork for both subsequent doctrinal rigidity and the pursuit of naval power as regional infrastructural power (chapter 4). The obsessive quest for military victory, the cult of the decisive battle, and visions of large-scale battle came to define operational planning that focused on big-power wars in regional maritime settings, such as the North Sea, the North Atlantic, the Caribbean, and the Pacific (chapter 5). Naval strategists stressed the importance of the economic dimension of naval warfare, as they prepared their navies for the contest of battle fleets, but they adhered to a regime of limitation when they conceptualized naval warfare as a war of economic pressure targeting the opponent's civilian trade (chapter 6).

Part 3 focuses on matters of state formation and national governance, the third axis of analysis. The two naval elites strove to position themselves as the organizing center of a warfare state and to minimize their subjection to civilian control in maritime matters, underwritten in the United States by a full-fledged adulation of the German military state (chapter 7). With considerable success, they also engaged in multifarious activities to transform the contested terrain of naval policymaking to their own advantage. These ranged from lobbying and pressure-group politics to public relations work and propaganda, and traversed the realms of civilian politics, civil society, and popular culture (chapter 8). As an intensely nationalist proposition, the navalist project also was an exercise in social imperialism, relating naval expansion to matters of governance and reform and aiming at the forging of a cohesive nation in the crucible of global power (chapter 9).

Part 4 elucidates the professional politics of the two naval elites that underwrote the making of navalism as a distinct set of ideas, agendas, and practices concerning global politics, maritime warfare, and nation-state formation, the fourth axis of analysis. Positioning themselves as servants of their nation-states, naval officers claimed to have acquired special knowledge in maritime and global affairs, based on their sciences of sea power and military strategy and a large, active embrace of the military professionalism and "strategic science" that had become identified with the Prusso-German army (chapter 10). In each country, full cohesion eluded the two navies: the pursuit of their navalist project was riddled, in varying ways, by conflict over turf and policy priorities (chapter 11).

I emphasize the central role played by naval elites and their distinctive politics in the militarization of Germany and the United States.

Participating in current efforts to "globalize" and "internationalize" modern German and U.S. histories, I demonstrate how transatlantic developments in military thinking opened the door for the pursuit of world power and maritime force in a new global age. The rise of navalism in the two most dynamic nation-states of the North Atlantic world at the beginning of the twentieth century was part of a common history of professional militarism, a history that eludes narratives of national exceptionalism and isolation.[73]

Part I

MILITARY FORCE, NATIONAL INDUSTRY, AND GLOBAL POLITICS

Naval Strategies of World Power

Chapter 1

World Power in a Global Age

At the beginning of the twentieth century, American and German naval elites used the language of "world power" to describe their own nations' changing places in the world. "Either by reason of our material wealth, force of circumstances, or manifest destiny, we have become a world power," declared Rear-Admiral George Melville to an American public in 1903.[1] On the other side of the Atlantic, Alfred von Tirpitz, the German secretary of the navy, told the emperor (*Kaiser* in German) in 1899 that Germany was one of only "four world powers" that would shape the globe's destiny in the next century.[2]

The notion of "world power" figured prominently in the two naval elites' approach to global power, foreign policy, and empire, as it congealed into a distinct set of ideas and practices around the turn of the twentieth century. Devising their brand of militarism, naval officers offered broad views of the direction of geopolitics, the pursuits of big powers, and the trajectories of their own countries. Based on a distinctive understanding of global politics, navalists charted coherent strategies of world power that anchored their pursuit of maritime force. These strategies addressed themselves to the (perceived) expansionist needs and global dependencies of the United States and Germany as fast-developing industrial nations in a world dominated by intense interimperial conflict and ferocious economic competition involving big powers. Fusing the causes of the navy and global power, they aimed to make their countries into cohesive world powers in control of their own destinies.

National strategies of world power took on particular emphases. German and U.S. maritime militarists shared a set of assumptions about the nature of international politics, economics, and sea power. In each country navalists fused these shared ideas to particular concepts of national destiny, empire, and the world, which permeated the expansionist discourses among the national intelligentsia in each country. German navy leaders such as Tirpitz imagined their country as an activist world power pursuing interests and shifting alliances across the globe and as a global empire in command of vast colonial holdings and global spheres of influence. Setting themselves up against alleged British aspirations, naval officers viewed German power as part of a continuing plurality of world powers and global peoples. Theirs was a proposition for Germany as one global imperial player among several, not a proposition for a German-led world order. Expanding on previous U.S. imperial imaginings, American officers emphasized the regional limitations of contemporary U.S. global-geopolitical interests while maintaining distance from European-style colonial-empire-building and alliance politics. Projecting ongoing competition among big powers into the future, U.S. naval leaders advanced universalistic notions of world domination that contrasted sharply with the particularistic outlook of limited German global aspirations. Visions of eventual U.S. global supremacy shaped their views of American global power in the (distant) future.

Economic Geopolitics

German and U.S. naval elites offered a clear rationale for world power, which reverberated with the larger geopolitical-expansionist thought shared by members of the political classes and the intelligentsias of the major powers in the age of global empire before 1914.[3] The rationale was bounded by the tenets of economic geopolitics. According to this cluster of ideas, commercial strife between imperial powers and peoples had become the most pressing issue of present and future global politics. The rivalries between these powers were economic in origin: mutually exclusive national policies of imperial assertion responded to domestic economic pressures and promoted the cause of national industry. Accordingly, war appeared as the continuation of commercial rivalry by other means, as "the ultimate form of economic competition," to use a phrase that enjoyed great popularity among members of the American naval elite.[4]

References to the primacy of economic conflict and pressures in international politics abounded in the two navies' policy papers. "World history now stands under the sign of economic struggle. It rages across the whole globe," a prominent German officer, the future Admiral Georg Alexander Müller, argued in 1896.[5] In 1902, Captain French E. Chadwick, then president of the U.S. Naval War College, expressed the conventional wisdom when he referred to the "contest for commercial supremacy" that would shape current and future global events and identified it as "the chief, if not almost the only cause [of war] in the future."[6]

The main powers would employ military force and diplomatic power in global settings to secure economic advantage, mostly by creating and expanding formal and informal spheres of influence and, if necessary, safeguarding them from unrestrained international industrial and trade competition. The "increasing imperialist strife for commercial purposes" among occidental powers, which Alfred Thayer Mahan invoked in 1897, would trigger a carving up of the globe as these powers strove for territory, not just for access to markets.[7] From the perspective of naval strategists, the "scramble for Africa" in the 1880s and 1890s had set the tone for things to come. The struggle among imperial powers and peoples was bound to marginalize the smaller powers and their economies, and it would threaten the integrity and very existence of old empires (for example, the Portuguese, Spanish, or Chinese).

By necessity, the accumulation of military force and its use (actual or threatened) moved to center stage. World power required massive armaments, argued members of the two naval elites, because military force would ultimately mediate the relations among powers. In Germany, Tirpitz perhaps put it most eloquently in 1896, declaring that though political "acumen" and moral questions "play an important role in the conflicts of interest among nations, the strongest basis nevertheless remains power, and above all military power."[8] In the United States, Mahan struck the same chord. "In diplomacy, in international negotiation," he argued time and again, "force underlies every contention as a possible final arbiter, and of force war is simply the ultimate expression."[9]

It was, of course, maritime force that was uppermost in the mind of naval officers. Only sea power would truly count in the new age of global politics, with its transoceanic spaces of economic competition and imperial conflict. The policies of naval expansion that all major powers embarked on by the turn of the twentieth century demonstrated more than anything else that naval power had become the central currency of diplomacy and empire-building.[10]

The United States and Germany could not afford to stand aside in twentieth-century global politics. They had made themselves into industrial and commercial powerhouses, with an inherent need for continuous economic expansion, and thus needed to prevent other powers from carving up the globe and controlling markets and resources. The main emphasis was on the tremendous productive powers of the respective national industries for which the capacities of home (and neighboring continental) markets would no longer suffice.

In the United States, concern about the new global dependence of national industry had come into focus during the 1890s. The economic depression of the mid-1890s acted as an important catalyst, as it was believed to underscore dramatically the perils of overproduction and the paramount importance of trade expansion. Officers began to stress the increasing saturation of domestic markets and the importance of distant markets and overseas trade. Mahan, for example, presented his own country as an "outward-looking" nation that depended on the successful acquisition of new markets, trade opportunities, and raw materials across the globe. The "productive energies of the country, and its advent to the three seas," would "impel it necessarily to seek outlet by them and access to the regions beyond," he wrote in 1893.[11] In 1898, Lieutenant-Commander Richard Wainwright, a future top-billed naval planner, summarized the mainstream view when he wrote that the United States was forced to seek "markets in all portions of the globe" because "our farms and factories produce more than we can consume or export without new markets."[12]

By the late 1890s, the German naval elite's view of their country as an ever-expanding industrial nation had come into its own as well. The Germans used the notion of "maritime interests" (*Seeinteressen*) to describe these developing global ties, among which they most prominently listed export industries, seaborne trade, and shipping. These interests were rapidly growing; by the turn of the century, they had already developed "into the factor contributing the most to the increase of German wealth," concluded Captain August von Heeringen, a confidant of Admiral Tirpitz, in January 1900.[13] The "increasing interconnectedness" of German national industries with the "global economy" was now vital to Germany's economic reproduction; the Germans would be choked to death in their own country "without the expansion and strengthening of our maritime interests." Such were the conclusions reached by Ernst von Halle, the man who masterminded the effort to document the development and significance of Germany's maritime interests.[14]

Germany was also allegedly plagued by economic pressures of a different sort. The problem of overpopulation, which had not been relieved by earlier mass emigration, would cast a long shadow over Germany's future. Global economic expansion alone could not provide enough employment and adequate wages for a fast-growing population. In order not to be stifled by its "surplus population" Germany needed to create "natural outlets," Tirpitz and others explained time and again.[15]

While leaving space for complementary justifications of empire in civilizational terms (which will be discussed later), the two naval elites' will to global power expressed itself in stark terms. Cast within the mold of their economic geopolitics, their strategies were founded on the idea that the pursuit of global empire was a matter of national survival, of "life" and "death," often couched in a "Social Darwinist" or Spencerian vocabulary of evolution and perpetual conflict. This vocabulary lent harsh existential meanings to the overall analysis and magnified its sense of urgency.[16]

German World Power

The desire to turn Germany into what Tirpitz called a "major world power" that would be present in all spaces of imperial rivalry was central to the approach of the German navy.[17] Tirpitz and other navy leaders sought markets, spheres of influence, and diplomatic power around the globe and they demanded an explicit say in all matters of global politics. The particular German will to world power came with a distinctive outlook on the developing world order, the *Weltreichslehre,* that is, the notion of the emergence of a small number of global empires: Britain, Russia, the United States, and, perhaps, Germany, within the context of an ongoing, conflict-ridden subdivision of the world. "4 world powers. Russia, England, America and Germany," Tirpitz told the emperor in September 1899; "Salisbury's saying: the big states become bigger and stronger, the small ones smaller and weaker, [is] my opinion as well."[18] Two years earlier, in 1897, Tirpitz had made the case for German global power by invoking the "ruthless advance of Pan-Americanism, the tremendous success of Russia, and the entirely astonishing strength of the British Empire idea," which he claimed he had observed in "close proximity" in China.[19]

The *Weltreichslehre* was a globalizing perspective on international politics and Germany's place in it.[20] Considerations of the European state system were of secondary importance. Most notably, France played no important or independent role in this view of the world. True, naval writers often listed France among the global empires of the present, as one of the "great global-political and global-economic units."[21] Yet ultimately Germany's western neighbor was viewed as economically too weak to compete on the world market and gain parity with the world powers of the twentieth century. On its own, French military power was also too small to matter very much. In short, France was viewed as an empire in decline, following the downhill path already taken by other "dying" empires such as the Spanish.[22]

In contrast, officers integrated their previously held perception of Anglo-Russian antagonism into the more encompassing *Weltreichslehre*. By the early 1890s, the idea of an irreconcilable and economically motivated conflict between Russia and Britain taking place mostly across Asia had become a staple within the foreign policy elite of Germany, as well as that of other European nations.[23] This conflict also had captured the imagination of German naval officers, who spent considerable time thinking about its ramifications for Germany.[24] The "entire configuration" of power politics would be "dominated by the antagonism between Russia and Great Britain," claimed one analysis of global politics after the other. The confrontation between these two "great rivals" would condition German imperial options; yet it would also create spaces for a resourceful German strategy of world power.[25]

Notions of a "yellow peril," and of Japan as an equal world power, were not central to this image of global politics.[26] To be sure, on occasion naval officers raised the possibility of the rise of Japan as a world power. In 1897, Tirpitz did so himself when he conjured up the specter of the "amassing of the giant nations, Pan-America, Greater Britain, the Slavdom, and possibly of the Mongolian race, with Japan in the front seat," which could destroy a Germany that did not become a world power.[27] By 1900, and to an even greater degree after the Russo-Japanese War of 1904–05, Japan figured prominently in any discussion of imperial rivalries in the Far East.[28] In fact, German observers of the Russo-Japanese War such as Admiral Albert Hopman heralded the outcome of the war as the "beginning of a new world historical epoch," characterized by the collapse of white racial supremacy in Asia and the formation of Japan as a dominant East Asian power.[29] In subsequent years, the Germans, led by their service attachés in Washington and Tokyo, cast the developing Japanese-American antagonism as a momentous development involving two powerful imperial protagonists and a "naval arms race similar to that between Germany and England," as one naval attaché wrote in April 1912.[30]

Still, the Japanese Empire was viewed primarily as a regional power, however formidable, not as a world power on par with the other global empires. Before 1904–05, Japan played a minor role in German mental maps of world powers. In the long run-up to the Russo-Japanese War, most officers, including Hopman, approached the impending war through the lens of the Anglo-Russian antagonism. After the war, the Germans accorded more prominence to the Japanese Empire as a great power in its own right but still discussed its place in world politics through the lens of the relations among the major world powers, that is, in terms of the impact of U.S.-Japanese enmity on Germany's relations with the United States and Great Britain.[31]

The *Weltreichslehre* was an exercise in agenda-setting. The German Empire faced a stark choice, namely, either global diplomacy, economic self-assertion, and imperial consolidation, or economic decline and political marginalization. Germany was approaching a "crossroads," Tirpitz claimed, "either forward or downhill such as France, Spain, Italy."[32] It needed to become a world power and a "global industrial and trading state" that could stand on its own against Britain, Russia, and the United States, or it would face "ruin" and "decline rapidly."[33] The "signature of the twentieth century" would "culminate in the question" of whether Germany could muster enough strength for that purpose.[34]

The *Weltreichslehre* followed the script of economic geopolitics. World power and a global economic empire were viewed as "inseparable," as many an analysis explicitly stated.[35] But central to this notion were also more abstract notions of power politics. Only the pursuit of global empire and maritime force could preserve Imperial Germany's prominence and independence as a great power at a time when world powers were redistributing and accumulating political and economic resources on a massive scale. In short, the will to world power was also related to the pursuit of diplomatic standing and what Tirpitz called "power as such," as opposed to economic necessity in the strict sense.[36] The German Empire would "abdicate" as a great power "if it did not claim its place in the council of those nations that decide over the destiny of the word," stated an analysis of Germany's new global role offered by the Imperial Naval Office in 1900.[37]

In short, there was a distinct imperial and political edge to German naval thinking about German global power. In Germany, the will to world power absorbed prevalent and highly potent notions of power politics and diplomatic greatness by fusing the *Grosse Politik,* the high diplomacy of great powers, to the causes of national industry, imperial expansion, and global competition. The *Weltreichslehre* transposed conventional views of a European state system organized around a few great powers onto a global stage.[38]

Thus navy leaders also embarked on a colonial project to create a "Greater Germany" in command of a vast formal empire. Going well beyond the quest for a global infrastructure of naval bases, they envisioned a policy of colonial aggrandizement.[39] The projected acquisition of new settlement colonies as sites for a state-led emigration of the surplus population was central to this plan. Yet new colonies and their equivalent, quasi-colonial "spheres of influence" served other purposes as well. They were to furnish protected markets for German manufactured goods and trade, become special sites for German overseas capital and investment, and provide privileged access to raw materials and primary production.[40]

But the *Weltreichslehre* was not simply a prescription for an extension of colonial possessions or the pursuit of empire as a self-contained economic space, as is often assumed.[41] The German talk about world empires did not negate the continuing existence of global economic relations and competition among the various states and peoples of the earth; it went hand in hand with clearly stated commitments to the cause of the German export industry in global markets and the pursuit of "Open Doors" for German goods and capital.[42] In the present and future, the German Empire continued to confront other powers in spaces of open economic competition, operating as one of the three "main competitors on the world market," next to the United States and Britain, as Ernst von Halle, the navy's in-house economist, put it.[43]

The naval elite cast the "Greater Germany" it desired as a site of a globally dispersed people. The community of overseas Germans, of *Auslandsdeutsche,* was a necessary part of the pursuit of a self-sustaining German global empire, whether they lived under direct German dominion or not. The "labor, intelligence, and capital of Germans abroad constitute an important, in some regards the most important part of our overseas interest," Tirpitz once explained to the imperial chancellor.[44] According to the navy's discourse, *Auslandsdeutsche* were the most "valuable elements of the German people" as they manned the "outposts" of Germany as a superior nation-state with global ambition.[45]

Such thinking was framed by deep-seated emigrationist anxieties that were etched into the navy's will to global power.[46] These anxieties focused not only on the pressures of overpopulation and the need to create outlets for excess people under German control, as already noted. Central to these anxieties was also a sense of loss. A fear that German emigrants were renouncing their "Germandom" in favor of new national loyalties and strengthening Germany's imperial rivals in an age of intense international competition, as they had done in the past, haunted the likes of Tirpitz.[47] The German state thus needed to get involved directly in the business of emigration, acquire settlement colonies, and forge close bonds between native Germans abroad and their home country. Such action would allow the German Empire to tap into "the one overabundant resource that Germany possesses in its production of people (*Menschenproduktion*)," as Tirpitz argued in 1896.[48] In the case of Tirpitz, it was a tour of service in East Asia in 1896–97 that brought this concern into sharp focus. Based on first-hand experience, Tirpitz complained bitterly about the waning loyalty to the fatherland of Germans in China, and their propensity to enter into either the British or the Russian "camp."[49]

Navy leaders combined their general desire to become a major world power with clearly stated objectives and regional emphases.[50] The Far East and South America were designated as privileged "areas of interest" for Germany, as one planner phrased it.[51] These were the two regions of the world that, by the turn of the century, explicitly figured as the primary areas for Germany's imperial expansion, in terms of both confidential planning and public presentation. Tirpitz referred to "shifts in power" in these regions when he made his case for an accelerated arms buildup after the passage of the Naval Bill of 1899.[52] The fleet of overseas cruisers requested in 1899–1900 was meant for service in East Asian and South American waters.[53] Unlike Africa, these chunks of the globe were not yet carved up by the imperial powers. They held great promise as gigantic markets and primary producers, and, in the case of South America, with its "favorable" climate and existing communities of ethnic Germans, as sites of future German settlement colonies. By contrast, Africa did not play an important role in the navy's imperial designs at that time. The idea of a huge German colonial empire in Africa, to be gained by a policy of imperial takeover, did not attract strategists until World War I.[54]

The consolidation of German economic power in Central Europe through some sort of economic or political union with neighboring countries was also to the liking of the navy's planners. Around the turn of the twentieth century, Tirpitz and von Halle, the navy's chief economist, championed the cause of such unions in personal conversations and public writing, even if they did so, in part, with an eye on the colonial possessions of such countries as the Netherlands and Denmark.[55] Such support did not end in subsequent years. In 1913 Admiral Hopman approvingly recorded a conversation with Tirpitz in which the navy secretary developed "very generous thoughts about the economic union of the European continental states" and presented it as the only appropriate course of action to counter the "economic dominance" of the United States, Russia, and Britain.[56] No doubt, navy leaders believed in the promise of *Mitteleuropa,* of Central Europe, or, for that matter, of landed empire-building in Eastern Europe or the Middle East, as long as empire by land was not couched as an alternative to the pursuit of German overseas interests as a global empire. Navy leadership kept a considerable distance from visions of a German continental empire in the Eurasian realm as the primary destiny for the German Empire in the twentieth century, visions that became prominent among the army leadership and parts of the national intelligentsia during World War I. Only a few officers suggested a rethinking of the navy's previous approach in favor of an increased emphasis on landed empire covering Eurasia and Africa, yet even they did not jettison ideas about German transoceanic power.[57]

Germany: An Equal among Others

The strong infusion of economic geopolitics with notions of great-power politics lent the navy's thinking about global empire its particular shape. The German Empire was to be a full-fledged world power among others, in command of a vast formal and informal empire. But this was not a prescription for global domination or the establishment of some sort of Pax Germanica, a German-led regime of global ordering, as is often argued.[58] The overall emphasis remained on the multiplicity of global empires and equal relations among a few world powers.

This outlook manifested itself in the language of equality that permeated the ways in which the Germans conceptualized their country's interest vis-à-vis the British Empire, the dominant world power of the nineteenth century. The self-professed goal of the German pursuit of maritime force and global power was not to challenge the very existence of the British Empire but to assure Germany's parity as a global empire by coercing the British into accepting the German Empire's aspirations as a developing world power. Germany needed to create so powerful a fleet, Tirpitz explained in 1899, that Britain would lose any propensity to attack Germany "and, instead, concede such maritime power (*Seegeltung*)" to that nation as to enable it to pursue a "great overseas policy."[59] Ten years later, Tirpitz struck the same chord when he wrote, in a letter to the Prussian crown prince, that the "question of whether Germany will rise to become one of the major states or sink down to become one of the small states must be decided upon in the course of this century. If one believes in the future of Germany, then such a degree of sea power becomes necessary so as to attain 'fair play' from England."[60] "Equality among the great global empires" had been the goal of the German pursuit of maritime force, summarized Captain Gerhard Widenmann, another officer close to Tirpitz, in 1916.[61]

Indeed, a destruction of the British Empire, the occasional object of speculation among reckless officers, did not fit into the mold of the *Weltreichslehre*, nor did it sit particularly well with German navalists' admiration of the British Empire.[62] Moreover, it was at odds with a sense of Anglo-German affinity prevalent among many officers. Prominent admirals Müller and Hopman, for example, invoked the notion of an Anglo-German "racial community" set against the Latin, Slavic, and Asiatic peoples to argue explicitly on behalf of close cooperation between the German and British empires. These officers even raised the possibility, as a temporary measure, of a German junior partnership. Such thinking traced its ideological lineage all the way back to Friedrich List, an early proponent of German global power in the first half of the nineteenth century.[63]

Considerations of geopolitical alliances loomed large in the navy's calculus of German global power. The accumulation of maritime force would turn the German Empire into a world power in its own right, capable of standing on its own against any other world power and making a difference in any combination of powers. This ability would translate into the much cherished "alliance value" vis-à-vis any other world power, which were bound to consider "German allianceship" as an "extraordinarily valuable good," as Tirpitz explained in 1899.[64] Far from being an idea invented for propagandistic reasons, the notion of "alliance value" was crucial for the German navy's reckoning.

Such thinking directly expanded on existing concerns among German foreign policy elites about the developing global conflict between the British Empire and Imperial Russia in the late 1880s and 1890s. This concern centered on the fear that the German Empire, a landed power based in Europe, was in the process of being permanently pushed to the margins of global politics, because it could not present itself as a valuable ally to either of the two sides. So low was Germany's value as an ally and so fragile its status as a great power that Tirpitz assumed in the 1890s that his country, even if it stayed neutral, would be in grave danger once an Anglo-Russian war broke out. Then it would be in the British Empire's best interest to launch a surprise attack against a peaceful Germany. Tirpitz reckoned that the British Empire could not afford to let a neutral Germany strengthen its overall position. After all, the British did not stand to lose anything from such a course of military action.[65]

Imperial Germany's "alliance value" was an open-ended proposition for the future. At the beginning of the twentieth century, navy policy makers such as Tirpitz did not draw up a scheme of alliances with other big empires. They emphasized the fluidity of future relations among the big powers. They never grew tired of emphasizing that "political constellations" could "entirely" change "within a short amount of time," a fact that would hold true with regard to relations with Britain and also other "transoceanic" powers such as the United States.[66] Tirpitz himself did not engage in explicit considerations of future alliances, at least none that can be found in the record. He was more interested in the pressure exerted on other world powers by Germany's sea power and its generally increased appeal as an ally rather than in committing himself to any particular alliance in advance. Already in 1899, Tirpitz was eager to read the first traces of such influence into some of British and Russian diplomacy (for example, in regard to the Samoan question) and credited German naval plans for this development.[67]

The idea of a future German-Russian alliance against Britain enjoyed considerable support among some officers, however. In 1898–1901, two senior Admiralty Staff officers, Admirals Otto von Diederichs and Felix Bendemann, talked about a future alliance with Russia and called for a continental union between Germany, France, and Russia against what they called the "Anglo-Saxon World."[68] An alliance with Russia seemed attractive because it provided an ideal means to check Britain, the country most immediately feared by them. The Russian Empire threatened the British position and interests in India, Asia Minor, and East Asia while not being vulnerable to British sea power.

But such thinking never became official policy, even as the idea of an alliance with Russia continued to attract the attention of some officers.[69] By the turn of the twentieth century, Tirpitz consistently argued against any schemes for an alliance with Russia in the present or near future. Tirpitz had offered highly favorable descriptions of Russia, its navy, and interests when stationed in East Asia in 1896–97, and he had stressed a German-Russian community of interest in the face of British imperial policy.[70] Yet in 1899–1900 he explicitly ruled out the idea of a Continental union as contemplated by Diederichs and Bendemann.[71] When the question of a German-Russian alliance was on the table during the Russo-Japanese War, the navy secretary spoke out against it.[72] Tirpitz's opposition to any open alignment with the Russian Empire at that time was driven by a strong sense of maritime vulnerability vis-à-vis the British Empire; it would provoke its policy makers and invite a strike against Germany. Still, Tirpitz's views on the whole issue were not only a matter of timing (or of feasibility for that matter); they also reflected a long-term orientation.

So capacious was the navy's notion of "alliance value," and so open-ended in relation to the British Empire, that in 1911–12 top officers in the Imperial Naval Office celebrated what they falsely believed to be the impending conclusion of an alliance with the British Empire as a crowning achievement of the previous German pursuit of maritime force, as a "world historical moment in our position as a global power."[73] By that time, the Germans, led by Tirpitz, craved British recognition of Germany as an imperial equal and geopolitical partner. They did so in the face of the formation of geopolitical blocs, including the making of the Triple Entente, which had rendered problematic previous assumptions about geopolitical fluidity and Germany's ever-increasing appeal as an ally.[74]

By contrast, during World War I, Tirpitz and most naval officers came to advocate a separate peace with Imperial Russia, and, possibly, a Eurasian alliance among the German, Russian, and Japanese empires under anti-British (and anti-American) auspices. They did so in response to the exigencies of the war itself and the search for a war-winning strategy against Britain, the power they believed to be the real instigator of war.[75] A few weeks before the outbreak of war, on 11 July 1914, Tirpitz had already set the tone for such advocacy. At a time when he assumed that the British Empire was actively promoting a war between the German and Russian empires, he suggested that Germany should make common cause with Russia, rather than accepting an "alignment with England," as proposed by the German chancellor and most members of the foreign policy elite.[76]

The overall emphasis on Germany as an equal world power among many was evident also in the nationalist cultural imperialism that permeated naval thought. The will to world power was imbued with notions of a distinct German cultural-imperial project, separate from the general "civilizing" mission that Germany shared with other occidental nations. The making of Germany as a world power was always cast as a matter of great importance for its continued development as a state with a superior culture, a *Kulturstaat*. "If we want to become a great people, we must advance forward. If our language, our German character (*Wesen*), our faith and our morals are worthy to stand, as equals, next to those of other peoples," wrote Tirpitz in 1902, "we must make them accessible to foreign peoples."[77] It would be Germany's duty to promote the "ideas and goals of its culture vis-à-vis the other giant empires" and carve out a global space for German culture and people, explained an article published in the *Nauticus*, the navy's in-house yearbook.[78] It was no coincidence that Paul Rohrbach, a leading liberal-nationalist theorist of Germany's "cultural mission" in the world, worked, for a while, for the German Imperial Naval Office.[79]

Strong as it was, the emphasis on the mission of the Germans as a global people, a *Weltvolk*, in Rohrbach's diction, and the merits of their *Kultur* remained limited. The emphasis did not come with a universalistic desire to remake the entire world in a German cultural image. This held true even during the war itself, when prominent naval officers confirmed their commitment to continue "the great work: to carve out a proper space in the world for German character and being" and assure the "expansion of German culture and civilization in all its forms" in the postwar world.[80]

American World Power

By the turn of the twentieth century, the American naval elite, too, emphatically defined its own country as a new world power, yet, in contrast to the situation in Germany, the navy's claims to global presence and influence were spatially and politically restrained. Although going far beyond the pursuit of the territorial integrity of the United States and its newly acquired colonial empire, the quest for world power did not involve claims to participate in all matters of global politics; it did not translate into demands to intervene directly in inter-European diplomacy or to become entangled in the European pursuit of empire in Africa or western Asia. Rather, before World War I, naval strategists focused their attention on particular parts of the world—the Western Hemisphere, the Pacific Rim, and China—as the primary playing fields for American imperial ambition and economic expansion.[81] Within these regional contexts, they attended to challenges posed by other powers to U.S. imperial policies, that is, the Monroe Doctrine, control of the Isthmian Canal and mastery of the Caribbean, and the "Open Door." Time and again, strategists phrased discussions of their country's global imperial stakes as a world power in terms of these specific, geographically bounded policies.

In the immediate aftermath of the Spanish-American War, in August 1898, the navy's War Board mapped out the spatial approach to world power taken by the U.S. Navy in subsequent decades. The board singled out the Pacific Ocean and the Western Hemisphere as the areas in which the United States would have "great political and commercial interests." These, then, were the key sites of American imperial assertion and the "possible scenes" of future imperial conflict. At the same time, the board explicitly circumscribed the arena for the exercise of American global power. It advised that the United States should "keep [its] hands off Europe and all regions fairly included within the exclusively European polity, as we require European hands kept off the two Americas." It was Africa that was explicitly alluded to in this context, for it "may be considered to belong wholly to the European system of polity."[82] But such restraint also involved other portions of the globe. Speaking for his peers, Alfred Thayer Mahan, who served on the Naval War Board, explicitly referred to "the Levant and India, and the countries between them" as regions situated outside the realm of U.S. primary "interest and influence" as a global power.[83]

To a remarkable degree, the constrained globalism of the U.S. Navy coincided with a curiously disjointed outlook on global politics. The navy's strategists were prone to focus on, and isolate from each other, the specific spaces of imperial conflict and military competition with other imperial powers. This approach provided little room for a more substantial recognition of interlocking structures of imperial rivalries and relations around the globe.

Mahan proved to be an exception as he offered more panoramic perspectives.[84] Around 1900 he conjured up an image of interimperial rivalry that pitted Russia (and its French ally) against Great Britain, the United States, Germany, and Japan. These powers were locked in an all-engulfing struggle for domination, from the Near East to Manchuria and China, triggered by Russia's relentless expansionist drive. This confrontation organized the relations of the world powers around the globe. So pervasive was its pull, so evident the common interests among the opposing set of powers, as to make other configurations of imperial conflict fall into line.[85] The momentous geopolitical developments between 1904 and 1907 propelled Mahan to redirect his views. He now moved to center stage the dynamics of inter-European politics. Noting the weakening of Russia as a world power and the rise to "predominance of Germany in Europe," Mahan identified the "rivalry" between the British and German empires as a new key "danger point, not only of European politics, but of world politics as well."[86] Its repercussions would be felt across the globe. By 1911, Mahan was busy reminding his naval peers that they would be "under the necessity" of closely studying European politics and the "swayings" and "oscillations" of its "Balance of Power."[87]

Mahan's panoramic perspectives aside, the main emphasis of the navy's view of the United States as a developing world power was on the Western Hemisphere and the Pacific. These regions were viewed as both the primary areas of U.S. global interest and the paramount playing fields for imperial rivalries in the twentieth century. Practically all officers shared the assessment that the (North) Pacific region and Far East were emerging as privileged sites for economic competition and, thus, a new "storm centre" of imperial rivalry and global politics, to use an expression offered by Rear-Admiral Stephen B. Luce in 1903. They also agreed that the "wealth and prosperity" of the United States lay "in the conquest of the commerce of the Pacific and markets of the great Asiatic continent," as one naval captain put it in 1909.[88] Such views were part of practically any discussion of the emergence of the United States as a "world power" after the war of 1898.[89]

The view of the Western Hemisphere as a region of primary U.S. interest and site of intense imperial conflict drew its strength not simply from an interest in the economic opportunities that beckoned to the south of its borders (and turned the shores of Central America and the Caribbean isles into a stomping ground for U.S. Marines).[90] Rather, this view resulted from a strong sense that the Western Hemisphere was becoming a primary area of territorial interest for newly expansionist powers, such as the German Empire, that were being forced to seek overseas markets and settlement colonies in an age of intense economic pressure. As important, the transformative promises of the coming transisthmian canal molded the navy's thinking about the region and its greater significance. In the eyes of the naval elite, the construction of the canal promised to dramatically advance the productive powers of the United States and their global reach, turn the Caribbean into a primary hub of world commerce, and attract the imperial attention of outside powers. In fact, the specter of a transisthmian canal played a pivotal role in naval officers' thinking about the future supreme importance of transpacific commerce and Far Eastern markets.[91]

The interest in the canal grounded the navy's view of the Caribbean Sea as a region of paramount significance for the United States, clearly overshadowing South America in importance. In August 1898 the Naval War Board expressed this view in a most forceful fashion when it defined the Caribbean Sea as one of the "most vital regions in the world" for the United States and argued that it would assume "surpassing influence" in world affairs after the completion of the canal.[92] In 1902, Rear-Admiral Taylor referred to the Caribbean as the "American Mediterranean," in which the United States acted as the "big policeman on the corner watching the smaller folks to see that they do not get too noisy at their sports."[93] The General Board declared in October 1910 that the sea was situated "peculiarly within the sphere of interest of the United States."[94] Much like protection of the canal itself, the claim to mastery of the Caribbean was a defining part of any explication of U.S. policies and interests as a world power from the 1890s onward.[95]

Within the framework of a constrained globalism, then, the U.S. Navy committed itself to the cause of open economic competition in global markets. While turning a blind eye on economic protectionism at home, the American pursuit of global empire self-consciously set itself against policies of colonial aggrandizement and protectionist empire-building. The commitment of the U.S. Navy to the Monroe Doctrine and the "Open Door" in China shared the same anticolonialist intent. They were all explicitly directed against any attempt on the part of other powers to set up colonies and quasi-colonial "spheres of influence" that granted privileged, if not exclusive, access to exports from their national industries. Semantically, the idea of the "Open Door" in China most visibly enshrined the desire for "unrestricted trade and equal commercial opportunity" for U.S. industry, to use the words of a lecturer at the Naval War College in 1902.[96]

Demands for colonies, which could serve as sites of settlement and economic exploitation, were conspicuously absent from the wish lists of naval officers and, particularly, the policy recommendations of the General Board after 1900. But officers were by no means opposed to the idea of acquiring colonial territories. Their search for imperial possessions focused on the acquisition of locales scattered across the Caribbean and Pacific in order to create an infrastructure of naval and coaling stations, which would support the use of military force and the control of maritime lines of trade and communications. This was a formal empire made up of naval colonies without immediate economic or demographic value. Its main purpose was to serve the purposes of military projection and the pursuit of economic advantage elsewhere.[97] In his first book on *The Influence of Sea Power Upon History,* published in 1890, Mahan provided the conceptual lead. Not only did he distinguish clearly between the different economic and military functions of colonies, but he also took great pains to present them as "the surest means of supporting abroad the sea power of a country" and of supporting the wartime operations of a navy in particular.[98]

The acquisition of the Philippines, Hawaii, and other Pacific island groups in 1898–99 found approval precisely for these reasons. These places interested naval officers for their intermediate value as "stepping stones to what is beyond," as Captain Charles H. Stockton, a two-time president of the U.S. Naval War College, wrote in 1898.[99] Control of these islands was deemed essential to what the Naval War Board in August 1898 called "our transit to Asia," that is, to the projection of force in the Pacific and, thus, for the use of threat and deterrence against other powers, a prerequisite for U.S. commercial expansion and the Open-Door policy in China.[100]

In the case of Hawaii, Mahan and other naval representatives had already championed annexation in previous years for the same reason, casting Hawaii as an indispensable way station for U.S. transpacific projections of trade and military force. Naturally, such advocacy entailed a defensive component as well, whether it was offered in 1893 or 1897–98: annexation would secure the one island group in the eastern Pacific that appeared as a "stepping stone" for any power intent on challenging American policies and claims to preponderance in the Western Hemisphere.[101] In the case of the Philippines, prominent naval officers, such as Mahan and Admiral George Dewey, the victorious commander of the U.S. Asiatic Squadron, did not favor seizing them as a whole in the summer of 1898. Their primary interest was to gain a naval base and overall military control, which, at most, would require the takeover of one island, Luzon.[102]

A constrained globalism and a muted (military) colonialism circumscribed the U.S. Navy's strategy of world power. This orientation spoke to the infusion of naval thinking with a strong sense of distance from the European world of power politics and colonial empire. Such sense also expressed itself in a profoundly unilateralist outlook that drove the U.S. pursuit of maritime force and global power. To be sure, the thinking of the navy was not entirely immune to considerations of the U.S. partaking in multipower coalitions or a clear alignment with another power.[103] Still, the navy imagined the United States as a self-reliant world power capable of pursuing its interests and exercising maritime threat and deterrence on its own. The navy's calculus of U.S. global power and maritime force did not entail any anticipation of a future powerful alliance or the quest for "alliance value." In their many discussions of U.S. national interest and sea power in the official context of war planning and naval programs, the officers at the General Board and the Naval War College emphasized the principle of "no foreign entanglements" and took it as their starting point. "Our policy of no entangling alliances is traditional," the General Board explained its long-standing outlook in 1915; "we have never left ourselves to any diplomatic log rolling for other powers."[104]

The navy's branch of geopolitics was an extension of previous policies, economic agendas, and imperial desires, put to new uses. The Monroe Doctrine was a case in point. It prefigured the claim to political and military preponderance in the Western Hemisphere. From the 1890s forward, the navy set the Monroe Doctrine against what it perceived to be a newly developing desire for transatlantic territorial expansion, whether this expansion was triggered by the commercial promises of the coming canal or a straightforward interest in settlement colonies and markets in the Americas; and it mobilized this doctrine with its anticolonialist language to justify its demands for imperial control of the Caribbean and military dominion over the canal.[105]

By the same token, the navy's emphases on the Pacific and control of markets, not of territories, were grounded in a long-standing policy of economic expansion. The navy had promoted an oceanic "commercialist vision" for most of the nineteenth century, with South America, Africa, and the Pacific Far East as the most important areas. By the 1880s and 1890s, naval officers had rhetorically staked out the overarching economic interest of the United States in the Pacific basin, and the Chinese market in particular. Well before 1898, the Pacific was defined as a primary site for the U.S. quest for economic opportunity abroad.[106] This definition had informed repeated calls for naval predominance in the entire ocean; it had permeated the gathering talk about the transisthmian canal; and it found its way into the rationale for the annexation of Hawaii, as laid out by Mahan and others in the early 1890s and again in 1897–98.[107]

Coming into full view by 1900, the naval elite's aspirations for U.S. global power in the present remained remarkably stable in subsequent years. They remained, by and large, unaffected by the outbreak of World War I. Navy leaders did not change their views when they staked out, for the first time, official claims to a navy "second to none." The members of the General Board set the tone in the summer of 1915. They assumed that the struggle for "industrial and commercial supremacy in the world" would continue after the war and involve the United States in "disputes in the regions south and west of the United States." Committed to its long-standing policies such as the Monroe Doctrine and the Open Door, the United States needed to muster the maritime force capable of fighting a big-power war against any imperial comers in the Atlantic, Caribbean, and Pacific. While facing the prospects of "simultaneous" action by two big powers in pursuit of empire "in two widely separated theaters" the United States could "expect little or no support" from "other powers" and needed to act alone in line with its long-standing "policy of no entangling alliances."[108]

The navy's top strategists did not change their minds when they entered World War I and then planned for the brave new world of the postwar period. "We may assume that the broad outlines of the national policies of the world powers will remain unchanged," declared a key memorandum on the goals of future U.S. naval policy in the spring of 1918. Big-power confrontations over empire and economic interest would continue to shape postwar global politics, regardless of the possible creation of a League of Nations. As in the past, war would remain the "ultimate form of economic competition." The U.S. pursuit of "political and economic self-preservation" involved a familiar set of policies, including the Monroe Doctrine and "non-interference in European affairs" as its "corollary," the "control of the Panama Canal and of the Caribbean Sea," and the "equality of trade opportunity" as expressed in the Open Door in China. The memorandum also reiterated the long-standing emphasis on American geopolitical unilateralism by stressing the investment in "no entangling alliances." On that basis, the authors of the document defined the "basic naval policy of the United States" as the pursuit of self-contained national maritime power to achieve a "commanding superiority of naval power" in the Pacific and a "defensive superiority of naval power" in the Atlantic.[109]

The United States: Visions of Global Mastery

The naval elite's thinking about America's global power was shot through with far-reaching visions of future economic preeminence and global mastery. They infused the restrained globalism, muted colonialism, and economic expansionism of American strategies of world power with unlimited long-term ambition. Indeed, a language of supremacy permeated the navy's discourse about global economics in the twentieth-century world. Economic competition among the major powers was consistently conceptualized as a struggle for "commercial supremacy" around the globe, and not simply for a share (however huge) in the world's economy and trade.[110]

This struggle would leave a clear winner. "Following the teachings of all history," the "great competitors for the world's trade" would be over time "practically subordinated" to one of them, the strategists of the General Board explained in 1913.[111]

There was, then, a clear expectation of future American economic preeminence. The navy's discourse presented the United States as one of the three contenders in global trade rivalries and economic competition, alongside Germany and Great Britain, while also referring to Japan as a contestant for "commercial supremacy" in the Pacific. There was hardly any doubt that the United States was destined to emerge victorious out of the global economic struggle, as long as any pursuit of war or conquest did not dramatically alter the struggle's direction. Time and again, officers stressed the superior productive powers of the United States, casting their country as the "greatest producer on the earth" and the "richest and most advanced nation" on the planet.[112] The United States was bound "to dominate the world commercially" on account of its superior industrial production and cheap access to coal, Captain Chadwick lectured at the Naval War College in 1901. "One thing at least" would "appear inevitable," he insisted, "that we shall be manufacturing, on a basis of cheap fuel, at a rate and cost before which the rest of the world will be powerless."[113] Writing ten years later, another influential admiral left no doubt that the United States was bound to emerge victorious from the "world-wide race for wealth," that it "holds the best hand" in the "grand game now going on for the stakes of the commercial supremacy of the world."[114]

It was left to World War I to further strengthen such a view of the trajectory of U.S. economic power. The sheer scale of U.S. economic mobilization for the war magnified the Americans' sense of their own country's superior productive powers. Moreover, with great pride, American naval planners heralded the emergence of the United States as one the world's principal "Ocean Carriers" of freight during the war. Here finally was the one remaining area of economic activity in which the United States was finally closing the gap on its transatlantic competitors.[115]

The prediction of future dominance was not just a matter of comparative economic statistics, nor was it phrased only in terms of productive powers, shipping tonnage, and economic geopolitics. Rather, it also articulated itself in a language of destiny, with its own nationalist subtext.[116] On several occasions, prominent officers invoked the notion of the "westward course of empire," according to which the United States was emerging as a new "seat" of empire. Admiral Henry C. Taylor, perhaps the most influential naval strategist in the early 1900s, argued that his country would "bid fair to occupy a high place among the nations," as the "centres of trade activity, of agriculture and the industries" were moving "steadily westwards" and the "centres of military power" were following, "in the nature of things," that "universal movement."[117] Rear-Admiral Stephen B. Luce lectured at the Naval War College in 1903 that "'Westward the course of empire takes its way'" could "never become, to us, a hackneyed phrase." "Its truth" would be receiving "fresh proofs every day," as the "laws of motion" would be "immutable, in the one case as in the other—in the flow of the great river, and the very onward current of human progress."[118]

Fittingly, Josiah Strong and Brooks Adams, who were the most prominent proponents of this destinarian notion at the beginning of the twentieth century, had their own personal ties with prominent naval officers. In his preface to his book on expansion, published in 1900, Strong thanked Mahan for assistance in the preparation of the book.[119] Adams lectured at the U.S. Naval War College in the early 1900s and his lectures were published in the key journal of the navy, the *Proceedings of the U.S. Naval Institute*. Adams made such a powerful impression that Admiral Taylor bombarded his fellow officers on the General Board with summaries of Adams's personal remarks to him.[120]

The civilizational imperialism that attached itself to the navy's discourse on economic geopolitics and world affairs was another case in point. Like their German peers, many American naval officers equated the cause of U.S. global power and economic expansion with a distinct American civilizing project. The American national mission was about the spread of the U.S. embodiment of "Anglo-Saxon" civilization and its assertion against the cultural projects of other imperial peoples. There was a universalistic tone to this mission, which manifested itself in the use of an imagery of a struggle for supremacy and the expectation of eventual success. Mahan was the most verbose articulator of this sense of mission. "To the full expression of this political force, great alike in its ability and in its vitality," he wrote in 1900, in reference to the superior merits of the political and cultural values embodied in Anglo-Saxon America, "the United States owes to mankind her due contribution."[121] "I believe," Mahan had written two years earlier, "that the United States has duties to the world outside, as well as to herself—that in a general way the extension of 'Anglo-Saxon' control is a distinct benefit to the world."[122]

Mahan also added his own note to the navy's civilizing mission. From the mid-1890s to the early 1910s, he set a special agenda for the United

States as a new Roman Empire on the Pacific and central mediator of the encounters of "East" and "West," offering a distinct narrative of a clash of civilizations.[123] According to Mahan, the "general outward impulse" of the imperial occidental states was in the process of irrevocably drawing the "nations of the oriental civilization" into the vortex of a new global politics. The biggest question of the twentieth century, argued Mahan, would be "whether Eastern or Western civilization" was "to dominate throughout the earth and control its future." The "great task now before the world of civilized Christianity, its great mission, which it must fulfill or perish," would be "to receive into its own bosom and raise to its own ideals those ancient and different civilizations by which it is surrounded and outnumbered,—the civilizations at the head of which stand China, India, and Japan."[124] In Mahan's view, this task increasingly fell to his own country as it became the most exposed, and powerful, agent of Christian civilization in the new meeting places of "East" and "West" across the Pacific. The mission of an expanding United States was twofold: it was to contain the "stirring" of Asiatic civilization and to bring its nations slowly into the spiritual and intellectual orbit of Christian civilization. The example of the Roman Empire and its civilizing interaction with the Teutonic tribes served as the explicit model in this context.

Preferring a language of economic geopolitics, most naval strategists did not share Mahan's musings about Christianity and East-West civilizational conflict. But they all were convinced that the United States was destined to rule the world. A group of naval planners at the Naval War College expressed this view in 1909 in an unequivocal fashion. Predicting that the United States. would eventually attain unmitigated naval supremacy in the Pacific and Atlantic oceans, they wrote that their country "will then be at the zenith of her power and will control the world."[125] The "mission" and "true strategy" of the United States, its destiny, was to "command" the world, as it was "great and rich enough" to be in a position "to do so," a president of the college had explained some seven years earlier.[126]

The naval elite's understanding of global politics allowed for clear visions of U.S. global supremacy as a proposition for some distant future. These visions coexisted with more limited aspirations for American global power in the present, which by and large fit with the new "paradigm" of American diplomacy that had emerged among other civilian elites by 1900.[127] In the early twentieth century, naval officers set the realities of limited American global power against the long-term expectation of eventual U.S. economic supremacy and, thus, global mastery. This orientation characterized the strategy of world power fashioned by American navalists. It also contrasted with the outlook of the German naval elite, which otherwise offered a similar understanding of the nature of global affairs and big-power confrontations over empire. In Germany, naval strategies of world power stressed the global reach of German interests and influence, yet aspirations to global empire remained bounded by an emphasis on the continuing plurality of world powers and the quest for parity, not world domination. Particular national conjunctures of expansionist thought left their imprint on the navalism of the two naval elites and their visions of the destiny of their own respective countries as world powers.

Chapter 2

Big-Power Confrontations over Empire

In the German naval elite's collective imagination, the United States figured as an exemplary world power. Admiral Diederichs, the chief of the German Admiralty Staff, noted admiringly in 1900 that America had "quietly" built so powerful a navy that it was now "well-entitled" to "have a powerful say in matters of global politics." Two years later Admiral Tirpitz explained that America "moves forward in enormous strides (namely: politically)"; it would manage to keep abreast of the overall "development towards a few gigantic empires."[1]

U.S. naval officers painted a similar picture of Germany. "With keen foresight" and the support of an entire people, declared a lecturer at the Naval War College in 1900, the German government was "preparing" to project naval power "to the uttermost parts of the earth." "Germany will be in the bidding," he added, "wherever and whenever" big powers will jockey for colonies or spheres of influence.[2] Germany had made "enormous strides" for "commercial and maritime interests" and made itself into a leading contender in the "race" for "naval supremacy" and, thus, "for greatness," read another analysis offered in 1901.[3]

Images of other world powers on the move and predictions of big-power confrontations over empire surrounded the two naval elites' pursuits of global power and maritime force under navalist auspices. These pursuits assumed that the making of the United States and Germany as nation-centered world powers rendered inevitable direct confrontation with other global empires and required the accumulation of maritime force for big-power war. The maritime militarists of the two navies offered remarkably similar views of the policies and interests of the other world powers. Moving within the self-contained conceptual world of economic geopolitics, navalists advanced an analysis of the causes of their imperial adversaries as structurally alike and natural, if not entirely legitimate. From their perspective, all powers were driven into imperial expansion in response to, and in recognition of, their larger "objective" economic and imperial needs. In each imperial country the will to global power was not a matter of idiosyncratic rulers (such as the German emperor) and arbitrary fantasies of self-aggrandizement and domination; rather, it reflected the enlightened interest and aspirations of the entire people. At the same time, racial categories attached themselves to the tenets of economic geopolitics and colored the analysis of particular powers and their imperial projects. A sense of race and racial commonality and difference helped to shape the particulars of navalists' strategies of world power.

Germany as an Imperial Adversary

The U.S. naval elite defined the Western Hemisphere and the Pacific basin as the two primary spheres of U.S. global interest. Within this framework, the claim to political and military preponderance in the Western Hemisphere, as encoded in the Monroe Doctrine, assumed "first place," to quote Rear-Admiral Henry C. Taylor.[4] At the turn of the twentieth century, the German Empire moved to the very center of maritime threat and deterrence because it was strongly assumed to be the one world power that intended to gain colonies and naval bases in Latin America and the Caribbean and, thus, challenge the Monroe Doctrine. As the General Board explained in 1906, "Germany is desirous of extending her colonial possessions. Especially, it is thought, that she is desirous of obtaining a foothold in the western hemisphere, and many things indicate that she has her eyes on localities in the West Indies, on the shores of the Caribbean, and in parts of South America."[5]

Indeed, by 1900, the Americans viewed the German Empire as a most probable opponent of the United States. "Our next war will be with

Germany," Admiral Dewey told his audiences when he returned from Asia in 1899.[6] Germany would be "more likely than any other nation to come into naval collision with us," the service attaché in Berlin reported in the same year.[7] The country became the object of intense American war planning, the navy's "most important war study," as was noted in 1903, and planners started to measure their navy against the German fleet.[8]

The image of an expansionist Germany bent on acquiring overseas possessions in the Western Hemisphere was part of a larger view of that country as a thriving industrial nation that competed with the United States for economic supremacy in its need to expand. Germany would face the economic pressures of overproduction and, particularly, overpopulation, which could only be relieved by securing markets and proper "outlets" in the form of settlement colonies. Such thinking was most forcefully expressed in the political section of the official war plan against Germany, drafted in 1913: "The steady increase of [German] population; harder conditions of life as the home population becomes denser—no possible expansion being practicable in Europe; the steady expansion of [German] home industries which must find a protected market abroad; the desire of Imperial Germany for colonial expansion to satisfy imperial needs; and the pronounced distaste of the Imperialists for the absorption of [German] emigrants by other nations"—all these factors would induce Germany to seek overseas territories.[9]

The U.S. Navy's perception of the German Empire and its drive for imperial expansion congealed between 1897 and 1900. The events surrounding the Spanish-American War and the subsequent dissolution of the Spanish Empire in the Pacific triggered the turn against Germany. The encounter between U.S. and German naval forces in the Philippines after the destruction of the Spanish fleet, during which a nervous (and outgunned) Dewey lost his temper and threatened the Germans with war, proved formative for the sense of future German-American antagonism.[10] Against this backdrop, the multifarious German diplomatic and commercial activities in the Western Hemisphere fed concerns over German imperial intent, however overblown (if not paranoid) they were. The country's massive naval buildup after 1898 and the debates surrounding it colored the perception of Germany as an expansionist imperial power as well.[11]

Suspicion of German intentions in the Western Hemisphere had spread among U.S. naval officers before the war of 1898. In the fall of 1897, planners at the Naval War College raised the possibility of a war with Germany over an attempt to gain territory in the Caribbean.[12] Around the same time,

Mahan thought of Germany as the "probable element of future trouble for us"; the United States with its Monroe Doctrine would "threaten to stand in the way of" the German emperor and people's "very natural (and very proper) ambition" to gain settlement colonies in South America.[13]

After 1900, the perception of the German Empire's drive for imperial expansion was well entrenched. With Admiral Dewey, the president of the General Board between 1900 and 1917, as its staunchest supporter, it stayed remarkably stable over time. Between 1900 and 1904, strategists were most absorbed by the German threat and believed that an attempt to gain a foothold (first a naval base, then a colony) in the Western Hemisphere was imminent. In subsequent years, by contrast, fears of immediate German action lost some of their urgency, mainly because the military balance of power had shifted in favor of the Americans.[14]

Not all officers subscribed to the mainstream perception of Germany as a geopolitical adversary scheming, in the present, for an empire in the Western Hemisphere. Between 1899 and 1904, Mahan, for example, offered a different view of Germany in the context of his analysis of the political situation in Asia.[15] He advocated active cooperation between the United States, Great Britain, and the German Empire to contain Russian expansion in the Far East. This plea was also cast in racial terms, for Mahan argued that the Anglo-American and German peoples were all part of the Teutonic race. Noting actual German hostility toward Britain and the United States in the present, Mahan expressed considerable faith that, led by their emperor, the Germans would come to their racial senses and cooperate with their fellow Teutons against the Slavs. So invested was Mahan in this idea that he openly supported the cause of German colonies in South America so that the country could resolve its economic pressures.[16]

Other officers also contested the mainstream assessment of Germany. Retired Admiral Luce let it be known in 1903 that he no longer shared the "common apprehension of Germany" because its hands were too tied by Europe's "balance of power" to engage in any transatlantic military action.[17] Between 1907 and 1912, a larger number of planners at the General Board and the Naval War College openly called into question the likelihood of German imperial action against the United States. These strategists did not doubt the reality of the economic pressures on Germany or the existence of imperial desires on its part; yet they followed in Luce's footsteps by highlighting the implications of the political alignments in Europe and the Anglo-German antagonism in particular. Imperial Germany had "longing eyes towards South America," yet "her relations with England are so strained as to prohibit other interests," as one of their analyses noted.[18] References to the Anglo-German naval race played a pivotal role in this context. "Like two bar magnets of equal strength placed side by side with poles reserved, each with all its force clinging fast to the other and the two just joined together forming a single mass incapable of serious disturbing influence exterior to that mass, so today, firmly locked together appear the British and German fleets," concluded Naval War College planners in 1910.[19]

This fairly realistic evaluation of the German Empire's options fell on deaf ears.[20] In fact, talk about Germany as a power strongly inclined toward territorial expansion in the Western Hemisphere attained new intensity in the early 1910s, with Mahan joining in as well.[21] Shortly before World War I began, expectations of German imperial transgressions in the near future were as powerful and widespread as ever.[22] This sort of alarmism mobilized existing images of Germany as an aggressive empire on the move. It was also fueled by other considerations. Among them was a clear recognition of a newly developing disparity between the German and U.S. navies. In addition, the navy's strategists feared that the flourishing American-Japanese antagonism invited German imperial action in the Western Hemisphere.[23]

Navy leaders clung to their firmly held views of the German Empire after the outbreak of World War I. They came to be haunted by the specter of a future naval challenge posed by a victorious Germany in a postwar pursuit of territories in the Western Hemisphere. On August 1, 1914, the General Board set the tone by arguing that "many indications exist that Germany desires a foothold in American waters, and it is well known that she does not concur in the Monroe Doctrine." If Germany were to emerge victorious from the war, the Board also stated, "the temptation will be great to seize the opportunity for obtaining the position she covets on this side of the ocean."[24] A year later, the agency reiterated the belief that a victorious Germany was bound to challenge the United States in the Western Hemisphere when it adopted its policy of a "navy second to none." Its members also magnified the sense of threat by raising the specter of joint German-Japanese pursuits of empire. A "rapprochement" between the German and Japanese Empire could be in the making, "with the possible result that we may be called upon to face an alliance between those powers" bent on imperial expansion "in regions south and west of the United States."[25] Such analysis attained its special valence from the fact that for most of the war the majority of officers (including Admirals Fiske and William Shepherd Benson, who were officially the navy's top strategists) assumed that Germany would emerge a winner from the war, or, at least, avoid decisive defeat. It took Allied victory in the summer of 1918 to change the navy's discourse on Germany.[26]

Conflict over Empire in the Far East

The navy's strategy of world power also concerned itself with the Pacific and East Asia, the part of the world defined, by the beginning of the twentieth century, as both a primary region of U.S. global interest and a new "storm centre" of imperial rivalry between the world powers. After 1900, it was Imperial Russia that appeared as America's primary adversary in considerations of military threat and deterrence in this regional context. This was the power whose pursuit of territorial empire and commercial exclusion in China was believed to represent the biggest threat to the U.S. Open Door policy.[27]

The specter of the Russian policy of conquest and war came to haunt naval strategists. Given its geopolitical position and the advantages offered by the developing trans-Siberian railways, Russia's "ultimate control" of Manchuria, northern China, and, possibly, Korea would be merely a matter of time, one alarmed captain (who had just returned from service on the Asiatic Station) explained to the General Board in 1903.[28] Two years earlier, the same officer had suggested that one better not talk about an ongoing "partition" of China "as that might imply that some nationality other than Russia was getting a share, which is not the case."[29]

This view of Russian-American antagonism was embedded in a larger analysis of interimperial alignments in China. Whereas Russia and France wanted to carve up China, Great Britain and Japan would jointly "advocate the integrity of China and equal commercial privileges for all nations."[30] Imperial Germany was sitting on the fence, for it had not committed itself to either cause. The volatility of this situation was exemplified by the escalating tensions between the Russian and Japanese empires. The Russo-Japanese War of 1904–05 did not surprise the Americans. And when it broke out, the same Americans knew where their sympathies were. Japan was "fighting out our battles" against Russia, summarized Captain William M. Folger, soon to be commanding officer of the Cruiser Squadron of the U.S. Asiatic Fleet, two days after the Japanese declaration of war on February 8, 1904.[31]

The navy's prescription for a strategy to uphold the Open Door in the face of Russia's policy of territorial expansion rested on this analysis. Navy strategists adhered to the vision of a natural anti-Russian alliance between the Japanese, British, and U.S. empires in China, which was grounded in common advocacy of the Open Door. Together, these three empires would be in a position to keep Russia and its French ally in check and muster enough maritime and land-based force to wage a war in Far Eastern waters and on mainland China. The idea of such a multiempire war (with Germany as a possible ally of Russia and France) shaped the navy's thinking about the Far East. Warmly endorsed by most officers, it was the Anglo-Japanese alliance treaty of 1902 that underwrote this approach.[32]

Strategists also racialized the clash between the empires in the Far East. When discussing the situation in Asia and the direction of global politics, many officers tended to conjure images of the confrontation between the "Slavic race" and the "Anglo-Saxon race." Racial imagery sharpened the sense of hostility toward Russia well before the Russo-Japanese War brought it into sharp focus.[33] Among his peers, Mahan offered the most systematic analysis of the clash of "races" in the Far East.[34] Confessions of a "deep-rooted distrust of the Slav" were combined with a strong sense of the superiority of the Anglo-Saxon "race" and "civilization" to shape Mahan's thinking about the different "racial traits" of these two subsets of the "white race" and their "concrete expressions" in "fundamental" differences "of political institutions, of social progress, and of individual development."[35] In addition, Mahan advanced a favorable view of the Japanese as a "race." Presenting Japan as a proxy for white Anglo-Saxon civilization, Mahan argued that the Japanese were "racially Asiatic" yet "adoptively European."[36]

The American–Japanese Antagonism

The Russo-Japanese War revamped the geopolitical landscape of the Far East. After a brief period of transition, the victorious Japanese Empire turned from a "sure friend" to a "possible enemy" of the United States, as Admiral Dewey explained in 1906.[37] From that point on, strategists assumed that their country confronted Japan in the Pacific and Far Eastern spaces of interimperial competition. Planners began to devote as much energy and time to planning for an armed encounter with Japan as for one with Germany. References to Japan as a "probable enemy" became a fixture of naval planners' discussions of naval programs and the peacetime deployment of the fleet. A most spectacular expression of the turn against Japan was the decision to send the U.S. battle fleet on a trip to the West Coast and then across the Pacific. The "world cruise" took place on the heels of a full-blown "war scare," which peaked in the summer of 1907. Resurfacing in 1913, fears of imminent war punctuated the navy's assessment of Japanese-American confrontations.[38]

The Americans viewed the Japanese Empire in much the same way they viewed its German counterpart. As a developing industrial nation with a fast-rising population, Japan would face severe economic and demographic pressures and be thrust upon a course of expansion. Repeatedly, strategists drew explicit parallels between the Germans and the Japanese. "Each is both a military and naval power of the first rank. Each has a rapidly increasing population with developing industries seeking new markets. Either nation is likely, when led by the pressure of population and the need of markets, to come to collision with the United States, either in America or in Asia," concluded a group of planners in characteristic fashion in 1909.[39]

Japanese expansionist pursuits posed a direct threat to the United States in a number of ways. First, the Japanese Empire was bound to challenge the Open Door in China even as it officially adhered to its principles. More than any other power, Japan wanted "to do away with the 'open door' and establish the 'spheres of influence,'" wrote the authors of the Naval War College's war plan against Japan in 1911.[40] Several years earlier, in 1907, planners at the same college had expressed their belief that the Japanese, while currently engaged in "the complete acquisition and development of Korea," always had "the ultimate conquest of China in view."[41]

According to the Americans, the Japanese Empire also considered schemes to seize U.S. territorial holdings in the Pacific as a way to meet mounting population pressures. The "fertile" Philippine Islands and Hawaii, with its large number of Japanese residents, were "ideal places of Japanese colonization," explained Rear-Admiral Fiske.[42] The strategic section of the official Orange War Plan, approved by the General Board in May 1914, suggested that the Japanese would view the Philippines in particular as a "natural part" of their empire while Hawaii and other islands such as Guam attracted attentions as necessary "outposts" to enhance Japan's strategic position and advance trade.[43]

This perception of Japanese imperial intent harkened back to the past. In 1897–98, strategists had imagined a war with Japan in the context of diplomatic quarrels over a possible U.S. annexation of Hawaii and Japanese immigration to that island. A view of Japan as an expansionist power seeking dominance in the Pacific region, and bent on the conquest of Hawaii and transoceanic expansion, had surfaced and found its expressions both in confidential correspondence and public writing. This imagery extended to dire predictions of the Japanese colonization of Mexico and other places in Central America.[44]

In subsequent years, a staff member at the Naval War College, John Ellicott, cast Japan as an imperial power thrust upon a course of "territorial expansion," either targeting "continental Asia" or taking a "southward" direction. While eschewing any direct alarmism, he also noted that the United States stood "in the way" of Japan's "natural insular territorial aspirations" in the Pacific, including the Philippines and Hawaii. It was no coincidence that Admiral Taylor, who had aided Ellicott's career, expressed some uncertainty about the future relationship with Japan in May 1904.[45]

Beginning in the summer of 1906, officers also identified another source of conflict: Japanese immigration to the United States. Indeed, this had become a source of considerable diplomatic friction between the two countries as the ever-increasing presence of Japanese immigrants was met by a white nativist response, which was punctuated by acts of violence. Such friction provided the immediate occasion for the navy's war panics in 1906–07 and 1913.

Planners talked about a flourishing "racial antagonism" that would magnify the hostility between two "race-conscious" empires. In 1911, the Naval War College defined this "racial antagonism" and the "inflammation produced by this friction" as a cause for possible war.[46] Racial discrimination was bound to inflame the Japanese, for it "hit" them "in their tenderest spots—their sense of honor; their pride of race and their patriotism," summarized Rear-Admiral Fiske two years later.[47] Planners also offered more panoramic visions of racial conflict sparked by the transpacific migration of the Japanese and white responses to it. This move involved the invocation of racial solidarity among the English-speaking people of the United States, Australia, New Zealand, and other parts of the British Empire. The Pacific crossing of the U.S. battle fleet in 1907–09, with its visits to Australia and New Zealand, combined with anticipation of the opening of the Panama Canal to galvanize this sentiment, which Mahan articulated at great length.[48]

Planners also repeatedly raised the possibility that the Japanese would pursue settlement colonies in the Americas. Already in 1897–98, there was talk about Japanese schemes for territorial expansion targeting Mexico and Central America.[49] In the context of their war panic in 1906–07, strategists contemplated the possibility of a Japanese seizure of U.S. Pacific states and related it to Japanese migration to the West Coast. By the early 1910s, the General Board repeatedly argued that the United States would have to defend the Monroe Doctrine against Imperial Japan, pointing to South America as a "field" for "Japanese emigration" and casting Japanese immigration to the United States as acts of colonization.[50]

The notion of a flourishing Japanese-American antagonism attained the status of common sense in naval circles. Only a few officers, such as Rear-Admiral Charles S. Sperry, who had commanded the U.S. battle fleet on most of its global cruise, took a more benign view of the Japanese Empire. Dismissing many fellow senior officers as irresponsible "war fiends" of questionable "intelligence," Sperry doubted that the Japanese were bent on any policy of war and conquest that could lead to a direct confrontation with his own country. Japan had fought "for life" against Russia to meet its pressing economic and population needs. With the acquisition of Korea, the empire had become more of a saturated power. Standing out among his peers, Sperry, in fact, imagined Japan, Britain, and his own country as three powers capable of sharing control of the Pacific and ensuring peace in that region.[51]

The mainstream assessment of Japan was of course capacious enough to allow for significant differences in analysis and emphasis. Most important, planners were divided in their assessments of the actual likelihood of war. During the "war scares" of 1906–07, for example, a good number of officers believed war to be imminent.[52] Other strategists, including Admiral Dewey, did not indulge in this alarmism. Significantly, the head of the Office of Naval Intelligence and the two officers on successive tours as naval attachés in Tokyo during this entire period offered similar assessments.[53] In the early 1910s, the General Board repeatedly viewed a war with Japan in the present as "improbable," yet in 1913 another "war scare" gripped most naval planners.[54]

Strategists also offered differing assessments of Japan's likely imperial behavior. Views varied according to changing assessments of the constraints set by Japan's economic exhaustion after its war with Russia, its absorption of Korea, continuing interimperial conflicts in the Far East, and the evolving Japanese-American military balance of power. There was no consensus as to whether Japan would seek its fortune on the Asian continent (and thus challenge the Open Door) or pursue a "southward" strategy (and thus move against the Philippines and Hawaii). The war plans drawn by the Naval War College and the General Board usually just sampled the possibilities without choosing among them.[55]

Assessments of the intensity of "racial antagonism," too, differed considerably. While framing the "war scares" in 1906–07 and 1913, this particular conflict came to be viewed by some analysts as a "side issue" of no "paramount interest" to a Japanese Empire pursuing territorial empire and commercial expansion in the Pacific and on mainland Asia.[56] The opening of the Panama Canal magnified such thinking, as the accelerated peopling of the western U.S. by white Americans would allegedly "lessen the chance of race friction."[57] Yet other officers continued to insist that it was precisely the issue that could make Japanese leaders seek war, regardless of their country's economic woes or U.S. military superiority.[58]

All planners agreed that Japan was a formidable power. The dramatic Japanese pursuit of military and industrial catch-up with Western powers in the late nineteenth century and the victorious pursuits of war against China and Russia captivated the Americans in this context. They also suggested a willingness to risk an open conflict with the United States. Notions of race strengthened this perception. The Americans ascribed racial traits to the Japanese that they believed to be well suited to the pursuit of empire. "Superb courage, intense patriotism, frugality and perfect probity in governmental expenditures" were all racial traits of the Japanese, insisted Rear-Admiral Fiske in 1913.[59]

Japan continued to loom large in the navy's imagination throughout World War I. Expectations of postwar conflict with Japan helped to anchor the navy's discourse about its naval programs and the postwar order.[60] The U.S. Navy required a "commanding superiority in the Pacific" in the face of the "growing need of Japan for an opportunity to expand" and a Japanese desire "to gain supremacy in the Pacific," summarized a key planning document in May 1918.[61] The thinking of the navy about the direction of the Japanese-American antagonism followed well-trodden paths, even allowing for continuing differences in emphasis concerning the direction and timing of possible Japanese action. But the war also provided fresh grist for the intellectual mills of the navy. The Japanese occupation of German holdings in the Pacific, for example, fueled concerns about Japan's expansionist leanings.[62] But what weighed most heavily on American minds was a sense that Japan was placing itself in a most advantageous position vis-à-vis the United States. Japan would be "assuring her future freedom of action with regard to the United States no matter which side is victorious in the present war," explained the General Board in 1915.[63] Japan would be assuring future British goodwill through its participation in the war. It would also cultivate friendly relations with Germany, which could eventually result in some sort of postwar German-Japanese combination. In fact, the specter of a victorious Germany making common cause with Japan haunted planners for most of the war.

The Threat of the British Empire

While the American naval elite focused on big-power confrontations in two distinct regions of the world, the German navy's strategy of world power centered on the desire to become a world power in control of global spheres of interest (including a vast colonial empire) and present in all arenas of world politics. The Germans emphasized threat and deterrence against the British Empire, the world's premier sea power: projection of force against this empire held the key to Germany's destiny in the twentieth century.[64]

The navy's turn against Britain dated from the mid-1890s. The crisis in Anglo-German relations over South Africa in the winter of 1895–96 served as an important watershed. The crisis triggered the first discussions of military operations against Britain in German naval circles. In the case of Tirpitz, the thinking about Britain took its final form during his service in East Asia in 1896–97 when he observed Anglo-German relations on the imperial spot.[65]

In his first policy statements as secretary of the navy, Tirpitz defined "England" as Germany's "most dangerous enemy" against which as many battleships as possible were needed, and cast "the increase of our political power and position toward England" as his overarching goal.[66] In a wartime review of German naval policy, Admiral Hopman, a close confidant of Tirpitz, summarized the anti-British rationale succinctly when he wrote that the "enlargement of our fleet pursued the goal of preventing a power-political intervention of England against the development of Germany's sea and world power."[67] So strong was this anti-British orientation that Admiral Eduard von Capelle, yet another key figure, granted, in 1911, the entire German fleet "only a right of existence against England."[68]

The navy conceptualized the Anglo-German antagonism in the present and future in the terms of economic geopolitics. According to Tirpitz, Britain considered Germany as its major economic rival and felt increasingly threatened by Germany's "real and unavoidable competition on the world market."[69] The sharpening economic competition in the world market and British envy of German commercial successes would give rise to ever-increasing political disputes. "My chief is of the opinion," a close aide to Tirpitz reported in 1897, "that the economic conflict of interest with England will become bigger and bigger, that we need to be prepared for everything."[70]

Tirpitz and others postulated the existence of Anglo-German economic rivalry and political antagonism in rather general terms. The competition would affect all areas of the global market, be they in Africa, America, or Asia. In particular, Britain and Germany would clash over their opposing, mutually exclusive economic interests in the Far East. Based on his own firsthand experience, Tirpitz defined China, with its gigantic market, as the site of an especially fierce Anglo-German economic rivalry. Already in 1896–97, Tirpitz warned of growing British resentment against Germany's commercial success in China. British toleration of German activities, he predicted, would come to an abrupt end and give way to exclusion once the German share of the Chinese trade was equivalent to 30 percent of the respective British share.[71]

Fears of war complemented this gloomy view of Anglo-German relations. Officers not only interpreted British resistance to German schemes for colonies and spheres of influence in Africa, Samoa, and Turkey as the first manifestation of British efforts to fend off the German economic challenge but considered Britain to be ruthless enough to launch a war to eliminate Germany as a rival.[72] "The development of German trade has led to a strong competition between England and Germany for the world market," a memo by the Imperial Naval Office noted in 1900. "The resulting conflicts of interest have created tensions and raised the danger of an attack by England against us."[73]

Fears of an imminent British attack intensified after 1900 when the German naval buildup was fully under way. The Imperial Naval Office declared in the fall of 1905 that "even a quiet and reasonable English policy must come to the decision to eliminate such an opponent before he attains a military strength too dangerous for England's position as a world power."[74] The Office did so in the wake of a serious "war scare" in 1904–05, occasioned by the Russo-Japanese War, when the Germans assumed that if the British Empire became involved in a war with Russia it would attack Germany.[75] So powerful was this concern that it did not escape the eye of foreign observers: "I am convinced that the fear of a war with Great Britain is very real," the British naval attaché in Germany reported in June 1906 after talking to Wilhelm II and numerous German officers in Kiel.[76]

The German angst was fueled by an overblown reading of the sentiments expressed by British radical nationalists and a portion of the British press. But it was the analysis of past British behavior that brought this angst into focus and provided its own semantics. The Royal Navy's strike against the neutral Danish fleet in Copenhagen in 1807 had captured the fertile

German imagination. With that action, Britain had demonstrated, Admiral Diederichs noted, "that it knows no moral scruples, when it becomes necessary to paralyze a future opponent."[77] Historian Jonathan Steinberg has fashioned the term "Copenhagen Complex" to capture the German nightmare: the fear of an unprovoked British military strike.[78]

Such assessments of British policy sat well with an overall perception that viewed Britain as a global empire. Tirpitz and others looked with envy across the Channel. Britain had what they coveted for Germany: world-power status, an empire, a first-rate navy. It was the prime example of an industrial and trading state whose policies were dictated purely by economic ends. "Policy in England is guided by trade interests," Tirpitz noted time and again with considerable admiration. "The 'City' makes English policy."[79] Based on a broad social consensus, British policy makers had always pursued a comprehensive imperial agenda on a global scale. British diplomacy had always acknowledged the interdependence of commerce, military might, and empire-building; ingeniously, it had maintained the "balance of power" in Europe in order to expand overseas and it had held down commercial and political rivals, if necessary through the ruthless use of military force.

This, then, was a world power fiercely determined, in the present, to protect its position of preeminence. Britain had already dramatically increased its political and economic position around the globe after 1850. In the present, it had started to rise to new challenges, as represented by the "determined" efforts of all the "other great civilized nations" to become "full competitors in global politics and world trade," one senior admiral commented, capturing the gist of German thinking on this issue in 1899. This "enormous exertion of force" expressed Britain's resolution not "to accept any significant restriction of its predominant position in global politics and in world trade without a fight, let alone to surrender it entirely." Within this context, the spread of protariff sentiment in Britain also appeared as important proof of British efforts to shore up its global position. Confronted with superior economic competition, the British were shedding commitments to free trade in favor of imperial protectionism.[80]

Conflict with the United States

If the focus on Britain served as an "elixir of life" for the German navy (as one officer put it right before World War I[81]), that navy was not only built as a lever against Great Britain. According to the navy's discourse, Germany's future as a nation with global aspirations also depended on the use of threat and deterrence against the United States.[82] By the turn of the twentieth century, strategists emphasized that the rising German navy would be used against both the British Empire and the United States. "If we want to pursue overseas policy and secure valuable colonies in the future," stated one planner in 1903, "we need to be primarily prepared for a confrontation with either England or America."[83]

Tirpitz put this double rationale succinctly in his notes on a crucial meeting with the emperor in September 1899: "4 world powers: Russia, England, America, and Germany. Because 2 of these world powers can only be reached over the sea, maritime state power moves to the foreground."[84] Fittingly, Tirpitz justified his legislative plans on several occasions in 1899–1900 by referring to the United States as an opponent.[85] This was the case even though the Imperial Naval Office had decided to focus exclusively on Britain as the strongest maritime adversary in its public presentation of its naval programs.

Navy leaders offered a dark view of future German-American relations. They predicted inevitable conflict over empire, firmly grounded in economic rivalry and the quest for markets and colonies. Considerations of tariff and commercial policy and of the direct economic relations of the two countries played only a minor role in this context.[86] The primary field of interimperial conflict with the United States was Latin America, the region defined as a primary area of imperial interest as both a gigantic market for Germany's export industries and as an ideal place to create settlement colonies for surplus population.[87] Strategists recognized that their country's schemes for South America stood at cross-purposes with American commercial interests and U.S. official policy. Predictably, it was the Monroe Doctrine that irked the Germans most. They denounced this doctrine as a self-aggrandizing "legal pretension" without parallel.[88] By the same token, planners looked with disdain at the impending construction of a transisthmian canal under American control and were haunted by the specter of full U.S. hegemony in the Caribbean. Views of the German-American antagonism and its stakes were forcefully expressed in the concise summary of German war aims that the navy's war plan against the United States offered in 1903: A "firm position in the West Indies," a "free hand in South America," and an official "revocation of the Monroe Doctrine" would provide a solid foundation for "our trade to the West Indies, Central and South America."[89]

Strategists realized that any anti-American course of imperial action required the tacit acceptance, if not assistance, of the British Empire and a free hand in Europe.[90] They watched the course of Anglo-American relations with concern after 1898, which circumscribed Germany's diplomatic options in the present. Picking up on Anglo-Saxon "race patriotism" and the diplomatic rapprochement between the two English-speaking empires, Admiral Bendemann offered in 1899 a gloomy picture of an "Anglo-Saxon fraternization" occurring in spite of "strong competition in the industrial sector" and the "undeniable and numerous political fields of tensions."[91] During the Venezuelan crisis of 1902–03 Tirpitz had to acknowledge the emergence of some sort of Anglo-American understanding about U.S. claims of preponderance in the Western Hemisphere.[92]

The momentous geopolitical events between 1904 and 1906, and the breaking open of the Anglo-German antagonism in particular, put an end to any efforts to imagine an isolated confrontation with the United States over empire. Subsequently, long-term anti-American intent was overshadowed by an interest in improving German-American relations in the present.[93] On occasion, some officers fantasized about some sort of German-American alliance that would improve Germany's position vis-à-vis the British Empire and perhaps create an opening in the future for German colonial schemes in South America. Admiral Wilhelm Büchsel, the chief of the Admiralty Staff, for example, stressed the desirability of a German-American geopolitical pact in 1905. Although skeptical of its feasibility in the present, the admiral banked whatever hopes he had on a future conflict of interest between the United States and a British Empire allied with the Japanese in the Far East.[94]

Büchsel set the tone for subsequent interest in the developing American-Japanese tensions in the Pacific, which, it was hoped, would turn into a long-lasting irreconcilable antagonism raising the specter of war. Within this context Tirpitz and other officers remained attracted to the idea of a German-American rapprochement, regardless of their awareness of the anti-German orientation of the U.S. naval elite. The navy secretary promoted the idea of German-American cooperation in public as late as December 1914 when he gave an interview to an American journalist and stressed in racially charged language the common German-American interests vis-à-vis Japan.[95] Only in 1915 did Tirpitz and other naval leaders shelve this idea in favor of counseling a separate peace, if not an outright alliance, with Japan to enhance Germany's chances to win the war.[96]

By that time, the notion of Anglo-American unity had moved to center stage within the navy's discourse. Whereas, before the war the United States had mostly figured as a world power on its own, Tirpitz and other navy leaders now stressed the close ties between, and shared interests of, these two empires, based on the "feeling of racial kinship" and "the cartellization (*Vertrustung*) of Anglo-Saxon economic and cultural life in its English and American forms."[97] The "Anglo-Saxon world" had "united itself for good," declared Tirpitz in 1915. The elimination of Germany as a world power would be at the center of the Anglo-American pursuit of global domination.[98]

Escalating Anglo-German Enmity

As the United States faded into the background as an immediate object of German threat and deterrence after 1906, the fixation on the Anglo-German antagonism grew even stronger. Tirpitz and others now focused all energies on managing the escalating Anglo-German arms race, which the German Naval Bill of 1908 and the so-called British Naval Scare in 1909, the public panic over the German naval threat that led to a massive construction program, brought into sharp focus. More than ever, what Tirpitz called, in 1897, "the increase of our political power and position toward England," appeared as the one key to Germany's future as a world power.[99]

Making sense of the open Anglo-German rift after 1906, naval officers all agreed that Anglo-German relations had now entered a period of open enmity. The British had identified the German Empire as their "national foe," a new "hereditary enemy," engaging against it in what Gerhard von Widenmann, the service attaché in London from 1907 to 1912, called a "latent struggle."[100] What had been, in 1900, a dire prediction for the future, had become reality in the present. Tirpitz and his peers explained the open Anglo-German rift in familiar terms. Its "natural explanation" and "ultimate reason" would be Germany's "economic development," "population growth," and "trade-political situation," British "unease about economic and political competition," and so on.[101] Accordingly, the deterioration of Anglo-German relations would not stem from German naval expansion, even as Tirpitz and others conceded, on several occasions, that this expansion had directly contributed to British enmity toward Germany.[102] Among his peers, Karl von Coerper, who served as attaché to London from 1898 to 1907, with a brief interlude in 1903–04, was isolated with his prescient views of the issue of the German buildup as the "key" cause of the "poor relations" between the two nations.[103]

According to the German naval elite, in this era of open antagonism British enmity against Germany's aspirations expressed itself in many ways. Most immediately, there was the persistent struggle against the advance of Germany's national industry. Everywhere on the globe, the British were allegedly hard at work denying what Tirpitz and other Germans referred to as an "Open Door for our commerce and our industry."[104] The British were also moving down the road toward full-throttle imperial protectionism, regardless of continuing professions of free trade or the immediate political fortunes of Joseph Chamberlain's plans for an imperial tariff union. Britain was "ruthlessly" pushing Germany and its industry out of such countries as China, Turkey, or Spain, warned Tirpitz in November 1913.[105]

But the British turn against Germany expressed itself most forcefully in the geopolitical realm. The making of the Entente Cordiale and the Triple Entente in 1904 and 1907, respectively, appeared as the product of a clever politics on the part of an empire bent on enhancing its geopolitical position and isolating its German rival. "England" has "striven" now "for years" to forge "Ententes" that were to "encircle" Germany, or at least to "politically paralyze" it, summarized Tirpitz in 1908.[106] So strong was the understanding of the anti-German meaning of British alliance politics at that time that Tirpitz and his peers began to assume that any war with Britain would automatically involve France and Russia.[107] By the time of the Second Morocco Crisis, they speculated that British policy makers either considered launching a war against Germany with its French or Russian allies or using its specter to both intimidate Germany and force her to increase the army at the expense of naval expansion.[108] On the eve of World War I, the making of an Anglo-Russian naval convention brought this concern once more into clear focus.[109]

British alliance politics, in turn, created the space for an increasing concentration of the Royal Navy in British home waters. It also anchored other measures that aimed directly at the growing German fleet. British policy makers allegedly also pursued a policy of "bluff," of intimidation and deception, to make Germany abandon its quest for maritime power.[110] Seeking to manipulate existing German fears, the British would deliberately engage in public talk about a preemptive military strike. The warmongering rhetoric of Sir John Fisher, the First Sea Lord from 1904 to 1910, captured the most attention in this argumentative context.[111]

British policy makers sought to trick the Germans into limiting their naval buildup. The search for an Anglo-German "agreement" over fleet strength and imperial issues would aim at reducing German armaments in return for meaningless assurances of political goodwill and empty promises of support for German demands for overseas possessions in the hypothetical case of a redistribution of smaller European empires. Here, allegedly, was a blatant attempt to swindle the Germans out of their pursuit of maritime force, as evidenced in British unwillingness to accept a clear limitation for their own navy or to disavow explicitly anti-German alliance politics. Accordingly, Tirpitz and the navy's other top policy makers insisted that Germany should not make any unilateral military concessions but rather insist on the principle of strict reciprocity in any arms control treaty and on a binding political agreement addressing fundamental questions of geopolitical allegiance.[112]

This reading of British intentions remained in place after the winter of 1911–12 when the Anglo-German explorations of maritime arms control had run their unsuccessful course. According to the Germans, the British would continue their efforts "to divert our attention" and "isolate us" through a "sham agreement" as they engaged in negotiations over an Anglo-German détente and colonial agreements after 1912.[113] Similarly, the proposal for a "naval holiday," that is, the suspension of new construction of capital ships, which Winston Churchill, then the head of the British Admiralty, made in 1912 and 1913, was dismissed as a propagandistic ploy. In fact, Churchill began to replace Fisher as an iconic figure personifying British ill intentions.[114] In the spring of 1914, Tirpitz and other navy leaders chafed at the British navy secretary's proposal to visit Kiel to meet his German counterpart in office.[115]

In the eyes of Wilhelmine officers, the anti-German activities of the British Empire bore the imprint of the collective will of the "City of London," the national intelligentsia, and the entire political nation, a will that German observers saw reflected in the remarkable unanimity of the British press on the "German issue."[116] Tirpitz and his peers were also eager to point to the deliberate manipulation of the "German threat." In 1909–10, for example, these self-proclaimed experts on Britain expressed great outrage at what they believed to be a mischievous politics of vested fleet interests, the *Flotteninteressenten*, civilian and military. This grouping, they charged, had fabricated lies about the tempo of the German naval buildup (of an alleged secret acceleration, which, in fact, had not taken place) to launch a "navy scare" and secure high naval appropriations.[117]

Central to the navy's view of Anglo-German relations was the sense that the British Empire did not deal with Germany from a position of unassailable strength. The British, Admiral Capelle insisted in 1912 and 1913, could "sustain an arms race much less than us"; they were "at the limit of their strength in terms of finances, politics, and naval technology."[118] The Germans took the British interest in arms control treaties, naval holidays, and (facile) colonial agreements to mean that British policy makers had realized they could not afford their current high level of armaments. British efforts to get the Dominion nations directly involved in major naval construction for the defense of the imperial realm, which were closely followed by the German naval attachés in London, signaled British weakness as well.[119] There were also clear limits to the British politics of alliance. The various ententes and the rapprochement with the United States had not done away with existing lines of conflict across the globe, which demanded continuous attention. The focus on Germany could only be a temporary measure.[120]

The British Empire also no longer held the ultimate trump card in its hand. Beginning in 1907–08, a preemptive military strike against Germany was ceasing to be a viable option. Germany was entering a period, Tirpitz suggested in 1908, in which the "conviction" took hold in "England" that "war against Germany" had become "a bad business."[121] Britain did not want war, Capelle noted in October 1912, because "already today" the "military and political risk" was simply "too high."[122]

On this issue, however, there was considerable disagreement within naval circles. Acute anxieties about imminent war surrounded the drafting of the Naval Bills of 1908 and 1912. "Worries of war" dominated the mood among planners in the Admiralty Staff and the active fleet in 1908–09.[123] So concerned was Admiral Friedrich von Baudissin, the chief of the Admiralty Staff, that he made his views known to Chancellor Bülow.[124] Three years later, the chiefs of the Admiralty Staff and the High Seas Fleet again left little doubt that a war with Britain had become a distinct possibility. And such fears persisted until the outbreak of war in 1914.[125] Tirpitz and his various lieutenants were not entirely immune to concerns about a coming war with Britain either. While dismissing the specter of imminent war, they postulated the existence of a "war party" within Britain, connected to the Conservative Party and the Royal Navy and waiting for its chance to take their country to war with Germany.[126]

The navy elite's view of the direction of the Anglo-German antagonism remained ambiguous before 1914. The British Empire posed a clear and present danger to the German Empire. Yet at the same time, Tirpitz and others also believed that British policy makers could and would eventually acquiesce in the German Empire's aspirations of global power. The supposed preeminence of the "City of London" allegedly ensured that Britain acted as a kind of "businessman" and that sober business calculations shaped British decision making.[127] Once the British realized the limits of their power vis-à-vis Germany, Tirpitz prophesized in 1908, "then the natural consequence will be that England will be inclined to seek 'from the outset' an agreement with Germany on all questions and thus shape 'from the outset' its behavior toward Germany, and to avoid constant needling, affronts, and even 'bluffing.'"[128]

So genuine was this belief that for a brief moment in February 1912, top officers in the Imperial Naval Office believed that Britain had decided to recognize Germany as its imperial equal and geopolitical partner. They developed this belief in the context of the visit of the British secretary of war, Lord Haldane, to Berlin. In their mind, Haldane had come to offer the "alliance of friendship" they had craved. According to Admiral Capelle, the British would seek a "free hand" through "dependence on us" as the "one country that it feared and through which it is bound." At a time when many fellow officers ruminated about a possible imminent war with Britain, these admirals heralded the imminent Anglo-German alliance as an "enormous success" and triumphant result of the previous German pursuit of maritime force. Even Tirpitz, who had originally suspected foul play on Haldane's part, accepted this view for a moment, if grudgingly.[129]

When subsequent Anglo-German interactions proved this assessment wrong, these officers wrote off the "Haldane mission" as a British attempt to throw a wrench into German naval expansion on the occasion of the upcoming Naval Bill of 1912. Still, the entire episode affirmed the belief that the British would eventually accept German global power. "England must and will come towards us," declared Eduard von Capelle in the fall of 1912 when he cast an "agreement" with Britain as the likely outcome of current Anglo-German tensions.[130]

Until that moment, however, Tirpitz and others argued, only the determined pursuit of force coupled with expressions of an iron will were bound to leave an impression on hard-nosed British policy makers. "Our behavior: to show a cold shoulder and not run after England!" counseled Capelle in October 1912. "We have to let them come and not seek them out. They will come for sure," seconded Tirpitz a year later.[131] Any action smacking of weakness, by contrast, promised to stiffen the British desire to keep down the pesky German rival. Premature arms control treaties, colonial agreements, or even a formal entente would only smother Germany's global aspirations and create some sort of "Societas Leonina" (where the German Empire would be permanently subordinated to its British counterpart), unless, of course, they included a recognition of German sea power, a disavowal of the entire edifice of anti-German ententes, the promise of British neutrality in a European war, and, ideally, the conclusion of a robust treaty of alliance.[132]

Meanings of World War I

Tirpitz and other navy leaders ended up viewing World War I through the lens of Anglo-German antagonism. They cast the war as the product of this antagonism and related its origins to British pernicious intent toward Germany and its national industry. The British Empire appeared as Germany's chief opponent and the head of the enemy coalition. "The most inner origins of the current European war lie in England's wish to subjugate the strongest competitor on the European continent, if possible through political measures, if there is an opportunity, through war. To summarize this thought graphically, the cause of war resides in the City of London," explained Tirpitz in January 1915.[133] "Our main enemy is England," noted another admiral in the same year. "Its grim jealousy of our political and industrial development, of our ever-increasing trade and growth, started with the formation of the German Empire and grew from year to year, until the decision was reached to brutally destroy by war the newly-emerged rival and competitor on the world market, which could not be eliminated by superior business practices, by greater competence, industriousness and intelligence."[134]

This fantastical interpretation fell into place at the end of the "July Crisis," after it had become clear that the British Empire would enter the upcoming big-power war on the side of France and Russia. Until the end of July, navy leaders had not assumed that Britain would take part in a possible war.[135] In fact, on August 1, Tirpitz joined the emperor and the imperial chancellor in a futile effort to stop the invasion of Luxembourg and Belgium to ensure British neutrality.[136]

This interpretation, then, expanded on previous thinking about the Anglo-German antagonism, a self-contained thinking that had always favored simple truths. Images of the British Empire as intent on eliminating the German rival, if necessary by means of war, had permeated the navy's discourse since the late 1890s. By the fall of 1911, the idea of a British-led war of coalition against Germany had entered the navy's collective imagination. A year later, Tirpitz predicted "that within the foreseeable future we will either come to war or to an agreement with England."[137] Subsequently, the Germans had little doubt that the British were fostering geopolitical tensions on the continent and accelerating the drift toward war, without necessarily wanting to get involved directly. In June 1914, Tirpitz conjured the specter of a British Empire driving its German and Russian counterparts into a "great continental war."[138]

The view of World War I as a direct outgrowth of British enmity charged the navy's analysis of the British Empire and the direction of the German pursuit of global power with new, aggressive meanings. The British had raised the stakes by committing themselves irrevocably to the idea of eliminating the hated German rival by force, either through all-out victory in the current war, or, if necessary, through subsequent armed confrontation(s), in analogy to the model of the Punic wars in classical antiquity. Thus German global power required, at one point, a decisive victory against the British Empire, and possibly the United States. As the war unfolded, the long-standing goal of recognition as a coeval world power, of making Germany into what Tirpitz in the fall of 1915 called a "co-determining force in world affairs,"[139] took on a new self-transformative emphasis. The idea of a cataclysmic German-British showdown entailed visions of German global power and the subjugation of the British Empire beyond the previous (limited) quest for equality.[140]

The interpretation of World War I as the product of the Anglo-German rivalry reflected the rigid worldview of the Wilhelmine naval elite. But it was not its preserve. Viewing the war through this lens and the British Empire as an instigator fit well with U.S. naval officers' outlook on global politics. As the General Board explained in July 1915, the current conflict resembled a "world-wide war, where England and Germany contend for industrial and commercial supremacy in the markets of the world."[141] According to Rear-Admiral Austin Knight, the war had resulted from Anglo-German "commercial rivalry," from that "wide-spread and growing conflict of material interests out of which war was bound to come, sooner or later."[142]

The Americans also went a step further. They invoked a long-standing British tradition of eliminating imperial rivals. Captain Henry Huse, the chief of staff of the Atlantic Fleet, declared in February 1915 that Britain had been "quite ready when a legitimate excuse [was] offered to meet Germany in the present war," committed as "she" was to the "ambition to retain and extend the commercial supremacy on the seas she has held for two centuries."[143] "Four great powers have arisen in the world to compete with Great Britain for commercial supremacy on the seas—Spain, Holland, France, and Germany. Each one of these in succession has been defeated by Great Britain and her fugitive allies," summarized a group of naval planners in November 1918.[144]

Such thinking framed talk about future Anglo-American conflict that came to permeate the discourse of naval planners when they contemplated first the possibility and then the reality of German defeat. According to Huse, there was "no reason to believe that the United States as a commercial rival would receive any different treatment" from Britain than Germany.[145] In July 1915, the General Board stated that the United States needed to be prepared to take on either one of the victors of the war.[146] "A fifth commercial power, the greatest one yet, is now arising to compete for at least commercial equality with Great Britain," read the planning document from November 1918. "Already the signs of jealousy are visible. Historical precedent warns us to watch closely the moves we make or permit to be made."[147] Strikingly, in 1915 and 1916, the U.S. Atlantic Fleet repeatedly simulated a war with Britain in its exercises.[148]

Although some high-ranking officers such as Admiral William Sims, the naval commander in Europe, and Captain William Pratt, the assistant chief of naval operations, were somewhat skeptical of such talk,[149] the emphasis on new Anglo-American antagonisms represented an important departure from the navy's prewar views of the British Empire. By the turn of the twentieth century, the British Empire had undergone a considerable transformation in the navy's geopolitical imagination. Whereas preparing for a war with Britain had occupied the attention of strategists before 1898, the British Empire had metamorphosed into a friendly power and potential partner of the United States.[150] Admiral Taylor expressed the emerging consensus well when he wrote, in 1899, "that for a generation to come the relations of this country with England will be those of friends, if not of allies."[151]

Favorable views of the British Empire fed off many considerations. They involved the recognition that the empire's policy makers had recognized U.S. claims for preponderance in the Western Hemisphere and accepted U.S. expansion in 1898–99 after playing a supportive role during the Spanish-American War.[152] The Open Door and opposition to Russia's territorial expansionism marked common interests in the Far East.[153] More important, the British and U.S. empires had a shared interest vis-à-vis Germany, as Mahan never grew tired of explaining.[154] And generally speaking, to the Americans the British Empire was simply not an aggressive imperial power on the move; if at all, it faced the problems of overextension.[155]

This view of the British Empire as a friendly power was also an exercise in Anglo-Saxonism, the racial ideology that had provided a foundation for much of the diplomatic rapprochement between the United States and Great Britain around 1900.[156] Allusions to the existence of a common Anglo-American "race," culture, and politics, undergirded by what one admiral called "ties of blood," were a staple in naval circles.[157] The most eloquent writer on this subject was of course Mahan. A relentless emphasis on the unity of the "race loosely called Anglo-Saxon" grounded his plea for an Anglo-American community of interest and active partnership. According to him, this unity rested in part on "common tongue and common descent" and the "working of kinship"; ultimately it was embodied in a "common inherited political tradition and habit of thought," involving a "particular type of political freedom, of aptitude for self-government, and of tenacious adherence to recognized law—by which alone freedom and self-government consist with orderly progress."[158]

Nevertheless, the navy's view of the British Empire had always remained ambiguous. Although strategists looked favorably at the British Empire in their considerations of international politics and military competition in the present, they were still wedded to a view of Britain—both in the present and even more so in the future—as a premier rival engaged in the struggle for commercial supremacy.[159] Although economic competition did not translate into any direct imperial conflict in the present, it raised questions about the future (and also qualified any argument that transatlantic economic entanglement made for Anglo-American cordiality).[160] The emphasis on parallel interests and the absence of open policy agreements remained circumscribed by a belief in the primacy of selfish national interest in a world of fierce interimperial competition. Talk about a natural alliance between the two empires never blossomed into concrete policy. In fact, the Anglo-Japanese alliance became a source of major irritation after 1906–07, as planners contemplated the possibility of British assistance for Japanese war pursuits in the Pacific.[161]

The navy's official war plan against Germany, completed in 1913, brought into focus the presence of skeptical attitudes toward the British Empire on the eve of World War I. "History shows," its authors declared, "that trade rivalry brought about the successive humiliation of Holland,

France and Spain by Great Britain. The three great competitors for the world's trade are now the United States, Great Britain and Germany. Following the teachings of all history, two of them must in the sequel be practically subordinated to the third." In the present, the British Empire had considerable interest in a military showdown between Germany and the United States, for it could enhance its position in the struggle "for the world's trade," if it "stood aloof, suffering from no war exhaustion and husbanding her resources." There was even the possibility that the British Empire could enter an American-German war on the side of the German Empire. Both empires would share an animus against the "pretensions of the Monroe Doctrine" and U.S. control of the Panama Canal, regardless of any previous British acceptance of U.S. claims to preponderance in the Western Hemisphere and full control of the Caribbean.[162]

In short, the reading of World War I as a product of Anglo-German rivalry coupled with allusions to a possible British turn against the United States as the next major rival resonated with prewar thinking. It also directly echoed German views, laying bare the fundamental commonalities that underwrote the two naval elites' views of international politics. These navalists moved within a common intellectual universe when they offered views of big powers and their confrontations over empire in the new milieu of global power in the early twentieth century.

Chapter 3

Maritime Force, Threat, and War

In his history of the war at sea, published in 1906, Vice-Admiral (ret.) Curt von Maltzahn, the former director of the German Naval War College, the Marineakademie, wrote that an "armed peace" characterized the "state community of naval powers" in the current age. "As war aims at the imposition of peace on our terms, so the armed peace desires to provide for the means of war in such strength and war preparedness that the enemy, that is the state with which we have come into a conflict of interest, will remain in peace on our conditions."[1] Maltzahn was only one among many observers who felt the need to use a number of metaphors such as "armed peace" or "dry war" to describe how maritime militarization blurred the distinctions between war and peace. After 1945 historians could not help but notice the parallels between the decades before 1914 and their own troubled times. They found it fitting to apply the contemporary term "cold war" to capture the essence of the pre–First World War approach to diplomacy as it had been fashioned by navalists.[2]

The relentless accumulation of maritime force grounded navalist strategies of world power and their militarizing approach to big-power diplomacy. German and U.S. naval elites emphasized the balance of (military) force, as opposed to the balance of power broadly speaking. They committed themselves to a competitive arms buildup, that is, to the drive for margins of superiority within equations of comparative naval strength. Arms races became a substitute for war and armaments the key currency of great-power politics. The pursuit of maritime force appeared synonymous with what Alfred von Tirpitz once referred to as "methodical" *Weltpolitik,* pursuit of global power.[3]

The quest for a maritime arms buildup proceeded along the same paths in each country. The two naval elites devised and tenaciously pursued massive long-run building programs to attain first-rate navies second only, if at all, to the Royal Navy. Making a run for global power, these maritime militarists contemplated, in a single-minded fashion, the possibility of war and the prospects of their nations as world powers through the lens of the shifting balance of force, and they directly related imperial intent to military capability. In fact, in each country, the pursuit of maritime force remained a tenuous geopolitical proposition. Unfolding naval expansion catapulted the two navies to the forefront of any calculations of sea power, yet a position of superior strength eluded the two national communities of naval strategists. A sense of never-ending vulnerability surrounded navalists' bids for maritime force.

The German Naval Program

Naval programs were at the heart of the two navies' efforts to remake their respective countries into premier sea powers and, thus, self-reliant global powers. Future force levels were established to create battle fleets powerful enough to measure up well against probable opponents and to assure, if at all possible, margins of superiority in the overall balance of military strength. These programs aimed at the creation of homogenous battle fleets over a long period of time; yet they were also flexible enough to incorporate the dramatic changes in capital ship construction after 1906 and allow for shifting ideas about the number, makeup, and type of smaller vessels (such as torpedo boats, destroyers, and submarines).

As far as these fixed naval programs were concerned, the German navy set the tone at the turn of the twentieth century. The Naval Bills of 1898 and 1900 codified the future size of the German navy and laid out a course of massive naval expansion aiming at the creation of a navy second only to the British. Doubling the battle fleet envisioned by its predecessor, the 1900 Naval Bill set the future size of the German fleet at thirty-eight battleships, fourteen large cruisers, and thirty-eight small cruisers, to be effective in 1917 and organized around two double squadrons of sixteen battleships each. But this bill was never intended as a final word. As Volker Berghahn has documented, the navy's policy makers settled, by 1900, on a plan to build a navy of some sixty large ships, battleships, and large cruisers over the next twenty years, based on an annual construction rate of three ships per year. Mandatory replacement after twenty years of service would then provide for permanence.[4]

In 1903, naval planners offered a definition of the maximum goal of naval expansion that went even further. Projecting a continuous annual construction rate of three capital ships into the 1920s and a replacement period for them of thirty years, Harald Dähnhardt, of the Imperial Naval Office, laid out plans for the next round of naval legislation that aimed at the eventual creation of a third double squadron of battleships. This was a proposition for a fleet of about sixty battleships and twenty large cruisers by the late 1920s, as a direct extension of the plans for a sixty-ship fleet envisioned for the end of the previous decade. Its completion was defined as the "final goal" beyond which there was no further need for any additional naval increase or bill.[5]

The "idée fixe" of the entire program was a German-British force ratio in capital ships of 2:3.[6] The pursuit of this quantitative relation drove the entire buildup from the beginning, when that ratio stood at 1:3, according to German estimates. The notion of a future fleet of sixty capital ships rested on the expectation that such a fleet would face a British force of no more than ninety such ships, an expectation that was clearly stated in 1900.[7] Accordingly, the plans for an armada of eighty capital ships to be completed in the late 1920s assumed that it would face a British fleet in the North Sea amounting to not much more than one and a half times the German strength.[8] Significantly, the dramatic change in capital ship construction in 1905–06, which rendered previous battleships obsolete, did not change the 2:3 calculus. Providing Germany with a "new start," the change only raised the hope of securing the coveted force ratio in a more expedited manner.[9] His country's naval program, a key figure in the Imperial Naval Office explained in October 1910, "requires maintenance of a particular ratio to the English fleet," which would be 2:3. This requirement would be met once sixty capital ships were "available and war-ready."[10] A ratio of 2:3 represented the "raison d'être" of his entire naval policy, declared Tirpitz a year later when he suggested making public a commitment to this "quantitative relationship to the mightiest sea power," which, previously, had to be kept hidden.[11]

It was within this framework that the navy's policy makers approached the issue of an arms agreement with Britain, which was explored after 1908 by imperial chancellors Bülow and Bethmann-Hollweg, and most of the civilian foreign policy elite, in an effort to improve Anglo-German relations.[12] Tirpitz torpedoed any agreement that would codify too substantive a British numerical superiority in capital ships, let alone reduce the number of ships provided for in the Naval Bill of 1900 or its 1906 supplement, which had added six large cruisers. The navy leadership demanded the conclusion of an agreement based on a 2:3 ratio in capital ships, in terms of both ongoing construction and ultimate numbers. Moreover, Tirpitz and others combined this demand with an insistence on a continuous building rate of three capital ships per year.[13] In 1910–11, such insistence took on special meanings as it entailed, much to the chagrin of British policy makers, a commitment to the submission of another Naval Bill in 1912, when, according to previous bills, the building tempo would drop to a rate of two capital ships a year.[14] Tirpitz stuck to his line in the winter of 1911–12 when the British and the German imperial chancellor made a final substantive effort to reach an agreement in view of the looming Naval Bill of 1912.[15]

The Imperial Naval Office did not abandon its commitment to a 2:3 ratio when, in the spring of 1913, Tirpitz publicly announced a willingness to accept a force ratio of 10:16 as proposed by Winston Churchill, the head of the British Admiralty. Tirpitz only accepted a 10:16 force ratio in the shape of a 5:8 ratio of entire battleship squadrons, as opposed to single ships, the metric proposed by the British (who also did not want to count battleships deployed in non-European waters). Tirpitz's metric was a meaningless proposal because the Anglo-German arms competition was not simply a matter of adding entire battleship squadrons to the existing force. Moreover, Tirpitz purposively left out battle cruisers from his force equation.[16]

The investment in a force ratio of 2:3 did not prevent Tirpitz from openly suggesting more advantageous terms. When first confronted with the idea of an Anglo-German naval agreement in the winter of 1908–09, Tirpitz countered his chancellor's suggestion to slow down capital ship construction with a proposal to conclude a ten-year arms control agreement with Britain prescribing an annual Anglo-German building ratio of 4:3 capital ships.[17] In the summer of 1909, Tirpitz expressed an interest in an arms settlement that would have prescribed an annual construction rate of 3:2 over five years, yet due to previous naval construction it would have resulted in a force ratio of 4:3 among Dreadnought-type capital ships at the end of the time period.[18] But such proposals were short-lived, and each time, Tirpitz recognized that they stood no chance of acceptance by the British.

The German program served a clear purpose. It was to create a navy strong enough "to pose a genuine military challenge to Britain," to quote Volker Berghahn, the historian who first documented this.[19] More specifically, the completed battle fleet was to have a real fighting chance in a defensive war against the Royal Navy in the North Sea. According to the navy's military wisdom, any battle fleet required a numerical superiority of at least one third to engage in offensive warfare and exercise "command of the sea" in the face of an opposing fleet.[20] The coveted 2:3 ratio created a military capability to secure what Tirpitz and others called a "real defensive chance"; it allowed the completed German fleet "to conduct a defensive war against England with some promise of success," as Tirpitz wrote in 1909.[21] When, in 1903, a planner outlined a scheme for an eighty-capital-ship fleet he too articulated this consensus: such a fleet would make it impossible, he wrote, for the British "to strike a successful blow against Germany and impose a successful blockade," thus ruling out "an attack by England."[22]

The program was not a prescription for a war of aggression against Britain, which, by the Germans' own estimates, required a numerically superior fleet. Providing military safety against Britain, the completed navy was imagined as a defensive military deterrent that, in turn, could nonetheless also act as a geopolitical lever against Britain. As Tirpitz promised his emperor in 1899, the desired fleet would compel Britain not to attack Germany and thus concede to it enough "maritime power (*Seegeltung*)" as to enable it to pursue a "great overseas policy."[23]

The program was premised on a series of additional assumptions about British and German capabilities and behavior. Most important, planners assumed in 1900 that the British would be incapable of matching the German construction program and maintaining, in the long run, a numerical superiority of more than 3:2. Within this context, Tirpitz and his aides pointed to the tremendous financial expenses and the available shipbuilding facilities.[24] As importantly, there was the personnel issue. Unlike Germany, Britain had no draft, and thus it would never be able to muster enough manpower to man more ships. The "difficulties of the appropriate enlargement of active and reserve personnel constitutes the main limiting force," one planning document stated in 1903.[25]

The German program also rested on geopolitical calculations. According to its promoters, the British Empire could not amass its entire fleet against Germany in the North Sea because of its worldwide strategic interests and, particularly, its antagonistic relationship to Russia and its French ally. The North Sea would constitute the British Empire's "weakest point" from a geostrategic point of view.[26] Confronted with the increasing concentration of the British fleet in home waters and the formation of political alliances among France, Russia, and Britain, the Germans did not fully change their views on this issue. By 1908, they began to argue that British military concentration against Germany could only be a temporary measure. For geopolitical reasons, Admiral Capelle explained in October 1912, Britain could not afford to continue the "amassing of its armed forces in the North Sea" because the empire would otherwise give up "voluntarily" and "in peacetime" its "position of supremacy in the rest of the world."[27]

After the outbreak of war in 1914, Tirpitz claimed on a number of occasions that his ultimate goal all along had been to attain naval parity with Great Britain. In a letter from August 31, 1914, Tirpitz presented the construction of "a fleet equally strong as Britain's" as the "natural and only goal" of previous German policy, but which could not have been disclosed in the past decades.[28] In December 1915, the navy secretary told the chief of the Admiralty Staff that the "risk theory" (the public rationale for the buildup since 1900, according to which the completed German fleet would remain inferior enough to meet certain defeat in a war with Britain) had merely been a "political phrase," and that Germany "could only slowly attain an equally strong fleet, through time and money."[29] In 1915, the quest for full naval parity with Britain became the official goal in planning for a postwar period, only to be abandoned, by 1916, in favor of the idea of a "smaller battle fleet" of some forty big ships and a vast submarine fleet.[30]

But Tirpitz's wartime claims as to his long-standing intent (which have been echoed by historian Paul Kennedy[31]) should not be taken at face value. To be sure, on a few occasions Tirpitz gestured toward naval parity with Britain.[32] Still, such rhetoric did not have any bearing on actual naval expansion, as planners consistently identified a force ratio of 2:3 as their goal. Moreover, the entire calculus toward the British Empire did not depend at all on parity: a fleet of about two thirds of the strength of the British could act as a defensive deterrent against Britain and thus do its geopolitical work for a German Empire aspiring to become a world power. Judged by their own military estimates and geopolitical calculations, there was no reason for Tirpitz or his collaborators to be specially invested in creating a "navy second to none."[33]

Whether they believed that, in some distant future, Germany could acquire a fleet on par with the British, or superior to it, is a different, and moot, question. Maritime buildups, Tirpitz and others liked to insist, took time. Armies could be raised within a short period of time; fleets were the "work of a generation." The question of whether one would want to eventually create an "offensive fleet," an *Offensivflotte,* that is, create a navy superior to the British, Tirpitz explained in 1905, "could be entirely bracketed for the time being." But "such a change of our naval policy if it were to be viewed as appropriate," could only be introduced at "that moment in time when a defensive fleet was actually afloat."[34]

U.S. Naval Expansion

Like the Germans, U.S. naval officers proposed long-range schemes of naval expansion that were tailored to the demands of threat and deterrence. By the late 1890s, a chorus of voices emerged that demanded a more definite building policy and laid out possible numbers.[35] After the turn of the century, the General Board, the navy's new strategic agency, developed a building program that surpassed its German counterpart in numerical terms. In 1903, the board committed itself to the goal of creating a fleet of forty-eight battleships and a requisite number of lesser vessels and auxiliaries to be completed by 1919. The goal of a forty-eight battleship fleet became the focal point of the navy's official building policy in subsequent years; it provided the base for annual building recommendations, regardless of the dramatic changes in capital-ship construction or geopolitical orientation (as evidenced by the rise of Japan as a probable enemy); and it anchored the discussion about appropriate age limits for commissioned ships (which culminated in the decision, reached in 1910, to follow German practice and seek the mandatory replacement of any capital ships after twenty years of service). On the eve of World War I, on July 1, 1914, the General Board once more affirmed its call for forty-eight battleships.[36]

Planners clung to their ideas about a forty-eight battleship navy in the face of considerable opposition among civilian policy makers. Originally, the General Board had envisioned an annual building tempo of two battleships to provide for the desired fleet in 1919. Yet subsequently, the General Board revised these numbers upward, as Congress consistently authorized fewer ships than the agency wanted, providing, on average, about half of the ships sought by the navy between 1904 and 1908. Beginning in the fall of 1907, the board consistently recommended the new construction of four battleships each year. Eventually, the agency pushed back the completion date past the original date. In July 1914, 1923 was set as the year by which the fleet was to be completed.

The political obstacles the navy's policy makers encountered fueled a relentless focus on the construction of battleships. The General Board had originally emphasized the importance of large armored cruisers and envisioned an armada of twenty-four such cruisers to accompany its battleships. But, beginning with its recommendations for the Naval Act of 1905, the navy's strategists stopped asking for these ships and, eventually, dropped the cause of armored cruisers entirely, in favor of securing the highest possible number of battleships.[37] For the same reason, the General Board showed little or no interest in the battlecruisers when they emerged as a new sort of capital ship after 1906.[38]

The German naval program provided the point of reference for the General Board's drive for a forty-eight-battleship fleet. The Board's program expressed the desire to create a navy that would have a numerical edge on the emerging German fleet. The Americans closely studied the provisions and implementation of the German Naval Bills. As the General Board explained in July 1914, "it was to be prepared for any possible challenge from this [German] fleet ... that the number of 48 battleships necessary to our absolute security was fixed on; and the date of the completion of the German program in 1920 fixed the date when this fleet should be ready." On that occasion, the navy's planners went as far as to project German and U.S. force levels into the 1940s.[39]

In 1903, when the General Board settled on its official program, the will to match the German buildup had been the focal point of much thinking among naval strategists for some time. In October 1901, for example, Captain Charles D. Sigsbee, the head of the Office of Naval Intelligence, had proposed a building program "to keep pace with the authorized increase of the German navy."[40] Between 1900 and 1903, the General Board and the Board on Construction (another board that made suggestions for annual naval increases) consistently recommended the annual authorization of more battleships and large cruisers than provided by the German Naval Bills of 1898 and 1900.[41] By 1900, officers no longer measured the desired U.S. naval strength in relation to the portions of (unnamed) European fleets that could be employed in American waters, as they had done in the previous years.

The American program was a function of its German counterpart. The projected forty-eight battleships would give a clear margin of numerical superiority over the German fleet, estimated at about forty battleships. In

1903, the General Board turned down proposals to fix the future size of the battle force at either thirty-six or forty-two battleships. On the other hand, the number fell short of the conclusions of a study by the Naval War College in 1903 about the desirability of attaining a 50 percent superiority over the German fleet to compensate for Germany's advantageous strategic position, defined by its ability to strike either in the Atlantic or Pacific at its own discretion.[42]

The exact number of forty-eight battleships struck a chord for another reason. This number was good politics, for it promised a battleship for each state of the union. Suggestions to make the number of battleships congruent to that of the states were a staple among naval officers after the turn of the twentieth century. In fact, during the meeting of the General Board that approved the number of forty-eight battleships, two members favored "recommending a gradual increase in the number of battleships until we have one for each state in the Union."[43] The number forty-eight accommodated such a wish. In 1903, the United States had forty-five states and three territories that were commonly believed to be destined for eventual statehood. It was no coincidence that the General Board supported the idea of naming all battleships, and only battleships, after the states.[44]

The desire to keep pace with ongoing German naval expansion colored the General Board's subsequent pursuit of its program. Concerns about developing German-American force differentials lent special flavor to the frustration of naval planners over their civilian policy makers' limited embrace of their demands. At a time when the transition to "Dreadnoughts" rendered previous battleships obsolete, the pace of naval construction continued unabated and then quickened in Germany, whereas in the United States authorization of new ships slowed down. Between 1908 and 1911, Germany began the construction of twice as many capital ships as the United States (sixteen versus eight). In response, the General Board issued one clarion call after another for accelerated naval construction "to meet the increased power of the German fleet."[45] By 1912, the General Board drew up a special "emergency program" to bring the U.S. fleet up to the strength of thirty-two capital ships of the new Dreadnought type by 1920, when the Germans were expected to field thirty-nine comparable ships.[46]

From the vantage point of 1903, the naval program devised by the General Board held out great promise. It promised enough force to deal with the German Empire. But the creation of a fleet of forty-eight battleships also promised to meet the demands of threat and deterrence in the Far East both before and after Japan's emergence as a probable opponent. After 1906, close attention to the Japanese maritime buildup became an integral feature of any discussions of construction policy. Planners were mesmerized by the geopolitical challenges posed by the Japanese Empire; yet it was also clear that their existing program would ensure the maintenance of a fleet that could outgun the Japanese by a wide margin. Facing the specter of Japanese-American conflict, the General Board clung to prior ideas about the ultimate size of the navy until World War I.[47]

Still, the emergence of Japan as the United States's probable adversary alongside Germany introduced a powerful logic that pointed beyond the existing program. The double challenge the United States faced suggested the desirability of some sort of two-power standard in relation to the German and Japanese navies. By 1907, the planners at the General Board suggested that the best way to deal with this challenge was the creation of a fleet so powerful that it could be safely divided between the two oceans and still project sufficient military power in each of them.[48] By 1910, the agency openly argued that the "combined strength of the German and Japanese fleets" represented a yardstick for the annual pace of naval construction.[49] Yet prior to World War I the board stopped short of arguing for numerical parity as the appropriate expression of such a two-power standard, nor did it challenge the goal of a fleet of forty-eight battleships, which was bound to fall short of such parity due to the sheer size of the developing German and Japanese navies.

Officers at the Naval War College were less circumspect in their discussion of the appropriate strength, even as they paid lip service to the forty-eight-ship program as a proposition for the present. The conference of officers that gathered at the college in 1907 argued that the United States should have a Pacific fleet "decidedly superior to that of Japan" and, in addition, an Atlantic fleet "equal to that of Germany."[50] In 1910 and 1911, officer committees envisioned a future navy composed of separate fleets in the Pacific and Atlantic, each stronger "than any probable adversary" in each body of water.[51] Only in 1912 did the officer conference criticize the position taken in previous years as "more drastic than the conditions justify," suggesting instead that parity with the German navy was sufficient.[52]

Arguments for a "two-ocean" navy were driven by the assumption that the United States needed to simultaneously project military strength against both Germany and Japan. The double challenge raised by these empires raised troubling questions in part because of the separateness of these two maritime regions (a problem the much-anticipated completion of the transisthmian Panama canal promised to alleviate); yet it also did so because in the minds of naval planners it raised the possibility of some sort of simultaneous German-Japanese action (a problem the completion of the canal would not solve). The expectation that if one of the two powers was involved in a conflict with the United States the other was likely to turn against the United States became a staple among planners. The officers at the Naval War College predicted in 1909 that Japan and Germany would support each other by "benevolent neutrality, if not by more positive methods."[53] The General Board warned on many occasions that "the existence of an issue between the United States and one of them would give the other an opportunity to press its own claim."[54] Rear-Admiral Fiske put it more bluntly in 1911: "If either country should consider itself compelled to declare war," he wrote, "the other could not possibly be so blind to her opportunity as not to declare war simultaneously."[55] The nightmare of some sort of concurrent Japanese-German action haunted strategists by the 1910s, regardless of the absence of any direct evidence supporting this prediction.

The naval program the General Board had devised was of a more transient nature for another reason. From the beginning, long-term visions of naval preeminence permeated the navy's discourse, driven by the sense that the United States was a rising world power, with superior levels of national production. Rear-Admiral Taylor hit that note in 1903 when he wrote that "providence seems to have ordained that the world's history for many centuries shall be strongly affected by ... the American navy; by the quality of the weapon which the great republic wields in its imperial path of progress and development."[56] In 1905, the article chosen as the annual prize essay by the U.S. Naval Institute made the case that the U.S. Navy should ultimately be "larger than Great Britain's" as "national greatness and naval greatness co-exist."[57] As the "richest and most advanced nation," the United States needed a big navy "at least equal to that of another nation," suggested another officer in response to this essay.[58] When, in 1909, planners at the Naval War College pinpointed the future need for two separate, self-contained fleets, a "strong" one in the Atlantic and a "paramount" one in the Pacific, they noted that the United States would "then be at the zenith of her power and will control the world."[59]

It was therefore no surprise that after the outbreak of war in Europe 1914 the General Board revised its building policy. In July 1915, the board abandoned its previous program in favor of a numerically open-ended policy to build a fleet that should "ultimately be equal to the most powerful maintained by any other nation of the world," and it set 1925 as the target date by which that goal was to be attained.⁶⁰ The one dissenting officer wanted his navy to become the most powerful in the world.⁶¹ This decision formalized what the members of the General Board had come to agree upon ever since the beginning of war in Europe. In September 1914, the General Board had reached a "consensus opinion" in favor of "a Navy second to none" and made a recommendation to that effect to Navy Secretary Josephus Daniels. But Secretary Daniels had disapproved and asked his navy leaders to refrain from voicing this position in public.⁶² Accordingly, in the congressional hearings in the winter of 1914–15, senior officers such as Rear-Admirals Frank Fletcher (who commanded the Atlantic Fleet) and Charles Badger (who acted as the official representative of the General Board) emphasized that they did not want parity with Britain.⁶³

The new policy set in the summer of 1915 was a natural culmination of previous thinking under the conditions of an ongoing world war. Its explicit premise was that the United States needed to muster enough maritime force to engage on its own, that is, without any reliance on support from other big powers in a vigorous postwar politics of military threat and deterrence. The primary object of this politics would be both the war's main winner, most likely Germany but perhaps Britain, and, of course, the Japanese Empire, the power that was likely to seek cooperation with the war's winner. The new policy formulated in the summer of 1915 anchored the subsequent thinking and building recommendations of naval planners.⁶⁴

Yet the goal of parity with the world's largest navy did not remain the final word. Over time, planners developed a different metric when they defined desirable force levels. Expanding on previous thinking about the double challenge posed by the German and Japanese empires, they promoted, by 1917, a multipower standard according to which their navy needed to match up well against the combined German-Japanese fleets in the future.⁶⁵ As German defeat became a reality, considerations of parity with Britain moved to center stage. When this shift happened, references to the possibility of future Anglo-Japanese cooperation against the United States suggested yet another two-power standard. In September 1918, the General Board championed the completion of a future fleet of sixty-one capital ships that, according to its own estimates, about equaled the current combined capital-ship strength of the British and Japanese navies, set at sixty-two.⁶⁶ In short, by the end of the war, the pursuit of parity with the world's mightiest fleet no longer encompassed all the ambitions of strategists, driven as they were by the relentless logic of their thinking about global politics and America's place within it.

The Making of a Panic

German and U.S. navalist discourse set the promise of national military power against the specter of geopolitical confrontations between big powers over empire. Intensely aware of the ever-shifting balance of force and their country's own specific geopolitical interests, the two naval elites did not aggressively clamor for a big-power war. In fact, in each country the navies' policy makers were prone to "war scares" and extensive expressions of grave concerns about military inequities that were unfavorable, in the present or near future, to their own nation as a developing world power. It was left to the Germans, by the mid 1910s, to start to panic over the very prospects of their pursuit of maritime force and global power. U.S. naval elites, too, grew increasingly alarmed over an alleged lack of military strength on the part of their country. Their concerns acquired a distinct urgency in response to the coming of a big-power war in Europe. Yet such alarmism stopped short of any existential panic, as the service's policy makers made the case for a rapid military buildup in relation to postwar geopolitics.

A sense of continuing vulnerability set the tone for the German maritime arms buildup throughout the entire prewar period. From the vantage point of 1900, the German naval program promised self-sustaining military power and almost unbounded imperial opportunity. Yet until its completion, Germany remained highly vulnerable as it was traversing what Tirpitz called a maritime "danger zone."[67] During this span of time the expanding German fleet remained weak enough that it could be destroyed by a vastly superior, and willing, British navy. More so, such weakness made for a period of acute risk, for it invited a military strike to discard the pesky German challenger at no substantial peril to Britain itself. So invested was Tirpitz in the notion of a "danger zone" that he counseled a policy of geopolitical restraint during the period of the initial buildup. "The gaining of time and naval buildup," argued Tirpitz, would be in Germany's interest as it was supposed to exercise imperial moderation and sit out the "danger zone."[68]

By its own estimates, the Wilhelmine navy failed to leave behind the "danger zone" it had officially entered with the Naval Bill of 1900. In February 1905, the Imperial Naval Office suggested that the next five years represented the "main danger zone."[69] By 1909, Tirpitz insisted that the danger zone would stretch out another five to six years before it came to an end.[70] In the following years, he and other senior officers identified on several occasions the years 1914 and 1915 as the moment when their fleet would be ready for a war with Britain. They did so while disagreeing over whether there was any acute risk of an imminent British war against Germany.[71]

The years 1914 and 1915 were cast as a key moment of transition for several reasons. The German-British force ratio as measured in Dreadnought battleships and battlecruisers was in the process of nearing the coveted 2:3 ratio by that time, with the British numerical advantage slightly above that ratio.[72] The German fleet was also bound to reach a new level of operational readiness by then, because it could then field three full squadrons of post-1906 capital ships and an entire squadron of battlecruisers. The projected completion of fortifications at Heligoland and Wilhelmshaven promised to improve Germany's maritime position as well. More important, there was the scheduled completion of the massive expansion of the Kaiser Wilhelm Canal in 1914. The expansion of this waterway, which allowed for the movement of the fleet's ships between the North and Baltic seas, had begun in 1907 in response to the recognition that the capital ships built after 1906 were too large to pass the canal as it existed.[73]

Still, the claims about war readiness in 1914–15 should not be taken at face value. Navy leaders remained deeply aware of the limits of the navy's wartime capabilities. In fact, in April 1914 Tirpitz suggested that it would take many more years to prepare the fleet for war.[74] The existing force ratio, which fell short of 2:3, hardly assured victory. The specter of defeat still loomed on the horizon, as the operational planning, fleet exercise, and wargaming the navy engaged in between 1912 and 1914 made painstakingly clear.[75] Allusions to the mid-1910s as the moment of war readiness always served a clear instrumental purpose. They were part of stalling tactics that Tirpitz and other navy leaders used to fend off the General Staff's gathering talk about the desirability, in the present, of a big-power war.[76]

Moreover, any talk about the end of the "danger zone" remained bounded by another consideration. By its own estimates, the navy could not win a war against Britain. Even in the best case, that of a successful defense against a British fleet imposing a blockade and seeking battle, the navy still lacked any capability to impose its will on Britain. On the navy's own terms, any war readiness attained in 1914–15 (or later) did not turn a war with Britain into an attractive proposition.

Prior to 1914, the Wilhelmine navy's leadership did not advocate a big-power war, which, in its view, was bound to include Britain. With considerable consistency, Tirpitz and other navy leaders counseled against any big-power war in the present, or any aggressive diplomacy that risked it. In the crises of 1904–05 and 1908, when parts of the German political and army leadership contemplated a major European war, the admirals were not interested, consumed as they were by the specter of certain defeat in a war with Britain.[77] In the summer of 1911, the navy secretary and other senior officers were critical of the policy of brinkmanship pursued by Secretary of State Alfred von Kiderlen-Wächter in the context of the Second Morocco Crisis, and spoke out against any policy that bore the risk of a war with Britain, which the navy could simply not afford at the moment.[78] When confronted with talk about Germany's interest in initiating a big-power war on the Continent in early December 1912, the navy secretary demurred once more, insisting that the navy was not ready for war.[79]

In July 1914, Tirpitz and other high-ranking officers did not take a front seat in the decision making that paved the road to war. The civilian leadership of the Empire under Chancellor Bethmann-Hollweg was responsible for the policy of brinkmanship that aimed at a local Balkans war and a devastating diplomatic defeat of the Entente while self-consciously risking a big European war.[80] Still, this time around, Tirpitz and other service leaders willingly accepted a big-power war that involved British participation, after they had not striven to prevent this possibility from developing, as they had in previous years. The biggest concern for the navy's policy makers had not been the prevention of a major European war (as opposed to a "local" war in the Balkans) but rather the fear that the German and Austrian governments would suffer diplomatic defeat. The specter of "weakly backing down" haunted Tirpitz and others in late July, not the (high) probability of a continental war with France and Russia, let alone the possibility of British participation. Tirpitz and other leaders of the navy did not change course, as they began to confront the possibility of war on the last days of July.[81] Strikingly, on July 29, Tirpitz and other admirals responded angrily to Bethmann-Hollweg's suggestion to secure, in the future, British cooperation by offering a reduction of their naval program.[82]

The navy's acceptance of a big-power war that involved Britain was tied up in a sharp sense of crisis that had come to grip its policy makers. Their pursuit of maritime force had reached a critical moment. By spring 1914, Tirpitz and other navy leaders such as Georg Alexander von Müller, the head of the Naval Cabinet, openly talked about the impending "fiasco" of the entire previous naval policy and anticipated an imminent "declaration of bankruptcy."[83] They did so as they were facing up to the insight that their service might be losing the arms race with Britain.[84] While, after 1912, Britain was annually authorizing more than double the number of German capital ships and passing one massive naval budget after the other, the German naval budget, by contrast, was "cracking at the seams," to quote historian Michael Epkenhans.[85]

Such a sense of doom also fed off the recognition that the navy had lost its hold on the making of Germany's foreign and defense policy. Army leaders had reclaimed the priority of landed military power, supported by the chancellor, most of the foreign policy elite, the national public, and the political parties.[86] Strikingly, the making of the massive Army Bill of 1913 unfolded directly at the expense of new naval legislation. The Imperial Naval Office had to drop plans for a new Naval Bill, which was to raise more money and increase the current construction rate of capital ships to a tempo of three through an accelerated construction of battlecruisers.[87] "In general, this decision is of enormous importance," summarized one admiral; it would suggest the end of any real effort to "slowly catch up to England." From here forward, the navy would be reduced to "begging" for "charitable givings" from a "wallet" the army had first dibs on.[88]

An ever-deepening rift with the chancellor informed the navy's sense of doom. Bethmann-Hollweg's interest in better relations with Britain ran counter to the service's priorities. To the likes of Tirpitz, negotiations about an Anglo-German détente suggested that the chancellor wanted to sacrifice the navy for vapid promises of political cooperation or territorial gain and thus irretrievably compromise Germany's position as a global power.[89] Bethmann-Hollweg also fought tooth and nail against any demands for naval increases. He forced the navy to compromise on its Naval Bill in the winter of 1911–12 after he had previously spoken out against any new naval legislation to increase the fleet.[90] He thwarted the submission of another bill a year later, and continued to signal that he would not accept additional demands from the navy.[91] The task of catching up with the British through new armaments could not be met "with the current Imperial Chancellor," an exasperated Tirpitz noted in April 1914.[92]

While sparked by the adversarial situation the navy faced in 1913–1914, the sense of crisis was ultimately a product of previous thinking. At its center loomed the long-standing belief that Germany's entire destiny hinged upon successful military threat and deterrence against the British Empire. On the eve of World War I, it was such thinking that informed the constant exhortations of Tirpitz that "only permanent strength" in the shape of a powerful navy could prevent Germany's decline to a regional European power of limited political importance and industry.[93] The same belief system also underwrote the claim offered in April 1914 that only the "pressure on England" generated by the "presence of our fleet" prevented "grave conflict" among the existing alliances in Europe.[94]

In the summer of 1914, the navy secretary and his fellow planners did not have clear ideas as to what was to come next. At the end of April, Tirpitz identified two courses of action necessary to remain competitive with the British: a further "enlargement" of the fleet or "growth and inner consolidation" within the "existing framework" of legislation. He also noted that, from a political point of view, the first option was out of the question. But the other option was not a self-evident proposition either. It required new, massive taxation over the next few years. In May and June the navy secretary pursued this second option. Rebuffed by the chancellor and his finance secretary, Tirpitz did not simply give in.[95] In mid-June he decided to gear up for a fight, in the fall, over the entire issue of naval expansion with a chancellor who was likely, by Tirpitz's own estimate, to put his political future on the line over this issue.[96]

The impasse the navy reached in 1914 also bred another response among its leaders. This was a willingness to go to war. In an important speech to senior officers of the Imperial Naval Office in October 1913, Tirpitz raised this possibility as he reviewed the direction of Anglo-German relations and the implications of the most recent army bill. He argued that his country was at a crossroads, because it was falling behind in the arms race with Britain while the chancellor was seeking to give away the fleet at the negotiation table. The empire would be left with nothing other than a failed naval policy if it did not attain a navy strong enough to deter a British maritime strike against Germany. According to Tirpitz, "the question whether Germany should fight, if necessary, for its global position against England—with the high stakes that such a fight entails, or whether it should be content with the status of a second-rate European continental power [was] a matter of political conviction." It would be "more honorable for a great nation to fight for the highest goal and perhaps to go down instead of ingloriously renouncing the future."[97]

Such sentiment fed off previous existential talk. The pursuit of maritime force and global power had always been cast as a matter of life or death: Germany could either thrive as a great nation with global ambitions or languish and face rapid decline. Discursively, this left little space for any acceptance, without a fight, of the second possibility, the imagined ruin of Germany. As Tirpitz explained in October 1911, the German Empire had the choice "to either abdicate as a world power or take risks."[98] To consider a big-power war from this angle also resonated with premonitions of inevitable war that had become widespread in the 1910s. These premonitions involved talk about war as one possible direction in which Anglo-Germans relations were heading. They also developed around a more general sense of a larger drift toward war on the European continent (whether the British stoked the fire of rising tensions or not), which mobilized deep anxieties, expressed most vividly by army leaders, about the viability of the German Empire's continental power. Thus, in August 1914 navy leaders willingly entered a big-power war involving Britain without any firm belief that the navy could fend off the British fleet in the North Sea, let alone any plan to defeat the British Empire, a striking absence it shared with army strategists and civilian elites.

American Insecurities

Like the Germans, American strategists negotiated the promise of their naval programs with the realities of the day. Like them, they knew their own extended periods of maritime weakness and were subject to both expectations of imminent imperial transgressions by other powers and outright war panics. The pursuit of maritime force and global power did not translate into mongering for war. Such absence primarily fed off considerations of force ratios and military prospects, or the lack thereof. Yet it also reflected the particular configuration of imagined U.S. global interests and possible causes of war, with their emphasis on the reactive nature of any U.S. pursuit of war in response to imperial action by other powers in the Western Hemisphere or the Pacific.

After 1900, naval strategists were intensely aware of the limitations of U.S. maritime military capabilities in the present. In their estimate, the Germans held a clear military edge in the first few years of the new century.[99] During the same time period, the Americans had few illusions about the consequences of the limited U.S. military presence in the Far East that restricted their country to little more than the status of an interested bystander in Far Eastern big-power politics. The rise of Japan as a probable opponent after the Russo-Japanese War raised troubling questions as well. Before the completion of the Panama Canal, U.S. victory in a naval war with Japan remained a tenuous proposition at best.[100] After 1909, planners also faced a newly developing American-German disparity of force that once more raised dire questions as to the outcome of a war in the Atlantic. Considerations of possible parallel German and Japanese action against the

United States further compounded the sense of vulnerability that naval planners experienced by the 1910s.

Strategists recognized that the relative maritime weakness circumscribed America's options in the present. This was the case in relation to Open Door interests in China. Yet the lack of a commanding strength also affected claims to empire in the Western Hemisphere. Concerns over insufficient military capabilities led the General Board to advise its government to qualify the claim of preponderance in the Western Hemisphere. By the summer of 1901, the agency recommended a suspension of the Monroe Doctrine for sub-Amazonian South America, for it would be impossible "to maintain naval control by armed force beyond the Amazon" in a "war against any probable European enemy or coalition."[101] Although this was not taken up by the navy's civilian superiors in the White House, such a limitation remained a matter of subsequent discussion among naval officers, including Mahan, who repeatedly raised this possibility.[102]

Navy leaders did not clamor for war during the crisis in German-American relations over Venezuela in the winter of 1902–03.[103] The plans of the German government to use military force against the Venezuelan government in pursuit of debt collection raised alarm among strategists who already firmly believed that the Germans were intent on seeking territories for bases and colonies in the Americas. In response to the first official German communication concerning possible action against Venezuela in December 1901, the General Board promptly sent one of its officers on a special mission to Venezuela and began to prepare plans "for a sudden descent on the Spanish Main should this be necessary," as Admiral Taylor informed the White House in January 1902.[104] In the summer, Taylor and other navy leaders took other measures to increase the fleet's preparedness. Most important, they went ahead with existing plans for joint maneuvers of the battle forces of the Atlantic and European stations in the Caribbean, which had initially been made during the previous winter when the navy had received the first news about possible German intentions toward Venezuela. Simulating German-American war in its likely theater of war, these exercises took place off the island of Culebra in December 1902 and early January 1903, thus coinciding with the start of the Anglo-German naval blockade of Venezuela. Dewey, who was well known for his anti-German views, assumed command.[105]

Navy leaders engaged in military threat and deterrence in the winter of 1902–03. According to their analysis, impending German action in response to the Venezuelan debt crisis could result in the South American country's "complete political dependence" on Germany either through a cession of territory or financial control, unless, of course, the United States intervened, as Taylor explained.[106] The fleet maneuvers were meant to both improve the fleet's military-operational readiness and display strength against the Germans. The decision to keep the entire fleet assembled off the islands until early February assured a continuous naval presence until the diplomatic crisis was resolved. In late December, Taylor wrote his secretary that he was "pleased" that the presence of the fleet in the Caribbean would be a "convenience" to his administration "in discussing the Venezuelan situation."[107] In mid-December and then again in late January, when events on the diplomatic front reached critical turning points, navy leaders watched the situation with great tenseness. One officer who attended the meetings of the General Board in late January later suggested that these meetings had felt as if they had been taking place on the eve of war.[108]

Still, navy leaders were not eager for war. The main purpose of their show of force was to prevent the Germans from taking drastic action against Venezuela. The General Board tabled the issue of a German-American war at the end of January, as soon as it became clear that a diplomatic agreement between the United States and Germany had been reached.[109] More important, throughout 1902, Dewey, Taylor, and other planners offered the same dire analyses of the course of a hypothetical German-American war as they had in the previous year, when such a war scenario had been studied for the first time in a systematic fashion. When the General Board discussed the matter of a German-American war in late January 1903, one officer raised the specter of successful enemy action against Washington, D.C., itself.[110]

A strong sense of vulnerability underwrote the navy's two outright war panics before 1914. Taking place between the fall of 1906 and the summer of 1907 and again in the spring of 1913, these panics focused on the specter of military conflict with Japan. They followed the same pattern, as naval planners conjured the specter of imminent Japanese decisions for war and geared up for what they considered a war of self-defense in the Pacific. Far from self-confidently counseling war, strategists were disconcerted about the prospects of war. Displaying a defensive mind-set, they wanted to take immediate steps to prepare the navy for war and shore up Pacific lines of defense.

The war scare in the spring of 1913 brought the thinking of the U.S. naval elite into sharp focus.[111] The protests of the Japanese government against white nativist legislation in California prompted intense fears of war as strategists (and their army counterparts) believed that a Japanese attack on the Philippines and Hawaii could be imminent. "It looks as if the Japanese are determined to find a reason for declaring war on us," reasoned Admiral Dewey in late April. It would be "conceivable" that Japan "may conclude" or had "already concluded" that it should go to war and seize U.S. territories across the Pacific, Rear-Admiral Fiske explained at the height of the service's panic in early May. Fiske and other planners urged their government to take immediate action to put the navy on a war footing, including the concentration of all Pacific and Asian fleet units at either Hawaii or the Philippines and the readying of the Atlantic battle fleet for a transfer to the Pacific.[112] The navy pushed for such immediate war preparations at a time when the General Board had just completed the "strategic section" of its plan for a Pacific war. This work had once more underscored the dire prospects of a war with Japan in the present, that is, before the upcoming opening of the Panama Canal.[113]

The navy's war panic was both self-made and profound. Japanese diplomatic protests against nativist politics on the West Coast mobilized already-existing images of an expansionist Japan bent on imperial war in the Pacific. Ideological verities trumped other assessments, such as those offered by a U.S. naval attaché in Japan who suggested that most Japanese leaders did not want war.[114] So alarmed were Fiske and fellow planners in late April and May that their activism in making their case prompted an open conflict with their civilian superiors in the Navy Department and the White House.[115]

Whereas the war scare of 1913 highlighted the sense of maritime vulnerability in the Pacific before the opening of the Panama Canal, World War I sparked acute anxiety about the state of armaments and the future prospects of U.S. global power in general. Led initially by Rear-Admiral Fiske, navy leaders responded to the war with great alarm. They expressed grave concerns about U.S. force levels and, thus, called for a rapid expansion of naval power in the name of military "preparedness" and self-reliant national power. These calls focused on maximizing the readiness of the existing fleet for war. Fiske and the General Board greeted the news of war with the demand for the prompt withdrawal and refitting of the battleships then deployed in Mexican and Caribbean waters to support U.S. interventionism in Mexico.[116] But their plea for fleet readiness also went far beyond the demand for the concentration of the available force on the Atlantic coast. According to Fiske, the navy suffered above all from three main problems: a dramatic shortage of personnel, insufficient fleet training, and the lack of a naval general staff to direct the operations of the fleet and take responsibility for its state of readiness.[117]

Accelerated naval expansion constituted the other cornerstone of the navy's agenda. In September 1914, Fiske and the General Board revised their prewar naval program in favor of an accelerated arms buildup and the new goal of a "navy second to none." Yet the agency reconsidered in the face of Secretary Daniels's opposition and promoted new construction that was in line with previous prewar recommendations (plus demands for more personnel and special funding for naval aviation).[118] In the summer of 1915 the General Board committed itself to the creation of a "navy second to none" within fewer than ten years. On that basis, the agency championed a massive construction program built around eight capital ships in the next year alone (as opposed to the four demanded in each of the previous years). In interaction with Rear-Admiral Benson, the newly appointed chief of naval operations, the board then developed a five-year building program centered on the construction of ten battleships and six battlecruisers. This program, in turn, served as a way station for further demands, after Congress had approved it and compressed it into three years.[119]

The agendas and anxieties created by the coming of World War I pertained mostly to the prospects of U.S. global power in the period after the conclusion of the ongoing conflict. The premise of the navy's alarmism was the anticipation of big-power confrontations in a postwar period, which would set the United States against either Germany or Britain as the war's main victor and/or a Japanese Empire emboldened by its wartime pursuits in the Pacific. By 1915, the early 1920s defined the time horizon for the accumulation of maritime force.[120] Expectations of imminent German victory to be followed by swift imperial action in the Western Hemisphere had fueled the case for maximizing fleet readiness in August 1914.[121] In November 1914, when it had become clear that an end to the war was not immediately in sight, the General Board raised the specter of unnamed belligerent powers coming to an agreement about the acquisition of territories "which lie on or near the American continent or flank our ocean routes to the Panama Canal or across the two oceans."[122]

Service leaders did not expect, or promote, an intervention into an ongoing war they expected Germany to win. Beginning with a specially convened meeting of the General Board on August 1, 1914, the navy's strategists assumed U.S. nonparticipation in the war. The General Board declared in mid-September that there was "neither reason nor necessity for the U.S. becoming involved in the present general war."[123] The expectation of any immediate involvement in the war was so low in December 1914 that the official update of the navy's formal plan for a war with Germany identified the maltreatment of U.S. citizens in German-controlled territories as the most "probable reason" for an armed conflict under the current conditions of a world war.[124]

On the issue of an armed intervention, the navy leadership did not change course until early 1917. Neither Admiral Benson nor other top-ranked naval officers were part of U.S. decisions to enter the war. As late as February 1917, Benson expressed his "abhorrence" at the thought of "becoming enlisted with either side of combatants." The United States should keep its "equipoise" and avert the "calamity" of war.[125] Accordingly, Benson proposed to counter the specter of German unconditional submarine warfare with means short of war amounting to some sort of armed neutrality.[126] In previous years, the navy's concerns about the violation of U.S. rights as a neutral power had targeted both Germany and Britain. Already in November 1914, the General Board had warned that all the belligerent powers, that is, both the British and German empires, had advanced "new and hitherto unrecognized" readings of the strictures of maritime law, which would "seriously interfere with our legitimate trade interests and with our national prosperity."[127]

All in all, the navy's alarmist response to World War I drew upon its previous thinking. The war magnified existing views about the pivotal importance of maritime threat and deterrence. Expectations of future confrontations with big powers such as Germany continued in the footsteps of previous views of global politics and U.S. national interest. The push for fleet readiness and naval expansion also directly fed off particular preoccupations that had been developing in the 1910s. They involved concerns about declining U.S. strength relative to the German and Japanese fleets. They also entailed a developing unease about the combat readiness of the existing fleet, sparked, in part, by the deployment of fleet units against Mexico, which had prevented any joint fleet exercises in 1913 or 1914.[128]

There were clear limits to the navy's alarmism. It did not rise to the level of existential angst that came to beset a German naval elite fearing that their country could not succeed in the competitive milieu of global power. Raising alarm, American navy leaders were looking toward some "postwar future," as historian George W. Baer has written,[129] a future following a war whose end was no longer in sight by the end of 1914. Fears of big-power confrontations lacked the urgency that came with firm expectations of imminent policy failure, let alone direct participation in a big-power war. The separation from a global conflict was combined with the opening of the Panama Canal and a continuing awareness of the superiority of American productive power to circumscribe any anxieties concerning the future. Moreover, the decision by President Wilson's administration to embrace the cause of preparedness in the summer of 1915 alleviated any profound concerns on the part of navy leaders. The Naval Act of 1916, which committed the United States to a massive, multiyear naval construction program that went beyond the General Board's initial demands, pleased the navy's strategists enormously. Fittingly, the piece of legislation was not meant as a preparation for an intervention into the ongoing war.[130]

The naval elite carried its postwar orientation, and, with it, concerns for the fortunes of U.S. maritime power, into the war, which it entered in April 1917. Naturally, the case for a ratcheting up of American sea power lost none of its force with participation in the war or the prospects of Allied victory in 1918. On the eve of U.S. entry into the war, in February 1917, Admiral Benson set the tone. His country needed to fight "mainly" to "secure guarantees for the future" and make sure "to develop the full military and naval strength of the United States as fast as possible." The key to the future was a superior fleet. The "possible combinations, of powers and circumstances," were "too numerous" and "too pregnant with possibilities adverse to our interest" to predict the shape of postwar politics, except that the United States would "have to act alone" in the world.[131]

Such an outlook permeated naval thinking about the wartime alliance with Britain and the first round of construction recommendations the General Board offered in wartime. The momentous decision reached in the summer of 1917 to concentrate all efforts on the mastery of German submarine campaigns and fight the war in closest possible cooperation with the British displaced the focus on postwar dangers and self-sustaining national power only temporarily. By the spring of 1918, strategists once more started to make the case for a massive arms buildup to commence as soon as possible to secure the flourishing of the United States in the postwar period. From their point of view, the war had not made the world safer for their own country. What beckoned, instead, was an ever-more dangerous postwar world of big-power conflict over empire. High armaments remained the requirements of world power.

Although U.S. navalists remained anxious about the prospects of American sea power, they had no reason to panic in 1918 (or, for that matter, in 1914). Unlike the Germans, the Americans did not confront the possibility of imminent geopolitical failure or existential war. By the time of World War I, diverging outlooks about the viability of national global power marked the otherwise common paths along which the U.S. and German navies and their militarist projects had moved since the turn of the twentieth century.

Part II

THE CULT OF THE BATTLE

Approaches to Maritime Warfare

Chapter 4

War of Battle Fleets

No other navy invited comparison to the German navy as much as the U.S. navy, noted Admiral Alfred von Tirpitz in a special presentation to the emperor in March 1902. Both navies had "reached the same conclusions about strategy and tactics," regardless of diverging attitudes toward "organization, training, and administration." For that reason a "careful observation" promised to yield most "instructive suggestions." The emperor agreed. "That is the key point," the *springende Punkt,* he scribbled in the margins of Tirpitz's presentation right next to the observations about German-American commonality in tactical and strategic matters.[1]

Much commented on by German and U.S. naval officers, such a commonality in outlook was striking. Indeed, the two naval elites moved along similar paths, as they claimed mastery of maritime warfare and strove to remake their navies into military instruments of big-power wars that were not dominated by landed military power. The common approach of these maritime militarists was marked first and foremost by a firm investment in the same paradigm of naval warfare. It encompassed the pursuit of military success and maritime control in regional concentration; and it extended to the shared adherence to a regime of military and legal limitation in regard to the economic dimension of war at sea. These properties lent a distinctive shape to the military imagination of naval militarists in Germany and the United States.

The concept of battle fleet warfare grounded the universe of operational thought and culture, which navalists had fashioned in each country by the close of the nineteenth century. Placing the nation's regular naval force at the center of the operational calculus of war, this paradigm of war moved battle-driven combat between fighting fleets to center stage. The expectation of a decisive naval encounter involving squadrons of battleships became the regulative idea of naval strategy, which imagined victory through climactic combat in temporally confined wars. The making of this paradigm of war was based on the self-conscious adoption of mainstream principles of contemporary land warfare. The embrace of battle fleet warfare entailed the rejection of strategies of coastal defense and cruiser warfare as alternate ways of waging war. It also laid the groundwork for subsequent doctrinal rigidity. The relentless attachment to battle fleet warfare, in turn, combined with geopolitical consideration to drive the pursuit of sea power as a spatially limited infrastructural power to fight wars and project force in distinct regional settings.

The Concept of Battle Fleet Warfare

The approach of the two navies to matters of naval warfare and fleet operations coalesced in the late 1880s and 1890s, and by the turn of the century it had become firmly embedded in operational doctrine, war plans, naval programs, and the curricula of naval academies and war schools. This understanding of warfare moved to center stage the "combat of fleets against fleets," to quote the foundational text for the Germans, the *Service Memorandum IX*, written in 1894.[2] Battle fleet warfare served a clearly defined purpose, namely, to gain "command of the sea" by defeating the enemy's naval forces and driving them off the sea. Such a control would prevent the enemy from using the sea; for the victorious fleet, it would also provide the necessary precondition for subsequent operations to force the enemy into submission. The purpose of navies was simple: to take the offensive and to engage the enemy's fleet in a big battle on the open sea. In a typical formulation, the U.S. General Board explained in 1906 that "the main dependence of any nation at sea will always be upon its fighting fleet, and the chief object for each belligerent to attain will be for his fighting fleet to meet the enemy and by a decisive action settle the question of control of the sea."[3]

Theorists of naval warfare subordinated all operations to the pursuit of command of the sea. Concentration of force became the most important operational and tactical principle of naval warfare, which in turn gave rise to a wide array of second-order propositions about the proper deployment of forces. By contrast, substantive discussions of the exercise of command of the sea did not figure prominently in naval thinking and war planning. Once that command had been established by crushing the opposing fleet, it was assumed that a war's outcome would be de facto decided, with one side rendered defenseless and incapable of raising new fleets to compensate for losses.

To a remarkable degree, the proponents of battle fleet warfare cast naval warfare in the image of contemporary army warfare, stressing the confrontation between organized military forces and the pursuit of decisive battles of annihilation. The two key theorists of naval warfare, Alfred Thayer Mahan and Alfred von Tirpitz, explicitly took their ideas from the works of the theorists of land warfare who were most influential in their respective countries. Mahan drew on the Swiss strategist Antoine-Henri de Jomini, while Tirpitz, with the same results, turned to Karl von Clausewitz.

In the United States, Mahan laid the groundwork for the concept of battle fleet warfare in the late 1880s. At the behest of his mentor, Rear-Admiral Stephen B. Luce, Mahan set out to identify the "principles" of naval warfare by drawing "entirely upon works devoted to land strategy" and then reading them back into past naval campaigns.[4] The original promise Mahan made to Luce in 1886, to "keep the analogy between land and naval warfare before my eyes," encapsulated the conclusion reached later, that is, the insight that the "principles" that the "recognized authorities upon land warfare" claimed "to be of general application in their own specialty received also ample and convincing illustration in naval warfare."[5] In short, as Mahan argued until his death in 1914, the "fundamental principles of warfare are the same on land and on sea."[6]

Specifically, Mahan primarily drew on the writings of Jomini on land warfare to devise his system of naval strategy. From Jomini, Mahan professed later, he had "learned the few, very few, leading considerations in military combination."[7] The turn to Jomini was hardly surprising. It reflected the enormous standing that the Swiss general enjoyed in the United States as a military authority and official interpreter of the Napoleonic wars. In particular, Jomini was read and taught at the United States Military Academy. Mahan's father, Dennis Hart Mahan, an influential instructor at West Point before the Civil War, played a pivotal role in the favorable reception of the Swiss military writer in America.[8]

The key principles of Mahan's edifice of naval strategy were all Jominian in nature. Mahan followed Jomini in stressing that the destruction of the enemy's armed forces was the primary goal of any military campaign and could be accomplished by aggressive pursuit of battle. "Jomini's dictum," Mahan explained, "that the organized forces of the enemy are ever the chief objective pierces like a two-edged sword to the joints and marrow of many specious propositions."[9] Thus, Mahan defined as the "object of all naval action" the "destruction of the enemy's organized force and the establishment of one's own control of the water."[10]

This emphasis, then, bounded Mahan's discussion of the principles of the proper conduct of naval warfare. They included the concentration of force, the value of a central position and of interior lines of movement, and the close interrelationship of combat and logistics, that is, the "bearing of communications upon military tenure and success," to use Mahan's own phrase.[11] While stressing the importance of bases and strategic lines, Mahan railed against any static understanding of war at sea as a war of position. Success is "wrought less by the tenure of a position than by the defeat of the enemy's organized force—his battle fleet. ... Decisive defeat, suitably followed up, alone assures a situation."[12] In short, what mattered most in naval warfare was swift action, based on the clever use of strategic lines and bases, to secure victory in battle. Echoing Jomini's own fixation on this point, Mahan elevated concentration of force to what he referred to as the "ABC" of any strategy.[13] "Being superior to the enemy at the decisive point, whatever the relative strength of the two parties on the whole" figured as the "one great principle" in a system of naval strategy, which defined the destruction of the enemy's organized force in combat as war's paramount objective.[14]

In Germany, the paradigm of battle fleet warfare was developed between 1892 and 1895 when Tirpitz was chief of staff of the Naval High Command. Tirpitz had defined the key principles of the new naval strategy and tactics in advance, that is, in a number of memoranda written in 1890–91.[15] In these texts, Tirpitz demanded that the navy should gratefully "lean on" the army "as much as possible" in its development of strategy and tactics.[16] Echoing the operational doctrines of the Prussian and Imperial German armies, the future secretary of the navy argued that the course of the war at sea depended almost entirely on "victory in the first great sea battle."[17] Tirpitz was so obsessed with the idea of decisive battle that it became an end in itself; he envisioned the war at sea in the image of land warfare so strongly that he characterized it as the "battle of armies (*Heerschlacht*) on water."[18]

Tirpitz enshrined the analogy between land and sea war and his belief in a decisive battle as the primary means of naval warfare in *Service Memorandum IX,* the foundational text for subsequent naval thinking, completed in 1894. He argued that the "natural mission" of the navy was the "strategic offensive" to secure "command of the sea"; only an "arranged mass battle" would decide the course of this offensive, and thus, "of the naval war in general." Explicitly drawing comparisons between wars on land and at sea, Tirpitz wrote that land warfare "seeks primarily to reach its objective through the destruction of the enemy's army and the occupation of the enemy territory." Defining the conduct of bombardments, blockade, and landings as the maritime equivalents of the occupation of enemy territories in land warfare, *Service Memorandum IX* regarded the destruction of the enemy's main fleet through a decisive battle as the main purpose of the strategic offensive. "As long as the opposing fleet still exists and is ready for battle, that is to say as long as it has not been decisively beaten," it would be impossible to create "a situation" near the enemy's coast "analogous to the occupation of enemy territory in land warfare."[19]

As an analyst of land and sea warfare, Tirpitz presented himself as a "student of Clausewitz," as historian Rudolf Stadelmann has observed.[20] Tirpitz's understanding of land warfare was informed by a typical late-nineteenth-century reading of Clausewitz that viewed him as a leading theorist of battle-oriented Napoleonic warfare and approached *On War* as a military manual.[21] Clausewitz was also the only theorist of war Tirpitz referred to by name in his military writings during the 1890s. *Service Memorandum IX,* for example, quoted Clausewitz on the concentration of force as the only sound principle of offensive warfare.[22]

Tirpitz followed the example set by Captain Alfred Stenzel, the first teacher of naval strategy and history at the Marineakademie. In his lectures on the principles of naval warfare (published after his death), Stenzel had applied the central tenets of land warfare to its counterpart on the sea and extensively borrowed definitions, phrases, and even whole passages from Clausewitz's *On War.* Stenzel had planned to turn his lectures, which insisted on the centrality of climactic naval combat, into a book entitled *On War at Sea.*[23]

But the transfer of principles of land war as abstracted from its leading theorists to the war at sea was a tension-ridden intellectual enterprise. Within the bounds set by the emphasis on offensive battle fleets and command of the sea, both Mahan and Tirpitz suggested important differences between land and naval warfare, which undercut their insistence on the paramount importance of the decisive battle and the destruction of the opposing force. Take, for example, the German *Service Memorandum IX*. Its emphasis on a decisive naval encounter coexists uneasily with arguments about the difficulty, if not impossibility, of imposing such an encounter on the enemy. In land warfare, the attempt to occupy the enemy's territory would usually force the defending army "to offer battle and, thus, to run the risk of being annihilated." But the war at sea would be different. The opposing fleet could refuse battle and still contest the enemy's full exercise of command of the sea, which entailed more than the simple presence of a fleet in hostile waters.

In fact, *Service Memorandum IX* predicted that an inferior fleet was likely to avoid battle, stay in port, and act as a "fleet in being," because it could not compensate for inferior numbers by using defensive tactics in battle, a military option that would simply not exist in naval warfare. In such a case, the attacking force had to begin to exercise the command of the sea without the destruction of the enemy's force in battle. Predicting such a course of action, Tirpitz concluded that a significant numerical superiority, of at least a third, was the precondition for the strategic offensive, not the least so because naval operations in enemy waters imposed heavy strains on matériel and personnel.[24]

Mahan, too, knew about the unlikelihood of decisive naval combat. The American advanced a similar argument about the likely action of a weaker fleet in the event of war. Its aim would be to refuse combat with the superior enemy fleet, to keep concentrated, and to avoid being neutralized in one particular harbor. Although skeptical of the concept of the "fleet in being," Mahan nevertheless was forced to consider its prescriptions as a likely and reasonable course of naval action.[25] At the same time, on several occasions, Mahan identified as a fundamental characteristic of naval warfare the impossibility of a strictly defensive operational posture as a way to protect one's country and its "great national *external* interests": its maritime trade, shipping, and overseas possessions.[26] The only appropriate course of action was to take the offensive by denying the use of the sea to the enemy through the containment or neutralization of the opposing fleet near its base. Such control would be best accomplished by a blockade, which, in turn, did not require a battle, as command of the sea automatically fell to the superior force. In short, such reasoning suggests a view of naval warfare that defined the blockade as the primary means of warfare and stressed the control of enemy forces, and not their destruction, as the key challenge of naval warfare.[27]

Tirpitz and Mahan never acknowledged the tensions inherent in their writings on the conduct of the war at sea. Like most of their fellow officers, they ignored these tensions in favor of a firm belief in a big sea battle. Before World War I, it was left to the British theorist Sir Julian Corbett to elaborate on the differences between land and naval warfare as glossed over by Mahan and Tirpitz. In *Some Principles of Maritime Strategy,* published in 1911, Corbett openly questioned the contemporaneous cult of the decisive battle, in favor of a more nuanced understanding of command of the sea and battle fleet warfare.[28] Fittingly, Corbett's book elicited a lengthy critical review in the Germany navy's house magazine, the *Marine-Rundschau.* In no uncertain terms, the review's author chided the book for its lack of enthusiasm for the notion of climactic combat and compared it unfavorably to Mahan's book on naval strategy, published in the same year.[29]

Competing Paradigms of War

Moving along common paths and engaging in acts of mimicry in relation to terrestrial military-professional warfare, Mahan, Tirpitz, and other officers set the paradigm of battle fleet warfare against other concepts of maritime defense and naval warfare that had been enshrined in official policy and strategy in both countries. In so doing, they cast their own paradigm as the answer to what Tirpitz referred to as the "uncertainty" about the "nature and function of the fleet" among naval officers, an uncertainty caused by the ever-accelerating industrialization of naval warfare, with its dramatic changes in naval architecture and weaponry.[30] Before 1890, the U.S. and German navies had been hit particularly hard by this lack of clarity as they did not have the resources to afford costly experimentation with new types of ships. In each country, naval policy makers had adopted a cautious wait-and-see stance toward the construction of large armored ships. During the 1880s, they had emphasized building torpedo boats (Germany) and a handful of steel cruisers (United States) to meet immediate needs of national defense and await the formation of some sort of consensus about ship types and naval technology among the naval authorities of major sea powers.[31]

The notion of battle fleet warfare set itself up against the concept of a navy strictly designed for coastal defense, as opposed to combat on the open sea. In Germany, a strategy of so-called mobile coastal defense had prevailed in the 1870s, 1880s, and early 1890s. It appeared attractive because it fitted well with the service's secondary mission in a two-front war against

France and Russia that would be decided by the army.[32] In the United States, the idea of a coastal defense system based on a combination of land fortifications, floating batteries, mines, and smaller coastal vessels had been widely popular throughout the nineteenth century. As coastal defense vessels, monitors had captured the public imagination because of their successful exploits during the Civil War. An ambitious comprehensive scheme for coastal defense of this sort had been outlined as late as 1886.[33] Notions of "costal defense" resonated, in part, because they matched well with a sense of distance from European military geopolitics. So prevalent was the attachment to the ideal of a nonaggressive "coastal defense" that the battleships authorized between 1890 and 1899 carried the designation of coastal defense vessels.

The presentation of the doctrine of battle fleet warfare also entailed the explicit rejection of a second paradigm of naval warfare, namely, a cruiser-based strategy of commerce-raiding. This approach placed cruisers and their use as commerce-raiders at the center of naval warfare (and building policy for that matter). It cast cruisers' direct operations against the enemy nation's seaborne trade as a war-winning proposition, paying little attention to the contest between fighting fleets on the open sea as the primary course of naval action. Cruiser warfare had been the primary operational mission of the U.S. Navy throughout the nineteenth century.[34] Notions of cruiser warfare against the enemy's commerce had also gained considerable grounds within the German navy during the 1860s, 1870s, and early 1880s. Drawing on the experiences of the U.S. Civil War and then the Franco-Prussian War, many officers had championed cruisers as an important means of waging war because they could deny essential supplies to the enemy's armed forces.[35] The popularity of the idea of cruiser warfare in the 1890s rested on this tradition; yet it also drew directly on another source, the teachings of the Jeune École, a French school of naval thought that emerged by the 1880s and then framed subsequent debate about commerce-destruction among the navies of the world.[36]

A strategy of cruiser warfare complemented a system of coastal defense by adding an aggressive, war-winning dimension. Yet the primary appeal of this operational doctrine for war was that it also fit perfectly with the peacetime mission of cruisers to protect commerce and trade overseas. When the various U.S. Naval Advisory Boards recommended the construction of cruisers in the early 1880s, they stressed the peacetime commercialist mission of cruisers.[37] By the same token, German champions of cruiser warfare in the 1890s all stressed the correspondence between the concept of cruiser warfare and the peacetime use of cruisers under commercialist auspices.[38]

Mahan and Tirpitz offered straightforward critiques of commerce-raiding as a prescription for the primary conduct of maritime war.[39] Invoking the lessons of past naval wars, they argued that cruiser warfare was only a subsidiary form of warfare. Commerce destruction through cruiser warfare would promise only limited and fleeting success unless supported by a battle fleet in control of the sea. Tirpitz also did not hesitate to point out that a commerce-raiding strategy was not feasible because of Germany's geostrategic position and limited colonial empire. Time and again, Tirpitz explicitly dismissed cruiser warfare "because of [Germany's] geographical position and the lack of naval bases."[40] Germany would lack direct access to the open sea and a chain of naval bases and coaling stations, covering the major oceans, on which to base a cruiser war on commerce. This limitation, argued Tirpitz after the mid-1890s, would be especially evident in a war against Britain, whose geostrategic position, formidable overseas fleet, and numerous well-placed naval bases all over the globe ensured easy victory in a transoceanic cruiser war.[41]

For Mahan, Tirpitz, and others, a cruiser-based strategy of commerce destruction was only a meaningful course of action in particular cases. It was viewed as a legitimate secondary action *before* gaining "command of the sea," as long as it did not become a parallel action that violated the principle of the concentration of force. Cruiser warfare against the opponent's trade and commerce also appeared as the only viable military option for a weaker belligerent. Cruiser warfare would be "the last or the only available means for either the defeated or the side which had been powerless from the outset," as *Service Memorandum* IX stated.[42] Mahan expressly cast "commerce-destruction by cruisers on the high seas" as the "only possible reply" by a weaker power to "commerce-destruction by blockade"; while Tirpitz referred to cruiser warfare against trade as the "right of blockade of the weaker party."[43]

Some German thinkers, such as Admiral Curt von Maltzahn, theorized the cruiser-based *Handelskrieg,* war of commerce, as an important "side operation" in the struggle "against," and not "for," the command of the sea. Maltzahn did so as part of an attempt to fill the notion of the "strategic defense" with concrete meanings, recognizing that the "strategic offensive," the true calling of any fleet, was not an option in a war with Britain, the key operational scenario his navy faced after 1897. Maltzahn suggested that a weaker fleet, which could not hope to attain favorable conditions for a defensive battle that bore any chance of success, needed to weaken the grip of the blockade and to limit immediate enemy action against the coast. This struggle against the enemy's command of the sea involved the use of battleships and other supporting craft in coastal waters, but cruiser operations against commerce were also important. According to Maltzahn, such operations were to put pressure on the enemy, forcing him to divert attention and resources away from Germany's coast to protect trade lines and hunt down cruisers.[44]

Theorists of battle warfare rejected cruiser warfare as the dominant strategy for a war between great powers on operational terms. Yet they also radically undercut this type of warfare on other grounds, precisely by transforming the understanding of the navy's peacetime commercialist service and prioritizing big-power wars over gunboat diplomacy as the focal point of strategies of maritime control in a global age. The pursuit of imperial opportunity and economic interest had become a matter of great-power rivalry; it would require sea-power based on threat and deterrence that targeted rival global empires. To continue their commercial peacetime mission navies had to project force directly against these empires, not against "local" rulers and peoples across the globe.[45] This logic obviated the need for a large number of overseas cruisers in the global imperial-maritime peripheries. Such a presence, Tirpitz once explained in characteristic fashion, mostly required small cruisers and gunboats, which would rely "more on the flag" than on their "actual capability" or "on whose military mission (for example, against savages or unfortified land positions) minor force sufficed."[46] U.S. officers agreed. Small cruisers and gunboats sufficed to meet the demands of "cruising and police duty," whereas battleships provided "protection against major nations," explained the General Board in April 1907 when it laid out its policy on the deployment of the entire U.S. Navy.[47]

New Ways of War?

The adoption of the concept of battle fleet warfare laid the groundwork for subsequent doctrinal rigidity. It manifested itself in the failure to consider seriously newly developing alternative military strategies, as they were explored by Admiral John Fisher and other British naval planners prior to World War I. Premised on technological innovation, these strategies bade farewell to battle fleets and their quest for control of the sea. They featured a new kind of large armored cruiser, the battlecruiser, for oceanic warfare against or in defense of trade lanes, and so-called flotilla warfare for "sea denial" organized around submarines and other torpedo-carrying smaller vessels. For Fisher, the future belonged to battlecruisers, as a single, multirole, high-tech capital ship that could both outgun and outrun any conventional battleship, and to submarines capable of paralyzing any naval operations by surface vessels.[48]

The promise of the submarine boat also captured the imagination of several retired naval officers in Germany. Animated by a sober assessment of the course of an Anglo-German war, critics such as retired Admiral Curt von Galster doubted the promise of battle fleet warfare. Instead, they stressed the ability of the submarine to attack battleships and other surface vessels, to deny them the use of the sea, and to prevent a blockade. Some of these naval writers also presented submarines as an ideal means of a war against trade and commerce that would simply bypass the enemy surface fleet to directly target Britain's seaborne imports.[49]

By contrast, German and U.S. naval strategists fitted the submarine and the battlecruiser into notions of battle fleet warfare. Thus, in each navy, submarines came to play a role as an adjunct to the contest between fighting fleets. Under the leadership of Admiral Tirpitz, the German navy had initially adopted a conservative wait-and-see attitude toward the construction of submarines and then never forcefully promoted their development. The first U-boat was commissioned only in 1906. Citing the lack of any practical experience, a *Service Memorandum* on the development of submarines, published in 1910, was forced to refrain from discussing their military potential. It was only in 1912 that the submarine arm gained a secure footing when the new Naval Bill fixed the arm's future size at seventy-two and envisioned the annual construction of six boats. In July 1914, there were only twenty-eight boats, only ten of which were seaworthy, compared to a total of sixty-eight British boats.[50]

Before 1914, strategists viewed submarines as a so-called *Nebenwaffe*, a secondary weapon.[51] They assigned to it a strictly supportive, albeit ever-expanding, role within the framework of battle fleet warfare. They did so in the three years before the outbreak of war in 1914 when submarines became a matter of substantive discussion, war games, and maneuvers. Expanding on initial ideas about submarines as coastal defense weapons, this role first involved operations within German home waters against attacking or blockading enemy forces. By 1912, submarines were also to engage, on their own or in conjunction with torpedo boats, in offensive, long-distance operations across the North Sea and on the British coast to attack and decimate the British main fleet. These plans for offensive action, which were boosted by the introduction of the diesel engine, which created the first generation of reliable oceangoing submarines, led to plans for an immediate attack on the British Home Fleet at its gathering place at the outset of the war.[52]

By 1914, the U-boat (from U-Boot, the German word for submarine, itself an abbreviation of Unterseeboot, or undersea boat) had become a fixture of naval thinking as an "important means of combat," to quote the German chief of Admiralty Staff;[53] yet it was to play only a subsidiary role in the contest of the battle fleets. The navy's wartime submarine campaigns represented a clear break with prewar naval strategy and planning.[54] Their pursuit also did not lessen the overall commitment of the naval leadership to battleships as the key ingredient of maritime force. The mission of the battle fleet now also extended, but was by no means limited, to safeguarding the conduct of successful submarine warfare.[55]

U.S. strategists, too, carved out roles for submarines as new means of war that subordinated them to the tenets of battle fleet warfare.[56] After a phase of initial experimentation, which saw the commissioning of a first submarine in 1900, submarines became an official part of the naval strategy and program by 1905. They came to feature as a weapon of coastal and harbor defense, imagined as the main tools, besides torpedo boats, of a maritime "mobile defense." The submarine allegedly held great promise in this context as a weapon of choice for the local defense of the newly acquired imperial possessions across the Pacific.[57] By September 1912, the General Board called for a fleet of one hundred submarines to defend U.S. coastlines and sea territories. The purpose of this vast fleet was to ensure the "strategic freedom" of the main fleet, of which submarines expressly were not a part.[58]

As in Germany, by the early 1910s officers carved out more extended roles for submarines as an offensive, oceangoing weapon and part of the contest of fleets. They included operations against the enemy either "in connection with" or "as part of" the "battleship fleet," to quote a key General Board memorandum, written in 1911.[59] Their tactics ranged from scouting missions to concentrated attacks on the enemy's battleships to attacks on shipping in enemy ports. These roles were initially proposed by officers serving with the submarines, who complained bitterly about the conservatism of most of their peers while stressing the vast improvements in submarine technology and construction.[60] The General Board asked for the first so-called fleet submarine in the summer of 1913 and for three more the following year. Within another two years the agency asked for an armada of at least thirty fleet submarines.[61]

Such plans for fleet submarines remained bounded by the firm conviction that submarines were, and would remain, a supporting weapon incapable of denying the use of the sea to battleship squadrons and whose very usefulness depended on the support of a battleship fleet. Accordingly, in June 1914 the General Board launched a blistering critique of the ideas put forward by the British admiral Sir Percy Scott, who had suggested publicly that submarines were in the process of displacing battleships and other surface vessels.[62] Strikingly, on those few occasions when officers raised the possibility of using submarines against enemy merchant shipping, as in the case of the officer classes at the Naval War College in 1911 and 1912, their main emphasis was on action against shipping in ports.[63] The war itself, and even the submarine crisis of 1917–18, did not fundamentally alter this mind-set. Time and again, the navy's strategists went out of their way to pronounce on the superior promise of the battle fleet, the sturdiness of fast battleships, and the strictly supportive role of submarines. Naval programs between 1916 and 1919 championed the construction of a vast battle fleet and embodied the continuity of thinking within the U.S. Navy.[64]

As in the case of submarines, the commitment to battle fleet warfare shaped the two navies' response to the rise of so-called battlecruisers. Neither in the United States nor in Germany did strategists embrace the battlecruiser's potential for independent operations against trade lanes before the war. Nor did anyone recognize Admiral Fisher's vision of the battlecruiser as the future capital ship and radical alternative to the conventional battleship.

Confronted with the construction of the first British battlecruiser in the summer of 1906, the Germans followed suit and built a new battlecruiser each year. But they nevertheless defined the cruiser's purpose in terms of battle fleet warfare, not cruiser warfare. Battlecruisers would find their "natural mission" as a "fast formation" operating in "close tactical conjunction" with the main force of battleships, explained Admiral Henning von Holtzendorff, commander of the High Seas Fleet in September 1911.[65] Their tactics were worked out in the next few years in maneuvers and war games, as the number of available battlecruisers increased from two to five in 1914, with three more in construction. In the spring of 1914, the chief of the German Admiralty Staff and the commander of the active fleet granted the battlecruiser "a practically decisive role in battle" as the fast wing of their battle fleet.[66]

The Germans saw in the battlecruiser a new capital ship that promised to dramatically improve the Anglo-German balance of forces while directly strengthening the rising German battle fleet on the maritime battlefield. The main debate about battlecruisers within the German navy concerned their ability to muster as battleships and be employed with them in battle. Some officers viewed the battlecruiser as a fast battleship, arguing that its use against battleships in combat ought to become the "norm" for design and the "goal" for its entire future development.[67] In contrast, others, Tirpitz among them, stressed the differences between battlecruisers and battleships, with the former trading armor and armaments for superior speed. Constituting the fast arm of the battle fleet, the cruisers' main mission was reconnaissance and "the life or death struggle" with opposing battlecruisers, not full-scale participation in open combat between battleships.[68] Such thinking directly expanded on previous views about the supporting role of the heavy cruiser in battle fleet warfare, as originally laid out during the 1890s.[69] By 1913, the second position had officially lost out.[70] Yet well before then, and in spite of Tirpitz's misgivings, the construction of German battlecruisers had already been guided by the effort to ensure their high combat value vis-à-vis other capital ships and, thus, enhance the overall "combat value of our [battle] line," as a memo from the construction department of the Imperial Naval Office noted.[71]

Before 1914, strategists did not stress the opportunities for independent cruiser warfare that the battlecruisers, with their speed and radius of action, presented.[72] When in the spring and summer of 1914, Admiral Eduard von Capelle promoted the accelerated construction of battlecruisers, he still did so in the spirit of offensive battle fleet warfare.[73] Only the wartime crisis of battle fleet strategy created a space for new ideas. Already in the fall of 1914, some strategists discussed novel roles for battlecruisers as well as for fast battleships, which centered on transatlantic warfare against trade lanes.[74] Even Tirpitz was not immune to such thinking. In late August 1914, the navy secretary raised the possibility of using one or two of these ships "for a trade war against Britain in the Atlantic" in a "later phase of the war."[75] Yet such ideas remained marginal to the service's continuing commitment to battle fleet warfare. The battleship remained the cornerstone of all planning for a postwar future.

U.S. strategists shared the impulse to consider the promise of battlecruisers within the paradigm of battle fleet warfare. Unlike their German peers, however, they evinced little interest in them until 1915. To be sure, the potential of this ship occasioned considerable discussion at the General

Board and the Naval War College, the navy's key planning institutions. But the navy did not press for their construction. Only in 1912 did the General Board ask for two battlecruisers, tying their authorization to approval of the battleships it also wanted, while placing its demands for battlecruisers in the context of their construction in Germany and Japan. There was no demand for battlecruisers in 1913 and 1914.[76]

American officers saw little immediate need for battlecruisers. As in Germany, the main debate about their military purpose centered on their contributions to battle fleet operations, not on cruiser warfare or trade protection. There was general agreement that one possible purpose of the battlecruisers would be independent operations against enemy trade lines and long-distance raiding. But overall references to commerce destruction and action away from the battle fleet remained secondary and inconsequential. As ardent an advocate of the battlecruisers as Captain William S. Sims made his case based exclusively on their value in climactic combat; the importance of their contributions to the fighting line of the battle fleet would preclude any other use.[77]

As in Germany, efforts to define the military value of battlecruisers in relation to the contests of fleets expanded on the previous discussion of the purpose of the armored cruiser. Strategists debated two primary missions for battlecruisers as part of battle fleet warfare. These ships could either serve as a superior scouting and screening force for the main fleet or they could be deployed as the latter's "fast wing" in combat and as part of the "fighting line." The relentless pursuit of a defeated force after battle constituted an additional minor mission. The debate over these roles of battlecruisers became controversial at times: subsequent officer classes at the Naval War College reported a "marked diversity of opinion" on this subject.[78]

Before 1914–15 the majority of strategists agreed on the secondary value of battlecruisers. Their military value was "problematical," pronounced the General Board on repeated occasions. Because of their design characteristics, which sacrificed "gun power" and "protection" in favor of speed, battlecruisers could never be more than a "temporary adjunct" to the battle line; they would prove a "failure" when they confronted enemy battleships.[79] Worse, because of their prohibitive cost, the former appeared as a "luxury" the navy could not afford to pursue, as long, that is, as it was lagging in battleships.[80] Precisely that attitude had already informed the policy of the General Board toward the building of armored cruisers. The agency had not asked for the authorization of a single one of them after 1904.

Strategists changed their minds on battlecruisers in 1915. Invoking the lessons of the ongoing war in Europe, the General Board now began to lament the lack of these cruisers and to clamor for the authorization of a large number of them. Typically, their use value was still very much defined in terms of battle fleet warfare, as both a superior scouting and screening force and the fast wing of the main battle force facing off with the enemy's force of battlecruisers. Yet their other main mission now lay outside the contest of battle fleets. Battlecruisers appeared as key purveyors of a cruiser war of raiding that involved attacks on, and the defense of, coastlines and maritime lanes of trade and communications. The specter of long-distance raids by either Japanese or German battlecruisers against the United States in some future war haunted planners in this context.[81] But such reorientation had its clear limits. Pleas for battlecruisers were always bounded by affirmations of the centrality of the battleship fleet. The embrace of battlecruisers cooled off, when their vulnerability in main combat became well known after the battle of Jutland in 1916.[82]

U.S. Strategies of Maritime Control

As rigid as they were tenacious, German and U.S. naval elites clung to a paradigm of battle fleet warfare. Such adherence to battle fleet warfare, in turn, shaped strategies of maritime control. Preparing to fight major wars in particular regional spaces, the Germans and Americans pursued sea power as spatially circumscribed infrastructural power. These regional bids for maritime force shaped naval programs, operational planning, peacetime deployment, infrastructural pursuits, and technological choices. They also set German and U.S. approaches apart from the truly global strategy of maritime control that British Empire policy makers had originally pioneered at midcentury, a strategy based on a relay of global networks of force, communications, supply, and repair, and to which they remained committed throughout (and beyond) the entire prewar period.[83]

The U.S. Navy stressed military concentration in distinct regional settings. The northern Atlantic, the Caribbean, and the Pacific became the primary spaces of maritime projection, reflecting the navy's desire to defend U.S. spheres of interests and territories in the Western Hemisphere and across the Pacific. By the beginning of the twentieth century, naval strategists took the necessary steps toward fleet concentration as a key element of this approach. By 1903 all battleships were concentrated in the North

Atlantic Fleet, with the exception of those ships already serving in the Far East. Their deployment dated back to the war in China in 1900–01. All other naval stations were reduced in strength.[84]

The organization of the navy's battle force into a single concentrated fleet was nonetheless not a self-evident proposition. After 1900 the navy's strategists intensely debated the terms of regional concentration as they strove to square battle fleet warfare, military threat and deterrence, and geostrategic reality. These strategists recognized that the anti-German orientation of the navy, both short- and long-term, required the peacetime concentration of the entire (and ever-growing) battle force on the Atlantic. Yet planners were forced to reconcile this insight with perceived imperial needs in the Pacific.[85] Before 1906 the plea for Atlantic concentration against Germany faced off against arguments on behalf of a strong naval presence in the Far East. On the one hand, naval planners outlined the principle of the peacetime stationing of the entire battle fleet in the Atlantic to assure threat and deterrence against Germany. On the other hand, after the end of the war in China in 1901, the imperial advantages of a strong show of force in the Far East weighed heavily on the minds of naval strategists. Concerns over political instability in Asia and ever-increasing Japanese-Russian tensions prompted the continuing deployment of battleships in the western Pacific.[86]

After much discussion (during which the retired naval authorities Admiral Luce and Captain Mahan were consulted), the General Board decided in December 1903 to keep a battleship squadron in the Pacific to bolster U.S. interests while also affirming, in general, the principle of battle fleet concentration in the Atlantic. The agency fixed the strengths of the naval forces in the Atlantic and Pacific at 70:30 for the time being.[87] This compromise stayed in place until the end of the Russo-Japanese War. After the Naval War College had again presented the case for Atlantic concentration in 1905, all battleships were withdrawn from the Pacific in 1906. The General Board officially affirmed this policy in April 1907.[88]

The emergence of Japan as a geopolitical adversary created a new set of problems. The concentration of the entire fleet in the Atlantic threatened to make successful conduct of war in the Pacific impossible. The question as to whether the battle fleet ought to be deployed in the Atlantic or Pacific or divided up provoked intense discussion among strategists at the General Board, Joint Army and Navy Board (the Joint Board), and the Naval War College between 1907 and 1910. This discussion took place against the backdrop of the sending of the battle fleet to the Pacific, which navy leaders urged in June 1907, and its subsequent cruise across the Pacific and back to the Atlantic.[89]

Between June 1907 and early 1910, most planners made the case for either the peacetime concentration of the available battle fleet in the Pacific, or dividing it up between the two oceans. The General Board and the Joint Board officially championed a policy of full Pacific concentration in various communications in 1908, after their official vote for the assembly of the battle fleet in the Pacific "at the earliest practicable date" in June 1907.[90] By summer 1908, the idea of a possible division of the fleet attained prominence as well; some planners had championed the dispatch of a substantial part of the battle fleet to the Pacific in the spring and summer of 1907. The General Board, which otherwise stressed the necessity of concentration, introduced the idea that once the U.S. fleet reached thirty battleships it could be safely divided into separate fleets, an idea already aired by one of its committees in December 1904. In February 1909 the agency stated that this time had come and advised a splitting of the fleet.[91]

But planners met with official disapproval. Presidents Roosevelt and Taft insisted on full concentration in the Atlantic, a position urged by Mahan as well.[92] The General Board, in turn, adopted this position wholeheartedly. The agency turned down proposals for Pacific concentration made by the Naval War College and some of its own members in the spring and fall of 1910. Even a stationing of older battleships in the Pacific, suggested in 1912 by one prominent rear admiral, was ruled out.[93] In response to the news of European war in 1914, the General Board affirmed the principle of military concentration in the Atlantic. Yet by that time, the imminent opening of the Panama Canal had also taken the heat out of the discussion about proper concentration. Fittingly, in May 1914 the General Board had reopened the deployment issue. Without reaching any official conclusions, it had considered dividing up the battleships equally between the Atlantic and Pacific in the future, when squadrons could easily move from one to the other using the new transisthmian waterway.[94]

While debating the terms of concentration, planners simultaneously pursued other prerequisites for the wartime projection of military force in the northwest Atlantic, the Caribbean, and the Pacific. Most important, they tailored the ship characteristics and composition of the battle fleet to the particulars of their strategy of maritime control. After 1898 battleship design came to value steaming radius and fuel economy above both cruising and battle speed; it emphasized the construction of long-range, oceangoing ships with maximum armor and the largest possible guns; and it stressed the importance of onboard repair capabilities such as a special machine shop, and extensive onboard spaces for spare parts and supplies. During the 1890s, by contrast, battleships had been designed to operate within coastal waters for the anticipated defense of the Atlantic coast against the Royal Navy.[95]

The navy's spatial priorities manifested themselves in other ways, too. Its strategists put great emphasis on a large, efficient reconnaissance force as they envisioned transoceanic confrontations of opposing battle fleets in search of one another. For that purpose, the General Board consistently championed the construction of fast, lightly armed scout cruisers.[96] The Board displayed a keen interest in creating a large force of special colliers to accompany a battle fleet engaging in long-range oceanic operations. Such a fleet could not depend on chartered foreign ships and commercial purchases, as the U.S. fleet did during its global cruise in 1907–09. It was in the same spirit that the General Board proposed the outfitting of specially designed repair ships and endorsed plans to provide subsidies for U.S. merchant shipping, on which it could then rely in war.[97] Navy leaders decided to pursue conversion from coal to oil fuel in 1908, not only because of oil's easy availability in North America but because the use of petroleum promised to increase the endurance and range of U.S. battleships.[98]

The desired projection of maritime force depended on another type of infrastructural power. By 1900, strategists all agreed that this projection required the acquisition of a string of naval bases and coaling stations outside the continental United States. The seizure of new territories in 1898–99 had already been driven by this recognition. The Naval Strategy Board had vigorously asserted this need during and after the Spanish-American War in 1898. Other officers agreed and presented their own wish lists. The General Board then took up this issue systematically and, within a few years, proposed a list of military bases that were required to support battle fleet operations in the Western Hemisphere and across the Pacific.[99] The desire to deny possible bases to other powers provided an additional impulse for the General Board's military colonialism. Angst over a possible German takeover of the Danish West Indies, for example, drove an interest in the American purchase of these strategically placed islands, which eventually bore fruit in 1917.[100]

Over time, strategists came to focus their energies on the development of a few key bases in the Caribbean and across the Pacific. This shift, which made the General Board reject suggestions to acquire more, resulted from a mix of domestic constraints (in particular, the unwillingness of Congress to appropriate the necessary funds), diplomatic conjunctures (which limited attempts to gain foreign bases), and strategic considerations (an increasing emphasis on the dangers of military overextension).[101]

In the Caribbean, the navy focused its attention on the creation of a major naval station at Guantánamo Bay in Cuba, in addition to the development of Culebra as an "advance base" and projected fleet anchorage location. In the Pacific, the navy first concentrated its efforts on the creation of a major naval base at Subic Bay in the Philippines, a quest that was abandoned in 1908 in the face of army opposition and congressional refusal to grant funding. The General Board then decided to make Pearl Harbor its major overseas base in the Pacific. Navy leaders nevertheless also expressed, by the early 1910s, a strong interest in creating a "naval base of the first order," if not an American "Gibraltar," in the western Pacific, with Guam as an object of desire.[102] Between 1900 and 1906, strategists had desired another base in the western Pacific, when they had sought, in vain, to attain a foothold on the Chinese coast.[103]

The pursuit of powerful naval bases in the Pacific extended to the western United States. In their quest for adequate shore support, planners settled on the development of two principal fleet bases in Puget Sound and in San Francisco Bay while also promoting naval shipbuilding on the West Coast to boost maritime industrial facilities. In the 1900s and 1910s, the Pacific coastal states lacked the naval bases and repair facilities to support a fleet concentrated there for a long period of time.[104] Proponents of Atlantic concentration stressed that this deficiency ruled out a Pacific solution. Their opponents argued that the only way to force Congress to fund proper naval facilities on the Pacific was to station the fleet, or at least a part of it, there.[105]

Another cornerstone of the infrastructure sought by the navy was, of course, a transisthmian canal. Led in the 1890s by Mahan, officers (who had played a prominent role in the initial exploration and also became involved as investors in the private companies interested in the construction of the canal) demanded the construction of this waterway as a national priority, involving U.S. governmental action and direct control. In so doing, they not only stressed the transformative economic promises of the canal. They also always highlighted the promise of the canal for the projection of force. In fact, considerations of military usages increasingly dominated the navy's interest in the canal while also underwriting the interest in direct U.S. control.[106] From the navy's point of view, the canal's military use value increased exponentially after 1906 when Imperial Germany and Japan were both viewed as imperial adversaries. When, in the 1910s, the completion of the canal neared, officers constantly reminded themselves and their audiences that the opening of the canal should not be taken as an invitation to slow down naval construction.[107]

Finally, strategists were not ignorant of the need to acquire communications capabilities to sustain projections of maritime force. At the turn of the century, officers such as Rear-Admiral Royal B. Bradford, the chief of the Bureau of Equipment, advocated the development of a U.S. national cable connecting the newly acquired imperial possessions on the Pacific to the West Coast. Fresh on Bradford's and others' minds was the experience of Admiral Dewey's squadron during the past war, which had depended on British-controlled cables for their communications with home. This wish bore fruit in 1903, when a privately owned U.S. Pacific cable reached Manila from the U.S. west coast.[108] By contrast, the navy only hesitantly explored the opportunities offered by wireless telegraphy. Only in 1913 did the commanders of the active fleet embrace radio as a key tool for its actual operations at sea. And only after 1914 did the navy acquire both high- and low-powered radio stations on shore lines that enabled long-distance communications between a cruising fleet and command centers at home.[109]

Regional Concentration German-Style

Like the Americans, the Germans emphasized the principle of concentration. In many ways, their entire enterprise was an extreme example of a regional strategy of maritime control. The approach fused geopolitical thinking about an Anglo-German antagonism, the tenets of battle fleet warfare, and a deft sense of politico-financial possibilities into a self-contained whole. It focused on the expansion of the battle fleet in home waters and its preparation for a war in the North Sea. Germany needed to develop and deploy its fleet in such a way that it could maximize its military power "between Heligoland and the Thames," opined Tirpitz in July 1897 when he laid out the agenda for the German navy's subsequent approach.[110]

The emphasis on home deployment left no room for a large or separate overseas fleet.[111] The navy only deployed a small force of cruisers and gunboats on various overseas stations. Because the emphasis on home deployment was powerfully reinforced by a desire to keep down expenses, Tirpitz showed little to no interest in sending significant forces on temporary overseas missions.[112] The deployment of a substantial force of both battleships and large cruisers to China during the Boxer War remained an exception.

Only in the early 1910s was there a new yet limited emphasis on overseas cruising, as evidenced in transatlantic cruises of one battlecruiser each in 1911 and 1912, and the South American cruise of two battleships in 1913–14. In March 1914, Tirpitz also approved the idea of creating a "flying squadron" composed of one battlecruiser and three smaller cruisers, while senior officers and the emperor were debating whether to attend the upcoming International Exposition in San Francisco to honor the opening of the Panama Canal.[113] But, contrary to Tirpitz's claims in his memoirs, none of this represented a shift in policy away from the principle of battle fleet concentration at home.[114]

The fixation on the North Sea expressed itself in many other areas beyond deployment patterns. Among them was ship design. Constructing battleships for combat in the North Sea, designers valued high battle speed above a high steaming radius, which in itself never became a top priority. They also provided for intermediate batteries for battleships at a time when the "all-big-gun ship," with its emphasis on long-range naval gunnery, dominated capital ship construction elsewhere, including the United States. Such intermediate artillery would be useful because of the particular weather conditions in the North Sea that made combat at closer range a likely occurrence.[115]

Likewise, German torpedo boats were laid out for a steaming radius of about 500 to 550 nautical miles, in line with expectations of a battle near home waters as they had originally shaped views of defensive war against Britain.[116] So limited was their radius that they could not even operate in the northern North Sea, much to the chagrin of an increasing number of planners who suggested fighting the British fleet there.[117] The expectation of a battle off the German coast made Tirpitz and other planners downplay the importance of a formidable cruiser scouting force. As in the case of torpedo boats, the underdevelopment of cruiser scouts eventually caused great concern among strategists. The few battlecruisers and the slow development of the naval airship arm did not compensate for the lack of a strong force of powerful small cruisers.[118]

Adherence to the principle of regional concentration limited the quest for sea power as global infrastructural power. Between 1895 and 1900, navy leaders had pursued a string of military bases and coaling stations to provide a supportive network for the deployment of maritime force, in addition to already existing colonies.[119] While engaging in a fundamentally opportunistic search, they had staked out clearly defined, by no means limitless, interests, driven by the identification of South America and East Asia as primary spatial focal points for German global ambition.[120] In the Western Hemisphere, these efforts had focused on the takeover through purchase of Danish or Dutch-owned insular possessions in the West Indies, with the island of St. Thomas as the key object of desire.[121] In East Asia, the navy had seized a colony in northern China in 1897. Subsequently, planners pursued projects to acquire naval stations on the route to Kiaochow from Germany, such as on the Farasan Islands in the Red Sea or Pulau Langkawi in the Indian Ocean. Likewise, territories for naval stations had been sought in the Pacific to ground projection of force in both East Asia and the Western Hemisphere. The Spanish-American War had prompted the Germans to jockey for a foothold in the Philippines.[122]

After 1900, the pursuit of naval bases to provide, in the present, the necessary territorial infrastructure to project force across the world's seas ran its course. To the chagrin of many planners, Tirpitz ended most of these highly visible activities, especially those in the Western Hemisphere.[123] Germany needed to keep a low geopolitical profile and focus its resources on the naval buildup. Characteristically, the navy showed no particular interest in gaining a naval station on the North African coast when the opportunity presented itself in the context of Franco-German disputes over Morocco. Kiaochow was not turned into a giant naval base in analogy to British Gibraltar, as originally envisioned by Admiralty Staff planners.[124] Only during World War I did military colonialism and global military capabilities become once again a present-day concern. The navy's war aims included an extensive shopping list of places for military bases around the globe.[125]

The suspension of the quest for military colonies highlighted the lack of global military infrastructural power. Before 1914 the navy's limited overseas presence rested on commercial purchases in foreign locales and the good will of others, mostly the British. The German naval squadron that sailed to China in 1900, for example, depended primarily on the British for its logistical support.[126] In their plans for the overseas use of cruisers in a war with either Britain or the United States, planners relied on networks of special agents who would secretly purchase supplies and find ways, through prepositioning and the purchase of vessels, to deliver them to German ships.[127]

Navy leaders also did not forcefully develop the communications capabilities that could underwrite a strategy of global maritime control. To be sure, talk about the desirability of a German "world cable" permeated the discussions about military footholds across the globe in the late 1890s; subsequently, strategists often debated the importance of a German-controlled submarine cable network spanning the globe. But its attainment did not become a matter of any urgency. Although the navy supported an expansion of German cable lines in general, its strategists realized the limitations imposed by geostrategy and cable politics. Their country could not attain an exclusive network that would remain impervious to interruption and monitoring by the British Empire in the event of war.[128] By the 1910s, strategists began to view wireless telegraphy, which by that time had already been introduced into their fleet at home, as a global communications alternative, or supplement, to Germany's weak cable network. The navy collaborated with the imperial government to create an intercontinental wireless telegraphy network based on powerful long-distance stations in Germany, Africa, and the United States, linking Germany's overseas possessions and reaching German vessels across the globe. These efforts bore some fruit by 1914 even if their results still remained somewhat limited.[129]

From a military point of view, these kinds of newly developed communications capabilities did not matter much in the context of an overall approach that strove to achieve its goals through regional military concentration, an orientation that the Germans shared with U.S. planners on the other side of the Atlantic. Underwritten by shared and increasingly rigid commitments to the tenets of battle fleet warfare, these regional bids for naval power helped to define German and American pursuits of maritime force under navalist auspices.

Chapter 5

Planning for Victory

The decisive battle between the German and U.S. battleship fleets took place off the coast of New England. A German battle force of twenty-two battleships, five battlecruisers, forty-four torpedo boats, and about fifty submarines had rapidly crossed the North Atlantic after the declaration of war. In its wake a fleet of transports carrying an invasion force of more than 150,000 troops had followed. A U.S. Atlantic Fleet consisting of sixteen battleships, two battlecruisers, thirty-two torpedo boats, and twelve submarines had moved to intercept the advancing German fleet. In the ensuing showdown, the Americans suffered catastrophic defeat, due to inferior numbers, matériel, and organization. The outcome of the battle gave the Germans command of the sea and cleared the way for the subsequent invasion of the northern United States, including the occupation of major cities such as Boston and New York.

This battle was an imaginary event. German and U.S. battle fleets never directly confronted each other in combat. Set in 1920, this operational scenario of an American-German war, with its decisive battle at the outset, was concocted by J. Irving Hancock, a prolific author of juvenile fiction in the United States that tended toward military themes; it was laid out in the first volume of his *The Invasion of the United States* series, published in 1916.

This series belonged to a flourishing fictional literature about future wars that surrounded the campaign for "preparedness" between 1914 and 1917. This literature, in turn, was part of a larger genre of tales about the next war that enjoyed great popularity in both Europe and North America.[1]

The writers of this genre were not the only people in the business of imagining future wars. Naval officers, too, drew up plans for imagined battles. In fact, Hancock's scenario followed the same script of battle fleet warfare and climactic combat as those of his professional military counterparts. In its basic premises, the scenario mirrored thinking about an imaginary German-American war by German and U.S. naval planners at the beginning of the twentieth century. The scenario did so even as these professional strategists eventually discarded the idea of immediate German action against New England in favor of an emphasis on the Caribbean as the initial key theater of war. The lines between popular fantasy and military thinking were blurry.

Preparing for war was central to the navalist enterprise of the German and U.S. navies in the global age. Operational planning functioned as the interface between the geopolitical agendas and military imagination of the two naval elites. On the one hand, thinking about maritime warfare became embedded in war plans. On the other hand, war plans served the purposes of threat and deterrence and envisioned geopolitical confrontation with other major powers. Welding together aggressive and defensive motives with political and military ones, naval strategists tailored their scenarios to the specific geopolitical and operational conditions characteristic of individual theaters of war. Yoking their tenets of warfare and global politics to national geostrategic and imperial circumstances, German and U.S. maritime militarists moved within the same self-contained conceptual world, which was defined by shared notions of war, strategy, and politics. Thus, in the case of an imaginary American-German military confrontation, the plans devised on both sides of the Atlantic mirrored each other.

Operational planning provided the ultimate field of enactment for the commitment to battle fleet warfare and climactic combat. Casting the war at sea as a discrete, calculable undertaking, navalists strove to assure wartime military success in their scenarios, regardless of which fleet would be on offense or defense. The cult of the decisive battle and visions of large-scale fleet operations became the hallmark of the war plans devised by both navies for big-power wars. By seeking to achieve their operational goals in regional concentration and concerned with operations until the decisive military showdown, plans for big-power wars limited war both temporally and spatially.

In each country, doctrinal attachments combined with a relentless devotion to victory to shape the rationality of navalists' operational planning. Strategists developed scenarios that assumed symmetrical commitments to battle fleet warfare on both sides and strove to promise wartime success even against the greatest odds. Both navies struggled to create plausible scenarios to ensure successful outcomes, even within the contexts of war planners' own premises and estimates. Claiming mastery of maritime warfare, navalists took great pride in their hard-nosed military professionalism; yet the war plans that naval strategists created were marred by mismatches between operational ends and logistical-military means and a general inability to allow for scenarios beyond the script of short, battle-driven wars and climactic combat.

Planning for War with Germany

U.S. strategists came to focus on three distinct scenarios after the turn of the twentieth century as they planned for victory in war. These scenarios reflected their thinking about their country's relations with other big powers and the requirements of maritime threat and deterrence. The specter of a German-American military encounter mesmerized planners after the turn of the twentieth century. At the same time, naval strategists also sketched plans for a multipower war in the Far East that pitted the United States, Britain, and Japan against Russia and France (and, possibly, Germany as well); but these plans were rendered obsolete by the Russo-Japanese War. In its wake, considerations of a Japanese-American war moved to center stage and vied for importance with planning for a possible German-American military confrontation. The U.S. Navy's plans for war against Japan and Germany eventually matured into the official war plans "Orange" (Japan) and "Black" (Germany) as the war-planning process itself grew more elaborate.

Starting in 1900, the development of war plans against Germany fused the geopolitical, strategic, and military elements of the maturing U.S. navalist enterprise.[2] In this case, the pursuit of U.S. interests combined the aggressive assertion of empire and hegemonic power with hemispheric military defense. According to the navy's reasoning, a German-American war would break out over a German attempt to acquire colonial possessions in the Western Hemisphere, which would first manifest itself in schemes to obtain a "permanent intermediate base" in the Caribbean, as the U.S. Navy's chief naval intelligence officer predicted as early as May 1900.[3] Germany's pursuit of its imperial goals would hinge on its transatlantic use of force to seize territories in the Western Hemisphere. Conversely, U.S. objectives required successful operations against German forces as they crossed the Atlantic, not an offensive, transoceanic war against Imperial Germany itself. Only occasionally did a strategist suggest offensive operations against Germany in European waters.[4]

Developing plans for a war against Germany laid out a rather fantastical scenario of transoceanic warfare. They focused on battle fleets, the struggle for command of the sea in the Caribbean and western Atlantic, and the quest for a decisive battle in West Indian waters within the first two months after mobilization. Strategists presented their operational scenario in stark terms. They assumed that the Germans would send their whole fleet, with a train of colliers and merchantmen transporting an invasion force of at least twenty-five thousand men, first attempting to seize a military base in the Caribbean. After (and only after) securing a base, the German fleet would seek a decisive engagement with U.S. naval forces to establish permanent "command of the sea" in the waters of the Western Hemisphere and end the war. The U.S. fleet was to seek a "decisive military engagement" with the enemy as well, either at the "entrance to the Caribbean," that is, before the German seizure of a base, while the German fleet was still "encumbered with train," or somewhere else in Caribbean waters, after the German adversary had securely established itself in the West Indies.[5]

Strategists debated and then dismissed other operational scenarios and theaters of war. In the early 1900s, some planners raised the possibility of direct German military action against the American East Coast itself, with the aim of establishing a base on U.S. shores. But this scenario was quickly dismissed as a proposition for war planning, because it was calculated that the German invasion force would be sandwiched between U.S. forces on land and the concentrated American fleet operating near its home bases.[6] In 1905, the Naval War College assumed a "raid" of German naval forces against New England after the Germans had secured bases in the Caribbean but before a battle had taken place. Seven years later, Naval War College strategists believed it possible that the German fleet would feint an attack on New England before descending into West Indian waters.[7] The "elimination of the continental coast line as a factor of the problem" was the "striking result" of the hypothetical study of a German-American war, as the official "War Plan Black" explained in 1913.[8]

Planners paid some attention to the likelihood of German action in the Pacific. In 1903, when the Naval War College studied a German-American war, it assumed that the Pacific would be the main theater of war. The whole German fleet would strike against the Philippines, not the West Indies.[9] But this particular scenario remained short-lived. It was never taken up again, because the concentration of the German fleet in the North Sea suggested otherwise. "War Plan Black" dismissed the possibility of any significant fleet action in the Pacific. The Germans would need to use all their available forces for operations in the Caribbean, which would decide the war.[10]

The geographical specifics of the scenario of combat in the Caribbean were a matter of considerable discussion. Starting in 1900, planners debated where the Germans would attempt to create a military base in the West Indies. Originally, the question was decided in favor of the Dominican Republic, with Puerto Rico remaining a distinct possibility.[11] After 1906, strategists came to believe that Germany's primary targets would be along the southeastern edge of the Caribbean and on the Margarita Islands (near Venezuela) in particular.[12] The initial point of concentration for the American battle fleet changed accordingly. The best possible strategy would be to gather American forces off the island of Culebra to strike against the German fleet as it arrived in West Indian waters. But there was a good chance that the Americans would be unable to concentrate enough force there in time. Their point of concentration would then lie elsewhere, depending on the movement of German forces after their projected seizure of a base.

Planners strove to promise military success in their plans for a war with Germany. From the very beginning, strategists identified the issues that vexed their war plans. One of them was the changing overall balance of force. Between 1900 and 1905 the German fleet enjoyed a noticeable, yet slowly diminishing, numerical superiority that would put it in a strong position in the early stages of a campaign.[13] Although American naval construction tipped the balance in favor of the United States after 1905, Germany's subsequent accelerated buildup provided it again with a significant numerical advantage between 1910 and 1914.[14] Perhaps more important, there were vast differences in the comparative readiness of the two fleets. Germany's capabilities to mobilize and deploy its forces were far superior to those of the United States. While it would take at least thirty days to mobilize the whole U.S. fleet, it would take only seven days for Germany to deploy its maximum force. Throughout the period between 1900 and 1914, planners calculated that the German fleet would enjoy "command of the sea" in the Caribbean for a period of up to three weeks, regardless of the exact numerical balance of force. Thus, the Germans had enough time to seize a base and engage the American battle force on their own terms. In short, German preparedness trumped U.S. proximity to the relevant theater of war.[15]

Considerations of the balance of force and comparative readiness raised troubling doubts about the promise of victory. In the war games played at the Naval War College in 1901 and 1902, success in the decisive battle usually belonged to the German fleet.[16] Admiral Henry C. Taylor, a key war planner, went so far as to dismiss as a "fairy tale" a Naval War College study of 1900 that had predicted a U.S. victory.[17] The rise of Japan as a military opponent magnified the problems American war planners were facing after 1910 when the Germans once again enjoyed a numerical advantage in capital ships, in addition to their superior readiness. If the battle fleet or only portions of it were deployed in the Pacific at the outbreak of hostilities with Germany, the situation for the United States would be "desperate" and "almost hopeless," the official "War Plan Black" explained in 1913.[18]

Planners reached their disquieting conclusions about the course of a German-American war through a rigorous application of the idea of the aggressive combat of battle fleets. In so doing, they downplayed the tremendous risks and logistical problems the German fleet and its train would face on their transatlantic voyage, which would eventually lead to a showdown with the enemy's main force. To be sure, strategists paid considerable attention to the logistical aspects of the projected German campaign plan. They predicted that the Germans would make a stop at either the Azores or the Cape Verde Islands to resupply; and they stressed that the Germans could only afford a battle after setting up a base in the West Indies.[19] But expectations of German capabilities for transatlantic warfare were overly optimistic, if not outright fantastical, even though they were shared by German officers. According to U.S. planners, the Germans would be able to fully supply their fleet on its transoceanic voyage, keep up its combat readiness, and, in addition, orchestrate the transport of at least twenty-five thousand troops in the train of the German battle force. "War Plan Black" even raised the possibility that the Germans could move up to two hundred thousand troops across the Atlantic within two months after the outbreak of hostilities.[20] These assumptions were well in place before the 1907–09 world cruise of the U.S. "White Fleet," with its sixteen battleships and nearly fifteen thousand sailors, could have been construed as lending some credence to them.

War in the Pacific

While U.S. strategists were preparing for a climactic combat in the Caribbean, they also planned for a war in the Pacific. At the turn of the century, such plans revolved around the idea of an alliance war in the Far East.[21] Prompted by Russian territorial expansion in Manchuria and China, which presented a direct threat to U.S. interests in China, such a war would pit Japan, Great Britain, and the United States against Russia and its ally, France (and possibly Germany). From an operational point of view, U.S. discussions of such a war entailed less dramatic scenarios than those for a war with Germany. Cast in a supporting role, U.S. naval forces would not see major combat. Command of the sea would automatically fall to the superior joint Japanese-British-American navies, without substantive fleet action. These navies would entrap Russian and French (and, if necessary, German) naval forces in their Far Eastern bases and make raids against other enemy territories in the Far East, such as French Indochina. They would also support the operations of the Japanese army, for example, by attacking enemy positions on the Russian and Chinese coastlines or by controlling the Yangtze River.[22] Another task of U.S. forces was to seize an "advanced base" on the Chinese coast. This intent reflected the service's overall desire to attain such a base in order to complement the buildup of a major base in the Philippines and strengthen the American position in China itself.[23]

A war with Japan became the central scenario for a military conflict in the Pacific after 1906. Plans for war centered on the operations of the American battle fleet and its quick advance to the western Pacific leading to a climactic battle, which, in turn, would end a war that would not last more than six to twelve months total. Like its German-American counterpart, this would be a transoceanic and temporally confined war. Yet in this case, the U.S. fleet would launch a transoceanic campaign to bring the war to a successful conclusion. The defense of American empire in the Pacific entailed a full-scale war against Japan in the western Pacific and its military subjugation.[24]

By contrast, when the possibility of war with Japan had been first raised in 1897–98, the overall scenario had been different. Operations would focus on Hawaii and, if necessary, the defense of the U.S. West Coast. Militarily, this defensive scenario reflected the overall weakness of the navy and its primary deployment in the Atlantic. Politically, this was a war of self-styled hemispheric defense against Japanese ambitions, with Hawaii belonging to the U.S. sphere of influence; it was not triggered by the mutual pursuit of imperial interests in the western Pacific.[25]

Successful transoceanic warfare against Japan proved to be a big challenge, the superior numerical strength of the U.S. Navy notwithstanding. Planning for a war against Japan became a highly charged, tension-ridden endeavor, surrounded by speculations of defeat. Strategists struggled to develop operational scenarios that promised military success in a temporally confined war against Japan. Belief in offensive battle fleet warfare and climactic combat dominated these scenarios yet glossed over any possible difficulties.

Envisioning a war with Japan, planners assumed a distinct sequence of military events and operations.[26] At the outset of war, with the main U.S. force deployed in the Atlantic and only some cruisers and smaller naval vessels in the Pacific, command of the sea in most of the Pacific would fall to the Japanese for at least three months. The Japanese navy and expeditionary forces (of up to one hundred thousand troops) were bound to attack and seize the Philippines, Guam, and all other American possessions in the western Pacific. The Japanese would also be able to take the Midway Islands and overrun Hawaii in the eastern Pacific. Any main Japanese advance, it was assumed by 1910–11, would end there. Japan would then withdraw its fleets to home waters in expectation of an American transoceanic offensive. It was likely to hold on to and to fortify its new positions in such a way as to make their retaking a costly, time-consuming affair. In previous years, American strategists had invoked the specter of Japanese military raids against the Alaskan coastline, the U.S. West Coast, and the Panama Canal. There even had been grim prophecies of an outright Japanese invasion of the western United States, an apocalyptic scenario shared by Mahan and already imagined by strategists in 1897–98. A Japanese bombardment of the West Coast was not entirely ruled out even in 1911.[27]

While the Japanese were moving around in the Pacific, the U.S. battle force would be sent to the western Pacific. Once the numerically superior U.S. fleet reached western Pacific waters, the tide of war would irrevocably turn against the Japanese, it was believed. The U.S. force would establish an improvised "advance base" in the western Pacific, using war materials carried by ship, and then seek a decisive naval encounter with the Japanese fleet in one way or another. With its outcome sealed by battle, the war would end with the U.S. fleet exercising command of the sea in Japanese home waters and engaging in the "blockade and commercial isolation" of Japan.[28] There were no scenarios for a military invasion of the Japanese home islands. But military operations against the Japanese Empire on mainland Asia, in conjunction with China and, possibly, Russia, were part of the "War Plan Orange" approved by the Naval War College in 1911.

After 1906, planners intensely debated the exact contours of U.S. offensive operations. They offered various scenarios that reflected their full commitment to the most aggressive, long-distance campaigning and their will to deliver victory as rapidly as possible. In one scenario, which the General Board laid out in its first sketch for war in late 1906, the fleet was to cross the Atlantic, proceed via the Suez Canal through the Indian Ocean, and then advance toward Philippine waters. After three months, the fleet would be positioned to seize a base and meet the Japanese fleet.[29]

The Naval War College offered a different scenario in the war plan it drafted in 1911. At that time, planners had discarded the Suez route as the course of the main American advance to the western Pacific. They had decided that it was better to have the fleet sail around South America and then across the Pacific. In 1909–10, U.S. planners had settled on this route, which had been originally suggested in 1907, for several reasons.[30] The cruise of the fleet to the Pacific coast had convinced them that this route would place the fleet in the western Pacific in less than three months, and not the 120 days previously assumed. A cruise around South America seemed advantageous for political and logistical reasons as well. Its states were much more likely to cooperate with an advancing U.S. fleet, which, in addition, would also need to call in foreign ports less often than on the other route. The American route also promised to render the battle fleet less vulnerable on its travel to the Pacific, reducing, in the words of one naval planner, exposure to the "latent animosity and jealousy of European nations."[31] Attached to the choice of this route in 1910 was also the hope entertained by several planners that it would be possible to retain control of Hawaii in the opening months of the war, an optimistic assumption that was not widely accepted before 1914.

Assuming Japanese control of Hawaii, the Naval War College, in 1911, wanted the U.S. battle fleet to sail across the Pacific on a southern route, foregoing the reconquest of any U.S. insular possessions such as Hawaii or Guam.[32] After a replenishing stop at the Panama Canal Zone, it would sail to Philippine waters via the Marquesas Islands and Samoa, secretly stopping at neutral islands for intermediate coaling. It would establish an improvised base in the southern Philippines, which would receive its continuous supplies through the Indian Ocean and the Pacific. While seeking a decisive fleet action against the Japanese fleet, the Americans would engage in a "protracted" campaign, with the help of an arriving army, to attain full control of the Philippines, seize other islands, such as Guam, and slowly secure and exercise command of the seas in western

Pacific waters, eventually cutting off Japanese overseas communications and trade.

By 1914, the navy's strategists on the General Board developed a new campaign plan for a war with Japan. The imminent opening of the Panama Canal and new thinking about the outer line of the Japanese advance combined to change the planning equation. In contrast to the 1911 Naval War College plan, the new plan's basic premise was that Hawaii lay beyond Japanese reach. More than two thousand miles west of San Francisco, Pearl Harbor could now ground the movement of the fleet across the Pacific. After passing the canal (or rounding South America, if necessary) the battle fleet was to cross the Pacific on a "direct" central route that spanned San Francisco, Hawaii, Midway, Guam, and the Philippines. The (re)seizure of Guam would put the U.S. fleet within reach of the northern Philippines and vital Japanese overseas communications and allow it to "bring" the Japanese fleet "into action," resulting in its catastrophic defeat. If a Japanese-held Guam could not be easily retaken, the fleet was to bypass the island and sail directly to Manila Bay or to southern Philippine waters, making one or two secret coaling stops in sheltered waters at some German island.[33]

Although shifting in shape, the U.S. scenarios for the operations of the U.S. fleet enacted the same strategy. They all prescribed the instantaneous, by and large uninterrupted advance of the battle fleet to the western Pacific and a culminating event in a climactic naval battle.[34] A key premise of this prescription was the fleet's ability to engage in extended operations across vast distances, to master the logistical challenges posed by long, improvised lines of communications and supply, and to maintain a high level of combat readiness throughout. The key purpose of the dispatch of the U.S. fleet to the Pacific coast in 1907 and its subsequent return to the East Coast was precisely to test the ability of the fleet to engage in long-distance fleet action. The experiences of the "global cruise," in turn, grounded the optimism of planners concerning its feasibility. The cruise not only revised upward previously held ideas about the maximum steaming range of a nonrefueling battle fleet. More important, it demonstrated the fleet's high "power of self-maintenance," which enabled it to engage in wartime operations after oceanic crossings, or so key officers such as Admirals Dewey and Sperry summarized the lessons of the cruise.[35]

With great ardor, planners sought victory against Japan in a short war. A profound devotion to the idea of a relentless battle fleet offensive pervaded the navy's plans, glossed over any possible problems, and kept any criticism at bay. Before 1914, strategists frequently expressed considerable skepticism, if not outright doubt, about the viability of existing war plans and their anticipation of victory. Several planners, for example, offered devastating critiques of the initial scenario worked out by the General Board and raised the possibility of defeat. In their view, on arrival in Philippine waters the fleet would not be able to force the Japanese fleet into battle. Without immediate access to coaling stations or to a base with repair facilities, the U.S. force would be limited in its operations and face an enemy in control of superior lines of communications. Far from seeking an early battle, the Japanese could wage a war of attrition to wear down the U.S. fleet. Even in the case of a successful battle action, the U.S. fleet would hardly be able to exploit its victory because it would be hampered by the lack of a major war base and an expeditionary force to (re)conquer the Philippines.[36]

In the early 1910s, prominent strategists mounted similar critiques of the plans for a transpacific advance. Captain Bradley Fiske argued in 1911 that the Naval War College had "failed to produce any war plan" that offered a reasonable chance of success. According to Fiske, the college had not demonstrated how the U.S. battle fleet, which had just ventured across the Pacific to southern Philippine waters, would be in a position to force the Japanese into a major battle to secure command of the sea.[37] A few years later, in 1913, Fiske argued that the United States was bound to fight an "inglorious and expensive war" with Japan, with no real chance of military success, assuming as he did that the Japanese would seize the Philippine and Hawaiian islands and then render them impregnable.[38]

Not surprisingly, logistical challenges were a constant source of concern for naval planners. Time and again, strategists identified the lack of sufficient logistical capabilities as a key problem vexing their campaign plans. The logistical requirements were indeed stupefying, especially in the absence of naval bases and the initial territorial conquests by the Japanese. The plans first devised in 1906–07 for the fleet's journey across the Atlantic and Indian Oceans, for example, envisioned commercial purchases of coal abroad, the chartering of foreign merchantmen, and continuous coaling on the move. The plans also rested on equally questionable assumptions concerning the ability to provide for continuous supplies in the theater of war and the promise of an "improvised base." The shift to a transpacific route and concerted efforts to enhance the navy's logistical capabilities did not dramatically alter this picture. The transpacific advance adhered to the chimera of a logistically self-sustaining advance across thousands of miles.[39]

Moreover, planners failed to meet the logistical goals they had set for themselves. In the early 1910s, the navy did not store the amounts of coal on the Pacific coast and the Panama Canal Zone that, by its own estimates, were needed to support the transpacific advance of the fleet. Colliers and other auxiliary ships were also in short supply. In 1913, for example, the Bureau of Supplies and Accounts reported that the navy lacked more than three-quarters of the fleet colliers required for its war plans in the Pacific.[40] In short, the U.S. Navy did not attain the logistical capabilities to make its strategy credible on its own terms.

Most planners were cognizant of the many problems inherent in "War Plan Orange." This was indicated by their strong, yet unsuccessful advocacy for the creation of well-fortified bases in the western Pacific, first in the Philippines (until 1908), then later on Guam (after 1911), which could hold out against the initial Japanese onslaught and then serve as an "advanced base" for the U.S. battle force.[41] The plans for fortifying Hawaii and developing it into a major naval base, which gathered full steam by 1908–09, spoke the same language.[42] In fact, a significant number of planners were so fearful of the prospects of a war with Japan that they openly demanded, albeit in vain, the peacetime deployment of either the whole U.S. fleet, or a substantial portion thereof, in the Pacific, which would alter, with one stroke, the strategic landscape of the Pacific.[43]

Still, plans for a war with Japan clung to the tenets of aggressive battle fleet warfare and speedy victory. Such a seemingly unshakeable commitment perhaps best showcased itself in the reaction to the impasse reached in the early 1910s when planners had found it reasonable to assume that Japan had the ability to seize Hawaii, Midway, and Guam. One common response was to assume this problem away in the planning process; another was to hope, against all odds, that these islands could be held if the cruisers stationed in Asiatic waters rushed to Hawaii.[44] Mahan, the iconic navalist, offered yet another solution in 1911: he wanted the fleet to proceed to the Aleutians after it had arrived on the West Coast. This move alone, he intimated, would force the Japanese to abandon both Hawaii and Guam.[45] A fourth response was the "War Plan Orange" the Naval War College crafted in 1911. Dismissing the possibility of recapture of Hawaii, the planners advised the immediate advance of the fleet across the Pacific, with the Panama Canal Zone as the starting point. The U.S. fleet was to thrust itself directly across the Pacific into southern Philippine waters and create an "improvised base," with supply lines extending across the Indian and southern Pacific Oceans, to anchor subsequent operations.[46]

Only a few planners offered, on occasion, a rather different perspective that broke with the dominant mold. These men did not expect a short war, based on the rapid advance of the fleet to the western Pacific. Stressing the logistical challenges of a transpacific campaign, they envisioned a long war of attrition, with the Americans slowly advancing across the Pacific and making the best use of the superior productive capabilities of a mobilized war economy. This vision of a carefully orchestrated military campaign revolved around the seizure of islands and the setting up of powerful intermediate bases in a methodical, step-by-step approach. Of course, there would still be a decisive naval encounter, and ultimate victory would belong to the Americans.[47]

By 1914, the war planners at the General Board felt fully confident about the military promise of their vision of transoceanic battle fleet warfare against Japan. Firm expectations of victory in a temporally confined war ruled the day at a time when the geostrategic situation shifted in favor of the Americans with the completion of the canal and the expectation of secure possession of Hawaii. The "War Plan Orange" that the General Board approved in 1914 predicted war-deciding military success within six months.[48]

Plans for an Anglo-German War

Like their American counterparts, German naval strategists prepared for big-power wars and championed regional concentration. Their thinking about future military encounters focused on the British Empire and the United States, the two most important German adversaries in the new age of global politics. Planning for an Anglo-German naval war became the central preoccupation of German war strategists between 1897 and 1914. Preparations for war with the United States, which began in earnest in 1898, matured into Operations Plan III by 1903; they were abandoned three years later for political reasons that lay outside the realm of German-American relations themselves.

By contrast, operational planning for a war against France and Russia, which previously had been the central concern for planners, faded into the background as the political tenets of navalism cohered. In the wake of the Anglo-French Entente, such planning made little or no sense. In a war that involved Britain on the other side, French and Russian naval forces would hardly matter at all. Between 1905 and 1909, the Admiralty Staff wasted no time on planning for a war against only France and Russia.[49]

By 1900, strategists had become obsessed with the inevitability of an Anglo-German armed confrontation. Tirpitz's assessment in 1897, that

"England" would be Germany's "most dangerous enemy," was reflected in the vast scale and scope of German preparations for the eventuality of a war with that country.[50] According to navalist logic, successful military self-assertion in a war of defense held the key to threat and deterrence against Britain. A hypothetical war with Britain thus required the ability to fight off a naval attack by the Royal Navy and prevent it from exercising command of the sea in the North Sea. Such ability, in turn, did not entail military capabilities to launch a naval war of aggression against Britain and pave the way for invasion.

By the turn of the century, Tirpitz developed a scenario for a future Anglo-German war that promised victory in a future war of self-defense to take place after the buildup of the German battle fleet. This scenario informed the Imperial Naval Office's subsequent long-term pursuit of a naval program; it also set the stage for the ongoing planning efforts for an Anglo-German war that might occur in the present. The specter of such a war terrified German officers, especially in the early 1900s, when the balance of maritime force was most uneven. Until 1914, planners struggled to develop operational plans that they thought could ensure military success in a convincing manner. Fittingly, operational planning was a site of considerable controversy and lacked stability.

Looking ahead, Tirpitz and like-minded strategists self-confidently promised future German victory attained by a big battle off the German coast.[51] The script for this war was straightforward. The Royal Navy would carry the "strategic offensive" to Germany's coast. Its battleship squadrons would actively seek a decisive battle to annihilate the opposing naval force and impose a close blockade of the German coastline. The numerically inferior German navy would adopt a defensive posture and then fight a "defensive battle" under favorable conditions.[52] In *Service Memorandum IX*, Tirpitz had concluded that any battle fleet needed a numerical superiority of at least one-third over the opposing fleet to engage in offensive warfare against the enemy's coast. Thus, Tirpitz fixed the force ratio between the German and British battle fleets necessary for a German victory at two to three. This was exactly the balance of force that the Imperial Naval Office wanted to attain through the construction of a fleet of sixty capital ships by 1918, as discussed previously.[53]

A German fleet two thirds the size of the opposing British force could expect to win a "defensive battle" against an attacking Royal Navy. As the defending force, the German fleet could choose the time and place of the battle and ensure the presence of its entire force. Ideally, the latter would first engage only a part of the British forces before taking on the remainder in the ultimate military showdown. Taking the strategic offensive would take its toll on the Royal Navy. Long lines of supply and communication and blockade duty would impose heavy strains and require a dispersal of naval forces. Operating in enemy waters, these forces would be vulnerable to instruments of defensive naval warfare, such as mines and torpedo boats. Furthermore, German numerical inferiority was to be compensated for by better naval training, organization, and ship construction. In September 1899, Tirpitz summarized such thinking when he noted that his naval program was to create "so powerful a force, that only England [will be] superior. But also against England we undoubtedly have good chances through geographical position, military system, wartime mobilization, torpedo boats, tactical training, planned organizational development, and the unified leadership of the monarch."[54] Belief in superior German military effectiveness grounded predictions of victory.

This overall scenario presumed symmetric commitments to the same kind of warfare on both sides. Specifically, the scenario also rested on assumptions about British offensive warfare and blockade tactics. The British navy was to adhere to the paradigm of aggressive battle fleet warfare, as laid out in *Service Memorandum IX*. This assumption was also based on a keen sense of the operational concepts that guided British naval strategy and armaments in the 1890s and were expressed in such documents as the so-called *Three Admirals Report,* published in 1888. The latter had provided the military rationale for the subsequent British battleship naval programs.[55]

But the expectation of British aggressive military tactics also fed on the perception of a particular predilection of the British navy for strategic offense and for seeking out a decisive battle. Time and again, Tirpitz and other strategists pointed toward the offensive spirit and doctrines of a British navy supposedly steeped in "Drakian" and "Nelsonian" traditions, the arrogant sentiment of the British as a people who expected glorious naval action, and an overall British interest in a short war for diplomatic reasons.[56] Convinced of the particularly aggressive inclinations of the Royal Navy, most planners continued to expect an attack on the German fleet and coast at a time when they had already concluded that such a British attack no longer made much military sense and was unnecessary for command of the sea itself.[57]

The turn-of-the-century scenario for the course of an imaginary Anglo-German war in the future framed the planning for an actual war in the present. This scenario occasioned considerable anxiety and debate among planners, who strove to come up with plans for any reasonable military action in the face of a superior British navy.⁵⁸ So intent were planners on providing for some sort of self-defense that they prescribed military action against neighboring neutrals to shore up Germany's position vis-à-vis Britain. Disregard for smaller countries and their neutrality was not only a prerogative of army planners; it also characterized naval strategy and fit well with the overall navalist emphasis on big empires.⁵⁹

When planners had first faced the specter of an imminent war with Britain in 1895–96, they had sought to solve the conundrum of an Anglo-German war by means of highly aggressive military behavior. They had developed daring schemes to exploit a presumed initial German superiority in the North Sea. They had advocated offensive strikes against the British coastline (especially the River Thames area), considered an invasion of the British Isles, and advocated the military occupation of the Netherlands to enhance their country's military position. By the end of the 1890s these reckless schemes had fallen into disrepute, and were officially dropped in 1899. When one planner expressed renewed interest in them in 1902 he was roundly condemned by his peers.⁶⁰

By the turn of the century, planners all agreed that the promise of success through battle in a war of maritime defense could only be a proposition for some future time. In view of the disparity in military strength in the present, the strategists of the Admiralty Staff, the key planning agency after 1899, prescribed a strictly defensive strategy that did not envision any major battle. Its main purpose was to ensure the survival of the fleet and, if at all possible, to limit somewhat the impact of the British exercise of command of the sea in the North Sea. This strategy assumed both a close British blockade of Germany's coastlines and a direct strike against Germany's small but ever-growing fleet. Ruling out the possibility for any successful initial reduction of the British naval forces that could perhaps allow for climactic combat with any chance for success, planners developed two main scenarios for the defensive posture they prescribed. The first entailed the concentration of the battle fleet in the Elbe estuary. The second involved a plan to deploy the main part of the fleet in the Danish Belt and then prepare for a defensive military action in the Baltic approaches.⁶¹

First suggested in 1899, this second plan moved to the center of the planning process in the early 1900s. It was premised on the military occupation of most of Denmark, which occasioned considerable negotiations with the army. To the naval planners' chagrin, the General Staff under General Alfred von Schlieffen viewed the occupation of Denmark with considerable reticence, if not outright opposition. Assuming that any war would most likely involve the French and the Russians, army planners did not want to deploy a substantial body of troops to occupy Denmark.[62] The hostility of the General Staff forced the Admiralty Staff to cancel its plans for the Baltic approaches and the occupation of parts of Denmark in the spring of 1905.[63] The navy subsequently refocused its attention on the North Sea as the main theater of war, with the fleet deployed in, or out of, the Elbe estuary.

The shift itself took place in the context of acute concern about an imminent war with Britain in 1904–05. Across the board, planners were terrified by the prospects of such a war. They expected the British to descend on Germany's coast, destroy its maritime trade and shipping, and impose a relentless blockade while a vulnerable German fleet could do nothing and faced the risk of complete destruction. A blockade was bound to have a catastrophic impact on the German economy and food supply, creating a "financial and social crisis" and sparking domestic unrest among the working class, explained various memoranda.[64] The outlook of planners was so grim that some of them, including Admiral Büchsel, the head of the Admiralty Staff, discussed a successful invasion of France as the only military option to relieve the pressures of a blockade and exercise threat and deterrence against the British opponent.[65] Admiral Hans von Koester, the commanding officer of the active battle fleet, favored an immediate battle action against the superior British Royal Navy. Koester recommended an early battle off Heligoland, which would result, he recognized, in the certain destruction of his own force.[66]

Imagining an Anglo-German war after the crisis of 1904–05, when operational planning focused again on the North Sea, strategists confronted an entirely new set of concerns in their search for success. Although continued enlargement of the fleet and the accelerated development of coastal defenses were improving Germany's maritime position in the North Sea, a new analysis of the probable course of a war nonetheless undermined their entire script for successful maritime self-defense against Britain as it had been defined by the turn of the century. The viability of the ideas about a strategic defense in the North Sea as a proposition for either the present or future was at stake as planners had to revise their assumptions about likely British behavior.

Until then, most planners had expected the British to take the most aggressive military action, including a narrow blockade of Germany's coastline, direct attacks on coastal ports and shipping, and immediate action against the fleet. But in 1907 views of how the British were to conduct a blockade underwent revision. Now, planners assumed that the Royal Navy would resort to a more flexible form of blockade, a blockade maintained only by light naval forces operating off the German coast, with the undivided battle fleet itself securely deployed further back, most likely in the proximity of Britain. Planners based such thinking on what they learned about new British plans for an "observational blockade." They also relied on their own estimates about proper action in the face of the increased strength of the German fleet and coastal defenses.[67]

By 1908, planners offered another scenario. They raised the possibility of a distant blockade at the entrances to the North Sea.[68] Tirpitz and all planners agreed in general that the prospects of such a blockade threatened to undercut any hope of success in a war with Britain. In this case, their battle fleet could hardly hope to fight a successful battle to break the blockade. It could not rely on a strategic defense to compensate for inferior numbers. A blockading navy had no reason to send substantive forces to the enemy's coastline or seek a decisive naval encounter. Rather, to break a distant blockade, the German battle fleet would need to take offensive action and seek battle under less advantageous conditions. There was little hope of diminishing the superiority of the Royal Navy in order to achieve an equalization of force before a main battle.[69]

In previous years, there had been several references to the possibility of a long-distance blockade yet they had remained inconsequential. Such warnings had become more common between 1904 and 1906 so that in the operation plan for 1906 the Admiralty Staff had felt the need to explicitly discount the possibility of a distant blockade.[70] Tirpitz himself had remained guarded on this issue. In 1907, the navy secretary accepted the notion of an "intermediate" blockade. But he also predicted that in a few years the sheer strength of the German fleet would force the British to institute a distant blockade at the Atlantic approaches.[71] Ten years earlier, Tirpitz had discussed the possibility of such a distant blockade in the context of a Franco-German war. France would be well advised, he had argued, to institute a blockade of the German coast at the North Sea entrances in the event of such a war. Not requiring offensive fleet action, such a blockade would be disastrous for Germany while protecting the French coastline.[72]

Hence the period after 1908 was one of crisis and dissent among planners as they were forced to imagine a course of war that still promised victory. In response to revised thinking about British blockade warfare and the formidable strength of the German fleet, operational scenarios went beyond previous commitments to the strategic defense. They provided a field of enactment for pent-up desires regarding offensive fleet action among officers schooled in the tenets of *Service Memorandum IX*, which defined the strategic offensive as the natural mission of a battle fleet.[73] The two heads of the Admiralty Staff between 1908 and 1911, Admirals Friedrich Graf von Baudissin and Max von Fischel, championed aggressive action. They devised plans for an immediate offensive by the entire concentrated fleet against the British coast, to take the Royal Navy by surprise and bring about a battle in the northern part of the North Sea. These proposals moved to center stage precisely at a time when another "war panic" involving a British preemptive strike against a rising German fleet gripped planners in the context of the Naval Bill of 1908.[74]

Although these proposals received Tirpitz's tacit approval, they remained contested. Under the leadership of Admiral Henning von Holtzendorff, the command of the High Seas Fleet also advanced its own views. Skeptical of the promise of an immediate offensive across the North Sea, the command suggested a concentration of the fleet off the city of Skagen, located at the northern end of the Jutland Peninsula, to both await British action and threaten an attack across the North Sea. The main purpose of the fleet was to pull the British main fleet in, then to withdraw into the Baltic Sea, and engage a pursuing British force in battle under the most favorable conditions.[75] This proposal had considerable appeal, in part because it addressed itself to yet another problem that beset planners by 1909–10. The capital ships built after 1906 and stationed in the Baltic Sea could not navigate the Kaiser Wilhelm Canal, thus ruling out an immediate concentration in the North Sea for offensive action.

The will to assure success through eventual battle in a war against a superior British fleet reigned supreme when operational planning entered a new phase in the winter of 1911–12. After much debate and intense wargaming, the search for what Admiral August von Heeringen, the new head of the Admiralty Staff, called a "militarily useful chance against England" again involved the strategic defense in the North Sea and the pursuit of a battle against the Royal Navy in the vicinity of the German Bight.[76] This approach dominated planning until the outbreak of war. It entailed an analysis of British blockade tactics that allowed for successful German action. It also expanded on the scenario originally devised by Tirpitz at the turn of the twentieth century. Not coincidentally, the Anglo-German balance of maritime force approximated the 2:3 ratio in capital-ship strength that strategists had aspired to since the late 1890s.

Tested in war games and fleet maneuvers, this scenario rested on a number of premises.[77] Overall British superiority in capital ships combined with the threat posed by British mine, submarine, and torpedo-boat warfare to rule out any long-range, battle-seeking operations by the German battle fleet. Germany's own maritime strength, in turn, imposed limits on British action. It rendered unlikely an all-out attack on the German coastline and ruled out the conduct of a close British blockade maintained by battleship squadrons patrolling the German coast. Anticipating a British blockade, planners remained cognizant of the specter of a distant blockade at the entrances of the North Sea. In fact, they studied its possible ramifications in numerous war games but they took French and British maneuvers in 1912 and 1913 to mean that it was not certain to happen.[78] Throughout, they assumed that any British blockade, however distant, would always involve light forces operating in the vicinity of the German Bight, either as a "guarding force" or as an "observational force," backed up by the entire fleet deployed further back, based on the British northeastern coast. They also postulated that the Royal Navy was unlikely to surrender most of the North Sea to the Germans or allow them to strike against the British coastline.

Under these circumstances, the navy's strategists convinced themselves that their fleet could fight a "defensive battle" in the southern North Sea, close to the German Bight, after successfully diminishing the existing force differential. Such diminishment, it was argued, could be obtained by continuous action against British "guard" or "observation" forces, which stood to be continually reinforced by the British. These attacks, in turn, were bound to draw in the bulk of the British fleet and expose it to German attacks before a big battle. The attacks were to involve the clever use of both capital ships and smaller vessels. Within this context, much hope was also put on long-range operations of U-boats and mine-ships across the entire North Sea. The result of all of this was an erosion of British strength, paving the road to climactic combat. Such combat, planners insisted, was inevitable: eventually, the British would either seek it or, at least, not avoid it.

The official operations orders for the fleet issued on August 1, 1914, reiterated this belief. They stated that the first "goal of operations" should be to "damage the English Fleet" through "offensive action" against the "guard or blockade forces in the German Bight" and a "relentless offensive mine and submarine offensive extending to the British coast." Once this warfare had produced an "equalization of forces" (*Kräfteausgleich*), the concentrated German fleet was to seek a battle "under favorable conditions." If an opportunity for combat presented itself beforehand, the order added, it should be exploited right away.[79]

In 1914, strategists promised success through decisive battle within the vicinity of the German Bight in a war of maritime self-defense against Britain. But their optimism in that regard was fraught with enormous tension. Most directly, planners were deeply aware of the adversity they faced in a hypothetical war. The specter of failure loomed large in the planning efforts the navy engaged in between 1912 and 1914, as it had always done. Strikingly, in the last war game planners had played before the war, the German fleet had suffered catastrophic defeat at the hand of a superior British fleet.[80] "Surely," summarized Admiral Müller on August 1, 1914, "England" had "no reason to fear the risk that her fleet encountered in a war against us. Rather the opposite."[81] Planners glossed over some of their own insights when they promised success in a more general way. On the one hand, they discussed the possibility of a British blockade at the entrance to the North Sea, and recognized that its success did not depend on any substantive British maritime presence in the North Sea itself (let alone any climactic combat with the Germans). On the other hand, planners assumed that the British were bound to employ enough light forces for guard or observational duty in the southern North Sea, and that they were ultimately willing to accept a big battle there, too, thus providing the Germans with a convenient opportunity to first attain an "equalization of forces," a *Kräfteausgleich,* and then a battle on their terms.

Moving within a self-contained universe, operational planners did not prepare for the possibility of a scenario that did not conform to their assumptions and expectation of victorious combat embedded therein. Admiral Heeringen remarked in 1912 that if the British were to institute a distant blockade at the entrances to the North Sea, the role of the German battle fleet would be a "very sad one" and that all then depended on the use of submarines. Yet the admiral did not follow up on this insight with any substantive action.[82] When in May 1914 Tirpitz asked Admiral Friedrich von Ingenohl, the officer in command of the High Seas Fleet, about any contingency plans in case British forces were not employed in the German Bight, he did not receive a positive answer.[83] Against their own better knowledge, strategists did not properly anticipate British fleet action. They tenaciously stuck to the idea of success in an armed conflict with Britain and clung to the script of battle fleet warfare that they had first developed at the turn of the century.

Transatlantic Warfare

In contrast to scenarios for an Anglo-German war, planning for a hypothetical war with the United States involved bold, if not fantastical, visions of transoceanic warfare. Strategists prepared for a hypothetical war to impose the German imperial will on U.S. policy makers and to protect German interests in the Western Hemisphere and the Far East against American encroachments.[84] In such a war, the German navy needed to engage in aggressive transatlantic warfare to secure and exercise command of the sea in the Western Hemisphere. Such warfare depended on German numerical military superiority. At the turn of the century, planners felt confident that their fleet was already stronger than its American counterpart.

Developed between 1898 and 1903, the plans for war with the United States clung to the tenets of offensive battle fleet warfare. They focused on a climactic military showdown between the German and American fleets in the western Atlantic or Caribbean within two months after the outbreak of hostilities. A German victory would then enable the German fleet to exercise "command of the sea" in the Atlantic by means of a close blockade, bombardments, and commerce-raiding. The destruction of the American battle fleet would also provide the conditions for landing German troops on North American soil and their deployment against major cities and "commercial and industrial centers" in the American Northeast, New York and/or Boston in particular. All planners agreed that operations against these centers were the "only means" to make the United States sue for peace and accept German terms.[85]

The exact contours of anti-American war plans were the subject of considerable discussion. They took their final shape in Operations Plan III, which was finished in 1903. Planners settled on the idea that their fleet needed to gain a base of operations in the Caribbean after crossing the Atlantic; they selected Puerto Rico and the small adjacent island of Culebra for that purpose. The arrival of the German fleet in the Caribbean, the seizure of these islands, and the immediate threat to American possessions in that region would force the American fleet to seek the battle the Germans coveted as a prerequisite for landing troops and successfully concluding the war. If the Americans eschewed battle in the Caribbean, the German fleet would descend on the North American coast and attack American coastal cities and commerce to impose a battle of annihilation on the American fleet off its own coast. Originally, in 1898–1900, German naval planners had discussed a different course of action. They had wanted their fleet to proceed directly to the U.S. coast, seize a base, preferably at Frenchman Bay in Maine, and then seek a decisive battle with the American fleet.[86]

Strategists strongly believed in their bold vision for a campaign against the United States in the Western Hemisphere. Their plans glossed over the enormous logistical difficulties of sending the German battle fleet into transoceanic waters and of organizing the transport of a sizeable number of German ground troops to America. The German force would have to exceed the thirty thousand men that Germany had sent to China in 1900 while receiving the open assistance of the other major powers. Planners also realized that their armada would consist of battleships built for warfare in European waters. Vice-Admiral Diederichs, then the head of the Admiralty Staff, did not even hesitate to include obsolete ships in the German fleet that would cross the Atlantic, ships that in his own judgment were hardly a match for the most recent battleships.[87] So committed was the Admiralty Staff to its operational design that it continued to plan for an attack on the American coast long after the General Staff under General Schlieffen had dismissed the idea of deploying German ground troops on North American soil and failed to cooperate in any meaningful way with naval planners.[88]

While eschewing operational realism, the Admiralty Staff recognized that any naval campaign against the United States required certain political preconditions. In order to send a fleet across the Atlantic, there had to be a political situation in Europe "which leaves the German Empire an entirely free hand abroad," as the authors of Operations Plan III stated.[89] Transatlantic warfare required the goodwill of Britain, the country otherwise defined as Germany's "most dangerous enemy."[90] By 1906, open Anglo-German antagonism forced the Admiralty Staff to cancel its planning for a German-American war, which had, up to that point, instantiated the major tenets of navalism and its professional obsessions.[91]

Plans for an American-German naval war devised by the Germans mirrored the scenarios envisioned by the Americans for the same war. Such symmetry was not surprising. Operational planning produced strikingly similar conclusions precisely because its protagonists embraced commonly shared notions of war, strategy, and politics. In each country, the tenets of battle fleet warfare combined with notions of threat and deterrence and the unmitigated desire to promise success to shape navalists' war planning and its rationality. The result was the same on both sides of the Atlantic: belief in victory in temporally confined wars trumped any other considerations.

Chapter 6

Commerce, Law, and the Limitation of War

After World War I, the German political theorist Carl Schmitt was quick to argue that maritime warfare had helped to pioneer so-called total war, a new practice of war among the great powers.[1] The conduct of such "total war" had dissolved the boundaries between combatants and noncombatants, soldiers and civilians: it was built around the potentially unlimited use of force across the civil-military divide. During the First World War, the Allied and German naval blockades had been the manifestations of this new type of war. "A hunger blockade," noted Schmitt, "targets indiscriminately the entire population of the blockaded area, and, thus, the military and civilian population, men and women, the elderly and children."[2]

For Schmitt, naval warfare had contained defining "elements" of such a "pure war of extermination" between states well before 1914.[3] Since the seventeenth century, war at sea had not been subjected to the same sort of *Hegung des Krieges* (regulation of war) as its counterpart on land (which, at least in theory, had been turned into a well-regulated armed contest between states, fought out by regular armies). "Naval war," wrote Schmitt, "not only has its own distinct naval strategic and tactical methods and parameters. In its entirety, this war has always been, to a remarkable degree, a war against the opponent's trade and economy; and thus a war against noncombatants, an economic war, that also affected neutral trade through the legal institutions and practices of prize, contraband, and blockade."[4] From Schmitt's perspective, the hunger blockades of the First World War simply pushed the peculiarities of Western naval warfare to their logical extreme.

Indeed, the official Allied blockade of Germany and the German submarine campaigns played a pivotal role in the "de-bounding of warfare" in World War I, enacting a professional-military war against civilian populations outside existing regimes of military limitation and legal restraint.[5] The conduct of a maritime war of economic strangulation transformed previous meanings of naval blockade and commerce-destruction by turning them into a means of potentially starving entire societies to death and destroying their wartime capabilities for economic and social reproduction, as opposed to causing limited economic dislocation and shortages and, possibly, political and social turmoil.[6] Wars of maritime extermination pursued victory by turning the entire enemy nation into the object of military force and targeting its infrastructure, cohesion, safety, and, ultimately, collective will.

To a remarkable degree, the practice of maritime wars of extermination during (and after) World War I was, however, at odds with prewar U.S. and German naval approaches to warfare. Prior to 1914, German and U.S. naval elites moved within a regime of military and legal limitation when they conceptualized maritime warfare as a war of economic pressure and prepared for the application of military force targeting the opponent's civilian trade. Far from enacting a predilection for unlimited destruction (a predilection that some scholars have described as a distinctive feature of either American or German "ways of war"[7]), these maritime militarists kept within clear limits the potentially unrestrained nature of naval warfare, as identified by Schmitt. In fact, such investment in the limitation of war lent a distinctive shape to the military thought and practice of the U.S. and German navies; much like the rigid adherence to the concept of battle fleet warfare and the pursuit of regional military power, it, too, set them apart from their British counterpart.[8]

Considerations of waging war against the opponent's maritime trade were nonetheless absolutely central to the thinking of German and U.S. navalists before World War I. While preparing their navies for the contest of battle fleets, planners did not discard those features of the war at sea that had always straddled the civil-military divide. Commerce-destruction and commercial blockades occupied an important place in their thinking; in fact, maritime strategists were adamant about the enormous promises (and grave dangers) of a war of economic pressure given the ever-increasing maritime-economic vulnerabilities of industrial nation-states in a globalizing world. Economic dislocation and social and political turmoil were part of the two navies' calculus of war. Accordingly, policy makers of the two navies strove to safeguard a proper (legal) space for waging war against the opponent's trade when they were confronted with the issue of the legal delimitation of maritime warfare after 1900. In short, the embrace of wars of maritime extermination required a leap, which was nevertheless also rooted in the prewar thinking of German and U.S. navalists.

War of Commerce and Trade

Battle fleet warfare anchored the universe of the military-operational thought and practice that German and U.S. naval elites fashioned at the beginning of the twentieth century. Yet these navalists' visions of naval warfare nonetheless always transcended the contest between battle fleets. Naval war was still a war of commerce and economic pressure that involved a more expansive use of military force. Supposedly, this remained a peculiar feature of maritime warfare, reflected, in turn, in the special meanings of the notion of "command of the sea," which lacked a direct equivalent in the realm of army combat. If we believe theorists such as Mahan and Tirpitz, this command was never an end in itself; rather, it was a means to a larger end in a war that involved more than the destruction of the enemy's fighting fleets. According to this view, command of the sea was a necessary precondition for subsequent naval operations to bring a war to a successful conclusion.

The "struggle" over "command of the sea" would be the "first task," the German *Service Memorandum IX* had explained in 1894, "because only once the command of the sea is gained, the actual means become available that force the enemy to sue for peace." The list of these means included commercial blockades, operations against enemy transoceanic trade and colonies, bombardments of enemy shorelines and coastal cities, and the landing of troops and creation of bases for the army.[9] In 1899, a lecture on naval preparations for war by Captain Charles Stockton, then the president of the U.S. Naval War College, summarized U.S. thinking on this issue. Stockton divided maritime warfare into three "general forms of action," that is, the "war of fleets and squadrons," the "war against commerce," and "maritime expeditions, combined or naval." The "war of fleets and squadrons" would secure "command of the sea" and, thus, be the "greater movement," which, in turn, would "give freedom for and allow or accompany the minor movements of commerce destroying and territorial attack." These so-called minor movements would "of course" be the "element[s] making for successful termination of war."[10]

Opposition to a cruiser-based strategy of commerce-destruction on the high seas as a primary strategy thus did not amount to general opposition to the very idea of operations against the enemy's seaborne trade. In his writings on naval strategy, Mahan, for example, was most adamant about the overall significance of the war of commerce and trade. "For what purposes, primarily, do navies exist?" Mahan asked in 1894. "Surely not merely to fight one another,—to gain what Jomini calls 'the sterile glory' of fighting battles in order to win them. If navies, as all agree, exist for the protection of commerce, it inevitably follows that in war they must aim at depriving their enemy of that great resource; nor is it easy to conceive what broad military use they can subserve that at all compares with the protection and destruction of trade." "Blows against commerce" would be the "most deadly that can be struck"; they would be "blows at the communications of the states; they intercept its nourishment, they starve its life; they cut the roots of its powers, the sinews of its war."[11] The "stoppage of commerce, in whole or in part," Mahan explained a few years later, "compels peace."[12]

Mahan had little doubt that the commercial blockade, based on "command of the sea," was the superior form of a war of trade and economic pressure, as opposed to cruiser warfare on the open sea. According to Mahan, the blockade of the enemy coast would be "the most systematic, regularized and extensive form of commerce-destruction known to war."[13] Sharing the same thoughts, Tirpitz expressly characterized the blockade as the "natural course of action" for the superior maritime power that also "commands a strong position."[14] Both writers identified the same advantages of a blockade, namely, its relentless concentration of force and its comprehensiveness, as it cuts off the enemy's seaborne trade at its very source, enemy ports, and also affects neutral trade.

Maritime commercial warfare had its firm place in operational planning. Strategists may have marginalized operations against the opponent's commerce in their operational planning when they imagined American-Japanese, Anglo-German, and American-German wars, focusing on the struggle over "command of the sea" and seldom looking beyond the battle of annihilation. Yet this was primarily a matter of priorities as defined by the emphasis on the crucial importance of climactic combat. In addition, the marginalization of commercial maritime warfare also reflected the specific political and military objectives in particular war scenarios. In a hypothetical German-American war, for example, the U.S. pursuit of victory depended on securing command of the sea only in the Western Hemisphere against possible German transatlantic military action.

The war of commerce and trade cast its long shadow over the two navies' war strategies. Although not mapped out in much detail, it was given a war-ending significance whenever one side was in a position to exercise command of the sea and force the enemy to sue for peace. The specter of British economic warfare, based on the Royal Navy's control of the North Sea, for example, rightly haunted German planners. According to U.S. planners, the commercial isolation of Japan would end a Japanese-American war. Their German counterparts envisioned raids against American trade and commerce, the blockade of ports on the East Coast, and amphibious attacks against major industrial and commercial centers as the means to bring a war against the United States to a successful conclusion. By the same token, American plans for a multination war in the Far East also prescribed commercial maritime warfare against Russian and French territories and trade in the region.[15]

Official German war plans included designs for limited cruiser-based commercial maritime warfare as a parallel action to the operations of the battle fleet. The handful of regular cruisers and other naval vessels deployed abroad in peacetime were to engage in "ruthless warfare" against trade and enemy possessions, as one planner put it in 1901.[16] The major naval force abroad, the cruiser squadron based in Kiaochow, was to proceed against the enemy's lines of communication, shipping routes, and colonial possessions and inflict maximum damage in the event of war against Britain and the United States. The envisioned field of operations spanned the Pacific and Indian oceans. Some schemes for a German-American war provided for a German cruiser force sailing across the Pacific to bombard American coastal cities such as San Diego and San Francisco and intercept merchant vessels off the U.S. coast. Provisions for an Anglo-German war included, for a while, similar strikes against the Canadian Pacific coast. The primary focus of plans for this war became operations against British shipping lanes in East Asian waters, with a special emphasis on Australia.

Tirpitz and other strategists generally agreed on the principal value of cruiser warfare against trade lines if an Anglo-German war broke out while the German battle fleet was still too weak to effectively challenge the British battle fleet. Tirpitz stressed such warfare's many values in 1907. After a lost battle, a campaign against Britain's trade routes would be "the only means of war that is left to us to fight successfully for somewhat satisfactory terms of peace."[17] The threat "of most ruthless war against English commerce" was Germany's only chance to exercise any military threat and deterrence against Britain. Only the possibility of cruiser warfare, in turn, would raise the bar for any British decision to go to war against Germany in the first place. If we believe Tirpitz and others, a campaign against Britain's trade and coastline was also the only promising course of action in case the British eventually decided to institute a distant blockade of Germany at the Atlantic approaches. In this instance, however, the German battle fleet, or parts thereof, would get directly involved, for Germany would then exercise command of the sea in parts of the North Sea.[18]

U.S. strategists did not offer extensive discussions of a cruiser-based war of commerce but they believed in its principal value. The General Board expressly advised it on one of the rare occasions after the turn of the century when it addressed the case of an Anglo-American war. Vigorous cruiser-based commercial warfare against the Royal Navy would be the only maritime military option left for the U.S. Navy, with its weaker battle force, the General Board reckoned in 1906. On that occasion, the agency also stressed the value of a cruiser-based war of commerce and trade against other commercial nations including Japan, Germany, France, and Italy.[19]

Between Danger and Opportunity

German and U.S. strategists agreed that the benefits of a successful war of economic pressure were enormous, if properly conducted according to the tenets of battle fleet warfare. In their historical works, Mahan and other writers had demonstrated the importance of commercial maritime warfare as a wartime strategy during the naval wars of the early modern period and the Napoleonic era. Britain's successful pursuit of a war of economic pressure against France after 1792 dominated Mahan's second book on the *Influence of Sea Power upon History*.[20] More recently, the American Civil War was believed to have taught the same lesson. The commercial blockade imposed by the North had conditioned the final outcome of the Civil War by profoundly interfering with the war economy of the South. Mahan himself published two books that dealt with the Civil War and appraised the effectiveness of the blockade.[21]

The two navies' strategists had little doubt that the economic dimension of naval warfare was gaining more significance than it had ever had, precisely because of the tremendous growth of maritime interests and the ever-increasing dependency of industrial economies on maritime trade. Like other military and economic writers across the Western world, U.S. and German naval officers pondered the ramifications of these developments. Rapid industrialization and the ever-increasing international division of labor within a flourishing world economy were creating unprecedented opportunities for maritime warfare targeting an opponent's seaborne imports.[22]

Viewing a war with Britain as a real possibility, the Germans took a particularly strong, if not obsessive, interest in this development, for it was fraught with tremendous danger for their own country. Germany was faced with the prospect of a successful blockade of its coast due to a mixture of geographical circumstance, diplomatic alignments, maritime weakness, and the ever-increasing importance of maritime trade for the German economy. Tirpitz and other strategists worried that a British blockade would interrupt the seaborne supply of raw material and foodstuffs. Their anxieties came into sharp focus during the "war scares" and political realignments of 1904–06, which raised the specter of a combined German naval and land war against Britain and France, and perhaps Russia. In such a case, everything depended on whether an enemy blockade would shut down Germany's ability to receive foodstuffs and other imports through neutral Dutch, Belgian, and Scandinavian ports. If Germany could rely on neighboring neutrals for continuous supplies, Tirpitz and others anticipated economic problems of only "more or less local importance" that would not pose a serious threat to the sustenance of wartime Germany.[23] But if the Germans could not count on trade through neutral countries, they would face great adversity. In 1906–07, the Imperial Naval Office investigated the issue closely. The agency concluded that if Germany could not use the seaborne trade of its neighboring neutrals during a war, feeding its armies and its population would become a major problem within a period of nine months.[24] In April 1907, Tirpitz expressed the dominant view among his fellow officers when he wrote that his country would not be able to bear the economic pressure of a full blockade "in the long run," without, however, going into any detail.[25]

Consideration of industrial Germany's need to keep open its maritime routes of trade and communication in times of war had emerged as a major issue in the early 1890s when war planners envisioned a two-front war against Russia and France that could turn into a long war of attrition. In such a war, military writers across the service lines, led by Imperial Chancellor

General Leo von Caprivi, and assisted by economists, argued that Germany could not afford to be cut off from world markets by a successful maritime blockade of its coastline. Continuous seaborne supplies of raw materials and foodstuffs were of vital importance for Germany's war effort. And so was a strong navy itself that could prevent a close Franco-Russian blockade of Germany's coastline.[26]

Yet German naval discourse about new economic vulnerabilities stressed not only dangers but also opportunities. Great Britain would be vulnerable, too, as its industries and subsistence rested on continuous supplies of foodstuffs and raw materials from abroad. Ernst von Halle, one of Tirpitz's close collaborators, concluded that Britain was "absolutely dependent on an unbroken and undisturbed continuation of its maritime traffic. If this were effectively cut off, it would be forced to conclude peace at any price."[27] Sharing this view, Tirpitz and other naval strategists explicitly identified the "Achilles' heel" of Britain as the "seaborne imports of foodstuffs and raw materials" on which hinged continued industrial production and the sustenance of the population.[28] An Admiralty Staff memorandum, written in 1905, drove home the same point. Britain could be defeated, it noted, either by a military invasion or by a full blockade, which would cut off "imports of foodstuffs, without which the population is bound to starve to death."[29]

Such views were advanced as officers followed the public discussions in Britain about the nation's ever-increasing economic dependency and the need for the military protection of vital import routes in times of war. The findings of the British Royal Commission on Supply of Food and Raw Material in Time of War, which were published in 1905, captured the German imagination.[30] References to the commission's findings became a staple in German planning documents. Vice-Admiral Günther von Krosigk, for example, extensively referenced them in his long 1911 memorandum on the promises of cruiser warfare against Britain. His long appendix on British wartime food supplies offered a battery of statistics and assessments culled from British sources.[31]

Against this backdrop, strategists predicted that even a limited cruiser-based *Handelskrieg,* designed as a secondary operation and adjunct to battle fleet warfare, could make a tremendous impact on Britain. In 1907, Tirpitz calculated that such military action against Britain's import routes could create economic dislocation, shortages, and moral panic, in his words: "inflation, perhaps famine, layoffs, unrest and similar things." The campaign, Tirpitz left no doubt, could inflict enough losses to pose a "considerable" danger especially to the economic interests of the "City," the community of British trading and financial interests in London, which would direct British policy.[32]

In their planning documents for the use of the handful of existing cruisers overseas, strategists struck the same tone. Even if limited in means and relegated to a secondary role, commerce destruction would disrupt the opponent's economic life, striking a blow to the enemy's war morale, and tying down substantial naval forces that otherwise could be deployed against the German battle fleet. In 1911, the commanding officer of the German cruiser squadron, for example, envisioned a "considerable disruption" of the "English economy" and "major interference" of British trade, including a collapse of Australian exports to Britain, when he discussed the wartime operations of his force. German overseas cruisers could provoke a "panic" that would force the British to send a "large" number of ships to hunt them down, thus relieving "pressure on our home front."[33] "The goal of the war against commerce is to create anxiety among the English people through damaging English shipping and interference with trade, to induce price hikes—especially for foodstuffs, and to bring about the transfer of a part of the trade and shipping to neutrals," a file note by the Admiralty Staff stated in 1913.[34]

U.S. planners did not study the new economic vulnerabilities and their implications for warfare in the same depth as did the Germans. After all, their country was hardly affected by them. But strategists nonetheless advanced perceptive views on the issue. When, in 1906, the General Board reviewed the U.S. approach to maritime law and commercial warfare, it stressed the ever-increasing economic dependency of Britain, Germany, and Japan on their seaborne commerce, which would open up tremendous opportunities for any opponent. The agency also explicitly noticed British discussions about this matter.[35] Germany's particular vulnerability to British commercial maritime warfare emerged as a central theme in Mahan's thinking after 1904–05. His recognition of Germany's dependence on its "carrying trade," and not just the latter's sheer volume, prompted Mahan to view the British wartime ability to shut down Germany's maritime trade lines as "the strongest hook in the jaws of Germany that the English speaking peoples have."[36] The findings of the Royal Commission on the Supply of Food and Raw Material in Time of War were well known within the U.S. Navy.[37]

U.S. naval thinkers repeatedly identified the import of foodstuffs and raw materials as the key vulnerabilities of the major powers. Admiral Stockton explained in 1908 that it was the "stress upon food supply" that would bring an end to any future war at sea.[38] In 1911, Rear-Admiral Fiske argued that for a "great manufacturing nation" the "stoppage of her over-seas trade by blockade" qualified as the "greatest danger from outside" (besides an invasion, that is); its effect would be "so great that it can hardly be estimated." He concluded that the prevention of a blockade must be the "primary use of a navy."[39] It was no coincidence that planners envisioned Japan's complete commercial isolation by seaborne blockade as the final measure in an imaginary Japanese-American war that would leave Japan no other choice than to surrender.

Altogether, German and U.S. naval officers offered expansive understandings of the economic vulnerabilities of major industrial powers that resulted from ever-increasing seaborne trade and global economic dependency. Well before 1914, there was little doubt about the great promise of economic pressure and its far-reaching impact. Images of lethal economic strangulation began to permeate the naval elites' discourse, even as the German and U.S. navies prepared themselves for battle fleet warfare and climactic naval combat.

Defining Maritime Law

By definition, an attachment to commercial warfare showcased itself in the realm of maritime law, a key domain of naval policy and strategy. The conduct of a war of trade and economic pressure was not simply about military strategy and national preference. It was also a matter of international law and consent, precisely because the conduct of a blockade and the seizure of ships and goods directly threatened the rights and trade of neutral powers and their citizens. In fact, neutral powers had a stake in a belligerent's conduct of a naval war and frequently expressed a determination to demand adherence to commonly accepted notions of maritime law. During the Boer War, for example, the United States and Imperial Germany had intervened to circumscribe the conduct of the British maritime blockade. Any breach of international conventions and standards of maritime law required neutrals' open or tacit acceptance.[40]

The second Hague Peace Conference and the subsequent naval conference in London in 1908–09 put the issue of the legal boundaries of maritime warfare squarely on the table of international diplomacy and maritime politics. The participants in these conferences set out to codify internationally recognized laws of maritime warfare and to create an International Prize Court to administer them. These efforts involved the attempt to refine, concretize, and extend the basic framework established by the Declaration of Paris in 1856, which had become accepted by all major powers, whether they had originally signed it or not. Besides abolishing privateering, the accord had prohibited the seizure of enemy goods on neutral vessels and of neutral goods on enemy vessels, respectively, with the exception of contraband of war. The accord had also made the legal validity of a blockade dependent on its actual enforcement by a naval force in place and capable of preventing any access to the enemy's coastline and ports.[41]

At stake at The Hague and London conferences was the promise of successful commercial maritime warfare. This promise conditioned all attempts to specify the legal rules governing the conduct of blockade and the seizure of ships and cargoes, enemy and neutral, on the open sea within the overall framework set by the accord of Paris. The Hague conference also provided a forum for a far-reaching proposal to confine the maritime war of commerce, trade, and economic pressure to a bare minimum by providing for the security of all private vessels and cargoes, enemy and neutral, except in cases of contraband and blockade-running. Clothed in the language of classic liberal commercialism and humanitarianism, the demand for the "immunity" of all "private property" represented the official position taken by the U.S. government and sat well with long-standing U.S. official policy toward international trade and maritime rights.[42]

Any attempt to radically diminish the possibility of commercial maritime warfare as a viable military strategy through the means of maritime law violated naval reasoning in Germany and the United States. Thus, on both sides of the Atlantic, naval policy makers opposed the providing for immunity of private property as it would do away with commerce-destruction on the high seas. Preventing the abolition of the *Seebeuterecht,* the right to seize enemy ships and goods and contraband on neutral ships, emerged as the dominant, if not obsessive, concern of Tirpitz and the other officers in charge before and during the conference at The Hague in 1907. It did so because the Germans expected the British, and not just the U.S. government, to propose such abolition. Taking the issue directly to the emperor and the imperial chancellor, the German secretary of the navy forcefully enshrined his view on this matter as official policy, even though he faced considerable opposition from representatives of the Foreign Office and other ministries.[43] Tirpitz did so after had already intervened in 1904 during a first round of interministerial preparations for the second Hague Peace conference in response to an initial decision, made without him, to accept private immunity.[44] In 1907, the Germans were enormously relieved when they realized that their fears about a British advocacy of private immunity were groundless, that the *Seebeuterecht,* and thus the viability of commercial maritime warfare, was not in jeopardy at the Hague conference.[45]

In the United States, strategists also came out strongly against abolishing a belligerent's right to seize ships and cargoes, except in the cases of blockade-running and contraband, as proposed by their own government. Mahan felt so strongly about this issue that he raised it first with President Theodore Roosevelt and the secretary of state in 1904 and 1906, then prompted the General Board into action, and eventually, in 1907, asked Roosevelt to allow him to present his views on the subject in public, which he did. As could be expected, Admirals Stockton and Sperry, the two naval delegates at the conferences in The Hague and London, concurred with the General Board and Mahan. The two delegates, who made their own views on the matter known to their colleagues from other countries, were pleased when the official proposal of their own government to provide for the immunity of private property failed at the Hague conference and did not surface at the follow-up London conference.[46]

American and German strategists reiterated their views on private immunity when they discussed it as a possible item on the agenda for the upcoming Third Hague Peace Conference. Scheduled for 1915, the conference was supposed to expand on the Declaration of London and create a formal international code of maritime warfare. The Germans were particularly disturbed by the prospects of yet another round of discussion about private immunity because they realized that many German policy makers and critics of the navy would support immunity. The Germans would be in a bind, reasoned a memorandum prepared by the Imperial Naval Office in March 1911, because in the past the navy's representatives had hidden their true views on the issue in public. They had publicly supported, in principle, the notion of immunity at previous Hague conferences, and proposed conditions, such as the complete abolition of a commercial blockade, which they knew would never be met. The memo suggested that the navy needed to adopt a new line of argument that reversed naval discourse on threat and deterrence against Britain. The ban against commercial maritime warfare would invite British economic action against German trade and shipping in peacetime through "preferential tariffs" and the "walling off" of the empire, precisely because a war would then no longer promise military success against Germany and vice versa.[47]

Beyond the issue of private immunity, the particulars of the two navies' reasoning about legal restraints on the use of force across the military-civil divide varied noticeably from country to country. The two navies staked out somewhat different positions concerning the rules governing the conduct of a commercial blockade and commerce-destruction on the open sea. The Americans promoted the cause of the blockading power while striking a clear balance between commercial warfare on the open sea and neutral trade.[48] By contrast, the Germans strove to impose restrictions on blockade warfare while seeking to enhance the prospects of cruiser-based commercial warfare.

In 1906, the U.S. General Board had declared that henceforth it would "resist any attempt to further limit the rights of blockaders."[49] The naval agency and the two U.S. naval delegates at the conferences consistently upheld the effectiveness of a blockade, as what one delegate called "one of the most valuable instrumentalities of naval warfare."[50] Thus they championed less rigid criteria for establishing the "effectiveness" of a blockade that the Declaration of Paris had defined as the official key requirement for its legal validity. The mere risk of capture of incoming or outgoing ships by blockading forces, and not its certainty, would suffice to assure the legality of a blockade.

The Americans also argued for the broadest possible rights to seize ships suspected of blockade-running. Seizures were to be allowed during these ships' entire trips from and to their home ports or final destinations, anywhere on the world's seas, and not just in the localized area of the blockade itself, before and after the actual act of breaching. Recognizing the need for a compromise between opposing views on this subject, the naval delegates supported a highly liberal understanding of the operational radius, the *rayon d'action,* of the blockading force. They suggested leaving it sufficiently indeterminate to allow for what Sperry called a "widely extended blockade."[51]

Most important, the General Board and the two naval delegates demanded the application of the principle of "continuous voyage" to blockade law. According to this notion, a blockade would also affect ships heading toward, and cargoes landed in, neutral ports whose ultimate destination was the neighboring belligerent power under blockade. During the London conference, the navy's delegate strongly resisted efforts to radically limit, if not abolish this notion, even if it could result in the failure of the entire conference. He successfully insisted on the application of this doctrine to the exercise of a blockade even if only restricted to cargoes bound to a neutral port that involved goods of direct military use destined for a neighboring belligerent.[52]

On the issue of how to regulate commercial warfare outside the confines of the blockade, U.S. naval delegates took positions that combined favorable attitude toward commercial warfare with considerations of neutral trading rights. This approach informed the treatment of the issue of contraband. In its review of U.S. policy toward maritime rights in 1906, the General Board had originally demanded "an increase in the list of contraband goods."[53] The position the U.S. naval delegates took, and that the Board then backed, was different. On the one hand, Admiral Sperry rejected the abolition of any contraband law, as initially proposed by the British in 1907. Sperry and Stockton, his successor in London, also insisted on the inclusion of the "doctrine of continuous voyage" in contraband law, that is, on the right to seize goods that were carried in neutral ships heading toward neutral ports as contraband of war if their ultimate destination was believed to be the opposing belligerent power. On the other hand, the Americans argued against any expansive understandings of contraband. They favored specific and narrow lists of contraband, defining absolute contraband as goods "exclusively adapted to military use," and its conditional counterpart as articles of dual purpose clearly destined for the enemy's military use.[54] In fact, Sperry had initially favored even the abolition of the entire category of conditional contraband. The Americans also supported the idea of a "free list" of goods, not to be declared contraband under any circumstances, including raw materials for industrial manufacturing and supplies for agricultural production.

The Americans' views on commercial warfare also became apparent in relation to several other issues discussed at both conferences. With the support of their superiors back home, the naval delegates accepted as a matter of principle the belligerents' rights to sink or destroy their prizes on the open sea, yet they wanted to limit the exercise of this right to cases of clearly defined military necessity. The Americans also wanted to allow for the conversion of merchantmen into warships on the open sea, but only for ships that were leaving their own national ports. And finally, the Americans championed clear restrictions on belligerents' conduct of mine warfare, such as the prohibition of unanchored contact mines, so as to not threaten the safety of neutral ships. Mines were also expressly not to be used for the purpose of commercial warfare, as opposed to their use in military defense in coastal waters, which was an important element of U.S. naval strategy in relation to the contest of battle fleets.[55]

German naval policy makers staked out clear positions in relation to the war of economic pressure: the quest to minimize the institution of the blockade combined with the desire to maximize the potential of cruiser-based commercial warfare on the high seas defined the German navy's agenda at the two conferences.[56] The imposition of restraints on the exercise of blockades received top priority; it was viewed as the one "truly decisive issue," as Tirpitz put it in a letter to Rear-Admiral Rudolf Siegel, the German naval delegate at the Hague Conference.[57] It was absolutely crucial to the Germans that a blockade was limited to the enemy coastline and, thus, did not extend to neutral neighbors. Seaborne trade between neutral ports was to be off limits to a blockading power.

The Germans sought to render most difficult the "conduct of a legally valid blockade," to quote the official instruction for the navy's delegate in London.[58] They offered restrictive readings of the principle of "effectiveness," which served as the official criterion for the legal validity of a blockade. In their view, such "effectiveness" required the continuous presence of blockading forces near the blockaded coast that were capable of preventing, in actuality, both outgoing and incoming maritime traffic. By the same token, the right to seize ships for blockade-running was to be restricted to the vicinity of the blockaded coast and, if necessary, the steaming radius of the blockading force.

To facilitate successful attacks on commercial shipping on the open sea, the Germans sought legal sanction for particular practices. Among them the right to destroy prizes on the open sea ranked first: its acceptance was deemed nonnegotiable. Its prohibition would render "illusory" any commercial warfare by a power such as Germany that lacked a globe-spanning chain of naval stations and depended on the agility and stealth of its commerce-destroyers.[59] The Germans also promoted an expansive reading of the right of belligerent warships to call at neutral ports and receive supplies there. The Germans also vigorously opposed any substantive restrictions on the conversion of merchantmen into auxiliary cruisers outside of home waters. They argued so strongly about the latter issue that they refused to compromise. The issues of conversion remained unsettled at London.[60]

The desire to expand the scale and scope of commerce-destruction on the high seas also informed the approach to contraband. Yet in this case the desire was circumscribed by the interest in not jeopardizing in any fashion Germany's ability to profit from neutral trade in wartime. On the one hand, the Germans opposed the abolition of contraband, as proposed by the British during the Hague conference. Moreover, they favored a broader definition of contraband goods that could become targets for German commercial warfare, including both foodstuffs and raw materials meant for the enemy's armed forces. On the other hand, the Germans adamantly insisted on the suspension of the doctrine of continuous voyage to protect any goods heading toward neutral ports, a suspension that conveniently did not affect military operations against the seaborne trade of the British Isles. From the German point of view, the doctrine was "unacceptable."[61]

To ensure such suspensions, the Germans were willing to accept carefully crafted, specific lists for both absolute and relative contraband and for free goods. The eventual settlement reached in London resonated with German definitions. In the face of U.S. objections, the Germans eventually consented to the application of the notion of "continuous voyage" to goods of absolute contraband. But this concession did not affect their core interests concerning this doctrine. Fittingly, the Germans managed to place items they considered particularly valuable on the "free list," including key industrial raw materials and agricultural machinery. They also succeeded in extending the key destination criterion for "relative contraband" to include goods destined for the enemy state, not simply for its armed forces. The inclusion of foodstuffs resonated with German interests precisely because of the explicit exclusion of this kind of contraband from the realm of "continuous voyage." In other words, this arrangement did not threaten to undermine Germany's ability to receive seaborne imports of foodstuffs through neighboring neutrals. It was for all those reasons that the Germans were most happy with the London Declaration, which, in their view, reflected German military interests.[62]

Military Necessity, National Interest, and Legal Limitation

The differences in emphasis and detail between German and U.S. strategists reflected varying definitions of national interests. Their positions were based on a careful analysis of military opportunity and geopolitical circumstance. The specter of a hypothetical Anglo-German war shaped the views of Tirpitz and fellow officers about the regulation of the commercial aspects of naval warfare. Economic pressure through a British maritime blockade posed the gravest danger. In the event of an Anglo-German war, "overseas imports of foodstuffs and raw materials are of the greatest importance for us," summarized one policy paper written in preparation for the upcoming London conference.[63] Such an observation, with its emphasis on the key importance of continuing trade through the maritime ports of neighboring countries, informed the Germans' desire to weaken the effectiveness of a blockade by legal means, to protect the seaborne trade of neighboring neutrals, and to suspend the doctrine of "continuous voyage." The prospect of cruiser warfare against Britain's vast and vital seaborne commerce, its alleged "lifeblood," underlay the vigorous German opposition not only to the demand for "private immunity" but to any substantive restriction imposed on commerce-destruction by cruisers.[64] This warfare could be Germany's only chance to exert direct pressure on Britain and attain a negotiated peace with that island nation.

U.S. strategists also arrived at their views of commerce-destruction on the basis of a careful study of specific war scenarios involving the United States as a belligerent. In 1906 the General Board outlined its position after a study of specific war scenarios with other powers. The agency stressed the prospect of commerce destruction in hypothetical wars against Germany, Japan, and Great Britain, while also giving nominal attention to possible armed conflicts with France and Italy. In all of these cases, the numerical weakness of an American-owned merchant marine and reliance on other nations' vessels to carry U.S. imports and exports minimized U.S. vulnerability while enemy seaborne trade offered rich targets for the U.S. Navy. Moreover, the Board and Mahan also explicitly cast commercial warfare as the most promising course of action for the British Empire in a possible war with Imperial Germany, whether or not the United States was involved as a third party. The emphasis on German vulnerabilities also informed their interest in strengthening the rights of blockaders.[65]

Ultimately the Americans' particular investment in commercial maritime warfare evolved from a general analysis of U.S. interests as a maritime belligerent. As a matter of principle, Sperry, Stockton, and others wanted to reserve the right to conduct a war of commerce and trade as an open-ended proposition for the future. Far from being a matter of life and death in war scenarios (as with Germany), it offered an attractive military option that bore little risk for the United States. Its navy was bound to be a powerful offensive and defensive weapon. The U.S. merchant marine was small. The riches of the vast North American continent ruled out the imposition of an effective blockade even by an overwhelmingly superior enemy. The United States, in short, should keep open its future military options, rather than behaving in what Admiral Stockton, the U.S. naval delegate to the London conference, referred to as an "altruistic" manner and promoting neutral rights.[66] It was no coincidence that Admiral Sperry explicitly cast maritime rights as a "matter of policy" that did not involve existential issues in the present.[67]

By and large, American strategists approached these issues from such a direction. There were of course exceptions. A committee of officers at the Naval War College in 1907 took a different view of U.S. interests as a maritime belligerent, one that was doomed to remain inconsequential. The committee favored the abolition of contraband, the principle of continuous voyage, and an overall weakening of the rights of a blockading power in order to assure easy and quick access to "arms, ammunitions and like munitions" in the event of war. The committee also argued that the United States could not hope to engage in any warfare to cut off the imports of European nations, including Great Britain. Yet it would also not be necessary. The United States could invade Canada in the event of a war with Britain; it could force Japan to peace by ensuring the "fall" of its "vital interests in Korea and Manchuria"; and it would secure its wartime goals vis-à-vis Germany by taking military action against a German fleet approaching the United States.[68]

Overall, German and U.S. officers operated in the same conceptual world in relation to the regulation of maritime warfare. One key element was a utilitarian reading of the interests of Germany and the United States as belligerent powers. These considerations resonated well with the officers' constructions of their own countries as self-reliant world powers in an antagonistic world of big-power conflict. Their future depended on their own capacity for the exercise of military threat and deterrence, not on restrictions on belligerent rights and cooperative security.

In each country, the navy's approach to commercial warfare and maritime rights broke new ground. In the American case, to imagine the United States as a warring power and to emphasize its belligerent rights amounted to a strong demand for a fundamental change in policy. During the U.S. Civil War, the Lincoln administration had stressed its broad rights as a belligerent power, including a rigorous application of the concept of "continuous voyage." Yet aside from this moment, U.S. conventional policy had always been conceived from the point of view of the United States as a neutral power, which had a vested interest in restricting the rights of belligerents. The demand for the immunity of private property, the official plank of both the McKinley and Roosevelt administrations that U.S. naval officers so strongly opposed, had evolved from this very approach.[69] Accordingly, in 1898 the United States had taken a more restricted approach to its rights as a belligerent power than it had during the Civil War.

In Germany, too, the navy's emphasis on belligerent rights and self-sustaining aggressive war-making broke with existing policy traditions. In the past, Germany had viewed maritime rights from the perspective of a minor sea power; it had pursued limited maritime force within a framework of cooperative security and extensive neutral rights. In the late 1880s and early 1890s, maritime strategists such as General Caprivi, the chancellor, and Captain Stenzel had followed this approach when they faced their own country's maritime vulnerability, its dependence on seaborne trade in a two-front war with Russia and France. In fact, at the turn of the twentieth century, German naval strategists, including Tirpitz, had followed the traditional approach. Seeking maritime security by restricting belligerent rights, they had initially endorsed the idea of private immunity, as it was put on the table in the context of the first Hague Peace conference.[70]

Approaching maritime rights from the point of view of a belligerent power, German and American naval strategists defended, as a matter of principle, the practice of commercial maritime warfare in the debates over maritime law. Both wished to assure a legal space for the conduct of a war of economic pressure. Stripping naval warfare of its economic dimension was unacceptable. Refusing to limit the war at sea to a contest between naval vessels, bombardments, and troop landings, naval officers such as Mahan and Tirpitz even explicitly denounced the allegedly misguided sentiment to "humanize" warfare by restricting it to the contest between armed forces. If successful, such limits would only prolong war and, possibly, make its outbreak more likely by softening its immediate impact on society. Preventing war depended on the specter of its very destructiveness, or so they claimed.[71]

While taking their utilitarian approaches to maritime law, the Germans and Americans nonetheless accepted the framework of maritime law as a defining and unalterable feature of military geopolitics. For them, the delineation of the legal boundaries of naval warfare in peacetime was not mere window dressing, that is, not simply an exercise for public consumption. Rather, maritime law was viewed as a serious matter that set firm rules. To be sure, the notion that in wartime belligerent powers would review and, possibly, bend the laws of warfare because of military necessity was accepted within naval and military circles. But officers who closely examined legal matters concerning naval warfare nonetheless ultimately considered maritime law as inviolate in its bounding of the pursuit of military necessity in wartime. The "weight of neutral power" would always "compel" adherence to the commonly agreed upon legal rules of warfare as they were expressed in the Declaration of London; their future recognition would not require any "additional force for police," explained Admiral Stockton.[72] The Germans were unsettled by intense public outrage at the Declaration of London in Britain that culminated in its nonratification by the House of Lords. "In any case" (*so oder so*), the planks of the Declaration would become the "foundation for the modern international maritime law" and circumscribe British behavior, they nonetheless reassured themselves.[73]

It was for the same reasons that, originally, the Germans had fretted over the prospects of these conferences. They expected Great Britain to impose its own agenda and codify legal rules to its own advantage, which would then bind the hands of the Germans and put them at a great disadvantage in war. It would be better to prevent any agreement than to accept one that was bound to put Germany at a serious disadvantage in war.[74] Indeed, the German navy took maritime law seriously. It did not approach that law with the same restrictive and dismissive attitudes as the army and legal experts approached the laws of land war. These latter experts explicitly and categorically placed *Kriegsnotwendigkeit,* military necessity, as a matter of principle, above any laws of war.[75]

The Germans and the Americans did not anticipate breaking these rules in the event of war. The stipulations of the Declaration of London were incorporated into both navies' legal codes for the conduct of naval warfare.[76] When, in the spring of 1914, the head of the German submarine inspection outlined a plan for a future submarine campaign against British trade, this proposal, which was the first of its kind, assumed that the campaign would be waged within the confines of existing maritime law.[77] This respect for the law become enshrined in the operations orders with which the German navy went to war in August 1914.[78]

The Road to Maritime Extermination

In striking contrast to their British counterparts, the U.S. and German naval elites conceived of, and prepared for, a war of commerce and economic pressure within clearly defined military and legal confines. Plans for commercial warfare remained a sideshow within the overall planning processes that relentlessly focused on the contest between battle fleets and the struggle for command of the sea. Military reasoning prioritized battle fleets and climactic combat and emphasized the temporal confinement of war, in explicit analogy to mainstream practices of terrestrial professional-military warfare. This orientation shaped naval strategy and understandings of new technological tools of war, such as submarines and battlecruisers. The naval operations against an enemy's economy and its seaborne connections, which American and German naval planners envisioned, instantiated a regime of military limitation and legal restraint that complemented the strictures of battle fleet warfare. They thus aimed at economic dislocation and political and social turmoil, not at mass death and starvation, or the destruction of an enemy society's very ability to reproduce itself.[79]

Moreover, the strictures of maritime law circumscribed the U.S. and German navies' approach to commercial warfare and their notions of what would be feasible and desirable. With its emphasis on the protection of neutral trade, a restrictive understanding of contraband and blockade law, and due process concerning search, condemnation, and legal recourse, maritime law de facto ruled out wars of maritime extermination, as historian Rolf Hobson has argued convincingly.[80] Perhaps most important, the Declaration of London heavily circumscribed the possibilities for a war of economic pressure that targeted foodstuffs for civilian populations: the declaration defined them as conditional contraband liable to seizure only when there was absolute proof that it was destined for enemy armed forces or the enemy state administration, as opposed to civilians.

Prior to World War I, German and U.S. strategists did not develop plans for a maritime war of extermination that aimed at civilian mass death and starvation. These navalists' eventual embrace of such a war represented a departure from their previous thinking and military practices. Only specific political and military junctures produced the wartime turn toward exterminist warfare. The turn took place in the context of the totalizing conditions and exigencies of the war itself after the collapse of the "short-war illusion" advanced by military planners across the Western world and the breakdown of the framework of maritime law occasioned by the British blockade in the fall and winter of 1914–15 and its toleration by the Wilson administration.[81]

The shift to maritime wars of extermination also unfolded differently in the case of each navy. The German navy waged a maritime war of extermination against Britain in the form of an unrestricted submarine campaign against all shipping, whether enemy or neutral, military or civilian, armed or unarmed, within an officially declared war zone (*Kriegsgebiet*) surrounding the British Isles. This war was unleashed on 1 February 1917, after the official decision for it had been made on 9 January 1917. The U-boat campaigns of 1917–18 followed on the heels of more restricted submarine campaigns that had served similar purposes but had followed the prewar protocol of commerce warfare, with its rules concerning the search and seizure of ships, cargoes, and contraband, in relation to neutral shipping. The naval elite chose exterminist warfare as a way of winning a war that had spiraled out of their control by the fall of 1914 and turned into a long, drawn-out war of attrition that raised the possibility of defeat. Settling on submarines as a new "wonder weapon," the navy's strategists promised victory against Germany's alleged chief opponent, the British Empire, which (allegedly) had caused the war and was conducting an "economic war of extermination" against Germany.[82]

The U.S. Navy came to wage a war of maritime extermination indirectly through its participation in the British "hunger blockade" of Germany after the U.S. official entry into the war in 1917. But the U.S. Navy's support of the latter was not unconditional. In the early stages of the war, its strategists were unwilling to sacrifice the "freedom of the seas" on the altar of any one party's conduct of a seaborne exterminist strategy of starvation. Already in the fall of 1914, strategists raised concern about the British conduct of war. In 1915, the General Board urged its government to take action against the British because their blockade violated U.S. rights as a neutral power.[83] After the American entry into the war, planners remained critical of their British ally's interpretation of maritime law, with its de facto denial of any neutral maritime rights. Setting a U.S. commitment to "freedom of the seas" against British ruthlessness, they expressly predicted conflict with Great Britain over this issue after the war.[84]

While championing battle fleet warfare and envisioning a maritime war of economic pressure conducted within clear, nonexterminist limits, prewar U.S. and German naval militarism nevertheless also prepared the ground for the turn to maritime wars of extermination. The wars of economic strangulation that the British, German, and other allied navies waged after 1914 both radicalized earlier notions of maritime commercial warfare and fed on prewar understandings of maritime economic vulnerabilities and images of lethal strangulation that had begun to permeate discussions of naval economic warfare. Operations against the enemy's trade and seaborne imports could easily move to center stage within the existing framework of naval strategy once its basic premise about a climactic military showdown between the fleets, which would practically end the war, proved wrong and the system of maritime law collapsed, as both happened in 1914. It was only fitting that British naval war planners, who had planned for an unlimited war of economic strangulation against Germany since the spring of 1904, drew directly on Mahan's writings when they described the war's imagined impact. When, for example Vice-Admiral Charles Ottley, the secretary of the Committee on Imperial Defense, wrote in 1908 that "grass would sooner or later grow in the streets of Hamburg and wide-spread death and ruin would be inflicted," he expanded on a line from Mahan's first book on the *Influence of Sea Power Upon History,* first published in 1890.[85]

German and American navalists' reasoning also contained political seeds of maritime wars of extermination. It cast global politics in harsh existential terms that pointed beyond the limitation of war, as identified later by Carl Schmitt, which had bounded maritime warfare among big powers in the nineteenth century. Naval officers thought about international politics and war in terms of an existential contest between competing empires. War appeared as the continuation of economic rivalry by other means between enemies that harbored exterminist considerations and exhibited, if necessary, a ruthless disregard for humanity.

Schmitt has insisted that different types of war require different types of enemies and vice versa: a "total" war comes, he argued, with a "total" enemy. To a considerable degree, the worldview of the two naval elites construed this enemy in advance. German officers' perception of Britain was perhaps the clearest manifestation of understandings of enmity and political conflict, which coexisted uneasily with commitments to the military limitation of war. They viewed the British Empire as a world power capable of exterminist sentiment, that is, willing, if necessary, to destroy Germany as a commercial and political rival. This image also included a pessimistic analysis of the British "military character," its deeply enshrined "tradition of war" built around a supposed propensity for unprovoked military attacks on maritime opponents and the use of any type of "brutality," if necessary, to achieve victory.[86]

Prewar German and U.S. navalism and its approaches to maritime big-power wars were thus part of the genealogy of maritime wars of extermination that became a crucial part of the pursuits of the German and U.S. (and other) militaries in the great-power wars of the twentieth century. These ways of waging wars against civilian populations swept away the regimes of military restraint and legal limitation within which German and U.S. naval strategists had operated when they imagined the war at sea before World War I.

Part III

THE QUEST FOR POWER

The Navy, Governance, and the Nation

Chapter 7

Naval Elites and the State

In 1904, the Republican assistant secretary of the U.S. Navy, Charles H. Darling, appeared before the House Naval Affairs Committee to denounce a plan for a change in the organization of the Navy Department. This plan, Darling argued, "savors too much of militarism to be consistent with the spirit of our institutions, even in the administration of the Navy Department." The officers who promoted this measure would "ape the monarchies of the Old World."[1] Other high-ranking civilian policy makers in Progressive Era administrations agreed. John D. Long, the navy secretary from 1897 to 1902, decried the "tendency" among naval officers "to seek undue control and secure legislation that would supplant the authority of the Secretary" and pave the way "towards a military head" of the department."[2] The navy secretary in the Wilson administration, Josephus Daniels, accused officers of being intent on "Prussianizing" the navy. Such officers, Daniels warned, wanted "to name some Von Tirpitz to rule the Navy" and "place the Secretary of the Navy at the top of the Washington Monument without a telephone."[3]

Such charges were an active response to the agendas of the U.S. naval elite. While officially paying tribute to the principle of republican governance, officers strove to renegotiate the subjection of the military to civilian supremacy in American representative government. They demanded a dramatic reorganization of the Navy Department that would enshrine the dominance of navy leaders and radically reduce the power of the civilian officials at the top. Such demands, in turn, drew explicitly on the example of the German Empire and the space its system of governance allotted to the military. Using the German General Staff as their model, American officers self-consciously set out to remake their naval institutions and politics in a German image.

Before World War I, both German and U.S. naval elites combined their call for large battle fleets with far-reaching demands for influence in the domestic area. These navalists not only demanded a massively increased allotment of societal resources and manpower for naval purposes; they also strove to attain independence from politics and minimize their subjection to any outside control in matters of grand strategy, military policy, and funding. This was a far-reaching agenda although it was not a plea for what political scientist Harold Lasswell would later call a "garrison state," a state, that is, in which military elites (and their corporate peers) would control the entire state and society for the purposes of national security.[4] The "enemy" of the navies' militarist claims to power was not civil society as such, but civilian participation in the making of naval policy and strategy and the supervision of the inner workings of the navy.[5]

As state-builders who fused together the causes of the navy, elite rule, and global power, the two naval elites pursued a common agenda; yet their terrains and emphases were different. The difference between the makeup of civil-military relations in the German imperial polity and the American civilian republic structured the specifics of navalists' quest for institutional power and policy control. The political strength and institutional separateness of the German imperial state and the extraordinary autonomy of its armed forces contrasted sharply with the lack of a strong, politically insulated administrative state in the United States and the institutional subordination of its armed forces. To a considerable degree, American officers were forced to seek institutional conditions comparable to those that already existed in Germany and that served as the point of departure for Admiral Tirpitz and his fellow officers.

Against the Reichstag

In Germany, the navy enjoyed considerable independence from civil society and parliamentary politics as part of the imperial state. To be sure, the navy did not control the sources and amount of its funding, the ultimate decisions over its use in war, or the process of negotiation among various governmental agencies that preceded the formulation of official policy initiatives. But apart from that, the German navy was by and large a self-governing institution outside civilian oversight, with a sailor at the helm of the Imperial Naval Office. Officers operated a network of established professional institutions that the constitution of the empire placed firmly within the monarchical sphere of influence.[6] Although this arrangement hinged on the institution of a military monarchy, it was underwritten by the acceptance, as a matter of principle, of military professionalism and the institutional separateness of the armed forces, as defined by the Prussian army during the "military revolution" of the 1860s. It also fed off the transformation of the military into a highly charged "charismatic institution" central to national identity politics, whose institutional independence was linked to the promise of superior performance.[7]

But naval officers were not content with this situation. Rather, they sought to expand their semiautonomous position and eliminate any remaining points of dependency. This desire united an officer corps that otherwise was prone to engage in internecine infighting; it became the obsessive concern of Tirpitz as soon as he was appointed secretary of the Imperial Naval Office. Almost by necessity, the quest for autonomy was directed chiefly against the Reichstag, constitutionally the one political institution that imposed limits on the independence of the navy. The national parliament had a say over funding, the very lifeblood of the navy. Such control put decisions about the size of the navy in the hands of political parties and (potentially) provided a venue for interference on the part of civilians in the inner workings of the navy. The Reichstag was also known to use its budgetary rights in military matters. In the mid-1890s, it had been reluctant to provide for the escalating naval expenses sought by the emperor and the Imperial Naval Office, a reluctance that had helped to precipitate a crisis of governmental politics.[8]

In the eyes of the navy, the Reichstag was therefore a major obstacle that denied it the autonomy and development it deserved. All of its officers shared the desire to disempower this institution. Considerations about the best way to minimize the parliament's influence in naval matters were the central themes of all intraservice deliberations about the proper organization of naval institutions in the 1890s (and beyond). In the jurisdictional disputes among naval agencies all parties involved argued that their task was only to provide the best way of saving the navy from parliamentary incursions.[9]

Riding on the crest of the navy's antiparliamentary sentiment, Tirpitz wanted to disempower the Reichstag as a political institution with a substantive say in naval matters as he embarked on his quest for naval expansion and German global power.[10] The Imperial Naval Office wanted to remove the navy from any meaningful budgetary control by the Reichstag. It did so by seeking to enshrine the naval program into law and creating what was called an "Iron Budget," a martial term with clear antiparliamentary connotations. The legal codification of the size of the fleet and the automatic replacement of each warship after a fixed period of time would bind the legislators to make annual provisions for the navy. The goal was to turn the navy "into such an untouchable entity" that "no party politics" could "interfere with it in the future."[11] The institutional position of the army and the practice of long-term cycles of military appropriations that fixed the strength of the army for longer periods of time served as the model for this attempt. The establishment of an "Iron Budget," argued Tirpitz, was to provide for "a similar protection against parliamentary majorities as is already in place for the army through the constitution and the military bills."[12]

As Volker R. Berghahn has demonstrated, the intent to diminish the influence of the Reichstag combined with the desire to build a large navy of some sixty big ships. This combination laid the groundwork for the scheme of naval expansion that the Imperial Naval Office devised under Tirpitz's leadership.[13] The policy makers of that agency decided to proceed in a carefully calculated manner in order to attain their antiparliamentary goals. An incremental approach appeared as the only way to create an "Iron Budget" with the consent of a Reichstag that stood to lose from it. A succession of naval bills would cumulatively fix the size of the fleet and the replacement age for ships at the appropriate level and would continually expand the construction rate of three big ships. A final "stabilization bill" would lay the "cornerstone" for the "solid edifice constructed, in a systematic fashion, according to one and the same plan."[14]

The Imperial Naval Office wanted to write the strength of the fleet into law to diminish the budgetary powers of the Reichstag. Yet the Iron Budget would not have entirely eradicated them. The actual provision of the funds for the navy remained part and parcel of annual budgets always under parliamentary jurisdiction. The legal codification of the number, type, and replacement of ships still left open the question of how much money should be appropriated over what period of time and of the exact specifications for each ship. Moreover, before the attainment of the Iron Budget, the navy's developing system of legal codification did not prescribe the exact rate of annual construction beyond the automatic replacement of existing ships once they reached the end of their active service. The Reichstag was not legally bound to accept any particular tempo of capital ship construction, as it committed itself only to the creation of a fleet of a certain size by a fixed target date and the automatic replacement of ships of a particular age. In short, there remained limitations to the legal obligations the Reichstag incurred both before and after a final "stabilization" bill. Still, Tirpitz and others assumed that the Reichstag would act according to their wishes, "morally bound" as it was to construct ships that were worthy of their classification and that compared favorably to their counterparts in other navies.[15]

From the beginning, the pursuit of permanent legal codification was as important as the naval buildup itself. During his first year in office, Tirpitz forcefully staked out his priorities. First he insisted successfully on the principle of legal codification against key policy makers within the government who considered the barely veiled attempt to minimize the budgetary rights of parliament as politically infeasible.[16] He and his aides then showed the same resolve in their dealings with the Reichstag, explaining that the naval legislation would stand or fall with the idea of a *Flottengesetz* ("fleet law" that established an ongoing legal basis for battleship construction), and that they would rather see the Reichstag dissolve than accept high naval appropriations without any permanent codification. Thus Tirpitz reacted forcefully in March 1898 to the request by politicians of the Center Party to give the Reichstag discretion to change the stipulations about mandatory replacement and threatened them with his resignation.[17]

Tirpitz tenaciously stuck to his priorities until the outbreak of war in 1914. In the run-up to the Naval Bill of 1906 the navy secretary bitterly fought attempts by the emperor and German Navy League activists to accelerate naval armaments without any regard for the stipulations of the *Flottengesetz* and the projected permanence of the fleet.[18] In 1907–08, the planners in the Imperial Naval Office accepted a higher construction tempo to protect the principle of legal codification against their own better geopolitical judgment. To save the *Flottengesetz* in the face of exploding armaments costs, they decided to submit a new bill that increased the annual rate of construction from three to four capital ships for a period of four years. Previously, Tirpitz and his aides had explicitly denounced any such increase because it would bring the Anglo-German naval rivalry out into the open and place the onus for the escalating arms race on Germany. Even more, the officer in charge of the Budgetary Department presciently pointed out in

February 1907 that the temporary pursuit of a "tempo of four" was bound to provoke a British response, which "through enormous expenditures for the fleet" could "take away from us any chance to close up to England in terms of naval power for the foreseeable future."[19]

The will to protect the *Flottengesetz* and to amend it so as to assure legal permanence of a "tempo of three" remained a leitmotif in Tirpitz's and fellow officers' thinking in subsequent years. In the winter of 1911–12 the Imperial Naval Office advocated for a new Navy Bill to ensure a continuous "tempo of three" for either the entire period until 1918, or at least for as many of the following six years as possible.[20] It was through the same lens that Tirpitz approached the issue of a naval agreement with Britain after 1908. The formulas for Anglo-German force ratios and building tempos that the navy secretary suggested did not call into question the framework of the *Flottengesetz*.[21] After 1912, ever-growing expectations of a coming war did not lead to prioritizing short-term readiness over the long-term pursuit of an "Iron Budget" and the scheme for a naval buildup contained therein.[22]

Such fanatical fixation on the *Flottengesetz* carried into the First World War. Time and again, Tirpitz insisted on the law's absolute centrality and conjured up the catastrophic consequences of its abandonment. Tirpitz's grave wartime concerns about the future of his own "life's achievement" extended to the *Flottengesetz* itself, and not simply the cause of a big navy.[23] But the attachment to the law was so widespread among navy leaders that it outlasted Tirpitz's tenure as secretary of the navy. When the Imperial Naval Office discussed future naval policy in 1916, the memoranda that were submitted (with only one exception) rose to the defense of the principle of an "Iron Budget" and the "eternal obligation" that the *Flottengesetz* provided.[24] Admiral Capelle, Tirpitz's successor, concluded that the "legal codification must remain in place."[25] Admiral Adolph von Trotha, one of the navy's most influential officers, concurred. It would be his firm conviction, he wrote in April 1918, that "the rebuilding of the navy needed to proceed on the foundation of the old *Flottengesetz*," which had received "fullest justification" by the war.[26]

Inside the State

The navy's quest for bureaucratic autonomy and policy control reached beyond the Reichstag. Demands for full control over strategy and military policy also targeted the imperial state and any interference emanating from within it. They stood at cross-purposes with Wilhelm II's neoabsolutist aspirations to "Personal Rule" and his aspirations to act the part of a military monarch who could wield sweeping power as a supreme warlord. Inside the navy, Admiral Gustav von Senden-Bibran, the chief of the Naval Cabinet between 1889 and 1908, was the most important exponent of this conception of monarchical power.[27] "People would seek to curtail more and more the Emperor's power," was one of his routine complaints, directed against both members of the Reichstag and top government officials; he, Senden, needed "to make sure that such curtailment would not take place."[28] Here was an officer who favored "an absolute monarchy" with the emperor deciding how large the navy had to be and who believed that the emperor "commands" and everyone else "obeys."[29]

Led by Tirpitz, the Imperial Naval Office asserted its exclusionary claim to control at the direct expense of Wilhelm II. The agency sought to shut the emperor out of policy deliberations and leave him with only ceremonial power to ratify decisions already made elsewhere. This quest came first into view during the run-up to the two Naval Bills of 1898 and 1900. Tirpitz carefully submitted his naval plans to the emperor in various personal presentations. Although styling himself as a loyal servant of His Majesty, Tirpitz left Wilhelm II with no choice other than to agree. He confronted the emperor either explicitly or implicitly with the threat of his resignation if he did not have his way. In this spirit, Tirpitz began his career as navy secretary in June 1897 by imposing his battleship plans on Wilhelm II, who had initially favored a large cruiser fleet for overseas service but then accepted Tirpitz's proposals right away.[30] By July 1898, Prince Henry of Prussia noted, with considerable disgust, that Tirpitz continually blackmailed his brother by threatening to resign in case he did not get his way.[31]

Tirpitz was adamant about warding off any interferences and suggestions on the part of the emperor, which were usually at odds with the navy secretary's naval programs and political calculations and often, but not always, marked by incompetence.[32] In the run-up to the Navy Bill of 1906, for example, the emperor caused great grief among Tirpitz and his aides when he demanded a massive naval increase that they considered to be a self-defeating legislative proposition bound to call into question future naval expansion. Just as worrisome, Wilhelm II had a particular proclivity for fast heavy cruisers and fast battleships, which threatened to disrupt Tirpitz's schemes. In this context, the system of legal codification served the planners in the Imperial Naval Office well: it placed the essentials of the navy (such as size, organization, ship types) beyond the reach of an emperor, who credited himself, already by 1901, with almost fifty personal contributions to the development of his navy.[33]

The disdain for the Kaiser's continuous interventions in naval affairs and his pompous treatment of his naval subordinates was shared by most officers. The "interventions of the Emperor" would create major "difficulties" and be a source of "great concern" among senior naval officers, a member of the emperor's entourage noted in 1904. He also recorded the despair of another high-ranking officer, Prince Henry of Prussia, the brother of Wilhelm II: "Must this man [the emperor] always meddle in such things?" the prince had exclaimed after yet another incident of intervention in 1904.[34] So obvious was the contempt for the emperor's antics that even a British naval attaché picked up on it: "I am of the opinion that the German naval officer views the Emperor's activity as regards the fleet with grave doubt, and even some resentment, especially fearing that he would attempt personally to conduct operations in time of war."[35]

Guarding its own space against outside interference, the navy also insisted on keeping its distance from the army, the bedrock of the imperial state. The specter of perpetual junior partnership haunted the entire naval officer corps, which claimed full equality with its fellow service in terms of political leverage, institutional position, and strategic importance. To maintain distance, the navy was not interested in any close coordination in matters of security policy and military planning. The Imperial Naval Office showed no interest in finding a replacement for the National Defense Commission, which had brought together the two military branches and other ministries before it had been dissolved in 1897.[36]

Some strides toward cooperation with the army were of course made in the field of operational plans. But bids for joint planning institutions remained rare. In 1904, Vice Admiral Büchsel, the head of the Admiralty Staff, proposed the establishment of a strategic council to include the emperor, senior army and navy officers, and the chancellor to discuss the current diplomatic crisis and operational planning against France and Britain. But his proposal went nowhere. Subsequent heads of the Admiralty Staff did not issue comparable calls.[37] On occasion, other officers broached the idea of creating a new permanent entity for defense policy by referencing British institutional practice; yet such discussions remained inconsequential. In 1913, when the naval attaché in London submitted a report that praised the British Committee on Imperial Defense and proposed a similar institution in Germany, he was told, in no uncertain terms, to drop the matter and that failure to do this would jeopardize his career.[38]

The search for independence targeted still another site of possible interference. This was the process of intragovernmental coordination on the top level. As a secretary of state, Tirpitz was officially answerable to the imperial chancellor in his dealings with the Reichstag yet he nonetheless demanded a free rein in the pursuit of his naval plans. He refused to submit his scheme for naval expansion for serious negotiation by the imperial chancellor and other members of government. In fact, by 1900 he had successfully reduced the process of intragovernmental coordination to a formality, henceforth simply asking Wilhelm II and the chancellor to rubber-stamp his legislative agendas, until this approach collapsed in the early 1910s.[39]

The navy's policy makers also strove to define the success of the naval legislation Tirpitz sought as a top priority of all governmental policy.[40] To ensure full governmental assistance, Tirpitz sought full membership in the then-powerful Prussian Ministry of State, a membership that the emperor granted in 1898, much to the chagrin of most of its members.[41] Tirpitz also asked that governmental politicking, the handling of other delicate political and legislative issues (such as the Courts Martial Bill), and the relations to crucial parties (such as the Center Party) should be subordinated to the imperatives set by his ministry's legislative endeavors.[42]

These demands lost some of their urgency once the Reichstag had committed itself to a policy of naval expansion with the Naval Bills of 1898 and 1900. Still, the Imperial Naval Office continued to insist on the support of the new chancellor, Bernhard von Bülow, who had played a crucial role in parliamentary politicking in 1897–1900, when he had been secretary of the Foreign Office.[43] In the winter of 1905–06 Tirpitz even forced the chancellor to abandon his preference for a massive naval bill. Bülow had wanted to use a possible legislative defeat of the bill in subsequent general elections, to shore up a new pro-government political coalition in parliament and rally together the major nonsocialist parties under nationalist auspices.[44]

Officers' claims for the primacy of their naval plans were also directed against the army. They involved nothing less than the subordination of future army bills to the cause of naval expansion. The government needed to concentrate all its resources on the cost-intensive creation of a first-rate navy as its top priority. Tirpitz openly demanded that there would be no substantive army increases during the period of the proposed naval buildup, that is, for at least fifteen to twenty years.[45] He did so in full recognition of the fact that most senior army officers were skeptical of the promises of a naval buildup and viewed the "development of the fleet" as a detriment to the future of their institution.[46]

Limitations of Power

No doubt, the navy's policy makers desired their service to become a "force," a *Macht,* in the German state, as Tirpitz wrote in his memoirs.[47] This quest was fear-reaching yet it was also defined by its limits. The navy secretary did not argue for an expanded role for the military beyond existing constitutional prerogatives or in favor of some kind of direct domination of state and society by the military. By the same token, he and his fellow officers made next to no effort to control governmental processes outside the field of naval policy broadly defined. In spite of its vested interest in fiscal matters, the Imperial Naval Office did not get fully involved in the various financial reforms to increase national revenues that were debated and passed after the turn of the twentieth century. This was the case even as Tirpitz supported Finance Secretary Stengel's reform plans in the Prussian State Ministry in 1905 and spoke out in favor of the dissolution of the Reichstag in 1906 to enhance the chances of their parliamentary approval and even if his agency encouraged some of its civilian allies, including the German Navy League in 1908, to work for this cause.[48]

Initially, however, Tirpitz had taken a different approach. Before the turn of the twentieth century, he advocated the extension of the jurisdictional authority of naval experts outside the military realm. At that time he argued in favor of the creation of a department, with him at the top, in charge of all maritime interests, that is, of shipping, fishing, export industries, colonies, and Germans living abroad.[49] Already during his first campaign for the office of the secretary of the navy in 1895–96 and then again in 1897–98, Tirpitz called for the "concentration of the maritime interests" in a reorganized Imperial Naval Office and for its emergence as a strong "central agency" in charge of all such interests.[50] As a first step in that direction he proposed the transfer of specific branches and offices from the Department of the Interior to the Imperial Naval Office, including the Ship Statistical Office, the Canal Department, and the Commissionership for Emigration.

Such a maritime superdepartment, Tirpitz explained, would provide an ideal state institution to promote German maritime interests, which he, at least in 1895–96, considered underdeveloped. A new maritime ministry was bound to eliminate interdepartmental friction and ensure a high degree of managerial efficiency. Such a new ministry would reflect the functional relationship between the navy and maritime interests, underscore the self-stylization of naval officers as the true representatives of industrial and trading Germany, and prevent them from becoming a self-absorbed caste.

Furthermore, a maritime department could directly assist the naval buildup; according to the "*do ut des* principle" ("I give so that you may give," the principle of reciprocity), it would also create a "larger nexus of interest and influence for the strong development of the fleet itself."[51] While imagining the proposed new Department of Maritime Affairs as the developmental agency of a strong activist state, Tirpitz had also anticipated a dismantling of the new maritime superagency in the future, that is, once Germany's maritime interests, including a powerful fleet, had been well developed.

Although it expanded on ideas previously offered by Admiral Albrecht von Stosch, the chief of the Admiralty before 1883, this particular grab for power was not successful. From the very beginning, it encountered stiff opposition from the emperor and the other ministries. By 1898, Tirpitz was forced to drop it for good, reserving for himself and the Imperial Naval Office the right to have a say in important matters of maritime interests and transatlantic policy, which would have fallen under the jurisdiction of the proposed maritime superministry.[52] Tirpitz and the Imperial Naval Office acted accordingly. Starting in 1898, they became involved in the long ministerial deliberations that preceded the making of the new Citizenship Law of 1913. The provisions of this law were of crucial interest to the navy because they regulated the legal status of Germans overseas, a community that featured prominently in the navy's imagination of a global Germany.[53] Tirpitz's ideas about a maritime superministry also left their direct mark in the realm of colonial administration. In the winter of 1897–98, Tirpitz ensured that the newly seized colony in China, Kiaochow, would fall under the jurisdiction of the Imperial Naval Office, as opposed to the Foreign Office.[54]

Although limited in some ways, the navy's primary emphasis on control over its policy agenda was far from innocuous, and not only because it came with the demand that this agenda be granted top priority in governmental policy. The same emphasis also had enormous ramifications for the overall direction of foreign policy, which transcended the navy's demand to have a voice in important matters of war and peace. Tirpitz and other naval policy makers placed themselves squarely at the center of the formation of German diplomacy because they strove to remove the matter of the massive maritime buildup itself, and the strategy of world power embedded therein, from the control of the (civilian) foreign policy establishment. They also claimed the right to shape public opinion according to their view of global politics and, if necessary, to exploit diplomatic crises for the purposes of naval legislation.[55]

In fact, Tirpitz went even further by openly demanding a reorientation of German foreign policy according to the world-power strategy that he championed. When Bülow became secretary of state in 1897, with the expectation of soon becoming chancellor, he was confronted with this demand and accepted it.[56] Tirpitz insisted on control when Bülow reconsidered his position in 1908. Supported by key officials of the Foreign Ministry, the chancellor expressed interest in slowing down the naval buildup and in attaining an arms control agreement with the British Empire. But the navy secretary opposed any such attempts to shake off the grip that the navy's arms program exerted on Anglo-German relations. To the emperor and chancellor, Tirpitz insisted on both the superior validity of the navy's view of the Anglo-German antagonism and the separateness of the domain of military considerations, which included the assessment of acceptable force levels and ratios. The chancellor and the diplomatic elite were supposed to bow to the navy's ultimate authority in these matters.[57] It was precisely this attitude (and Tirpitz's willingness to back up claims to control with resignation threats) that continued to shape the navy secretary's dealings with Theobald von Bethmann-Hollweg, the chancellor who followed Bülow, and who continued in the footsteps of his predecessor in his quest for better relations with the British Empire.[58]

Ultimately, it required the action of the army to break the navy's hold on foreign and security policy. So determined was the navy in its claims to policy control inside the state and so well did these claims comport with the imperial system of governance, that the critics of the navy's pursuit of maritime force in the Imperial Chancellory, Foreign Office, and Imperial Treasury had to resort to extraordinary means in pursuit of their cause. In the fall of 1911, Bethmann-Hollweg had to count on the army to hold in check a navy that continued to pursue its policy of naval expansion and veto any meaningful naval agreement with the British. The Army Bill of 1912 (for which the initiative came from the chancellor, not the military leadership, as navy leaders realized only too well[59]) and its successor in 1913 changed the direction of the German armaments policy. A new emphasis on Germany's landed power combined with ever-increasing talk about a coming war with France and Russia to impose radical limits on the continuous pursuit of maritime force. The navy's claims to power and resources faltered in the face of a politics of army expansion (and the apparent futility and skyrocketing expenses of arms competition with Britain). The navy could not commandeer the imperial state in the 1910s.[60]

American Claims to Power

The U.S. naval elite looked enviously across the Atlantic at the position of the German military. At the close of the nineteenth century, these officers were not part of a self-governing body beyond direct civilian oversight. In the republican polity of the United States, the military fell under civilian oversight at various levels. The navy answered to civilian superiors, to the president as commander-in-chief, and to the secretary of the navy. Congress was in control of appropriations. No important naval matter was outside the realm of substantial civilian interference.

Moreover, administrative decentralization and "weak" military institutions characterized the organization of the naval realm. By law, the Navy Department was subdivided into a number of separate and formally equal bureaus. These bureaus concerned themselves primarily with administration, ship construction, and the material and human infrastructure of the navy. Most of the bureau chiefs belonged to the staff corps, not the regular line officer corps. The department also lacked a central policymaking military body, or an office or board at the top, headed by a senior officer, which represented professional interests to the secretary of the navy and the bureaus in charge of providing the material tools of war. Certainly, the Bureau of Navigation was charged with the supervision of the fleet and its personnel. But there were no permanent entities in charge of operational planning and the movements of the fleet, or responsible for devising policy on naval strategy, tactics, and building programs. The practice of the Navy Department had been to appoint, on occasion, special committees to review matters of naval strategy and building policy, or engage in operational planning.[61]

The makeup of the Navy Department exemplified the absence of both an extensive bureaucratic state and a powerful executive in the United States. In the post–Civil War American "state of courts and parties," Congress was at the very center of the political system.[62] "Congressional government" implied that Congress claimed a dominant say in naval affairs and exerted a remarkable influence on the inner operations of the Navy Department itself. The pluralistic structure of independent bureaus and the absence of strong military institutions resulted in a high degree of congressional control over the allocation of funds for the public works aspects of the naval establishment.[63] The organization of the naval realm was also the product of a particular political culture permeated by considerable skepticism regarding the promises of military professionalism. Such skepticism drew on a long-standing republican critique of large "standing" military establishments as threats to the liberty of the people—a critique that was fed by antipathy toward a strong federal state. Rejection of the military inclinations and "war-mongering" of the Old World and a strong emphasis on civilian supremacy was central to American political discourse.[64]

Officers nevertheless openly began to strive for barely circumscribed institutional power and policy control. This quest focused on the attempt to create self-governing professional institutions, which would establish the primacy of military officers and wrest control away from civilian policy makers. Going beyond departmental affairs, navy leaders sought to gain control over the whole naval political process and to delimit the powers of Congress. They did so as they explicitly recognized the principle of democratic governance and civilian control. This pursuit of power was interwoven not only with the goal of a military buildup but also with the project of military institution-building itself and the promotion of new practices of military preparedness in peacetime (such as systematic planning for war). It was the intention of the navy's state-builders to expand the scale and scope of the professional capacities of the navy and to gain control over their operations and direction. This quest faced as much "inwards" as "outwards," for it involved the curtailment of the powers of the bureaus and was thus at odds with the desires of those officers, mostly of the staff corps, with a vested interest in these institutions.

The efforts of the naval elite to ensure institutional empowerment and policy autonomy came to focus on the creation of a naval general staff with sweeping powers. Under the initial leadership of Admiral Henry C. Taylor, a one-time president of the Naval War College who became chief of the Bureau of Navigation in 1902, this drive consumed the U.S. Navy from the mid-1890s through the 1910s. It closed off a long-standing debate within the navy about institutional reform and the faulty organization of the Navy Department.[65]

The call for an all-powerful naval general staff embodied the naval elite's claims to power. According to Taylor, the general staff would be in charge of naval strategy and tactics, naval movement, fleet exercises, war plans, and building policy, independent of any civilian interference from within or outside the department.[66] The chief of staff would be the senior military adviser of the secretary of the navy and dispense authoritative advice "on all questions of general naval policy." Situated directly under the secretary, the chief would also be the highest authority within the naval establishment and endowed with commanding powers, for he would direct the work of the entire department to ensure the war readiness of the navy and overall "fleet efficiency." Equipped with legal authority to act on its own, the general staff was to wield control over the various bureaus on all issues relating to fleet logistics, naval construction programs, warship design, force levels, and naval bases. Supervised by this agency, the administrative and technical bureaus would go about their business in the fields of construction, maintenance, and supply.

Taylor took a long view of the creation of a general staff with such great powers. He anticipated considerable opposition to his plans by civilian policy makers and those officers with a vested interest in the prerogatives of the administrative bureaus. Unlike some of his more impatient peers, Taylor championed a piecemeal approach to the implementation of his plan. The general staff would "probably have to grow slowly by a process of natural evolution," Taylor explained at the very outset in 1896.[67] His approach was first to create a miniscule professional body within the existing institutional framework of the department to engage in more narrowly defined general staff work, and then to extend the scale and scope of its activities and powers.

Supported by other navy leaders, Taylor started his campaign for the creation of a powerful general staff well before the war of 1898. He first made the case in 1896 with Democratic secretary of the navy Hilary Herbert and his assistant secretary, William McAdoo, and then again with their Republican successors in office, John D. Long and Theodore Roosevelt, a year later.[68] It took until the winter of 1899–1900 for Taylor and his collaborators to find the ear of their civilian superiors, when Long created the General Board. Officially designed to prepare the navy for war, the duties of this board were to engage in operational planning and to advise the secretary of the navy on the size and composition of the fleet and on naval stations. The General Board was set up as a statuary, purely advisory board that lacked any authority over the bureaus and consisted of only eleven officers, including officeholders such as the chief of the Bureau of Navigation, the chief intelligence officer, and the president of the Naval War College.[69]

Deeply aware of such limitations, Taylor saw the creation of the General Board as a first step in the right direction, hailing it as the "nucleus of a great general staff" and working hard to expand its spheres of authority.[70] Backed by Admiral Dewey, the Board's president, Taylor now vigorously argued for transforming the General Board into a full-fledged general staff, with its chief assuming a most prominent role in the Navy Department. As a next step toward that larger end, Taylor and his associates pushed for legislation to gain official congressional sanction for the General Board. They did so as early as 1901 but Secretary Long, who remained wary of the aspirations of his naval subordinates, refused to act.[71] With Long out of office in 1902, Taylor renewed his efforts. After extended negotiations with the new navy secretary, William Moody, a bill to provide a legislative footing for the General Board was presented to Congress in the winter of 1903–04. The bill was also intended to free all the board's members from outside administrative duties. Another provision allowed for the appointment of a chief military adviser to be chosen from the ranks of the board and to hold the rank of senior rear admiral. Without specifying their exact duties, the bill positioned this officer and the board directly under the secretary of the navy. Appearing before Congress in April 1904, both Taylor and Dewey underscored the importance of a general staff and the need for a responsible body of military advisers.[72] This legislative endeavor met with failure in the face of stiff opposition from Congress, the assistant secretary of the navy, and the chiefs of most bureaus. Taylor himself was so upset by this turn of events that he suggested to his peers to stop asking for further naval expansion until the issue of reform was resolved.[73]

The navy's quest for institutional power and policy control did not come to an end in 1904. The matter of reform was merely put on hold. Demands for a reorganization of the Navy Department and the formation of a full-fledged general staff abounded in the naval press.[74] For the time being, most officers simply acquiesced to what was politically feasible; they were willing to settle, at least temporarily, for less than they preferred and to focus on other tasks. Some activist officers entertained the possibility of creating the position of a "chief of staff" in a disguised form by some executive means and subsequent legislative confirmation.[75] Others, including the later Admiral William S. Sims, a protégé of President Roosevelt, sought to reopen the issue of large-scale institutional reform by accusing the bureaus in charge of ship construction with incompetence.[76]

When the issue was reopened in 1909, representatives of the navy toned down their claims to power in their proposed schemes for reorganization. Led in this instance by Mahan and Luce, who were the key players on a special commission, the so-called Moody Board (named after its titular head, former secretary of the navy William Moody), they proposed to reorganize the naval department into loosely coordinated, functional divisions (Operations, Personnel, Inspection, Material), which were placed above the bureau level. The Division of Operations would be the home for a general staff whose actual work would be shared by its own operational staff, the

General Board, the Naval War College, and the Office of Naval Intelligence. Its chief would serve as the principal adviser of the navy secretary in all naval matters; as such, he would head the council of division chiefs. On the other hand, the chief of operations lacked any executive authority outside his own division. While oriented toward interdivisional coordination, the council of chiefs only provided a forum for interaction and advice. The chiefs alone were responsible for all activities that fell under their divisional purview.[77]

This scheme, which was echoed by another specially convened board made up of active officers, the so-called Swift Board (named after Captain Swift, its chair), expressed demands for a general staff with all-encompassing powers in a compromise fashion.[78] Still, if put into practice and legally enshrined, the scheme promised to provide the chief of operations with enough authority to exert influence throughout the whole department and speak to the navy secretary in an authoritative fashion. His status was reflected in the provision for his appointment by the president, with the Senate's consent, for a three-year term and his eligibility for another term.

In 1909, the proponents of institutional reform did not get their way. Incoming Republican secretary of the navy George Lengerke von Meyer accepted their proposals only in a limited way. He appointed four senior officers as his personal advisers in the areas of operations, material, inspection, and personnel. Although these "aides" were to coordinate the work of bureaus in their field, they lacked both their own authority and congressional sanction. The new system of aides was welcomed by most officers as yet another step in the right direction.[79]

Dedicated to the idea of a general staff with sweeping powers, the navy's representatives campaigned for it again in 1914. This time, Rear-Admiral Bradley A. Fiske, the aide of naval operations, set out to attain the long-term goals as originally defined by Taylor with one single stroke. Fiske had been a vocal advocate of an all-powerful naval general staff before he became the navy's top strategist in 1913.[80] Against the backdrop of the war in Europe, Fiske sought to create, by law, a new office, that of a chief of naval operations, in charge of a reorganized and vastly expanded apparatus performing the tasks of a general staff. The chief of naval operations and his staff were to become the new directing center and policymaking body of the Navy Department. The plan was to put the chief in control of all naval matters and invest him with broad executive powers and command authority above and beyond all other service institutions. Appointment by the president for a multiyear term, after confirmation by the Senate, would further solidify the preeminent position of the chief of naval operations and his intended insulation from the civilian secretary at the helm of the department.[81]

This scheme for a chief of naval operations authorized to direct the workings of the entire department met with the approval of Fiske's naval peers. Only a few officers (such as Dewey and Rear-Admiral Chester Badger, the General Board's chairman between 1915 and 1921) felt strongly attached to the General Board and opposed its loss of authority.[82] Most naval officers viewed the provisions of the act that created the position of the chief of naval operations in 1915 as insufficient, as only another "step" in the right direction, as Admiral Austin Knight, the president of the Naval War College, told the House Naval Affairs Committee in 1916.[83] When offered the new position in the spring of 1915, Rear-Admiral Cameron Winslow, Knight's predecessor in Newport, declined: the new position, he explained, lacked the necessary authority and would be no substitute for the needed creation of an all-powerful naval general staff.[84] Due to the massive intervention of Secretary Daniels, the act had fallen short of what Fiske and his peers had originally proposed. It restricted the responsibilities of the chief of naval operations and denied him independent executive powers and direct authority over the bureaus. The bill charged him, "under the direction of the Secretary of the Navy," with the "operations of the fleet" and with "the preparation and readiness of plans for its use in war." By contrast, Fiske had wanted the bill to make the chief of naval operations to be directly "responsible for the readiness of the Navy for war and be charged with its general direction."[85]

The subsequent wartime enhancement of the authority of the chief of naval operations did not satisfy most naval officers either, including Admiral William S. Benson, the first holder of the office. New legislation in 1916 granted the chief the right to issue executive orders on his own, elevated his formal status to that of the highest-ranking officer (that is, besides the Admiral of the Navy, the rank bestowed upon Dewey in 1899 and bound to fall away with his death), and provided him with a large body of assistants.[86] The sentiment among high-ranking officers was perhaps best expressed in their testimonies during hearings of the Senate Naval Affairs Committee in 1920 that officially investigated the charge of insufficient military preparedness of the navy before the war. Almost all of these officers (including Benson and his successor, Admiral R. E. Coontz) spoke out in favor of enhancing the institutional responsibilities and legal authority of the chief of naval operations to the level proposed by Fiske in 1914–15.[87]

Meanings of a Naval General Staff

For more than two decades, the quest for a naval general staff with sweeping powers embodied the naval elite's interest in institutional control and independence from politics, inextricably interwoven as it was with the quest for increased professional military capability. It was the powers of the German military state that served as the explicit point of reference for the Americans' quest for unmitigated institutional power. Taylor and the Naval War College had settled on the German General staff as their model for the reorganization of the Navy Department in the mid-1890s.[88] This choice shaped the subsequent thinking and agendas of most officers who set out to mold American naval institutions and politics in a German image. These officers admired the power of the German state to harness military force without undue intervention from civilian authorities. The "German methods, nearer than any other, are what are needed for us," summarized Taylor in 1903.[89]

The Americans filled the model of the German General Staff with their own particular meanings. Like their counterparts in the army, naval officers barely took notice of the limits of the German staff's actual institutional power in peacetime. True, they were not ignorant of the pluralistic structure of the top army agencies in Imperial Germany, and they were also aware of the institutional framework of the German navy, which had come to resemble that of the army after the dissolution of the Admiralty in 1889.[90] But ultimately, the German model was taken to mean that the general staff was in control. Such a reading comported with a desire to commandeer the administrative and "technical" bureaus.

The belief in the German model circumscribed the esteem with which officers held the British Admiralty. The British Board of Admiralty had commanded much attention in the debates about changes in the institutional makeup of the U.S. Navy Department in the 1880s and 1890s (as had the French Naval Ministry, with its naval general staff).[91] But the British institutional model was of interest primarily as a possible institutional model for the creation of a powerful German-style general staff, with its chief in overall control. This was the position that Captain Chadwick, president of the U.S. Naval War College, explicitly took in 1902.[92] Both Luce and Mahan, who used the British Admiralty as their template in 1909, shared this position. As Luce wrote in 1911, the "most important office in the Navy Department" is the "office of naval operations," that is, the office of the chief of the general staff. "All other offices in the navy are merely subsidiary to that one particular office."[93]

The champions of an all-powerful naval general staff modeled along German lines all claimed that its creation was compatible with U.S. representative government and the subjection of the military to civilian supremacy. To be sure, these officers recognized that there were substantial differences between German and American systems of governance that limited, and rendered politically delicate, any attempt to copy directly German arrangements of power. Taylor, for example, took great paints to emphasize that "German methods" needed to be "modified to suit the different political conditions existing in this country," for "a system that well fits a monarchy may not be desirable for the navy of a republic."[94] But the adoption of a general staff, like that of the Germans, Taylor and others maintained, would present no threat to the constitutional prerogatives of the president, the navy secretary, and Congress, as the general staff and its chief would always remain under their direction in terms of policy, funding, and ultimate authority.

Indeed, from this perspective, the German model was not about "militarism" or monarchical government, but simply a matter of proper organization.[95] Taylor, Fiske, and others eschewed the word "militarism" to describe the German model or their own ideas about an all-powerful general staff. The German armed forces were still subordinate to "civil authority," they explained. Civilian authority would set the larger political goals and then leave their implementation in the hands of naval subordinates. Although in Germany the "central authority of government" happened to be the emperor, it could also be any other political force or institution.[96]

Still, the plans for an all-mighty general staff amounted to nothing less than a takeover of the Navy Department and the disempowerment of its civilian secretary. These plans were premised on limiting the navy's subordination to civilian institutions and policy leadership. Civilian officials would determine national foreign policy goals. It would be left to the navy itself to concretize these goals in terms of naval strategy, preparations, and programs. The general staff would determine the military needs of the country based on those predetermined goals and then seek the funds, which were allotted by the legislative branch of government. Within this conception, there was hardly any room left for civilian leadership inside the Navy Department. The chief of the general staff would be legally entitled to direct the workings of the department in pursuit of the overall military readiness of the navy for war. The secretary would merely accept and pass on authoritative advice on matters of overall naval strategy and (building) policy, which he received from the only "responsible" authority of the navy, the chief of the general staff (or the chief of operations, in Luce and Fiske's schemes). If overruled by the navy secretary, the chief could take his case directly to Congress or the president. There was no substance to the claims of naval institution-builders that they wanted to put the secretary of the navy in a position to make the ultimate decisions.

The desire to eliminate civilian control within the department was all too apparent. On occasion, officers followed their demands to their logical end. Going beyond oft-heard calls to make a high-ranking officer the official assistant secretary of the navy, they endorsed the notion of a military man at the helm of the Navy Department.[97] So widespread was the support of this idea that in 1911 Fiske felt the need to defend the idea of a civilian secretary of the navy in public against what he perceived to be its many naval critics.[98] Some years later Fiske took a different position in public. In congressional hearings in 1916, he supported the notion of a sailor serving as navy secretary.[99] In his memoirs, published in 1919, Fiske wrote that only as long as the country wanted the navy to remain a "political asset to successive administrations," and not a "navy simply," a "politician should be at the head of it."[100] It would be "utter folly," Fiske had confided to his diary in August 1914, "to put a civilian at head of army and Navy in any country. Not only useless, but dangerous."[101]

Outside the Navy Department

In their quest for power and independence, the navy's policy makers looked beyond the Navy Department. Congress was to bow to the navy's ultimate authority as well. Thus, by the turn of the twentieth century, officers called upon all civilian policy makers to commit themselves to a long-range naval program, based on the proper calculations by naval planners. In particular, the idea was to make Congress commit to a fixed policy of a continuous maritime buildup, with fixed annual naval increases. The program for such a buildup would be devised by the navy itself according to supposedly purely military requirements; its scale and scope would be bounded by the foreign policy goals set by civilian policy makers, which, not incidentally, were believed to be already well established and encoded in the principles of the Monroe Doctrine and the "Open Door" in China. This arrangement, the argument went, would end "short-sighted" congressional policy-making driven by domestic concerns, antimilitary sentiment, and pork barrel politics.

After 1900, demands for a long-term naval program and adherence to a fixed naval policy invaded the pages of the *Proceedings of the United States Naval Institute,* the navy's pivotal print media. Officers pinpointed the navy's need to "develop a definite, continuous and progressive building program" that could then be presented to civilian policy makers in an authoritative fashion.[102] This, then, became the main concern of the General Board. By 1903, the agency worked out a coherent long-term program that combined figures for the ultimate size of the fleet with those for an annual building program.[103]

It was again the German example that provided the point of reference. American naval officers were captivated by the long-run program devised and pursued by the German navy, and based on legal codification. They offered the most glowing descriptions of the stipulations of the German Naval Bills of 1898 and 1900 (with their clauses about the size and composition of the navy, and the automatic replacement of ships after a specified time) and the "systematic, steady, and rapid" maritime buildup that their subsequent execution guaranteed.[104] All officers agreed: the "result has been marvelous," and particularly so because the German system bound the legislature in its decision making, thus suspending divisive partisan politics in favor of the (alleged) requirements of foreign policy and military strategy.[105]

As in the case of the general staff, naval officers suggested that German practice needed to be modified to fit American political conditions. They did not suggest that their naval construction program should be written into law. To be sure, Congress was supposed to adopt the naval program as devised by the navy, with its stipulations for annual increases. One naval intelligence officer suggested in this context that the legislature ought to set aside a "proper share of the estimated revenues of the governments" for the purpose of naval expansion over an extended period.[106] But congressional adherence was envisioned as a matter of substantive commitment, not of legal obligation, which needed to be renewed each year as the annual naval budgets were drafted. It would be the "business" of the navy to present Congress with a well-crafted naval building program and to provide authoritative guidelines; "afterwards" it would still be "the business of Congress" to legislate and to "decide whether it can afford the money," or so someone like Fiske argued.[107]

Confronted with the refusal of Congress to bind itself to a long-term naval program and follow the building recommendations of the General Board, officers sought out other ways to make congressional policy makers commit to their policy demands. By the early 1910s, they promoted the idea of a Council of National Defense. The council was to consist of key policy makers in the administration and in Congress. Its civilian members would include the secretaries of war and navy and the chairmen of the Appropriations, Military Affairs, and Naval Affairs committees of the U.S. House and Senate. The military representatives would be the chief of the Army General Staff, the naval aide of operations, and the presidents of the U.S. Army and Naval war colleges. The official purpose of the council was to set overall official "policy" and provide civil-military coordination at the top level. By setting political ends and then relating them to military means, the council would fuse diplomacy, military strategy, and armaments policy into a self-contained whole. It would present Congress with long-term military programs on that basis. According to the navy's rhetoric, the overall "policies" would be set by the civilians "as the custodians or the directors of the policies of the people," yet they would do so after consulting with the naval and army authorities about military capabilities and requirements. These authorities, in turn, would devise and coordinate arms plans and military strategy accordingly, which would then reflect the will of their civilian superiors, explained Captain F. K. Hill, of the Naval War College, in 1912.[108]

Officers championed the Council of National Defense because it promised to better align the positions of civilian policy makers with the navy's policy definitions and arms programs. The council would force these civilians to commit themselves to general national policies, such as the Monroe Doctrine and the Open Door Policy, that were, from the navy's own view, well established and that the navy had already committed itself to upholding. The same civilians, then, would be left with little choice but to accept the long-range military and financial ramifications of these policies as defined by the military. Such acceptance would have ended an alleged congressional refusal to provide the military means for officially stated policy ends, a refusal that, according to the navy's representatives, compromised the legislature's approach to naval matters.

Prominent officers openly argued that the Council of National Defense would strengthen congressional commitment to a maritime buildup and long-range policies on naval terms. Rear-Admiral Richard Wainwright explained during a congressional hearing in January 1911 that the "object is to better bring before the Members of both Houses the requirements of the country, and then they would determine how much their resources were to be turned into preparation."[109] A Council of National Defense would be "desirable to educate Congress as to the relation between the policy laid down by the people and the forces necessary to maintain it," yet another high ranking officer wrote in 1911, summarizing the conclusions reached by the "summer conference" at the Naval War College.[110] Mahan made a similar point. The council promised to overcome the natural tendency of "representative government" to put short-term material interest and the "welfare of the local voters" above considerations of general interest, military preparedness, and foreign policy.[111]

Although Congress did not act on these plans for a Council of National Defense, they showcased naval hostility toward actual civilian policymaking. The same plans also spoke to navy leaders' interests in civil-naval-military coordination in terms of both policies and institutions and the full recognition of military leaders in the formation of policy. Ultimately, the navy's plans for such a council and their political fortunes were emblematic of the difficulties the U.S. naval elite encountered as it sought bureaucratic autonomy and policy control before World War I. Confronted with a civilian politics fearful of military aggrandizement, these efforts met with little success.[112]

The "war scare" in the spring of 1913 brought some of the limitations within which the navy operated into sharp focus. At that time, the navy's strategists and their representatives on the General Board and the Joint Army and Navy Board vigorously made their case before skeptical civilian superiors in the Navy Department and White House. In fact, the officers continued to press the issue after the president and navy secretary had decided not to heed their advice. They even went public by leaking one of their strategic assessments to the press. Incensed by this behavior, President Woodrow Wilson lectured his naval subordinates on the supremacy of civilian leadership and threatened to abolish the two boards, which were statuary institutions without permanent legal standing. In fact, Wilson eventually suspended the work of the Joint Board. It only reconvened in the fall of 1915.[113]

Although the naval elite had not attained the power it coveted and also ascribed to its German counterpart, it nonetheless yielded more influence in the corridors of power in Washington, D.C., than its own intimations suggested. By the mid-1910s, civilian policy makers had expanded the professional capacities of their navy and created institutions, such as the General Board, that could articulate the navy's opinions on matters of policy and strategy with great authority. Lacking the sort of bureaucratic autonomy they wanted, navy leaders had nonetheless carved out for themselves an important space in a developing warfare state that had amassed a first-rate battle fleet navy. Their claims and definitions had become an important part of the equation of executive policymaking and strategy formation. It was only fitting that the Wilson administration took a more favorable view of the demands of the navy for power and resources over time. By the winter of 1915–16, the administration came around to support the case for a navy "second to none" and increased overall readiness for war; and it also eventually acquiesced in the creation of the Office of Naval Operations and its subsequent accumulation of more institutional powers.

By the 1910s U.S. navy leaders had come a long way in their militarist quest for enhanced institutional power and policy control in which they had explicitly drawn on the example of the German Empire and the space its polity allotted to the military. Still, important differences in the makeup of warfare states and civil-military relations continued to exist between Germany and the United States. On the eve of World War I, German navalists may have suffered a severe crisis of acceptance and no longer controlled naval politics. But their navy nonetheless enjoyed an institutional independence and absence of immediate civilian control that their American counterparts found both desirable and unattainable.

Chapter 8

Manufacturing Consent

In an important article on German-American naval competition before World War I, published in 1939, Alfred Vagts, a German émigré historian in the United States, insisted on the commonality of the two navies' approaches to politics and propaganda. Both had recognized, claimed Vagts, "that they had to make and keep their peoples 'navy minded'; hence the interest in the 'navy leagues', pressure groups useful against the sometimes hesitant parliamentarians or governments; hence the wide and constant use of the mass of newspapers." To persuade the "great masses," both navies had even felt the need to invent "virile and reckless" enemies to concretize their "sea power doctrine." Such commonality, in turn, had stemmed from close mutual observation between two navies that considered each other probable opponents. "Imitating the enemy" and "improving on his lines" had "engaged a large part" of the "political and technical efforts of the two navies," extending in particular to the mobilization of public consent.[1]

As Vagts suggested, U.S. and German naval elites strove to promote the cause of maritime expansion and transform the contested terrain of naval policymaking in strikingly similar ways. Navalists' quest for power and resources entailed the vigorous pursuit of political opportunity and domestic consent, which, in turn, fed on a keen sense of the realities of participatory politics and the power of public opinion. Traversing the realms of national politics, civil society, and popular culture, officers engaged in a wide array of activities to further the cause of their navy. They ranged from parliamentary lobbying to public relations work and pressure-group politics. Seizing upon the opportunities opened up by new modes of mass communication and the profound changes in the public spheres in the two countries, the two navies' policy makers engaged in propaganda efforts and strove to forge a navalist public.

By 1900, the Imperial Naval Office under Tirpitz came to set the tone for the two navies' efforts to play politics and shape public opinion. The Americans openly admired the German example and sought to emulate it. But well before the Germans could provide inspiration, the Americans had already been intervening in the political arena and entering the public and literary spheres to promote the cause of naval expansion. U.S. naval militarists did not need the German example, or any other for that matter, to recognize that the pursuit of maritime force did not take place in a "professional vacuum."[2]

Points of Departure

The two navies pursued different institutional approaches to the matter of naval propaganda and politicking, which were emblematic of the different landscapes each group of navalists navigated in its quest for power and resources. In Imperial Germany, the navy followed a bureaucratic model. The organization of the navy and the structure of the state favored the formation of a cohesive, far-reaching, and aggressive strategy by a powerful naval agency.[3] Most directly, the navy was part of a strong imperial state that was prone to exert pressure on the parliament, shape public opinion, and involve itself in electoral politics and civil society.[4]

The Imperial Naval Office created a framework that allowed its officers to fuse policy, lobbying, and public relations work into a seamless whole. Already during his first campaign for the office of the secretary of the navy in 1895–96, Tirpitz had given this issue considerable thought, sharing in a growing consensus among senior naval officers and the emperor about the need for increased public agitation to prepare the ground for new navy bills.[5] The propaganda campaign for the army bill in 1893 served as a major source of inspiration.[6] The immediate reason was the opposition of the Reichstag to massive naval expansion, which had come to the fore in the debates surrounding the naval budgets of the mid-1890s. The imperial state, it once again became evident, could not command the parliament at will.[7]

Yet the Germans were also intensely aware of the examples set by other navies. British methods of naval propaganda cast a long shadow on the thinking of Tirpitz and his aides. When Tirpitz took office he commissioned a report by the German naval attaché in London about the "movement among the English people, which led to a large increase of the English Navy during the past 10–20 years." The 141-page report that the attaché presented in November 1897 laid out the ways in which the British navy had worked closely with the British press to orchestrate the "fleet scares" of 1884, 1888, and 1893, while also pursuing a long term strategy of educating an "ignorant" and "indifferent" British "nation" about the pivotal necessity of a strong fleet. With its clever publicity policy and its careful preparation of parliamentary debates, the British Admiralty had succeeded over time, the attaché stressed, in rallying the "Nation" behind the cause of the navy, without any regard for party.[8] The report's description of the specifics of British practices anticipated much of the subsequent publicity work of the German navy. Until the war, a stream of attaché reports continually kept the Germans apprised of the Royal Navy's activities in the field of naval agitation.[9]

The example of the U.S. navy was also on the mind of Germans. Time and again they praised the work of Mahan as an enormously successful propagandist of sea power who "attracted an increasing number of collaborators and fellow champions" over time until "most of the nation" had finally stood "behind him," as one analysis declared in 1902.[10] But precisely because of such a fixation on Mahan, the look across the Atlantic remained of limited importance and did not provide a source of inspiration for concrete action.

Once appointed, Tirpitz acted quickly to lay the institutional foundation for his approach. In June 1897 a new "Bureau for Information and General Parliamentary Affairs," known as the Nachrichtenbureau (Information Bureau), was set up and put in exclusive charge of naval propaganda and public relations, thereby also ending the involvement of any other naval agencies in that area. Tirpitz also created an independent Budget Bureau within the administrative department of his ministry; and this particular bureau moved to the center of naval planning and direct parliamentary lobbying. The first chiefs of these two bureaus, Eduard von Capelle and August von Heeringen, rose to immediate prominence. Capelle eventually succeeded Tirpitz as navy secretary. Heeringen ended his career as chief of the Admiralty Staff.[11]

Setting up this apparatus, the naval politicians had no intention of allowing any outside interference in its lobbying and public relations efforts. When, for example, in 1898, the Prussian minister of the interior issued a call for a coordination of official press policy, Tirpitz insisted, in response, on the independence of his Information Bureau in all matters relating to the Navy.[12] In 1912–13, when Chancellor Bethmann-Hollweg sought to establish his control over the government's press work and toyed with the idea of creating an Imperial Press Bureau, the Imperial Naval Office balked and handled the matter in a dilatory fashion.[13] The agency also showed little interest in any cooperation when the Prussian War Ministry created a special Press Bureau in 1913. "We have to not let anyone peek at our cards," explained the officer in charge of the Information Bureau.[14]

The U.S. navy took a different route. Its approach was less directed, less coordinated, and less formal. The overwhelming powers of Congress and the lack of a central directing military body shackled the formation of a well-orchestrated and unitary military politics, like that at work in Germany. The late-nineteenth-century U.S. national state did not provide a strong repertoire of statist capacities from which officers (or any state officials) could draw to make their case publicly.[15] In the 1880s and 1890s, the Office of Naval Intelligence and the Naval War College nevertheless emerged as institutions that provided a base for publicity work. The growing prominence of the newly created General Board then created new opportunities for a more cohesive approach after 1900.[16]

Overall, the navy lacked the institutional apparatus for a coherent and well-oiled pursuit of political opportunity. The service's direct interactions with Congress were extensive, but until after World War I no naval office fostered legislative dealings. Officers were heavily involved in influencing public opinion but often on their own initiative and without central direction.[17] Although there were many recruitment offices that also publicized the navy, there was no press bureau, a lack that became an issue of much debate in the 1910s.[18]

The General Board's public voice remained severely muffled. Navy secretaries took care to prevent the agency from having direct (meaning both official and independent) contact with the press and Congress. Only in 1913 was the agency allowed to formally insert its views into the public record. Setting a new precedent, Secretary Daniels decided to publish a comprehensive memorandum on naval policy authored by the General Board as part of the Navy Department's Annual Report and then allowed a representative of that board to testify before Congress in an official capacity.[19]

Still, navy leaders attached great importance to publicity work. The absence of a special bureaucratic apparatus did not necessarily render efforts at propaganda less effective. After all, the British Admiralty did not set up a separate office in charge of publicity either.[20] Thus it was only fitting that, by the early twentieth century, navy-press relations became a special subject of lectures at the Naval War College. Prominent journalist John Callan O'Laughlin (who wrote, in successive order, for the *New York Herald,* the *Chicago Tribune,* and the *Chicago Herald* before 1914) stressed the importance of publicity for the navy and of close contacts with press correspondents.[21]

Lobbying Efforts

The activities of the two navies to muster majorities for their legislative agendas followed a similar logic and stressed similar themes. Broadly speaking, naval elites pursued the same practices. The first was direct interaction with civilian policy makers. German and American naval officers shared an interest in lobbying and creating good working relationships with civilian policy makers in their respective legislative bodies.

In Germany, Tirpitz and his aides displayed a spirit of cooperation and accommodation vis-à-vis the nonsocialist parties in the Reichstag. It would be highly advisable, Heeringen wrote, reflecting the consensus among Tirpitz and fellow officers in June 1897, "not to affront the Reichstag as has happened often."[22] In their appearances before the Reichstag, the representatives of the navy therefore avoided personal attacks and behaved in a calm, nonconfrontational manner. The representation of professional rationality dominated public presentation. "We need to explain the necessity, purpose, goal and limit of the fleet clearly," Tirpitz demanded in March 1897 in regard to the naval bills in the Reichstag.[23]

Tirpitz and others forged close contacts with leading politicians. Tirpitz even invited selected groups of parliamentarians to his house for social gatherings.[24] The Imperial Naval Office enlisted the support of other officials of the government such as Bernhard von Bülow, whose lobbying played a crucial role in the deliberations over the Naval Bills of 1898 and 1900. Such activities targeted in particular the liberal parties and, most important, the Center Party. This was the party that almost singlehandedly decided the fate of naval legislation, with the possible exception of the period between 1906 and 1909, when the Conservative and Liberal parties formed a short-lived political bloc. Capelle and others used their contacts with politicians to scout out the mood in the parties and to fine-tune their handling of critical issues in the Reichstag. Sharing information and (seemingly) seeking advice, they sought to create an atmosphere of trust and mutual respect and to win over those politicians who might believe that they were privy to secrets of the Imperial Naval Office.[25]

The courting in 1897–98 of Ernst Maria Lieber, the head of the Reichstag delegation of the Center Party, exemplified the new direction. Tirpitz and Capelle sought a meeting with him as early as the fall of 1897 when the first draft of the naval bill was in its final form but not yet submitted. They invited Lieber to Berlin for secret negotiations. There they discussed with him the forthcoming legislation and showed him a draft of the bill, which, in turn, was revised according to Lieber's suggestions. These initial negotiations—the navy reimbursed Lieber's travel expenses—set the tone for subsequent cooperation during the Reichstag's negotiations on the bill. Lieber would be the "notary of the bill," a courteous Capelle informed the Center politician in October 1897, before the Imperial Naval Office had publicly announced its legislative program. Capelle expressed his confidence that Lieber would see to it that his "child" would not be stranded in the Reichstag.[26] When the bill was finally passed, Tirpitz sent a signed photo of himself to Lieber together with a flattering thank-you letter. It must fill Lieber with much pride, he wrote, "to have played such a great part in the development of the new Germany."[27]

After 1900, the officers of the Imperial Naval Office all agreed on the indispensable nature of what Capelle referred to in 1912 as "non-official interaction with the parliament."[28] Contacts between these officers and Reichstag politicians became routine. Members of the Reichstag were allowed to visit naval installations and ships. The Imperial Naval Office eventually extended such courtesies to a deputy of the Social Democratic Party, the putative enemy of the empire, even if mutual handshakes and common dining remained off limits for the officers present. The deputy in question was Gustav Noske: he sat on the Naval Affairs Committee of the Reichstag after 1907 and became the official co-reporter of the annual Naval Budget in 1912.[29]

In 1907 and 1908, the Imperial Naval Office organized large-scale inspection tours for the members of the legislature. Tirpitz's cheers for the Reichstag at the end of a speech to the parliamentarians in an officer casino in Wilhelmshaven in 1908 was indicative of the warm atmosphere on these trips.[30] A precursor for these so-called parliamentary study trips had taken place in summer 1902 when, on the invitation of the Imperial Naval

Office, fifteen Reichstag members not only attended a British fleet revue at Spithead but also visited the German fleet and naval installations in Kiel.[31]

In Germany, the emphasis on direct exchanges and cordial relations between the military and the parliament represented an important departure from the past military practice of maintaining a distance. In the United States, by contrast, intense interactions between civilian policy makers and the navy were the natural order of the day. In the American system of governance, officers had little choice but to lobby, and be amicable to, their civilian superiors inside and outside the administration.

The activities of Admirals Taylor and Dewey and their collaborators between 1902 and 1904 to promote their plan for the creation of a naval general staff exemplify the U.S. Navy's approach to civil-military interaction. This approach maximized the use of official channels of civil-military contact. Taylor and Dewey communicated with, and submitted memoranda to, the secretary of the navy and the president. Taylor inserted pleas for a naval general staff in his yearly reports as the chief of the Bureau of Navigation. These reports then became part of the annual reports of the Navy Department, which were submitted to Congress. President Roosevelt agreed to endorse the idea of a general staff in his annual message to Congress, and, in fact, he used a paragraph drafted by Taylor himself. Taylor and Dewey also took their case before Congress during a specially arranged hearing for the pending bill on the General Board in 1904.[32]

The officers around Taylor pulled other strings as well. With the support of Secretary Moody secured, their energies focused on informal lobbying Congress through a "campaign of education," as one member of the General Board wrote.[33] Retired Admiral Stephen Luce was approached to use his influence with the "pen" and with "the politicians," which he did.[34] A pamphlet containing articles in support of a general staff was issued.[35] Legislators were sought out directly by individual officers. At one point, the members of the House Naval Affairs Committee were dined and briefed aboard the *Dolphin,* the secretary's yacht.[36] Previously, a boat ride on the *Dolphin* to inspect naval locales on the Atlantic seaboard and the Caribbean had created a chance to broach the topic of the general staff with the chairmen of the Naval Affairs committees of the House and Senate.[37]

In the early twentieth century, officers practiced and benefited from new forms of military-civilian interaction. The General Board provided a new institutional channel of communication inside the Navy Department and became the navy's central authority on naval policy and strategy. In particular, the General Board devised the official building program of the navy and submitted recommendations for annual naval increases to the secretary. Usually, the secretary passed on these recommendations to Congress while keeping the board's reports to himself. As already noted, this practice changed when Secretary Daniels made them available to Congress, starting in the winter of 1913–14.[38]

When Roosevelt became president in 1901, the White House became a new base for pronavy lobbying. While expanding the role of the presidency in general, Roosevelt aspired to policy leadership in the field of naval affairs in particular. A former assistant secretary of the navy (and an in-law of a high-ranking officer), Roosevelt solicited and welcomed the opinions of the General Board and other navy men.[39] Taylor, for example, was in frequent touch with his commander-in-chief. Mahan exchanged letters with Roosevelt after 1901.[40] Roosevelt also listened to, and promoted the careers of, upcoming younger officers. William S. Sims, who, at the president's behest, served as the inspector of target practice and also as presidential naval aide between 1901 and 1909, was a prominent example. For several years after the death of Taylor, Sims was among the most ardent crusaders for a full-fledged naval general staff.[41]

The increased importance of the White House as a clearinghouse was tied to Roosevelt, the person. Under President William Howard Taft, an assertive navy secretary, George Lengerke von Meyer, kept a tight lid on the politicking of the navy.[42] So did his successor in office, Josephus Daniels, a southern Democrat with an instinctive distrust of any self-aggrandizing pretensions on the part of navy leaders. Moreover, while Roosevelt had opened up a new space for lobbying within the political system, navy leaders never lost sight of Congress. If necessary, they were ready to appeal directly to congressional allies.

This was precisely what happened in 1914–15, when Fiske lobbied for the creation of the position of a chief of naval operations. Having failed to impress his views on Daniels, Fiske first turned to big-navy proponents on the House Naval Affairs Committee to share his views on the issue and make arrangements for upcoming hearings in mid-December, during which he aired his disagreement with his civilian superior. Fiske then went a step further. In open defiance of the authority of the navy secretary, the admiral and a number of other officers met secretly with a member of the committee in January 1915 to draft a bill for the position, which they knew would not find the approval of their civilian superiors. Subsequently, Fiske followed the course of the bill and repeatedly urged his congressional allies to fend off the changes Secretary Daniels ultimately achieved.[43]

The German Navy and Publicity

In both countries, naval officers ventured energetically into public relations work in an effort to create a navalist public. The main purpose was to put pressure on policymaking bodies and convince Congress and the Reichstag that the "people"—the public, voters, and interest groups—demanded approval of the navies' agendas. No doubt, the Germans excelled in naval propaganda.[44] They also attached the highest importance to this line of work. To the dismay of the Civil Cabinet, navy leaders pressed the emperor to shower decorations on those who assisted them in appealing to the broader public.[45] "We must not leave public opinion, and the site of daily political struggle in the press and literature, to itself," summarized Heeringen, the man first in charge of publicity work.[46]

The Information Bureau of the Imperial Naval Office engaged in a wide array of propagandistic activities. What Heeringen called the "immediate work" with the press ranked highest.[47] It included the methodical observation of the print media. The Information Bureau developed ties with newspapers, journals, and news agencies around the country, usually based on close personal contacts with journalists and writers. The agency fed them with carefully prepared material; it proposed articles and suggested, if necessary, who should write them; and it floated all kinds of ideas and interpretations concerning naval issues. Beginning in 1913, the Bureau compiled special "Notes for the Press" to send to a wide circle of journalists and publicists.[48] A historian of the agency, Wilhelm Deist, has asserted that before 1914 almost every non–Social Democratic newspaper in Germany eventually came into contact with the Information Bureau at one point or the other.[49] One of the chiefs of the Bureau boasted in 1912 that it would not be difficult at all "to direct public opinion into a particular direction"; he also defined as "success" in his line of work the ability to plant an idea in the press in such a way that the civilian "authors" expressing it believed that they had come up with it on their own and that "public opinion," in turn, expected it as "self-evident truth."[50]

Starting in 1908, the agency systematically found positions for retired officers as regular writers at important newspapers and as press correspondents.[51] This policy expanded on the previous practice of recruiting retired officers to write pieces on special occasions and finding proper publication outlets for them. Between 1907 and 1909, for example, the officers of the Information Bureau had used this approach to counter, in public, the writings of retired Vice-Admiral von Galster, who had dared to openly critique official policy.[52]

The Imperial Naval Office put out its own publications, going well beyond the editorship of the naval magazine *Marine-Rundschau,* which targeted primarily, but not exclusively, the officers of the navy.[53] To do so, the Information Bureau enlisted the support of academics. Tirpitz hired Ernst von Halle, since 1899 professor for "the sciences of the state, with particular consideration of maritime traffic" at Friedrich-Wilhelms University in Berlin.[54] Under Halle's leadership, the Information Bureau focused on what Heeringen referred to as "the publication of academic works about the maritime interests of the state and their protection, namely in the historical, economic and maritime-military fields."[55] These publications included official memoranda that documented Germany's maritime interests.[56]

Beginning in 1899, the Information Bureau also edited a special "Yearbook for Germany's Maritime Interests" called *Nauticus* after it had, under the same name, published three separate volumes on the fleet issue. *Nauticus* pretended to be a private publication that was only assisted financially and materially by the navy. It was designed as a handbook for Reichstag members and public opinion makers, setting itself up initially against the prominent political guide put out by Eugen Richter, a prominent Left Liberal critic of the navy. The unsigned articles in *Nauticus* were written by naval officers, Halle himself, or other civilian writers. Thematically, the yearbook featured articles on all kinds of maritime matters, technical issues, global politics, and naval armaments. It also extensively documented Germany's maritime interests overseas.[57]

On top of this, the Imperial Naval Office sought to initiate and assist "efforts" of all sorts, as Heeringen put it, "which would point out to the German people, in spoken word, writing, and image the importance and purposes of the navy."[58] Such activities were wide ranging, targeting such diverse sites as schools, theaters, exhibition halls, popular magazines, and, even if belatedly, belletristic literature.[59] Special attention was also paid to the rather popular genre of fictional accounts of future wars, with the navy actively involving itself in the creation of such fantastical texts.[60]

The theatrical display of maritime force played an important part in such publicity efforts. Beginning in the late 1890s, the Imperial Naval Office, and the emperor, took tremendous interest in staging warship launches as major public events. Previously rather modest affairs, these launches became ever-more elaborate, carefully orchestrated pageants for public consumption, with the "launch speech" becoming a key site of navalist speechifying in public. This was one of the few areas in which the Imperial

Naval Office departed from its usual emphasis on economy in expenditures, much to the chagrin of the Imperial Audit Office.[61]

The Imperial Naval Office developed an interest in staging the active fleet in front of the nation. One early instance occurred in May 1900 when a squadron of torpedo boats was sent up the River Rhine, with Karlsruhe as its final destination.[62] In subsequent years, the attention was more and more directed toward regularly held fleet reviews. The official parade of the fleet in front of the emperor developed into an annual event and became an integral part of the annual naval exercises in the fall. Over the years this parade grew more elaborate and into a prominent public ritual. In 1911, it involved more than a hundred ships and drew about forty thousand seaborne spectators. By that time, high-ranking officers started to complain that the emphasis on the theatrical, on the fleet review as a "show piece," was slowly seeping into the conduct of naval maneuvers.[63]

Such naval spectacle was situated at the intersection between politics and mass culture and entertainment, as historian Jan Rüger has cogently argued.[64] In its efforts at publicity, the Imperial Naval Office did not stop short of the world of popular culture, the popular press, and the cinema. The Information Bureau paid much attention to visual representations of the navy through photography and film. Its officers recognized the increasing power of the "Cinematograph" as a "new means of propaganda," as one of them explained in 1914.[65] Commissioning its own cameramen, the navy provided footage for distribution to traveling exhibitions and movie houses. The navy forged ties with the advertising industry, which discovered the appeal of naval images, and it collaborated in the commodification of the navy through naval games and miniature model shows, which were a considerable commercial success.[66]

To create a navalist public, Tirpitz and Heeringen also took other, more drastic measures. The Imperial Naval Office contacted numerous professors, the so-called fleet professors, and asked them to present the navy's cause through public lectures and writings. As in the case of the press, the navy provided these professors with materials; it proposed themes and sketched lines of argumentation.[67] The Information Bureau also helped to coordinate and provide adequate settings for professorial activities. It supported collective publication endeavors. In 1898, it suggested, for example, a large survey by the *Allgemeine Zeitung,* a liberal daily in Munich, that polled professors and prominent public figures about the pending naval legislation. The Information Bureau also helped to found another association, the "Free Association for German Fleet

Lectures," which bore the brunt of professorial agitation for the Naval Bill of 1900.[68]

While the direct mobilization of the German academy took place mostly between 1897 and 1900, the Imperial Naval Office called upon another constituency, the so-called maritime interests, to support the navalist cause. Tirpitz and Heeringen engineered a massive display of business opinion in favor of the navy. They helped to organize waves of pronavy resolutions by chambers of commerce from all around Germany and solicited similar public declarations from other economic organizations.[69] Tirpitz and Heeringen were particularly interested in forging close ties to the Hanseatic shipping community and to heavy industry.[70] In the run-up to the Naval Bill of 1898, this effort culminated in a massive meeting of more than one thousand representatives of trade and industry in Berlin in January 1898. It endorsed a strong pronavy resolution.

From the beginning, nationalist pressure groups figured prominently in naval agitation schemes. Tirpitz and his aides assigned an important role to two existing so-called patriotic societies, the German Colonial Society and the Pan-German League. They enlisted the support of their leadership, which had previously agitated in favor of the navy. The Information Bureau assisted them during the naval campaigns of 1897–1900, supplying information, pamphlets, speakers, visual materials, suggestions for activities, and also financial subsidies.[71] But from the very beginning, the naval professionals looked beyond these societies.[72] The major focus of these societies lay elsewhere, and they appealed only to narrow segments of the public. The Pan-German League, in particular, was too independent minded, and, in addition, too polarizing a political force.[73]

Inspired, in part, by the British example, Tirpitz and his aides regarded a separate Navy League as a central and "indispensable" tool for their agitation strategy.[74] Such a league could become the key institution of a navalist public, allow the Information Bureau to orchestrate propaganda from a less exposed position, and render obsolete the need for the continuous direct mobilization of business and the academy. Tirpitz and others thought about the Navy League in strictly utilitarian terms. Once the naval buildup was completed, the Iron Budget attained, the navy secretary confided to the imperial chancellor in 1905, the League would be "superfluous."[75] This was a vision of a Navy League as an instrument of the state, not as an independent political actor. The Information Bureau would prescribe the general demands, the tone, and the lines of argumentation for the league's naval agitation. The League, in turn, was to present itself as a nonpolitical organization devoted to a single national cause. Only such an organization could attract a mass following across partisan, sectional, or confessional divides, while profiting from the support of the representatives of Germany's maritime interests: the industrial, trading, and shipping communities.

The Imperial Naval Office strongly encouraged and assisted in the official founding of the German Navy League in April 1898 by a group of heavy industrialists, merchants, and shipbuilders. The new Navy League received massive support from the imperial state and the Imperial Naval Office specifically. Such assistance enabled the League to become a mass organization whose membership—almost a million by 1900—soon outnumbered that of all other self-styled "patriotic societies."[76]

The politicians of the navy wanted to use the Navy League for their purposes. But almost from the outset, they had to realize that this might entail conflict with naval enthusiasts in the League. They did so after they had weathered a political controversy, in 1899, surrounding the league's highly visible ties to heavy industry.[77] By 1900, Heeringen expressed grave concern "that the activities of the League could be harmful." Its agitation "goes far beyond the goals set by the government." The general public would assume that the League's agitation reflected official desires and thus hold the government accountable. The League's leaders would display a determination "to go their own ways and not seek the council of the Information Bureau for their own measures"; they would seek "to free themselves in every way from the direct interference of the relevant state agencies, without abandoning their good relations with them."[78]

Within a few years, such concerns acquired new significance, as historians Geoff Eley and Wilhelm Deist have superbly shown.[79] The relationship between the navy and the League deteriorated, as the Imperial Naval Office faced an emboldened leadership that refused to be a mere instrument of the state. Directed by General August von Keim, the League's leaders began to massively criticize the plans of Tirpitz and his agency and counter them with own demands. Moreover, the League's radical nationalist leadership attacked the Center Party in a manner reminiscent of the *Kulturkampf* era. This course of action ran counter to the priorities of the Imperial Naval Office. On one level, the League's agitation called into question the authority of the naval agency while also threatening to find the supportive ear of Wilhelm II and other naval enthusiasts inside and outside the state, as it did in 1905–06, when Tirpitz faced an emperor who favored the League's program over that of his navy secretary.[80] The efforts of League activists, on another level, posed a threat because they alienated the Center Party and were bound to tear apart the League itself. Its Catholic minority repeatedly threatened to walk out.

Managing an unruly Navy League became a matter of constant concern for the officers of the Imperial Naval Office. In 1907–08, these officers had had enough. Strongly believing that they had "all reason" to "keep" the Navy League as an indispensable means of agitation, they took radical steps beyond their previous policy of limited intervention.[81] With the help of the emperor, they openly forced the League's political leadership out of office in favor of more pliable leaders.[82] In subsequent years, the navy continued to enlist the League for its purposes. Yet they realized that the League's political value had been compromised. The Imperial Naval Office wanted the Navy League's new leadership to keep a low profile and thus prescribed a limited and subdued level of agitation.[83] Although the Navy League was asked to swing into action in the run-up to the Naval Bill of 1912, the Information Bureau primarily banked on its contacts with individual publicists and the national press in its publicity strategy for that bill.[84]

On the eve of World War I, the navy's propagandists reconsidered their entire approach. Highlighting the fickleness of pronavy convictions among the parties and within civil society and the limited value of the Navy League as a tool for agitation, they not only reemphasized the paramount importance of press work but also called for renewed efforts to deepen the proper "understanding of the nature of the world economy and global politics, and thus of maritime interests and sea power," among both the "educated" and representatives of trade and industry as the key constituency of influential opinion makers. Only serious, high-brow "work of enlightenment and education" could lay a more permanent foundation for the future.[85] In short, the navy's propagandists remained committed to their entire project of forging a navalist public while realizing that after fifteen years of intense propaganda most of the work still needed to be done. The work of persuasion remained an open-ended proposition. It did so at a moment when the naval elite was simultaneously beginning to panic over the prospects for German global power.

The U.S. Navy and Publicity

By the turn of the twentieth century, U.S. naval observers were dazzled by German naval lobbying and propaganda and their alleged success, as evidenced by high naval expenditures and the spread of pronavy sentiment among the German populace. The German Navy League aroused the most astonishment. Its growth "has been almost phenomenal," a naval intelligence officer wrote in 1901. "It has been in keeping with the enormous strides Germany has made for commercial and maritime interests, and in great measure has been the cause of those strides."[86] The German Navy League was in a class all its own, outperforming those of other countries, including its British counterpart.

The look across the Atlantic, at the country that was remaking itself rapidly as a global power, lent new urgency to previous efforts to beat the navalist drum in public. By 1900, naval officers were fully engaged in propaganda. According to their own account, the limited naval buildup of the previous two decades had already been, in good part, the product of the "public opinion" created by the navy itself.[87] The navy needed to gain "the intelligent sympathy of the people," summarized one winter in 1907; if done successfully, "we shall have no more trouble in getting sufficient money from Congress, proper support from the daily press, and freedom to develop the navy along correct strategical lines."[88]

Officers employed various means to create a navalist public. Most important, they inserted their voices directly into public discourse to shape public opinion. Publications by naval officers, active or retired, especially books and magazine articles, were one central means. These publications took naval writers beyond the military press itself, which had only limited appeal to a broader civilian audience. Still, founded in 1874, the quarterly journal of the U.S. Naval Institute served as one important venue for publishing, for it was well known to civilian policy makers.[89] There was also the weekly *Army and Navy Journal*. Although institutionally independent, this service magazine understood itself as a print platform for the armed forces. Drawing directly on information and stories provided by officers, its reports were also likely to be picked up, or commented upon, by the press at large.[90]

The officers-turned-writers strove to directly reach a broad national elite and middle-class public. They published books on naval history and contemporary naval matters, which were printed by commercial publishing companies. They also aggressively entered the world of magazines and journals, which was undergoing profound transformations by the end of the nineteenth century. The latter created a national public, with general-interest magazines emerging as an expanding national media reaching a nationwide (literate) audience. Naval officers covered the entire range of these media. With great frequency, they wrote for the more elite, "quality" magazines (such as the *North American Review, Harper's Weekly*, the *Atlantic Monthly*, and the *Forum*); but they also strove to publish in the more "popular," mass magazines (such as *McClure's, Scribner's, Collier's Weekly*, or *World's Work*).[91]

As his German admirers had recognized, Mahan was the most prominent example of the navalist as writer and public proponent. He published nineteen books and more than 150 magazine articles between 1890 and 1914 (as well as many articles in the *New York Times* and other newspapers). By the mid-1890s, Mahan stepped away from writing naval history in heavy tomes toward writing magazine articles on matters of naval policy and global politics, often in serialized form as a prelude to their publication as a book.[92]

But Mahan was not alone as a publicist. His mentor, Admiral Luce, was a prolific writer with a similar orientation. He published widely not only in the *Proceedings of the U.S. Naval Institute* but also in other places such as the *North American Review* and popular youth magazines.[93] Rear-Admiral Henry C. Taylor placed important articles in *Forum* and *North American Review*.[94] Admiral Chadwick, an influential naval figure, wrote articles for *Scribner's, Collier's Weekly*, and *Munsey's* between 1898 and 1905, to give yet another example.[95]

The navy's collaboration with the world of national magazine publishing extended to the publishing industry's more sensationalist methods. When, after 1905, the campaign for a naval general staff came to a temporary halt, Sims and some other officers enlisted the new reform-oriented journalistic politics of moral outrage and scandalizing, so-called muckraking. They collaborated with Henry Reuterdahl, a noted maritime painter and American editor of *Jane's Fighting Ships,* on an article on what they considered to be the grave defects in the design of the newest American battleships. Their goal was to pry open a political space for another push for a naval general staff by galvanizing the public and instigating an official investigation into the charge. The article was published in *McClure's Magazine* in January 1908 under the title "The Needs of Our Navy." As intended, it created a public stir, leading to congressional hearings and a specially arranged "conference" of naval officers convened by President Roosevelt himself. In the meantime, Reuterdahl accompanied the U.S. fleet as an official guest on its cruise to the Pacific coast.[96]

Officers devoted considerable attention to public relations work through the national press. The attempt to shape public opinion capitalized on the rise of mass-circulation newspapers that no longer clung strictly to partisan roles.⁹⁷ The Office of Naval Intelligence supplied important newspapers with information, yet direct contacts with the press were also forged by other naval institutions and by individual officers across the board, with the exact scale and scope of these interactions with the press remaining difficult to gauge. Until 1904, the Office of Naval Intelligence also published annual handbooks that made available prepackaged information on "Naval Progress Abroad," that is, on recent developments in other countries in naval policy, programs, operations, and construction.⁹⁸

Officers promoted their cause before the public in other ways. The theatrical display of the fleet, or parts thereof, was a most prominent way of calling attention to the navy and demonstrating its power. Modeled after ever-expanding European practices, the U.S. Navy repeatedly staged massive naval pageants for public consumption and press coverage. So enamored was one officer by the propagandistic promises of naval pageantry on the eve of World War I that he wanted his service to increase naval reviews and port visits even if it meant interrupting fleet operations and exercises.⁹⁹ To great public acclaim, the Office of Naval Intelligence had first organized such a spectacle in 1892 when it hosted an international naval rendezvous in New York Harbor, in official celebration of Christopher Columbus's voyage to the Americas.¹⁰⁰ But it was after 1900 that large-scale naval reviews and pageants became frequent and much publicized events that were carefully staged in advance (as was U.S. participation in international naval pageants abroad). A fleet review in Oyster Bay that took place in Roosevelt's presence in August 1903 set a new precedent.¹⁰¹ In September 1906, another Oyster Bay naval review in Long Island Sound that included twelve battleships drew a crowd of more than one hundred thousand spectators.¹⁰² In April and June 1907, an even larger U.S. fleet, numbering sixteen battleships, staged two official naval parades, one strictly national and the other also involving warships from other nations, as part of the 1907 Jamestown Exposition.¹⁰³

Spectacular displays of the fleet were crucial to the cruise of the U.S. fleet around the globe in 1907–09, which was a gigantic propaganda exercise. The voyage of the "Great White Fleet" was framed at the beginning and the end by two massive naval reviews on the Atlantic seaboard; it also involved a massive naval parade in San Francisco Bay in May 1908 (which attracted more than a million spectators) and a string of ceremonial visits to other cities on the U.S. Pacific coast, as well as subsequent visits to places such as Honolulu, Auckland, Melbourne, Manila, and Yokohama.¹⁰⁴ Carefully chosen by Roosevelt, press correspondents were accredited to the battle fleet (such as Franklin Matthews, who worked for the *New York Sun* wire service and reached an audience of thirty million readers with his nationally syndicated column) and wrote extensively about its voyage.[105] Accounts by officers complemented the coverage by civilians; thus *Harper's Weekly,* for example, sent its own correspondent and also lent its pages to two officer writers who published a slew of story-driven accounts of a U.S. fleet on the move.[106]

The reviews of the fleet, and the global cruise as a whole, provided a stage for Roosevelt to beat the navy's drum by addressing the American people through the mass press. In fact, Roosevelt became the navy's foremost propagandist during his presidency. The navy profited directly from his practice of the "rhetorical presidency," which relied on popular speaking and direct contacts with members of the press as a technique of (newly claimed) presidential leadership.[107]

The use of large-scale naval pageants continued after Roosevelt left office in 1909. In the fall of 1909, for example, the navy's battleships were at the center of a huge international naval parade as part of the Hudson-Fulton celebration in New York. A year later, half of the Atlantic fleet was on public display for the dedication of the Pilgrim's Memorial Monument in Provincetown, Massachusetts.[108] Reviews of the entire Atlantic fleet for public consumption were staged in the falls of 1911 and 1912, carefully timed with an eye toward the opening of congressional sessions and attracting mass audiences.[109] Beginning in 1911, the navy was involved in plans for a gigantic review of fleet detachments of all maritime nations at the International Exposition in San Francisco in 1915. A public review of the entire U.S. Atlantic fleet on the Atlantic seaboard was also scheduled to take place before its journey to the West Coast. These plans for giant naval spectacles fell victim to the outbreak of war in the summer of 1914.[110]

As in Germany (or Britain for that matter), the deliberate use of naval pageantry brought together the realms of participatory politics and popular culture. Indeed, in their public relations efforts, navy leaders paid attention to the world of mass entertainment and consumption and the possibilities it offered. It was for that reason that officers were drawn to world's fairs: according to one count, the U.S. Navy had participated, with its own displays, in nearly fifteen world's fairs by 1907.[111] Likewise, the navy developed an early interest in the use of film to promote its popularity. By the mid-1900s, the navy had become both a producer and purchaser of newsreels and films, using them both at official expositions (such as in St. Louis in 1904) and as traveling exhibitions, and eventually providing them to cinemas and pronavy civic organizations. Well before World War I, the navy collaborated with a fast-growing film industry on the making of dramatic movies while also creating official regulations concerning the filming and use of its ships, installations, and personnel.[112]

Like their German peers, U.S. naval officers focused much of their attention on mobilizing key representatives of civil society. The Americans evinced a strong interest in enlisting economic constituencies for their cause. Representatives of the navy busily reached out to leaders of industry, commerce, and shipping to enlist their public support and to urge them to exert influence on civilian policy makers. "I am trying to sow the seed all over the country," Captain Taylor wrote in 1894 when he served as president of the Naval War College. "I am beginning to work up Boards of Trade, Chambers of Commerce and other commercial bodies all along our coast and lake frontiers."[113] By 1900, this practice of enlisting the support of broad economic interests for political purposes had moved to center stage, drawing increasingly on the industrial and commercial constituencies directly involved in naval construction and the sprawling infrastructure of navy stations and yards. With clear intent, officers seized "every opportunity to tell interest groups of the importance of the navy to each special interest," summarized historian Peter Karsten.[114]

By the early 1900s, plans to orchestrate public support for the navy came to focus on the formation of a special, single-issue civilian pressure group. Many officers evinced a strong interest in a U.S. Navy League, modeled along European lines. The League was to engage in a continuous "campaign of education" directed at the American people at large and act as the navy's political lobby in legislative battles. Based on his study of European practices, Lieutenant-Commander John Gibbons, for instance, outlined a "general scheme of educational work for a Navy League." There were tasks of "important missionary work of spreading the naval propaganda among the people at large; of creating a strong public opinion that should begin in the school-room and end with 'the man in the street'; and, finally, of establishing that community of interest which makes preparation for the maritime defence of vital importance to every good American." Gibbons's scheme for the League's duties was extensive. It included "conferences with superintendents of public instruction, principals of schools, and other educators" to consider the best way to bring navalism into the classroom. He also proposed lecture courses, the distribution of books and pamphlets, extensive press work, a new commemorative politics focusing on honoring naval anniversaries through monuments, statues, and elaborate ceremonies, and active cooperation with chambers of commerce and other organized economic interests.[115]

Institutionally, officers conceived of a Navy League as a free-standing voluntary association, independent of direct control by the navy, yet following its lead. The League would engage in public activities from which officers were debarred; it would openly champion a policy of naval expansion as suggested by the officers in charge of devising policy. The navy, in turn, was to support the League in every possible way.

The navy's policy makers celebrated the creation of the U.S. Navy League in 1903. Its founders and honorary officials came primarily from the political and corporate classes, many with an affiliation or vested interest in the navy. Initially, the League fell short of the original expectations. But by 1910, the League had expanded enough to count as a viable political pressure group. Its journal had become a fixture in public discourse; its national office circulated press releases to newspapers across the nation and engaged in mass mailings and the distribution of agitational material on special occasions. By 1914, the League commanded resources comparable to those of the German League, as its agitation for preparedness demonstrated.[116]

In contrast to its fellow German service, the U.S. Navy faced no problems with the League, which acted in line with naval expectations. Thus, the League came to support fully the naval building programs of the navy; it also promoted the cause of an all-powerful general staff.[117] Within its means, the navy, in turn, assisted the efforts of the League, for example, through the sharing of information and materials (including navy-produced motion pictures), the mass subscription of its periodical, and providing occasional access to naval facilities. Prominent officers spoke at the annual conventions and other staged events. After 1907, active officers could join the League, albeit without full membership rights. So close were the connections that the League's journal doubled as the alumni magazine of the Naval Academy between 1907 and 1915.

As in Germany, there were, however, clear limits to the League's effectiveness. The League had a polarizing effect on public opinion. Moreover, this interest group did not command the means to change the equations of civilian policymaking, that is, the particular configurations of sectional orientations and regional interests that lent shape to the congressional politics of naval buildup.[118] In the early 1910s, when the League finally came of age, many officers articulated their concerns about what they considered to be the limited effectiveness of their previous publicity and education strategies.[119] The General Board chimed in as well. In the winter of 1913, the agency deplored the current situation as the outgrowth of "an inadequately expressed public opinion"; and it presented the "support of the people" and their "full understanding of the meaning of and the reasons for naval power," which, in turn, would force the hands of "the legislative branch," as a proposition for the future.[120] This sense directly fed off the political fortunes of the navy's massive naval programs in Congress. Between 1907 and 1914, Congress authorized less than half of the battleships the General Board asked for.[121]

As in Germany, the navy remained wedded to the promises of publicity work on the eve of World War I. Officers issued one clarion call after another for more public agitation and education on behalf of the navy, drawing on the repertoire of existing practices. These calls also grounded the plea for a Council of National Defense as an institutional means to "educate" civilian policy makers.[122] After 1914, frustration with alleged public ignorance carried directly over into the campaign for increased "preparedness." The navy participated in this campaign along pathways it had charted in previous years, including cooperation with the Navy League. It also profited from both the efforts of army leaders and, as importantly, the mostly self-propelled mobilization of civilian elites and associations such as the National Security League.[123] Eventually, the U.S. entry into the war offered additional possibilities for the navy, and the Office of Naval Intelligence in particular, to shape public opinion and sustain the public it wanted. These possibilities were created by wartime measures that ranged from massive censorship and official state-sponsored propaganda to domestic surveillance and persecution.[124]

Elite Politics

In the United States and Germany, the multifarious activities of naval officers cohered into a distinctive style of elite politics. This elite politics was primarily interested in directly influencing the decision-making process within Congress and the Reichstag and focused its publicity work on elite and middle-class publics. This approach recognized the importance of participatory politics and the public sphere yet it also assumed that the two could be mastered through the proper combination of politicking, propagandizing, and the careful calibration of demands.

In Germany, navy leaders sometimes employed a much fiercer rhetoric. Frequently, Tirpitz and his aides invoked the "nation," the "people," and the "masses" and mobilized them, in a plebiscitary fashion, against the Reichstag. "The pressure must come from the nation, otherwise the Reichstag will reject [the new Naval Bill]," Tirpitz, for example, explained in October 1899.[125] Tirpitz used almost the same language during the run-up to the Naval Bill of 1912, saying the navy needed a "slogan for the masses" to rally parliamentary support.[126] But such rhetoric should not be taken at face value.[127]

In its activities, the Imperial Naval Office focused on the mobilization of all sorts of "educated" and economic elites. Its considerable interest in the realm of popular culture and entertainment notwithstanding, the Information Bureau defined public opinion in terms of notables and educated opinion makers; it orchestrated propaganda that primarily targeted an elite audience of parliamentary politicians, the educated, and the well-to-do. It would be of utmost importance, declared Tirpitz in 1899, for the "legislative powers" and the "entire German people in its educated and insightful parts" to approve his naval plans.[128] The "educated," that is, "the men of the practical world of business, the realm of politics, of substantive public writing and teachers of all kind," were the principal "bearers" of the idea of sea power and, thus, the focal point of any work of persuasion, explained an officer with the Information Bureau in March 1914.[129]

When the Imperial Naval Office made an explicit effort in 1899–1900 to reach out to a working-class audience and "broader popular segments," it did so halfheartedly and within the parameters of notable politics, with respected "fleet professors" seeking to educate workers at Social Democratic Party rallies. "Overall, the masses are not yet laid hold of," Heeringen noted after this effort.[130] This was a failure that officers attached to the Imperial Naval Office often identified yet did remarkably little about, despite the navy's fast-developing interest in the public uses of ship launches and naval parades, or its backing of various efforts by the Navy League to reach mass audiences beyond middle-class populations.[131]

Operating inside the semiautonomous imperial state and outside any substantive civilian control, officers inserted a manipulative streak in their style of elite persuasion that was not available to their American colleagues. To be sure, U.S. officers engaged in a number of rather transparent tactics of misrepresentation as they made their case in public. With great care, and led by the Office of Naval Intelligence, officers represented comparative naval strength in public in ways that downplayed the strength of their own navy and maximized that of their rivals.[132] Naval spokespeople also offered sensationalist depictions of imaginary foreign naval actions against the

United States that conjured up dire images of catastrophic defeat, unlimited devastation, and national ruin. It was in this vein that Rear-Admiral Fiske proposed, in early 1915, the staging of carefully rigged maneuvers in which a defending U.S. fleet would suffer catastrophic defeat at the hands of an imaginary enemy fleet and subsequent publicity about the results, to make the case for increased maritime "preparedness."[133]

In Germany, by contrast, systematic deception emerged as a defining feature of the political pursuits of the navy. On a large scale, Tirpitz and his fellow naval politicians concealed their real intentions from the national parliament and the public. They offered a rationale for the naval buildup that did not reveal the extent to which its fleet was built against Britain; they denied the very existence of a long-term plan to expand the navy in finely tuned stages; and they took great pains to deflect attention away from the antiparliamentary goals embedded in their pursuit of legal codification.[134]

Although such efforts at deception were not particularly successful, the manipulative tactics included yet another component: outright intimidation. This involved the threat that the emperor would dissolve the Reichstag over defeat of naval legislation and that in subsequent elections the fleet issue would be used against those parties which had voted against the provisions sought by the navy. To make this threat more effective, the Imperial Naval Office packaged its legislation carefully. Much emphasis was laid on finding catchy slogans, a selling strategy in line with the flourishing practices of commercial advertising. The navy had forced the Reichstag in 1897–98, Tirpitz explained in 1905, to "decide the question, whether, as a matter of principle, Germany should have a fleet at all, or not. This course of action created the possibility, in the case of rejection, of appealing directly to the nation through the dissolution of the Reichstag." According to Tirpitz, the slogan "the doubling of the fleet" had given the Naval Bill of 1900 a similar significance; "once again," the Reichstag "could either only turn it down in its entirety or accept it, and that in the former case dissolution was made inevitable."[135]

The threat of dissolution was not mere rhetoric. But its valences varied. The political situation in 1897–98 weakened the threat as new elections were already scheduled for the summer of 1898. Nevertheless, after some hesitation, Tirpitz insisted on the dissolution in case the Reichstag rejected the idea of a "fleet law" while still voting for a naval increase, and he conveyed this determination to the parties in parliament.[136] In fact, for quite some time, Tirpitz seemed to have pinned his hopes for approval of his "fleet law" on a newly elected Reichstag that would be more susceptible to a dissolution threat.[137] In 1899–1900, the Imperial Naval Office confronted the Reichstag with the same threat, although the navy felt confident of getting a parliamentary majority through political negotiations.[138]

After 1900, the dissolution threat became less important. Its appeal had been diminished by the recognition that during the elections of 1898 and 1903 those mass parties did well that had managed to present themselves as either principled opponents of armaments expansion (the Social Democrats) or as a constraining force (the Center Party).[139] But the navy's policy makers never lost sight of this sort of pressure tactics.[140] This became evident when, in 1911, they entertained, for a brief moment, the idea of exploiting the domestic political fallout of the diplomatic crisis over Morocco to submit a massive Navy Bill. Tirpitz suggested, in late August, that a bill be submitted in October, that is, before the upcoming national elections, and that it be made part of the political campaigning of the parties and the imperial government.[141] Subsequently, Tirpitz and his aides spent a considerable amount of time searching for the proper "slogan for the masses" that could turn the bill into an existential national issue and lend credibility to the threat of electoral campaigning over this issue.[142]

Although they were willing to put political pressure on the Reichstag, the navy's policy makers did not contemplate taking more drastic measures. They were not interested in a strategy of intimidation that mobilized the memory of the constitutional conflict of the 1860s. After becoming navy secretary, Tirpitz had explicitly set himself up against any policy of confrontation that included the threat of a coup d'état, a fantasy held by Wilhelm II and Admiral Senden in the 1890s.[143] This acceptance, as a matter of principle, of constitutional government and its framework of participatory politics was the point of departure for the entire pursuit of political opportunity, with its emphases on cooperation, manipulation, and mobilization. It was also this acceptance that underlay the fundamental commonality of the efforts of German and American naval elites to garner support for their navalist agendas. Remaining an open-ended proposition in each country, these efforts fed off the keen insight that the work of continuously manufacturing consent was essential to any pursuit of maritime force in the German and U.S. nation-states.

Chapter 9

A Politics of Social Imperialism

In an oft-cited letter from December 1895, Alfred von Tirpitz wrote that Germany needed to create a powerful navy and promote its maritime interests "not the least so because in the new great national goal and the associated economic gain lies a strong palliative against educated and uneducated Social Democrats."[1] In so doing, the future navy secretary offered a social-imperialist rationale for the pursuit of German global power and maritime force; he also directly borrowed language from an article published the previous year by Alfred Thayer Mahan. In "The Prospects of an Anglo-American Reunion," which appeared in the *North American Review* in November 1894, Mahan had written about the beneficial impact of U.S. active engagement in geopolitics and presented it as an anti-socialist endeavor. Only such engagement, he had argued, could foster a "reviving sense of nationality, which is the true antidote to what is bad in socialism."[2]

In each country, makers of navalism offered social-imperial formulations that related the pursuit of global power and maritime force to matters of national governance, reform, and societal order. Transcending the two navies' pursuit of institutional power, societal resources, and public prominence, these formulations centered on the (re)making of Germany and the United States as integral nation-states. They set the cause of the nation against its alleged enemies from within, be they socialist or otherwise, and fused it to nondemocratic elite rule, centralized state power, and national industry. Such linkages saturated navalist discourse. No doubt, the navies' pursuit of global power and maritime force was always an exercise in domestic policy and political domination, to invoke the mantra of all those analysts of German maritime militarism who follow in the footsteps of radical historian Eckart Kehr.[3]

But there were also significant differences in the connections that the two national communities of naval militarists drew between maritime force, global empire, and a proper order at home.[4] The Germans envisioned the forging of a cohesive nation in the crucible of global empire within the framework of a monarchical nation-state, decisive governmental leadership from above, and limited social reform. These emphases reflected the presence of both a vigorous socialist labor movement and of a powerful monarchical-bureaucratic state with a long-standing tradition of social intervention. In the United States, the absence of a strong national bureaucratic state and the relative weakness of a distinct working-class politics ensured that a primary emphasis of any social-imperialist project was on the creation of a strong administrative state insulated from participatory politics and electoral pressures. Thus, American officers tied their nationalist case for world power to a bid for bureaucratic expert government within the constitutional shells of republican governance. At the same time, they elaborated on the domestic benefits of empire within the framework of a politics of moral reform, racial exclusion, corporation-dominated industry, and reactionary welfarism (that is, the promise of material prosperity through empire without redistributive politics).

German Visions of the State

Fusing the causes of global power, the nation, and elite rule, Tirpitz and his fellow officers promoted the making of a "new" Germany under nationalist, technocratic, and industrial auspices.[5] Their vision of governance cohered around several elements. The commitment to Germany as a nation-state, and not to the Prussian state, or any subnational particularism, ranked most prominent among them. Tirpitz and other naval policy makers all promoted strengthening the powers of the national state. The plans for a powerful national ministry of maritime affairs, which Tirpitz advanced at the turn of the century, exemplified this orientation.[6] So did the consistent support of new direct taxes on the national level, which was to end the empire's fiscal reliance on the federal states and advance the costly naval buildup and the expansion of other national services.[7]

Such fixation on the nation-state was evident in the self-image of the navy as an exemplary national organization and custodian of the German nation as a global people. This view emphasized that the navy served and represented the nation-state as a whole: it would function as a nationalizing "melting pot" that recruited its personnel from all walks of life, regions, and confessions.[8] Moreover, the navy was forging, through overseas service, special bonds with Germans abroad. It was the key "link" between "the German fatherland at home" and the "great Germany out there in the far world," as stated by the admiral in command of a battlecruiser that was calling in ports in West Africa and Latin America in 1913–14.[9]

Officers combined their allegiance to the nation-state with an attachment to the idea of a national monarchy. Their concept of a monarchical state restricted the monarch to the official guardianship of the separateness of the imperial state from the Reichstag, and to matters of representation, ceremony, and formal ratification. The naval elite's "ideal" emperor was Wilhelm I, a "passive" monarch, not his grandson, Wilhelm II, with his neo-absolutist aspirations to "personal rule." In fact, Tirpitz himself considered these aspirations of Wilhelm II, and the rhetoric surrounding them, as idle talk not grounded in political reality. Germany was simply not an "absolute" monarchy, he insisted. It would never be, "whether that is pleasant or not."[10]

Tirpitz and practically all other officers who had firsthand experience with the emperor were also critical of him as a person.[11] Tirpitz found only harsh words for the emperor's careless and martial talk of imposing his will on the nation, if necessary by force, and in violation of the constitution. "The Emperor makes many utterances that demonstrate that he lives outside the realm of reality," Tirpitz noted in August 1897 after a conversation during which Wilhelm II had once again stated his conviction that the Germans "just needed to be shaken up soundly and feel the reins."[12] The emperor's inflated sense of himself and his pompous behavior was most irksome as well. "What is sad and troubling about the able monarch, is that he puts appearance above substance. It is not the substance itself that matters, but whether he can appear as the only master," a subdued Tirpitz noted in 1903;[13] a year later he noted that it was impossible to have a serious discussion with the emperor when more than two people were present.[14]

Other officers agreed. Admiral Müller, the chief of the Naval Cabinet from 1906 to 1918, for example, was a sharp critic of Wilhelm's preference for the "decorative," his dislike for actual work, and his ignorant self-aggrandizement. "It requires enormous courage (*eine Mordsstirn*), to talk so much amateurish nonsense in front of so many experts," he noted in 1912, reviewing, with anguish, the emperor's action as a critic of naval maneuvers.[15] "I have the impression that the Emperor is insane," exclaimed another Admiralty Staff officer in 1912.[16] Although being endowed with remarkable intelligence, the "main trait" of the emperor's "character" would be "vanity and self-aggrandizement," observed Rear-Admiral Hopman, then a senior officer in the Imperial Naval Office: "thus the continuous talking, lecturing, and storytelling, the communication of and emphasis on his superiority, the indignation toward any objections, in short his caesardom."[17] At the end of World War I, Hopman, considered for a while a possible successor to Tirpitz, expressed officers' disenchantment with their Supreme Warlord (which had reached new highs during wartime) when he wrote in his diary that Germany's monarchical ruler had been a "fool bursting of vanity and hubris."[18]

Well before the war, the navy's policy makers did not treat the emperor as a serious person and developed sophisticated methods to handle an "All-Highest" person increasingly considered a sad, childlike figure. That "knowledgeable people" avoided sitting next to the emperor was a well-known if harmless secret among officers with firsthand experience.[19] Repeatedly, Tirpitz openly treated the emperor as an immature person. When in 1905 the emperor yet again bombarded the Imperial Naval Office with ship designs and ordered it to act on them, Tirpitz instructed the Construction Department to provide the emperor with material about ship designs to give him something to play with until he lost interest in the matter.[20] Tirpitz and many other officers all agreed: the emperor was approaching their navy as a "mechanical toy," not as a war-fighting machine.[21]

But such disenchantment did not call into question the monarchical form as such. Critics of the emperor remained committed monarchists. Indictments of the All-Highest Person were balanced by warm appreciation for other members of the Hohenzollern dynasty, such as the crown prince and his wife. Schemes to declare Wilhelm II unfit and replace him with his eldest son as new regent, which were drawn during the war, remained bounded by a deep-seated monarchical outlook. Admirals Tirpitz and Trotha and others involved all concurred that their country's future depended on what they called a "strong monarchy."[22]

Navy leaders saw the monarchy as an ideal framework for the rule of technocratic elites. They placed themselves in the tradition of the Prussian state and monarchy. Tirpitz articulated this sense most strongly. He embraced what he (and others) believed to be the peculiar Prussian ethos of public service and officialdom. "We all are only links in a chain," he told a group of high-ranking fellow officers in October 1899; "the individual can disappear from the surface at any moment."[23] While commenting unfavorably on the emperor's emphasis on appearances in 1903, Tirpitz referred to himself as the emperor's "helper" who, according to Prussian tradition, did not expect public recognition for his hard work.[24]

According to this conception, the officials of the state, both civilian and military, pursued the general interest of the nation, standing above party or selfish economic interest. The imperial chancellor was to provide authoritative national leadership from above. The political figure of Bismarck as an ideal national leader towered over this conception of governmental politics. It was no coincidence that Tirpitz went to visit Bismarck after his appointment to the helm of the Imperial Naval Office to receive the blessing of the national hero and claim the mantle of his political authority.[25] Such admiration of Bismarckian leadership combined with an insistence on the autonomy of the military. For many years, Bülow was the navy's chancellor of choice precisely because he acted, by and large, according to the service's script, until he reconsidered in 1908–09. His successor, Bethmann-Hollweg, earned the navy's scorn for his disagreement with the Imperial Naval Office over the maritime arms buildup and his willingness to move against it. Here was a man, Tirpitz and others insisted, who had a flawed understanding of geopolitics and viewed as his "life mission" the attainment of an agreement with Britain "at the expense of the fleet."[26]

The conception of an authoritarian leadership from above was premised on a critique of participatory politics and explicit opposition to any parliamentary form of governance. The navy's policy makers derided the Reichstag for its divisive, short-sighted interest group politics, its endless, futile debates, and its inability to provide leadership on issues of true national importance. On the other hand, such reasoning did not question the legitimacy of the Reichstag as a representative body of the German nation as such. Tirpitz in particular recognized the Reichstag as a viable political institution. This view lent shape to the explicit rejection by Tirpitz of the talk about revising the existing constitution, as it had been engaged in by the emperor and members of his entourage in the mid-1890s; it was also a foundational premise of the navy's entire pursuit of resources and influence.[27] So natural was the recognition of the Reichstag as an important political body that when, in 1911, the navy's policy makers discussed the desirability of having the demand for a new Navy Bill emanate "out of the midst of the nation," they alluded to the Reichstag and the parties represented therein.[28]

Tirpitz and other navy leaders, then, adhered to an inclusive albeit antisocialist vision of the political nation. The so-called national parties represented the political constituency of this state, as opposed to the working-class-based Social Democratic Party of revolutionary socialism and internationalist orientation. They included the Conservative, Liberal, and Center parties. The imperial state's pursuit of policy "with" these parties constituted the navy's ideal of national politics, as expressed by the navy's policy makers, and this ideal guided their practices until well into the war.[29] The vision of the political nation emphatically extended to Catholic Germany and its political expression in the Center Party. Tirpitz promoted a broad policy of conciliation and cooperation with the Center Party, which went beyond isolated concessions in return for the party's approval of naval expansion. Rather, the overall counsel was to treat the Center Party as some sort of "governing party" and to fully integrate it into national politics.[30]

Accordingly, Tirpitz and others were strictly opposed to the intensifying anti-Catholic politics of the nationalist pressure groups after the turn of the century and the massive political mobilization against the Center Party during the so-called national elections of 1906.[31] While Chancellor Bülow subsequently defined his parliamentary base as the bloc of the Conservative and Liberal parties, the Imperial Naval Office continued to cultivate ties with the Center Party; it also forced the anti-Catholic radical nationalist leaders out of the German Navy League. So committed was Tirpitz to the Center Party that he was one of the few top state officials who before the war were willing to do away with the legal prohibition of the Jesuit order in Germany (which then happened during the war itself).[32]

Commitments to the Industrial Nation

The navy's entire pursuit of maritime force and global power was premised on a commitment to the notion of Germany as an industrial nation and the close nexus between military power, productive forces, and maritime interests. Couched in the language of economic geopolitics, this attachment had an uneasy relationship, at best, with the imperial state's particular ties to Prussia's East Elbian landed society and agrarian-conservative interests.[33]

The view of Germany as an expanding industrial and commercial society left little room for agriculture, a minor, if not a nonexistent, player in maritime interests. "The transformation of Germany into an industrial and trading state," Tirpitz told the emperor in 1899, "is irreversible like a law of nature. If one would seek to dam it, the process would flow on regardless. That does not rule out the view that one can seek to preserve other interests like agriculture as much as possible. Yet they are not a part of the great development."³⁴ Strikingly, in 1905, the Imperial Naval Office abandoned plans for an official documentation of the maritime interests of East Elbian Germany, which it had explored in the context of the upcoming Naval Bill. It had proved too difficult to muster enough authoritative material to make the case.³⁵

The navy's proindustrial outlook emerged into full view during the political juncture of 1897–1902 when the future place of proagrarian politics became a site of intense contestation that involved competing views of the future of Germany as a fast-developing country. Most directly, Tirpitz and his collaborators rejected any protectionist proagrarian tariffs that would hinder German foreign trade. They stressed that the case for a navy and agricultural protectionism were antagonistic. "If it were really the intention of the ministries in charge to inaugurate a commercial policy that is likely to diminish our trade and export industries to a substantial degree," Tirpitz wrote in August 1897, "this Naval Bill and for that matter any other one would constitute a contradiction to this policy. Any success would appear to be impossible because the fleet is after all a function of our maritime interests."³⁶ When one of Tirpitz's aides suggested two years later that the parliamentary passage of future naval legislation hinged on governmental acceptance of agricultural protectionism, Tirpitz scribbled in the margins "that one ought not to abolish the ends in order to get the means."³⁷ Tirpitz and his aides favored only modest agrarian tariffs that would be compatible with the primacy of industrial over agrarian interests in all matters of economic policy.³⁸ It was within the same spirit, which was shared by most officials of the imperial state, that the navy secretary approached other issues that pitted proagrarian politics against proexport trade policy, such as the politically contentious construction of a new east-west waterway, the Mittellandkanal (Midland Canal). Strongly opposed by East Elbian elites and organized agrarian pressure groups, the navy's policy makers officially supported it.³⁹

The Imperial Naval Office, then, advanced its agenda in contradistinction to key proagrarian policy makers within the government and, in particular, to the Prussian finance minister and vice president of the Prussian State Ministry, Johannes von Miquel, whose *Sammlungspolitik* (politics of rallying together) represented an important strand of governmental politics after 1897. This *Sammlungspolitik* sought to reconsolidate the alliance between heavy industry and agrarian interests and resurrect the party alliance of National Liberals and Conservatives, with the tacit addition of the Center Party, under protectionist, antisocialist, and repressive auspices.[40] Once in office, Tirpitz first asserted his naval plans against the initial opposition of Miquel and demanded that he officially support the navy's legislative agenda.[41] In 1899–1900, Tirpitz then sought to fight off Miquel's efforts to use the naval buildup for proagrarian *Sammlung* purposes by making the passage of the pending naval bill dependent on the introduction of high grain tariffs in the new tariff law that was being prepared. Tirpitz's opposition to this attempt became most evident during the Navy League's so-called first crisis in 1899. At that time a temporary alliance of Pan-Germans, naval professors, and Left Liberals denounced the dominance of the interests of heavy industry in the Navy League, and the activities of the League's initial secretary, Viktor von Schweinburg, a close associate of Miquel and the industrialist Friedrich von Krupp. Tirpitz, who complained confidentially that Schweinburg had been willing to act according to Miquel's wishes and to tie naval matters to the increase in grain tariffs, sided with Schweinburg's opponents and forced him out of office.[42]

At the same time, Tirpitz and his lieutenants engaged in political mobilization and naval propaganda that directly undercut Miquel's proagrarian policy. Initially, the Imperial Naval Office had considered welding the naval cause to the case against agricultural protectionism and creating an associational framework for that purpose.[43] The Office was responsible for propaganda that stressed Germany's transformation into an industrial state and, thus, had strong antiagrarian undertones. It forged a coalition between industry and commerce and cultivated ties with those political forces, such as Left Liberals and Hanseatic merchants, which were strictly opposed to Miquel's policies and to the preservation of the dominance of preindustrial (landed) elites.[44]

In 1899–1900, Tirpitz did not surrender to the demands of the proponents of a proagrarian *Sammlungspolitik*. To be sure, Secretary of Finance Max Freiherr von Thielmann promised during deliberations by the Budget Commission of the Reichstag over the Naval Bill of 1900 that the government would protect agrarian interests in the making of new tariff laws and commercial treaties; and he did so in full accordance with Tirpitz.[45] But this promise, which was elicited mostly by the leadership of the Center Party, was meaningless. A tactical move to ensure parliamentary approval of naval legislation, the assurance only reiterated a rhetorical position already taken by the government. It played no recognizable role in the actual making of the new tariff legislation, which in itself did not lose sight of the interests of exporting industries and trade.[46] In short—and despite the interpretive claims of Kehr and his followers—there was no strategic linkage between naval legislation and the tariff issue; and this reflected the trajectory of the navy's politics and economic imagination.

On the other hand, the Imperial Naval Office was politically savvy enough not to ignore some constraints set by the special ties of the imperial state to the Conservative-agrarian camp, which "has always been of utmost importance for the success of governmental policy initiatives and which, to a certain degree, will remain so in the future," as two of Tirpitz's top aides noted in 1900.[47] Thus the Imperial Naval Office did not engage in an explicit political effort "to become master" of the agrarians, an idea that had been entertained by at least one of its officers.[48] After discussion, the agency also decided not to get involved in the contentious debates surrounding the new tariff laws and commercial treaties.[49] Strikingly, the navy's official economist, Ernst von Halle, took a guarded position in public. He signaled support for the recognition of "legitimate" agricultural interests as represented in a "moderate" increase of grain tariffs, as long as it did not affect in any negative way the export interests of Germany's industry.[50]

Promises of National Unity

Naval reasoning placed the pursuit of maritime force and global power in the context of national integration and the orchestration of domestic consent to the nation-state, bourgeois society, and industrial capitalism. The emphasis on the material, socially integrative, and nationalizing promise of global empire was an integral aspect of a politics that hitched global power to an explicitly antisocialist politics of nationalist identification and limited social reform. August von Heeringen, the first chief of the Information Bureau, explicitly expected that the pursuit of maritime force was destined to develop a "people-unifying power."[51] Using a language of the nation, Tirpitz himself conceived of a German global empire, and the naval expansion it implied, as a "strong palliative against educated and noneducated Social Democracy."[52]

This strategy of national integration focused on an attempt to "nationalize" German workers and dissociate them from the Social Democratic Party and its revolutionary socialism. Accordingly, prominent officers never grew tired of arguing in public that the pursuit of maritime force and global power reflected workers' real interests and that the Social Democratic leaders were betraying their followers. Some officers displayed a remarkable optimism about their ability to win over the workers. In 1899–1900, Heeringen informed Tirpitz on several occasions that "understanding for the necessity of a strong fleet" would increasingly gain ground among workers, with the exception of only "very determined Social Democrats." He believed that the more intelligent Social Democrats were already in the process of rethinking their socialist convictions.[53]

According to the navy's representatives, the promise of Germany's rise to a prosperous global industrial and trading state were enormous. It could eliminate economic hardships at home, which, in turn, was bound to provide for social integration and national unity. The navy could make a substantial contribution to the "solution of the social question" by ensuring the "profitable expansion" of all the "energies" of the German people, Captain Curt von Maltzahn wrote Tirpitz in August 1895.[54] Heeringen argued along the same lines when he stressed the "high social political importance" of the naval buildup.[55] Tirpitz himself openly speculated about the political benefits of the "economic gain" from which all Germans and the "welfare institutions in an enlarged sense" would profit.[56]

Such thinking also focused on the immediate economic benefits of naval armaments. The construction of a battle fleet would facilitate growth, increased employment, and higher wages in those private industries involved in the construction of warships. Continuous construction at a steady pace appeared as a countermeasure against uneven economic growth and temporary economic downturns.[57] There was an acute awareness that the buildup would serve as a stimulant for the emergence of a military-industrial complex that in turn would foster the growth of the economy at large and of the shipbuilding industry in particular.[58] With great consistency, the navy's policy makers employed arguments about the nexus between naval orders, employment figures, and economic growth after the battle fleet buildup was under way.[59] Pleas for a continuation of the naval buildup were couched in this language of a proto–naval-military Keynesianism, which otherwise went hand in hand with efforts to retain the upper hand in naval-industrial relations to keep expenses at an "acceptable" level.[60]

This, then, was a reformist social imperialism of sorts.[61] Tirpitz and his fellow naval politicians combined their belief in the material benefits of global empire and naval buildup with an interest in limited social reform, that is, for redistributive welfare politics and tangible improvements in wages and working conditions. According to this conception, naval expansion was no substitute for concrete social reform measures at home; rather, they were mutually inclusive.[62] To promote the workers' reconciliation with the state and the capitalist economy, someone like Tirpitz recognized, at least in principle, that labor had legitimate demands and endorsed as a matter of principle ameliorative welfare policies and new social policy initiatives. The officers-turned-politicians in the Imperial Naval Office took a special interest in recruiting for naval propaganda the so-called academic socialists (*Kathedersozialisten*), that is, those professors who advocated some kind of state-led social reform.[63]

Much like these professors, the same officers also opposed any repressive legislation directed against the Social Democratic Party and the unions that would restrict the freedom of association and the workers' right to strike.[64] Politically, such conciliatory antisocialism, which coincided with aggressive antisocialist rhetoric within navy yards, was part of a general investment in constitutional government, the sanctity of the public sphere, and civil society.[65] To a considerable degree, the navy's politics of the industrial nation, global power, and social integration shared ground with the tenets of bourgeois technocratic reformism engaged in by Liberals, academic social reformers, and civilian officials of the imperial state.[66]

The pursuit of global empire and maritime force also appeared in itself as a truly nationalizing endeavor that, facilitated by clever propaganda, could serve as a rallying point for forging new, all-transcending national identities. Tirpitz made the case himself when he located the antisocialist "palliative" of naval expansion as much within the "new big national task" itself as in its "economic gain."[67] Present at the creation of the navy's navalist project and lending rhetorical shape to it subsequently, this emphasis attained a new urgency in the wake of the elections of 1912, which saw the Social Democrats emerge as the nation's largest party in the Reichstag. Invoking images of a "red flood," Tirpitz and other naval policy makers pronounced, in an alarmist fashion, the necessity of strong national leadership and goal-setting from above and associated that with a renewed commitment to the cause of global empire.[68]

The navy's discourse foregrounded the nation as the focal point of primary allegiance in a globalizing world. The proposition of "*civis*

Germanus sum" ("I am a German citizen"), which Tirpitz offered in the winter of 1895–96 when he first made the case for German global power, was central to this politics of identity.[69] The latter saturated the entire discourse surrounding the community of Germans abroad, *Auslandsdeutsche*, and its links to the navy and the entire nation at home. And of course, naval talk consistently presented the act of facing up to the world of geopolitical rivalry and the threat posed by a nationally united British Empire as an ultimate object lesson in the primacy of the national interest.[70]

No doubt, naval policy makers attached great national political goals to the pursuit of global power and maritime force. But this was primarily a matter of general emphasis, rather than a comprehensive strategy of national politicking. True, Tirpitz told the emperor in the fall of 1899 that the navy could serve as a "focal point" for the "rallying-together (*Sammlung*) of the National Parties."[71] Still, there was no effort by the Imperial Naval Office to follow up on such rhetoric and engage in national politics to engineer a sort of hegemonic political bloc through the naval-imperial cause. The navy's policy makers concentrated on the buildup of a battle fleet and the assertion of their claims to power in the field of naval policy. The Imperial Naval Office resisted any suggestions to aggressively use the issue of the navy for the rallying-together of the "national parties" in electoral politics (even if Tirpitz did raise this possibility briefly in August 1911 to make his naval bill attractive to the imperial chancellor[72]); and it did its utmost to separate naval legislation from other controversial issues as long, that is, as they did not impinge in some direct way on the pursuit of maritime force and the rationale for global power. A politics of self-conscious limitation shaped the navy's practices in the realm of national politics.

Social Imperialism U.S.-Style

Like their German peers, U.S. officers articulated a social-imperialist politics that hitched the arms buildup and global empire to particular conceptions of the state, productive forces, and social order. This politics combined an attachment to elite rule, national state power, and corporate industrialism with the promulgation of national renewal within the bounds of moral reform, racial exclusion, and reactionary welfarism. Broadly speaking, these emphases placed the navy's agendas inside an ever-shifting civilian politics of reform in Progressive Era America. The navy's social imperialism was of the complex world of (white) elite and middle-class reform that evolved between the late 1870s and 1910s and had, by the beginning of the twentieth century, spawned the Progressive movement, a loosely knit, rather heterogeneous configuration of actors and causes.[73]

The navy's social imperialism was a state-building proposition. The vision of a strong national state and the political insulation of its officials anchored the navy's political agendas. The call for naval expansion and a maximum degree of military self-governance amounted to the demand for a powerful warfare state manned by decision-making elites committed to the national interest and impervious to domestic political pressures. This statist project set the nation, and international considerations, against electoral politics and the alleged fallacies of short-sighted rule by party politicians. The navy, the core institution of an envisioned American *Machtstaat*, would owe its allegiance to the "point of view of the Nation's need, free from other influences," summarized the General Board in 1913. "The Navy, like our foreign policy and diplomacy, is broadly national, and has no relation to party or parties; and hence, should not be affected by changes of the administration."[74] "Our Cabinet and party system of government makes us, as a nation, weak in both 'preparing for' and 'carrying on' a war," as the conclusions of the "military experts" who were exclusively committed to the nation's interests in the world did not carry enough weight in a "democratic state," explained a high-ranking officer in 1914.[75]

Mahan himself offered an extensive critique of representative government. "Fits and starts" would be the attributes of "government by party ... in which regard to the voters takes precedence of regard to the interests of the voters—that is, of the nation," he explained in 1912.[76] "To prepare for war in time of peace," he noted on another occasion, "is impracticable to commercial representative nations, because the people in general will not give sufficient heed to military necessities, or to international problems, to feel the pressure which induces readiness."[77]

The national state envisioned by naval officers was an institutional apparatus committed to the cause of national industry. Going beyond the pursuit of economic interests abroad, this conception of a "promotional state" was wide ranging.[78] It was particularly evident in regard to domestic maritime industries. With great consistency, officers championed the cause of a state-sponsored revival of the U.S. oceanic merchant marine. Material aid to U.S. shipping emerged as a key platform during the 1880s. In subsequent years, prominent navy leaders expressed their favorable views of direct governmental action when they supported legislative efforts on behalf of the merchant marine, for example, in the context of the 1903–05

Merchant Marine Commission of Congress. The navy's support of an activist state policy culminated in the service of Admiral Benson, the first chief of naval operations, on the U.S. Shipping Board, which was created in 1916, and his role in the passage of the Merchant Marine Act of 1920.[79]

At the same time, naval officers championed a political economy of warfare built around the promises of private firms and corporate industrialism. The officers involved in naval construction and procurement stressed time and again the advantages of private companies. U.S. "naval strength" resided in the productive capacities of its "ship-building" and "armor plants" as private "corporations," summarized Rear-Admiral George W. Melville, the navy's engineer-in-chief, in 1903.[80] While assigning clear roles to governmental navy yards as key installations for repair and maintenance (and occasional construction) and to the Navy Gun Factory as a (limited) manufacturer in the ordnance field, officers such as Melville did not jockey for navy yards and the government armor plant as substitutes for private industry, as suggested by the many Democratic and Populist critics of the emerging naval-industrial complex. It was no coincidence that in the 1880s and 1890s the navy's interest in creating an industrial infrastructure for future naval construction was framed in part as developmental aid for the U.S. steel industry.[81]

Supporting a close nexus between the national state and private productive forces, the navy's social imperialism breathed the "corporate liberal" current of Progressive thought and reform.[82] Prominent naval officers were captivated by the example of big business and its model of large-scale managerial organization. They invoked a "corporate metaphor," that is, the example of private corporate institutions, whenever they discussed the organization of the Navy Department.[83] When the Naval War College investigated this issue closely in the mid-1890s, it set an example by exploring the "organization of great commercial companies."[84] After 1900, naval officers continued to invoke the example of corporations, with their boards of directors and functional organization, in their pleas for a naval general staff. "It would be a "world-wide policy, in large organizations of every kind," such as "industrial companies," to "direct the organization by special bodies," explained Commander Fiske, the future rear admiral, in 1905.[85]

The navy's "corporate liberalism" was evident in other realms as well. It included the turn toward industrial-shop management methods in the navy yards even if officers disagreed over the merits of the principles of "scientific management" as associated with Frederick Taylor.[86] The navy's personnel policy was another case in point. Seeking long-term employment for its enlisted force, the navy self-consciously engaged in the same tactics as large-scale private enterprise.[87]

It was within these parameters that naval discourse attached central importance to the promise of state power in general. Officers celebrated the promises of a strong national state and set them against both individualism and the fallacies of representative government, as represented by Great Britain and the United States. The imperial German state and its superior organizational power figured as the key (positive) point of reference. But the example of Imperial Japan was invoked as well. The Americans painted that empire in the same image as Germany and ascribed the same features of political, military, and social organization to them both. They cast Germany and Japan as "military nations" led by strong governments committed to the pursuit of force and imperial expansion.[88]

Among his peers, it was Mahan, perhaps the most Anglophile American naval officer, who articulated views on the state and "national efficiency" and elaborated on the comparative strength of the imperial German state (and, on occasion, its Japanese counterpart) and its significance in more detail. "Great executive efficiency," he argued time and again, would characterize the German Empire and its pursuit of military force and imperial power. Here was a modern-day Sparta, a model type of society historically dominated by a "system of state control, not only highly developed but with a people accustomed to it." German "organization of energy" through and with the state would surpass that of other countries. This would be true in particular for those countries such as Great Britain and the United States that clung to the idea of the "liberty of the individual, undirected and unrestrained by the community."[89] According to Mahan, the future belonged to the system of strong and efficient state power that in the present gave the German Empire, and its Japanese counterpart, the competitive edge over other empires in the international arena. "The control of the individual by the community—that is, by the state, is increasingly the note of the times. Germany has in this matter a large start. Japan has much the same."[90]

Mahan offered a pessimistic view of the long-term ability of the British Empire to harness national power and remain competitive with its German rival. British naval politics was bound to take a turn for the worse, he insisted, as the importance of participatory politics rose. As early as 1890, Mahan gave expression to such fear. "Great trade, large mechanical industries, and an extensive colonial system" would still provide the conditions to keep British sea power at maximum strength. But it remained "an open question" whether the current "democratic government," as opposed to the landed aristocracy that had ruled Britain in the early modern period, "will have the foresight, the keen sensitiveness to national position and credit, the willingness to insure its prosperity by adequate outpouring of money in times of peace, all of which are necessary for military preparation."[91] In 1911, Mahan predicted a bleak future for the British Empire "if social and political conditions in Great Britain develop as they now promise."[92] It was such thinking about the empire's possible decline that provided a subtext for Mahan's calls for a close Anglo-American union.[93]

The navy's vision of the superior "executive efficiency" of the "State" focused on the organization of military force and the promotion of national industry. It was not a proposition for a welfare state. Officers envisioned long-lasting material prosperity through global power but in none of their many discussions of national industry and economic needs did they link it with state-led welfare schemes and redistributive politics. Mahan even voiced serious reservations about the pursuit of social welfare programs in Britain.[94] Such reactionary welfarism came with denunciations of any independent labor politics; it bounded dismissals of the agenda of William Jennings Bryan, the Democratic presidential contender in 1896 and 1900, as a harbinger of socialism and anarchy (not to even speak of the presidential candidacy of Eugene Debs); and it went hand in hand with general laments about creeping egalitarianism that would erase the proper distinctions among different classes of citizens.[95]

The navy's vision of the state fused the cause of the industrial nation to the cause of elite rule and technocratic governance. Navy leaders were part of what historian Stephen Skowronek has described as an "emergent intelligentsia" of state-builders "rooted in a revitalized professional sector and a burgeoning university sector."[96] Service leaders used the same antidemocratic language of "expertise," "efficiency," and "effectiveness" as Progressive Era state-builders and reformers in the civilian realm, when they made the case for a powerful (warfare) state and its political insulation.[97] The demand for a general staff with sweeping powers was consistently presented as a matter of putting the professional expert in charge. According to this reasoning, creating such an institution would only imply "recognizing" naval officers "as members of real professions, in the same sense that doctors and clergymen and lawyers are recognized as members of real professions," as Rear-Admiral Fiske, for example, argued on more than one occasion.[98]

Remaking the Nation

American navalists linked the pursuit of maritime force and global power to the cause of moral reform and national regeneration. This linkage entailed the promise of a newly reinvigorated militant nationalism to stave off perceived civilizational decline and rising socialist ideals within the existing framework of republican governance, civil society, and corporate capitalism. Explicit concerns about gender figured prominently in this analysis, which associated domestic regeneration with the reassertion of both martial spirit and manly resolve while presenting a crisis of manhood as a key marker of societal malaise and civilizational decay. Remasculinization appeared as essential to the future of a reforged U.S. nation and its self-assertion against enemies from within and without.[99]

Acting as the key ideologue, Mahan forcefully explicated this social-imperialist politics of moral reform and national reinvigoration. On the one hand, he outlined a rationale for the pursuit of maritime force in terms of both economic geopolitics and an unfolding clash of civilizations. On the other hand, he tied the cause of naval expansion to the reassertion of the proper moral fiber, martial assertiveness, and combative national sentiment in the face of soulless materialism, rising socialism, and emasculation at home.[100]

Indeed, the specter of "socialism" in the "current age of anarchy and insubordination" haunted Mahan. So did the materialist pursuit of happiness in "our modern times of infrequent war," with its "worship of comfort, wealth and general softness," which was bound to lead to a loss of the proper "spiritual convictions" and "strong masculine virtues" of the nation. To reinvigorate the nation in the crucible of violent geopolitics, by contrast, promised the right kind of (moral) order at home. Only the pursuit of maritime force and global power could remasculinize the United States and foster a strong "sense of nationality" as the "true antidote to what is bad in socialism," argued Mahan. "In the rivalries of nations, in the accentuation of differences, in the conflict of ambitions, lies the preservation of the martial spirit" that, allegedly, held the key to the future of the nation, or, for that matter, European civilization as a whole. "Control of the sea" not only meant "predominant influence in the world," summarized Mahan. "The greatest of the prizes for which nations contend, it too will serve, like other conflicting interests, to keep alive that temper of stern purpose and strenuous emulation which is the salt of the society of civilized states, whose unity is to be found not in flat identity of conditions—the ideals of socialism—but in a common standard of moral and intellectual ideas."[101]

It was within this spirit that Mahan vehemently dismissed any attempts to "civilize" geopolitics through the introduction of binding means of arbitration in the arena of international politics. Arbitration, with the prospect of eliminating competitive arms buildups and war itself, was at odds with the primacy of strife and manly assertion as organizing principles of national and international worlds; it was bound to weaken the manly "energy" and "moral muscle" of the white peoples of Europe and North America. Fittingly, Mahan directly linked arbitration to the much-dreaded socialism. The latter appeared as a prescription for a "socialistic community of states" that flattened the salutary differences between nations in favor of an "artificial equality among members" and resulted in the atrophy of the "powers of individual initiative, of nations and of men, the greatest achievements of our civilizations so far." The result of arbitration would be a "flood of socialistic measures" at home: in an age of mass politics, resources previously spent on armaments were destined to be redirected toward welfare programs and thus to "demoralize" entire peoples, or so Mahan predicted.[102]

Mahan did not stand alone in his advocacy of national regeneration and moral reform. Other prominent officers waved the same flag in public. Admiral Luce stressed the redeeming qualities of the pursuit of military force and war, which would "chasten" the nation and the individual; and contrasted them with the "destructive" and emasculating nature of peace and prosperity. "As adversity and opposition toughen the mental and moral fibre and temper the spirit of man," he explained in an influential article on the "benefits of war," "so riches and easily-acquired success enervate the strongest character and unfit it for protracted efforts. It is the same with nations." Admiral Taylor emphasized the enormous promises of military preparedness and armed confrontation for the "moral nature" of the nation. Only they could protect it against the degradations of the "corrupt ease," "luxurious immorality," and "race decadence" that came with a period of both long-lasting peace and material prosperity. Both Luce and Taylor agreed that the United States was in need of martial regeneration under nationalist auspices. And, much like Mahan, they invoked the "degeneration" and "corruption" of the Roman Empire as the key negative example.[103]

As a discursive proposition, the notion of national regeneration through moral reform was central to the case for maritime force and global power as it congealed in the 1890s. Its open articulation became less prominent in the years after the turn of the century, at a time when Mahan diagnosed a "conversion of spirits and of ideals" in the United States and celebrated its "new national resolve."[104] But the emphasis on martial manhood and a militant nation remained a potent force. It exerted a defining influence on the self-stylizations of the navy as a model institution and the identity naval officers fashioned for themselves and their enlisted force. These officers presented their own service as an exemplary national and nationalizing institution that could turn people from different classes, sections, and religions into proper American men and citizens. The service was cast as a prominent site for the production and enactment of a new martial yet "civilized" manhood that combined a rugged physicality with moral strength and national identification.[105]

The corollary of the navy's emphasis on the nation and moral reform was a politics of white nativism. This policy expressed itself most forcefully in the defense of an imagined white nation against Asian migrants. Before 1914 (and after), officers supported the coalescing policy of "Asiatic exclusion" that strove to preserve the racial and cultural integrity of white Anglo-Saxon America. In the 1870s and 1880s prominent naval officers had embraced anti-Chinese immigration platforms. The eminent Admiral John Rodgers, for example, had publicly spoken out in favor of the cause of so-called Chinese exclusion in the years leading up to foundational federal legislation in 1882.[106] In the 1890s, such anti-Chinese white nativist sentiment expressed itself in naval discussions of the U.S. interest in Hawaii. In 1893, Mahan promoted the annexation of Hawaii as a measure against the Chinese peopling of the island group and the transpacific advance of what he referred to as the "comparative barbarism of China."[107]

In direct continuation of such nativist sentiment, representatives of the navy promoted the cause of anti-Japanese "Asiatic exclusion" as it attained prominence as a political proposition after the turn of the twentieth century. Interwoven with the understanding of imperial conflict with Japan, this support was built around a sense of racial conflict sparked by the transpacific migration of the Japanese (which accelerated after 1900) to the West Coast of the United States (and elsewhere).[108] In every single discussion of naval strategy and policy after 1906–07, the navy's strategists defined "Asiatic exclusion" as one of the key policies their service served to uphold. Officers rallied to the defense of an imagined white nation against an alleged Japanese racial threat. Japanese immigration appeared as a hostile act of "colonization within our own borders," wrote Captain J. D. McDonald, an officer assigned to the Naval War College in 1914.[109]

Mahan himself articulated this position most forcefully and in a fashion echoed by his peers. Raising the specter of large-scale Japanese settlement in the western United States and their eventual takeover by the Japanese race, he argued that "with the black race question on our hands," the United States could not afford "a further yellow one."[110] It would prove impossible to assimilate the Japanese into dominant Anglo-Saxon civilization. "The question," he wrote, would be "one of age-long differences, proceeding from age-long separations producing variations of ideas which do not allow intermingling, and consequently, if admitted, are ominous of national weakness through flaws in homogeneity. The radical difference between the Oriental and the Occidental, which is constantly insisted upon, occasions incompatibility of close association in large numbers for the present, and for any near future."[111] By 1906–07, Mahan backed away from his earlier assessment of the Japanese race as "adoptively" European, which he had offered at the turn of the century as part of his analysis of global geopolitics and civilizational conflict.[112]

The navy's allegiance to racial exclusion was firm. It was also in plain view in the concerted efforts to make the emerging battleship navy into an exemplary national institution. The navy leadership wanted native-born white U.S. citizens, preferably from rural areas, to man the navy; and it tailored its recruiting efforts and imagery of naval service accordingly. Breaking with previous enlistment practice, this effort was directed not only against the kind of international maritime labor that had always helped to make up the ranks of the U.S. Navy, but also against African Americans and the new immigrant populations from eastern and southern Europe. Between 1900 and 1914 the navy raised the share of native citizens from about 60 percent to 90 percent. The share of noncitizens dropped from 20 percent to 1 percent. African Americans had comprised about 10 percent of the enlisted force in the 1870s and 1880s; by 1910, that number stood at less than 3.5 percent, to further sink to about 1.4 percent at the end of World War I. "The Great White Fleet," one historian of the navy's enlisted force has noted, "was aptly named for both its racial makeup and its paint job."[113]

New Departures

In both countries, the priorities of the two navies took on a new urgency during the mid-1910s. Continuing differences in emphasis coexisted with fresh convergences to shape the social-imperialist politics of navalists as their technocratic authoritarianism and nationalist commitments radicalized. Whereas the Germans reconsidered previous commitments to constitutional government and political limitation in favor of dictatorial governance and broad political intervention, members of the American naval elite made the case for all-encompassing "preparedness" and explicitly endorsed the cause of "militarism" as they argued for making the United States truly competitive with the German Empire.

In Germany, the navy's ideas about the nation and global power came under intense pressure when the navy's policy makers first faced an adversarial national politics and then confronted war. Between 1911 and 1914, the navy lost control over both governmental and parliamentary policy-making concerning the maritime arms buildup and related matters of foreign policy.[114] Moreover, the previous period of governmental stability and parliamentary normalization, which had shaped the navy's policy pursuits after 1900, had run its course. The formation of the "National Opposition," the dramatic success of the Social Democratic Party in the 1912 elections, and cross-cutting polarities among the Reichstag parties marked severe political instabilities. They raised troubling question about the future of the imperial polity.[115]

Under these circumstances, the navy's commitment to a strong *Machtstaat* capable of harnessing national power attained new valences. Agreeing that the entire political regime was heading toward disaster, that the empire was moving "down a slippery slope," the navy's policy makers called for a new national government led by an assertive Bismarckian figure.[116] He was to instill new life into the pursuit of global power and maritime force and rally the nation in order to create a stable political basis for governance, contain the socialist threat, and fight the specter of future parliamentary governance. To many officers, Tirpitz was a candidate of choice as the leading figure of a new national leadership. Here, allegedly, was the "only" person in government who "in a manly fashion promoted and stood for the honor and greatness of Germany" and who could "save the situation" and "set great goals for a nation instead of the currently common small-minded criticisms," explained Rear-Admiral Hopman.[117] Characteristically, such aspirations to high political office were also entertained by at least one other senior officer. Admiral Henning von Holtzendorff, a well-connected critic of Tirpitz who commanded the High Seas Fleet until 1913, also thought of himself as a possible candidate for the imperial chancellorship.[118]

The case for Tirpitz as chancellor involved a critique of the existing governmental leadership, not of the political parties. The main responsibility lay with Wilhelm II and the imperial chancellor. Hopman opined in December 1912 that Germany lacked "a firm hand and a clear head endowed with a hard-nosed realism, at the top. In its stead, confusion, personal interest, and partisan interest ruled the day."[119] In the admiral's view, the product of this was "partisan business" and "democratic conditions," with the socialist threat posed by the Social Democratic Party looming ever more darkly on the horizon.[120]

Such views placed the navy in the vicinity of those radical nationalist forces on the right that moved within a discourse of an authoritarian "national efficiency" and positioned themselves as a "National Opposition" to the imperial state, its civilian leadership, and the emperor. In fact, Tirpitz became the chancellor of choice among the extraparliamentary right-wing nationalist public because of his reputation as an assertive statesman committed to the cause of the militant nation and unmitigated power. More so, Tirpitz figured prominently in the plans for a national dictatorship, which were drawn up by radical nationalists associated with the Pan-German League in 1913–14.[121] In the early 1900s, by contrast, the relationship of the Imperial Naval Office to the radical nationalists had been conflict ridden precisely because of their challenge to the professional authority of the navy secretary (and his more inclusive vision of the political nation).

But there were limits to such convergence, at least as far as the naval circle around Tirpitz was concerned. Prior to the war, its members still remained committed to the imperial polity in its given constitutional form.[122] Moreover, before 1914 the navy's political representatives did not abandon their previous politics of limitation. Their interest in a new national government notwithstanding, they continued to focus their political energies on matters of maritime force. Such a focus fit well with the recognition that the talk about Tirpitz as chancellor stood little chance of realization, for it lacked the necessary support within the imperial executive, in the broader public, or among the parties. Strikingly, Tirpitz himself expressed his unwillingness to become chancellor whenever he discussed this issue in the years leading up to war.[123] To fight the general drift of national politics, Tirpitz ultimately left vague assurances that he would support any effort to help "bring together" the "state-supporting bourgeois parties" as long as he could do so within the bounds of his departmental domain.[124]

World War I altered the direction of the navy's politics. The pursuit of victory left little room for political restraint or constitutional niceties, or so it seemed from the navy's point of view. Tirpitz led the charge, starting in the spring of 1915, after he had talked about the necessity of replacing Chancellor Bethmann-Hollweg in the fall of 1914.[125] With the support of other navy leaders, the navy secretary worked toward the creation of a wartime military dictatorship to supplant civilian governmental leadership and limit any monarchical powers. Although on several occasions he suggested other candidates, Tirpitz primarily promoted himself as a possible chancellor with dictatorial powers and he engaged in intrigues to end the reign of Wilhelm II in favor of a regency by the crown prince.[126] Simultaneously, Tirpitz and other navy leaders orchestrated a massive political campaign, which included the mobilization of public opinion and nationalist notables, in favor of the pursuit of a victorious peace (*Siegfrieden*), unrestricted submarine warfare, and massive annexations.[127]

Placing themselves in open opposition to the imperial chancellor and Wilhelm II, Tirpitz and others officers now staked out a common ground with radical nationalist politics. They did so after they had first flirted, for a moment, with the idea of combining strong national leadership and limited political reform in the direction of greater political inclusion as the best way to fight the war with a fully mobilized nation. In the fall of 1914, Admirals Tirpitz, Hopman, and Müller had endorsed the idea, proposed by naval-officer-turned-diplomat Admiral Paul von Hintze, of providing Social Democratic leaders with positions in government and reforming the plutocratic Prussian suffrage to promote the unity of the nation and exploit its enormous enthusiasm, its "colossal drive."[128]

Aiming at the highest degree of "national efficiency" in the pursuit of victory in war, the officers ultimately rallied around the cause of the imperial state and unadulterated authoritarian rule. "The path to democracy is wrong. A middle position does not exist in the field of domestic policy," summarized Tirpitz.[129] When, in 1916, Admiral Franz Hipper, one of the key commanding officers in the active fleet, proposed dictatorial governance in the context of the ongoing crisis over the "Peace Resolution" in the Reichstag and the governmental promise of a reform of the Prussian electoral system, he articulated a position then prevalent among his peers.[130]

It was left to the creation of the nationalist Fatherland Party in September 1917 to showcase the navy's wartime priorities. The party's platform promoted the unity of the "nation" by setting the causes of unconditional victory, authoritarian governance, and an annexationist peace against proponents of negotiated peace, political democratization, and socialist subversion.[131] The Fatherland Party met with great enthusiasm among naval officers. In retirement, Tirpitz became the first chairman. Navy leaders pledged their support. Many officers joined; others served as speakers for the party. Its officials were allowed to propagandize inside of naval installations, to the chagrin of many sailors. No doubt, the Fatherland Party struck a chord with the naval elite. According to one captain, the party's first rally at the Berlin Philharmonic in September 1917 ranked as a "third great day" of the entire war, next to the declaration of war and the battle of Jutland: "It was as if in the twelfth hour a new star arose, on which everyone pinned his hopes. Because what we miss, that is national unity and a will to victory."[132]

As the Germans radicalized their commitments to the nation and decisive leadership from above, American officers, too, articulated their own political commitments with new intensity. Their pursuit of "preparedness" in the mid-1910s brought their priorities into sharp focus. Navy leaders pushed for a massive arms buildup and more professional-institutional power. But officers did not lose sight of their politics of moral reform and national regeneration, which, in fact, emerged as a key pillar of the navy's talk about "preparedness." Such a plea for the remaking of the American body politic mobilized images of rampant materialism, pleasure-seeking individualism, disrespect for authority, and sagging martial energies, which harkened back to those invoked in earlier years by Mahan and others. But the same plea also expanded on the growing frustration among naval officers in the early 1910s with the alleged indifference of both civilian policy makers and the "American people" toward the navy's policy prescriptions. Writing in the *Proceedings of the U.S. Naval Institute* in the summer of 1914, Admiral Fiske set the tone as he bitterly complained about the flourishing of an "anti-military spirit" in the United States. The "requirement of business, society, and pleasure" was in the process of "monopoliz[ing] the attention of the nation" while "military character" was "deteriorating" and the "martial spirit" was being "smothered." Only the development of the much-needed "martial power" promised to foster the "character and health" of the "American people," ensure "law" and "order," and turn "honor" once more into a "watchword."[133]

The navy's investment in moral reform attained a new quality in the context of "preparedness" and the subsequent war mobilization. It became a proposition for national rejuvenation by means of mandatory military service. In previous years, Mahan and other officers had offered admiring portrayals of European regimes of military conscription and, with barely concealed envy, touted their beneficial impact as an agent of moral uplift, social discipline, and patriotic instruction.[134] They had done so in clear recognition of the political infeasibility of a draft in the United States.[135] But officers now faced a new playing field due to the campaign for compulsory military training that was launched by a broad-based movement of elite figures, the army leadership, and middle-class reformers.[136] In the *Proceedings of the U.S. Naval Institute,* writers waxed eloquent about the promises of universal military training beyond its immediate function of generating manpower for geopolitical conflict. Such training was bound to make for "better citizenship" and a "stronger and finer manhood," bringing the latter up to a "higher level of physical and moral fitness" and imbuing male adults with much-needed "ideas of patriotism and subordination," summarized Lieutenant-Commander John P. Jackson.[137]

Such talk about moral reform and national regeneration articulated fears about the loyalties and pursuits of (white) immigrant and working-class populations and lent itself to open denunciations of labor radicalism and socialist subversion. The same talk also addressed concerns about the proper orientation of the white middle classes. It was no coincidence that particular vitriol was heaped upon organized pacifism and female suffrage politics. There was little sympathy for what one rear admiral referred to as those "long-haired men with white ties and the short-haired women with glasses" who denounced "militarism" with a "line of stuffed words and inflated language."[138]

Overall, the "preparedness" campaign provided the space for the open articulation of the vision of a powerful national state, elite rule, and a reforged militant nation. It was within this context that some officers took their long-standing commitment to making the United States competitive with the "military nations" of Germany and Japan to its logical conclusion. "Properly considered," learned the reader of the *Proceedings of the U.S. Naval Institute* in 1915, "militarism" was "merely preparedness" and the "business of best using the national resources to overcome an enemy."[139] "If the current war were not to result in long-lasting peace and universal disarmament," noted Commander A. W. Hinds in the same pages, and in the same year, "the quicker the country is saddled with an efficient militarism the better."[140] Rear-Admiral Bradley Fiske, the initial leader of the navy's "preparedness" campaign, followed suit. In his memoirs, published in 1919, Fiske finally owned up to the term he had eschewed, with care, in previous years. "Militarism," he wrote, does "not menace the liberties of the people but it does menace the irresponsible powers of politicians. The correct meaning of the word militarism has the same connection with the word military...that any noun ending with 'ism' has with its corresponding adjective. Militarism, *in its correct meaning,* stands for something that is good and strong and honest and efficient in a country."[141]

Part IV

A MILITARISM OF EXPERTS

Naval Professionalism and
the Making of Navalism

Chapter 10

Of Sciences, Sea Power, and Strategy

In his *Science of the Army,* published in 1872, the German historian and administrative scholar Lorenz von Stein proclaimed the transformation of the officer corps into a corporate body of experts. The corps had become "the holder and representative of the real military professional education and in the latter lies its true and higher justification." Officers devoted their entire lives to military service and the science of war "in such a way, that both elements are as closely linked with each other as possible." On a political-institutional level, the officer corps required a high degree of separation from outside interference to accomplish its occupational task. Stein viewed the independence enjoyed by the armed forces within Imperial Germany as a matter of true military professionalism, and not of aristocratic privilege or antiliberal authoritarianism.[1]

A few years later, Emory Upton, a U.S. Army officer, painted a similar picture of European officer corps in his *The Armies of Asia and Europe,* a book that helped set the agenda to remake the American armed forces in relation to an image of an idealized European model, which was mostly abstracted from the Prussian-German military. Upton went to great length to emphasize the professional orientation of the officer corps, reviewing the selection, training, and promotion of its "specially educated" members.

Constant study, postgraduate education, regular performance reviews, and preferential treatment of all officers "who manifest decided zeal and professional ability" ensured high standards of excellence. The general staff and the war academy figured as the key institutions for the intellectual elite of the officer corps to acquire and practice their expertise in the art of war.[2]

While offering highly normative accounts, Stein and Upton captured the professional projects of Western officer corps in the aftermath of the Prussian "military revolution" of the 1860s.[3] It was this project, as pursued by naval officers, which drove the rise of navalism in the United States and Germany. This militarist formation did not simply reflect the selfish interests of self-aggrandizing officers in institutional growth, career advancement, or social standing, as some historians have suggested.[4] Rather, navalism represented the interests and definitions of naval elites who viewed themselves and acted as a group of professionals who laid claim to a distinctive body of thought and practices and demanded recognition on that basis.

As makers of navalism, naval officers positioned themselves as a science-based "epistemic community" of experts.[5] This community claimed to have acquired a special knowledge in naval affairs and global politics and to have uncovered the laws governing the conduct of navies, economies, and states. The sciences of sea power and of strategy were at the heart of these claims. These two sciences also fed directly into a transatlantic movement of ideas between its adherents. Their development was underwritten by a shared attachment to the type of military professionalism that had become associated with the Prussian-German army. This general attachment further differentiated the professional militarism of the U.S. and German navies from their British counterpart. Its key point of reference was the "strategic science" of the German General Staff that had emerged as a "startlingly new and genuine professional ideology" at mid-nineteenth century, as Michael Geyer has suggested.[6]

The Science of Sea Power

The navalists' science of sea power fused military strategy, naval history, and imperial ideology into a self-contained whole. It produced large historical narratives of states, diplomacy, and war that claimed to offer the analytical tools and vocabulary for understanding the present and the future. These analyses emphasized the importance of sea power and military preparedness for the rise and fall of great powers. By doing so, they stressed the interdependence of national industry, maritime force, and great-power rivalry and they provided a language to explain the meanings of sea power and maritime interests in general. This language, in turn, both marked and shaped the naval elites' participation in the "ideological consensuses"—the loosely knit configurations of arguments, languages, and themes among national intelligentsias—that shaped the fast-developing interest in empire and global power in each country.[7] And it allowed navy leaders to define geopolitical agendas for their nation-states, claim discursive mastery over the definition of their universal interests, and demand control over the pursuit of policy.

Mahan provided the groundwork for this approach in his series of books on *The Influence of Sea Power upon History*. The first installment, published in 1890, promised to deliver "an estimate of the effect of sea power upon the course of history and the prosperity of nations."[8] He assumed that the history of sea power would be "a narrative of contests between nations, of mutual rivalries, of violence frequently culminating in war"; in short, it was "largely a military history."[9] Mahan's analyses focused on the grand strategies and military operations of the major maritime powers in the age of sail, the seventeenth through the nineteenth centuries. The first chapter of the first tome laid out a series of general arguments on behalf of sea power, economics, and power politics and grounded them historically. Mahan's discussion provided a set of terms and ideas to define the constituents of "sea power" and the "conditions" affecting it. Outlining his rationale for "sea power," Mahan naturalized an early-modern "mercantilist" rationale for empire-building and yoked it to a classic European conception of a system of great powers.[10]

In the most general terms, Mahan's historical narrative argued that "sea power" and maritime affairs mattered greatly. They had exerted an "immense determining influence" on "the history of the world" and played a pivotal role as a "principal factor" in shaping the "general advance and decay of nations which is called their history."[11] More specifically, a nation's prosperity, its "greatness and wealth," depended on the flourishing of maritime economies. The latter included production, shipping, and colonies, "in a word: sea power."[12] As Mahan explained, "In these three things—production, with the necessity of exchanging products, shipping, whereby the exchange is carried on, and colonies, which facilitate and enlarge the operations of shipping and tend to protect it by multiplying points of safety—is to be found the key to much of the history, as well as of the policy of nations bordering upon the sea."[13] Their very prominence, in turn, made these three elements of "sea power" primary objects of the rivalry between powers. Nations would "decay" without them, that is, "when cut off from external activities and resources which at once draw out and support their internal powers."[14] Time and again, Mahan argued forcefully that throughout history only superior maritime force guaranteed the promotion and protection of a nation's maritime interests during both peace and wartime. In Mahan's scheme, maritime economies could not flourish without a powerful fleet. Eschewing conceptual consistency, Mahan defined maritime force either as a servant of "sea power" or directly as a constituent part.

Mahan's exposition identified six "principal conditions" that affected the development and pursuit of sea power. They ranged from geographical and natural factors to the "number" and "characteristics" of the people and the "character of government."[15] Mahan used this discussion as a "foil for his governmental argument, which was about the appropriate role of state action with respect to naval development," as historian Jon Sumida has explained convincingly.[16] History demonstrated how important it was for a government to build up a strong navy and an infrastructure of naval bases as a means to promote its national industries and to ensure its access to seaborne commerce and overseas markets. Even if the "principal conditions" largely shaped the "history of seaboard nations," the "shrewdness and foresight of governments" nonetheless made a huge difference.[17]

Mahan's historical narratives and arguments set the tone in U.S. naval circles. Mahan had given "sea power" the "logical supremacy in the minds of men" that it deserved and, thus, had a "revolutionizing effect in international politics," declared a president of the Naval War College in 1901.[18] Expressing a widespread consensus, Admiral Fiske stated in 1911 that "Mahan proved that sea power has exercised a determining influence on history. He proved that sea power has been necessary for commercial success in peace and military success in war."[19] Fiske also noted that Mahan had not been the first to make this case.

Indeed, Mahan's narrative and larger findings were hardly original. They were the work of a highly imaginative synthetic thinker who welded together the insights, ideas, and scholarship of others into a cogently argued, well-crafted narrative. In his memoirs, published in 1906, Mahan himself credited Theodor Mommsen's *History of Rome* as the major inspiration for his insight about the importance of sea power. He also admitted that his historical work drew primarily on the literature on the naval conflicts of the seventeenth and eighteenth centuries that was available to him in the United States.[20] The recognition of the interrelationship of navy, maritime trade, and manufacturing, and of sea power, national wealth, and great-power status, had been a staple of naval discourse in the United States and elsewhere well before the 1890s. Most directly, Mahan drew on arguments advanced by fellow officers in a number of articles in the *Proceedings of the U.S. Naval Institute* in the early 1880s. Writing on the decline and the future of the U.S. merchant marine, these officers had discussed the sources and elements of maritime greatness within a historical context. Isolating the factors that determined the "rise and fall of the great maritime nations of the past," these authors had furnished all the analytical categories that Mahan employed in his own narrative of sea power and history.[21]

Mahan's history-based exposition of sea power served a purpose. It provided a historical framework to make sense of present-day developments and lay out an agenda for the United States and the outward projection of its productive power in the present and future. The "practical object" of his "inquiry" was "to draw from the lessons of history inferences applicable to one's own country and service," declared Mahan in the first volume of his history of sea power.[22] Casting himself as a "naval officer in full sympathy with his profession," Mahan, the historian, explicitly made the case for the pursuit of American sea power to ensure his nation's prosperity in the twentieth century.[23] Strikingly, this move not only reflected a belief in the unity of history and the forces shaping it; it was also a product of a particular view of the goals of writing history. According to Mahan, historical narratives were written for public consumption.[24] Fittingly, Mahan deliberately employed the term "sea power" to maximize the popular accessibility, and, thus, the use-value of his study, while privately admitting to its conceptual vagaries.

A history-based science of sea power blended into the analysis of the United States and the geopolitics of war and empire in the present. Presenting himself as a public voice of the navy, Mahan made himself into a key shaper of American expansionist discourse and a prominent analyst of global politics. Published in 1897, the collection of Mahan's first series of essays as an imperial thinker was appropriately entitled *The Interest of America in Sea Power, Present and Future*.[25] At the beginning of the twentieth century, the history-based analytic of sea power associated with Mahan underwrote any effort by the navy to make sense of ongoing geopolitical events for its own policy purposes.

Mahan became the official high priest of the new history-based naval science of sea power in the United States and beyond.[26] It was in the shadow of his first two books on the influence of sea power in history that German naval officers produced their own historical narratives of sea power and advanced their understandings of maritime force, international politics, and economic struggle.[27] Already by 1893, the German Naval High Command (Oberkommando der Marine) urged all officers to study the "works of Captain Mahan."[28] Apparently, the command did so on the prodding of its chief of staff, Alfred von Tirpitz, who had been discussing Mahan's works with his friends and colleagues and on whose fertile mind these works made a "lasting impression," as his son explained in 1918.[29] In his hyperbolic manner, Wilhelm II claimed in 1894 that he was "not reading but devouring" Mahan's first book on the *Influence of Sea Power*, a "first-class work and classic in all points," which "is on board of all my ships and constantly quoted by my captains and officers."[30]

Tirpitz himself proved instrumental in the German translation and distribution of Mahan's "epochal" volumes on sea power in history.[31] Becoming available to a German-language audience by the mid-1890s, Mahan's work cast a long shadow on the massive histories of maritime conflict that were written after the turn of the century by several officers associated with the Marineakademie. Their analysis of sea power from the mid-seventeenth century to 1815 drew on Mahan's analysis as a primary source of information and interpretation.[32]

Early on, in 1895, an influential article published in the navy's own journal, the *Marine-Rundschau*, written by Ludwig Borckenhagen, a teacher of naval history at the Marineakademie, brought the navy's appropriation of Mahan into sharp focus. The American had "stated in clear, unassailable sentences the importance of naval history, its foundations, the eternal value of its lessons and its broader meaning, which includes the domain of naval strategy." Which "new law do we owe to Mahan?" the article asked. "It is in a few words the following: sea power, or the command of some part of the sea, secures for its holder, depending on its extent, an eventually dominant position in relation to all countries which border with their coasts on that sea." Borckenhagen enthusiastically embraced Mahan's conception of sea power as both a historical analytic and proposition for the future. The American's insights applied to Germany. His own country, Borckenhagen surmised, had just been catching up to the leading "maritime sea states" in regard to "production, trade, and maritime shipping" and it now confronted the necessity of creating a first-rate navy, expanding overseas, and acquiring colonies.[33]

A year earlier, in 1894, *Service Memorandum IX,* authored by Tirpitz, mapped out central ideas and terms of the navy's new thinking about sea power, international politics, and economic conflict in the past, present, and future. This memorandum offered an analysis of maritime interests and the function of the fleet that echoed Mahan's analysis. Fittingly, it invoked the past, namely the decline of Germany and Holland as preeminent trading states after the collapse of Hanseatic and Dutch (military) sea power, to validate its central observation that a "state which has sea interests or—what is equivalent—world interests must be able to represent them and to make its power felt beyond territorial waters. National world trade, world industry, and to a certain extent high-seas fisheries, world transportation, and colonies are impossible without a fleet capable of taking the offensive." The "most important purpose of the fleet in general" was to provide a "backbone" for the maritime "expressions of life by a state." Characteristically, the memorandum then jumped from the past to the present and future. Although Germany had declined as a "naval and world power when the sea power of the Hanseatic League collapsed" and the Dutch trade empire had collapsed with "the defeat of De Ruyter's fleets," one could see today "how mercantile North America builds up an offensive war fleet to attain seaborne trade and sea interests."[34]

Adopting Mahan's basic terms and historical claims, *Service Memorandum IX* offered a comprehensive interpretation of sea power that stressed the peacetime political importance of maritime force, that is, of a powerful battle fleet, while invoking the historical record. The adoption of Mahan's history-based science of sea power anchored what historian Rolf Hobson has analyzed as a newly emergent "ideology of sea power."[35] This ideology stressed the close interrelationship between the size of a nation's overseas interests and maritime force and postulated that the "starting point of the development of a fleet needs to be the sea and the maritime interests of a nation." Command of the seas in the shape of a first-rate navy was essential for the growth of national industry and trade in peacetime. The proper understanding of the "nature and purpose of the fleet" required a nation's recognition that "already in peacetime a navy creates economic advantages for the fatherland," as defined by the nexus between overseas interests and maritime force.[36]

Mahan proved crucial in defining the parameters of the German navy's history-based science of sea power and the ideological commitments it sparked. He provided an analytical and semantic framework within which Tirpitz and others advanced their own historical narratives of maritime conflicts and interpreted contemporary developments from the mid-1890s onward. In so doing, they also drew on sources other than Mahan to develop their views toward naval power, national industries, and empire. They poured old wine into new Mahanian bottles by drawing on other existing accounts of power politics, wars, and the rise and fall of states and rearticulating previous arguments offered on behalf of German sea power by liberal nationalists since the early nineteenth century, beginning with Friedrich List.[37]

Within this context, the thought of historian Heinrich von Treitschke ranked most prominently as an intellectual source. With his lectures and writings on the science of politics, German history, and global affairs, Treitschke exerted a considerable influence on officers such as Tirpitz. Tirpitz fondly remembered in his memoirs that "wonderful man," his lectures, and their private meetings.[38] With his early advocacy of German global power and mission, critique of British naval supremacy, and elaboration of force-based power politics, Treitschke preconfigured the German navy's views of naval power, national industries, and empire as they took shape in the 1890s.

Most important, Tirpitz and fellow writers fused their history-based understanding of sea power with contemporary debates among national economists and other writers about trade policy, global economic rivalry, and their political consequences. The talk about the formation of a few "great world empires" and Germany's place in a globalizing world, which occupied a central role in the imaginings of the German intelligentsia from the mid-1880s onward, underwrote the formation of the navy's discourse.[39] One of the early participants in this debate was Alexander von Peez, an Austrian economist, industrialist, and politician. His most important pieces on the topic were published in 1895 at a critical moment in the formation of the navy's new outlook. Looking back in 1914, August von Heeringen, a key officer close to Tirpitz, considered Peez's contribution to Tirpitz's and his own thinking to be as important as that of Mahan. Tirpitz, too, singled out Peez in his memoirs as a thinker of extraordinary importance. He compared the man's global perspectives favorably to the narrow perspective of most historians before 1900 who had simply failed to think in terms of "continents."[40]

Other direct connections existed as well. Gustav Schmoller, the eminent historical economist and social reformer, was a prominent case in point. Schmoller and Tirpitz were long-time acquaintances. They had many conversations about German industry, colonialism, trade policy, power politics, and the British Empire. According to Schmoller, they were by and large in agreement on the main issues. The analyses of the currents of global politics and their historical foundations that Schmoller offered resonated with and influenced the direction of the navy's thinking.[41] As previously discussed, Tirpitz hired a student of Schmoller's, Ernst von Halle, as an in-house academic to promote a proper scientific understanding of sea power. Halle proved instrumental, either as author or editor, in publishing a wide range of articles about global empires and sea power in the past and present that continually shaped the thinking of the navy and refined its narratives of sea power in public.[42]

In short, the Germans embraced Mahan's history-based science of sea power as they staked out claims to their mastery of the historical laws governing the conduct of states and navies in past and present. Offering an overall analytic for historical narrative and contemporary analysis, this science was so capacious as to absorb the tenets and propositions of expansionist discourses in each nation. The Americans and the Germans could effortlessly combine it with particular understandings of global politics and economics that circulated among their national intelligentsias.

The Science of Strategy

In Germany and the United States, naval elites created their own system of military strategy through a distinct, historically grounded approach. The formation of the paradigm of battle fleet warfare was informed by the rise of scientific strategy. This science defined strategy as a field of scientific inquiry that uncovered universal principles that remained more or less constant, regardless of changes in technology and tactics, and which applied to both land and maritime warfare. These principles could therefore be abstracted from the study of military history, of previous land and naval wars. They could also be found in the work of leading military theorists and writers such as Antoine-Henri de Jomini and Carl von Clausewitz. The careful examination of past military campaigns thus moved to the forefront. The tenets of naval strategy were forged in the crucible of history.

In the United States, Rear-Admiral Luce and Mahan mapped out this approach in the 1880s and early 1890s. Past naval history could "furnish a mass of facts amply sufficient for the formulation of laws or principles which, once established, would raise maritime war to the level of science," explained Luce.[43] According to him, the study could yield laws of strategy because the latter would be "less affected by the mutations of time and the advance of learning." There thus would be "certain general principles which are just as applicable to the management of a sea army of the nineteenth century as they were in the days of Salis or Actium, of Trafalgar or Lake Erie." Whereas the "Science of War" involved "immutable principles," the domain of the "Art of War" did not as it pertained to the "proficiency" that involved the actual conduct of a fleet in battle. The realm of tactics presented "such a variety of conditions as to defy all rules."[44]

Mahan fleshed out this particular approach. He placed the study of strategy at the center of his history-based science of naval warfare. Mahan elucidated the principles of naval warfare through an analysis of past military campaigns. The examination of contemporary wars, such as the Spanish-American War of 1898 or the Russo-Japanese War in 1904–05, complemented this course of action and validated his strategic insights based on the study of past naval wars. Mahan spelled out the premises of his approach clearly. There would be "certain teachings" in the "school" of military history "which remain constant, and, being, therefore, of universal application, can be elevated to the rank of general principles," he wrote in his first sea power book. They would concern primarily (but not exclusively) the "wider operations of war, which are comprised under the name of strategy."[45] The "considerations and principles" that fell into the "province of strategy" belonged to the "unchangeable, or unchanging, order of things," remaining "the same, in cause and effect, from age to age"; they "belong, as it were, to the Order of Nature, of whose stability so much is heard in our day."[46]

By the turn of the twentieth century, this history-based science of naval strategy had become dominant.[47] Mahan's lectures on naval strategy were used for instruction at the Naval War College after he left that institution and retired from active service. The idea that "the principles of warfare remain the same, and only the conditions change" had become "our accepted creed," another prominent naval officer, Bradley A. Fiske, summarized in 1908.[48]

Fiske belonged to a younger generation of naval strategists who fully embraced this creed, yet deemphasized the contemporary utility of the scientific study of past naval history. They did so by elaborating on the distinction between the universality of principles and their particular applications. Unlike Mahan and Luce, they put the emphasis on the study of the application of principles to the "conditions" of contemporary naval warfare, rather than on the history-based theoretical study of the principles themselves. The principles of naval strategy were few and "have been known for so long a time, and are so clearly set forth in books, that the student can learn them as easily as he can learn geometry," commented Fiske. By contrast, the machinery and technology of naval warfare had been completely transformed and created entirely new conditions for the war at sea. To prepare for war in the present, "we must study the conditions and then the applications of the principles to the conditions," Fiske argued, stressing that the study of naval history did not provide the tools for that endeavor.[49]

Luce and Mahan developed their history-based scientific strategy under the influence of contemporary military-professional thinking, with its emphasis on history, strategy, and universality. As noted before, they drew directly on the work of Antoine-Henri de Jomini, a most revered authority in the United States. When Luce set the task of developing a scientific system of strategy, he expressed his hope of finding "that master mind who will lay the foundations of that science and do for it what Jomini has done for the military science."[50] He then heralded Mahan, whom he had steered toward the study of Jomini, as precisely that master mind, a maritime "Jomini."[51]

But Luce and Mahan took some of their inspiration from naval theorists in Britain who, in the 1870s and 1880s, were discovering history as the foundation for the study of naval strategy and tactics. Most prominent among them was John Knox Laughton, who forcefully argued on behalf of the scientific study of naval history as a useful tool for the development of strategic principles and operational doctrines. Both Luce and Mahan were familiar with Laughton's work, especially his seminal article on "The Scientific Study of Naval History," published in 1875.[52] Both Luce and Mahan became personally acquainted with Laughton and exchanged letters with him. Mahan explicitly acknowledged Laughton's influence on his own thinking in his memoirs, published in 1906.[53]

Developing their science of strategy, Luce and Mahan also drew on the example of civilian sciences.[54] When Luce laid out the parameters for the study of naval strategy as a history-based science in search of universal principles, which Mahan then adopted, Luce developed his ideas by invoking civilian theorists of science. Luce leaned in particular on the writings of the British historian Thomas Buckle and the German philologist Friedrich Max Müller to make the case for a "science of naval warfare" aiming at the "formulation of laws or principles" by an "inductive process" that utilized a "comparative method" as the principal mode of investigation. In short, the science of naval strategy, with its emphasis on laws, history, and universality, fitted within late-nineteenth scientism and its "formalism."[55]

Unlike their American peers, German officers did not need to argue aggressively for the legitimacy of history-based scientific strategy. Its very principles were taught at the Marineakademie, founded in 1872. Lectures on strategy and the history of naval warfare thus occupied a prominent role in the school's curriculum from the very beginning.[56] The most prominent instructor for naval strategy and history between the 1870s and 1890s, Alfred Stenzel, enthusiastically espoused the principles of scientific strategy. In his lectures, he laid out a strategic theory of naval warfare that assumed the universal validity of its core principles and their derivation from military history. This assumption informed his work on a multivolume history of naval wars, which devoted a full tome to the naval battles of antiquity.[57] Stenzel commanded wide respect among his fellow officers. After 1890, he even became an object of favorable comparisons to Mahan as a theorist and historian of naval warfare.[58] His lectures helped shape the intellectual outlook of the generation of naval officers who pieced together the navy's concept of battle fleet warfare in the 1890s and then became the strategists of the developing battle fleet.

Tirpitz ranked first among them. As an exemplary scientific strategist who deduced universal principles of operations from the study of military history, Tirpitz prided himself on his extensive knowledge of naval and land wars, knowledge he claimed was not equaled by any other naval officer in the 1880s and 1890s.[59] Tirpitz's key military writings and, particularly, *Service Memorandum IX,* insisted on the universal validity of the core principles of naval strategy. His discussion of battle fleet warfare constantly referred to the lessons of past naval conflicts. "As the history of all past naval wars demonstrates irrefutably," he wrote, for example, "the war of [battleship] squadrons is the most effective type of offensive fleet action and thus of maritime warfare in general and this war's outcome resides in battle." The "struggle for command of the sea," he also explained, would be resolved through battle "as much today as at all times in the past." By the same token, Tirpitz styled himself as a follower of Clausewitz, whose science of war, in his view, supported the notion of the universal character of strategy.[60] In fact, a number of fellow officers had no doubt that that the tenets of *Service Memorandum IX* had been the product of Tirpitz's study of naval history, rather than the product of the analysis of the actual fleet maneuvers upon which the memorandum purported to base its conclusions.[61]

By the turn of the twentieth century, Rear-Admiral Curt von Maltzahn further developed the history-based scientific strategy and its "theory of naval war." A student of Stenzel and onetime friend of Tirpitz, Maltzahn taught naval history and strategy at the Marineakademie and assumed its directorship in 1900. He retired in 1903 and used his time to write extensively about naval warfare, including a detailed study of the Russo-Japanese

War and a history of German naval tactics.⁶² Maltzahn "decisively influenced the strategic thinking of our navy until the world war and the postwar period," recalled Rear-Admiral Wilhelm Michaelis, an officer who attended Maltzahn's lectures before he rose to prominence during the war and became the chief of the Naval High Command in 1920.⁶³

Maltzahn expanded on the analytical framework and substantive conclusions of Tirpitz and Stenzel. He also combined his appreciation for Clausewitz with the findings of Mahan. The critical examination of "the history of the naval war" had created "the theory of the war at sea, which provides our current strategy with its foundational rules," Maltzahn wrote in summary of the basic concept.⁶⁴ The notion of the "laws" of naval warfare and their universal validity was central to Maltzahn's thinking and his interest in the history of maritime warfare. "In brilliant discussion, using convincing examples from the history of naval war, Maltzahn taught, based on Clausewitz, and the American naval theorist Mahan, that the struggle between battle fleets was the only thing that mattered decisively in the war at sea," remembered Michaelis.⁶⁵

Maltzahn also explicitly incorporated the work of Friedrich Ratzel, the pioneering practitioner of an emerging academic discipline of geopolitics.⁶⁶ According to Maltzahn, Ratzel's entire project of a "Geography of States, Traffic, and War" amounted to a "military science" in the making, focusing on the "laws" of naval strategy. Ratzel's writings provided "a rich source of instruction," a "scientific foundation" for naval officers "even down to questions of tactics." Stressing the peculiarities of the geographical medium of the sea, Ratzel in particular had identified immutable laws of naval warfare and the command of the sea, which stressed concentration of forces and decisive fleet action within compressed space and time. Ratzel's science naturalized the notion of universal strategic principle and lent additional scientific proof to the validity of the concept of battle fleet warfare. Ratzel, explained Maltzahn in 1905, had drawn attention to the "highest maxim of naval strategy" by declaring that the "sea is the site of great decisions from one single location because he herewith casts the enemy fleet as a primary object of attack and demands a concentration of effort on this great decisive moment."⁶⁷

The Model of the Army

Belief in the autonomy and universality of strategy was part of a larger embrace of the kind of military professionalism that had become identified with the German army and its General Staff after the 1860s. This professionalism combined an emphasis on the methodical preparation for war in peacetime with the theory and practice of a new science of war. This science focused on operational knowledge (that is, the mastery of the laws of military strategy and of the deployment of armies and navies) and its implementation in the planning and conduct of war. This knowledge could be acquired through the study of history and through military exercises and various types of war games; its primary institutions were general-staff organizations and a special war school, a Kriegsakademie, for the advanced study of the science of warfare.[68]

Laboring in the shadow of the Prusso-German General Staff, German naval officers strongly believed in the applied operational science of its fellow service. The making of navalism as a system of naval strategy directly fed off the navy's embrace of this science and its increasing translation into professional-military practice. The Naval High Command created its own Admiralty Staff department in charge of operation plans, tactics, maneuvers, and intelligence in 1892.[69] Subsequently, the practice of fleet drills and war-gaming and their coordination with operational planning and the formulation of doctrine took off after war games, including the practice of so-called staff rides, had first been introduced in the previous decade.[70] The development of the doctrine of battle fleet warfare rested on a systematic approach that combined the study of strategy through the use of history with methodical military work based on fleet exercises and practical experimentation, and the simulation of war on the board. Tirpitz himself had first practiced this approach when he had developed operational and tactical doctrines for the torpedo arm between 1877 and 1889.[71]

By the turn of the twentieth century, the navy stressed its newly gained operational knowledge, its mastery of the principles of naval warfare. Newly created in 1899, the Admiralty Staff set itself an ambitious agenda of expanding the practice of continuous planning for war, which the Naval High Command had already put on a more solid foundation in the previous decade. Under the leadership of Maltzahn, the Seekriegslehre (the Science of Naval War) became a key part of the school's curriculum as both a theoretical-historical and applied science of war, complemented by Admiralty Staff service as a distinct subject.[72]

The naval elite nonetheless adopted the army's operational science only in a modified form. There was no powerful naval general staff or a separate (elite) Admiralty Staff officer corps. Exactly that was proposed by successive chiefs of the Admiralty Staff and officials of the Marineakademie between

1899 and 1908. These officers wanted to copy the general staff system and turn the Admiralty Staff and the Marineakademie into institutions comparable in every aspect to their counterparts in the army. Vice-Admiral Diederichs took the lead at the turn of the twentieth century. An avid admirer of Helmuth von Moltke, the longtime chief of staff of the Prussian Army, he had responded to his appointment as the first regular head of the Admiralty Staff by attaching himself temporarily to the Greater General Staff before assuming his new post. Between the fall of 1899 and his resignation in the summer of 1901, Diederichs not only insisted on his prerogatives as the chief strategic adviser to the emperor. He also envisioned the Admiralty Staff as a powerful agency in charge of war planning, intelligence gathering, the training of officers in operational matters, and the further elucidation of the history-based strategic science of naval war. Central to this vision was the institutional expansion of the Admiralty Staff (which counted only eight officers and four clerks on duty in 1899), spread out over multiple sections for operational planning, intelligence, naval history, and administrative matters.

Following the model of the army, Diederichs also suggested the creation of a separate corps of admiralty staff officers, marked by a special career track, distinct uniforms, and a separate chain of command with the chief of the Admiralty Staff at the top. These officers were to be trained at the Naval War College in operational science and admiralty staff duty and rotated between the Admiralty Staff and the various commands of the navy from the active fleet to technical inspections. Accordingly, the vice-admiral wanted to place the college under his command (and even move it from Kiel to Berlin, where his agency resided). The school's graduates were to serve as members of the Admiralty Staff in Berlin, as chiefs of staff and staff officers for other independent commands, and as instructors at the school itself.[73]

Diederichs's successor in office, Vice-Admiral Wilhelm von Büchsel, committed himself to the same cause. Invoking the model of the army and seeking close contact with the General Staff, Büchsel set himself the task of attaining "a most substantive approximation of the arrangements of the General Staff," as he explained in November 1906.[74] Büchsel worked tirelessly toward this goal. As a result of his prodding, an imperial decree in 1904 made the chief of the Admiralty Staff responsible for the training and continuous service of the navy's admiralty staff officers as a clearly defined group. The chief of the Admiralty Staff gained direct influence over the promotion of these officers as well by becoming involved in the annual assessment reports, which played an important role in shaping an officer's career stations.[75]

Viewing this decree as an important first step, Büchsel continued to argue for a further extension of his control over all admiralty staff officers and their elevation to an exclusive corps of elite professionals on par with their counterparts in the army general staff. He combined these demands with a call for more personnel and resources for the Admiralty Staff (which counted thirty-four officers in 1906, up from seventeen five years earlier). And he asked for an official recognition of the Naval War College as an exclusive feeder institution for all officers performing Admiralty Staff duty, whether in the Admiralty Staff itself or in the other commands of the navy.

In 1907–08, Tirpitz and Admiral Müller, the chief of the Naval Cabinet, put an end to any efforts to adopt the institutional model of the army. The "development" of the Admiralty Staff "in analogy to the General Staff of the army needs to be prevented," summarized Müller.[76] He also described the Admiralty Staff as nothing more than a "study agency for war with an intelligence section."[77] Tirpitz agreed, casting the Admiralty Staff as a "depository for all experiences in the domain of naval tactics."[78] The two admirals thus forced Büchsel into retirement and brought about a reduction of the Admiralty Staff's personnel. Key provisions of the 1904 decree were revoked. The Marineakademie was made subordinate to the Imperial Naval Office. Tirpitz and Müller also reaffirmed the principle that college attendance was to neither mark an officer for service in the Admiralty Staff nor serve as a prerequisite for higher command and staff positions in the navy.[79]

The unwillingness to copy the institutional arrangements of the army had many sources. Generally speaking, the cause of a powerful naval general staff ran afoul of the conflict over turf between various naval agencies.[80] Most officers also agreed that there was no room for a small elite corps within an overall corps that numbered only a thousand officers in 1900 and little more than twenty-three hundred in 1914.[81] Ultimately, Tirpitz, Müller, and other officers also stressed differences between the army and navy in regard to operational expertise. They highlighted the pivotal importance of the immediate leadership of officers commanding naval units from the bridge of their flagship and their mastery of operations, which lacked a counterpart in army warfare. "The leader in the navy arises from within the Front," declared Müller; central to naval command, the application of operational expertise was "only the practical experience that could be gathered at a command bridge," he insisted.[82] Accordingly, Tirpitz and Müller assured that the Naval War College would not only teach strategy, tactics, and the operational science of war but also provide a substantial knowledge of naval technology as a requirement for the successful mastery of the "practice" of naval command and combat.[83]

In short, the Wilhelmine navy appropriated the operational science of its fellow service, the army, yet it also filled it with its own meanings. The Admiralty Staff never acquired the kind of stature that the General Staff enjoyed in the army. Its chief figured as the chief strategic adviser yet he lacked the prerogatives of his army counterpart who was destined to take overall operational command in war. Separated from the leadership positions of the battle fleet, the navy's general staff did not even gain a monopoly over operational preparations for war. Operational planning became the domain of two institutions, the Admiralty Staff and the official command of the active fleet, the High Seas Fleet. Under Tirpitz's leadership the Imperial Naval Office also claimed a right to review the operations plans and directly intervened in operational matters if it saw fit.[84]

It took World War I to draw renewed attention to the Admiralty Staff as the navy's key operational agency. At the end of the war, the Admiralty Staff enhanced its formal position when it was put in charge of the navy's entire conduct of war. The creation of a new Supreme Naval Command, Seekriegsleitung, in August 1918 under the command of Admiral Reinhard Scheer as the newly appointed chief of the Admiralty Staff created a planning and command center under single professional leadership. Scheer attained the authority to issue orders to naval commanders and he claimed control over officer appointments in his domain. Moreover, on Scheer's behest, an imperial decree officially recognized the Admiralty Staff as being on par with institutions such as the Foreign Office or the General Staff. With the arrangement, the Admiralty Staff attained a position comparable to that of the General Staff and the so-called Supreme Army Command, even if there was no effort made to create a separate elite corps of naval staff officers.[85]

As Scheer, the new man in charge, candidly admitted, the new arrangement was related to the case for a powerful Admiralty Staff, as it had been previously made.[86] Beginning in the summer of 1916, the chief of the Admiralty Staff, Admiral Henning von Holtzendorff, had, in fact, made yet again the case for a transformation of the Admiralty Staff into the navy's central institution on par with the army's General Staff in all respects, without any immediate success.[87] Ultimately, the formation of the Seekriegsleitung was the product of an intense, if not acrimonious, wartime debate over the splintered organization of the navy's high command, the lack of an overall commander-in-chief other than the emperor. This debate had opened at the very beginning of the war, when Tirpitz himself strove to attain overall command.[88] Yet it also traced its origins to prewar calls for command unity at the top. Previous chiefs of the Admiralty Staff such as Admirals Büchsel and Heeringen, for example, had suggested creating a commander-in-chief of all naval forces, who sat above the commanding officer of the High Seas Fleet and assumed the responsibilities of a true chief of the naval general staff.[89] As commander of the High Seas Fleet, Admiral Holtzendorff had suggested a similar arrangement in 1911–12, a few years before he clamored for the authority to issue commands to the fleet as the wartime head of the Admiralty Staff.[90]

The German Model and Its Promise

On the other side of the Atlantic, the U.S. Navy's enthusiasm for the German military's operational science of war, and its central agency, the General Staff, knew next to no bounds at the beginning of the twentieth century. If we believe American naval officers, the Germans had rewritten the book of war in the 1860s and 1870s. "In the Franco-German war, warfare took on a phase entirely new; and the incident is as clearly marked as the invention of gunpowder or the sextant," summarized Bradley A. Fiske in 1908. The Prussian-German army had set new standards of military preparedness and warfare that no country could afford to ignore.[91]

The Americans took an almost obsessive interest in the German General Staff. They enthused about the competence of this agency, touted time and again as a "most perfect military engine,"[92] and stressed how it ensured the superb workings of the German war machine in past and present. According to Rear-Admiral Taylor, the "Franco-Prussian conflict plainly indicated the value of the German General Staff"; its effectiveness would not only be reflected in superior military planning in peacetime but also in the "trained readiness of officers' minds," that is, "that familiarity with war situations, acquired in the staff work of peace," which would enable officers "from Generals down to Majors" to "confront all emergencies of the campaign with ready energy and composure of mind."[93]

Here, in short, was an institution that taught the world how to prepare for war in the best possible manner and thus had been copied by militaries everywhere.[94] Accordingly, the Americans sought to collect as much information as possible about the workings of the German staff organization. The English translations of key texts by German general staff officers, such as Paul Bronsart von Schellendorf's *The Duties of the General Staff* and Otto von Griepenkerl's *Letters on Applied Tactics,* became key readings. Another was the account of the German General Staff by the British radical nationalist Spenser Wilkinson, first published in 1890, the most influential study of the subject in the English-speaking world (which also served as the key referent for British military reforms along Germanic lines).[95]

For the Americans, the present and future belonged to the German general staff system and its operational science. They were so convinced that most of them expected that the German Empire would win the First World War on account of the professional superiority of its military.[96] The navy's interest in increased military "preparedness" between 1914 and 1917 once more brought favorable views of the German model of military professionalism into sharp focus. So strong was this continuing infatuation that one officer alluded to the current "fetishism to refer excellence in military training and preparation to German methods."[97]

The veneration for German military professionalism was in place before the German naval buildup began. The Americans then projected their favorable views of the German army onto its fellow service. The German navy was regarded as a highly effective, well-directed military organization that had adopted the military methods and professional standards of the army.[98] This favorable view extended to all aspects of German naval practices, even the most mundane, with the General Board willing to view a rumored German designation of "starboard" and "port" as "left" and "right" as a possible instantiation of superior military efficiency.[99] The esteem in which the German navy was held invited favorable comparisons to the British navy. In fact, Rear-Admiral Fiske argued in the 1910s that in naval matters the German Empire had changed places with the British Empire: its navy had become the "preceptor" of its former "preceptor," the Royal Navy. Second in numerical strength, it was "perhaps the first in efficiency in the world."[100]

The admiration for German military-professional approaches circumscribed the respect that the British navy commanded. Naturally, the Royal Navy was held in high esteem as a fighting force that set standards of excellence. In such diverse fields as seamanship, naval construction, or gunnery (to name just a few), British ideas and procedures served as a benchmark, closely studied and often adopted.[101] Still, there was a clear sense that the Royal Navy was deficient in the key areas of military professionalism. The present and future belonged to scientific strategy and general staff organization, which had been theorized and practiced in an exemplary fashion by the Germans, not the British.[102] By 1900, the lack of a naval general staff in Britain had become a key theme among American observers.[103] Ten years later, a leading officer such as Fiske attributed the high "efficiency" of the Royal Navy in the present precisely to its increasing turn toward the "ideals" of the German army and navy.[104] Typically, William Sims, the ardent Anglophile naval reformer, too, wanted to remake his service in a Germanic professional image.[105]

The fast-developing Japanese Imperial Navy captured attention as an exemplary military institution that had attained the highest levels of operational proficiency and military readiness. Here was a navy that had adopted the same approach as the Germans, stressing scientific strategy, general staff organization, and managerial control. Naturally, the Japanese pursuit of war in 1904–05 galvanized admiration for the professional conduct of the Japanese navy and its operational science, which first had come into view in response to the Sino-Japanese War in the mid-1890s.[106] In 1909, one officer referred to the Japanese navy as a "perfectly organized and war-seasoned navy, and with a general staff, not exceeded in excellence and perfection by that even of Germany."[107]

The Japanese navy riveted the Americans' imagination. But its direct appeal as a subject of borrowings and imitations was circumscribed precisely because Germany was (allegedly) already teaching the same lessons. In military matters, the Japanese appeared as a direct copy of a German original that thus lost none of its luster as a primary referent. Strikingly, exposure to the methods of the Japanese operational science could just provide another point of entry to German approaches. The adoption, after 1910, of a new method of instruction, the so-called applicatory method, at the Naval War College, which was modeled after the German practice of studying operational problems, owed itself in part to direct encounters with Japanese practice. An officer who played a pivotal role as a prime mover at the Naval War College, Frank Marble, first acquired direct experience with this method during his tour of service as naval attaché in Tokyo from 1905 to 1907.[108]

By the 1890s, navy leaders explicitly set out to adopt German operational science including its institutional embodiment, a powerful general staff. "We must naturally look forward to development upon the lines which the long and successful experience of such a military expert among nations as is Germany has laid down for all us," explained Captain French Chadwick, the president of the Naval War College in characteristic fashion in 1901.[109] The Naval War College was a case in point. Founded in 1884 after an investigation of European war schools as an institution for the professional study of maritime warfare as an applied science, the college strove to approach the study of war and the professional training of officers in the "art and science" of war "in the best manner possible, viz. the manner of Clausewitz and Von Moltke," as one of its presidents, Captain Caspar F. Goodrich, explained in 1897.[110] The specifics of the work of this self-styled "school of naval warfare" were directly informed by a constant dialogue with and borrowing of German practices of war-gaming and staff exercises, from the first use of board-based war games in the 1890s to the introduction, after 1910, of the "applicatory system," which then moved to the core of the college's curriculum. The latter system resembled a case method approach to the study and teaching of the "art" of naval warfare by concrete example and with an emphasis on so-called estimate of the situation and subsequent order writing in the context of hypothetical military scenarios.[111]

Officers charted their own pathways as they strove to enact their applied science of strategy. The general staff that navy leaders from Taylor to Fiske envisioned, for example, was a distinctive institution in terms of size, scope, and power. None of these officers promoted the creation of a separate corps of general staff officers in analogy to German army practice. But they suggested that assignment to the General Board and attendance at the Naval War College should mark officers, and ideally only them, for higher command and staff positions and serve as a prerequisite for any promotion to flag rank.[112]

American practitioners of scientific strategy forged their own institutional style. In the early twentieth century, they worked within a triangular set of institutions with overlapping functions, and even personnel: the General Board, the Office of Naval Intelligence, and the Naval War College. In the 1890s, the College had shouldered many of the functions of a war planning agency, based on its development of the technology of war gaming. In fact, even after the creation of the General Board, the college continued to be directly involved in operational planning, a field of activity not engaged in by the German Kriegs- and Marineakademien. The school's participation in war planning diminished severely in the early 1910s. In the fall of 1911, Secretary of the Navy von Lengerke Meyer decided that the college's involvement was to be confined to those activities that could be performed as part of the college's educational mission and that its primary task within this context was to test the war plans drawn by the General Board in its gaming exercises.[113]

Lengerke Meyer had reached his decision in 1911 after the president and staff of the Naval War College had drawn attention to the fact that the college could no longer combine the professional training of officers in the science of naval warfare with any war planning responsibilities unless its personnel were enlarged and a separate planning division created.[114] But the secretary's decision was also prompted by severe disagreement between war planners at the General Board and the Naval War College over key tenets of the formal plan for a war with Japan that the College had completed in 1911.[115] A year earlier the two agencies had offered diametrically opposed opinions on the issue of the proper peacetime deployment of the battle fleet.[116]

Unlike their German counterparts, navy leaders endorsed the cause of joint planning with the army. Set up in 1903 as a statutory institution, the Joint Army and Navy Board provided a forum for officers from the General Board and the army's General Staff to confer on matters of overlapping policy. Presided over by Admiral Dewey, yet with no separate staff of its own, the Joint Board dealt with war plans, schemes for bases, and preparations for armed interventions in the Americas.[117]

All in all, there were clear limitations to the development of scientific strategy and mastery of operational warfare in the first two decades of the twentieth century.[118] The modest size of the General Board, the Naval War College, and the Office of Naval Intelligence as the three key institutions bounded the development of the navy's operational science. The General Board, for example, had on average fewer than ten members during its first ten years of existence. Its committee in charge of war plans consisted of three officers in 1910. An institution like the Naval War College scrambled for applicants for its classes and could not count on a regular influx of a fixed number of students each year until 1913, when Secretary of the Navy Josephus Daniels became a champion of the college and oversaw its massive expansion.[119] Before this elevation of status, attendance at the Naval War College did not mark an officer for higher rank in the navy nor was it viewed as a prerequisite for promotion to flag rank, as it eventually was, by and large, in the 1920s and 1930s.[120] The navy acquired a more substantive war-planning apparatus only with the creation of the Office of the Chief of Naval Operations in 1915 and the subsequent creation of a separate War Planning Division within it. In fact, a demand for fifteen assistants tasked with the preparation of war plans had been central to Fiske's original plans for such an office as they took shape in 1914.[121]

Such institutional weakness influenced the quality of war planning. Until the early 1910s the existing plans were thinly scripted operational scenarios that provided only the broadest possible directives. When

Rear-Admiral Fiske was made head of the war plans section of the General Board in 1910, he found that the war plans "were so general in character as hardly to be war plans at all, and to consist mainly of information of all kinds concerning various countries, accompanied with suggestions for the commander-in-chief of the fleet."[122] "The condition of the navy as regards war plans must be regarded as deplorable. A safe full of so-called 'war plans' consists really of plans for a landing party seizing certain ports," complained another officer in the same year.[123] In fact, the proper making of war plans became a subject of intense study at the Naval War College in subsequent years;[124] the General Board engaged in a concerted effort to overhaul the entire planning process, which resulted, by 1915, in the drafting of more comprehensive and detailed plans.[125] This development, in turn, coincided with the introduction of the "applicatory method" to study operational issues at the Naval War College, which contributed to the increasing technical sophistication of war planning efforts during the decade that eventually saw U.S. entry into the war in Europe.[126]

By the same token, during the 1910s, carefully orchestrated fleet exercises to address larger issues of operational warfare and test the scripts of war plans remained a proposition for the future.[127] Only in 1914–15 did the navy turn toward the official creation of "naval doctrine," and its inculcation through instruction at the War College and fleet exercises.[128] Strikingly, the field of operational logistics, too, remained a "barely studied field" until around the same time, as a recent historian of early twentieth century naval logistics has noted.[129]

All these American shortcomings did not escape foreign eyes. German naval observers agreed that the United States lagged behind in its mastery of strategy and operational warfare. To be sure, naval attachés reported proudly that U.S. naval circles took the "example of our navy" as a "model."[130] Repeatedly, they also found words of praise for the professional orientations of their American peers, their "patriotism and professional dedication," which, in turn, were contrasted to the alleged evils of U.S. congressional rule.[131] Still, German analyses ultimately stressed American professional limitations. Thus, in February 1913, Karl Boy-Ed, the naval attaché in Washington, summarized such thinking when he reported on the critique of the current state of U.S. naval readiness that Captain William Sims had offered in public. The Americans, Boy-Ed suggested, had good reasons to view themselves as "beginners" in the realms of "tactics and strategy." Recent fleet maneuvers had not been impressive. The "lack of tactical and strategical schooling" was only too apparent. The Americans still had much to learn, the German concluded.[132]

In contrast to their Americans counterparts, German navalists were not looking across the Atlantic for direct professional inspiration for their operational science of war and its proper application on the eve of World War I. German officers viewed the efforts of the American practitioners of operational warfare as a study in professional development still falling short of excellence. And they took this sense with them into the war, flagrantly misjudging the capabilities of the United States and its navy to project maritime force across the Atlantic in 1917–18.

Chapter 11

Between Leadership and Intraservice Conflict

In his memoirs, written in 1918, Alfred von Tirpitz stressed the harmonious relationship among the navy, nation, and parliament that had existed during his tenure as secretary of the navy before World War I. "Almost all differences between Reichstag and government" had vanished early on as the cause of the fleet had become a "natural property of the nation." Tirpitz contrasted this approval with the opposition he had eventually encountered from the Empire's top civilian governmental leadership. He also complained about the constant meddling in his affairs by the kaiser and his entourage. Yet according to his account, conflict among the naval elite itself had created clear obstacles on the road to German sea power. Unbeknownst to the public, continuous divisions within his own service had sapped much of his energies as the policy maker in charge. More often than not, they had forced him to compromise, that is, to "negotiate" with his peers rather than just to "take action." "Intraservice tensions," Tirpitz claimed, "had been more demoralizing over the course of the years than, for example, the parliament or actual work itself (*hervorbringende Arbeit*)."[1]

Tirpitz set the image of a fractured and multivocal intraservice politics against his own decisive leadership from above. But contrary to the impression Tirpitz gave, it was precisely Tirpitz's exercise of power (coupled with his longevity in office) at the beginning of the twentieth century that lent a distinctive shape to the making of navalism in Germany and the intraservice politics sustaining it. The constitutional makeup of the state and the personal inclinations of the emperor created the space for a single man to become the director of the entire pursuit of maritime force before World War I.[2]

In the United States, the work and desires of individual officers such as Alfred Thayer Mahan, Henry C. Taylor, and George Dewey, who provided leadership and sought to act on behalf of their peers, also left a recognizable imprint on the navy's professional politics that underlay the making of navalism. Like the German navy, the U.S. Navy had its organizing centers of power and authority that ensured more centralized direction and provided its leaders with considerable influence. But ultimately in the U.S. system of governance there was no room for a single officer to wield a comparable degree of individual agency or to assure the navy a similar amount of policy control and continuity as in Germany.

In each country, the navies' militarism had its own nationally specific dialectics of leadership, cohesion, and disunity. The pursuit of navalism involved conflict-ridden processes of intraservice negotiation and contestation, which differed from country to country. In Germany, such conflicts centered on Tirpitz's claims to absolute leadership yet they also came to involve substantive disagreement over priorities in the pursuit of the naval buildup itself. Intraservice conflict in the U.S. Navy was primarily a matter of bureaucratic politics, which, in turn, was mediated by the powers wielded by civilian policy makers and cross-cutting civil-military alliances.

Intraservice disputes along such lines (not to speak of personal animosity or career competition that divided officers and could lead to bitter disputes[3]) coexisted, however uneasily, with shared commitments to a common universe of thought and practice, and, thus, to the flourishing of navalism as a new "organizational ideology."[4] The officers also remained bounded by a strong sense of shared collective identity within each officer corps, forged through naval service, reinforced by a distinct lifestyle, and further underwritten by a shared social profile.[5]

The Influence of Tirpitz

As secretary of the navy, Tirpitz wielded unparalleled power within his service. In office for almost twenty years, from 1897 to 1916, he styled himself as a pivotal authority within the navy who set overall policy and could demand strict adherence in all important matters. In his view, forceful leadership from above over a long period of time was required to accomplish the "great task" of creating a battle fleet capable of ensuring German global power in the twentieth century.[6]

This approach cohered in the particular context of service politics, shaped as it was in the 1890s by open conflict among officers and their various agencies. The tripartite system of top naval institutions that Wilhelm II had created after the dissolution of the admiralty in 1889 had become a breeding ground for bureaucratic infighting and personal animosity among senior officers. The jurisdictions of the various naval agencies were ill-defined and caused endemic conflict. The final word was left to an emperor incapable of providing consistent leadership; the chief of the Naval Cabinet could serve as a key power broker because he controlled access to the All-Highest Person. For most of the 1890s, the Naval High Command and the Imperial Naval Office claimed to have a final say in matters of overall naval policy and strategy.[7]

The officer corps was also divided over important substantive issues. Disputes over jurisdictional matters attained special significance by 1895–96 when they directly involved different views of naval warfare and building programs. At that time, the Naval High Command began to call for a long-term naval program, based on the previous development of the battleship doctrine under the tutelage of Tirpitz.[8] But Navy Secretary Friedrich von Hollmann did not heed these calls in the schemes for naval increase he submitted to the Reichstag, which stressed the construction of new cruisers. For two years, there was no resolution to the conflict. The paradigm of battle fleet warfare dominated operations plans, fleet exercises, and service memoranda, but not the actual building policy.[9] Only the appointment of Tirpitz as navy secretary put an end to this conflict. And it took until 1900 for an aide of Tirpitz to note that his peers supported "almost unanimously" the creation of a battle fleet as "the foundation of the increase of the navy."[10]

Fittingly, Tirpitz confronted a plurality of opinions when he assumed control of the Imperial Naval Office. Navy leaders such as Admirals Eduard von Knorr and Hans von Koester, the influential heads of the Naval High Command and the Kiel Naval Station, respectively, critiqued the navy secretary's particular plans for rapid fleet expansion. They suggested that these plans did not pay sufficient attention to personnel needs, training, present-day naval preparedness, or the continuous need for an armada of overseas cruisers as an important complement to the battle fleet at home. None of the seven admirals who had reviewed his schemes for what became the Naval Bill of 1898 had agreed with them, complained Tirpitz in 1899.[11]

As head of the Imperial Naval Office, Tirpitz sought to put an end to any multivocal professional politics by staking out claims to supremacy. His ministry was to enjoy a position of preeminence among the various agencies and commands of the navy. It was to be in sole charge of the entire pursuit of maritime force and all policy decisions affecting it, extending to maritime arms control with Great Britain.[12] Likewise, the Imperial Naval Office took the lead in the deliberations over maritime law.[13] It was no coincidence that the ministry also claimed exclusive control over the correspondence of naval attachés within the service.[14]

The Imperial Naval Office was to be the directing center of the entire development of the navy and its officer corps. Applying to practically all service matters, the quest for control extended to matters beyond the ministry's official purview. For example, Tirpitz evaluated operations plans on a regular basis; on occasion, his agency crafted its own operational studies; and the navy secretary attempted to impose his particular operational vision on the Admiralty Staff and fleet leadership, as he did successfully in 1911–12 when a momentous decision was made to deploy the High Seas Fleet in the German Bight. The Imperial Naval Office went so far as to take interest in the development of fleet tactics, even as its ability to influence decisions here was more limited.[15]

The navy secretary's pursuit of overall control expanded upon the possibilities created by the particular constitutional makeup of the German Empire and the personal aspirations of Wilhelm II, the emperor. The framework of a military monarchy did not only provide the navy with a remarkable degree of institutional independence and policy control within the system of governance. The same framework also made it possible for a resourceful navy secretary to attain a position of preeminence (and longevity in office) by relying on the direct support of the emperor.

Serving directly under an emperor who had already appointed him for the express purpose of masterminding the making of Germany as a first-rate naval power, Tirpitz enjoyed immediate access to Wilhelm II. Going well beyond his annual audiences in the fall of each year about upcoming naval legislation, Tirpitz continually sought to enlist the emperor's authoritative support through personal communications and to solicit his commands, which then proved essential in any dealings within the service. The emperor intervened time and again when his navy secretary had disagreements with other officers. At Tirpitz's behest, Wilhelm II also issued a series of imperial decrees that proclaimed the primary authority of the Imperial Naval Office as the agency in charge of the naval buildup and with the best overall perspective on all naval matters.[16]

Capitalizing on the emperor's support, Tirpitz also sought dominance by other institutional means. After taking office, he moved to expand the official prerogatives of his ministry and assure its paramount position. He successfully pressed the emperor to abolish the Naval High Command in 1899. Previously, he had already excluded the command from any say over the making of the Naval Bill of 1898 and promoted various measures to diminish its standing, much to the chagrin of practically all other senior officers, whether they served in the High Command or not.[17] After 1899, the Imperial Naval Office worked hard to curtail the development of other naval commands or agencies into competing institutional centers of power. Tirpitz insisted that he alone, and not the chief of the Naval Cabinet, was to make formal reports to the emperor on all matters that fell within the domain of his ministry, broadly conceived. The navy secretary set himself up against the transformation of the Admiralty Staff into an institution comparable in power, prestige, or size to the Prussian-German General Staff. Tirpitz resisted as long as possible the establishment of a special command for the entire active battle fleet and then insisted on curtailing the powers of the officer in charge of it. Thus, the commanding officer of the active fleet (or High Seas Fleet, as it was called after 1907) never attained a large staff or gained an official say in any matters that did not directly pertain to the operations of the fleet itself. Until 1912, the same officer also lacked a formal right to make a personal presentation to the emperor, on his own initiative, and without any mediation.[18]

To enhance his preeminence, Tirpitz acted as an aggressive, if not ruthless, infighter. The navy secretary routinely employed the threat of his resignation to make the emperor conform to his wishes.[19] On occasion he even used this threat to enlist the support of top civilian officials.[20] By the same token, Tirpitz adopted a most assertive, often confrontational approach in his dealings with other senior officers. On occasion, his close advisers had to implore him to show more respect.[21] Under Tirpitz's leadership, the Imperial Naval Office not only excluded the heads of the Admiralty Staff or the fleet command from important decisions concerning the pursuit of maritime force; it was also always willing to take unilateral action or take uncompromising positions on issues that involved other naval agencies.[22]

Tirpitz almost never shied away from conflicts with his peers and when they arose he never hesitated to turn to the emperor to decide the issue in his favor. In so doing, Tirpitz also managed to push many senior officers, including several chiefs of the Admiralty Staff and the fleet command, into retirement. This was done so blatantly that it did not escape the notice of outside observers. Admiral Tirpitz "appears to have the whole Navy absolutely under his thumbs," the British naval attaché reported back home in October 1910; "for although theoretically the various Admirals who command stations, fleets, &c., are responsible to the Kaiser alone, it seems that if they differ from Tirpitz, it generally ends in their losing their appointments."[23]

Until 1906, Admiral Senden raised Tirpitz's particular ire. The chief of the Naval Cabinet wielded enormous power that served as a real counterweight to Tirpitz's position of preeminence. Heading an office that lent decisive shape to the institution of military monarchy, upon which Tirpitz's own power depended, Senden enjoyed direct access to the emperor and viewed himself as a mediator of the relations between the senior officers and their Supreme Warlord.[24] Openly critical of Tirpitz's quest for complete control, Senden had close ties to higher officers and embraced some of their agendas in contradiction to Tirpitz. The two men became involved in intense clashes, surrounded by resignation threats and bitter personal recriminations. Playing out in front of the emperor, they began with the dispute over the institutional powers of the Imperial Naval Office in 1898 and climaxed in the falls of 1903 and 1904 when Senden supported Admiral von Koester, who was in command of the active battleships, against Tirpitz in a series of bitter arguments over the creation of a separate fleet command and the proper development of the battle fleet.[25]

Not surprisingly, Senden's successor in office, Admiral Müller, too, became an object of Tirpitz's scorn. Müller did so in the early 1910s, as he was striving to mediate between the navy secretary and his critics from within the service and viewed himself as protecting the interests of other naval institutions against the actions of a transgressive Imperial Naval Office.[26] By contrast, during his first years in office, Müller had, by and large, consistently supported Tirpitz in his dealings with the emperor and other senior officers.[27]

Tirpitz's style of leadership alienated many of his fellow officers. Former chancellor Bülow could claim in his memoirs that most naval officers strongly disliked Tirpitz.[28] Vice-Admiral Diederichs, a short-lived chief of admiralty who had lost a power struggle with the navy secretary, referred to Tirpitz as a "crafty Muscovite."[29] Such misgivings did not stop short of the emperor (or his brother, Prince Henry, a onetime commander of the active fleet[30]). Wilhelm II was known to complain that Tirpitz was a "neurasthenic" who was difficult to deal with, a Bismarck-like figure lacking in deference.[31] The emperor viewed "the man Tirpitz with suspicion," reported Admiral Müller, who himself repeatedly bemoaned the pettiness and "evil" machinations of the navy secretary.[32]

Tirpitz combined his confrontational pursuit of control and power with a strong emphasis on the necessity of intraservice unity. The navy was to present a common front in all naval matters and speak with only a single voice in policymaking and public debate. Tirpitz never grew tired of making this case, asking for the support of his fellow officers and, on occasion, relying on carefully arranged speeches in front of larger officer audiences.[33] Tirpitz appealed to the political instincts of his fellow officers when he made the case for uniformity of opinion. The public and the parties would support a policy of naval expansion, he insisted, only if "this course of action appears, in its material substance, as the only correct one"; officers ought not to create "confusion" among the lay public and raise doubts about the validity of official naval policy.[34]

But under Tirpitz's leadership the Imperial Naval Office did not just leave it at a rhetoric of unity. The agency also relied on force to repress dissenting voices in the public sphere. Although conceding the right of any officer to voice an opinion within the "private" realm of the navy, Tirpitz moved to regulate public utterances by officers that did not reflect official policy as defined by the Imperial Naval Office. In 1899, the navy secretary convinced a willing emperor to issue a decree that regulated the publications of active and inactive officers. The decree practically forbade the voicing of opinions that conflicted with the wishes of an Imperial Naval Office that attained far-reaching censorship prerogatives. The admiral in charge of the navy's educational system resigned over this entire affair.[35]

The Imperial Naval Office remained invested in policing public expressions among naval officers until 1914. This investment was on full display when in October 1907 retired Vice-Admiral Galster began to openly criticize the policy of the Imperial Naval Office, reaching an audience that included Chancellor Bülow, who had grown weary of Tirpitz's policy prescriptions.[36] In response, Tirpitz first suggested to Admiral Müller that the emperor simply order Galster to cease and desist. When this failed, Tirpitz agreed on another course of action. Enlisting the support of Admiral Koester, a former commanding officer of the High Seas Fleet, Tirpitz and

Müller orchestrated a campaign to ostracize Galster among his naval peers until he fell in line, which Galster eventually did.[37]

Tirpitz sought to gain direct control over the navy by pursuing his own personnel policy. He claimed some say, or at least veto power, in the appointment of officers to the senior positions in the navy.[38] He also strove to plant officers he respected in positions of power and to forge bonds with the most promising officers during their tours of service in the Imperial Naval Office. Many of the careers of top officers were made in this way, such as those of Admiral Reinhard Scheer, the commander of the active fleet between 1916 and 1918, and Admiral von Trotha, the first commanding head of the postwar navy.[39] Accordingly, the navy secretary insisted that promising graduates of the Naval War College would be directly assigned to his naval agency, and thus come under his direct influence.[40]

Tirpitz had established a precedent for such a personnel policy before 1897. Working within the torpedo arm, Tirpitz had created a closely knit group of fellow officers and co-workers, nicknamed the "torpedo-gang"; he had insisted on their transfer to the Naval High Command when he had moved to that agency in 1892. As secretary of the navy, Tirpitz continued to draw on the members of the group, whose careers flourished once their leader had climbed to the top of the naval hierarchy. Officers August von Heeringen and Gustav Bachmann were good examples. Rising through the ranks, they served with and under Tirpitz in the torpedo service, the Naval High Command, and then in the Imperial Naval Office; they eventually became admirals and chiefs of the Admiralty Staff.[41]

Within the office Tirpitz practiced a style of leadership that differed from his confrontational approach in his dealings with the service as a whole. He encouraged initiative and harnessed his subordinates' sense of responsibility. Although reserving ultimate decisions to himself, Tirpitz fashioned himself as a sort of "primus inter pares" who would listen to his collaborators and seek the best solutions in interaction with them.[42] Claiming naval politics and building as his domain, the navy secretary delegated authority and day-to-day affairs to others while relying on a circle of collaborators with whom he would discuss all matters of policy. "I used to 'roll the material about,' an expression I was often teased for and gave each of my co-workers a maximum degree of independence," he explained in his memoirs; large-scale "modern organizations" required such a course of action.[43]

All in all, Tirpitz's power drew on his particular style of leadership and a resourceful exploitation of the opportunities provided by the institution of the military monarchy. But ultimately, it depended on his authority as an officer with extraordinary talents. Dedicated to the naval profession, the Prusso-German state, and the industrial nation, this consummate professional stood out among his peers. During the 1890s, Tirpitz established himself as the navy's foremost professional authority, as he played a pivotal role in the making of navalism as a new body of professional thought and practice. He also earned such a reputation as an outstanding naval strategist who could command the navy in war that it stayed with him throughout the entire prewar period.[44] Masterminding the two Navy Bills of 1898 and 1900, the new navy secretary positioned himself as a man with superior competence as a naval politician and, thus, fostered a sense of his indispensability for the pursuit of maritime force, as he himself knew only too well when he employed the threat of his resignation. Such a sense had already prompted Admiral Senden to ensure Tirpitz's appointment as navy secretary despite his misgivings about an officer considered to be not "too choosy about his means" and "too self-conscious and convinced of his excellence."[45]

A Divided Navy

With remarkable success, Tirpitz imposed coherence on his service's professional politics and its pursuit of maritime force. Yet there were also clear limits to the navy secretary's exercise of leadership; by the early 1910s, Tirpitz no longer enjoyed the dominant position among his peers that he had originally gained after taking office in 1897. In fact, a high level of infighting marked the navy's professional politics before World War I. Neverending conflict characterized relations between the heads of the Imperial Naval Office and other naval agencies. It was astonishing, more than one officer observed, how much "time," "work," and "energy" was devoted to infighting in a navy whose heads were at odds with another.[46]

Such infighting was a product of bureaucratic politics within an institutionally fragmented navy. Disputes over turf attained some of their bitterness through personal rivalries among senior officers, which, in turn, were fueled by Tirpitz's claims to bureaucratic power and his imperious behavior. But ultimately, the lines of division did not simply stem from competing quests for institutional power or personal ambition.[47] They also entailed substantive conflict over the proper direction of the entire pursuit of force. It was the particular priorities of Tirpitz's overall approach and his unrelenting adherence to it that created a primary line of conflict and charged any institutional divisions with their special meaning. In contrast to the situation in the army where, by the early 1910s, intraservice dissension over an accelerated buildup concerned matters of class and political cohesion, competing time horizons became a divisive factor in naval policy debates.[48]

The navy secretary wedded his quest for supreme power within the navy to a particular approach to the pursuit of maritime force. He put the emphasis on the long-term creation of a powerful battle fleet and defined the eventual projection of maritime threat and deterrence at some point in the future as the top priority. By contrast, the present-day military capabilities, that is, the immediate combat readiness of the navy or other short-term naval defense needs (or, for that matter, its overseas presence) mattered less. Numerical expansion trumped high fighting power and military capability in the present when it came to the allocation of resources. Tirpitz laid out his priorities unequivocally as he assumed office and embarked on his quest for German sea power. In November 1898, for example, he informed his emperor that if he wanted to go ahead with his battleship program many "wishes and requests of the Front and perhaps of Your Majesty would have to be dropped" over a long period of time.[49]

Tirpitz tenaciously stuck to this approach. His policy, the navy secretary explained during the "war scare" of 1904, was to focus "to the utmost" on the effort "to push forward the battle fleet." It would be absolutely wrong to "put off the tomorrow for the 'today,'" he admonished.[50] In April 1909, when concerns about a possible war reached yet another high point, Tirpitz advised that his approach had not changed: he could not "sacrifice" the "future" by submitting to "daily fads" and "dilettantish wishes."[51] In the run-up to the Navy Bill of 1912, Tirpitz sounded precisely the same note as he defined the demand for more battleships beyond the existing framework of the *Flottengesetz* as the primary goal, and not the attempt to maximize the fighting value of the existing fleet.[52] When Tirpitz discussed in May and June 1914 the future needs of the navy and decided to risk open conflict with the imperial chancellor, he again expressly prioritized the long-term cause of continuous capital ship construction over the consolidation of the navy and its military capabilities.[53]

Over time, these priorities elicited ever-increasing animosity within the navy as concerns over present-day military capabilities flourished. Those officers attached to the active fleet and the Admiralty Staff placed the maximum readiness of the fleet in the present above considerations of its eventual size at some distant point in the future. They wanted to maximize the number of ships maintained in active service, to construct coastal fortifications, to build bigger and technologically superior battleships, to develop all arms of naval warfare from vessels like torpedo boats to weaponry such as mines, to provide for sufficient personnel, or to expand the institutions tasked with preparing the fleet for war such as the command of the active fleet or the Admiralty Staff, and so on.[54]

It took the specter of an Anglo-German war in 1904–05 to bring these priorities into sharp focus. Discussing the "current critical situation," Admiral Felix Bendemann, the commanding officer of the North Sea Station, suggested in December 1904 that his country needed to concentrate on strengthening the fleet within the given framework, including the "enlargement of our torpedo forces, our mine arm, our offensive and defensive coastal defense in general."[55] Captain August von Heeringen, a close confidant of Tirpitz, who headed a specially convened commission in late 1904 to study the war preparedness of the fleet, struck the same note. Conjuring the specter of a Anglo-German war in the future, Heeringen wanted his country to focus on maximizing the war preparedness of the fleet, its fighting power, in the present. Every new armament measure should be taken in view of "not what will be in the distant future, but what it will yield us in terms of the actual increase in maritime force in the period of time directly in front of us."[56] Confronted with the dramatic changes in capital ship construction, Heeringen became even more explicit several months later. In September 1905 he argued that the "maximization of the combat value of the fighting units" was the only appropriate course of action for a "smaller navy that might have to face a big navy." Concern for the combat value of the large ships and overall war preparedness trumped the long-term pursuit of larger numbers, "if, in the future, we want to lay any claim to maritime prominence and not remain permanently behind with the matériel of our navy."[57]

Despite such views, the Navy Bills of 1906 and 1908 adhered to Tirpitz's precepts. Successfully defending the primacy of his vision of the naval buildup, the navy secretary was nonetheless forced to make what historian Ivo Lambi has referred to as "major concessions" to his critics.[58] The Imperial Naval Office accepted the need to build bigger capital ships, which it did in the context of embracing the British building of Dreadnought-style battleships and battlecruisers; to strengthen coastal defenses in the North Sea, including the fortification of Heligoland; and to engage in other measures to increase the overall combat readiness of the fleet in the present.

In subsequent years, the open Anglo-German arms competition and continuing fears of imminent war continued to breed ever-increasing unhappiness among senior officers about Tirpitz's priorities. The concessions of the Imperial Naval Office hardly alleviated concerns about the fleet's state of war preparedness, its level of training, or its glaring shortage of personnel. There remained a consensus that in the present and foreseeable future the fleet lacked adequate strength for any "serious challenge," as the outgoing chief of the Admiralty Staff, Vice-Admiral Büchsel, phrased it in January 1908.[59]

These issues reached a boiling point in the winter of 1908–09 in the context of a veritable "war scare" when the heads of the Admiralty Staff and the fleet command came out in unprecedented open criticism of Tirpitz's policy. Prince Henry of Prussia, the commander of the fleet, who had already spent most of the previous year complaining about the preparedness of the High Seas Fleet (which after all was ready for war for only four months each year), questioned the "validity" of Tirpitz's "entire course of action regarding the further development of the fleet and the general maritime power of the Empire against an attack over sea."[60] Admiral Baudissin, the head of the Admiralty Staff, agreed. He charged Tirpitz with actively "inhibiting the fulfillment of military needs."[61] In fact, so strong was the unhappiness among senior officers that Baudissin made their views known not only to the emperor but also to the imperial chancellor. He even signaled support for Bülow's attempt to trim down the rate of German naval construction.[62] Tirpitz had good reasons to complain, in 1909, that he felt "deserted" by his "own Couleur" (fraternity), and to denounce the "secret counter-work" of the Admiralty Staff.[63]

The conflicts within the navy over the course of naval expansion reached another climax in the context of the Second Morocco Crisis and the making of what became the Naval Bill of 1912. This time Vice-Admiral Henning von Holtzendorff, the commander-in-chief of the High Seas Fleet, led the charge against Tirpitz. He asserted that the navy's insufficient state of preparedness was scandalous and set priorities in relation to any new naval legislation. Expressing a preference for slowing down the pace of capital ship construction in favor of meeting the navy's other needs, he urged a dramatic increase in naval personnel and "lesser" ships such as torpedo boats, submarines, and cruisers that were deemed essential for the proper operations of the battle force. His was also a plea for keeping as many of the available ships as possible in active service, and for a number of other measures to improve the fighting power of the fleet, including the development of the service's mine and air arms.[64]

Holtzendorff's agenda fed off an acute sense of vulnerability and the fear that any continuous attempt at "winning" the arms race with Britain could lead to war. In fact, the admiral expressed an interest in securing British goodwill by toning down German capital ship construction and entering into some sort of fleet agreement. He felt so strongly about this that he communicated his views to the British naval attaché.[65] Holtzendorff also sought contact with prominent diplomats and, following the precedent set by Baudissin a few years earlier, he took his case to the imperial chancellor, and not just the emperor.[66]

Holtzendorff articulated a larger consensus among most officers within the navy. Most strikingly, the head of the Admiralty Staff, Admiral Heeringen, agreed in substance with Holtzendorff's demands.[67] "Open opposition by the Admiralty Staff and Fleet Command," recorded the chief of the Naval Cabinet in October 1911 in relation to Tirpitz's original plans for a new naval bill.[68] The "entire front" would be "rebellious from the chief of the fleet to the youngest lieutenant," Deputy Secretary of the Navy Capelle had explained to his boss a month earlier.[69] In fact, many of Tirpitz's closest collaborators either shared or evinced sympathy for the demands of the "front."[70]

Differences over the direction of the pursuit of maritime force divided the navy until the summer of 1914. Sure, in the winter of 1911–12, the Imperial Naval Office had to heed its critics and compromise on the number of capital ships in favor of other needs when it finalized the new bill.[71] But the provisions of the bill did not meet all of the demands made by Holtzendorff and others. And after passage of the bill, the policy makers at the Imperial Naval Office continued to put off demands arising from within the fleet and the Admiralty Staff. The construction tables of the new bill could "only become reality, if greatest restraint is exercised in all areas," explained Capelle.[72] Between 1912 and 1914, the navy faced a severe shortage of personnel, material, and operating funds that cast a long shadow over the readiness of the available forces and even the day-to-day workings of the entire navy.[73] So fraught with tensions was this entire issue that in early 1914 Tirpitz urged Admiral Hugo von Pohl, the chief of the Admiralty Staff, not only to reconsider his demands for a dramatic improvement in the fleet's immediate preparedness for war but also to refrain from circulating them among the officer corps via service memoranda. In his response, Pohl defended his demands and suggested that they simply reflected the "unanimous complaints and sentiments" of the entire officer corps.[74]

On the eve of World War I, Tirpitz faced a severe crisis of acceptance. Most officers believed that the pursuit of maritime force had reached a crossroads and that their service needed a period of consolidation. The provisions of the Navy Bill of 1912 came close to the "limit" of "what the navy could digest" if it were to remain "at the height of its activity," as one observer summarized the sentiment of senior officers he had encountered in Kiel.[75] So critical were many officers of Tirpitz that there was open talk about the desirability of his leaving office. In 1912–13, the outgoing commander of the active fleet, Admiral Holtzendorff, openly lamented Tirpitz's detrimental impact on the navy and urged his fellow officers to work toward toppling the navy secretary.[76]

Tirpitz's crisis of authority extended to his ultimate power base, Wilhelm II. The emperor shared the view of his brother, Prince Henry, that Germany could no longer attain its armaments goals vis-à-vis Britain as defined at the beginning of the twentieth century.[77] To Tirpitz's chagrin, Wilhelm II visibly lost interest in the cause of further naval expansion. He failed to back plans for another bill in the winter of 1912–13, showed little desire to seriously discuss the future of the navy afterward, and did not support the navy secretary's armaments initiative in the summer of 1914. Tirpitz suspected that the monarch blamed him personally for Anglo-German tensions.[78] Strikingly, on a number of occasions, an erratic emperor heaped harsh criticism on his navy secretary for alleged shortcomings in naval construction and technology.[79]

Still, Tirpitz remained a powerful figure in 1914.[80] In fact, he responded to the coming of war by asking for ultimate power within the navy. Over the course of the first year of the war (and beyond), Tirpitz suggested that he should also wield overall operational command, preferably by also becoming the head of the Admiralty Staff, or, perhaps, the fleet command itself, or by heading a newly created Supreme Navy Command.[81] This bid attracted considerable support in naval circles, which in part reflected Tirpitz's continuing standing as the navy's foremost leadership figure. Yet ultimately this support stemmed from a new sense of crisis. In 1914–15 the enthronement of Tirpitz as a supreme navy leader appealed to some officers because they preferred to blame the disappointing course of the naval war on the timidity of their current operational leadership. In this situation, Tirpitz appeared as the one person who promised decisive leadership and a successful conduct of the war, even when he, in fact, had no answer to the operational dilemmas besetting the German fleet in the North Sea.[82]

Tirpitz's bid for power failed in the face of opposition from the emperor, Admiral Müller, and other service leaders who had crossed swords with him before.[83] And Tirpitz eventually resigned from his office over the issue of unconditional submarine warfare in 1916 at a time when the cataclysmic events of the war were transforming the landscape of the navy's professional politics. The ongoing war elevated the status of the Admiralty Staff and the fleet command at the expense of the Imperial Naval Office and moved the concerns of the "front" to the forefront in any debate over the direction of naval policy, whereas the course of the war raised questions about some of the priorities shaping the previous pursuit of maritime force. By the end of the war, the Imperial Naval Office enjoyed the status of a subordinate administrative agency whereas the creation of the Supreme Navy Command in the summer of 1918 created a new center of power in the navy.[84]

Intraservice Politics in the United States

There was no American Tirpitz. The U.S. Navy lacked the autonomy and institutional structure conducive to a single officer's rise to comparable prominence and power. During the 1880s and 1890s, the initial making of navalism rested on a larger collective effort of officers dispersed throughout the navy, with some institutional affiliations (such as with the Naval War College) and individual officers (such as Alfred Thayer Mahan) standing out. Only the creation of the General Board in 1900 provided a clear organizing center, which then clamored to be the navy's true professional representative. But its long-term president, George Dewey, lacked the authority and competence of Tirpitz.

As in Germany, the making of navalism pitted naval officers and institutions against each other. Yet it did so in very different ways. In the United States, the pursuit of maritime force under navalist auspices involved the demand for the wholesale reorganization of power and jurisdictional authority within the navy as it challenged the existing system of bureaus, with their mostly administrative and technical functions. Thus, demands for a full-fledged general staff with sweeping powers faced strong and continuous opposition from within the navy itself. The resistance came from members of the staff corps and the community of naval engineers (which was officially amalgamated with the line officer corps in 1899) who ran various bureaus (including Steam Engineering and Construction); it also extended to a good number of regular line officers who were strongly opposed to changes in the existing institutional makeup. These officers guarded the prerogatives of the bureaus with which they had been associated throughout their careers.

Considerable intraservice conflict surrounded the drive for an all-powerful naval general staff after 1898, during which both sides openly forged coalitions with civilian policy makers. In 1904, congressional hearings on a bill to expand the powers of the General Board and provide legal sanction for it brought such disunity into the sharpest possible focus. The secretary of the navy and Admirals Dewey and Taylor supported the bill strongly, as did the head of the Bureau of Equipment and the commanding officer of the U.S. Marine Corps. But the heads of the bureaus of Steam Engineering and of Supplies and Account came out in open opposition as did the civilian assistant secretary of the navy. The chiefs of the Bureaus of Ordnance and of Construction and Repair hedged their official support for the bills by insisting that any powers given to the General Board should only remain advisory, and thus not present a challenge to the authority of the existing bureaus. In fact, the behind-the-scenes lobbying efforts of Rear-Admiral William Capps, the head of the Bureau of Construction and Repair, proved pivotal in the defeat of the bill in Congress.[85]

By contrast, the basic parameters regarding battle fleet warfare, sea power, and imperial assertion were forged in a less conflict-prone process of consensus-building. They had already come into sharp focus by 1890 when a number of key texts capped a decadelong debate among naval officers about proper naval strategy and policy. These texts included an article, published by Rear-Admiral Luce, which advocated the immediate construction of a fleet of twenty battleships and laid out the basic operational premises of the entire concept of battle fleet warfare.[86] In January 1890, a committee of naval officers, the so-called Policy Board, outlined a more ambitious naval program and also enunciated some of the basic political premises of the navy's new geopolitical creed.[87] In May 1890, Mahan published his *Influence of Sea Power upon History, 1660–1783*; in December 1890, he published an important follow-up article, "The United States Looking Outward," which aired his broader views about the new direction of global politics and the changing destiny of the United States.[88]

Navy leaders embraced the pursuit of maritime force and global power. But not all of them endorsed the promises and practices of scientific strategy, in part because they had a vested interest in the autonomy of the bureaus. Until well after the turn of the twentieth century, anti-intellectualism and skepticism toward allegedly "abstract" academic training and scientific knowledge percolated among many officers who insisted on the primacy of the seagoing, ship-handling, and material-technological aspects of their profession. Strikingly, in the early 1890s, senior officers such as Admiral

Francis Ramsay, a chief of the Bureau of Navigation, which handled officer assignments, had viewed Mahan skeptically. They had insisted that he prove himself as a seagoing officer and as the captain of a ship, and abandon his study and teaching of sea power, naval strategy, and history.[89]

This oppositional current imposed heavy constraints on the initial development of the new strategic science, which was at the heart of the entire navalist enterprise. The Naval War College faced considerable opposition on the part of many officers. Minuscule in its operations, the War College was continuously haunted by the specter of institutional extinction in its early years. More than ten years passed before it became a more widely accepted institution within the navy and it would then take another ten or fifteen years, that is, until the mid-1910s, for the College to be viewed as a key institution providing expertise and training for all aspiring officers of the fleet.[90] The Office of Naval Intelligence was only formally incorporated in 1899; it attained its own civilian staff after it had existed for more than fifteen years.[91] It took the experience of war in 1898 and then the initial work of the General Board itself to dispel all doubts about the importance of continuous war planning and the systematic study of matters of naval strategy and programs within a fixed institutional framework.

Significantly, the integrity of the General Board as such was not at stake in the acrimonious debates over institutional reform after 1900. Within a few years, the General Board established itself as the navy's authoritative voice in all matters of naval policy, imperial policy, strategy, and building programs.[92] Substantive conflicts over turf within the navy focused on matters relating to naval construction and the material infrastructure sustaining the fleet. The rise of the General Board to a preeminent position within the Navy Department took place against the backdrop of the Board's continuously conflict-ridden engagement with the so-called technical bureaus over their control of ship construction and design. Starting in earnest in the fall of 1903, the General Board claimed a dominant say in the determination of the overall specification of ship types and their characteristics, which it eventually gained in 1909.[93] In the same year, the increased say of the General Board was also reflected in the abolition of the Board on Construction, the interbureau agency that had supervised the work of the technical bureaus since 1889. This board had previously rankled officers for another reason. At the behest of Secretary of the Navy John D. Long, it had also given official suggestions on annual building policy, starting in the fall of 1898. It continued do so after 1900, to the increasing dislike of the newly established General Board.[94]

The elevation of the General Board and dissolution of the Board on Construction capped off six years of acrimonious debate.[95] By 1907–08 this debate had reached a high level of publicity, including a congressional investigation and a specially convened meeting of naval officers at the Naval War College in 1908, which was attended by President Roosevelt himself. This struggle over the distribution of institutional power within the Navy Department was fought out over the issue of proper battleship design during a period of dramatic change in capital ship construction. Staking out claims in relation to the overall design and characteristics of ships, the General Board began to promote the cause of an "all-big-gun" battleship, which stressed the maximization of heavy artillery at the expense of any intermediate battery. Asked by the General Board to develop such a ship in the spring of 1904, the Board on Construction had not responded positively, even as a few years earlier the Bureau of Construction and Repair had briefly entertained the possibility of such a battleship.[96]

Tense negotiations followed in which officers from the General Board and the Board on Construction reached compromise decisions as to the construction of the next generation of battleships authorized in the Naval Acts of 1905 and 1906, which led to the construction of the first American "Dreadnought" battleships.[97] These negotiations took place against the backdrop of an open public debate over the merits of "all-big-gun ships" in the light of the lessons of the Russo-Japanese War, during which proponents of these ships, such as Bradley Fiske, publicly criticized the technical bureaus for their misguided conservatism while also arguing against Mahan, who championed the construction of smaller battleships.[98] The negotiations also entailed repeated suggestions by the General Board (which bore fruit in 1907) to use a special examination board comprised of officers to examine final battleship designs and open up the design process to civilian shipbuilders in order to break the hold of the Board on Construction on final design decisions.[99]

The debate shifted gears in 1907 and 1908 when two already prominent officers, William S. Sims and Albert Keys, with special connections to the president in their capacity as his previous or current naval aides, changed tactics. These self-styled "insurgents" decided to publicize what they considered to be the gross defects of most recent battleships as part of an all-out attack on the Board of Construction and the bureaus it represented. In their attacks, they employed the method of journalistic sensationalism in collusion with a civilian naval writer and also relied on their own public testimony. Prompting a Senate investigation and a subsequent special conference at the Naval War College, Sims and Keys succeeded in creating a stir. At its height, congressional allies of the Bureau of Construction such as Senator Eugene Hale, the chairman of the Senate's Naval Affairs Committee, worked hard to provide a stage for officers of the technical bureaus to present their cases and silence their critics. Treating Sims and Keys with open contempt, Hale even threatened to dissolve the General Board. So bitter was the tone that the General Board as an institution kept a low profile. Dewey, its president, did not even attend the Newport conference of officers.[100]

Although facing considerable adversity, Sims and Keys managed to bring about significant change. They may have raised only technical points of "debatable importance," as historian William McBride has convincingly argued, and on which most officers, including those in command of the fleet and its vessels, disagreed with them.[101] They also ignored the developing collaboration in preceding years between the General Board and Board on Construction, between line officers, naval architects, and engineering specialists across various institutional lines, on battleship design.[102] Yet the controversy they sparked created the space needed for the champions of the General Board to make the case for the agency as the true custodian of the interests of all seagoing officers. The officer conference at the Naval War College decided that it was up to the General Board to determine the overall characteristics for ships and then monitor the development of preliminary designs.[103]

In short, the General Board emerged victorious from the debate over the control of ship design as the navy's top policymaking agency. Its position was officially enhanced when the prerogatives of the abolished Board on Construction were transferred to it in 1909. This change took place as part of the introduction of the "Aide-System" in the same year, a system that established a handful of high-ranking officers as the secretary of the navy's top advisers for operations, materials, inspections, and personnel, to coordinate the work of the various agencies of the navy, with the operations and materials aides becoming ex officio members of the General Board. Strikingly, the aides and the General Board worked together harmoniously and with a remarkable "unanimity of purpose," or so Bradley Fiske, who briefly served as aide of inspection before becoming aide of operations in 1913, claimed.[104]

Still, by 1914 it also became clear that the position of the aide of operations as the navy's top professional authority could develop into a center of power in its own right and somewhat at the expense of the General

Board. As aide of operations, Fiske successfully interjected himself between the General Board and the navy secretary and would, on occasion, communicate only his own views to his civilian superior while not presenting the dissenting majority opinion of the General Board. Substantive differences in overall approach were not involved. But members of the General Board registered a sense of institutional decline by 1914, a year before the creation of the Office of the Chief of Naval Operations transformed the landscape of the navy's professional politics and imposed new limits on the authority of the General Board.[105]

While growing into a position of authority, the General Board was not dominated by a single officer in the same way as the Imperial Naval Office, and with it the entire navy, was in Germany. As the navy's senior officer (he had been given the lifetime rank of Admiral of the Navy in 1899), Admiral George Dewey served as the official president of the General Board from 1900 until his death in 1917. He did so while also serving as the chairman of the Joint Army and Navy Board and taking command of the entire fleet on special occasions.[106]

Dewey had become the president of the General Board because of his prominence as the result of his victorious exploits as the commander of the Asiatic Squadron during the Spanish-American War of 1898. But prior to the war, Dewey had not stood out or earned a reputation as a professional with extraordinary talents, as Tirpitz had in Germany. Dewey had not been known as an articulate naval thinker or strategist, nor as an outstanding commanding officer. He had not played a significant role in the making of navalism, nor did he belong to those officers who seriously studied the changing hardware of the navy and excelled as technological innovators.

Dewey fashioned his own style of leadership. His conception of his role as president of the General Board was that of a moderator and facilitator, not as the premier policy maker and agenda-setter. Dewey "handled the board with exceeding skill, keeping himself in the background, never taking part in discussions but keeping a tight rein which all of us felt," explained Fiske, who served as a staff assistant to the General Board.[107] So restrained was Dewey's notion of immediate control that, with only a few exceptions, he never sought to impress his views on any important issue on the members of the General Board. He usually supported the decision reached by its majority. Dewey's moderation provided the setting in which Rear-Admiral Taylor assumed a leading role until his death in 1904 and the Board's members collectively determined policy.

But Dewey nevertheless exerted considerable influence and shaped policymaking by the indirect means of personnel selection. As the president, it was his prerogative to select the officers serving on the Board, with the exception of the few ex officio members. Assignments to the Board became desirable billets of crucial importance to the careers of upcoming officers. The personnel policy surrounding the General Board, as overseen by its president, provided cohesion and a unity of purpose within the navy at large.[108]

Dewey, then, helped to ensure the institutional preeminence of the General Board by his sheer presence and advocacy. Dewey lent his authority to the board and he used his fame as a war hero as an important resource to impress civilian policy makers. In spite of his ill-advised, almost farcical foray into presidential politics in 1899 and another public relations disaster (he signed over the house, which had been bought for him through popular subscription, to his newlywed, second wife, a Catholic millionaire socialite), Dewey remained a noted public figure whose words as an officer commanded attention among civilians.[109] "The General Board's real status depends largely upon you and your influence. Your interest in its work and the value attached to your advice both in and out of Congress gives it a prestige which it otherwise would lack," wrote Captain Nathaniel Sargent, an officer attached to the board, to Dewey in 1905, even after Dewey had lowered his public profile in response to criticism of his talk about the possibility of an armed conflict with Germany in the winter of 1902–03.[110]

Dewey was an active promoter of the General Board and expected it to be recognized within the navy as the highest authority on all matters of naval policy. Yet as a naval infighter Dewey usually exercised restraint. He eschewed public rifts and controversy among naval officers. His emphasis was on professional cohesion and incremental change. Following the lead of Taylor, Dewey openly supported the evolutionary approach to the formation of the general staff. From the very beginning Dewey considered the General Board as the "natural center and head of a general staff,"[111] yet he toned down his language in public and avoided any appearance of hostility toward the bureaus. "Let us have neither cliques nor grudges, but all stand together for the good of the country and the service," declared the Christmas message the admiral sent to his naval peers in December 1906.[112]

Over time, Dewey's preference for consensus-building and his attachment to the General Board steered him in conservative directions. True, the Admiral of the Navy fully insisted on the existing prerogatives of the General Board and claimed a dominant say in determining the overall characteristics of ships. But the admiral refrained from pushing further the cause of an all-powerful general staff. He refused to actively support those officers (such as Sims and Fiske) who strove to keep the issue of further institutional reform alive and were willing to engage in confrontational tactics. Accordingly, Dewey did not openly attack the technical bureaus in 1907–08 when the debate over the design of capital ships reached its fever pitch. At that time, those officers intent on pushing the issue of a full-fledged naval general staff and a restriction of the bureau's jurisdictional powers perceived Dewey as a hindrance to their cause.[113]

All in all, Dewey was a big asset for the General Board and the navy's pursuit of maritime force after the turn of the twentieth century. Dewey's public and professional persona facilitated the rise to prominence of the General Board and the pursuit of the navy's agendas, which took place in the face of considerable skepticism about military claims to power within the wider political nation. At the same time, Dewey's conception of his role inside the navy enabled other, more competent officers to engage in the work of military planning and institution-building. It was only fitting that the decision reached by Secretary Long in the winter of 1899–1900 to create the General Board was indirectly related to Dewey. From Long's perspective, the new agency also solved the problem of what to do with Dewey after the Spanish-American War.[114]

Intraservice Conflict over Preparedness

Although the debate over the prerogatives of the General Board vis-à-vis the bureaus had run its course by the early 1910s, a heated debate over naval "preparedness" and civil-military relations erupted within the navy in 1914. In the face of an unfolding big-power war in Europe, a rift over the pursuit of maritime force and policy leadership opened up among top navy leaders. It did so as these officers engaged with a secretary of the navy, Josephus Daniels, who in the first year of World War I was neither particularly alarmed about the state of America's naval armaments nor perceived any immediate geopolitical emergency, and who had told the navy leadership to back off during the anti-Japanese "war scare" of 1913. In this situation, disagreement over policy among high-ranking officers became inseparable from the issue of the exercise of professional authority within a Navy Department headed by a civilian secretary, an issue that had always set U.S. Navy leaders and their professional politics apart from their German counterparts.[115]

In his capacity as aide of operations, Rear-Admiral Bradley A. Fiske forcefully articulated the alarm about the prospects of American naval power and current fleet capabilities. Unwilling to compromise, the navy's senior strategist confronted his navy secretary with demands for drastic measures to increase the fleet readiness and expand the military capabilities of the navy, including the creation of an all-powerful naval general staff with sweeping powers. He harangued his civilian superior on every conceivable occasion while continually pressing his fellow officers at the General Board and elsewhere into action. He also enlisted newspapers, such as the *New York Herald,* to make his case in public. Growing impatient with his secretary, whom he viewed as the "real obstacle" with his "silly handling" of his department, Fiske was willing to disregard any constitutional niceties to press his case.[116] He defied the secretary by offering public testimony before Congress that ran counter to the views expressed by Daniels and by actively colluding with like-minded congressional policy makers behind the secretary's back to attain the legislation he coveted.[117]

Fiske encountered significant opposition from within the service. Several senior officers, such as Rear-Admirals Albert Winterhalter and Victor Blue, the aide for materials and the chief of the Bureau of Navigation, respectively, lacked Fiske's obsessive sense of urgency. Winterhalter and Blue in particular counseled moderation, sided or sought compromises with their navy secretary on contentious issues, and supported his positions through public testimony. Yet their disagreement with Fiske concerned his methods and style more than his goals. It reflected a different sense of political propriety and opportunity. Typically, when in a meeting with Winterhalter, Blue, and Fiske, the navy secretary argued that navy leaders "should not submit" papers calling for more than the president and his navy secretary wanted and should "have answers ready, to be given when asked for," Winterhalter and Blue explicitly agreed and flatly denied that it was the navy's "business" to determine the "probability of war" and "advise" their secretary about it.[118]

Fiske's uncompromising behavior alienated many officers, who were simply unwilling to openly break with their civilian superior, let alone end their career. Their opposition involved a heavy dose of institutional politics as well. Winterhalter and Blue successfully aligned themselves with their navy secretary and thus enhanced their personal power within the Navy Department (whereas Fiske's officer career came to a premature end in 1915, with an irate Daniels telling him at one point that he, Fiske, could not "write or talk any more; you can't even say that two and two make four"[119]).

The centerpiece of Fiske's agenda, the creation of the Office of the Chief of Naval Operations, had its detractors also among other prominent officers associated with the General Board. They viewed the newly proposed office as a clear threat to the institution they identified with. Significantly, they also had not been too happy with Fiske's treatment of the agency prior to the outbreak of war in 1914.[120]

The most prominent among these dissenting officers was Admiral Dewey himself. Not only did his sense of accomplishment as the president of the navy's most important institution stand at cross purposes with any arguments about the fleet's glaring lack of readiness for war but he was also so invested in the General Board that he (like a few other officers) saw no real need for a chief of naval operations and viewed the creation of this position as an institutional threat to the continuing existence of the board. "It has been my opinion for many years that we have in the General Board of the Navy a better General Staff than the Army; and the work as conducted by the Board in its advisory character based upon mature thought and experience by the best talent in our Navy, I believe to be of inestimable value as an asset in times of peace or war," explained Dewey in the spring of 1915.[121] In fact, Dewey would treat the first chief of naval operations, Rear-Admiral William Shepherd Benson, with initial contempt precisely because he suspected him of undermining his own position and that of the General Board.[122]

Dewey used his authority to rein in his peers and pay obeisance to a civilian secretary who professed a great deal of personal admiration for the old admiral.[123] It was Dewey who ensured that in the fall and winter of 1914–15 the General Board complied with the wishes of the secretary to not go public with its far-reaching demands that ran counter to the priorities of the administration.[124] Dewey also let his reservations about the creation of an all-powerful chief of naval operations be known and went on record as saying that the General Board sufficed to prepare the navy's plans for war, thus providing important cover for Daniels to modify the legislation. Moreover, on several occasions, the old admiral defended the record of Secretary Daniels against his critics from within (and without) the navy and stressed the high level of readiness of the existing fleet.[125]

In 1914–15, Dewey may not have fully promoted the cause of "preparedness" as defined by most other members of the naval elite. But acting as an important mediating force in the conflict between the likes of Fiske and Secretary Daniels, the ailing admiral (who was no longer capable of fulfilling his role as the president of the General Board) nonetheless helped to pave the way for the embrace of this cause by the Wilson administration. Through his moderating behavior, Dewey helped to prevent a massive falling out between the naval elite and their civilian superiors. At the same time, the admiral made it clear that, in general, he supported a buildup of American naval power, thus outlining a case vis-à-vis Secretary Daniels that became official administration policy by late 1915. Strikingly, Dewey remained in high standing among officers such as Fiske.[126]

Ultimately, in calling for a ratcheting up of American naval power, Fiske acted on behalf of most his peers, including the vast majority of the naval planners at the General Board and Naval War College.[127] Secretary Daniels learned about the navy's majority opinion in the spring of 1915 when he was seeking to appoint the first chief of naval operations. Rear-Admiral Frank Fletcher, the commanding officer of the Atlantic Fleet, and the navy's other rear admirals all supported Fiske's case for preparedness, as he had outlined it before Congress in the previous winter, and they all suggested Fiske as the first chief.[128] More than ever in the summer of 1915, the navy leadership rallied around the causes of enhanced fleet readiness and an accelerated arms buildup. The General Board officially committed itself to the goal of a "navy second to none" (which it had already approved in September 1914, yet had not made it public in response to Daniels's request) and began to issue a series of ever-escalating demands.[129] These demands also found the support of the newly appointed chief of naval operations, William Benson. Strikingly, Benson himself (who had supported the creation of a naval general staff before the war) was as committed to "preparedness" as Fiske, including the enhancement of both the prerogatives and capabilities of the office that he now held. But unlike Fiske, he pursued this agenda in a more understated, yet remarkably effective, manner while maintaining a good working relationship with Secretary Daniels.[130]

The creation of the position of a chief of naval operations established an office that proved conducive to a more comprehensive exercise of professional leadership and bureaucratic coordination, if not control. The product of a long-standing effort to remake naval politics and institutions in an idealized Germanic image, this new institution came to be the center of a new institutional infrastructure of a more cohesive and directed politics, yet it nonetheless remained circumscribed by a framework of civilian control and continuing institutional pluralism.

In short, patterns of top leadership, professional cohesion, and intraservice conflict never converged on the German and American sides of the Atlantic, despite shared navalist commitments. Strikingly, the shift in the

U.S. Navy's professional politics after 1914 took place as German navy leaders, too, reconsidered the merits of their own multipartite institutional arrangements in favor of a more unified and hierarchical system. In the summer of 1918, the entire navy was placed under the control of the chief of a Supreme Navy Command, thus creating a position of formal power that Tirpitz, the seemingly all-powerful director of the German naval buildup, had never possessed.

Conclusion

Navalism and Its Trajectories

In his polemic *The Navy: Defense or Portent?* (1932), the eminent radical historian Charles Beard offered a scathing critique of the so-called naval expert. Beard traced the rise of this "new creature of modern civilization" back to the making of navalism in the United States and Imperial Germany before World War I. He related the formation of the "big-navy policy" directly to the activities of naval officers such as Tirpitz and Mahan, rejecting the idea that "capitalists and merchants" had been the prime movers. Beard painted a devastating picture of the "dark corner of navy specialism." On the one hand, the "naval expert" jockeyed for power, undermined the principle of civilian control, and strove to impose an "imperialist creed" on the nation. On the other hand, the same expert was highly "fallible." His exclusionary claims to special expertise in matters of maritime warfare, sea power, and global politics lacked any substance. In Beard's view, then, the "naval expert" was anything but a disinterested figure. Most important, "professional pride and zeal" made him impatient with any civilian interference in his domain. He also had other practical interests at stake:"more ships, more posts, bigger ships and bigger posts, more prestige, honor, salaries, stars and perquisites."[1]

Beard offered his critique as part of an antimilitarist politics.[2] It countered Depression-era calls for naval expansion, which made the case for a big navy in terms of anti-Japanese geopolitical alarmism, military Keynesianism, and superior professional expertise. Couched in a distinctive progressive-populist language that set the "people" against the "interests," and, thus, against the professional military and its corporate allies, Beard's critique of the "naval expert" traced its intellectual lineage back to critics of the navalists' pursuit of maritime force before World War I. It also resonated with the original meanings of the concept of militarism as it had emerged in the middle decades of the nineteenth century in the context of Prussia's "military revolution" and war-making in the 1860s. The charge of "militarism" had focused on the transformation of the military into an ever-expanding bureaucratic machine bent on a policy of continuous high levels of armament. This transformation, in turn, had been viewed as part of the rise of capitalist industrialization and institutional domination that were seen as transforming civil society and compromising its promises of peace and prosperity.[3]

Historically situated as it was, Beard's indictment of the "naval expert" and his ingenious critique of the central tenets of the naval elites' "expertise" may nonetheless strike a sympathetic chord with modern readers. What makes Beard's treatise so powerful is not simply his exercise in a kind of Marxist critique of ideology but also his identification of the "naval expert" as a central actor on the international stage of military politics. This profoundly antiexceptionalist emphasis corresponds with the self-understanding of naval elites before World War I, who considered their own times as the "day of the experts," to quote U.S. Rear-Admiral French Ensor Chadwick.[4] The same emphasis also presents a striking contrast to the celebration of the "professional soldier" as an antidote to militarism. At the time of Beard's writing, such celebration was slowly moving to the forefront in hegemonic discourse on the military, militarism, and civil-military relations in Western societies. In the 1930s and 1940s, it was perhaps most famously elaborated upon by Alfred Vagts, the liberal German-American scholar who sought salvation from "militarism" in the "scientific" and "functional" way of the professional military as he succumbed to a "moral panic" in the face of societal militarization in an age of mass politics and "total war."[5]

The Two Navies' Militarism

In *Militarism in a Global Age,* I have shared Beard's identification of the "naval experts" in uniform as key players in processes of global militarization.

German and American navalism, I have argued, was a professional militarism that stressed the paramount importance of sea power in a new global age. It was fashioned by German and U.S. naval elites who viewed themselves as professional experts in an industrial world and followed a "technocratic impulse" that permeated important sectors of civil societies in both nations.[6] Assuming a perfect harmony between superior maritime force, national industry, and institutional expertise, these officers set out to remake the United States and Germany as nation-centered world powers under the conditions of what historian Geoff Eley has referred to as "competitive globalization."[7] In so doing, they simultaneously engaged in a common transatlantic discourse among military elites and participated in the imaginings and consensuses among national intelligentsias in each country.

As makers of militarism, German and American naval elites took a broad, comprehensive approach that occupied a distinct space in the history of professional-military imaginaries. This militarist formation fused together considerations of international politics, maritime warfare, political rule, and national industry while also synthesizing naval strategy, operations, tactics, technology, and organization. This was a far cry from opportunistic professional-military approaches that viewed military matters in isolation and relentlessly focused on maximizing fighting power and the use value of weapons, at the expense of any larger vision of strategy and its fundamental parameters, or, for that matter, a holistic understanding of the uses and boundaries of war.[8]

Devising their brand of militarism, German and U.S. naval elites made the relentless pursuit of maritime force essential to the future of their industrial nation-states in twentieth-century global politics and economics. In contrast to understandings of European power politics that stressed the "concert" of powers and the many shared interests among them, navalist-style geopolitics emphasized the prevalence of direct conflict among big powers and revolved around threat, deterrence, and favorable armaments ratios.[9] Prioritizing military preparedness for interimperial conflict over gunboat diplomacy in imperial spaces overseas, the two navies' strategists championed the relentless national accumulation of maritime arms in preparation for big-power war and the massive extraction of societal resources to that end. At the same time, the two naval elites imposed clear boundaries on the pursuit of maritime force. Embracing the professional organization of military violence within the confines of a separate, clearly demarcated institution, the makers of navalism promised a limitation of war. Drawing directly on the example of land warfare, their paradigm of warfare envisioned decisive victory through climactic combat in temporally limited wars. Until World War I, it also accepted, as a matter of principle, the strictures of maritime law in relation to the economic dimension of naval warfare, thus imposing clear boundaries on the maritime war of trade and economic pressure.

Within each national system of governance, the makers of navalism sought control over all matters relating to the pursuit of maritime force, as they positioned themselves as the custodians of the two countries' interests as integral nation-states in a globalizing world. Their demand for independence from any politics or civilian interference involved the claim of the military's instrumental mastery of maritime warfare and its firm promise of victory. The two naval elites claimed broad knowledge of the rules governing the conduct of states, navies, and economies. In asserting such expertise, these professionals simultaneously defined, on their own, larger geopolitical agendas for their respective nation-states and demanded a maximum degree of policy control and institutional autonomy. This case for technocratic rule, in turn, translated into an activist approach in political and public arenas, which ranged from concerted lobbying to wide-ranging efforts at the mobilization of consent and the "education" of policy makers and publics. In short, the two navies engaged in a professional elite politics that acknowledged the realities of participatory politics and the power of public opinion as it sought to shape and manipulate them.

The professional militarism of the two navies operated within the same universe of military-operational thought and practice. It was defined by investments in the tenets of battle fleet warfare, the harnessing of maritime force in regional concentration, and the embrace of the sciences of sea power and strategy. German and U.S. naval cultures were cut from the same cloth. Its members shared the same levels of professional rationality, as expressed perhaps most visibly in the same cult of decisive battle, the same doctrinal rigidity, and the symmetry of the operational scenarios of war plans. They did so regardless of whether or not the navies functioned as "charismatic institutions" and highly charged national symbols within their own countries.[10] In fact, the particular outlook of navalist thought and culture along these lines set the German and U.S. navies apart from their British counterpart with its own distinctive approaches to military professionalism and maritime warfare. German-American commonality, in turn, was sustained by direct exchanges and shared referents. The example of the Prussian-German army provided a shared model for the naval elites of both countries. Their sciences of strategy and sea power drew on an active embrace of the science of war that had become identified with that army and its General Staff. Furthermore, the language, if not the "ideology," of sea power that Mahan laid out in public in the 1890s played a pivotal role in the development of navalist thought in Germany.

A common understanding of global politics, a common geopolitical *Weltbild* (conception of the world), further lent shape to the professional militarism of the two navies. Shared tenets of economic geopolitics bounded the reading of the direction of global politics and the interests of big powers. A Social Darwinist vocabulary of perpetual conflict added harsh existential meanings to an analysis that related the imperial pursuits of big powers to domestic economic pressures and identified commercial strife as the most pressing issue of global politics. Moving within the same conceptual world, German and U.S. naval elites offered remarkably similar views of particular powers, including their own countries. Such commonality eventually extended to the interpretation of World War I as an expression of the Anglo-German antagonism over empire and industry.

Although German and American naval elites pursued a common militarist project, the navalism they fashioned took on particular shapes and emphases in each country. Naturally, national configurations of power and knowledge left their imprint on the ideas, agendas, and practices of each navy. These two militaries operated in distinctive systems of governance and political cultures, each of which structured civil-military relations and the militaries' identity politics in their own ways. They worked within, and responded to, particular conjunctures of national politics and state-formation, of elite rule, participatory politics, and institutional domination. Visions of world power were colored by the particulars of imperial imaginations among national intelligentsias of the two countries. Strategies of geopolitical projection and operational scenarios for wars addressed themselves to the specifics of each state's peculiar geostrategic positioning and overall entanglements with the world.

From the beginning, differences in expression between the navalist projects of the two navies were particularly pronounced in three areas. To start with, bids for global power came with their own distinctive formulations. They fused the same sets of ideas concerning sea power, national industry, and international politics with specific notions of national destiny, empire, and race. Expanding on well-established discourses of great-power politics and colonial empire-building, the Germans sought diplomatic power, spheres of influence, and a vast colonial empire around the globe; and they imagined their country as a participant in alliance politics across the world. While directly challenging the world's premier sea power, the British Empire, they advanced an antiuniversalistic understanding of future global politics and the German Empire's place within it. Such understanding stressed the multiplicity of world powers and "global people"; it aimed at a "Greater Germany" as one global empire among many.

Influenced by previous U.S. expansionist approaches, the Americans made their case for global power and a first-rate navy within a framework of a restrained globalism and a minimalist colonialism. The former defined the Western Hemisphere and East Asia as primary regions of U.S. self-assertion; the latter prioritized projection of military force and economic power over acquisition of territory. While putting considerable emphasis on U.S. distance from the entanglements of big-power politics, members of the American naval elite articulated universalistic notions of world domination. Unlike the Germans, they advanced expectations of their own nation's global mastery.

Differences in expressions extended to the social-imperialist imaginings that were an integral part of the navalists' expansionist discourse. The two naval elites related the pursuit of global empire and maritime force to matters of governance, national cohesion, and social politics in nationally distinctive ways. In Germany, leading officers promoted a reformist social imperialism of sorts as they drew on the ideas of other civilian state officials and bourgeois proponents of social reform. Tirpitz and others envisioned the forging of a cohesive nation in the crucible of global politics within the framework of a constitutional monarchy, decisive governmental leadership from above, all-inclusive nationalist mobilization, and (limited) social reform. American naval officers, too, embraced the cause of the nation against its enemies from within and linked it to the defense of elite rule. Yet in line with civilian Progressive reformers, they elaborated on the promises of empire primarily within the confines of moral reform, reactionary welfarism, racial exclusion, and corporate industrialism. And they buttressed their case for national renewal with a bid for enhanced national state power and bureaucratic expert government, a linkage that was central to any American-style social imperialism, with its investment in building a strong administrative state.

Finally, there were noticeable differences in the self-presentation and exercise of power between the two navies. In Germany, the navy was part of a military monarchy. Its officers viewed themselves as the nation's first estate. Demanding control over their professional project and imbued with a strong sense of service to the state, the Germans advanced highly potent notions of civil-military separation. They both stressed the bonds between the monarch and his officers and used a self-referential language of expertise, the exclusive focal point of which was the military as a superior institution unto itself. At the same time, the political strength of the imperial state and the extraordinary autonomy of its armed forces endowed the navy with remarkable powers. They allowed its leaders to operate as independent actors outside substantive civilian oversight and engage in a cohesive professional politics to master the political process and shape public opinion.

The American naval elite worked with a different set of capabilities, resources, and languages. Lacking an exalted status within state and society, officers drew directly on civilian examples and presented themselves as a military extension of organizational society at large when they defined themselves as an expert group and demanded recognition of their agendas. Aiming at a maximum degree of policy control and self-governance, the navy's professional politics nonetheless continually paid official tribute to the principles of republican governance. Institutional independence (and, with it, the opportunity for decisive professional leadership from above) eluded the U.S. Navy. In fact, its policy makers admired the power of the German state to harness military force without undue civilian interference. Seeking institutional powers comparable to those already in existence in Germany, they self-consciously set out to transform U.S. naval politics and institutions in a German image.

Diverging Futures

What ultimately separated the common militarist projects of the two navies were the new trajectories they produced. Over time, the pursuits of these projects channeled the two naval elites in different directions: by the mid-1910s, navy leaders developed divergent outlooks on the prospects of their bids for world power and maritime force. On the eve of World War I, the Germans were in a state of panic. Fixated on the Anglo-German antagonism, the fortunes of their naval program, and the direction of German national politics, they self-consciously confronted nothing less than the specter of all-out failure and ruminated about an impending ruin of Germany as a big power and viable nation. In the early 1910s, the Americans, too, expressed grave concerns about the comparative "preparedness" of their country for big-power confrontations over empire. But their alarmism lacked the existential immediacy that plagued the Germans, and it developed alongside the conviction that the United States could ultimately succeed in the competitive interimperial milieu of global power.

World War I deepened these differences in outlook and pushed the naval elites further along diverging paths. The war dramatically raised the stakes for German navy leaders as they found themselves locked in what they considered to be an existential war that would decide the entire future of the German nation-state. Prewar panic gave way to wartime "extremism," to use historian Isabel Hull's term.[11] It entailed a relentless commitment to the pursuit of victory at all costs, and beyond previous regimes of limitation, an attachment that manifested itself in the conduct of a submarine-based maritime war of extermination, the imagery of a violent subjugation of the British Empire, and fierce opposition to the idea of a negotiated peace (except if it meant a separate peace with Imperial Russia as a prelude to German military success against Britain and France). But the German navy's new "extremism" also expressed itself in the radicalization of previous commitments to elite rule and an integral nation-state. The embrace of dictatorial governance and a radical nationalist politics took navy leaders well beyond their prewar adherence to constitutional government and political restraint.

World War I and eventual U.S. intervention in it raised the stakes for American navalists, too. Contemplating the growing requirements of self-sustaining U.S. global power in a postwar world of big-power conflict over empire, navy leaders made the case for a dramatic naval buildup, enhanced societal militarization, and increased bureaucratic autonomy within an expanding warfare state. The entry into the war then redirected immediate attention toward the conduct of a coalition war and the proper employment of naval power across the Atlantic, without, however, displacing previously articulated concerns about post-war dangers. But overall, World War I did not dramatically transform the professional militarism of the navy, let alone propel it in new radical directions, as in Germany. Far from being consumed by the threat of existential war, the U.S. Navy's wartime agendas remained circumscribed by a sense of distance from the big-power war in Europe, which, in fact, did not diminish with U.S. participation in 1917–18. At the same time, the new civilian politics of massive naval expansion and the sheer scale of wartime mobilization reassured the navy in its belief in the viability of American global power.

After World War I, both navies continued to move along different paths while remaining committed to their navalist projects. In the German case, wartime failure lent new urgency to the panic over the prospects of German global power that had first beset Wilhelmine navy leaders on the eve of war. In so doing, this failure fed an increasing fanaticism in pursuit of expanding goals by ever-more radical means. In the 1920s, the naval elite labored within a very restrictive environment in the wake of military defeat, regime change, and institutional diminishment. Despite the reduced roles and limited capabilities of their service, navy leaders never lost sight of their principal attachments to global power, elite rule, an integral nation, and a first-rate navy. When the navy finally managed to break free of its constraints, it entered a new path to war, imperial dominion, and militarization.[12] In the 1930s, the navy's leadership committed itself to the cause of a dictatorial regime that set out to create a united militant nation, harness military force, and respect professional expertise in pursuit of global empire. Firmly situated within the Nazi state and beholden to its promise of a militarized *Volksgemeinschaft* (people's community), the navy began to arm for and then willfully entered another big-power war to attain German global empire and what the navy's commander-in-chief, Admiral Erich Raeder, referred to in the fall of 1939 as a "final solution" of the "English question."[13] In so doing, the naval elite yoked their particular navalist commitments to the unfolding pursuit of genocidal war, racial empire, and unmitigated global power, which represented the radical end point of twentieth-century German bids for global empire and both the ambitions and panics sustaining them.

This trajectory contrasted sharply with the path along which the U.S. Navy moved after World War I. Much to the chagrin of antimilitarist critics like the venerable Charles Beard, the American naval elite clung tenaciously to the central tenets and practices of its navalist project in the interwar period. Resentful of the strictures of the international regime of arms control first established at the Washington Naval Conference in 1921–22, and dismayed by the limits imposed by civilian politics on the pursuit of an adequate level of maritime force, navy leaders navigated what they considered to be the limitations of the present. In so doing, they continually set the political realities and geostrategic challenges of the day against the promises of the nation's superior productive powers and the future possibility of global mastery, as they had before World War I.

The navy then took its long-standing navalist convictions into World War II and folded them into the larger U.S. pursuit of war and internationalist empire. While the service had already benefitted from a politics of naval expansion that had preceded U.S. entry into the war in December

1941, it was in the act of successful war-making and mobilization during the war itself that the U.S. Navy aligned its long-term aspirations with present-day realities (except, of course, in relation to the service's formal subordination to civilian authority). At the end of the war, navy leaders could claim to command the world's seas, and the United States had made itself into the world's preeminent global empire. In short, World War II reinforced the service's professional militarism. In contrast to the situation in Germany, navalism remained a viable proposition for the navy and a driving force of militarization in the second half of the twentieth century.

Notes

Introduction

1. Liebknecht, "Militarismus," 268.
2. Jefferson, *Men,* quotes: 6, 17, 5, 4, 9.
3. Conze, Stumpf, and Geyer, "Militarismus"; Berghahn, *Militarism*; Geyer, "Militarism"; and Stargardt, *Idea.*
4. Langer, *Diplomacy,* chapter 8, 415–44.
5. Kennedy, *Mastery*; Beeler, "Standard."
6. Geyer, "Militarism," 249.
7. Kennedy, *Powers,* 261.
8. On the notion of a "long" twentieth century, see Geyer and Bright, "World History"; Bright and Geyer, "Regimes"; Lang, "Globalization."
9. Osterhammel and Petersson, *Globalization*; Schroeder, "Politics"; Dülffer, "Mächtesystem."
10. I take the term "iron cage" from Max Weber, the German sociologist. A concise exposition of his views of the rise of bureaucratic machines and the military's contribution to it is Weber, "Parlament."
11. A starting point is McNeill, *Pursuit,* chapter 8.
12. One historian has written about the rise of an "armaments nationalism" in Imperial Germany: Berghahn, "Preparations."
13. Rüger, *Game*; Hart, *Fleet.*
14. Geyer and Bright, "Violence"; Förster and Nagler, *Road.*
15. Typical are Berghahn, *Rüstung*; Berghahn and Deist, *Rüstung*; and Epkenhans, "Outcome."
16. Boemeke, Chickering, and Förster, *Anticipating*; Sondhaus, *Warfare.*

17. Geyer and Bright, "History"; idem, "Violence"; Bright and Geyer, "World"; idem, "Regimes."

18. Mauch and Patel, *Wettlauf*; Fiebig-von Hase and Heideking, *Wege*.

19. The main studies of German-American confrontations over empire include Vagts, *Deutschland*; Herwig, *Politics*; Fiebig-von Hase, *Lateinamerika*; Schröder, *Confrontation*; Mitchell, *Danger*.

20. In other words, the militarism of naval elites was not the product of a self-enclosed military culture, or of a self-involved military technicism, in short, of the military's detrimental self-insulation from civilian society, politics, or statecraft. On notions of self-centered military culture and technicism, see Ritter, *Staatskunst*, and Hull, *Destruction*.

21. Bönker, "Aufrüstung"; Steinisch, "Path."

22. A classic example is Hintze, "Staatsverfassung."

23. Geyer, "Fictions"; Steinisch, "Path."

24. Welskopp, "Identität"; D. Rodgers, "Exceptionalism."

25. For a brilliant critique, see Geyer, "Militarization."

26. "Comparative analyses" of German militarism are still "a rare commodity," observes one recent survey of the literature: Wette, "Militarismus," 26.

27. Eley, "Army," 86. On "German militarism" as a master narrative, compare Kühne and Ziemann, "Militärgeschichte," and Maier, "War."

28. Geyer, *Aufrüstung*; idem, *Rüstungspolitik*; idem, "Strategy"; idem, "Past."

29. Vogel, *Nationen*; Becker, *Bilder*; idem, "Militarismus"; Rüger, *Game*.

30. Stevenson, *Armaments*; Herrmann, *Arming*.

31. Kuehne and Ziemann, "Militärgeschichte," 25.

32. Nipperdey, *Geschichte*, 250. For a most recent affirmation of this view, see Chickering, "Militarism."

33. Wehler, *Gesellschaftsgeschichte*; idem, "Revolution"; Kocka, "Ende," all insist on the continuing validity of the *Sonderweg* argument in relation to the imperial state and its military.

34. Horne and Kramer, *Atrocities*; Hull, *Destruction*; M. Anderson, "Way"; Cramer, "World." See also Roger Chickering's review of Hull, *Destruction*.

35. Geyer, "Space"; idem, "Germans"; Smith, "Sonderweg"; idem, *Continuities*.

36. Berghahn, *Tirpitz-Plan*; idem, *Rüstung*; idem, *Germany*; idem; and Berghahn and Deist, *Rüstung*.

37. Key contributions include Herwig, *Corps*; idem, *Politics*; idem, *Fleet*; Deist, *Flottenpolitik*; Lambi, *Navy*; Epkenhans, *Flottenrüstung*; idem, *Tirpitz*; Kelly, Tirpitz; and of course Paul Kennedy's work, such as "Strategieprobleme," "Development," and *Antagonism*. A superb guide to the literature is Bird, *History*.

38. Berghahn, *Tirpitz-Plan*, 424.

39. Berghahn, *Germany*, 53. Kehr, *Schlachtflottenbau*; idem, *Primat*; Wehler, *Bismarck*; idem, *Kaiserreich*.

40. Compare Funck, "Militär"; Geyer, "Geschichte."

41. Herwig, *Corps*; Bald, *Offizier*; Scheerer, *Marineoffiziere*; Bräckow, *Geschichte*; Sondhaus, "Spirit."

42. E.g., Nipperdey, *Geschichte*; Stürmer, "Flottenbau"; Hildebrand, *Reich*; Schöllgen, *Macht*.

43. Maier, "War," 546.

44. One important exception is Eley, "Sammlungspolitik," published in 1974. In this article, Eley challenged Berghahn's portrayal of Tirpitz as an agent of traditional elites by stressing his commitment to the industrial nation. But this important intervention was drowned out in subsequent controversies surrounding the domestic roots of Germany's naval policy. In this context

one should also note that Paul Kennedy has repeatedly suggested that historians take more seriously Tirpitz's radical nationalist and Social Darwinist commitments. His views are now summed up in Kennedy, "Levels."

45. On this scholarship, see Eley, "Introduction"; Dickinson, "Biopolitics"; Jefferies, *Empire*.

46. Hobson, *Imperialism*. By contrast, Rödel, *Krieger*, is less than helpful.

47. Schumpeter, "Soziologie"; Vagts, *Militarism*. In his new biography of Tirpitz, Patrick Kelly has accepted Hobson's interpretations, tying them to his portrayal of Tirpitz as a bureaucratic empire builder bereft of social imperialist inclinations. Kelly, *Tirpitz*.

48. John, "Institutions"; Katznelson, "Capacity"; Wilson, "Politics."

49. Sherry, *Shadow*. On the ever-increasing literature on U.S. militarization, see also Bönker, "History"; Kohn, "Danger."

50. E.g., Koistinen, *War*; Bristow, *Men*; Chambers, *Army*; Capozzola, *Uncle*; Schaffer, *America*; Keene, *Doughboy*.

51. E.g., McConnell, *Contentment*; Blight, *Race*; O'Leary, *Paradox*; Hoganson, *Fighting*.

52. Karsten, "Militarization," 30, 38, 43. For almost identical assessments, see Sherry, *Shadow*, 1–11; Kohn, "Danger," 182–90.

53. Typical is Koistinen, "Economy." For the older literature, see Sprout, *Rise*.

54. Galambos, "Synthesis"; idem, "Technology"; Balogh, "Synthesis."

55. Wilson, *Business*, quotes: 4, 208; idem, "Politics." Compare John, "Farewell."

56. An excellent guide to the literature is Higham, *Guide*.

57. E.g., Cooling, *Tracy*; idem, *Steel*; Shulman, *Navalism*; Trubowitz, *Interest*; Oyos, "Roosevelt." An outstanding study of civil-military relations in the context of foreign relations for the time period after 1898 is Challener, *Admirals*.

58. Karsten, *Aristocracy*; idem, "Progressives."

59. Karsten, *Aristocracy*, xiii.

60. Karsten, "Progressives," 259; idem, *Aristocracy*, 387, 353.

61. Williams, *Tragedy*; LaFeber, *Empire*; McCormick, *Market*.

62. Excellent surveys are Crapol, "Empire"; Rosenberg, "Interests"; Fry, "Imperialism."

63. E.g., Hagan, *Diplomacy*; Braisted, *Navy, 1897–1909*; idem, *Navy, 1909–1922*; Herrick, *Revolution*; Challener, *Admirals*.

64. See, for example, Hoganson, *Fighting*; Rosenberg, *Missionaries*; Kramer, *Blood*. An important cultural history of navalist thought is Stewart, "Gift."

65. Spector, *Professors*; Abrahamson, *America*. Compare Millet, "Professionalism"; Allin, *Institute*; Dorwart, *Office*; Stein, *Torpedoes*.

66. Typical are Livezey, *Mahan*; Herwig, "Influence"; Hobson, *Imperialism*, 165–89, 190–204, 223–27.

67. Dorwart, *Office*; Crumley, "System."

68. D. Rodgers, "Age," 260; compare idem, *Crossings*. An analysis of the "Atlantic crossings" that shaped the formation of U.S. navalism in the Progressive Era is Bönker, "Admiration."

69. For this phrase I have leaned in part on the editor's introduction, in Gillis, *Militarization*, 3.

70. Paulmann, "Vergleich"; Lingelbach, "Erträge"; Cohen and O'Connor, *Comparison*.

71. A major biography of Tirpitz is Kelly, *Tirpitz*. An excellent brief portrait is Epkenhans, *Tirpitz*. For biographical information, see also Tirpitz, *Erinnerungen*, and Hassel, *Tirpitz*.

72. Biographies of these figures are Spector, *Admiral* (Dewey); Seager, *Mahan*; Coletta, *Fiske*. There is no separate study of Rear-Admiral Taylor.

73. Conrad and Osterhammel, *Kaiserreich*; Conrad, *Globalisierung*; Geyer, "Germans"; Bender, *History*; Bender, *Nation*; Tyrell, *Nation*.

1. World Power in a Global Age

1. Melville, "Strength," 390.
2. Tirpitz, Notes for a presentation to the Emperor, 28 September 1899; BA-MA, RM 3/1.
3. A classic study is Gollwitzer, *Geschichte,* II: 23–82.
4. Adams, "War."
5. Görlitz, *Kaiser,* 37.
6. Chadwick, "Address," 263.
7. Mahan, "Outlook" (1897), 221.
8. Tirpitz, Draft for a Reichstag speech, March 1896; BA-MA, N 253/3.
9. Mahan, *Armaments,* 36–37.
10. E.g., Driggs, "Increase"; Peters, "Tendencies"; Howard, "Increase"; *Nauticus,* "Machtstellung"; idem, "Fortschritte."
11. Mahan, "Isthmus" (1897), 100.
12. Wainwright, "Power," 43.
13. August von Heeringen, "Notizen zum Immediatvortrag betreffend die Denkschrift über die Fortentwicklung der deutschen Seeinteressen seit 1896/97," 21 January 1900; BA-MA, RM 3/9632.
14. *Nauticus,* "Weltpolitik," 144, 143. Compare Halle, "Seeinteressen"; and idem, "Deutschland."
15. Heyking, *Tagebücher,* 185, about a conversation she had with Tirpitz in China on 3 August 1896. On this issue, compare *Nauticus,* "Auswanderung" and "Deutsche Auswanderung."
16. E.g., Ahlefeld to Tirpitz, 12 February 1898; BA-MA, N 253/19; Wainwright, "Power," 40–41; Hood, "Cable," 479–81.
17. Tirpitz, Notes for a speech before senior officers on 20 October 1899; BA-MA, RM 3/1.
18. Tirpitz, Notes for an audience with the Emperor, 28 September 1899, BA-MA, RM 3/1.
19. Tirpitz to Schmoller, 28 July 1897; quoted in Grimmer-Solem, "Socialism," 110. According to *Nauticus,* "Machtstellung," the German people had to decide whether their country was to join Russia, Britain, and the United States in becoming a primary force in global politics.
20. Neitzel, *Weltmacht.*
21. Halle, "Seeinteressen," 167. Other general assessments of France as a global empire are in *Nauticus,* "Weltreiche" and "Erstarken." See also Ratzel, "Mächte," esp. 936–39.
22. Such assessment was widely shared among the German elites: Hewitson, "France."
23. Canis, *Bismarck*; Winzen, *Weltmachtkonzept.*
24. Memorandum by Georg Alexander v. Müller from 1896 in Görlitz, *Kaiser,* 36–41.
25. *Nauticus,* "Machtstellung," 170; idem, "Weltpolitik," 137.
26. A classic study of the Yellow Peril is Gollwitzer, *Gefahr.*
27. Tirpitz to Amsler, 18 July 1897, BA-MA, N 253/166.
28. E.g., *Nauticus,* "Erstarken;" idem, "Chinesische Frage"; idem, "Erschliessung."
29. Hopman, Diary, 2 January 1905; compare his letters to his wife, 7 February and 25 April 1904; all in Epkenhans, *Leben.* A postwar analysis of the rise of Japanese power is Firle, "Entwicklung."
30. Retzmann to RMA, 8 April 1912; BA-MA, RM 3/2978. Compare Hebbinghaus to RMA, 12 November 1907 and 21 February 1908, BA-MA, RM 3/2978; and the analysis in *Nauticus,* "Rückblicke."
31. Mehnert, *Deutschland.*
32. Tirpitz to Hassel, 1902, in Hassel, *Tirpitz,* 172.

33. Tirpitz, Notes for an audience with the Emperor on 28 September 1899, BA-MA, RM 3/1.
34. Tirpitz to his daughter, 1903, in Hassel, *Tirpitz,* 223–24; *Nauticus,* "Weltreiche," 51.
35. *Nauticus,* "Weltpolitik," 141.
36. Tirpitz, Notes for the imperial audience on 28 September 1899, BA-MA, RM 3/1.
37. *Nauticus,* "Machtstellung," 167.
38. Dehio, "Ranke."
39. Tirpitz to Wilhelm II, 24 April 1898, BA-MA, N 253/39.
40. Ludwig Schröder, "Bedarf Deutschland einer Vergrösserung seines kolonialen Besitzstandes?" 21 April 1898; idem, "Braucht das Deutsche Reich Flottenstützpunkte?" 15 April 1903; BA-MA, RM 3/9625.
41. E.g., Neitzel, *Weltmacht.*
42. E.g., *Nauticus,* "Weltreiche"; idem, "Flotte"; idem, "Erstarken"; idem, "Weltpolitik."
43. Halle, "Hauptbeweber."
44. Tirpitz to Bülow, 10 November 1905; BA-MA, RM 3/4962.
45. "Stellungnahme der Vertreter des RMA in der Sitzung über das Staatsangehörigkeitsgesetz im Reichsamtes des Innern am 30.X.05," BA-MA, RM 3/4962.
46. Eley, "Empire." On the importance of the "population question" in German imperialist thinking, see Bade, *Fabri*; Smith, *Origins.*
47. Tirpitz, Memorandum, 3 January 1896, BA-MA, N 253/3; Maltzahn to Tirpitz, 28 August 1895; BA-MA, N 253/408.
48. Tirpitz, Memorandum, 3 January 1896, N 253/3. Compare *Nauticus,* "Auswanderung"; and idem, "Deutsche Auswanderung."
49. Tirpitz to Knorr, Fall 1896 (draft); Tirpitz to Knorr, 7 December 1896; BA-MA, N 253/45. In addition, see Tirpitz's letters from that time in Hassell, *Tirpitz,* 132–37.
50. By contrast, most historians of German *Weltpolitik* argue that it lacked a concrete objective, being either informed by a disposition for an "objectless expansion" (Joseph Schumpeter) or a vague desire to become a world power. E.g., Mommsen, *Grossmachtstellung*; Schöllgen, *Macht*; Hildebrand, *Reich.*
51. Schröder, "Braucht das Deutsche Reich Flottenstützpunkte?" 15 April 1903, BA-MA, RM 3/9625. For interest in China, see, for example: *Nauticus,* "Chinesische Frage"; idem, "Interessen;" idem, "Erschliessung;" idem, "Jahr." In 1904, Tirpitz argued that Germany had no interest in a Russo-Japanese war turning into a global conflict because "the English" would then take full possession of the Yangtze River. See Bülow to Holstein, 16 January 1904, in Rich and Fisher, *Papiere,* IV: 249–50.
52. Tirpitz to Miquel, February 1899. Quoted in Berghahn, "Zielen," 64.
53. Tirpitz, Notes for an imperial audience on 20 February 1899, BA-MA, N 253/4.
54. Herwig, "Admirals"; Epkhenhans, "Marine."
55. Hohenlohe-Schillingfürst, *Denkwürdigkeiten,* 497–98, recording a conversation with Tirpitz on 1 May 1899; Nowak and Thimme, *Erinnerungen,* 407; Halle, "Beziehungen."
56. Hopman, Diary, 23 October 1913; in Epkhenhans, *Leben,* 340.
57. Harald Dähnhardt, "In Welcher Richtung wird sich nach ehrenvollem Frieden die Weiterentwicklung unserer Flotte bewegen müssen?" BA-MA, RM 3/11624; Admiral Walter Freiherr von Keyserlingk, "Militärpolitische Richtlinien," 7 June 1918, BA-MA, N161/3.
58. E.g., Berghahn, *Tirpitz-Plan*; idem, *Germany*; Epkhenhans, *Flottenrüstung*; idem, *Tirpitz*; Herwig, *Fleet.*
59. Tirpitz, Notes for an imperial audience, 28 September 1899, BA-MA, RM 3/1.

60. Tirpitz to Crown Prince Wilhelm, 15 May 1909; BA-MA, N 253/8.
61. Gerhard Widenmann, "Die Weiterentwicklung der Marine," 1916; BA-MA, RM 3/10.
62. Such speculation is mentioned in Müller, Memorandum, 1896, in Görlitz, *Der Kaiser*, 36–41. On the naval elite's view of Britain, see chapter 2.
63. Müller, Memorandum, 1896; Hopman, Diary, 26 January 1901, 13 November 1907, 2 October 1911, 10 February 1912, in Epkenhans, *Leben*. On the genealogy of such thinking, see Fitzpatrick, *Imperialism*.
64. Graf Hohenthal und Bergen to the Secretary of the Saxonian Foreign Office, 2 November 1899, summarizing a conversation with Tirpitz from the same day; HSA Dresden, Ministerium für Auswärtige Angelegenheiten, File 4706. Compare the section on "Alliances and Political Power," in *Nauticus*, "Machtstellung," 170–74.
65. Tirpitz to Stosch, 13 February 1896; BA-MA, N 253/321. See also Tirpitz, Notes for an appearance before the Budget Commission of the Reichstag in 1900; BA-MA, N 253/19.
66. Tirpitz to Arnim, 30 November 1899, BA-MA, RM 3/2. Compare Admiral Senden's notes about the ideas of Vice-Admiral Valois from 1898, BA-MA, N 160/3.
67. See his conversation with the political plenipotentiary of Saxony, Graf Hohenthal und Bergen, on 13 December 1899, recorded in Hohenthal to the Secretary of the Saxonian Foreign Office, HSA Dresden, Ministerium für Auswärtige Angelegenheiten, File 4706.
68. Diederichs to Senden, 18 May 1898, BA-MA, N 160/7; Diederichs to Knorr, 19 and 29 October 1898 and 13 March 1899, BA-MA, RM 3/3156; Bendemann, "Die Defensive gegen England," 8 December 1899, including Diederichs's notes in the margins of this memorandum; BA-MA, RM 5/1603.
69. E.g., Hürter, *Hintze*.
70. Tirpitz, "Notizen zu einem Bericht über die Stellung Russlands in Ostasien," 26 October 1896, BA-MA, N 253/45; and his letters to his wife from summer and fall 1896, excerpted in Hassel, *Tirpitz*, 132–47.
71. Hohenlohe-Schillingfürst, *Denkwürdigkeiten*, 497–98, recording Tirpitz's views expressed in a conversation on 1 May 1899.
72. Tirpitz to Secretary of Foreign Office, Oswald von Richthofen, 1 November 1904, Notes about a top-level meeting chaired by Imperial Chancellor on 31 October 1904; both in BA-MA, RM 3/4. See also Tirpitz, *Erinnerungen*, 142–46.
73. Hopman, Diary, 10 and 12 February 1912, in Epkenhans, *Leben*.
74. For more on this, see the discussion in chapter 2.
75. Naval leaders favored the idea of a separate peace with Russia by late 1914. For example, see Hopman, Diary, 7 November, 10 November and 28 December 1914, in Epkenhans, *Leben*; Tirpitz, Notes about Conversation with Chief of the General Staff, 15 November 1915, and Tirpitz to Capelle, 16 November 1914, in Tirpitz, *Ohnmachtspolitik*, 166–69.
76. Tirpitz to Hopman, July 1914, in Berghahn and Deist, "Kaiserliche Marine," 45; Hopman, Diary, 11 July 1914, in Epkenhans, *Leben*.
77. Tirpitz to his daughter, 10 July 1900, in Hassel, *Tirpitz*, 222.
78. *Nauticus*, "Weltreiche," 64. For a similar emphasis, see idem, "Machtstellung, 173–74.
79. Rohrbach, *Deutschland*. Tirpitz sent copies of Rohrbach's 1903 book to several senior officers such as Admirals Bendemann and Müller who, in turn, were full of praise for it. Bendemann to Tirpitz, 18 December 1903, and Müller to Tirpitz, 11 December 1906; in BA-MA, N 253/16.
80. Trotha to Tirpitz, 24 April 1915; in Trotha, *Volkstum*, 33. For similar language, see, for example, Harald Dähnhardt, "In Welcher Richtung wird sich nach ehrenvollem Frieden die Weiterentwicklung unserer Flotte bewegen müssen?" BA-MA, RM 3/11624.

81. Challener, *Admirals,* esp. 12–44; Braisted, *Navy, 1897–1909;* idem, *Navy, 1909–1922.*
82. NWB to SN, 15–20 August 1898, Seager and Maguire, *Letters,* II: 582, 589.
83. Mahan, "Monroe Doctrine" (1908), 396–97. Compare idem, Retrospect" (1908).
84. Maurer, "Mahan"; Livezey, *Mahan.*
85. The key texts are Mahan, *Problem;* idem, "Considerations" (1902); idem, "Persian Gulf" (1902).
86. Mahan, *Interest, Conditions,* 69, 163.
87. Mahan, *Strategy,* 103.
88. Hood, "Doctrine," 665; Luce to Taylor, 7 December 1903; Taylor Papers, MD, LC.
89. Melville, *Future;* Hood, "Cable"; Mahan, *Problem.*
90. E.g., Wainwright, "Power"; Mitchell, "Trade."
91. In various essays, collected in *The Interest of America in Sea Power,* Mahan laid out this view in the 1890s. Compare C. H. Stockton, "The Inter-Oceanic Canal," Lecture, 23 July 1894, NWCA, RG 14; Crownshield, "Dream"; Melville, *Future.* So powerful was this particular view of the transformative promises of a transisthmian canal and U.S. regional interests that it was still shaping the discussions held among strategists about the impact of the imminent completion of the Panama Canal in the mid-1910s. See RC 1911 and 1912, Q 5, NCWA, RG; and the papers on the "Strategic Effects of the Completion and Fortification of the Panama Canal," in Long Course 1913–14, Class of January 1914, NWCA, RG 8, XSTZ.
92. NWB to SN, 15–20 August 1898, Seager and Maguire, *Letters,* II: 584.
93. Taylor to Moody, 14 December 1902; Moody Papers, LC, MD. See also Taylor, "Future."
94. GB, "Strategic Situation of the United States and its Possessions in the Atlantic," in "General Considerations and Data: Possible Plans of the Enemy," 19 October 1910; NA, RG 80, WP.
95. Yerxa, *Admirals;* Challener, *Admirals,* esp. 12–45.
96. James H. Oliver, "The Eastern Seas. A Brief Account of the Wars that Have Occurred in, and Their Causes," Lecture, 1902, NWCA, RG 14.
97. Compare LaFeber, "Note."
98. Mahan, *Influence, 1660–1783,* 82–87.
99. Stockton, "Comment."
100. NWB to SN, 15–20 August 1898, Seager and Maguire, *Letters,* II: 581–91.
101. Mahan, "Hawaii" (1897), quote: 47. On this issue, see also Hamilton, "Strategists," and Morgan, *Gibraltar,* 147–71.
102. On Dewey, see Palmer, *Eyes,* 110; Spector, *Admiral,* 83–100. On Mahan, see his letter to Lodge, 27 July 1898, in Seager and Maguire, *Letters and Papers,* II: 569; on the Naval War Board, see its report to SN, 15–20 August 1898, ibid., 582–83. It was the specter of a German colonial presence in the Philippines that clinched the issue of full-scale annexation.
103. See the discussion in chapters 2 and 3.
104. GB, Memorandum filed with letter to SN, 30 July 1915; NA, RG 80, SF 420-2.
105. On this approach, see Mahan, *Influence, 1660–1783,* 83–88; idem, "Looking" (1897); and Naval Policy Board, "Report."
106. Hagan, *Diplomacy;* Drake, *Empire;* M. Shulman, *Navalism,* 58–94.
107. Pre-1898 calls for naval predominance in the entire Pacific include Taylor, "Control"; C. H. Stockton, Strategic Features and Condition of the Southwestern Pacific with special attention to Australia, Lecture, 1895, NWCA, RG 8, XSTP.
108. GB, Memorandum filed with letter to SN, 30 July 1915; NA, RG 80, SF 420-2.
109. Planning Section Memorandum 21, 11 May 1918; NA, RG 80, GB, SF 420-6. On the importance of this memo, see Trask, *Captains.*

110. This imagery was invoked in every extensive discussion of the geopolitical-imperial scenery in either the official war plans or building program proposals drafted by the GB or the deliberations of the "summer conferences" at the NWC.

111. Black Plan, NA, RG 80, GB, WP.

112. Melville, *Future,* 33; Beehler, "Comment," 188.

113. French Ensor Chadwick, "Coal," Lecture, 1901, NWCA, RG 14. Compare Kelly, *Navy,* 9–12.

114. Fiske, "Power," 709, 712.

115. This is an important theme in the Planning Section Memorandum 21, 11 May 1918, NA, RG 80, GB, SF 420–6. On this entire issue see Safford, *Diplomacy.* For more, see the references in chapter 2 concerning expectations of future Anglo-American conflict that permeated the navy's planning discourse after 1914.

116. On this language, see Stephanson, *Destiny.*

117. Taylor, "Study," 189.

118. Luce, "Address," 541. Mahan, too, explicitly invoked the notion of the "westward course of empire": "Outlook" (1897), 269.

119. Strong, *Expansion.*

120. Adams, *Supremacy*; idem, *Empire*; idem, "War." For Taylor, see GB, Minutes, 4 December 190, NA, RG 80.

121. Mahan, *Problem,* 194.

122. Mahan to unidentified addressee, 29 May 1898, Seager and Maguire, *Letters,* II: 557–58.

123. Key texts are Mahan, "Outlook" (1897); idem, *Problem*; idem, *Interest, Conditions.* Compare Stewart, "Gift," 132–63.

124. Mahan, "Outlook" (1897), 243.

125. RRC on Q 16, RC 1909, NWCA, RG 12.

126. Chadwick, "Address," 267.

127. Beisner, *Diplomacy.*

2. Big-Power Confrontations over Empire

1. Otto von Diederichs, "Krieg Deutschlands mit den Vereinigten Staaten von Nordamerika," 22 January 1900, BA-MA, RM 3/6657; Tirpitz to Hassel, 1902; in Hassel, *Tirpitz,* 172.

2. John Morris Endicott, "Sea Power of Germany," 1900; NWCA, RG 14.

3. Knepper, "Leagues," 351.

4. Henry C. Taylor, "Memorandum," 31 May 1904. NA, RG 225, JB, SF 325.

5. GB to SN, 28 September 1906, NA, RG 80, SF 438.

6. Quoted in Clifford, "Dewey," 216. Theodore Roosevelt, the well-connected former Assistant Secretary of the Navy, wrote in 1899 that the navy was a "unit in wanting to smash Germany." Roosevelt to Spring, 11 August 1899, in Morison, *Letters,* II: 1050.

7. J. M. Barber to Bureau of Navigation, 23 January 1899, NA, RG 38, Entry 189.

8. GB, Memorandum enclosed in letter to NWC, 30 July 1903; NA, RG 80, SF 425.

9. Black Plan, NA, RG 80, GB, WP. Compare, for example, French Ensor Chadwick, "Coal," Lecture, 1901, NWCA, RG 14; RC 1907, Q 19, RC 1909, Q 16, both in NWCA, RG 12; and GB, "Possible War Situations in the Atlantic," 19 October 1910, NA, RG 80, SF 425.

10. Dewey's own account is in his *Autobiography,* 252–67; see also Sargent, *Dewey.*

11. E.g., Office, *Notes*; and the correspondence and memos relating to Germany in NA, RG 80, General Correspondence 1897–1914, SF 4581; and NA, RG 38, ONI, Entry 102, Memoranda of Information.

12. See "War with Germany," 1897, NWCA, RG 8, UNOpB. Compare Crowninshield to SN, 28 February 1898, NA, RG 80, GB, SF 414–3.

13. Mahan to Thursfield, 1 December 1897, Seager and Maguire, *Letters,* II: 529–30; compare his "Fallacies" (1899).

14. Compare Baecker, "Feindbild"; Costello, "Planning," 128–54.

15. The key text is Mahan, *Problem.* See also various essays in idem, *Retrospect.*

16. Mahan, *Problem,* 201–2; idem, "Monroe" (1908).

17. Luce to Taylor, 7 December 1903; Taylor Papers, MD, LC.

18. Answer of the First Committee to Question 10, August 16, 1910, RC 1910, Part III; NWCA, RG 12.

19. Final Action of the Conference on Question 10 (September 26, 1910), RC 1910, Part III; NWCA, RG 12. Other critiques of anti-German alarmism include Commander C. S. Williams, Memorandum, 16 March 1910, NA, RG 80, GB, SF 420–1; Minority Report of Reconciling Committee on Q 16, RC 1909, QQA, NWCA, RG 12; Rear-Admiral S. A. Staunton, Memorandum, 16 April 1912, NA, RG 80, GB, SF 420–1. On the improbability of German action in the present, see also GB, "Possible War Situations in the Atlantic," 19 October 1910; NA, RG 80, SF 425.

20. E.g., GB to SN, 17 November 1910 and 26 June 1912, NA, RG 80, SF 420–1.

21. Mahan, *Interest of America*; idem, *Armaments.* Compare Baecker, "Mahan."

22. The GB completed its first official plan for a war with Germany in 1913. In 1912 and 1913 the Naval War College devoted itself to the study of a war, and its officer classes stressed the reality of the German threat. Strikingly, the 1912 Prize Essay of the Naval Institute struck the same chord: Hunt, "Might."

23. On this, see the discussion in chapter 3.

24. GB to SN, 1 August 1914; NA, RG 80, SF 420–1.

25. GB, Memorandum file with letter to SN, 30 July 1915; NA, RG 80, SF 420–2.

26. Fiske, *Midshipman,* 546–48, 629, 636. A key planning document raised the possibility of German victory in May 1918. Planning Section Memorandum 21, 11 May 1918, NA, RG 80, GB, SF 420–6.

27. Braisted, *Navy, 1897–1909,* 115–90; Challener, *Admirals,* 179–224.

28. GB, Minutes, 8 May 1903, NA, RG 80. For assessments by other officers, see the Minutes for 28–29 May 1902, 7 May 1903. Compare Braisted, *Navy, 1897–1909,* 115–16, 136–53.

29. Sperry to unidentified admiral, 3 November 1901. Compare Sperry to Harris, 8 January 1901, 21 June 1901, and 28 October 1901; Sperry to Allen, 2 August 1902; Sperry to unknown, 23 August 1902; all in Sperry Papers, LC, MD.

30. James H. Oliver, "The Eastern Seas. A Brief Account of the Wars that Have Occurred in, and Their Causes," Lecture, 1902, NWCA, RG 14. For other more extended analyses, see GB, Minutes, 28–29 May 1902 and 7–8 May 1903. NA, RG 80.

31. Folger to Taylor, 10 February 1904; Taylor Papers, LC, MD. Compare GB, Minutes 25 May 1904, NA, RG 80; Henry C. Taylor, "Memorandum," 31 May 1904, NA, RG 225, JB, SF 325.

32. The NWC studied a war in the Far East in 1902: "Problems and Solutions 1902," NWCA, RG 12. See also Rear-Admiral Rodgers to GB, 13 May 1901, and the Memorandum that the board drafted in response, NA, RG 80, GB, SF 425–2. For an embrace of the Anglo-Japanese alliance, see Sperry to Charles Sperry, 9 October 1905; Sperry Papers, LC, MD.

33. French Ensor Chadwick, "Coal," Lecture, 1901, NWCA, RG 14; idem, "Address." For racialization in the context of the Russo-Japanese War, see Doenhoff, *McCully.*

34. The key texts are Mahan, *Problem*; idem, "Considerations" (1902), and "Persian Gulf" (1902).

35. Mahan to Maxse, 7 March 1902; Seager and Maguire, *Letters,* III: 12–13, 13; Mahan, *Problem,* 114.

36. Mahan, *Problem,* xix.

37. Quoted in Braisted, *Navy, 1897–1909,* 221.

38. Braisted, *Navy, 1897–1909,* 191–239; idem, *Navy, 1909–1922*; Challener, *Admirals,* 225–64, 270–87, 367–79. On the "world cruise," compare Reckner, *Fleet.*

39. RRC on Q 17, RC 1909, QQA; NWCA, RG 12.

40. NWC, "Strategic Plan of Campaign against Orange," 15 March 1911, NA, RG 80, GB, WP.

41. RC 1907, QGA, Q 19; NWC RG 12.

42. Fiske to SN, 14 May 1913, in Cronon, *Diaries,* 61.

43. GB, "Orange War Plan, Strategic Section," 13 March 1914; NA, RG 80, WP.

44. Barker to SN, 30 August 1897, NA, RG 45, SF U.S. Navy 1775–1910, entry 455; Goodrich to Roosevelt, 23 June 1897, NWCA, RG 8, XSTP; Crowninshield, "Dream"; Belknap, "Aspects," 283–84.

45. John M. Ellicott, "Sea Power of Japan," 1901, NWCA, RG 8, SF JN; idem, "The Strategic features of the Philippine Islands, Hawaii and Guam," 14 June 1900, NWCA, RG 8, XSTP; H.C. Taylor, "Memorandum," 31 May 1904, NA, RG 225, JB, SF 325. On Ellicott, see also Rivera, "Stick," 131–38.

46. NWC, "Strategic Plan of Campaign against Orange," 15 March 1911, NA, RG 80, GB, WP.

47. Fiske to SN, 14 May 1913, Cronon, *Diaries,* 61.

48. E.g., Mahan, "Value" (1908); Rear Admiral Charles S. Sperry, "The Cruise of the United States Atlantic Fleet," Sperry Papers, LC, MD; RC 1911 and 1912, Part I, Q 5; Class of January 1914, "Discussion of Strategic Effects of the Completion and Fortification of the Panama Canal," NWCA, RG 8, XSTX.

49. Barker to SN, 30 August 1897, NA, RG 45, SF U.S. Navy 1775–1910, entry 455; Goodrich to Roosevelt, 23 June 1897, NWCA, RG 8, XSTP.

50. GB to SN, 28 September 1910 (enclosed memorandum); compare GB to SN, "Building Program, 1913–1917," 25 September 1910; both in NA, RG 80, SF 420-2. For a wartime articulation of this fear, see ONI, Notes on the Japanese Question, March 1916, NA, RG 45.

51. Sperry to Strauss, "Control of the Pacific," 4 February 1907 (quotes), and his entire personal correspondence from 1907 to 1909. On Sperry's dismissal of the war-mongering peers, see his letter to his wife, 1 November 1908, and to his son, 9 January 1909. LC, MD, Sperry Papers.

52. GB, Minutes 15 and 17 June 1907, NA, RG 80; JB, Minutes 18 June 1907, NA, RG 225. According to Sperry, Rear-Admirals Wainwright and Evans believed a "row" with Japan to be "imminent." Sperry to his wife, 1 November 1909. LC, MD, Sperry Papers.

53. Dewey to Brownson, 15 January 1907, Dewey Papers, MD, LC; Sperry to Strauss, 4 February 1907, Sperry Papers, MD, LC; Brownson to Roosevelt, July 30, 1907, Roosevelt Papers, MD, LC; NWC, RC 1907, QGA, Q 19. For the naval intelligence officers, see Braisted, *Navy, 1897–1909,* 194–95, 198–99, 214–15. Compare Challener, *Admirals,* 243–64.

54. E.g., GB, Memoranda, 30 June and 25 September 1912; NA, RG 80, SF 420-2. On the War Scare of 1913, see the section on "American Insecurities" in chapter 3.

55. E.g., NWC, RC 1907, QGA, Q 19; RC 1909, QGA, CR, Q 16 and 17; RC 1910, Part I, CR on Q 10; RC 1911, Committee Solution to Q 1, Part I; RC 1912, CR on Q 1 and 4, Part I. NWCA, RG 12.

56. L. A. Cotten, "Far Eastern Conditions from the Naval Point of View," February 1915, NWCA, RG 8, XSTP; Strategic 35. Class of January 1915, Problem III, Discussion; Class of

January 1916, Problem III, Strategic 35, Modification 2, Discussion, NWCA, RG 4. Significantly, "racial antagonism" and "Asiatic exclusion" did not feature prominently in the two most prominent policy papers authored by naval strategists between 1915 and 1918. GB, Memorandum filed with letter to SN, 30 July 1915, NA, RG 80, SF 420–2; Planning Section Memorandum 21, 11 May 1918, NA, RG 80, GB, SF 420–6.

57. RC 1912, Part I, Q 1, First CR, NWCA, RG 12.

58. E.g., the various papers on "The Strategy of the Pacific" from 1915 in NWCA, RG 8, XSTP; and ONI, "Foreign Policies and Relations Affecting the United States, 20 January 1916," NWCA, RG 8, UR.

59. Fiske to SN, May 14, 1913, in Cronon, *Diaries*, 60, 63. Compare John M. Ellicott, "Sea Power of Japan," 1901; NWCA, RG 8, JN.

60. GB, Memorandum, filed with letter to SN, 30 July 1915; NA, RG 80, SF 420–2. Planners continued to prepare for a war with Japan. See, e.g., GB, War Plan, 15 January 1917, NA, RG 80, SF 425; Class of January 1915, 1916, and 1917, Problem III, Strategic 35, NWCA, RG 4.

61. Planning Section Memorandum 21, 11 May 1918, NA, RG 80, GB, SF 420–6.

62. Braisted, *Navy, 1897–1909*, 153–70, 289–309; Schilling, "Admirals," 70–75.

63. GB, Memorandum, filed with letter to SN, 30 July 1915; NA, RG 80, SF 420–2.

64. On the anti-British orientation, compare Berghahn, *Tirpitz-Plan*, esp. 173–201.

65. On the crisis in 1896, see Lambi, *Navy*, 113–18. On Tirpitz, see Tirpitz, Memorandum, 3 January 1896, idem, Notes for a presentation to the Emperor on 28 January 1896, BA-MA, N 253/3; Tirpitz to Stosch, 13 February 1896; Tirpitz to Senden, 20 January 1897, BA-MA, N 160/5.

66. Tirpitz, "Allgemeine Gesichtspunkte bei der Feststellung unsere Flotte nach Schiffsklassen und Schiffstypen," July 1897, BA-MA, N 253/4.

67. Albert Hopman, "Beantwortung der Fragen betreffend die Weiterentwicklung der Marine," 7 July 1916, BA-MA, RM 3/ 10.

68. Capelle to Tirpitz, 14 September 1911; BA-MA, N 253/25.

69. Notes by Tirpitz for a statement before the Appropriation Committee of the Reichstag, winter 1899–1900, BA-MA, N 253/19.

70. Capelle to Tirpitz, 7 August 1897, BA-MA, N 253/4.

71. Tirpitz to Knorr, Fall 1896 (draft) and 7 December 1896; BA-MA, N 253/45.

72. On Anglo-German relations, see Kennedy, *Antagonism*.

73. RMA, "Die Sicherung Deutschlands gegen einen englischen Angriff," February 1900, BA-MA, RM 3/6657.

74. RMA, "Motive für die Novelle von 1905," 1905, BA-MA, RM 3/29; Tirpitz to Bülow, 8 November 1905, BA-MA, N 253/6.

75. Wilhelm Büchsel, "Aufzeichnung," 20 November 1904, BA-MA, N 168/8; Waldemar Vollerthun, "Politische und militärische Betrachtungen über einen englisch-deutschen Krieg," 27 November 1904; Felix Bendemann, "Gedanken über die augenblickliche kritische Lage," 3 December 1904, both in BA-MA, N 253/21; August von Heeringen, "Schlußvotum des Vorsitzendens der R-Kommission," 14 December 1904; Wilhelm Büchsel, "Denkschrift über die Kriegführung gegen England 1905," both in BA-MA, RM 3/4. Compare Lambi, *Navy*, 241–68.

76. Philip Dumas, Germany N.A. Report 28/06, in Seligman, *Intelligence*, 14.

77. Diederichs to Senden, 18 May 1898; BA-MA, N 160/7.

78. Steinberg, "Complex."

79. Tirpitz to Stosch, 13 February 1896; BA-MA, N 253/321. Stosch, in turn, had used an almost identical phrase in his letter to Tirpitz from 2 February 1895, in Hassel, *Tirpitz*, 105–6.

80. Felix Bendemann, "Die Defensive gegen England," 8 December 1899; BA-MA RM5/1607. A general assessment of British Empire in history is *Nauticus*, "Entwicklung"; on protectionism, see also Halle, "Phase."

81. Hopman, Diary, 10 May 1912, in Epkenhans, *Leben*.

82. Compare Fiebig-von Hase, *Lateinamerika*, 385–506, and Herwig, *Politics*; idem, *Vision*.

83. Harald Dähnhardt, Memorandum, 2 November 1903, BA-MA, RM 3/6663. Compare Ludwig Schröder, "Braucht das deutsche Reich Flottenstützpunke im Ausland?" 15 April 1903; BA-MA, RM 5/5956.

84. Tirpitz, Notes for an imperial audience on 28 September 1899, BA-MA, RM 3/1.

85. Bülow, Notes about the secret meeting of the Reichstag's Appropriation Committee on 27 March 1900, BA. Koblenz, Bülow Papers, 24; Jagemann to Brauer, 20 December 1899, summarizing a conversation with Tirpitz from the previous day, in Fuchs, *Friedrich*, IV: 213–14.

86. On such considerations, see Halle, "Bedeutung"; idem, "Hauptbeweber."

87. E.g., Otto von Diederichs, "Krieg Deutschlands mit den Vereinigten Staaten von Nordamerika," 22 January 1900, BA-MA, RM 3/6657; Ludwig Schröder, "Braucht das deutsche Reich Flottenstützpunke im Ausland?" 15 April 1903, BA-MA, RM 5/5956; and the note of a German diplomat about a conversation with Tirpitz on 16 March 1898, in Bülow, *Denkwürdigkeiten*, I: 188–189. A discussion of German-American conflict in East Asia is in Admiralty Staff, Memorandum prepared for an imperial audience of the staff's chief, October 1902, BA-MA, RM 5/5960.

88. Ludwig Schröder, "Braucht das deutsche Reich Flottenstützpunke im Ausland?" 15 April 1903; BA-MA, RM 5/5956.

89. "O-Plan III," 21 March 1903, BA-MA, RM 5/5960.

90. Büchsel, Notes for presentation to the Emperor on 21 March 1903, "O-Plan III," 21 March 1903, both BA-MA, RM 5/5960; and Tirpitz, "Entwicklung unseres Großen Kreuzers," 29 January 1904, BA-MA, N 253/20.

91. Bendemann, "Die Defensive gegen England," 8 December 1899, BA-MA RM 5/1603. See also Diederichs to Senden, 18 May 1898, BA-MA, N 160/7; Diederichs to Knorr, 19 and 29 October 1898 and 13 March 1899, BA-MA, RM 3/3156.

92. Vagts, *Deutschland*, 1578.

93. Compare Fiebig-von Hase, "USA."

94. Bernhardi, *Denkwürdigkeiten*, 313. A plea for a "defensive military alliance" with the United States is in Waldemar Vollerthun, "Politische und militärische Betrachtungen über einen englisch-deutschen Krieg," 27 November 1904, BA-MA, N 253/21.

95. Mehnert, *Deutschland*, 234–35, 238, 242, 293. A version of this interview is printed in Tirpitz, *Ohnmachtspolitik*, 623–27.

96. Tirpitz, Notes about a conversation with the Chancellor, 8 August 1915, in idem, *Ohnmachtspolitik*, 398–400; Holtzendorff to Jagow, 11 December 1915, in Scherer and Grunewald, *L'Allemagne*, I: 237–38. Compare Mehnert, *Deutschland*, 296–318.

97. Tirpitz, Memorandum, 2 January 1916; Tirpitz to Wilhelm II, 27 April 1916; Tirpitz to Graf Hertling, March 1916; in Tirpitz, *Ohnmachtspolitik*, 450–55, 539–34, 514–17.

98. Quoted in Mehnert, *Deutschland*, 298. Compare Tirpitz, "Die Bedeutung Belgiens und seiner Häfen für unsere Seegeltung," 17 October 1915, BA-MA, N 253/231.

99. Tirpitz, Notes for an audience with the Emperor on 15 June, 1897; BA-MA, N 253/4. On the Naval Scare of 1909, see Seligmann, "Information," and the summary in O'Brien, *Power*, 73–98.

100. E.g., Tirpitz to Bülow 20 April 1907, Enclosure, *GP* 24; Müller to Tirpitz, 23 April 1908, in Tirpitz, *Aufbau*, 66; Capelle, Memorandum, 1 June 1909, BA-MA, N 253/54; Tirpitz,

Notes for an Imperial Presentation, 26 September 1911, BA-MA, N 253/25a; Widenmann to Tirpitz, 7 March 1912, *GP* 31.

101. Tirpitz to Bülow, 22 November, 25 November 1908, and 17 December 1908, and his remarks during a meeting with the Imperial Chancellor on 3 June 1909, *GP* 28.

102. E.g., Tirpitz to Müller, 6 May 1909, Tirpitz, *Aufbau*, 150–52; Widenmann to Tirpitz, 11 May 1909, Tirpitz, *Aufbau*, 153–55; Capelle, Memorandum, 1 June 1909, BA-MA, N 253/54. On this issue, see also the discussion in Epkenhans, *Flottenrüstung*, 50–51.

103. Coerper to Tirpitz, 14 March 1907, in Giessler, *Institution*, 283–84. On Coerper, see ibid., 137–50.

104. Tirpitz to Bethmann-Hollweg, Enclosure II, 25 August 1910, *GP* 28.

105. Hopman, Diary, 24–30 November 1913, in Epkenhans, *Leben*.

106. Tirpitz, "Notes," St. Blasien, Summer 1908; BA-MA, RM 3/8.

107. Tirpitz to Bülow, 4 February, 1909, *GP* 28.

108. Widenmann to Tirpitz, 28 October and 30 October 1911, *GP* 31; Heeringen to Bethmann-Hollweg, 7 December 1911, Tirpitz, *Aufbau*, 220–21; Hopman, Diary, 31 December 1911, in Epkenhans, *Leben*. On the Anglo-French Entente as an anti-German "offensive alliance," see also Tirpitz to Bethmann-Hollweg, 7 October 1911, BA-MA, RM 2/1764; Tirpitz to Müller, 8 February 1912, in Tirpitz, *Aufbau*, 282; Hopman, Diary, 10 January 1913, in Epkenhans, *Leben*.

109. Müller to Tirpitz, 18 February and 9 June 1914, in *GP* 31, and Tirpitz, *Aufbau*, 425–26.

110. E.g., Widenmann to Tirpitz, 2 March 1912, Widenmann to Wilhelm II, 28 July 1912, in Tirpitz, *Aufbau*, 311–13, 350–53; and his letters to Tirpitz, from February and March 1912, in *GP* 31.

111. E.g., Tirpitz to Bülow, 22 November 1908 and 4 January 1909, Tirpitz to Bethmann-Hollweg, 19 August 1909, *GP* 28; Tirpitz to Müller, 6 May 1909, Widenmann to Tirpitz, 11 May 1909 and 14 July 1910, Tirpitz, *Aufbau*, 139, 153–55, 178.

112. E.g., Tirpitz to Bülow, 20 January and 4 February 1909, Minutes of a Meeting in the Imperial Chancellory on 3 June 1909, *GP* 28; Tirpitz's letters from March and April 1909, in Tirpitz, "Flottenverständigung"; Tirpitz to Müller, 6 May 1909 and 25 July 1910, in Tirpitz, *Aufbau*, 150–52, 176; Tirpitz to Bethmann-Hollweg, 1 September 1909 and 4 November 1909, *GP* 28; Tirpitz, "Niederschrift über Unterredung mit Haldane am 9 February 1912," *GP* 31; Tirpitz to Chief of Naval Cabinet, 8 and 25 February 1912, Tirpitz, *Aufbau*, 284, 299–300; Müller, Diary Entries for January and February 1912, in Görlitz, *Kaiser*, 109–16.

113. Widenmann to Tirpitz, 2 March 1912, in Tirpitz, *Aufbau*, 311–313, 312. Compare Widenmann to Tirpitz, 19 March 1912, *GP* 31; various letter of his successor as attaché, in Tirpitz, *Aufbau*, 355–56; 400–404, 425–26; Hopman, Diary, 10 May 1912, 8 January, and 24–30 November 1913, and his letter to Rheinbaben, 10 January 1913, in Epkenhans, *Leben*.

114. E.g., Hopman to Müller, 11 June 1913, in Tirpitz, *Aufbau*, 395–97; Hopman, Diary, 7 and 11 June, 19 and 21 October 1913, in Epkenhans, *Leben*; Tirpitz, Notes for an imperial audience on 22 February, 1913, Capelle, "Notizen ü die Kieler Reise," 1913, both in BA-MA, N 253/28.

115. Hopman, Diary 4 May and 23 May 1914, in Epkenhans, *Leben*. On this episode, compare Epkenhans, *Flottenrüstung*, 363–64.

116. E.g., Widenmann to Tirpitz, 13 November 1908, *GP* 28; Tirpitz, Notes, St. Blasien, 1908, BA-MA, RM 3/8; Tirpitz to Bülow, 28 February 1907, in *GP* 23; Tirpitz to Bülow, 20 April 1907, Enclosure, *GP* 24.

117. E.g., Tirpitz, Notes about a Conversation with the British naval attaché in Berlin, 28 March 1909, and Widenmann to Tirpitz, 29 April 1910, in Tirpitz, "Flottenverständigung," 101–2, 111–14. On Tirpitz and the "acceleration crisis" see also Kelly, *Tirpitz*, 299–306.

118. Capelle, Memorandum, October 1912, BA-MA, N 253/25b; idem, "Notizen für die Kieler Reise," 1913, BA-MA, N 253/28
119. Von Krosigk, "Denkschrift über Immediatvortrag über die Reichsverteidigungspolitik Englands und seiner Kolonien," 8 January 1914; BA-MA, RM 3/2720. See also the many letters by the service attaché in London on this issue in *GP* 39 and Tirpitz, *Aufbau*.
120. E.g., Capelle, Notes, October 1912, BA-MA, N 253/25; idem, "Notizen für die Kieler Reise," 1913, BA-MA, N 253/28; Müller to Tirpitz, 18 February 1914, *GP* 39.
121. Tirpitz, "Notes," St. Blasien, Summer 1908, BA-MA, RM 3/8.
122. Capelle, Notes, October 1912, BA-MA, N 253/25.
123. Müller, Diary, 29 June 1908, BA-MA, N 159/3.
124. Tirpitz, Comments on a letter by Bülow, which dated from 25 December 1908; BA-MA, N 253/24. Compare Epkenhans, *Flottenrüstung*, 40–41.
125. Holtzendorff to Tirpitz, 25 October 1911, BA-MA N 253/25; Heeringen to Tirpitz, 6 December 1911, BA-MA, RM 3/6678; Tirpitz, Addendum to his notes for an imperial audience on 26 September 1911, BA-MA, RM 3/1; Müller, Note, 12 September 1911, and Diary, 13 September 1911, BA-MA, N 159/4. For the persistence of such fears, see Lambi, *Navy*, 375–84.
126. Tirpitz to Bülow, 4 January 1909, *GP* 28; Widenmann to Tirpitz, 11 May 1909, Tirpitz, *Aufbau*, 153–55; Tirpitz to Eisendecher, 25 November 1912, BA-MA, N 253/16.
127. E.g., Tirpitz to Bülow, 20 April 1907, Enclosure, *GP* 24; Widenmann to Tirpitz, 11 May 1909, Tirpitz, *Aufbau*, 153–55; Müller to Tirpitz, 14 March 1913, Tirpitz, *Aufbau*, 381–84.
128. Tirpitz, Notes, St. Blasien, Summer 1908; BA-MA, RM 3/8.
129. Hopman, Diary, 10 and 12 February 1912, in Epkenhans, *Leben*. Compare, Tirpitz, Notes before and after the meeting with Haldane, Tirpitz, *Aufbau*, 284, and *GP* 31.
130. Capelle, Notes, October 1912, BA-MA, N 253/25b. Compare Hopman, Diary, 26 February 1912, Hopman to Rheinbaben, 10 January 1913 in Epkenhans, *Leben*; and various letters by Widenmann from spring 1912, printed in *GP* 31, and Tirpitz, *Aufbau*.
131. Capelle, Notes, October 1912, BA-MA, N 253/25b; Hopman, Diary, 24–30 November 1913, in Epkenhans, *Leben*.
132. On the navy's demands for a "true" agreement with Britain, see Tirpitz, Notes for his Conversation with Haldane on 9 February 1912, Tirpitz to Müller, 8 and 25 February 1912, in Tirpitz, *Aufbau*, 282, 284, 299–300; Capelle, Notes, October 1912 ("Societas Leonina"), BA-MA, N 253/25b; Tirpitz to Eisendecher, 25 November 1912, BA-MA, N 253/16; Müller, Diary, 10–16 March 1912, in Görlitz, *Kaiser*, 117–18.
133. Tirpitz to Pohl and Müller, 25 January 1915, in Tirpitz, *Ohnmachtspolitik*, 198–200, 198–99.
134. Harald Dähnhardt, "In Welcher Richtung wird sich nach ehrenvollem Frieden die Weiterentwicklung unserer Flotte bewegen müssen?" BA-MA, RM 3/11624.
135. Hopman, Diary, 29 and 30 July 1914, in Epkenhans, *Leben*. On the navy in the July crisis, compare Epkenhans, *Flottenrüstung*, 400–407, and Lambi, *Navy*, 416–24.
136. Tirpitz, Notes, 1 August 1914, in Tirpitz, *Ohnmachtspolitik*, 16–18.
137. Tirpitz, Notes about a meeting on 18 December 1912, BA-MA, N 253/28.
138. Hopman, Diary, 11 June 1914, in Epkenhans, *Leben*. A month later Tirpitz suggested that any Anglo-German entente would lead to inevitable war with Russia. Tirpitz to Hopman, July 1914, in Berghahn and Deist, "Kaiserliche Marine," 45; Hopman, Diary, 11 July 1914, in Epkenhans, *Leben*.
139. Tirpitz, "Die Bedeutung Belgiens und seiner Häfen für unsere Seegeltung," 17 October 1915, BA-MA, N 253/231.

140. This can be traced in Tirpitz, *Ohnmachtspolitik*; Granier, *Seekriegsleitung*.
141. GB, Memorandum filed with letter to SN, 30 July 1915; NA, RG 80, SF 420-2.
142. Austin M. Knight, "Are Large Armaments Provocative of War?" Presentation at the Mohonk Conference, 17 May 1916; NWCA, RG 14. See also idem, memorandum, 28 July 1915, NA, RG 80, GB, SF 420-2.
143. Huse to Commander-in-Chief of the U.S. Atlantic Fleet, 10 February 1915. LC, MD, Daniels Papers. See also Schilling, "Admirals," 59. According to ret. Rear-Admiral Chadwick, the British Empire was the real driving force behind the war. Coletta, *Chadwick,* 151–72; and the admiral's letters and writings from that period in Chadwick, *Letters*.
144. American Naval Planning Section, Memorandum 65, "United States Naval Interests in the Armistice Terms," 4 November 1918; in NA, RG 45, VA.
145. Huse to Commander-in-Chief of the U.S. Atlantic Fleet, 10 February 1915. LC, MD, Daniels Papers. See also Schilling, "Admirals," 59.
146. GB, Memorandum filed with letter to SN, 30 July 1915, NA, RG 80, SF 420-2.
147. Planning Section, Memorandum 65: "United States Naval Interests in the Armistice Terms," 4 November 1918. NA, RG 45, SF, VA.
148. See the materials in NA, RG 80, GB, SF 434, including "Spring Exercise for the Atlantic Fleet," 13 March 1915; "Strategic Maneuvers for Department and Fleet," 19 August 1915; and "Strategic Maneuver #3," 9 October 1916. On this, compare O'Brien, *Power,* 121.
149. Morison, *Sims*; Wheeler, *Pratt*.
150. Crapol, "Anglophobia." On considerations of a war with Britain in the 1890s, see Spector, *Professors,* 86–89, 95, 104.
151. Taylor, "Future," 6.
152. Report of a Special Committee on Tactics, and the Strength and Composition of the Fleet, 21 September 1904, RC 1904, Part III, NWCA, RG 12; RRC on Q 16, QGA, RC 1909; Answer of the 2nd Committee to Q 10, August 18, 1910, RC 1910, Part III; all in NWCA, RG 12.
153. See my discussion of Russia as an imperial opponent in the Far East in this chapter's section on "Conflict over Empire in the Far East."
154. Mahan, *Interest of America*.
155. This is a key theme in Mahan, *Interest of America*. Compare Mahan, *Strategy,* 109–12. Major Earle H. Ellis, Lecture on Naval Bases, 1913; NWCA, RG 4.
156. Anderson, *Race*; Kramer, "Empires."
157. Typical are Herbert C. Stockton, "The Sea Power and Position of Great Britain," 21 July 1894, also read in 1898 and 1900, NWCA, RG 14; GB, "Possible War Situation in the Atlantic," 19 October 1910, NA, RG 80, SF 425; Sperry to his wife, 16 September 1908, Sperry Papers, LC, MD ("ties of blood").
158. Mahan, "Possibilities" (1907), 108–9; idem, *Problem,* 192.
159. Herbert C. Stockton, "The Sea Power and Position of Great Britain," 21 July 1894, also read in 1898 and 1900; NWCA, RG 14.
160. For example, RRC on Q 16, RC 1909; Answer of the Second Committee to Q 10, 18 August 1910, RC 1910, Part III. NWCA, RG 12.
161. H. S. Knapp, "War Between the United States and Japan. The Possibility of Great Britain Becoming Japan's Ally," 19 January 1907; idem, "Memorandum," 31 January 1907; NWCA, RG 8, XSTP.
162. Black Plan, NA, RG 80, GB, WP. Compare Albert P. Niblack, "Noticeable Tendency of Improved Relations between England and Germany, involving possibly the Monroe Doctrine," 15 April 1913; NA, RG 38, ONI, Naval Attaché Reports, c-9-d-2365.

3. Maritime Force, Threat, and War

1. Maltzahn, *Seekrieg* (1906), 115.
2. Dehio, "Gedanken"; Steinberg, *Deterrent*; Berghahn, *Tirpitz-Plan*; idem, *Rüstung*.
3. Tirpitz, *Aufbau*, 346. On the distinction between "balance of force" and "balance of power," see Herrmann, *Arming*; and Geyer, "Review."
4. Berghahn, *Tirpitz-Plan*.
5. Dähnhardt, Memorandum, 9 July 1903; idem, Draft for a new bill, July 1903; idem, "Sonderbegründung der Vorlage," July 1903; and, Memorandum, 2 November 1903; BA-MA, RM 3/6663. Compare Berghahn, *Tirpitz-Plan*, 309–25.
6. Epkenhans, *Flottenrüstung*, 17.
7. RMA, "Die Sicherung Deutschlands gegen einen englischen Angriff," BA-MA, RM 3/6657.
8. Dähnhardt, "Sonderbegründung der Vorlage," July 1903, BA-MA, RM 3/6663.
9. Michaelis, "Wirken," 407.
10. Capelle, Notes for a Presentation to the Emperor, 24 October 1910; BA-MA, N 253/24.
11. Tirpitz, Notes for an Imperial audience on 26 September 1911; BA-MA, N 253/25.
12. Epkenhans, *Flottenrüstung*, 52–82, 113–37, 313–24, 337–65; idem, "Race."
13. Tirpitz to Bülow, 4 November 1909, *GP* 28; Tirpitz, Notes for a Meeting with the Chancellor on 12 January 1910, in Tirpitz, "Flottenverständigung," 109–10.
14. Tirpitz, Draft for a letter to the Chancellor, 23 September 1910, RMA, Memorandum, April 1911, both in Tirpitz, "Flottenverständigung," 115–16, 117–19; Capelle, Notes for a Presentation to the Emperor on 24 October 1910, Tirpitz, Notes, 27 January 1911, Tirpitz, Notes about a Conversation with the Chancellor on 4 May 1911, all in BA-MA, N 253/24.
15. Tirpitz to Müller, 8 February 1912, Tirpitz, Notes before and after his meeting Haldane on 9 February 1912, Tirpitz to Müller, 25 February 1912, all in Tirpitz, *Aufbau*, 282, 284, 286–88, 299–300; Hopman, Diary, 8, 9, 10, and 26 February 1912, in Epkenhans, *Leben*.
16. Tirpitz, Note for a presentation to the Emperor on 22 February 1913, BA-MA, N 253/28; Dähnhardt, Memorandum, 7 May 1913, BA-MA, RM 3/6674; Hopman to Müller, 11 June 13, in Tirpitz, *Aufbau*, 395–97; and Hopman, Diary, 6, 7, 8, and 25 February, 7 and 11 June, 19, and 21 October 1913, in Epkenhans, *Leben*; Capelle, "Notizen für die Kieler Reise," 1913, BA-MA, N 253/28.
17. Tirpitz to Bülow, 20 January 1909, and Minutes of a Meeting at the Imperial Chancellory, 3 June 1909; *GP* 28. Compare Tirpitz to Bülow, 21 March 1909, Tirpitz to Plessen, 5 April 1909, and Tirpitz to Müller, 17 and 25 April 1909, all in Tirpitz, "Flottenverständigung," 98, 100–103.
18. Tirpitz, Remarks during a joint imperial audience with the Imperial Chancellor on 12 August 1909, in Tirpitz, "Flottenverständigung," 106–8; Tirpitz to Bethmann-Hollweg, 1 September 1909, in Tirpitz, *Aufbau*, 165–66.
19. Berghahn, *Germany*, 51.
20. E.g., "Allgemeine Erfahrungen aus den Manövern der Herbstübungsflotte," 16 June 1894, BA-MA, RM 4/176; Tirpitz, Memorandum, St. Blasien, Summer 1908, BA-MA, RM 3/8; Tirpitz to Bülow, 20 January 1909, in Tirpitz, *Aufbau*, 116–17, 116. See also Dähnhardt, "Sonderbegründung der Vorlage," July 1903, BA-MA, RM 3/6663: D. refers to the common assumption that the blockading force needed to be "one and a half times as strong as the blockaded."
21. Tirpitz to Bülow, 4 January 1909, *GP* 28; Tirpitz to Bülow, 21 March 1909, in Tirpitz, "Flottenverständigung," 98; Tirpitz, Notes for an Imperial Audience, 26 September 1911, BA-MA

N 253/25; Tirpitz to Bethmann-Hollweg, 7 October 1911, Heeringen to Bethmann-Hollweg, 7 December 1911, in Tirpitz, *Aufbau,* 220–24.

22. Dähnhardt, "Sonderbegründung der Vorlage," July 1903; BA-MA, RM 3/6663.

23. Tirpitz, Notes for an imperial audience on 28 September 1898, BA-MA, RM 3/1. In his *Imperialism at Sea,* historian Rolf Hobson has also stressed that Tirpitz saw the emerging fleet as a defensive military deterrent. Michael Epkenhans and Holger Herwig, in turn, have critiqued him for downplaying Tirpitz's aggressive intentions. Epkenhans, *Tirpitz,* 34; and Herwig, "Review."

24. Imperial Naval Office, "Die Sicherung Deutschlands gegen einen englischen Angriff," February 1900, BA-MA, RM 3/6657; Tirpitz, "Stärkevergleich zwischen England und Deutschland," 1900, BA-MA, N 253/19; Otto von Diederichs, "Betrachtungen über die Kriegführung Deutschlands zur See gegen England in den Jahren 1904 und 1920," and Admiralty Staff, "Denkschrift zum Immediatvortrag betreffend Ausarbeitungen zur Flottenvorlage über Operationen gegen England und Amerika," 20 January 1900, both in BA-MA, RM 5/1945.

25. Harald Dähnhardt, "Sonderbegründung der Vorlage," July 1903; BA-MA, RM 3/6663. Compare the two letters on this issue by successive attachés in London to Tirpitz from 19 August 1897 and 3 January 1900, BA-MA, RM 3/9615 and RM 3/10221. For the persistence of this belief on the eve of World War I, see Müller to Tirpitz, 18 January 1913 and 28 March 1913, in Tirpitz, *Aufbau,* 365–67, 383–86; Müller to Tirpitz, 19 and 29 March, BA-MA, RM 5/1109; A, "Offiziersmangel in der englischen Marine," 15 April 1913, BA-MA, RM 3/2719.

26. Tirpitz to Büchsel, 29 July 1899, BA-MA, N 253/16.

27. Capelle, Notes, October 1912, BA-MA, N 253/25. Compare idem, "Notizen für die Kieler Reise," 1913; BA-MA, N 253/28.

28. Kennedy, "Strategieprobleme," 210.

29. Notes about a meeting between the Secretary of the Imperial Naval Office and the Chief of the Admiralty Staff, 6 December 1915, BA-MA, RM 5/2153.

30. On the initial goal of parity, see Admiral Dähnhardt, "In Welcher Richtung wird sich nach ehrenvollem Frieden die Weiterentwicklung unserer Flotte bewegen müssen?" 26 January 1915, BA-MA, RM 3/11624; on the decision for a "smaller battle fleet" in 1916, see the material in BA-MA, RM 3/10.

31. Kennedy, "Strategieprobleme."

32. Hohenlohe-Schillingfürst, *Denkwürdigkeiten,* 464; Nowak and Thimme, *Erinnerungen,* 194; Kühlmann, *Erinnerunngen,* 292.

33. Compare Scheck, *Tirpitz,* 9–10; Hobson, *Imperialism,* 247–60.

34. Tirpitz, Memorandum, 13 November 1905, BA-MA, RM 3/6.

35. E.g., Ellicott, "Composition"; Wainwright, "Power"; Taylor, "Future."

36. GB to SN, 9 February and 17 October 1903, GB, Minutes, 30–31 January and 16 October 1903; in NA, RG 80. The GB's annual building recommendations are in NA, RG 80, SF 420–2.

37. GB to SN, 28 October 1904; NA, RG 80, SF 420–2. In April 1907, the Board talked about the desirability of having one armored cruiser for each battleship. GB to SN, 25 April 1907; NA, RG 80, Letter Book.

38. On this, see chapter 4.

39. GB to SN, 1 July 1914; NA, RG 80, SF 420–2.

40. GB, Minutes, 29 October 1901, and BC, Minutes, 28 October 1901; NA, RG 80.

41. GB to SN, 12 October 1900 and 30 October 1901, NA, RG 80, Letter Book; BC to SN, 14 November 1898, 16 November 1899, 1 and 5 November 1900, 31 October 1901, 15 October 1902, NA, RG 80, Letter Books.

42. Washington Irving Chambers, "Memorandum," circa September 1904, NA, RG 80, GB, SF 420–2; GB, Minutes, 31 January 1903, NA, RG 80.

43. GB, Minutes, 31 January 1903; NA, RG 80.

44. GB to SN, 27 July 1905, NA, RG 80, SF 420. Demands to use the number of states as the basis for the battleship program include Rear-Admiral Higginson to SN, 26 June 1905, NA, RG 45, SF US Navy, 1775–1910, Box Number 674; Rodgers, "Extent"; Stirling, "Comment."

45. GB, Memorandum for SN, 28 September 1910; GB to SN, 21 April 1909. NA, RG 80, SF 420–2.

46. GB, "Building Program, 1913–1917," 25 September 1912; see also GB to SN, 25 May 1911. NA, RG 80, SF 420–2.

47. E.g., GB to SN, 28 September 1910, 25 May 1911, 25 September 1912, and 1 July 1914; NA, RG 80, SF 420–2.

48. GB to SN, 25 April 1907 and 2 August 1907; NA, RG 80, SF 420–1.

49. GB, Memorandum for SN, 28 September 1910; NA, RG 80, SF 420–2.

50. RC of 1907, QGA, Q 19; NWCA, RG 12.

51. Final Action of the Conference on Q 10, September 26, 1910, Part I, RC 1910; First Committee Solution, Part I, Q 1, RC 1911; compare RRC on Q 16, RC 1909, NWCA, RG 12.

52. Second CR on Q 1, Part I, RC 1912; NWCA, RG 12.

53. RRC on Q 17, RC 1909; NWCA, RG 12.

54. GB, Memorandum for SN, 28 September 1910; GB, "Building Program, 1913–1917," 25 September 1912; see also GB to SN, 25 May 1911. NA, RG 80, SF 420–2.

55. Fiske, "Power," 705.

56. Taylor, "Fleet," 801.

57. Fiske, "Policy," 3, 10. See also idem, "Profession."

58. Beehler, "Comment," 188.

59. RRC on Q 16, RC 1909, NWCA, RG 12.

60. GB to SN, 30 July 1915, and the memorandum filed with it; NA, RG 80, SF 420–2.

61. GB, Proceedings, 27 July 1915; NA, RG 80.

62. GB, Proceedings, 18 and 24 September 1914, NA, RG 80; Fiske, Diary, 28 and 29 September 1914, LC, MD, Fiske Papers; GB to SN, 17 November 1917 and 11 December 1914; NA, RG 80, SF 420–2.

63. *Hearings on Estimates, 1915*, 463–570.

64. GB to SN, 12 October 1915, 9 November 1915, 12 and 16 October 1916, NA, RG 80, SF 420–2; and the testimony of naval officers in *Hearings, 1916*, 1401-99, 1881-2118, 2271-2435, 3103-3283.

65. GB to SN, 20 April 1917, 29 August 1917 and 15 June 1918, NA, RG 80, SF 420 and SF 420–2; Planning Section Memorandum 21, 11 May 1918, NA, RG 80, SF 420–6. Compare Schilling, "Admirals."

66. GB to SN, 10 September 1918, see also GB to SN, 2 December 1918; all in NA, RG 80, SF 420–2; compare Planning Section, Memorandum 67, "Building Program," 21 November 1918; LC, MD, Benson Papers. This memorandum was written sometime in October.

67. "When the current policy was embarked upon, all the relevant decision makers recognized that we would have to pass through a danger zone," Tirpitz wrote to the Chancellor on 7 October 1911; BA-MA, RM 2/1764. Expositions of the notion of the "danger zone" are in Tirpitz, *Erinnerungen*; idem, *Aufbau*.

68. Tirpitz to Richthofen, 1 November 1904, BA-MA, RM 3/4. Compare Eckardtstein, *Lebenserinnerungen*, II: 40, and Hohenlohe-Schillingfürst, *Denkwürdigkeiten*, 464, recording conversations with Tirpitz from 1899 and 1897, respectively. On this entire issue, see Berghahn, *Tirpitz-Plan*, 380–415.

69. Tirpitz, Memorandum, 22 February 1905, in Tirpitz, *Aufbau,* 16–17; RMA, "Motive für die Novelle von 1905," 1905, RM 3/29; Tirpitz to Bülow, 8 November 1905, BA-MA, N 253/6.

70. Minutes of a Meeting at the Chancellory, 3 June 1909, GP 28; Tirpitz, Remarks during a joint imperial audience with the Chancellor on 12 August 1909, in Tirpitz, "Flottenverständigung," 106–8.

71. Tirpitz to Capelle, 13 September 1911, BA-MA, N 253/25; Holtzendorff to Tirpitz, 25 October 1911, BA-MA N 253/25; Heeringen to Tirpitz, 6 December 1911, RM 3/6678; Hopman, Diary, 9 December 1912, in Epkenhans, *Leben;* Müller, Diary, 8 December 1912, BA-MA, N 159/4.

72. Convenient summaries of numbers are in Sumida, *Defense,* and Sondhaus, *Warfare.*

73. On this issue, see Salewski, "Bedeutung," 341–64.

74. Tirpitz to Müller, 30 April 1914, BA-MA, 3/10; Müller, Diary, 3 May 1914, BA-MA, N 159/4.

75. On this, see chapter 5.

76. Hull, *Entourage;* Mombauer, *Moltke.*

77. A good account of these crises and German war talk is in Lambi, *Navy,* 241–68, 287–309.

78. Tirpitz to Capelle, 12 August 1911, Capelle to Tirpitz, 14 and 17 August 1911, Tirpitz, *Aufbau,* 203–4, 206–7; Müller, Note, 12 September 1911, idem, Diary, 13 September 1911, BA-MA, N 159/4. See also Hopman, Diary, 23 August and 2 October 1911, in Epkenhans, *Leben.*

79. Hopman, Diary, 9 December 1912, in Epkenhans, *Leben;* Müller, Diary, 8 December 1912, BA-MA, N 159/4.

80. Instead of many: Hewitson, *Germany.*

81. On the navy in the July crisis, see Epkenhans, *Flottenrüstung,* 400–407; Lambi, *Navy,* 416–24. On fears of "backing down," see Hopman, Diary, 27 and 28 July 1914, in Epkenhans, *Leben.*

82. Müller, Diary, 29 July 1914, in Görlitz, *Regierte,* 36.

83. Hopman, Diary, 31 December 1913, in Epkenhans, *Leben;* Tirpitz, Notes, undated, May 1914, Capelle, Notes for an Imperial audience, 17 May 1914, and Müller to Tirpitz, 27 May 1914, BA-MA, N 253/29.

84. Epkenhans, *Flottenrüstung,* 391–99.

85. Epkenhans, "Race," 126.

86. Epkenhans, *Flottenrüstung,* parts II and IV; Förster, *Militarismus.*

87. Tirpitz, Note, early December 1912, "Ausarbeitung von Kontreadmiral Dähnhardt für C," 5 January 1913, Tirpitz, Notes for a Presentation to the Emperor, undated, early January 1913, all in BA-MA, N 253/28; Draft for a letter to the Imperial Chancellor, 17 December 1912, BA-MA, RM 3/11624; Hopman, Diary, 11, 13, 14, and 16 December 1911, 1, 2, 6, and 11 January 1913, in Epkenhans, *Leben.*

88. Hopman, Diary, 7 January 1913; see also the entry for 2 January 1913, summarizing a conversation with Tirpitz, in Epkenhans, *Leben.*

89. See the discussion in chapter 2.

90. The struggle between Tirpitz and Bethmann-Hollweg over the Naval Bill of 1912 is documented in Tirpitz, *Aufbau.* A historian's account is Epkenhans, *Flottenrüstung,* 93–142.

91. Hopman, Diary, 16 December 1912, in Epkenhans, *Leben;* Bethmann-Hollweg, Note about a conversation with the Secretaries of War and Navy, 14 December 1912, Bethmann-Hollweg to Wilhelm II, 18 December 1912, all in GP 39; Tirpitz, Note, 19 December 1912, Müller to Tirpitz, 6 January 1913, both in Tirpitz, *Aufbau,* 370–71.

92. Tirpitz to Müller, 30 April 1914, BA-MA, RM 3/10.

93. Hopman, Diary, 24–30 November 1913, in Epkenhans, *Leben.*

94. Tirpitz to Müller, 30 April 1914, BA-MA, RM 3/10.

95. Capelle, Notes for an Imperial presentation, 17 May 1914, including Tirpitz's comments; Tirpitz, Notes for an imperial audience on 23 May, 1914, Tirpitz to Bethmann-Hollweg, 22 May 1914, Tirpitz to Kühn, 22 May 1914, Müller to Tirpitz, 27 May 1914, all in BA-MA, N 253/29; Bethmann-Hollweg to Tirpitz, 3 June 1914, Kühn to Tirpitz, 13 June 1914, in BA-MA, RM 3/10.

96. Hopman, Diary, 15 June 1914, in Epkenhans, *Leben*. For more on the Imperial Naval Office in the spring of 1914, see Epkenhans, *Flottenrüstung*, 391–99.

97. Tirpitz, Speech before senior officers, 9 October 1913; BA-MA, N 253/423. See Epkenhans, *Tirpitz*, 53.

98. Tirpitz to Bethmann-Hollweg, 7 October 1911, BA-MA RM 2/1764.

99. See chapter 5.

100. See chapter 5.

101. GB to SN, 25 June 1901, NA, RG 80, Letter Books; GB, Minutes, 24 and 26 April, 21–23 May, 25 June and 20 August 1901, NA, RG 80.

102. Mahan, *Problem*, 201–2; idem, "Doctrine" (1908). In 1909, one prominent officer published a plea for the Doctrine's restriction to the Caribbean Sea and the lands controlling the approaches to the Panama Canal: Hood, "Doctrine."

103. Fiebig-von Hase, *Lateinamerika*; see also Spector, *Admiral*, 137–47; Mitchell, *Danger*, 64–107.

104. Taylor to Cortelyou, 1 January 1902, LC, Roosevelt Papers; GB, Minutes, 23 April 1902, NA, RG 80; Taylor to Dewey, 31 January 1902; LC, MD, Dewey Papers.

105. Roosevelt to Dewey, 14 June 1902; LC, MD, Dewey Papers. For the navy's interest in fleet maneuvers, see GB to SN, 23 January 1902, NA, RG 80, SF 434–2; and the correspondence in NA, RG 80, GB, SF 434–3. For the Board's continuing discussions of the Venezuelan situation and possible naval action, see, for example, GB, Minutes for 27 May and 18 June 1902, NA, RG 80.

106. Taylor, Memorandum, no date, summer 1902, LC, MD, Roosevelt Papers.

107. Taylor to Moody, 25 December 1902, LC, MD, Moody Papers.

108. Taylor to Moody, 22 December 1902, LC, MD, Moody Papers; GB, Minutes, 27–31 December 1902, NA, RG 80, GB. For the planner, see Fiebig-von Hase, *Lateinamerika*, 1060.

109. GB, Minutes, 29 January 1902; NA, RG 80.

110. GB, Minutes, 29 January 1902; NA, RG 80. On this entire issue, see Spector, "Roosevelt." For more on plans for war against Germany, see chapter 5.

111. Braisted, *Navy, 1909–1922*, 123–49; Challener, *Admirals*, 367–78. For more on the previous scare, see chapter 2.

112. Dewey to his son, 19 April 1913, LC, MD, Dewey Papers; Fiske to SN, 13 and 14 May 1913, in Cronon, *Diaries*, 54–58, 60–64. Compare JB, Minutes, 8 and 15 May 1913, NA, RG 225; GB, Minutes, 29 April and 16 May 1913, NA, RG 80; and GB to SN, 29 April 1913 and 8 May 1913, NA, RG 80, SF 425.

113. GB, Minutes, 29 April 1913; NA, RG 80. For more, see chapter 5.

114. Braisted, *Navy, 1909–1922*, 131, 147

115. See chapter 7.

116. GB to SN, 1 August, 9 and 16 September 1914; NA, RG 80, SF 420–1 and 420.

117. Fiske summarized his demands in a letter to Daniels from 9 November 1914, in Fiske, *Midshipman*, 555–60; see also his testimony in front of Congress on 17 December 1914, in *Hearings on Estimates, 1915*, 999–1047. Compare Coletta, *Fiske*, 131–48. On the importance of the personnel issue, see also GB to SN, 14 November 1914, NA, RG 80, SF 421.

118. GB to SN, 17 November 1914; NA, RG 80, SF 420–2. On the action in September, see GB, Proceedings, 18 and 24 September 1914, NA, RG 80; Fiske, Diary, 28 and 29 September 1914, LC, MD.

119. GB to SN, 30 July 1915, and the memorandum filed with it; GB to SN, 12 October and 9 November 1915; NA, RG 80, SF 420–2.

120. This entire approach is explicated in GB to SN, 30 July 1915, and the memorandum filed with it. NA, RG 80, SF 420–2.

121. Fiske, *Midshipman*, 546–48, 550; Coletta, *Fiske*, 131–33.

122. GB to SN, 14 November 1914; NA, RG 80, SF 421.

123. GB to SN, 16 September 1914; NA, RG 80, SF 420–1; GB, Proceedings, 1 August 1914 NA, RG 80; GB to SN, August 1, 1914, NA, RG 80, SF 420–1.

124. Supplemental Plan for War against Germany, Austria and Turkey (January 1, 1915), GB, Black Plan, NA, RG 80, War Portfolio.

125. According to Daniels to Wilson, 2 February 1917, quoted in Klachko, *Benson*, 55.

126. William S. Benson, "Regarding Belligerents in Neutral Jurisdiction," 2 February 1917; Daniels Papers, LC, MD.

127. GB to SN, 14 November 1914; NA, RG 80, SF 421.

128. On concerns for "preparedness" on the eve of World War I, see GB to SN, 16 December 1913; and Dewey to Padgett, 23 April 1914; NA, RG 80, SF 420 and 420-6.

129. Baer, *Years*, 59.

130. Braisted, *Navy, 1909-1922*, 196–208. On the Naval Act of 1916, see also Kirschbaum, "Act." A succinct analysis of Wilson's shift is in O'Brien, *Power*, 116–21.

131. William S. Benson, "The Possibility of War," February 1917; Daniels Papers, LC, MD. Compare Klachko, *Benson*, 52–61; Trask, *Captains*, 42–52.

4. War of Battle Fleets

1. Tirpitz to Wilhelm II, 7 March 1902, BA-MA, RM 2/2405.

2. "Allgemeine Erfahrungen aus den Manövern der Herbstübungsflotte," 16 June 1894, BA-MA, RM 4/176.

3. GB to SN, 28 September 1906, NA, RG 80, SF 438.

4. Mahan, *Strategy*, 12. For the Luce-Mahan connection, see Seager, *Mahan*, 160–90.

5. Mahan, *Influence, 1793–1812*, II: iv. For the original promise, see Mahan to Stephen B. Luce, 6 January 1886, Seager and Maguire, *Letters*, II: 619.

6. Mahan, "Sea Power in the Present War" (August 1913), in Seager and Maguire, *Letters*, III: 706.

7. Mahan, *Sail to Steam*, 282. Compare Mahan, *Strategy*, 17.

8. Weigley, *Way*, 77–91, 167–91; Shy, "Jomini"; Gat, *Development*.

9. Mahan, *Sail*, 283.

10. Mahan, *Sea Power, 1812*, II: 51.

11. Mahan, *Strategy*, 25.

12. Ibid., 176.

13. Ibid., 6, 8.

14. Ibid., 296–97. "On no point is Mahan more emphatic" than on the point that "the primary mission of a battle fleet is to engage the enemy's fleet": Crowl, "Mahan," 458.

15. "Gründe, welche für die Beibehaltung eines Oberkommandos mit kräftigen Befugnissen sprechen," February 1891, BA-MA, N 253/39; "Unsere maritim-militärische Fortentwicklung,"

April 1891, BA-MA, RM 3/32; "Denkschrift über die Neuorganisation unserer Panzerflotte," Fall 1891, BA-MA, N 253/3.

16. Tirpitz, "Gründe," February 1891, BA-MA, N 253/39.

17. Tirpitz, "Denkschrift über die Neuorganisation," Fall 1891, BA-MA, N 253/3.

18. Tirpitz, "Unsere maritim-militärische Fortentwicklung," April 1891, BA-MA, RM 3/32. Compare Hobson, *Imperialism*, 194–200.

19. "Allgemeine Erfahrungen aus den Manövern der Herbstübungsflotte," 16 June 1894, BA-MA, RM 4/176.

20. Stadelmann, "Epoche," 106–7.

21. Marwedel, *Clausewitz*.

22. Tirpitz, "Unsere maritim-militärische Fortentwicklung," April 1891, BA-MA, RM 3/32; "Allgemeine Erfahrungen aus den Manövern der Herbstübungsflotte," 16 June 1894, BA-MA, RM 4/176.

23. Stenzel, *Kriegführung*. Compare Hobson, *Imperialism*, 136–47.

24. "Allgemeine Erfahrungen aus den Manövern der Herbstübungsflotte," 16 June 1894, BA-MA, RM 4/176.

25. On this, see Mahan, "Lessons" (1899); idem, "Principles" (1908); idem, "Retrospect" (1902). Such an argument should not be confused with Mahan's tendency to caution against undue eagerness to seek battle as an end in itself.

26. Mahan, "Blockade" (1895); idem, "Considerations" (1902).

27. On this, see also Hobson, *Imperialism*, 170–77.

28. Corbett, *Principles*, esp. part III. Compare Schurman, *Corbett*.

29. Maltzahn, "Seestrategie."

30. "Allgemeine Erfahrungen aus den Manövern der Herbstübungsflotte," 16 June 1894, BA-MA, RM 4/176. On the industrialization of naval warfare, see the summary in Sondhaus, *Warfare*.

31. Thiesen, "Professionalization"; Sondhaus, *Preparing*, 158–68; Petter, "Flottenrüstung," 130–36.

32. See the summaries in Petter, "Flottenrüstung," 103–45; Sondhaus, *Preparing*, 101–84.

33. Browning, *Two*.

34. Hagan, *Navy*.

35. Olivier, *Strategy*.

36. Bueb, *Schule*; Røksund, *École*.

37. Hagan, *Diplomacy*, 3–56; Buhl, "Maintaining."

38. See Dülffer, "Reich"; Winzen, "Genesis," 204–13.

39. Mahan's critique of a commerce-raiding strategy is fully developed in his writings on the naval wars of the sailing age. See, e.g., Mahan, *Influence, 1660–1783*, 8–9, 132–38, 148–49, 179, 193–96, 229–30, 539–40; idem, *Influence, 1793–1812*, I: 179–80, II: 197–201. For a concise summary, see Sumida, *Strategy*, 45–47. For Tirpitz's critique, see "Allgemeine Erfahrungen aus den Manövern der Herbstübungsflotte," 16 June 1894, BA-MA, RM 4/176; his comments on the excerpts from Curt von Maltzahn, *Seelehre*, unpublished ms., and an unsigned memorandum entitled "Erwiderung auf die Schrift von Valois," all in BA-MA, RMA 3/2.

40. Tirpitz to Büchsel, 29 July 1899, BA-MA, N 253/16.

41. Tirpitz, "Allgemeine Gesichtspunkte bei der Feststellung unserer Flotte nach Schiffsklassen und Schiffstypen," July 1897, BA-MA, N 253/4.

42. "Allgemeine Erfahrungen aus den Manövern der Herbstübungsflotte," 16 June 1894, BA-MA, RM 4/176.

43. Mahan, *Sea Power, 1812*, I: 286, 288; Tirpitz to Bülow, 20 April 1907, GP 23.

44. See Maltzahn, *Kampf*; idem, "Meer."
45. On this older approach, see Bönker, "Bürgerkrieg" 93–115; Sondhaus, *Preparing*.
46. "Allgemeine Erfahrungen aus den Manövern der Herbstübungsflotte," 16 June 1894, BA-MA, RM 4/176. Large cruisers could take the role of battleships in the case of "differences with small transatlantic nations," Tirpitz also noted.
47. GB to SN, 25 April 1907; NA, RG 80, SF 420–1.
48. Sumida, *Defense*; Lambert, *Revolution*.
49. F. Rust, *Marinesorgen*; Galster, *Seekriegsrüstung*; idem, *Küstenverteidigung*; Schleinitz, "Außen- und Kleinkrieg." See also Persius, *Menschen*.
50. Lakowski, *U-Boote*; Weir, "Tirpitz." On submarine construction, see Rössler, *Geschichte*. The service memorandum is Inspektion des Torpedowesens, "Der Stand des Unterseebootswesens," 1911; BA-MA, RM 3/10981. Compare the articles on the development of submarines that were published in *Nauticus* in 1904, 1908, and 1911.
51. *Nauticus* 15 (1913): iv, 187, as quoted in Schröder, *U-Boote*, 33.
52. E.g., "Zum Immediatvortrag über U-Boottaktik," 9 September 1912, BA-MA, RM 5/2062; "Das Kaisermanöver im Jahre 1912," BA-MA, RM 5/899; Admiralty Staff, "Fernverwendung der U-Boote im Kriege gegen England," 13 December 1912, BA-MA, RM 5/1615; "Militärische und technische Erfahrungen auf Unterseebooten während der Herbstmanöver in der Nordsee," 9 January 1913, BA-MA, RM 3/10992; Chief of Admiralty Staff to Tirpitz, 21 February 1913, BA-MA, RM 5/1615; Pohl, "Denkschrift zum Immediatvortrag uber das strategische Kriegsspiel des Admiralstabes Winter 1913/14," 5 May 1914, and Pohl's note after his presentation, 26 May 1914, BA-MA, RM 5/900; Pohl to Tirpitz, 30 July 1914, BA-MA, RM 47/414. Compare Kaulisch, "Klärung."
53. Pohl to Tirpitz, 29 May 1913, BA-MA, RM 5/2062.
54. In the spring of 1914 an officer, associated with the submarine branch, developed a war scenario for an Anglo-German war that used a vast, imaginary fleet of 222 submarines to impose a commercial blockade against Britain and bypass the confrontation between battle fleets over command of the sea. Presented with this scenario, Tirpitz flatly dismissed it. Spindler, "Handelskrieg," I: 153–54.
55. Typical are the memoranda on the future development of the navy from 1916, in BA-MA, RM 3/10; the memoranda on a same topic by Vice-Admirals Dähnhardt and Boedicker from 1915 and 1918, in BA-MA, RM 3/11624 and RM 3/11729; the letters and brief memos from wartime in Trotha, *Volkstum*; and, finally, Hollweg, *Aufgaben*.
56. Compare Friedman, *Submarines*.
57. E.g., "The Sphere and Scope of the Submarine in Coast Defense," approved by General Board on 14 April 1905, NA, RG 80, SF 420–15; GB to SN, 27 February 1907, 19 January 1910, ibid., SF 403; GB to SN, 6 June 1907 and 27 January 1909, ibid., SF 407. Compare RC 1904, Part IV, Q 31, RC 1905, Part III, Q 25–28, RC 1907, Tactical Questions, Q 5; NWCA, RG 12.
58. GB to SN, 25 September 1912, NA, RG 80, SF 420–2.
59. GB, "Submarines. Characteristics: Function in War: Numbers: Organisation," July 1911; NA, RG 80, SF 420–15.
60. R. McLean, "Submarines," 1911, D. C. Bingham, "The Military Value of the Submarine," lecture, Naval War College Conference 1910; Chester W. Nimitz, "Defensive and Offensive Tactics of Submarines," NWCA, RG 4, Files XTYU; and the discussions of submarines by the officer classes at the NWC in 1911, 1912, and 1913: RC 1911, Part III, Q 5, RC 1912, Part III, Q 6, both in NWCA, RG 12; Summer Conference 1913, Q 5, NWCA, RG 4.
61. GB to SN, 1 July, 17 November 1914, 30 July 1915, 12 and 16 October 1916, NA, RG 80, SF 420.

62. GB to SN, 17 June 1914; NA, RG 80, SF 420.

63. See the answers to Part III, Q 5 in RC 1911, and to Part III, Q 6, in RC 1912; NWCA, RG 12. See also Spector, *Professors* 148.

64. For views on the military value of submarines, see, e.g., GB to SN, 27 September 1915, NA, RG 80, General Correspondence File 8667; GB to SN, 9 November 1915 and 16 October 1916, both in NA, RG 80, SF 420–2; Planning Section, Memorandum 21, 11 May 1918, NA, RG 80, SF 420-6 On the wartime debate, see also McBride, *Change,* 119–27. On the submarine crisis, see the account in Still, *Crisis.*

65. Holtzendorff to Tirpitz, 16 September 1911, BA-MA, N 253/25.

66. Pohl, "Notiz zum Immediatvortrag," 20 February 1914, BA-MA, RM 5/900. On battlecruiser tactics, compare Maltzahn, *Geschichte,* II: 133, and Philbin, *Hipper,* 31–33.

67. "Denkschrift, betreffend Grosse Kreuzer für 1907 und folgende Jahre," 29–30 June 1906, BA-MA, RM 3/3691.

68. "Protokoll. Sitzungen über Linienschiffe und Grosse Kreuzer 1911," 6, 8, 11 and 17 May 1910, BA-MA, RM 3/15. See also "Protokoll. Sitzung vom 18. September 1906, betreffend Projekt des Grossen Kreuzers 1907," 1 October 1906, BA-MA, RM 3/3693.

69. Tirpitz, "Allgemeine Erfahrungen aus den Manövern der Herbstübungsflotte," 16 June 1894, BA-MA, RM 4/176; idem, "Allgemeine Gesichtspunkte bei der Feststellung unserer Flotte nach Schiffsklassen und Schiffstypen," July 1897, BA-MA, N 253/4; idem "Was ist ein Großer Kreuzer?" 29 January 1904, BA-MA, RM 2/1601; idem "Die Entwicklung unseres Großen Kreuzers," 5 March 1904, BA-MA, RM 3/357.

70. "Bemerkungen Seiner Excellenz des Herrn Staatssekretärs betr. Grossen Kreuzer 1914," 12 April 1913; see also "Notiz zum Immediatvortrag betreffend Grosser Kreuzer 1914," 29 April 1913; both in BA-MA RM 3/3695.

71. "Wünschenswertes und notwendige Verbesserungen am Grossen Kreuzer 1910 (J)," 8 March 1909 BA-MA RMA 3/3693. A superb study of battlecruiser construction is Grießmer, *Kreuzer.*

72. Compare Rahn, "Optionen," 201–2.

73. Eduard von Capelle, "Notizen zum Immediatvortrag," 17 May 1914, BA-MA, N 253/29. Capelle proposes the rapid creation of two battlecruiser squadrons ready for offensive warfare against Britain.

74. Hahn to Hipper, 6 November 1914; Hipper to Admiral Ingenohl, 12 November 1911; Ingenohl to Admiral Pohl, 14 November 1914, all in BA-MA, RM 2/2179; Hipper, "Operations-Vorschlag," 12 November 1914, in Philbin, *Hipper,* 92–95; idem, "Betrifft Schiffstypen," 7 July 1915; Captain von Levetzov, "Betriff Schiffstypen," 14 May 1915; Captain Hahn, "Betrifft Schiffstypen," 2 May 1915; idem, "Die bisherigen Kriegserfahrungen und ihr Einfluß auf die weitere Entwicklung der Kreuzer," 22 March 1915; Rear-Admiral Hebbinghaus, "Schiffstypen," 19 May 1915, all in BA-MA RM 3/5444; and the various memoranda in Wegener, *Strategy,* 133–98.

75. Quoted in Epkenhans, *Leben,* 413, footnote 278.

76. GB to SN, 25 September 1912; compare GB to SN, 25 May 1911, NA, RG 80, SF 420–2. On initial views of the battlecruiser, see GB to SN, 24 October 1906, NA, RG 80, SF 420–6; RC 1907, "Final Action of the conference on question 8," NWCA, RG 12; Special Committee to President of NWC, 24 August 1907, NA, RG 80, GB, SF 407. Compare Riggs, "Question," and GB to SN, 21 April 1909; NA, RG 80, GB, SF 420–2.

77. Sims to SN, 2 May 1912; NA, RG 80, General Correspondence, File 10580–135–14. According to Sims, officers of the summer conference at the NWC all agreed that European nations were building battlecruisers for commerce-destroying actions.

78. Summer Conference 1913, Q 5, Discussion of Papers Submitted, NWCA, RG 4. Compare RC 1911, Part III, Tactical Q 2, NWCA, RG 12; Summer Conference 1912, Discussion of the Use of Armoured Cruisers in Action; Summer Conference 1913, Discussion of the use of battlecruisers, armored cruisers, and scouts, R. H Robinson, "Battle Cruisers," 12 July 1912, all in NWCA, RG 8, XTYB.

79. GB to SN, 28 September 1910, enclosed memorandum; GB, Third Committee, "Building Program for the Period 1914–1920," July 17, 1912; both in NA, RG 80, SF 420–2. Compare W. L. Rodgers, "Notes Upon the Memorandum of the Third Committee Regarding Characteristics of Battle Cruisers of 1914 Program," 2 January 1913; Pratt to Rodgers, 26 December 1912; NA, RG 80, GB, SF 420–6.

80. The term "luxury" is from Captain Knepper's contribution in Summer Conference 1912: Discussion of the Use of Armoured Cruisers in Actions (Tactical Q 2), NWCA, RG 8, XTYB.

81. GB to SN, 30 July 1915 and 9 November 1915; both in NA, RG 80, SF 420–2. For subsequent demands for battlecruisers, see GB to the SN, 12 and 16 October 1916, 20 April and 29 August 1917, 15 and 10 September 1918; all in NA, RG 80, SF 420 and 420–2. On wartime debate about battlecruisers, see McBride, *Change*, 113–19.

82. E.g., Dinger to SN (Operations), 1 September 1916; Planning Section Memorandum 21, 11 May 1918, NA, RG 80, GB, SF 420–6.

83. Geyer and Bright, "Violence"; Lambert, "Macht"; Beeler, "Steam." On continuing commitment to global maritime control after 1900, see Lambert, "Transformation."

84. Taylor, "Fleet," and his reports as Chief of the Bureau of Navigation, in Navy Department, *Annual Reports, 1902 and 1903*. Compare GB to SN, 22 March and 22 August 1901, NA, RG 80, SF 434–1; GB to SN, 19 December 1901, NA, RG 80, SF 434–5; and the correspondence about the maneuvers in the winter of 1902–03 in NA, RG 80, SF 434–3.

85. Compare Maurer, "Concentration"; Costello, "Planning," 279–319.

86. On the NWC, see "Solution, Problem of 1903," Part IV, "Blue's Plan of Campaign," NWCA, RG 12. On the navy's interest in deployment in Asia, see GB to SN, 26 September 1901, NA, RG 80, SF 405; Commander Nathan Sargent, "The Disposition of Our Naval Forces," undated, LC, MD, Dewey Papers.

87. GB, Minutes, 20 November to 4 December 1903, in NA, RG 80; GB to SN, 5 December 1903, NA, RG 80, SF 420–1. On Luce and Mahan, see their letters to Taylor, both dated 7 December 1903, in LC, MD, Taylor Papers (Luce), and Seager and Maguire, *Letters*, III: 79–80 (Mahan). See also Taylor to Luce, 5 and 9 December 1903, LC, MD, Luce Papers; and Taylor to Dewey, 2 December 1903, LC, MD, Dewey Papers.

88. GB to SN, 25 April 1907, NA, RG 80, SF 420–1; GB, Minutes for 20 December 1904 and 24 January 1905, NA, RG 80; NWC, Problem 1904, Part 3, Reports of a Special Committee on Tactics, and the Strength and Composition of the Fleet, 21 September 1904; NWC, Solution, Problem 1905, Part III, Q 3, RC 1906. Solution of Problem, Part II, Q 25; all in NWCA, RG 12.

89. Challener, *Admirals*, 225–64. Compare Braisted, *Navy, 1897–1909*, 191–239.

90. GB, Minutes, 17 June 1908, NA, RG 80; JB, Minutes, 18 June 1907, NA, RG 225. On pleas for Pacific concentration, see GB to SN, 2 and 15 August 1907; GB, "Memorandum for the Guidance of the Naval Members of the Joint Board," 18 February 1908; all in NA, RG 80, SF 420–1; JB, Minutes, 19 February 1908, and JB to SN, 21 February 1908, NA, RG 225.

91. GB to SN, 24 February 1909; NA, RG 80, SF 420–1. On earlier discussion of fleet splitting, see GB to SN, 25 April, 2 and 15 August 1907, all in NA, RG 80, SF 420–1; GB, Minutes, 15 and 18 June 1908, NA, RG 80; Captain S.A. Staunton, memorandum, 23 June 1908, NA, RG 80, GB, SF 420–1. The summer conferences of the Naval War College endorsed the principles

of current concentration and eventual splitting in 1907 and 1909. On 1904, see GB, Minutes, 20 December; NA, RG 80.

92. Mahan to Roosevelt, 2 March 1909, in Seager and Maguire, *Letters*, III: 290; Roosevelt to Taft, 3 March 1909, in Morison, *Letters*, V: 1543.

93. GB to SN, 10 and 16 November 1910; Admiral George Dewey, "Memorandum," 26 June 1912; GB, First Committee, "Notes on Distribution of the Fleet," 7 May 1912; C. W. Williams, Memorandum, 16 March 1910, Sidney Staunton, Memorandum, 16 April 1912; all in NA, RG 80, GB, SF 420-1; RC 1910, Part I, Final Action of the Conference on Question 10, 26 September, 1910, NWCA, RG 12. After 1910, the summer conferences at the NWC endorsed the principle of Atlantic concentration. See RC 1911, Part I, Q 1, and RC, 1912, Part I, Q 1, NWCA, RG 12.

94. GB to SN, 13 May, 1 August, 9 September and 16 September 1914; NA, RG 80, SF 420-1 and 420.

95. Friedman, *Battleships*.

96. Between 1900 and 1914, the General Board asked for such cruisers almost every year, as evidenced by its annual building recommendations; NA, RG 80, GB, SF 420-2. Compare Costello, "Planning," 263-64.

97. E.g., GB to SN, 23 November 1905 and 3 August 1914; NA, RG 80, SF 420-5 and SF 442 respectively. On colliers, see, e.g., GB to SN, 11 September 1905 and 28 February 1910; NA, RG 80, SF 420. Compare Costello, "Planning," 267-70.

98. Snyder, "Petroleum."

99. NWB to SN, 15-20 August 1898, Seager and Maguire, *Letters*, II: 581-91; Bradford, "Stations"; GB to SN, 30 September 1902, NA, RG 80, Letter Books.

100. E.g., GB to SN, 12 November 1901 and 27 February 1902; NA, RG 80, Letter Books. For the rationale in 1915, see GB to SN, 10 December 1915, NA, RG 80, SF 427. In 1905, one senior officer proposed the purchase of all European territories in the Caribbean. Melville, "Elements."

101. On this, see Challener, *Admirals*; Costello, "Planning," 173-225; and the relevant passages in Braisted, *Navy, 1897-1909*; idem, *Navy, 1909-1922*. Between 1910 and 1914, the formulation of a coherent naval base policy was at the forefront of the discussions during summer conferences at the NWC.

102. Quoted from GB to SN, 4 December 1911; NA, RG 80, SF 403. Mahan referred to Guam as a "Gibraltar" in a letter from 24 September 1910, in Seager and Maguire, *Letters*, III: 352-58. On the navy's new interest in Guam after 1910, see Miller, *Plan*, 69-73.

103. Braisted, *Navy, 1897-1909*, 124-36; Challener, *Admirals*, 182-98.

104. E.g., GB to SN, 28 September 1910 and 28 September 1911, NA, RG 80, Letters. On this entire issue, see the excellent discussion in Braisted, *Navy, 1909-1922*, esp. 36-57, 209-30.

105. Captain Sidney Staunton, Memorandum, 16 April 1912; compare Commander C. S. Williams, Memorandum, 16 March 1910, NA, RG 80, GB, SF 420-1.

106. E.g., Wainwright, "Power"; NWB to SN, 15-20 August 1898; Seager and Maguire, *Letters*, II: 581-91; Stockton, "Canal." Repeatedly, the summer conferences at the NWC discussed the implications of the opening of the Panama Canal after 1900.

107. GB to SN, 28 February 1910, NA, RG 80, SF 420; Knapp, "Navy"; Commander J.S. McKean, *The Strategic Value of the Panama Canal to the Navy* (Washington, D.C., 1914), in NWCA, RG 8, XSTZ. Compare RC 1911 and 1912, Part I, Q 5, NWCA, RG 12; Class of January 1914, "Discussion of Strategic Effects of the Completion and Fortification of the Panama Canal," NWCA, RG 8, XSTX.

108. E.g., Stockton, "Cables"; Hood, "Cable"; Squier, "Influence." A historian's account is in Headrick, *Weapon*, 99-102.

109. Howeth, *History*; Douglas, "Navy."
110. Tirpitz, "Allgemeine Gesichtspunkte bei der Feststellung unserer Flotte nach Schiffsklassen und Schiffstypen," July 1897, BA-MA, N 253/4.
111. Ganz, "Policy."
112. Berghahn, *Tirpitz-Plan,* 271–304.
113. On the exposition, see Ingenohl to Tirpitz, 18 June 1914, Tirpitz to Pohl, 1 July 1914, both in BA-MA, RM 5/5503; Rear-Admiral Rebeur Pachwitz, "Abschlussbericht," 7 June 1914, BA-MA, RM 2/1779. On the flying squadron, see Tirpitz to Wilhelm II, 22 March 1914, BA-MA, N 253/29; Tirpitz to Wilhelm II, 13 October 1913, Ingenohl to Tirpitz, 23 October 1913, Tirpitz to Müller, 7 November 1913, Wilhelm II to Tirpitz, 15 November 1913; all in BA-MA, RM 2/1778.
114. Tirpitz, *Erinnerungen,* 67, 73, 131. On this entire issue, see Kloosterhuis, *Imperialisten,* 137–56. For a clear explication of Tirpitz's new interest in an overseas presence, see the protocol of the meeting at the Imperial Naval Office on 17 December 1912 about the trip of the battlecruiser *Von der Tann*; in BA-M A, RM 3/15.
115. On battleship design, see Gröner, *Kriegsschiffe,* and Grießmer, *Linienschiffe.* On the expectation of close combat in the North Sea, see Maltzahn, *Geschichte,* II, 122–23, 131–33.
116. On torpedo boat design, see Gröner, *Kriegsschiffe,* esp. 34–35. On Tirpitz's views of torpedo boats and fleet tactics, see also Besteck, *Line,* 57–60; Maltzahn, *Geschichte,* II: 120–23.
117. Holtzendorff to Tirpitz, 16 September 1911, BA-MA, N 253/25; Heeringen to Bethmann-Hollweg, 7 October, 1910, BA-MA, N 164/6; Holtzendorff to Tirpitz, 25 October 1911, BA-MA, N 253/25; Heeringen to Tirpitz, 16 September, 24 November 1911, and 6 December 1911, BA-MA, RM 3/6678; Heeringen to Capelle, 10 August 1911, and to Tirpitz, 8 July 1911, BA-MA, N 253/24. On this issue, see also the observations offered in Michaelis, "Wirken," 404, 410.
118. E.g., Tirpitz, "Allgemeine Gesichtspunkte bei der Feststellung unserer Flotte nach Schiffsklassen und Schiffstypen," July 1897, BA-MA, N 253/4. On concerns about their underdevelopment, see Michaelis, "Wirken," 410, and Philbin, *Hipper,* 21–36.
119. Tirpitz to Wilhelm II, 24 April 1898, BA-MA, N 253/39; Knorr to Wilhelm II, 20 April and 1 July 1898, BA-MA, RM 5/5954; Ludwig Schröder, "Braucht das deutsche Reich Flottenstützpunke im Ausland?" 15 April 1903, and the lecture on "Flottenstützpunkte und Flottenstützpunktpolitik," 7 March 1906, both in BA-MA, RM5/5956.
120. By contrast, Herwig, *Fleet,* 109, has suggested that the navy's desire for naval bases knew no limits, that "no island had been too small, no coral reef too insignificant for German planners, who had accepted fully the British premise that 'even the most unpromising detached ocean rock will, if kept long enough, develop some useful purpose.'"
121. Fiebig-von Hase, *Lateinamerika,* 429–72; Herwig, *Politics,* esp. 24–36, 68–76.
122. Gottschall, *Order*; Petter, "Marine."
123. Fiebig-von Hase, *Lateinamerika,* 428–31; Herwig, *Fleet,* esp. 99–103, 109–10; Kaulisch, "Stützpunktpolitik."
124. See the correspondence between the Admiralty Staff and the Imperial Naval Office from October 1907 in BA-MA, RM 5/5955. On Kiaochow, see Stingl, *Osten,* 431–39.
125. E.g., Holtzendorff to Bethmann-Hollweg, 26 November 1916 and 24 December 1916; idem to Wilhelm II, 18 May 1917; BA-MA RM 2/1983.
126. Petter, "Marine."
127. Walle, "Kreuzergeschwader"; and the documents collected in Tampke, "*Warfare.*"
128. Michaelis, "Verwendung"; Roscher, "Seekabelpolitik"; *Nauticus,* "Hilfsmittel." Compare the account in Headrick, *Weapon,* 105–10.

129. *Nauticus,* "Fortschritte"; Thurn-Coblenz, "Telephonie"; *Nauticus,* "Hilfsmittel." Compare the account in Friedewald, "Beginnings"; idem, "Funkentelegraphie."

5. Planning for Victory

1. Hancock, *Invasion.* On Hancock and "preparedness," see Frank, "Preparedness." On the literary genre of war tales, see Clarke, *Voices.*

2. Compare Fiebig-von Hase, *Lateinamerika,* 788–839; Mitchell, *Danger,* 53–63; Herwig and Trask, "Plans."

3. Captain C. D. Sigsbee, "Germany versus the United States—West Indies," 21 May 1900, NA, RG 80, GB, WP.

4. Washington Irving Chambers, "Memorandum, circa September 1906"; NA, RG 80, GB, SF 420-2.

5. "Black Plan"; see also the section on the "Possible Plans of the Enemy," in "General Considerations," 19 October 1910, NA, RG 80, GB, WP.

6. See GB, Minutes, 22–23 August and 26 September 1901, NA, RG 80; and the "Report of the Minority" in "Solution to the Problem 1901," NWCA, RG 8.

7. See "Conference of 1905. Solution of the Problem," in Problem and Solutions 1905; "Strategic Problems: Blue versus Black," in RC 1912; all in NWCA, RG 12. For the suggestion in 1912, see the summary in Appendix D in "Black Plan," NA, RG 80, GB, WP

8. "Black Plan," Appendix D: Studies and Conclusions of Naval War College, NA, RG 80, GB, WP.

9. See "Problems and Solutions 1903," NWCA, RG 12.

10. See the section on "Black and Blue Resources Available, July 1, 1915," in "Black Plan," NA, RG 80, GB, WP.

11. See Sigsbee, "Germany versus the United States"; GB, Minutes, 21 May 1900; GB to SN, 10 December 1900 and 12 November 1901; and "Plan for the Seizure and Defense by the Navy of Samana Bay, Santo Domingo, and Fort Liberty Bay, Haiti as Advanced Bases in Time of War," September 1905; NA, RG 80, GB, WP.

12. This is the scenario of the "Black Plan" and the "General Considerations." In 1901, 1903, 1905, 1912, and 1913, the NWC consistently stressed the paramount strategic importance of the Margarita Islands. In 1912 and 1913 the college assumed that the Germans would seize a base there. See the summary in Appendix D: Studies and Conclusions of Naval War College, "Black Plan," NA, RG 80, GB, WP.

13. On these concerns see, GB, Minutes, 19–20 December 1900, 20 March 1901, 23 April 1901, 21 May 1901, 29 October 1901, 26–28 March 1902, 25 April 1902; GB to SN, 27 March 1902; NA, RG 80, GB, Minutes and Letter Books, respectively.

14. After 1910, this became the central theme of the letters of the GB to the SN concerning the naval program. NA, RG 80, GB, SF 420-2.

15. See, e.g., the comparative assessments of readiness in "Black Plan," sections on "Black and Blue Resources available July 1, 1915" and "Assumed Conditions of Problem—3 Cases." NA, RG 80, GB, WP.

16. See Spector, "Roosevelt," 260–62.

17. Quoted in Mitchell, *Danger,* 60.

18. See the sections "Blue Estimate of the Situation—3 Cases" and "Blue Decisions—3 Cases" of the "Plan Black." NA, RG 80, GB, WP.

19. These assumptions are spelled out in the "Foreword" of "Plan Black" and in the section on "Possible Plans of the Enemy," in "General Considerations," from 1910; NA, RG 80, GB, WP.

20. See the sections on "Black and Blue Resources Available, July 1, 1915," of "Plan Black," and the appendix B: "Logistics of Blue and Black—Fuel and Train"; NA, RG 80, GB, WP.

21. E.g., "Problem and Solutions 1902," NWCA, RG 12; Rodgers to GB, 13 May 1901, and the undated "Memorandum" that the board drafted in response, NA, RG 80, GB, SF 425-2; and Henry C. Taylor, "Memorandum," 31 May 1904, NA, RG 225, JB, SF 325. See also Spector, *Professors*, 104–5.

22. In his *Problem of Asia*, Mahan attached great importance to the control of the Yangtze River by combined Anglo-American naval forces.

23. This desire is well documented in Braisted, *Navy, 1897–1909*, 124–36; Challener, *Admirals*, 182–98.

24. Compare Miller, *Plan*; Vlahos, "College"; Rivera, "Stick."

25. See NWB, "Plan of Campaign against Spain and Japan, 30 June 1897," NA, RG 80, GB, WP; Goodrich to Roosevelt, 23 June 1897, NWCA, RG 8, XSTP. In addition, see Spector, *Professors*, 95–96; Vlahos, "College," 24–26; Morgan, *Gibraltar*, 198–217. For a scenario for a U.S.-Japanese war from 1900, see John M. Ellicott, "Sea Power of Japan," 1901; NWCA, RG 8. On plans for a war against Spain, see Trask, *War*.

26. GB, "In Case of Strained Relations with Japan," September 1906, NWCA, RG 8, UNOpP; NWC, "Strategic Plan of Campaign Against Orange," 15 March 1911, and GB, "Orange War Plan: Strategic Section," 14 March 1914, both in NA, RG 80, WP. See also "Conference of 1906: Solution of Problem," which foreshadows the approach of the first formal war plan in 1907, NWCA, RG 12; GB, "Report of the Second Committee," 28 January 1908, NA, RG 80, Proceedings; GB, Second Committee to Executive Committee, "General Plan of Campaign for War against Japan," circa November 1910, NWCA, RG 8, UNOpP.

27. NWC, "Strategic Plan," 15 March 1911, NA, RG 80, GB, WP. For Mahan, see Mahan to Raymond P. Rodgers, 22 February, 4 March, 17 March 1911, in Seager and Maguire, *Letters*, III: 380–88, 389–94. For a scenario for a U.S.-Japanese war from 1900 that assumed a Japanese attack across the Pacific, leading up to the invasion of California, see John M. Ellicott, "Sea Power of Japan," 1901; NWCA, RG 8. It took until 1914 for U.S. naval logisticians to prove "conclusively" that Hawaii "lay safely beyond Japan's grasp." The main reason was the imminent opening of the Panama Canal. Miller, *Plan*, 46.

28. GB, "In Case of Strained Relations with Japan," September 1906, NWCA, RG 8, UNOpP.

29. Ibid.

30. Clarence Williams, "Proposed Routes Between the Pacific Coast and the Philippines," November 1907, NA, RG 80, GB, WP; GB, Second Committee to Executive Committee, "General Plan of Campaign for War against Japan," circa November 1910, NWCA, RG 8, UNOpP. On this issue, see also Miller, *Plan*, 87–90.

31. Commander Sargent, Memorandum, 15 June 1907; NA, RG 80, GB, Proceedings.

32. NWC, "Strategic Plan," 15 March 1911, NA, RG 80, GB, WP. See also "Notes on Comments of Rear Admiral Mahan," spring 1911; NWCA, RG 8, UNOpP.

33. GB, "Orange War Plan: Strategic Section," 14 March 1914, NA, RG 80, GB, WP. This scenario expanded on previous planning efforts and discussions among naval planners at the Naval War College and General Board. In 1910, they had developed similar plans for an offensive advance across the western Pacific, which took the assembled battle fleet at Hawaii at its point of departure. GB, Second Committee to Executive Committee, "General Plan of Campaign for War against Japan," circa November 1910; NWCA, RG 8, UNOpP.

34. Compare Miller, *Plan*, esp. 33–38, 77–82, 86–99, 100–109.

35. Dewey to SN, 8 November 1909, in JB, Minutes, NA RG 225; Rear-Admiral Charles S. Sperry, "The Cruise of the United States Atlantic Fleet," Sperry Papers, LC, MD.

36. See Commander H. S. Knapp, "Memorandum," 31 January 1907, which summarized the deliberations of a special joint committee consisting of officers from the General Board and the Army General Staff; Lieutenant-Commander W. D. MacDougall, "Study of Orange-Blue Special Situation of 1906–1907," 5 April 1907; NWCA, RG 8, Subject File XSTP. In fact, at least two planners even invoked the specter of defeat in an early battle.

37. Fiske to GB, 25 March 1911, NA, RG 80, GB, SF 408.

38. Fiske to SN, 13 May 1913, in Cronon, *Diaries*, 56, 58.

39. On these logistical issues, compare Maurer, "Fuel"; Miller, *Plan*, 87–99. A prescient discussion of the logistical challenges is Fiske to GB, 25 March 1911, NA, RG 80, GB, SF 408. Beginning in 1907, GB and NWC planners closely studied logistical issues. A striking early example is "Fleet Supply. Questions and Conclusions of Committees and of Conference of all officers," 1908; NWCA, RG 8, XLOG. All campaign plans include lengthy discussions of matters of supply and logistics.

40. Braisted, *Navy, 1909–1922*, 129. On coal storage, see, e.g., GB to SN, 27 April 1910, 8 July 1910; NA, RG 80, GB, Letters. Compare Maurer, "Fuel."

41. See Miller, *Plan*, 64–76; Braisted, *Navy, 1909–1922*, 58–76.

42. Miller, *Plan*, 44–48; Braisted, *Navy, 1909–1922*, 39–42, 209–30.

43. On this, see chapter 4.

44. GB, Second Committee to Executive Committee, "General Plan of Campaign for War against Japan," circa November 1910, Commander C. S. Williams, "Extract from Paper," November 1909, NWCA, RG 8, UNOpP; "Problem of 1907: Tentative Plan of Campaign and Strategic Problem," NWCA, RG 12.

45. Mahan to Rodgers, 22 February, 4 March, 17 March 1911, in Seager and Maguire, *Letters*, II: 380–88, 389–94, 395; and Seager, *Mahan*, 483–88.

46. NWC, "Strategic Plan," 15 March 1911, NA, RG 80, GB, WP.

47. E.g., Lieutenant-Commander James H. Oliver, "Memorandum Submitted to the President of the War College," 20 April 1907; idem, "Our Situation in the Pacific Ocean," 3 June; idem, "Our Situation in the Pacific," January 1911; all in NWCA, RG 8, Subject File XSTP.

48. Compare the characterization of the plans for the instantaneous advance to the western Pacific as a "failed strategy" in Miller, *Plan*, 86.

49. On planning against Russia and France, see Lambi, *Navy*, 68–86, 91–112, 193–208.

50. Tirpitz, "Allgemeine Gesichtspunkte bei der Feststellung unserer Flotte nach Schiffsklassen und Schiffstypen," July 1897, BA-MA, N 253/4.

51. The scenario for a future Anglo-German war has been described in Berghahn, *Tirpitz-Plan*, 173–205; Kennedy, "Strategieprobleme."

52. On the notion of "defensive battle," see also Maltzahn, *Kampf*; idem, "Meer"; idem, *Geschichte*, II: 22–25.

53. In his *Imperialism at Sea*, Rolf Hobson has pointed out the mathematical flaws in this reasoning. A force ratio of 2:3 between the numerically inferior German fleet and the superior British fleet leaves the latter with more than a superiority of one third. It is the central thesis of Hobson's entire discussion of German navalism that the military scenario for a future war with England, with the emphasis on the "defensive battle," was incompatible with the central tenets of *Service Memorandum IX*, which stressed the central importance of the "strategic offensive."

54. Tirpitz, Notes for an imperial audience, 29 September 1899, BA-MA, RM 3/1.

55. "Report of the Three Admirals." Compare "Naval Manoeuvres." On the *Three Admirals Report* and British naval thinking, see also the analysis in Marder, *Anatomy*.

56. E.g., Admiral Diederichs, "Betrachtungen über die Kriegführung Deutschlands zur See gegen England in den Jahren 1904 und 1920," 22 January 1900, BA-MA, RM 3/6657.

57. Lambi, *Navy*, 399–405.
58. Compare Lambi, *Navy*; Kennedy, "Development"; Gemzell, *Conflict*, 50–137; Nägler, "Vorstellungen."
59. The classic study for the army is Ritter, *Schlieffen-Plan*. For army-navy comparisons, see also Herwig, "Tirpitz Plan."
60. On these schemes, see August von Heeringen, "Gesichtspunkte für einen Operationsplan der feindlichen Streikräfte bei einem Kriege Deutschlands allein gegen England allein," 5 March 1896; "Grundzüge für einen Operationsplan Deutschlands gegen England allein," 20 May 1897; Admiral Knorr, "Immediatvortrag Betreffend Grundzüge für einen Operationsplan Deutschlands allein gegen England allein," 31 May 1897; idem, "Kriegführung gegen England," 12 September 1898, all in BA-MA, RM 5/1609. For Tirpitz, see his letter to Stosch, 13 February 1896, BA-MA N 253/321. Compare Lambi, *Navy*, 118–29; Kennedy, "Development," 172–77; Steinberg, "Plan." For 1902, see August von Heeringen, "Denkschrift betreffend den Krieg zwischen Deutschland und England," 12 April 1903; BA-MA, RM 5/1602.
61. The crucial memorandum is Rear-Admiral Felix Bendemann, "Die Defensive gegen England," November 1899; compare idem, "Zum Immediatvortrag. Defensive gegen England," 12 December 1899, both in BA-MA RM 5/1603. See also Admiral Büchsel, "Grundlage für Erwägungen, betreffend den Krieg zwischen Grossbritannien und Deutschland," undated, including Büchsel's statement at the end of the document from 24 November 1902, BA-MA, RM 5/1602; "Immediatvortrag Krieg England u. Deutschland," 1903, N 168/8; idem, "Zum Immediatvortrag," 2 December 1904, BA-MA, RM 5/1604.
62. See Lambi, *Navy*, 209–26, 241–57; and Kennedy, "Development," 177–81.
63. "Zum Immediatvortrag," 20 March 1905, BA-MA, RM 5/1604.
64. Waldemar Vollerthun, "Politische und militärische Betrachtungen über einen englisch-deutschen Krieg," 27 November 1904, BA-MA, N 253/21; Wilhelm Büchsel, "Denkschrift über die Kriegführung gegen England 1905," BA-MA, RM 3/4. Compare idem, "Aufzeichnung," 20 November 1904, BA-MA, N 168/8; Felix Bendemann, "Gedanken über die augenblickliche kritische Lage," 3 December 1904, BA-MA, N 253/21.
65. Büchsel, "Aufzeichnung," 20 November 1904, BA-MA, N 168/8; "Denkschrift über die Kriegführung gegen England 1905," BA-MA, RM 3/4.
66. Koester to Büchsel, 17 February 1905; BA-MA, RM 5/1603.
67. Kennedy, "Development," 183–84. On the British, see Martin, "Plan"; Partridge, "Navy."
68. The key memorandum is Taegert, "Wie wird der Feind voraussichtlich handeln?" 13 April 1908, BA-MA, RM 5/1613.
69. Compare Kennedy, "Strategieprobleme."
70. "Denkschrift über die Kriegführung gegen England 1906," BA-MA, RM 5/1603.
71. Tirpitz to Bülow, 20 April 1907, Enclosure, *GP* 23. See also Tirpitz's statement before the Budget Commission of the Reichstag on 17 March 1909. The protocol of the meeting is in BA-MA, RM 3/9757.
72. Tirpitz, Handwritten notes for a presentation to the emperor, 15 June 1897, BA-MA, N 253/4. Compare Hallman, *Weg*, 240–41; Kelly, *Tirpitz*, 133–34.
73. E.g., Hopman, Diary, 21 January 1905, 9 September 1908, 10 September 1911; in Epkenhans, *Leben*; Michaelis, "Wirken."
74. This approach is well explicated in Admiral Baudissin, "Immediatvortrag zur A.O. an den Chef der Hochseeverbände für den Krieg gegen England 1908," 12 March 1908; idem, "Denkschrift zum Immediatvortrag," 24 October 1908; and "Zum Immediatvortrag," October 1908 BA-MA, RM 5/1606; Fischel to Holtzendorff, 15 December 1909, BA-MA, RM 5/1607; "Zum Immediatvortrag," 18 December 1909, BA-MA, RM 5/1614; "Ostsee oder Nordsee als

Kriegsschauplatz," 18 August 1910, BA-MA, RM 5/1607. Compare Nägler, "Vorstellungen," 41–49; Lambi, *Navy*, 338–49; Gemzell, *Conflict*, 79–80; Kennedy, "Development," 184–86.

75. On Holtzendorff's approach, see Holtzendorff to Fischel, 5 October 1909; statement by the chief of the active fleet, 12 November 1909; "Denkschrift des Flottenkommandos," 5 November 1909; all in BA-MA RM 5/1606. Compare Lambi, *Navy*, 351–56; Gemzell, *Conflict*, 80–84; Kennedy, "Development," 186–87.

76. Heeringen to Tirpitz, 7 October 1911, in Tirpitz, *Aufbau*, 220–21. Compare "Zum Immediatvortrag. Strategische Kriegsspiele Winter 1911," June 1911, BA-MA, RM 5/899. On Heeringen, see also Nägler, "Vorstellungen," 49–50.

77. On this scenario, see "Zum Immediatvortrag," 24 October 1911, BA-MA, RM 5/1606; "Zum Immediatvortrag am 30. 1.1912," 28 January 1912, BA-MA, RM 5/1607; "Zum Immediatvortrag. Entwurf zum Operationsbefehl für den Krieg gegen England," 28 November 1912, BA-MA, RM 5/899; "Zum Immediatvortrag. Gesichtspunkte für eine Kriegführung gegen eine überlegene westliche Seemacht," February 1913, BA-MA, RM 5/899; "Zum Immediatvortrag," 6 March 1913, BA-MA, RM 5/899; Pohl, "Zum Immediatvortrag über das strategische Kriegsspiel des Admiralstabes Winter 1913/14," 5 May 1914, BA-MA, RM 5/900. Compare Lambi, *Navy*, 390–95, 399–405; Nägler, "Vorstellungen," 51–54.

78. "Zum Immediatvortrag: Die französischen Flottenmanöver im Sommer 1913," 30 September 1913; "Zum Immediatvortrag. Englische Flottenmanöver 1913," 17 December 1913, BA-MA, RM 5/900.

79. Operations Order, 30 July 1914, in Granier, *Seekriegsleitung*, I: 67–68.

80. "Denkschrift zum Immediatvortrag über das strategische Kriegsspiel des Admiralstabes Winter 1913/14," 5 May 1914, BA-MA, RM 5/900.

81. Müller, Diary, 1 August 1914, Görlitz, *Regierte*, 39.

82. Michaelis, *Wirken*, 412. Compare Capelle, Notes, 17 May 1914, BA-MA, N 253/28: Capelle raised the possibility of a distant blockade, which would then force the German fleet to engage in offensive action across the North Sea.

83. Hopman, *Logbuch*, 393.

84. Compare Fiebig-von Hase, *Lateinamerika*, 472–506; Lambi, *Navy*, 129–31, 226–31; Herwig, *Politics*, 13–92.

85. Hubert Rebeur-Paschwitz to Tirpitz, 26 January 1900, BA-MA, RM 5/5960. See "O-Plan III," March 1903; "Denkschrift zum O-Plan III," 21 March 1903; "Denkschrift zum O-Plan," 9 December 1902; "Denkschrift zu einem offfensiven Vorgehen gegen die Vereinigten Staaten von Nordamerika," 15 January 1902; all in BA-MA, RM 5/5960; "Denkschrift zum O-Plan," 7 September 1903, "Vermerk zum O.P. III," Winter 1904–05, BA-MA 5/5961.

86. See Felix Bendemann, "Entwurf einer Denkschrift," 2 February 1899; Admiralty Staff, "Denkschrift," March 1899; and idem, "Denkschrift für einen Operationsplan," December 1899; BA-MA, RM 5/5960.

87. See Diederich's memorandum for an imperial audience on 26 February 1900, BA-MA, RM 5/5960.

88. See the correspondence between Admiral v. Diederichs and General v. Schlieffen, March 1900-December 1901, and the memorandum for an imperial audience on 10 December 1900, with the notes about the decision reached by the Emperor that day; in BA-MA, RM 5/5960.

89. "O-Plan III," March 1903, BA-MA, RM 5/5960.

90. Alfred Tirpitz, "Allgemeine Gesichtspunkte bei der Feststellung unsere Flotte nach Schiffsklassen und Schiffstypen," July 1897, BA-MA, N 253/4.

91. Georg Hebbinghaus, "Der Marsch nach Westen," 1906; idem, "Memorandum," 10 September 1906; BA-MA, RM 5/5961.

6. Commerce, Law, and the Limitation of War

1. Schmitt, *Positionen*; idem, *Land*; idem, *Nomos*.
2. Schmitt, *Land*, 88.
3. Schmitt, *Nomos*, 294.
4. Schmitt, *Positionen*, 237. *Hegung des Krieges* is the crucial term in Schmitt, *Nomos*, 285–99.
5. Geyer, "Gewalt": idem, "Urkatastrophe."
6. The conduct of unconditional submarine warfare also involved the direct killing of civilians, of the crews and passengers of torpedoed ships.
7. Weigley, *Way*; Hull, *Destruction*.
8. On the British navy, see Offer, *First World War*; Lambert, "Great Britain."
9. "Allgemeine Erfahrungen aus den Manövern der Herbstübungsflotte," 16 June 1894, Part II. BA-MA, RM 4/176. Compare Maltzahn, "Meer," 412–24.
10. Stockton, *Preparation*. Compare idem, "Commerce Destruction," Two Lectures, 18 and 19 June 1894; NWCA, RG 14.
11. Mahan, "Possibilities" (1897), 128, 133.
12. Mahan, "Lessons" (1899), 106.
13. Mahan, *Sea Power, 1812*, I: 286.
14. Tirpitz to Bülow, 29 April 1907, *GP* 23.
15. See chapter 5.
16. Max Grapow, "Denkschrift die Kriegführung Deutschlands gegen England auf der Australischen Station betreffend," November 1901, BA-MA RM 5/6693. Compare two memoranda by commanding officers of the East Asian Cruiser Division, Vice-Admirals von Prittwitz and von Krosigk from March 1905 and April 1911, BA-MA, RM 5/6256 and 5/5925. On the following see also Lambi, *Navy*, 231–35, 408–10; Overlack, "Function"; idem, "Plans."
17. Tirpitz to Bülow, 20 April 1907, *GP* 23.
18. Ibid., 28 February 1907, *GP* 23. Compare Büchsel to Tirpitz, 27 March 1907, and the enclosure entitled "Gutachten des Admiralstabes der Marine über die Beibehaltung des Seebeuterechtes (vom Standpunkt eine uns aufgezwungenen Krieges gegen E)" BA-MA, RM 5/998.
19. GB to SN, 20 June 1906; NA, RG 80, GB, SF 438
20. Mahan, *Influence, 1792–1812*.
21. Mahan, *Navy*, and idem, *Farragut*. Compare Soley, *Navy*; Maltzahn, *Seekrieg*, 68–86, and *Nauticus*, "Blockade."
22. This is a main theme in Offer, *War*, and Hobson, *Imperialism*, part I.
23. Tirpitz to Einem, 13 March 1906, Reichsarchiv, *Kriegsrüstung*, 206.
24. Tirpitz to Posadowsky-Wehner, 28 January 1907, with enclosure entitled "Untersuchung des Reichsmarineamtes," in Reicharchiv, *Kriegsrüstung*, 218, 219–23. On the context of this investigation, see Burchardt, *Friedenswirtschaft*. For the nine-month figure, see also Schmidt, "Denkschrift über die Vorverhandlungen zur Londoner Konferenz," 3 June 1908, BA-MA, RM 3/3898.
25. Tirpitz to Bülow, 20 April 1907, Enclosure, *GP* 23. For similar assessments offered in previous years, see also Waldemar Vollerthun, "Politische und militärische Betrachtungen über einen englisch-deutschen Krieg, " 27 November 1904, BA-MA, N 253/21; and Wilhelm Büchsel, "Denkschrift über die Kriegführung gegen England 1905," BA MA, RM 3/4.
26. Kehr, *Schlachtflottenbau*, 251–59; Reinhardt, "Tirpitz," 27–67; Hobson, *Imperialism*, 113–31, 273–84.
27. Halle, *Handelsmarine*, 57; compare idem, "Seemachtpolitik."
28. Tirpitz to Bülow, 20 April 1907, *GP* 23; compare Tirpitz to Bülow, 28 February 1907, *GP* 23.

29. Büchsel,"Denkschrift über die Kriegführung gegen England," 1905; BA-MA, RMA 3/4.
30. Halle,"Seemachtpolitik."
31. Vice-Admiral Krosigk,"Denkschrift," April 1911; BA-MA, RM 5/5925.
32. Tirpitz to Bülow, 28 February 1907, *GP* 23. Compare Büchsel to Tirpitz, 27 March 1907, including the enclosure entitled "Gutachten des Admiralstabes der Marine über die Beibehaltung des Seebeuterechtes (vom Standpunkt eine uns aufgezwungenen Krieges gegen E)," BA-MA, RM 5/998.
33. Vice-Admiral Krosigk,"Denkschrift," April 1911; BA-MA, RM 5/5925.
34. A,"Handelskrieg: Fragen des Seekriegsrechtes," 4 December 1913; BA-MA, RM 5/1013.
35. GB to SN, 20 June 1906 NA, RG 80, SF 438.
36. Mahan to Roosevelt, circa July 20, 1906, in Seager and Maguire *Letters*, III: 165. See also several of his letters to Maxse between 1906 and 1907, ibid., 192, 204–16; his "Hague Conference: The Question of Immunity" (1907); and "The Hague Conference and the Practical Aspect"(1907); idem, *Interest, International Conditions*, 47–68, 79–83, 111–17.
37. E.g., Sperry to Bacon, 15 December 1906, NWCA, RG 8, XLAI; Sperry, "Interview with Capt. Ottley, R.N., Wednesday, August 21, 3 P.M.," and Sperry to Secretary of the State, 20 October 1907, all in LC, MD, Sperry Papers, SF "Hague Conference"; Stockton, "Immunity," 937–38.
38. Stockton,"Immunity," 942.
39. Fiske,"Power," 702, 700, 703.
40. My understanding of maritime law draws on Coogan, *End*, and Hobson, *Imperialism*, 57–76. On contest over the British blockade during the Boer War, see Coogan, *End*, 30–42.
41. Coogan, *End*; C. Davis, *Second Hague*, esp. 220–50, 303–26. On the Hague peace conference, compare Dülffer, *Regeln*.
42. On this long-standing policy, see Savage, *Policy*; Semmel, *Liberalism*, 152–71. The issue of the exemption of private property did not become an object of substantial discussion during the first Hague conference in 1899. The U.S. delegates had been instructed to support such an exemption. See C. Davis, *First Hague*, 80, 133–35.
43. Tirpitz to Bülow, 28 February 1907, 20 April 1907 (twice), 30 May 1907; all in *GP* 23; Tirpitz to Müller, 23 April 1907, BA-MA, RM 2/1760; Büchsel to Tirpitz, 27 March 1907, and Tirpitz to Büchsel, 23 April 1907, both in BA-MA, RM 5/998; Imperial Naval Office,"Punktation, dem Herrn Reichskanzler beim Vortrage am 24. May 1907 überlassen" and "File Note," 11 June 1907, both in BA-MA, RM 5/1000; official instruction for German naval delegation in 1907, enclosed in Imperial Naval Office to Admiralty Staff, 12 July 1907, submitting official instructions, BA-MA RM 5/998. Compare Dülffer,"Limitations."
44. Official minutes of an interministerial meeting on 12 November 1904 and their addendum, which noted Tirpitz's objections to the initial decision to accept private immunity; Tirpitz to Chief of Admiralty, 19 December 1904; Tirpitz to Foreign Office, 2 December 1904; all in BA-MA, RM 5/997. At the beginning of the second round of preparations in 1906, the navy's representatives took positions that reflected Tirpitz's wishes: "Aufzeichnung über das von der Russischen Regierung vorgeschlagene Programm der zweiten Haager Friedenskonferenz," including the enclosure on the position of the navy, July 1906; BA-MA, RM 5/998.
45. Siegel to Tirpitz, 17 and 21 June 1907, *GP* 23; Siegel to Tirpitz, 22 July 1907, BA-MA, N 253/9. Siegel was the German naval delegate at the Hague conference.
46. Mahan to Roosevelt, 27 December 1904 and circa 20 July 1906, idem to Elihu Root, 20 April 1906, in Seager and Maguire, *Letters*, III: 112–14, 157–59, 164–65, and idem,"Comments on the Seizure of Private Property at Sea," enclosed in the letter to Root, ibid., 623–26; idem, "The Hague Conference: The Question of Immunity" (1907) and "The Hague Conference and

the Practical Aspects" (1907); GB to SN, 20 June and 28 September 1906, NA, RG 80, GB, SF 438; Roosevelt to Mahan, 29 December 1904 and 16 August 1906, in Turk, *Relationship,* 136, 139; Stockton, "Immunity;" Sperry to Bacon, 15 December 1906, Sperry to Wainwright 20 December 1906; Wainwright to Sperry, December 24, 1906; all in Sperry Papers, LC, MD. See also C. Davis, *Second Hague,* 128, 138–40, 171; Coogan, *End,* 56–60. For German awareness of the views of the U.S. naval delegate, see Siegel to Tirpitz, 21 June 1907, *GP* 23.

47. "Denkschrift über Seebeuterecht," March 1911; BA-MA, RM 3/4919.

48. The following analysis of the U.S. positions is based upon the following material: *The Laws and Usages of War at Sea, A Naval War Code,* prepared by Charles H. Stockton (Washington, D.C., 1901), NA, RG 80; GB, SF 438; GB to SN, 20 June 1906, RG 80, GB, SF 438; Admiral Sperry, "Memorandum Upon the Articles of the Russian Programme for the Second Conference at the Hague Which Relate to the Laws of Maritime Warfare," 30 April 1908, Sperry, Reports to Secretary of State, 11 August, 12 August, 21 August, and 20 October, 1908, undated report on "Contraband," all in LC, MD, Sperry Papers, SF "Hague Conference"; Rear-Admiral Merrell to Secretary of the Navy, 29 September 1908, C. H. Stockton, extract from letter, 18 November 1908, Merrell to SN, 12 December, 1908; all in NWCA, RG 8, XLAI; GB to SN, 25 January 1909, and the many reports by Stockton to the State Department between 8 December 1908 and 18 February 1909, all in RG 80, GB, SF 438. Coogan, *End,* 95–98, 113–16, 122–23; C. Davis, *Second Hague,* 235–42, 310–11, discuss U.S. positions in the context of conference proceedings.

49. GB to SN, 20 June 1906, NA, RG 80, SF 438.

50. Stockton, Extract from letter, 18 November 1908, LC, MD, Sperry Papers.

51. Sperry, Memorandum, 30 April 1907, LC, MD, Sperry Papers.

52. Coogan, *End,* 113–17, shows how U.S. insistence almost prevented an agreement at the conference after the Germans and British had been able to find common ground.

53. GB to SN, 20 June 1906, NA, RG 80, SF 438.

54. Quoted from Sperry, Report to Secretary of the State, 21 August, LC, MD, Sperry Papers.

55. On the issue of conversion and submarine mines, see also President of the NWC to SN (Division of Operations), November 29, 1912, enclosed report; NWCA, RG 8, XLAI.

56. The following analysis draws on these explications of the German positions: "Aufstellung über Positionen der Marine und anderer Ressorts bezüglich der im Schreiben des englischen Botschafters vom März 1908 aufgeführten seekriegsrechtlichen Fragen, wie sie in den Vorverhandlungen zur II. Haager Konferenz festgesetzt wurden," BA-MA, RM 3/3897; "Übersicht über die Hauptunterschiede der Memoranden zur Londoner Konferenz," 1908, BA-MA, RM 3/3897; Schmidt, "Denkschrift über die Vorverhandlungen zur Londoner Konferenz," 3 June 1908, and "Denkschrift für die Vorverhandlungen zur Londoner Konferenz Teil II: Die Bedeutung der einzelnen Fragen und ihre gegenseitigen Beziehungen," 5 June 1908, BA-MA, RM 3/4919 and RM 5/1001; Kriege to Bülow, 5 January 1909, BA-MA, RM 2/1760; memorandum on the results of the London conference, 23 March 1909, BA-MA, RM 2/1760; Kriege to Bülow, 29 April 1909, the official instructions for the German delegation at the conference in London, BA-MA, RM 3/4919; and the correspondence of the naval delegates during the two conferences, RM 5/999–1000 (Hague), *GP* 23, 382–97 (Hague), BA-MA, RM 2/1760 (London), BA-MA, RM 3/4919 (London), and BA-MA, RM 5/1002 (London).

57. Tirpitz to Siegel, 27 June 1907; BA-MA, RM 5/1000.

58. "Instruktion für die Deutsche Delegation zur Londoner Seekriegsrecht-Konferenz," BA-MA, RM 3/4919.

59. For the term "illusory," see "Aufstellung über Positionen," BA-MA, RM 3/3897; Schmidt, "Denkschrift," 3 June 1908 BA-MA, RM 3/4919; and the minutes of an interministerial meeting, 8 July 1908 (statement by Uslar, the representative of the Imperial Naval Office), BA-MA, RM 3/4919.

60. "Ergebnisse der in London vom 4. Dezember 1908 bis zum 26. February 1909 abgehaltenen Seekriegsrechts-Konferenz," BA-MA, RM 2/1760; Kriege to Bülow, 29 April 1909, BA-MA, RM 3/4919. For an exemplary recognition of the importance of the conversion issue, see Müller, Note, 19 June 1907; in *GP* 23.

61. Kriege to Bülow, 5 January and 6 February 1909, BA-MA, RM 2/1760; "Aufstellung über Positionen," BA-MA, RM 3/3897.

62. "Ergebnisse," BA-MA, RM 2/1760; Kriege to Bülow, 20 April 1909, BA-MA, RM 3/4919; Starke to Bachmann, 17 February 1909, BA-MA, RM 5/1002; Tirpitz to Bethmann-Hollweg, 20 March 1909, BA-MA, RM 5/1002.

63. Schmidt, "Denkschrift über die Vorverhandlungen zur Londoner Konferenz," 3 June 1908, BA-MA, RM 3/3898.

64. "Stellung der Marine," July 1906, BA-MA, RM 5/998.

65. GB to SN, 20 June and 28 September 1906, NA, RG 80, SF 438; Mahan to Roosevelt, 27 December 1904 and circa 20 July 1906, and to Root from 20 April 1906 including the enclosure, Seager, *Letters,* III: 112–14, 157–59, 164–65.

66. Stockton, "Immunity," 942.

67. Sperry, "Memorandum," April 30, 1908, LC, MD, Sperry Papers, SF "Hague Conference." On dismissals of the specter of a successful blockade of the United States, see the same memo; Stockton, "Immunity," 941–42; Fiske, "Power;" 700–703; Mahan, *Influence, 1660–1783,* 86–87; GB to SN, 20 June 1906, NA, RG 80, SF 438.

68. NWC, "Report of the 2nd Committee on International Law Questions Proposed," 31 August 1908; NWCA, RG 8, XLAI.

69. This is also the argument in Coogan, *End,* and Semmel, *Liberalism,* 152–71. The traditional U.S. policy is well documented in Savage, *Policy.*

70. Hobson, "Prussia." On Tirpitz and private immunity in 1899, see Dülffer, "Limitations," 27–28.

71. Mahan, "Conference, Question" and "Conference, Aspects" (1907); and Tirpitz to Bülow, 28 February 1907 and 20 April 1907, in *GP* 23.

72. Stockton, "Conference," 614; idem, "Address, 1909," 80.

73. Widenmann to Tirpitz, 2 November 1910; Aiv, "Denkschrift über England und die Londoner Erklärung," 21 December 1910; both in BA-MA, RM 3/3898. Strikingly, Widenmann was a rabid Anglophobe. On him, see Widenmann, *Marine-Attaché.*

74. A case in point are the instructions for the German delegation at the London naval conference; BA-MA, RM 3/4919. On German concerns prior to the conference, see "Niederschrift über die erste kommissarische Vorbesprechung über das Programm der Londoner Konferenz, die am 22. April 1908 im AA stattfand," BA-MA, RM 5/1001; and the draft for an official statement by the Imperial Naval Office at an interministerial meeting, 19 June 1908, BA-MA, RM 3/4919. On similar concerns expressed in 1907, see Tirpitz to Bülow, 28 February 1907 and 20 April 1907, *GP 23*; and the "Punktation" that Tirpitz submitted to the imperial chancellor on 24 May, 1907, BA-MA, RM 5/1000.

75. Hankel, *Prozesse*; Hull, *Destruction,* 122–26; Messerschmidt, "Völkerrecht."

76. On the making of the German legal code governing commerce-destruction, the Prisenordnung, which Wilhelm II approved in September 1909, see the materials in BA-MA, RM 5/1004–1005. The Prize Order itself is printed in Pohl, *Seekriegsrecht,* 30–71. On the incorporation of the London Declaration into the U.S. naval war code, see NWC to SN, 31 January 1912,

NA, RG 80, GB, SF 438; NWC to SN, November 29, 1912, NWCA, RG 8, SF XLAI; Stockton, "Conference," idem, "Address, 1912." Compare Coogan, *End*, 126.

77. Spindler, "Handelskrieg," I: 153–54.

78. Operations Order, 30 July 1914; in Tirpitz, *Ohnmachtspolitik*, 35–36.

79. By contrast, Jost Dülffer has argued that Tirpitz's ideas about a cruiser-based war against British commerce, which he advanced in 1907, "tended towards a kind of total naval war in the event of a general war with Britain." See his "Limitations," 39.

80. Hobson, *Imperialism*, esp. 72–76. Compare Coogan, *End*; Hankel, *Prozesse*.

81. On the actions of the Wilson administration, see Coogan, *End*, 169–236.

82. Bönker, "Way," 308–322. The term "war of economic extermination" was used in Holtzendorff to Wilhelm II, 7 December 1915, in Granier, *Seekriegsleitung*, I: 339–42. On "wonder weapons" as applied to the German navy's embrace of submarines, see Hull, *Destruction*, 222–24, 295–98.

83. GB to SN, 24 March 1915, NA, RG 80, SF 438. Compare GB to SN, 14 November 1914, NA, RG 80, SF 421. In September 1914, Rear-Admiral Fiske predicted severe conflict with Britain as soon as the British started to treat foodstuffs as contraband. Diary entry, 28 September, LC, MD, Fiske Papers.

84. See especially U.S. Naval Planning Section, "Memorandum No. 70: Freedom of the Seas," 7 November 1918, Office, *Section*, 481–88; Benson to Daniels, 10 November 1918, MD, LC, Daniels Papers.

85. Offer, *War*, 232 (Ottley quote); Mahan, *Influence, 1660–1783*, 133. Compare Lambert, "Great Britain," 23, 33.

86. E.g., Tirpitz to Bülow, 20 April 1907, *GP* 23; Widenmann to Tirpitz, 2 March 1911, Tirpitz, *Aufbau*, 311–13.

7. Naval Elites and the State

1. *Hearings for a General Board*, 927, 935.
2. Long, *Navy*, I: 124, II: 182.
3. *Naval Investigation*, Hearings, 2099–2100; *Annual Report of the Navy Department, 1920*, 357.
4. Lasswell, *Essays*.
5. For this formulation I have drawn on Geyer, "Strategy," 533.
6. Förster, "Forces": Herwig, *Fleet*.
7. Geyer, *Rüstungspolitik*, 25–45; idem, "Past"; Förster, "Forces"; Wehler, *Gesellschaftsgeschichte*, 873–85, 1109–37; Becker, "Militarismus." In her *Absolute Destruction*, 93–109, 327, Isabel Hull characterizes the Imperial German military as a "charismatic institution."
8. E.g., Steinberg, *Deterrent*, 61–124; Kehr, *Schlachtflottenbau*.
9. E.g., Knorr to Wilhelm II, 19 December 1896, Hollmann to Wilhelm II, 21 January 1897, Knorr to Tirpitz, 30 January 1898, all in BA-MA, RM 2/2005; Tirpitz to Wilhelm II, 3 February and 24 April 1898, Knorr to Wilhelm II, 21 May 1898, Tirpitz to Kaiser, 28 May 1898, Tirpitz, "Motive für die Organisationsänderung," undated, 1898, Tirpitz to Wilhelm II, 10 March 1899, and Tirpitz, Notes for the imperial audience on 20 March 1899; all in BA-MA, N 253/39. Compare Berghahn, *Tirpitz-Plan*, 23–45, 531–34; and Lehment, *Kriegsmarine*, 100–126.
10. This is one of the main themes in Berghahn, *Tirpitz-Plan*.
11. Tirpitz to Wilhelm II, 7 September 1907, BA-MA, N 253/9. A good explication of Tirpitz's ideas is in Tirpitz, "Über die Entwicklung und Bedeutung des Flottengesetzes," presentation before senior officers, Kiel, 4 April 1910; BA-MA, RM 3/11690.

12. Tirpitz to Prince Henry of Prussia, 28 January 1907, BA-MA, N 253/9. Compare Tirpitz to Bülow, 14 August 1907; BA-MA, N 253/9.

13. Berghahn, *Tirpitz-Plan*.

14. Harald Dähnhardt, "Weiterer Ausbau des Flottengesetzes," 4 February 1907, BA-MA, RM 3/6677. Compare Harald Dähnhardt, Memoranda from 9 July and 2 November 1903, BA-MA, RM 3/6663; Tirpitz to Bülow, November 1905, BA-MA, RM 3/6.

15. Tirpitz, *Erinnerungen*, 109. Compare Tirpitz, "Über die Entwicklung und Bedeutung des Flottengesetzes," Presentation before senior officers, Kiel, 4 April 1910, BA-MA, RM 3/11690. Stressing the limitations of the Reichstag obligations, historian Patrick Kelly has suggested that Tirpitz's entire system of legal codification "to a degree, was a bluff." He also emphasized that the navy secretary had no doubts about the navy's never-ending dependence on the goodwill of the Reichstag. Kelly, *Tirpitz*, 191–95, 451–56 (quote: 193).

16. E.g., Tirpitz to Miquel, 5 August 1897; Heeringen to Tirpitz, 6 August 1897; Capelle to Tirpitz, 6 and 7 August 1897; Tirpitz, notes for an imperial audience on 19 August 1897; his notes about a meeting with the Imperial Chancellor on 15 September 1897; and the official minutes of the meeting of the Prussian Ministry of State on 6 October 1897; all in BA-MA, N 253/4.

17. On this incident, see Steinberg, *Deterrent*, 189–93.

18. Tirpitz to Bülow, 8 November 1905, and the enclosed summary of a conversation with leaders of the German Navy League, BA-MA, N 253/6; Tirpitz, Memorandum, 13 November 1905, BA-MA, RM 3/6; Tirpitz to Loebell, 16 November 1905, BA-MA, RM 3/6; and the documents in Tirpitz, *Aufbau*, 20–30. Compare Berghahn, *Tirpitz-Plan*, 491–504. So frustrated was Tirpitz with the emperor's behavior that he offered his resignation on April 6, 1906.

19. Harald Dähnhardt, "Weiterer Ausbau des Flottengesetzes," 4 February 1907, BA-MA, RM 3/6677; compare idem, Memorandum, 15 May 1906, and "In Welcher Richtung soll sich die Weiterentwicklung unserer Flotte bewegen?" 7 July 1906, both in BA-MA, RM 3/6677; Capelle, Memorandum, May 1906, BA-MA, N 253/23; Tirpitz to Prince Henry of Prussia, 28 January 1907, BA-MA, N 253/9; Harald Dähnhardt, Memorandum, 19 January 1907, BA-MA, RM 3/6677; and Tirpitz's correspondence from 1907 in BA-MA, N 253/9 and RM 3/7. Compare Berghahn, *Tirpitz-Plan*, 505–91; Kelly, *Tirpitz*, 263–92.

20. Tirpitz, Notes for and about a conversation with the Imperial Chancellor on 4 May 1911, Capelle to Tirpitz, 29 July 1910, Tirpitz, Notes, undated, May 1914, N 253/24; Capelle to Tirpitz, 11 and 14 September 1911, Tirpitz to Capelle, 13 September 1911, Tirpitz, Notes for a presentation to the Emperor, 26 September 1911, BA-MA, N 253/25. On the bill's making, see Epkenhans, *Flottenrüstung*, 93–142.

21. See chapter 3.

22. See chapter 11.

23. Tirpitz, *Ohnmachtspolitik*; idem, *Erinnerungen*, esp. 393–503 (wartime letters); and the many entries about conversations with Tirpitz in the diary of Hopman, Epkenhans, *Leben*.

24. See "Aufzeichnung Seiner Excellenz des Herrn Staatssekretärs in der Sitzung vom 13. April 1916," and the memoirs submitted in return, all in BA-MA RM 3/10. The quotes are from Admiral Hebbinghaus, "Gedanken über die zukünftige Entwicklung der Marine," 31 April 1916.

25. Capelle, Report about an imperial audience on 3 May 1916, BA-MA, RM 3/11599.

26. Adolf von Trotha, "Wie steht die Marine den neuen Aufgaben gegenüber?" 16 April 1918, in Trotha, *Volkstum*, 141–42.

27. A concise portrait of Senden is in Hull, *Entourage*, 178–81. There's a huge literature on the Emperor and his aspirations to personal rule, including the monumental multivolume biographies by John Röhl and Lamar Cecil.

28. Tirpitz, Notes about his imperial audience on 28 January 1896, BA-MA, N 253/3. Compare Holstein to Eulenburg, 9 February 1896, in Rich and Fisher, *Papiere*, III: 530–32.

29. Senden to Tirpitz, 13 February 1896, BA-MA, N 253/3; Senden to Tirpitz, 29 April 1898, BA-MA, N 253/39.

30. Tirpitz, Notes about the imperial audience on 15 June 1897, BA-MA, N 253/4.

31. Prince Henry of Prussia to Senden, 25 July 1898, BA-MA, N 160/4. In the spring and summer of 1898, Tirpitz used this pressure tactic to enhance the authority of the Imperial Naval Office among the various naval agencies. Tirpitz to Bülow, 25 April 1898, Wilhelm II, 28 May 1898, Tirpitz to Hohenlohe, 28 May 1898, Tirpitz to Wilhelm II, 14 June 1898, Tirpitz to Hohenlohe, 14 June 1898; all in BA-MA, N 253/39.

32. E.g., Röhl, *Wilhelm II*, 1109–52; Cecil, *Wilhelm II*, 291–318; König, *Wilhelm II*, 19–51, 250–52.

33. König, *Wilhelm II*, 252. The importance of the system of legal codification in relation to the emperor is emphasized in Tirpitz, *Erinnerungen*, 85–86. Compare Berghahn, "Flotte," esp. 187–88.

34. Trützschler, *Jahre*, 83, 100.

35. Philip Duams, Germany N.A. Report 20/6, 10 May 1906; in Seligmann, *Intelligence*, 11. For more on naval officers' attitudes toward Wilhelm II, see chapter 9.

36. On this commission, see Lambi, *Navy*, 50–56.

37. On Büchsel's proposal, see a note written by an Admiralty Staff officer, 26 October 1904; RM 5/1609. See also Lambi, *Navy*, 225–26.

38. Michael Epkenhans, presentation, German Studies Association Conference in San Diego, Fall 2007.

39. On Tirpitz's maneuvering in the run-up to the Naval Bills of 1898 and 1900, see Berghahn, *Tirpitz-Plan*, 108–29, 226–48, and Kelly, *Tirpitz*, 129–202. Strikingly, in 1897 Tirpitz had to present his plans to the Prussian State Ministry and engage in political negotiations with its powerful vice-president, Johannes von Miquel. See the Minutes of the meeting of the Ministry on 6 October 1897, and the correspondence among Tirpitz, two of his aides, and Miquel in the summer and fall of 1897, in BA-MA N 253/4. There was no equivalent in 1899–1900.

40. Tirpitz, Memorandum, 3 January 1896; idem, Notes about the imperial audience on 28 January 1896; BA-MA, N 253/3.

41. On Tirpitz's demands, see also his letter to Prince Henry of Prussia, 15 November 1898, BA-MA, N 253/39. On his appointment, see Goldschmidt, *Reich*, 105–6, 327–32; and the letter exchange between Hohenlohe and Wilhelm II, 23 and 27 March 1898, in Hohenlohe-Schillingfürst, *Denkwürdigkeiten*, 435–37.

42. Thus, Tirpitz intervened in the intergovernmental disputes over the Courts Martial Bill and asked Wilhelm to accommodate the wishes of the Reichstag. See his notes about an imperial audience on 18 August 1897, BA-MA, N 253/4; Hohenlohe-Schillingfürst, *Denkwürdigkeiten*, 390; Tirpitz to Grand-Duke of Baden, 14 November 1897, BA-MA, N 253/4; Bülow to Eulenburg, 22 August 1897, in Röhl, *Korrespondenz*, III: 1856–58.

43. On Bülow's role in 1899–1900, see Winzen, *Weltmachtpolitik*, 98–128. For Bülow's support of Tirpitz after 1900, see Lerman, *Chancellor*, 106.

44. On the Naval Bill of 1906, see the discussion in the previous section. On Tirpitz's demands in the context of the Bill of 1908, see Tirpitz to Bülow, 17 March 1907, Tirpitz to Bülow, 14 August 1907, in BA-MA, N 253/9.

45. Tirpitz, Notes for his imperial audiences on 28 January 1896 and 15 June 1897; BA-MA, N 253/3 and N 25/4.

46. Tirpitz to Hohenlohe, 28 October 1899; Hohenlohe-Schillingfürst, *Denkwürdigkeiten*, 536.

47. Tirpitz, *Erinnerungen*, 128.

48. E.g., Ernst Halle, Memorandum, 7 July 1899, with Tirpitz's comments; BA-MA, RM 3/1; Tirpitz, "Notizen über wichtige Ereignisse und Verhandlungen," 12 September 1904, BA-MA, RM 3/3; Tirpitz, Notes for imperial audiences on 9 March 1907 and 21 September 1907, BA-MA, N 253/9; Tirpitz to Bethmann-Hollweg, 30 August 1911, in Tirpitz, *Aufbau*, 207–8; idem, Tirpitz, Notes for an imperial audience on 26 September 1911, BA-MA, N 253/25. On the entire issue, see Witt, "Reichsfinanzen;" Berghahn, *Tirpitz-Plan*, esp. 370–74.

49. Tirpitz to Stosch, 21 December 1895, Tirpitz, Memorandum, 3 January 1896, Tirpitz, Notes for and about an imperial audience on 28 January 1896, all in BA-MA, N 253/3; Tirpitz to Senden, 8 February 1896, BA-MA, N 160/5; Senden, Notes about a conversation with chief of the Civil Cabinet, 13 February 1896, BA-MA, N 160/11; Senden to Tirpitz, 13 February 1896, BA-MA, N 253/3; Tirpitz to Senden, 15 February 1896, BA-MA, N 160/5; Tirpitz, Notes for an imperial audience on 15 June 1897, BA-MA, N 253/4; Tirpitz to Emperor, 24 April 1898, idem, "Motive für die Organisationsänderung," undated notes, summer 1898, Tirpitz to Prince Henry of Prussia, 15 September 1898; all in BA-MA, N 253/39.

50. Tirpitz, Memorandum, 3 January 1896; Tirpitz to Stosch, 21 December 1895; Tirpitz, Notes for an imperial audience on 15 June 1897, BA-MA, N 253/3 and N 253/4.

51. Tirpitz, Memorandum, 3 January 1896, BA-MA, N 253/3.

52. Tirpitz, "Motive für die Organisationsänderung," and Tirpitz to Prince Henry of Prussia, 15 September 1898; BA-MA, N 253/39. On Stosch and his ideas, see Sieg, *Ära*, 379–90.

53. On this, see the materials in BA-MA, RM 3/4961–4964. Compare Gosewinkel, *Einbürgern*, 278–327.

54. On the navy and Kiaochow, see Tirpitz, *Erinnerungen*, 61–78; Muehlhahn, *Herrschaft*. For Tirpitz's reasoning in 1898, see his notes for an imperial audience on 16 January 1898; and RMA, File Note, January 1898; BA-MA, RM 3/6699.

55. Compare Mollin, "Militär;" Kelly, *Tirpitz*, esp. 462–63.

56. See his own account in Bülow, *Denkwürdigkeiten*, I: esp. 108–17, 412–17; see also idem, *Politik*, esp. 20–21. Compare Winzen, *Weltmachtkonzept*, 61–128; Kennedy, *Antagonism*, 223–50.

57. See the correspondence between Tirpitz and Bülow from November 1908 to March 1909 and the Minutes of a Meeting at the Imperial Chancellor on 3 June 1909; all in *GP* 28. Compare the documents in Tirpitz, *Aufbau*, 38–162.

58. On Tirpitz's dealings with Bethmann-Hollweg between 1909 and spring 1912, see the documents in *GP* 28 and 31 and in Tirpitz, "Flottenverständigung." On resignation threats, see Tirpitz to Bülow, 4 January 1909, and Tirpitz to Bethmann-Hollweg, 4 November 1909, *GP* 29; Tirpitz, Note about a Conversation with Admiral Müller, 14 November 1911, and Tirpitz to Müller, 10 March 1912, in Tirpitz, *Aufbau*, 256–57, 323; Müller, Diary, 14 November 1911, in Görlitz, *Kaiser*, 100.

59. Tirpitz, Notes about a Conversation with Admiral von Heeringen, 30 November 1911, in Tirpitz, *Aufbau*, 266; Hopman, Diary, 30 November 1911, in Epkenhans, *Leben*. On the making of the Army Bill, see Förster, *Militarismus*, and Herrmann, *Arming*.

60. An exhaustive account is in Epkenhans, *Flottenrüstung*, parts II and IV.

61. On the Navy Department, see Paullin, *Paullin's History*, 205–18, 321–34, 364–85; Beers, "Development."

62. Skowronek, *Building*. Compare Bright, "State," and Skocpol, *Protecting*.

63. On "congressional government" and the post–Civil War navy, see Buhl, "Maintaining," and White, *Era*.

64. Still pertinent on this issue are Ekirch, *Civilian*, 1–123; Millis, *Arms*, 13–210.

65. Compare O'Connor, "Origins"; Costello, "Planning," 8–105; Spector, *Professors*, 130–43; Oyos, "Roosevelt," 227–50.

66. On the following, see Taylor, "Memorandum"; Admiral Dewey, "Memorandum for the President," 3 June 1902 (a text written by Taylor and then submitted to Roosevelt over Dewey's signature), Taylor, "Memorandum on the Necessity of a Naval General Staff and the Method of Supplying It," 13 October 1903, both in NA, RG 80, GB, SF 401; Taylor, "Fleet"; and Taylor's reports as the Chief of the Bureau of Navigation in October 1902 and 1903 in Navy Department, *Annual Report, 1902 and 1903*. The quotes are from Taylor, "Fleet."

67. Taylor to Luce, 13 January 1896; see also Taylor to Luce, 1 October 1896. LC, MD, Luce Papers.

68. Taylor to Luce, 13 and 22 January 1896, Luce Papers, LC, MD; Roosevelt to Taylor, 24 May 1897, and Roosevelt to Goodrich, 19 November 1897, in Morison, *Letters*, I: 617 and 718; Taylor to Luce, 3 December 1897, LC, MD, Luce Papers. In 1896, the chief of the Naval Intelligence Office included provisions for a General Staff in a first draft of the new Personnel Bill, which was eventually enacted into law in 1899. Cummings, *Wainwright*, 214.

69. See Navy Department, "General Order No. 544," 13 March 1900; Long to Dewey, 30 March 1900; "Brief Account of the General Board," 26 October 1903; all in NA, RG 80, GB, SF 401. For Taylor's lobbying efforts that led to Long's action in 1900, see Taylor to Long, 30 January 1900 and 14 February 1900, in Allen, *Papers*, 305–6, 311–12; and Taylor, "Memorandum."

70. Taylor, "Fleet," 803. On the GB, see Costello, "Planning for War."

71. Taylor to Long, 8 June 1901 and 12 August 1901, in Allen, *Papers*, 367–68, 387; Dewey to Long, 28 June 1901, NA, RG 80, GB, SF 40; Long to Dewey, 10 July 1901, Taylor to Dewey, 14 July 1901, Dewey to Taylor, 17 July 1901, all in LC, MD, Dewey Papers.

72. *Hearings for a General Board*. On the previous deliberations, see Taylor to Luce, 11 September 1903; Taylor to Moody, 10 April 1904; Taylor to Dewey, undated, in LC, MD, Luce Papers, Moody Papers, and Dewey Papers, respectively. Compare Heffron, "Moody."

73. Taylor to Luce, 29 June 1904, LC, MD, Luce Papers; Taylor to Barnette, 30 June 1904, NA, RG 45, SF 1775–1910, box 675.

74. E.g., Fiske, "Policy," the 1905 Prize Essay, and Luce, "Department"; and the official discussion of these articles in *PUSNI* 31 (1905): 179–96, 465–78, 478–85. Demands for a naval general staff abounded on the pages of *PUSNI* after 1900.

75. For these attempts, see Barnette to Luce, 15 October 1905, 3 May 1906, 16 May 1906, and 15 December 1905, in LC, MD, Luce Papers. Compare Costello, "Planning," 72–75; Spector, *Admiral*, 156–57. For another proposal to push the issue, see Luce to GB, 27 March 1905, NA, RG 80, GB, SF 446. See Luce to Taylor, 25 June 1904, in Gleaves, *Life*, 238–39.

76. A classic analysis is Morison, *Sims*, esp. 176–216. For a fuller discussion of this incident, see chapter 11.

77. Written by Mahan, the reports of the "Moody Board" dated from 20 and 26 February 1909. They were printed as *Senate Documents 740 and 743*, 60th Congress, 2nd session.

78. In NA, RG 80, GB, SF 446.

79. More extensive discussions of the aide system include Stirling, "Organization"; Crosley, "College"; Jones, "Details." Compare Beers, "Development."

80. Fiske, "Policy"; idem, "Authority"; idem, "Profession," esp. 480–82, 574–76.

81. For Fiske's agenda, see his own account in his memoirs: *Midshipman*, 550–71; and his statement before Congress on 24 March 1916; in *Hearings 1916*, 2887–2975. Compare Coletta, *Fiske*, 131–78.

82. See chapter 11. Already in 1909 Admiral Dewey and Rear-Admiral Sperry had voiced their concern that the schemes proposed by the Moody and Swift boards would diminish the

role of the General Board and strip it of much of its authority. Sperry, in fact, had suggested to the secretary of the navy the aide system as it was then set up. Sperry to Charles Sperry, 16 May 1909, LC, MD, Sperry Papers.

83. See Admiral Austin Knight's statement before Congress on 28 February 1916, *Hearings on Estimates 1916*, 2011. For the dissatisfaction with the law of 1915, see the statements by Admirals Winslow, Fiske, and Benson and Captain Sims during those hearings.

84. Daniels, *Era*, 244.

85. Quoted in Beers, "Development," II: 12.

86. Beers, "Development," II: 18–20.

87. *Naval Investigation. Hearings*, especially the "Appendix, Written Statements by Witnesses about Desirable Changes."

88. Taylor, "Fleet," 802–3. This choice was part of a larger veneration for the German model of military professionalism, which will be discussed in chapter 10.

89. Taylor, "Fleet," 803.

90. See, for example, W. L. Rodgers, "A Comparative Study of Naval Departmental Organizations," 2 January 1909, NA, RG 80, GB, SF 446; Stirling, "Organization."

91. Allin, *Institute*, 263–306.

92. Chadwick, "Address," 260–61.

93. Luce, "Relations," 83. For Luce, see also his "Administration" and his "Department." For Mahan, see his "Principles" and Mahan to Roosevelt, January 1909, in Seager and Maguire, *Letters*, III: 153–55.

94. Taylor, "Fleet," 803.

95. On this point, compare Steinisch, "Path," 38–39.

96. The best elaboration of this view is in Fiske, "Authority"; idem, "Profession," esp. 480–82, 574–76.

97. One example is Rear-Admiral Hendry McCalla who did so in his memoirs, written within seven years after his retirement from active duty in 1903. Coletta, *McCalla*, 155. Public endorsements are McKean, "War"; and Hinds, "Peace."

98. Fiske, "Power," 731.

99. See Fiske's statement before Congress on 24 March 1916; in *Hearings on Estimates 1916*, 2919–20.

100. Fiske, *Midshipman*, 632.

101. Fiske, Diary, 9 August 1914. Coletta, *Fiske*, 132.

102. Ellicott, "Design," 63. Other examples include Murdock, "Need"; Gibbons, "Need"; Poundstone, "Size"; Fullinwider, "Fleet."

103. As discussed in chapter 3.

104. Nulton, "Notes." See also Howard, "Increase."

105. Gibbons, "Need," 328. See also the following two lectures given at the Naval War College in 1899 and 1900: F. A. Traut, "The Sea Power of Germany," 1899, and John Morris Endicott, "Sea Power of Germany," 1900, both in NWCA, RG 14.

106. Gibbons, "Need," 331.

107. Fiske, "Ships," 550.

108. Hill, "Coordination," quote: 565. Compare idem, "Coordination Before and During War," 1910 and 1912, NWCA, RG 14; the reports of the first and second committees on the issue of a Council of National Defense, in RC 1911 and RC 1912, and Captain W. L. Rodgers, "RC Discussion—Q 1," in RC 1912, all in NWCA, RG 12; the statements by Admiral Raymond P. Rodgers and Admiral Wainwright before Congress on 24 January 1911, *Hearing on Council*; the statements by Mahan and Wainwright before Congress on 19 May 1911 in *Hearing*

on Council; Mahan to Lengerke-Meyer, 1 February 1911, Seager and Maguire, *Letters*, III: 374–75; idem, "Navies"; and Rear-Admiral Sidney A. Staunton, "War Plans and War Portfolios," 22 April 22, 1912, NWCA, RG 8, XSTAP.

109. *Hearing on Council of National Defense*, 1911, 14.

110. Captain W. L. Rodgers, "CR Discussion—Q 1," in RC 1912, NWCA, RG 12.

111. Hearing on Council of National Defense, 1912, 11. Compare Mahan to SN, 1 February 1911, in Seager and Maguire, *Letters*, III: 374–75.

112. On the naval elite's continuing interest in a Council of National Defense between 1914 and 1916, see McKean, "War"; Gatewood, "Preparedness"; Davis, "Thoughts"; Hinds, "Peace"; Cronan, "Need." The Council of National Defense that was set up in 1916 served the purpose of industrial mobilization and government-business coordination.

113. On this crisis see Cronon, *Diaries*, 52–69; Daniels, *Era*, 161–69.

8. Manufacturing Consent

1. Vagts, "Hopes," 523, 521, 522.
2. I have taken this term from Geyer, *Rüstungspolitik*, 73.
3. Deist, *Flottenpolitik*.
4. Eley, *Reshaping*, 206–12; Stöber, *Pressepolitik*.
5. Tirpitz, Memorandum, 3 January 1896, idem, Notes for an imperial audience on 28 January, BA-MA, N 253/3; All-Highest Cabinet Order from 28 May 1896, and the memorandum by Hugo Pohl, an officer with the Imperial Naval Office, about this order, BA-MA, RM 2/1730; Senden, Notes about a conversation with the Chief of the Civil Cabinet, 13 February 1896, and Senden, Notes on Admiral Hollmann, spring 1896, BA-MA, N 160/11. Compare Deist, *Flottenpolitik*, 31–69.
6. Keim, *Erlebtes*, 49–77.
7. E.g., Steinberg, *Deterrent*, 61–124; Kehr, *Schlachtflottenbau*.
8. Gülich to Tirpitz, 24 November 1897; BA-MA, RM 3/9618.
9. Geppert, *Pressekriege*, 233–45.
10. Borckenhagen, "'Seeoffizierstypen,'" 498.
11. Tirpitz, *Erinnerungen*, 81–82; Deist, *Flottenpolitik*, 71–73.
12. Tirpitz to Hohenlohe, 15 April 1898; BA, Akten der Reichskanzlei, R 43/1560.
13. Capelle to Tirpitz, 25 July 1912, Tirpitz to Capelle, 26 July 1912, Capelle to Tirpitz, 27 July 1912, Tirpitz to Bethmann-Hollweg, 16 August 1912, all in BA-MA, N 253/27. On Bethmann-Hollweg's initiative, see Stöber, *Pressepolitik*, 250–53.
14. Löhlein, Comments on a letter from the War Department to Imperial Naval Office, 12 February 1914, BA-MA, RM 3/9798; for more, see the correspondence in BA-MA, RM 3/9953, 3/9954, and 9/9798. On this issue, see Deist, *Flottenpolitik*, 322–23.
15. Skowronek, *Building*, 37–162; White, *Era*.
16. Albion, *Makers*, 212–14.
17. Ibid., 174–77.
18. Davis, *Lobby*, 266. For interest in a press bureau in 1912, see also "First CR Q1," Part I, RC 1912; NWCA, RG 12.
19. *Annual Reports of the Navy Department*, 1913, 30–33.
20. Geppert, *Pressekriege*; and Rüger, *Game*.
21. John Callan O'Laughlin, "The Navy and the Press, address," 13 July 1909; NWCA, RG 15; idem, "The Relations of Press Correspondents to the Navy before and during the War,"

Lecture at Naval War College Extension Course, Washington, D.C., 17 February 1913; NWCA, RG 4.

22. Heeringen to Tirpitz, 25 June 1897, BA-MA, N 253/407.

23. Tirpitz to Senden, 20 January 1897, BA-MA, N 160/5.

24. Kühlmann, *Erinnerungen*, 292.

25. Take, for example, Caprivi's notes about various conversations with Reichstag deputies in late 1897 and early 1898, and Fritz Hoenig to Tirpitz, 6 December 1897, all in BA-MA, N 253/4.

26. Capelle to Lieber, 30 October 1897, quoted in Gottwald, "Umfall," 194. On these negotiations and the subsequent cooperation, compare Kelly, *Tirpitz*, 140–52; Zeender, *Center Party*, 63–72; Winzen, *Weltmachtkonzept*, 108–19.

27. Tirpitz to Lieber, 23 April 1898, BA-MA, N 253/4.

28. Statement by Eduard von Capelle, Enclosure to Wahnschaffe to Capelle, 26 July 1912; BA-MA, N 253/27.

29. Noske, *Erlebtes*, 39.

30. For Tirpitz's cheers, see the prepared text for his speech; BA-MA, N 253/8. On these trips, see Fischer, "Faszination"; Raeder, *Leben*, 58–59. The trips were covered in *Marine-Rundschau* 18 (1907): 937–38, and 19 (1908): 779–80.

31. Bassermann, *Tirpitz*, 19–20; Deist, *Flottenpolitik*, 19.

32. Dewey, Memorandum for the President, 3 June 1902; Henry C. Taylor, "Memorandum on the Necessity of a Naval General Staff and the Method of Supplying it," 13 October 1903, both in NA, RG 80, GB, SF 401; Dewey to Roosevelt, 3 June 1902, and Roosevelt to Dewey, 4 June 1902, both in NA, RG 80, GB, SF 401; Taylor's reports as the Chief of the Bureau of Navigation in October 1902 and 1903, *Annual Report of the Navy Department, 1902*, 415, and *Annual Report, 1903*, 498–99; *Hearing on General Board, 1904*. On the paragraph, see Taylor to Roosevelt, 13 September 1903, LC, MD, Roosevelt Papers; Roosevelt to Taylor, 15 September 1903, in Morison, *Letters*, III: 601–2; Roosevelt, "Third Annual Message," 6806.

33. Barnette to Luce, 16 September 1903; LC, MD, Luce Papers.

34. Ibid., 26 September 1903; LC, MD, Luce Papers.

35. "Circular for the Information of Officers," dated 1903, NA, RG 80, GB, SF 446.

36. Barnette to Luce, 28 July 1903; LC, MD, Luce Papers.

37. See Heffron, "Secretary Moody," 42. For the *Dolphin*, see also Albion, *Makers*, 164–66; and Gleaves, *Admiral*, 61–64, 99–103.

38. *Annual Report of the Navy Department, 1913*, 30–33.

39. Oyos, "Roosevelt"; Arnold, "Policy Leadership"; O'Brien, *Power*, 47–72; Hendrix, *Diplomacy*. During Roosevelt's presidency, the realm of naval politics, too, was characterized by an "executive-professional reform coalition," as described in Skowronek, *Building*, 165–76.

40. Turk, *Relationship*.

41. A full-scale biography is Morison, *Sims*.

42. Wiegand, *Patrician*.

43. Fiske, *Midshipman*, 550–71.

44. The authoritative study is Deist, *Flottenpolitik*. Compare Kamberger, "Flottenpropaganda"; Meyer, *Propaganda*.

45. August Heeringen, "Denkschrift zum Immediatvortrag, betreffend Ordensverleihungen anläßlich der Annahme des Flottengesetzes," 13 June 1898; Lucanus to Hohenlohe, 5 August 1898; Hohenlohe to Wilhelm II, 18 August 1898; Wilhelm II to Hohenlohe, 31 August 1898; Lucanus to Hohenlohe, 2 September 1898; all in GSAPK Dahlem, Rep. 89, 32225.

46. August von Heeringen, "Denkschrift, betreffend die Erhaltung, die Aufgaben und die Organisation des Nachrichtenbureaus," 24 September 1900. BA-MA, RM 3/9551.

47. August von Heeringen, "Denkschrift, betreffend die Erhaltung, die Aufgaben und die Organisation des Nachrichtenbureaus," 24 September 1900. BA-MA, RM 3/9551.

48. These press notes are in BA-MA, RM 3/10397.

49. Deist, *Flottenpolitik,* 132.

50. Karl Hollweg, "Für die Übergabe an meinen Nachfolger," Fall 1912; BA-MA, RM 3/11703.

51. On these officers, see the materials in BA-MA, RM 3/9957; and Karl Hollweg, "Für die Übergabe an meinen Nachfolger," Fall 1912, BA-MA, RM 3/11703.

52. Deist, *Flottenpolitik,* 250–57.

53. Gunzenhäuser, "Marine-Rundschau."

54. Scholl, "Halle."

55. August von Heeringen, "Denkschrift, betreffend die Erhaltung, die Aufgaben und die Organisation des Nachrichtenbureaus," 24 September 1900. BA-MA, RM 3/9551.

56. Reichsmarineamt, *Die Seeinteressen* (1898), *Steigerung* (1900), *Entwicklung* (1906).

57. *Nauticus, Altes*; idem, *Neue Beiträge*; idem, *Beiträge*; idem, *Jahrbuch für deutsche Seeinteressen* 1–(1899–). For the concept, see N to Tirpitz, 10 June 1899, and the file note about the public announcement of the *Nauticus* yearbook, June 1899, BA-MA, RM 3/10001.

58. August von Heeringen, "Denkschrift, betreffend die Erhaltung, die Aufgaben und die Organisation des Nachrichtenbureaus," 24 September 1900. BA-MA, RM 3/9551. For the following, see Deist, *Flottenpolitik,* 96–100, 105–8, 140–45; Kamberger, "Flottenpropaganda," 48–70, 251–57.

59. On belletristic literature, see the materials in BA-MA, RM 3/10052–10057.

60. E.g., Bernstorff, *Flotte*. On Tirpitz's direct interest, see his letter to Hollweg, 16 October 1902, suggesting a brochure on a fictional Anglo-German war. BA-MA, RM 3/11679. Compare Deist, *Flottenpolitik,* 169–71.

61. Rüger, *Game,* 37–43; Epkenhans, "'Mund.'" "Launch" speeches are collected in BA-MA, RM 3/9958–9960. A superb analysis of these speeches is in Rüger, *Game,* 146–64.

62. See the materials in BA-MA, RM 3/7814.

63. Hopmann, *Logbuch,* 373–74; Gröner, *Lebenserinnerungen,* 124. On naval parades, see Rüger, *Game,* 27–33.

64. Rüger, *Game,* 50–92.

65. Gerhard Janson, "Denkschrift über die Aufgaben und die Tätigkeit des Nachrichtenbüros," March 1914; see also idem, Note, 30 November 1913, and Heinrich Löhlein, "Die Tätigkeit des Nachrichtenbüros," 19 March 1914, all in BA-MA, RM 3/9954.

66. On film, see also Loiperdinger, "Beginnings."

67. On the navy's interest in professorial agitation, see a file note from summer 1897 about a possible contribution of German universities to the naval campaign, BA-MA, RM 3/9617; and August von Heeringen, "Denkschrift, betreffend die Erhaltung, die Aufgaben und die Organisation des Nachrichtenbureaus," 24 September 1900. BA-MA, RM 3/9551. On the Imperial Naval Office's contacts with "fleet professors" in 1899–1900, see the correspondence in BA-MA, RM 3/10405–10407.

68. Deist, *Flottenpolitik,* 102–4, Marienfeld, *Wissenschaft*; Bruch, *Wissenschaft,* 66–92.

69. They can be found in BA-MA, RM 3/9621–9626.

70. Heeringen to Tirpitz, 10 September 1897, BA-MA, N 253/4.

71. On the naval agitation of these societies, see Kamberger, "Flottenpropaganda," 100–3, 110–12; Meyer, *Propaganda,* 164–74.

72. E.g., Heeringen to Tirpitz, 5 August 1897, BA-MA, N 253/4.

73. Chickering, *Men*, 57–73, 213–23.

74. Waldemar Vollerthun, Note, 9 November 1904, recording Tirpitz's views on the Navy League, BA-MA, RM 3/9914. Admiral Capelle stated in 1905 that "we needed to create the Navy League if it did not exist already." Holleben, Notes, 6 May 1905, BA-MA, RM 3/9914.

75. Tirpitz to Bülow, November 1905, BA-MA, RM 3/6.

76. Eley, "German Navy League," 35–63, 90–106, 120–42; idem, *Reshaping*, 75–85; Deist, *Flottenpolitik*, 147–63; Chickering, *Men*, 60–62. On the assistance the League initially received, see August von Heeringen, "Denkschrift zum Immediatvortrag betreffend die Unterstützung des Flotten-Vereins durch das RMA," 11 February 1899, BA-MA, RM 3/9907. To a considerable degree, the German Navy League became "virtually a semi-public institution," argues Chickering, *Men*, 60.

77. On the crisis, see Eley, "German Navy League," 64–83; idem, *Reshaping*, 85–94.

78. Heeringen, "Notiz zum Immediatvortrag betreffend des Flottenvereins," 31 March 1900; idem, "Notiz zum Immediatvortrag über Thätigkeit und weitere Aufgaben des Flottenvereins," 8 June 1900; idem, "Notiz für Seine Excellenz den Herrn Staatssekretär, betreffend Besprechung der Angelegenheiten des Deutschen Flottenvereins mit dem Herrn Reichskanzler und Präsidenten des Staatsministeriums," 6 November 1900. BA-MA, RM 3/9907 and RM 3/9908.

79. Deist, *Flottenpolitik*, 171–247; Eley, "German Navy League," 179–91, 260–317; idem, *Reshaping*, 267–79. Compare Grießmer, *Massenverbände*.

80. Tirpitz to Bülow, 8 November 1905, and the enclosed summary of a conversation with leaders of the German Navy League, BA-MA, N 253/6; Tirpitz, Memorandum, 13 November 1905, BA-MA, RM 3/6; Tirpitz to Loebell, 16 November 1905, BA-MA, RM 3/6; and the documents in Tirpitz, *Aufbau*, 20–30.

81. Tirpitz to Müller, 13 July 1908, BA-MA, N 253/9.

82. Deist, *Flottenpolitik*, 210–47; and Eley, "Navy League," 260–318.

83. Boy-Ed to Tirpitz, 4 July 1908, 10 July 1908, 16 July 1908, and 18 July 1908, Boy-Ed to Hans Koester, 24 September 1908, BA-MA, RM 3/9918

84. Deist, *Flottenpolitik*, 285–305.

85. Gerhard Janson, "Denkschrift über die Aufgaben und die Tätigkeit des Nachrichtenbüros," March 1914; see also idem, Note, 30 November 1913, and Heinrich Löhlein, "Die Tätigkeit des Nachrichtenbüros," 19 March 1914, all in BA-MA, RM 3/9954.

86. Knepper, "Navy Leagues," 351; see also Peters, "Tendencies," 16. Compare the two "Memoranda of Information" enclosed in ONI to SN, 16 and 23 November 1901. NA, RG 38, Entry 102.

87. Fiske, *Midshipman*, 88. Compare Shulman, *Navalism*; Karsten, *Aristocracy*, 362–79.

88. Fiske, "Profession," 497.

89. *Proceedings of the U.S. Naval Institute* 1–(1874–). Compare Allin, *Institute*.

90. Bigelow, *Church*.

91. Schneirow, *Dream*; Keller, *Affairs*, 289–92, 565–66.

92. On Mahan's writings, see Hattendorf and Hattendorf, *Bibliography*.

93. See the bibliography in Hayes and Hattendorf, *Writings*, 201–36.

94. Taylor, "Control"; idem, "Study"; idem, "Future."

95. See the bibliography in Coletta, *Chadwick*, 225–27.

96. Reuterdahl, "Needs of Our Navy." An account of this incident of navalist muckraking from the point of view of its key participant is in Morison, *Sims*, 176–200. For more, see chapter 11. For muckraking in general, see Filler, *Muckrakers*; for *McClure's*, see also Schneirow,

Dream, esp. 212–26. The rationale for muckraking is well expressed in Barnette to Luce, 19 October 1907, LC, MD, Luce Papers.

97. McGerr, *Decline,* 107–37.

98. A listing of the Office's publications is in Navy Department, *The History and Aims of the Office of Naval Intelligence* (Washington, D.C., 1920); in NA, RG 45, ONI, File ZU, 2–4. On ONI and its work, compare Dorwart, *Office;* and Shulman, *Rise.*

99. Yarnell, "Need," 26–28.

100. Office, *Rendezvous.*

101. *Annual Report of the Navy Department, 1904,* 524–25.

102. Oyos, "Roosevelt," 384–85.

103. *Official Blue Book;* Yarsinske, *Exhibition.* See also Schroeder, *Century,* 302–5.

104. For a description, see Reckner, *White Fleet.*

105. Hilderbrand, *Power,* 69–70; Hart, *Fleet,* 41–44. Matthews was one of the few reporters who made the entire trip. His accounts are *Battle-Fleet* and *Hampton Roads.*

106. A listing of the *Harper's Weekly* articles is in the bibliography of Reckner, *White Fleet.* An account by an officer is Miller, *World.* An analysis of public narratives of the fleet's world cruise is Dorsey, "Sailing."

107. Oyos, "Roosevelt," 369–410. On the "rhetorical presidency," see Tulis, *Presidency,* 97–116; Ellis, *Speaking.*

108. Hall, *Celebration;* Schroeder, *Century,* 394–401, 409.

109. *Annual Report of the Navy Department, 1911,* 28–31; idem, *Annual Report, 1912,* 15–20.

110. Woodward, "Participation."

111. Bogle, "Use." At the Chicago exhibition in 1893 the navy had displayed a full-scale model of a battleship: Rydell, *Fair,* 38–71.

112. Harrod, "Medium."

113. Taylor to Luce, 9 February 1894; LC, MD, Luce Papers.

114. Karsten, *Aristocracy,* 362.

115. Gibbons, "Leagues," 763–64; see also idem, "Need." Compare Dewey, "Force."

116. Rappaport, *League;* and Owens, "Warrior," 321–49.

117. See the league's journal (first entitled *Navy League Journal,* then *The Navy*) between 1903 and 1916.

118. Trubowitz, "Geography"; idem, *Interest,* 31–95.

119. E.g., First CR, Q 1, Part I; RC 1912, NWCA, RG 12; and Papers on Q 5, Class of January, 1914; NWCA, RG 8, UNU.

120. GB to SN, "Naval Policy," in *Annual Report of the Navy Department, 1913,* 30–33.

121. For a summary, see GB to SN, 11 December 1914; NA, RG 80, SF 420-2.

122. These calls are a subject of discussion in chapter 7.

123. Finnegan, *Spectre;* Ward, "Origin."

124. Dorwart, *Office;* idem, *Conflict.*

125. Tirpitz, Notes for an imperial audience, 23 October 1899, BA-MA, RM 3/1.

126. Ibid., 26 September 1911, BA-MA, N 253/25. See also Capelle to Tirpitz, 11 and 14 September 1911, BA-MA, N 253/25.

127. This has been done by Meyer, *Propaganda,* 25–26; Berghahn, *Tirpitz-Plan,* 120–21; Deist, *Flottenpolitik.* For a critique of such acceptance, see also Eley, *Reshaping,* 208–12.

128. Tirpitz to Arnim, 30 November 1899, BA-MA, RM 3/2.

129. See also Heeringen, "Denkschrift betreffend die Erhaltung, die Aufgaben und die Organisation des Nachrichtenbureaus," 24 September 1900, BA-MA, RM 3/9951.

130. Heeringen, "Sozialdemokratische Massenkundgebungen gegen die Flottenvorlage und Gegenmassregeln," 9 February 1900, BA-MA, RM 3/9831; Heeringen, "Denkschrift betreffend die Erhaltung, die Aufgaben und die Organisation des Nachrichtenbureaus," 24 September 1900, BA-MA, RM 3/9951.

131. Eley, *Reshaping*, 218–26.

132. A good example is the "Memoranda of Information" provided to the House Naval Affairs Committee by Captain Sigsbee, the chief intelligence officer between 1900 and 1902. NA, RG 38, ONI, Entry 102. On March 22, 1902, for example, Sigsbee informed the committee chairman, George E. Foss, that based on current naval authorizations the U.S. Navy should be considered "to be but one half of the strength of the German navy" and was in the process of falling further behind. Between 1898 and 1901 Congress authorized the construction of fourteen battleships and armored cruisers combined, while the German parliament approved the building of "only" twelve such ships.

133. GB, Proceedings, 5 March 1915, NA, RG 80; Fiske, Diary, 7, 8, 10, and 17 March 1915, Fiske Diary, LC, MD; Fiske, *Midshipman*, 576–79.

134. Berghahn, *Tirpitz-Plan*.

135. Tirpitz to Bülow, November 1905, BA-MA, RM 3/6.

136. Hohenlohe-Schillingfürst, *Denkwürdigkeiten*, 422–23 (conversation with Tirpitz on 1 December 1897). Compare Jagemann to Brauer, 20 January 1898, in Fuchs, *Friedrich*, IV: 9 (conversation with Tirpitz from previous day). In his conversations with Reichstag deputies of the liberal parties during the winter of 1897–98, Capelle raised the specter of dissolution. His notes are in BA-MA, N 253/4.

137. Tirpitz, Notes for a meeting with the Imperial Chancellor, 15 September 1897; and Tirpitz to Crailsheim, 22 November 1897; in BA-MA, N 253/4. In January 1896, Tirpitz had expected a similar scenario. See his notes for the imperial audience on 28 January 1896, BA-MA, N 253/3.

138. Jagemann to Brauer, 20 December 1899, Fuchs, *Friedrich*, IV: 213–14 (recording a conversation with Tirpitz on the previous day); compare Jagemann to Brauer, 31 December 1899 and 19 February 1900, ibid., 217–19, 225–26. Compare Tirpitz to Hohenlohe, 23 October 1899, BA-MA RM 3/1.

139. Fairbairn, *Democracy*.

140. A discussion of the threat in the run-up to the Naval Bill of 1908 is Müller to Tirpitz, 10 December 1907, BA-MA, N 253/07.

141. Tirpitz to Bethmann-Hollweg, 30 August 1911, in Tirpitz, *Aufbau*, 207–8.

142. Capelle to Tirpitz, 11 and 14 September 1911, Tirpitz to Capelle, 13 September 1911, Capelle, Note, 24 September 1911, all in BA-MA, N 253/25; Karl Hollweg, Notes, 23 September and 24 September, 1911, BA-MA, RM 11703.

143. For this fantasy, see Röhl, *Wilhelm II*, 1121–1237; Cecil, *Wilhelm II*, 303–12. On Senden, see chapter 7.

9. A Politics of Social Imperialism

1. Tirpitz to Stosch, 21 December 1895, BA-MA, N 253/321. Compare Tirpitz, Memorandum, 3 January 1896, BA-MA, N 253/3.

2. Mahan, "Possibilities," 122.

3. Kehr, *Schlachtflottenbau*; Berghahn, *Tirpitz-Plan*; Epkenhans, *Flottenrüstung*; Wehler, *Gesellschaftsgeschichte*.

4. On social imperialism, compare Eley, "Social Imperialism," and Kramer, "Reflex Actions."
5. I take the term "new Germany" from Tirpitz to Lieber, 23 April 1898; BA-MA, N 253/4.
6. See chapter 7.
7. For references, see chapter 7, section on "Limitations of Power."
8. Tirpitz, *Erinnerungen*, 127.
9. Trotha to Wilhelm II, 16 May 1914, in Trotha, *Wollen*, 145. Compare Kloosterhuis, *Auslandsvereine*, 137–56.
10. Tirpitz to Senden, 15 February 1896, BA-MA, N 160/5. Compare Tirpitz, Memorandum, 3 January 1896, BA-MA, N 253/3.
11. See also Berghahn, *Tirpitz-Plan*, esp. 354–59, 454–56.
12. Tirpitz, Notes about an imperial audience on 18 August 1897, BA-MA, N 253/4.
13. Tirpitz, Addendum to his notes for an imperial audience on 14 November 1903, BA-MA, N 253/20.
14. Tirpitz, Notes from 27 February 1904, BA-MA, RM 3/3.
15. Müller, Diary, 20 September 1912; in Görlitz, *Kaiser,* 166–67 (quote), 190–94 (the emperor's preference for the decorative), 159–67, 194–203 (general assessment).
16. Rahne, "Wilhelm II," 289.
17. Hopman, Diary, 18 September 1912, in Epkenhans, *Leben*. See also the diary entries for 28 November 1911, 12 May 1912, 2 October 1912, 31 December 1913, 6–9 May 1914.
18. Hopman, Diary, 6 October 1918, in Epkenhans, *Leben*. On wartime monarchism, see Wolz, *Warten,* 370–74, 397–400.
19. Rahne, "Wilhelm II," 289.
20. Tirpitz to Trotha, 11 July 1905, BA-MA, N 253/7.
21. Hopman, Diary, 16 November 1911, 4 January 1913 and 9 April 1913; in Epkenhans, *Leben*.
22. Trotha to Tirpitz, 24 April 1915, 25 August 1916, and Trotha to Eulenburg, 29 October 1916, in Trotha, *Volkstum,* 32–34, 74–77 (quote: 77), 96–99.
23. Tirpitz, Notes for a speech to senior officers on 20 October 1899, BA-MA, RM 3/1.
24. Tirpitz, Addendum to his notes for an imperial audience on 14 November 1903, BA-MA, N 253/20. After the war, Tirpitz expressed interest in writing a book about the Prussian tradition of state building. But this project never materialized.
25. Tirpitz, Note about his trip to Friedrichsruh, 22 August 1897, BA-MA, N 253/4; Tirpitz, *Erinnerungen,* 88–94. On Bismarck as the naval elite's political idol, compare Gottschall, *Order,* and the editor's biographical portrait of Albert Hopman in Epkenhans, *Leben*.
26. Tirpitz, Notes, May 1911, BA-MA, N 253/4. A year later, Tirpitz characterized his differences of opinion with the chancellor as both "profound and irreconcilable." Tirpitz to Hopman, summer 1912, BA-MA, N 253/27.
27. See chapter 8.
28. Karl von Hollweg, "Einbringen einer Flottennovelle," no date, and Notes, 20 October 1911, BA-MA, RM 3/11703.
29. Tirpitz, Notes for an imperial audience on 23 October 1899, BA-MA, RM 3/1; Tirpitz to Bethmann-Hollweg, 30 August 1911, Tirpitz, *Aufbau,* 207–8; Tirpitz to Hertling, September 1913, BA-MA, N 253/17.
30. Halle, Memorandum, 7 July 1899, with Tirpitz's comments; BA-MA, RM 3/1.
31. The best study of this entire issue is Smith, *Nationalism*.
32. E.g., Hohenlohe, journal entry for 1 May 1899, and Bülow to Hohenlohe, 25 October 1899, in Hohenlohe-Schillingfürst, *Denkwürdigkeiten,* 497–98, 533; Hopman, Diary, 5–7 February, 1914, in Epkenhans, *Leben*; Müller, Diary, 17 February 1914, in Görlitz, *Kaiser,* 131.

33. By contrast, Berghahn, *Tirpitz-Plan*, ignores this uneasy relationship and argues that Tirpitz acted as an agent of preindustrial landed elites.

34. Tirpitz, Notes for an imperial audience on 28 September 1899; BA-MA, RM 3/1.

35. See the materials in BA-MA, RM 3/9665.

36. Tirpitz, Draft for a letter to Imperial Secretary of Finance Thielmann, 8 August 1897. Tirpitz deleted this particular passage in the final copy of the letter; BA-MA, N 253/4.

37. Halle, Memorandum, 7 July 1899, with Tirpitz's comments; BA-MA, RM 3/1.

38. Halle, "Zur Einführung," in idem, *Volks- und Seewirtschaft*, I: vii–xiv.

39. E.g., Jagemann to Brauer, 3 October 1899, summarizing a conversation with Tirpitz, in Fuchs, *Friedrich*, IV: 172–73.

40. Eley, "Sammlungspolitik." Compare Deist, *Flottenpolitik*, 118–21; Fairbairn, *Democracy*, 69–109.

41. Tirpitz, Notes for the imperial audiences on 28 January 1896 and 15 June 1897, and the comments by Heeringen on Tirpitz's memoir from 3 January 1896; BA-MA N 253/3 and N 253/4. On Tirpitz's negotiations with Miquel in 1897, see his correspondence with Capelle, Heeringen, and Miquel in BA-MA, N 253/4. Compare Hallmann, *Weg*, 265–87.

42. On Tirpitz's complaints and behavior, see Tirpitz to unknown, 18 November 1899, BA-MA N 253/16; Tirpitz to Eisendecher, 21 November and 24 December 1899, PA AA, Nachlass Eisendecher; Tirpitz to Alfred von Krupp, 2 December 1899, Krupp to Wilhelm II, 3 December 1899, Krupp to Chief of the Civil Cabinet Lucanus, 19 December 1899, Viktor Schweinberg to Lucanus, 4 January 1900, all in GSAPK, Rep. 89 (2.2.1), File 32225. Compare Epkenhans, "Patriotismus"; Eley, "League," 84–83; idem, *Reshaping*, 85–94.

43. Heeringen to Tirpitz, 6 August and 10 September 1897; BA-MA, N 253/4.

44. This is emphasized in Deist, *Flottenpolitik*, 110–21; Eley, "Sammlungspolitik," 122–28.

45. The "classic" account is in Kehr, *Schlachtflottenbau*, 194–207.

46. Torp, *Herausforderung*; Bleyberg, "Government."

47. August von Heeringen, Memorandum on the work of the Information Bureau from 24 September 1900, and the first draft by Karl von Hollweg, BA-MA, RM 3/9951.

48. Karl Hollweg, Comments from 1901 on his draft of the memorandum on the work of the Information Bureau of the Imperial Naval Office, writte n in the summer of 1900; BA-MA, RM 3/9951. Böhm, *Überseehandel*, 196–201, has argued that Tirpitz had originally pursued a politics of "counter-rallying," a *Gegensammlung*.

49. This decision is recorded in Hollweg, Comments from 1901 on his draft of the memorandum on the work of the Information Bureau; BA-MA, RM 3/9951.

50. Halle, "Zur Einführung," in idem *Volks- und Seewirtschaft*, I: vii–xiv.

51. Heeringen, Memorandum on the work of the Information Section of the Imperial Naval Office, 24 September 1900; BA-MA, RM 3/9951.

52. Tirpitz, Memorandum, 3 January 1896; compare Tirpitz to Stosch, 21 December 1895. BA-MA, N 253/3 and N 253/321.

53. Heeringen to Tirpitz, 17 December 1899, BA-MA, RM 3/9620; idem, "Sozialdemokratische Massenkundgebungen," 9 February 1900, BA-MA, RM 3/9831; idem, Memorandum on the work of the Information Bureau of the Imperial Naval Office, 24 September 1900, BA-MA, RM 3/9951.

54. Maltzahn to Tirpitz, 28 August 1895; BA-MA, N 253/408.

55. Heeringen, Memorandum on the work of the Information Bureau of the Imperial Naval Office, 24 September 1900; BA-MA, RM 3/9951.

56. Tirpitz to Stosch, 21 December 1895, BA-MA, N 253/321; Tirpitz, Memorandum, 3 January 1896, BA-MA, N 253/3.

57. Karl Hollweg, Daft for a memorandum on the work of the Information Bureau of the Imperial Naval Office, summer 1900, BA-MA, RM 3/9951.

58. E.g., draft for a statement by the Secretary of the Navy to be made before the Appropriations Committee of the Reichstag, winter 1899, BA-MA, N 253/19; *Nauticus,* "Arbeiterinteressen," and idem, "Deutschen Arbeiterinteressen."

59. Typical is *Nauticus,* "Wirkung."

60. Epkenhans, *Flottenrüstung,* 143–312; Weir, *Building.*

61. The notion of reformist social imperialism draws on Eley, "Social Imperialism."

62. Halle, "Weltmachtpolitik," 211: "one group wants to divert interest from the expansion of social legislation at home, while the other hopes to benefit its ambitious policy at home precisely by means of a strong power politics abroad." Evidently, Halle sided with the second group.

63. E.g., Heeringen to Tirpitz, 30 July, 16 August, and 10 September 1897, in BA-MA, N 253/407 and N 253/4. Compare Deist, *Flottenpolitik,* 117, 126.

64. Heeringen to Capelle 13 August 1897; BA-MA, N 253/4.

65. On this, see Sondhaus, "Navy."

66. As analyzed in Eley, "Social Imperialism."

67. Tirpitz to Stosch, 21 December 1895; BA-MA, N 253/321.

68. For invocations of the "red flood," see Hopman, Diary, 5–7 and 17 February 1914, in Epkenhans, *Leben.*

69. Tirpitz to Stosch, 21 December 1895; BA-MA, N 253/321.

70. E.g., *Nauticus,* "Weltreiche," "Erstarken," and "Weltpolitik."

71. Tirpitz, Notes for an imperial audience on 23 October 1899; BA-MA, RM 3/1. Compare Tirpitz, *Erinnerungen,* 98.

72. Tirpitz to Bethmann-Hollweg, 30 August 1911, in Tirpitz, *Aufbau,* 207–8.

73. D. Rodgers, "Search"; Link and McCormick, *Progressivism.*

74. GB to SN, "Naval Policy," in *Annual Reports of the Navy Department,* 1913, 30.

75. McKean, "War," 6.

76. Mahan, *Armaments,* 59.

77. Mahan, *Strategy,* 447.

78. The term "promotional state" is from Rosenberg, *Spreading,* 38.

79. Calkins and others, "Merchant Marine"; Cooke, "Reserve"; *Report of the Merchant Marine Commission*; Benson, *Merchant Marine.* Compare Roberts, "Marine"; Ellsberg, "Revival."

80. Melville, "Strength," 390.

81. E.g., Cooling, *Steel*; Koistinen, *Mobilizing.*

82. Weinstein, *Ideal*; Kolko, *Triumph.*

83. I take the term "corporate metaphor" from Carpenter, *Forging*; idem, "Centralization."

84. Taylor, "Fleet," 802.

85. Fiske, "Policy," 74. Compare Stirling, "Organization."

86. Petersen, "Fighting."

87. Hussey, "Do," 47–62.

88. See, e.g., the discussions of Germany and Japan as U.S. imperial opponents offered by subsequent officer classes at the Naval War College: RC 1909, CR on Q 16 and 17, QGA; RC 1910, Reports on Q 10, Part I; Committee Solutions for Part I, Q 1, RC 1911; CR on Q 1, Part I, RC 1912; all in NWCA, RG 12.

89. Mahan, *Strategy,* 109, 110; idem, "Origin" (1915), 38–40; idem, "Predominance" (1915), 97–99.

90. Mahan, *Strategy,* 110.

91. Mahan, *Influence, 1660–1783,* 67.

92. Mahan, *Strategy*, 110.

93. E.g., the various essays in Mahan, *Interest, Conditions*. On this issue, compare Sumida, *Strategy*, 82–92.

94. Mahan, "Predominance" (1915), 64–68, and "Relations" (1902), 149–52.

95. E.g., Goodrich, "Esprit." Compare Karsten, *Aristocracy*, 203–13.

96. Skowronek, *Building*, 42. Compare Abrahamson, *America*. It was only fitting that the American Academy of Political and Social Science attracted the attention of the navy. In its ninth annual meeting in April 1905, for example, three high-ranking officers took the stage to discuss central matters of naval policy: *Annals of the American Academy of Political and Social Science* 26:1 (1905): 11–136, 137–45, 161–69 (papers), and 173–79 (meeting report).

97. On this language, see D. Rodgers, "Search." Typically, individual officers were involved in the municipal reform movement: Hays, "Politics."

98. Fiske, "Authority," 129. Fiske laid out his views of naval officers as members of a profession in his "Naval Profession," and his *Navy*, published in 1916. On this entire issue, see Spector, *Professors*.

99. Jackson Lears, *Place*; Bederman, *Manliness*; Hoganson, *Fighting*; Lears, *Rebirth*.

100. The two key texts are Mahan, "Possibilities" (1897), and "Outlook" (1897). Compare Stewart, "'Gift'"; and the perceptive remarks in Stephanson, *Destiny*, 84–86.

101. Mahan, "Possibilities" (1897), quotes: 119–22, 124–25.

102. Mahan, *Armaments*, 1–154, quotes: 5, 10, 13.

103. Luce, "Benefits," (1891) republished in 1904 as "War." Quotes: "War," 672, 673; Taylor, "Study," 183.

104. Mahan, "Retrospect" (1902), 16, 24.

105. See the excellent analysis in Hussey, "Do."

106. Chang, "Barbarism."

107. Mahan, "Letter" (1897), 31.

108. Mehnert, *Deutschland*; Gollwitzer, *Gefahr*.

109. Captain J. D. McDonald, Class of January 1914, Individual Question 4—Naval Base," NWCA, RG 8, XBAN.

110. Mahan to Maxse, 30 May 1907, in Seager and Maguire, *Letters*, III: 214.

111. Mahan, *Armaments*, 163.

112. Mahan, *Problem*. Mahan's racial views toward the Japanese after 1907 are laid out in his *Armaments*, esp. 8–10, 155–80, and his "Relations" (1915) and "Open Door" (1915). See also his various letters in his Seager and Maguire, *Letters*, III: 215–26, 447–53, 495–99.

113. Hussey, "Do," 31–47; Harrod, *Manning*; idem, "Jim Crow. The numbers are from Harrod," *Manning*, appendix, tables 4 and 5.

114. Epkenhans, *Flottenrüstung*, part IV; see also Berghahn, *Germany*, 97–219.

115. An excellent summary is in Eley, "Construction."

116. Tirpitz to Capelle, 8 July 1913; BA-MA, N 170/1.

117. Hopman, Diary, 31 December 1911 and 12–17 January, 1914, compare the entry for 30 June 1913, in Epkenhans, *Leben*.

118. Weizäcker, Diary, 18 March 1916, in Hill, *Papiere*, 196.

119. Hopman, Diary, 31 December 1912, in Epkenhans, *Leben*.

120. Ibid., 24 February 1913, in Epkenhans, *Leben*.

121. Thoss, "Rechte"; Strandmann, "Staatsstreichpläne." On the National Opposition, compare Eley, *Reshaping*, and Chickering, *Men*. On the cult of Bismarckian national leadership and its relation to right-wing politics, see Frankel, *Shadow*.

122. E.g., Hopman, Diary, 31 December 1913, in Epkenhans, *Leben*.

123. Hopman, Diary, 30 June 1913 and 12–17 January 1914, in Epkenhans, *Leben*. Already in the fall of 1911 Tirpitz had denied any ambitions to become imperial chancellor when the emperor had sounded out that possibility. Scheck, *Tirpitz*, 16. The Imperial Naval Office closely followed the talk about Tirpitz as a possible chancellor. An example is a report by the head of the Information Bureau from 8 August 1913. BA-MA, N 253/8.

124. Tirpitz to Hertling, September 1913, BA-MA, N 253/17; see also Epkenhans, *Flottenrüstung*, 394–95.

125. Hopman, Diary, 18 September 1914, 4 October 1914, 10, 13, 19, 20, and 27 November 1914; in Epkenhans, *Leben*. On Hopman's own thinking, see also entries for 15 and 17 September and 13 and 26 November 1914.

126. Scheck, *Tirpitz*, 35–64. On Tirpitz's first initiatives in March 1915, see Hopman, Diary, 22 and 27 March 1915, in Epkenhans, *Leben*. Compare Tirpitz's letters to his wife from March 1915, in his *Erinnerungen*, 455–62; Müller, Diary, 18 April 1915, in Görlitz, *Regierte*, 97.

127. A summary is Scheck, "Kampf."

128. Tirpitz to his wife, 19 September and 3 October 1914, Tirpitz, *Erinnerungen*, 404, 411–12; Hopman, Diary, 18 September 1914, in Epkenhans, *Leben*; Müller, Diary 19 September 1914, Görlitz, *Regierte*, 60.

129. Tirpitz to Trotha, 16 October 1916, in Tirpitz, *Ohnmachtspolitik*, 580.

130. On officers' attitudes, compare Wolz, *Warten*, 360–70.

131. Hagenlücke, *Vaterlandspartei*; Scheck, *Tirpitz*, 65–81.

132. Quoted in Deist, *Militär*, II: 1049, 1061. On the navy's overall response, compare Herwig, *Officer Corps*, 214–18; Scheck, *Tirpitz*, 65–81.

133. Fiske, "Duty"; see also Phelps, "Industrialism"; Gatewood, "Preparedness." On the growing frustration among navy leaders in the early 1910s, see chapter 8.

134. E.g., Mahan, "Possibilities" (1897), 119–20; idem, "Outlook" (1897), 231–34.

135. E.g., Staunton, "Reserves," published in 1889, and Gleaves, "Views," written in 1914.

136. Finnegan, *Spectre*; Chambers, *Army*; Pearlman, *Democracy*.

137. Jackson, "Preparedness," 1570; idem, "Plea," 310. Compare Williams, "Need"; Washburn, "Spot"; Frost, "Factor"; Hulbert, "Training"; Frost, "Role"; Rittenhouse, "Preparedness"; Foster, "Benefits."

138. Niblack, "Letters," 376. Compare Karsten, *Aristocracy*, 204–5.

139. Niblack, "Letters," 376.

140. Hinds, "Peace," 1419

141. Fiske, *Midshipman*, 374.

10. Of Sciences, Sea Power, and Strategy

1. Stein, *Lehre*, quotes: 67, 64, 31.
2. Upton, *Armies*, quotes: 319, 321.
3. On Prussia's "military revolution," see Geyer, *Rüstungspolitik*; Förster, "Armed Forces."
4. Karsten, *Aristocracy*; Hobson, *Imperialism*.
5. On the notion of an "epistemic community," see Holzner and Marx, *Knowledge/Application*.
6. Geyer, "Past," 189. On British naval professionalism, see A. Lambert, "History."
7. On the notion of an "ideological consensus," see Wehler, *Bismarck*; idem, *Aufstieg*; Eley, "Empire."
8. Mahan, *Influence, 1660–1783*, v–vi. Compare Mahan, *Influence, 1793–1812*, I: iii.

9. Mahan, *Influence 1660–1783*, 1.
10. Schluter, "Looking," 81.
11. Mahan, *Influence, 1660–1783*, 24, 90.
12. Ibid., 28, 71.
13. Ibid., 28.
14. Ibid., 200.
15. Ibid., 28–83.
16. Sumida, *Strategy*, 28.
17. Mahan, *Influence, 1660–1783*, 28.
18. Chadwick, "Explanation," 303.
19. Fiske, "Power," 683.
20. Mahan, *Sail*, 277, 279.
21. Calkins and others, "Marine," quote: 151. On Mahan's direct indebtedness to his naval peers, compare Allin, *Institute*; Hagan, "Mahan"; Karsten, *Aristocracy*; Drake, *Empire*. On naval discourse prior to the 1880s, see also Leeman, *Road*.
22. Mahan, *Influence, 1660–1783*, 83.
23. Ibid., vi.
24. Compare Mahan, "Subordination" (1908).
25. Mahan, *Interest of America in Sea Power*.
26. On Mahan's international reception, see Livezey, *Mahan*.
27. Compare Hobson, *Imperialism*; Berghahn, *Tirpitz-Plan*, 179–81; Lambi, *Navy*, 65–67; Herwig, "Influence."
28. Quoted in Sondhaus, *Preparing*, 196.
29. Wolfgang von Tirpitz (the admiral's son), Memoirs, in BA-MA, N 253/114. An example for the discussion of Mahan's work by Tirpitz and his fellow officers is Maltzahn to Tirpitz, 28 August 1895, BA-MA, N 253/408.
30. Quoted in Baecker, "Mahan," 14.
31. Mahan, *Einfluss, 1660–1783*; idem, *Einfluß, 1783–1812*. Halle, *Seemacht*, 6, characterized Mahan's volumes as "epochal." Mahan's analysis of the war of 1898 and its lessons was summarized in Galster, "Besprechung." Discussion of Mahan's works published after 1900 include Borckenhagen, "Seeoffizierstypen"; Hebbinghaus, "Biographisches"; and Maltzahn, "Seestrategie."
32. Rittmeyer, *Seekriege*; Kirchhoff, *Seekriegsgeschichte*, vols. II–VI.
33. Borckenhagen, "Studium," 171, 172, 174. See also idem, "Krieg." Another example for an early reception of Mahan is Maltzahn, "Seeherrschaft."
34. "Allgemeine Erfahrungen aus den Manövern der Herbstübungsflotte," 16 June 1894. BA-MA, RM 4/176.
35. Hobson, *Imperialism*, esp. chapters 4 and 5.
36. "Allgemeine Erfahrungen aus den Manövern der Herbstübungsflotte," 16 June 1894. BA-MA, RM 4/176.
37. Fitzpatrick, *Imperialism*; idem, "Fall"; Sieg, *Ära*; Sondhaus, *Preparing*, 19–45. *Nauticus, Altes, Neue Beiträge,* and *Beiträge* abound with references to previous supporters of the cause of German sea power.
38. Tirpitz, *Erinnerungen*, 96. On Treitschke's influence, compare Winzen, "Treitschke's Influence."
39. Neitzel, *Weltmacht*.
40. Tirpitz, *Erinnerungen*, 96–97, n. 1; Heeringen to Tirpitz, 28 June 1914, BA-MA N 253/407. Peez, *Handelspolitik*.

41. On the Schmoller-Tirpitz connection, see Grimmer-Solem, "Socialism."
42. Scholl, "Halle." A listing of important writings by Halle is in the bibliography.
43. Luce, "Study," 53. This essay was originally published in *PUSNI* 12 (1886): 527–46.
44. Luce, "Address," 2.
45. Mahan, *Influence, 1660–1783*, 2, 7.
46. Ibid., 88. Compare idem, *Strategy*, 2, 4, 10.
47. E.g., Goodrich, "College"; Wainwright, "Problems."
48. Fiske, "Profession," 485.
49. Fiske, "Profession," 485, 505, 503. Compare Fiske, *Midshipman*, 220–22. On this entire issue, see also Spector, *Professors*, 45.
50. Luce, "Study," 68.
51. Luce to Mahan, 16 July 1907, in Gleaves, *Life*, 295–96. See also Hayes and Hattendorf, *Writings*, 68, n. 71.
52. Laughton, "Study." On Laughton, see A. Lambert, *Foundations*.
53. Mahan, *Sail*, 280. Laughton's correspondence with Mahan and Luce is in A. Lambert, *Letters*. By contrast, the work of other prominent writers such as Admiral Philip Colomb, who published his own massive study on naval strategy and history in 1891, was less important in shaping Luce and Mahan's developing ideas. Colomb, *Warfare*, nonetheless became mandatory reading at the Naval War College.
54. For more see Hattendorf, "History"; idem, "Wars."
55. The key text is Luce, "On Study," esp. 51–57 (quotes: 53, 54). On formalism, see White, *Thought*.
56. Güth, *Admiralstabsausbildung*, 11–24; Bald, *Tradition*, 34–35, 138–52. In addition, see Tirpitz, *Erinnerungen*, 18–20; Hopman, *Logbuch*, 232–47.
57. Stenzel, *Kriegführung*; idem, *Seekriegsgeschichte*, I: 3–57. On Stenzel, compare Hobson, *Imperialism*, 136–47.
58. Vice-Admiral Kirchhoff, "Introduction," in Stenzel, *Kriegführung*, xxx.
59. Tirpitz, *Erinnerungen*, 41.
60. "Allgemeine Erfahrungen aus den Manövern der Herbstübungsflotte," 16 June 1894, BA-MA, RM 4/176. Compare Tirpitz, Notes for an Imperial audience, no date, 1898–1899, BA-MA, N 253/4: The "study of history" would demonstrate that a "battle" would "decide everything."
61. Michaelis, "Wirken," II: 15.
62. Maltzahn, *Geschichte*; idem, *Seekrieg* (1912–14).
63. Wilhelm Michaelis, "Erinnerungen," BA-MA, N 164/4, 7. On Maltzahn, compare Hobson, *Imperialism*, 284–95.
64. Quoted in Güth, *Admiralstabsausbildung*, 24.
65. Michaelis, "Erinnungen," 7. Maltzahn explicated his views on Clausewitz and Mahan in idem, "Buch"; idem, "Seestrategie."
66. Ratzel, *Geographie*; idem, *Meer*; idem, *Geographie* (second edition).
67. Maltzahn, "Ratzel," quotes: 218, 219; and idem, "Meer," 273–75.
68. Bucholz, *Moltke*. See also Geyer, "Past"; 189–90.
69. Hopman, *Logbuch*, 216–17; see also Lambi, *Navy*, 80; Gustav Bachmann, "Der Admiralstab der kaiserlichen Marine," 1936, BA-MA, RM 8/1272; Lambi, *Navy*, 191–240.
70. Maltzahn, *Geschichte*, I: 231. On the army's war gaming practices, see Bucholz, *Moltke*, 85–93.
71. Hobson, *Imperialism*, 147–53, 201–9. Compare Kelly, *Tirpitz*, 47–68, 81–102. Tirpitz summarized his work in the torpedo arm in a massive memorandum entitled "Über die Entwicklung des Torpedobootswesens," 18 April 1889, BA-MA, N 253/15.

72. Güth, *Admiralstabsausbildung*.

73. Diederichs to Tirpitz, 21 November 1899, BA-MA, RM 3/361; Diederichs, "Denkschrift zum Immediatvortrag betreffend Immediatbericht des Admiral von Koester über seine Kenntnissnahme in Admiralstabsarbeiten und Vorschlage über die Entwicklung des Admiralstabes," February 1900, and Diederichs, Notes for Imperial audience on 17 February 1899, both in BA-MA, RM 5/879; Diederichs to Tirpitz, 29 March 1900, Diederichs, Notes for an imperial audience on 12 January 1901 and 22 January 1901, in BA-MA, RM 2/1553; Diederichs to Senden, BA-MA, N 160/11; Diederichs, Notes for an Imperial Presentation on 16 April 1902, RM 5/918. On Diederichs, compare Gottschall, *Order*, 223–56.

74. Bachmann, "Admiralstab," 14. On Büchsel's agenda, see Büchsel, "Zur Weiterentwicklung des Admiralstabes," 2 March 1903, BA-MA, RM 5/600; Büchsel to Müller, 4 January 1904, RM 2/1553; Büchsel, Memorandum on the occasion of his imperial audience on 6 December 1906, BA-MA, RM 5/600; Büchsel, Notes for an Imperial Presentation on 8 January 1907, BA-MA, RM 5/891; Büchsel, Notes for his Imperial Audience on 8 June 1907, BA-MA, RM 5/892; Büchsel to Wilhelm II, 19 December 1907, BA-MA, RM 2/1553; Büchsel, Notes for an Imperial Presentation on 7 January 1908, BA-MA, RM 5/893; Büchsel to Wilhelm II, 26 January 1908, RM 2/1553.

75. The text of the decree is in Hubatsch, *Admiralstab*, 245–46. On the development of the Admiralty Staff, see "Die Pflege des Admiralstabsdienstes in der Marine," a history covering the years from 1903 to 1908, in BA-MA, RM 5/601; and Bachmann, "Der Admiralstab, der Kaiserlichen Manne," BA-MA, RM 8/1272. Compare Hubatsch, *Admiralstab*, 109–39.

76. Müller, Presentation to the Emperor, 22 January 1907, BA-MA, RM 2/1553. Compare his comments on presentations to the emperor by Admiral Büchsel, 8 January and 8 June 1907, and his letter to Büchsel, 1 February 1907; BA-MA, RM 2/1553.

77. Müller to Tirpitz, 3 June 1907, BA-MA, RM 2/1553.

78. Quoted in Hubatsch, *Admiralstab*, 137. On Tirpitz, see also his letters to Müller, 17 April and 8 June 1907; BA-MA, RM 2/1553.

79. A general account of these changes is in Hubatsch, *Admiralstab*, 133–39. For a discussion of the role of admiralty staff in a modern navy by an officer close to Tirpitz, see Hollweg, "Admiralstabseinrichtungen."

80. These claims will the subject of discussion in chapter 11.

81. Scheerer, *Marineoffiziere*, 129–30; for personnel numbers, see the tables on 260–61.

82. Müller, Presentation to the Emperor, 22 January 1907, BA-MA, RM 2/1553. On this line of thinking, see Tirpitz, *Erinnerungen*, 20–21; Görlitz, *Kaiser*, 48–49; and Raeder, *Leben*, 50–54.

83. On the Naval War College's curriculum and its (changing) emphases, see Scheerer, *Marineoffiziere*, 94–97; Güth, *Admiralstabsausbildung*; 11–24; Bald, *Tradition*.

84. Hopman, *Logbuch*, 272; Michaelis, "Wirken," 410–413.

85. Deist, "Politik"; Gross, *Seekriegsführung*.

86. Scheer to Müller, 9 August 1918, and Scheer, Notes for Imperial Audience on 10 August 1918, both in Granier, *Seekriegsleitung*, IV: 112. See also Scheer to his wife, 11 August 1918, in Epkenhans, *Schatz*, 83.

87. Holtzendorff to Wilhelm II, 13 August 1916, with an enclosed draft of an imperial decree, BA-MA, RM 2/1983; compare the correspondence in RM 2/2007 and RM 5/274 and 5/275 on this issue. A summary is in Hubatsch, *Admiralstab*, 174–77.

88. See references in chapter 11. On Tirpitz's opposition to this idea before World War I, see, e.g., Tirpitz to Wilhlem II, 10 March 1899 and 11 June 1911; BA-MA, N 253/39 and N 253/24.

89. Büchsel, Notes for an Imperial Audience, 15 March 1907; BA-MA, RM 5/891. On Heeringen, see Granier, *Seekriegsleitung*, I: 181; and Michaelis, "Wirken," 413–14.

90. E.g., Holtzendorff to Müller, 4 December 1911 and 14 June 1912, BA-MA, RM 2/994; Holtzendorff, Presentation to the Emperor, 27 July 1916, and his note about the course of the imperial audience, BA-MA, RM 2/1983.

91. Fiske, "Profession," 480. Compare Mahan, *Sail,* 266–67; Taylor, "Study," 185–87.

92. Hood, "Remarks," 389; Radford, "Organization," 1703.

93. Taylor, "Memorandum," 445.

94. Charles H. Stockton, "Preparation for War," 15 June 1894, NWCA, RG 14.

95. Wilkinson, *Brain.*

96. On this expectation, see Fiske, *Midshipman,* 546–48, 629, 636.

97. Gleaves, "Views," 1303.

98. Communications pertaining to the German fleet are in NA, RG 80, General Correspondence 1897–1914, SF 4581, and NA, RG 38, ONI, Entry 102, Memoranda of Information. The GB discussed the German navy and its practices in one meeting after the other in the early 1900s. On the reporting by the service attaché in Berlin, see Crumley, "System."

99. GB, Minutes, 23 May 1901, NA, RG 80; compare Mitchell, *Danger,* 43.

100. Fiske, *Navy,* 156, 160.

101. On respect for British accomplishments, see section entitled "Professional Notes" in the issues of *PUSNI* and ONI, *Notes.*

102. E.g., Taylor, "Fleet," 803; idem, "Study," 187.

103. E.g., Taylor, "Fleet," and idem, "Study." Compare the report by the naval attaché in London from 1903 on the "Need of a General Staff": Richardson Clover to Office of Naval Intelligence, 30 April 1903, NA, RG 38, RNA, Entry 98, Reports of Naval Attachés. On the reporting by Clover and the other attachés to London, see Crumley, "System."

104. Fiske, *Navy,* 159–60. Compare Luce, "College" (1910), and Knox, "Role."

105. Morison, *Sims.*

106. Luce, "Warfare"; Marble, "Battle"; Wainwright, "Battle"; Fiske, "Togo"; Schroeder, "Gleanings."

107. Hood, "Remarks."

108. Rivera, "Stick," 203–12.

109. Chadwick, "Explanation," 309–10. Compare, Taylor, "Fleet," 803.

110. Goodrich, "College," 682. Compare Taylor, "Address"; Chadwick, "Explanation"; idem, "Address"; 251–68; William L. Rodgers, "Subjects of Work at the Naval War College," Lecture, 1909, NWCA, RG 14; idem, "Field." On the vision of Admiral Luce, the College's founder, see his "War Schools," "College" (1885), and "Address."

111. Members of the NWC, "Notes"; W. McCarthy Little, "The Philosophy of the Order Form," Lecture, Summer Conference, 1913, and E. S. Kellogg, "The Estimate of the Situation," July 1914, NWCA, RG 14; and the discussions of "Estimate of Situations" and "Formulation of Orders" in part II of the RC 1910, 1911, and 1912, NWC, RG 12.

112. E.g., Chadwick, "Opening"; Cotton, "Elements"; Luce, "Relations," 83–86; Sims, "Cheer Up."

113. SN to GB, 26 October 1911; William Rodgers, Memorandum, 26 October 1911; Rear-Admiral Sidney A. Staunton, Memorandum, 22 April 1912; NWCA, RG 8 XSTAP. On the college's educational emphasis in the wake of this decision, see Knight, "Estimate," and his various "Remarks" and "Addresses" to officer classes, NWCA, RG 4. Compare Spector, *Professors,* 112–29; Hattendorf, Simpson, and Wadleigh, *Sailors,* 74–82, 86–91.

114. President of NWC to GB, 19 October 1911, and enclosed letters by a Special NWC Committee to the President of the NWC, 19 October 1911, on "Educational Work of War College as Related to War Plans," and "Method of Preparing Strategic Plans"; NWC, RG 8, XSTAP.

115. NWC, "Strategic Plan of Campaign Against Orange," 15 March 1911, NA, RG 80, GB, WP; Fiske to GB, 25 March 1911, NA, RG 80, GB, SF 408. GB to President of NWC, 22 March 1911, and President of NWC to GB, 19 October 1911, including enclosed letters by the Special Committee of the Naval War College Staff to the College's President from the same day; NA, RG 80, SF 425.

116. "Final Action of the Conference on Question 10," September 26, 1910, RC 1910, NWCA, RG 12; GB to SN, 17 November 1910, and its official endorsement by Meyer; both in NA, RG 80, SF 420–1.

117. JB, Minutes, Copy Book, and SFiles, NA, RG 225. On the Board as a planning agency, see Miller, *Plan*.

118. On the 1920s and 1930s, see Felker, *Testing*.

119. Hattendorf and others, *Sailors*, 80–82. On Daniels's high opinion of the Naval War College, see *Annual Report of the Navy Department, 1913*, 7–8, 34–46; and Daniels, *Era*, 269–72.

120. Until 1923, personnel boards promoted a number of officers who had not attended the Naval War College: Chisholm, *Waiting*, 553–623.

121. Fiske, *Midshipman*, 567–71.

122. Ibid., 477, 480.

123. Quoted in Costello, "Planning," 119.

124. E.g., the various officer papers on "Plan-Making" and "War Plans: Their Form and Substance," Long Courses 1912–13 and 1913–14; in NWCA, RG 8, XSTAP.

125. SN to GB, 26 October 1911, NA, RG 80, GB, SF 425; GB, "Black Plan," 1913, and GB, "Orange War Plan: Strategic Section," 14 March 1914, both in NA, RG 80, WP. The GB completed the "Administrative Section" of the Orange Plan on 29 May 1913 and a revised version in May 1915.

126. The importance of this development is stressed in Miller, *Plan*, 16–17.

127. Yarnell, "Need." Compare Fiske, *Midshipman*, 540.

128. A call to action is Knox, "Role." Compare Gleaves, "Views"; Sims, "Principles"; Knox, "Problem"; Cronan, "Need"; Sims, "Character." On the inattention to "doctrine" in the Navy Department and the lack of a "real general staff," see also the diary of Commander Joseph Knefler Taussig: Still, *Patrol*, 9–10, 11 (entries for 15 and 17 April 1917).

129. Shulman, "Empire," 199.

130. Rebeur-Pachwitz to RMA, 14 March 1903; see also Hebbinghaus to RMA, 8 August 1904; both BA-MA, RM 3/2978.

131. Boy-Ed to RMA, 4 November 1913, BA-MA, RM 3/2978. Compare Hebbinghaus to RMA, 26 October 1904; and Boy-Ed to RMA, 15 December 1913; all BA-MA, RM 3/2978.

132. Boy-Ed to RMA, 12 February 1913, BA-MA, RM 3/2978.

11. Between Leadership and Intraservice Conflict

1. Tirpitz, *Erinnerungen*, 121, 101, 125.

2. Compare Hobson, *Imperialism*, chapter 8.

3. E.g., Langley, "Schley"; Reckner, "Ollie"; Gottschall, *Order*.

4. On "organizational ideology," see Snyder, *Ideology*; Posen, *Sources*. But Snyder's and Posen's use of this notion is limited as they cast such ideology as a direct product of the overall material interest of an organization.

5. Herwig, *Corps*; Scheerer, *Marineoffiziere*; Karsten, *Aristocracy*. The two officer corps were recruited from the professional, commercial, and manufacturing elites of each nation.

Recruitment from other officer families accounted for between 10 to 20 percent of the membership.

6. Tirpitz to Wilhelm II, 10 March 1899, idem, "Motive für die Organisationsänderung," undated, 1898; BA-MA, N 253/39. Tirpitz's desire to become an all-powerful Secretary of the Navy is at the center of the analysis in Kelly, *Tirpitz*.

7. Berghahn, *Tirpitz-Plan*, 23–45; Lambi, *Navy*, 31–33; and Hubatsch, *Admiralstab*, 49–85.

8. Naval High Command to Secretary of the Navy, 14 February 1895, BA-MA, RM 2/2005; Naval High Command to Emperor, 28 November 1895, BA-MA, N 253/3; Tirpitz Memorandum, 3 January 1896, BA-MA, N 253/3; Naval High Command, "Aufgaben der Marine im Krieg und im Frieden," 2 May 1897, and Naval High Command to Emperor, 10 May 1897, BA-MA, RM 3/6634.

9. Berghahn, *Tirpitz-Plan*, 68–108; Hallmann, *Weg*, 137–248; Steinberg, *Deterrent*, 61–124.

10. August von Heeringen, "Denkschrift, betreffend die Erhaltung, die Aufgaben und die Organisation des Nachrichtenbureaus," 24 September 1900; BA-MA, RM 3/9551.

11. Tirpitz, "Motive für die Organisationsänderung," 1898, BA-MA, N 253/39. For the critique of Tirpitz's plans, see Gottschall, *Order*, 224–26.

12. When in June 1909 the fleet agreement with Britain became the issue of a specially convened conference of top military and civilian officials presided over by the chancellor, the chief of the army's General Staff attended whereas the head of the Admiralty Staff (and the commanding officer of the fleet) did not. See the protocol of the Meeting on 3 June 1909 in Tirpitz, *Aufbau*, 157–61.

13. Tirpitz took control over this issue in 1904: Minutes of an interministerial meeting on 12 November 1904; Tirpitz to Chief of Admiralty, 19 December 1904; Tirpitz to Secretary of State of the Foreign Office, 2 December 1904; all in BA-MA, RM 5/997.

14. Giessler, *Institution*.

15. On this, see the summary in Michaelis, "Wirken," 410–13.

16. Imperial decrees, 24 June 1901 and 9 January 1909, BA-MA, N 253/20, BA-MA, RM 3/8.

17. Tirpitz, Notes for Imperial Audience, 20 February 1899, Tirpitz to Wilhelm II, 10 March 1899, Tirpitz to Prince Henry of Prussia, 1 July 1899, BA-MA, N 253/39. For Tirpitz's previous demands, see his various letters and notes from 1898 in the same file. For the critical views of senior officers, see Bendemann to Tirpitz, 6 April 98, BA-MA, N 253/39; Prince Henry of Prussia to Senden, 25 July 1898 and 18 April 1899, BA-MA, N 160/4. Compare Berghahn, *Tirpitz-Plan*, 37–45; Gottschall, *Order*, 224–31; Kelly, *Tirpitz*, 155–65.

18. Forstmeier, "Geschichte." On Tirpitz's opposition to the creation of a powerful fleet command in 1902–03, see Tirpitz, Notes for an imperial audience, 16 September 1903, BA-MA, RM 3/2; RMA, File Note, June 1903, Tirpitz, "Über die organisatorische Weiter-Entwicklung unsere aktiven Schlachtflotte," no date, Tirpitz, Notes about his stay in Rominenten, 25–29 September 1903, BA-MA, N 253/20; Tirpitz to Hollman, 30 September 1903, BA-MA, N 253/16; Tirpitz, Notes about his visit in Hubertusstock, 12 and 18 October 1903, BA-MA, N 253/20. On the changes in 1912, see Scheerer, *Marineoffiziere*, 213–14.

19. See chapter 7.

20. E.g., Tirpitz to Bülow, 25 April, 1898, Tirpitz to Hohenlohe, 28 May and 14 June 1898, BA-MA, N 253/39; Tirpitz to Bülow, 22 May 1901, BA-MA, N 253/20. As discussed in chapters 7 and 9, Tirpitz resorted to the resignation threat in his direct dealings with imperial chancellors, using this pressure tactic to demand recognition of his policy priorities by top civilian governmental officials.

21. E.g., Capelle to Tirpitz, 11 September 1911, BA-MA, N 253/25.

22. Lambi, *Navy*, 164–70, 277–80, 363–68, 371–79; Epkenhans, *Flottenrüstung*, 322–24, 335–36, 392–94; Görlitz, *Kaiser,* esp. 132–33.

23. Herbert Heath, Germany, N.A. Report 27/10, 6 August 1910, in Seligmann, *Intelligence,* 263.

24. See the discussion of Senden in chapter 7.

25. On this, see the Senden-Tirpitz correspondence from 1898, in BA-MA, RM 3/33 and N 253/39; Tirpitz's correspondence from February to May 1901 and his various notes from September, October and November 1903, in BA-MA, N 253/20; Tirpitz to Prince Henry of Prussia, 6 May 1904, and Tirpitz to Senden, 23 June 1904, BA-MA, RM 3/3. Compare Berghahn, *Tirpitz-Plan,* 37–45, 287–96, 341–54, 359–69.

26. E.g., Görlitz, *Kaiser,* esp. 80–82, 89–94, 116–19, 124–28, 132–37; and Hopman, Diary, 16 October 1911, 13 and 30 January 1912, 15 September and 2 October 1912, 1, 4 and 18 January 1913, 24 February 1913, in Epkenhans, *Leben*. Compare Fischer, *Admiral,* who casts the admiral as an honest broker.

27. Strikingly, Tirpitz did not offer any criticism of Müller in either his *Erinnerungen* or in *Aufbau* pertaining to this time period.

28. Bülow, *Denkwürdigkeiten,* I: 109.

29. Gottschall, *Order,* 253.

30. Instead of many examples: Entry for 3 March 1911, in Hill, *Papiere,* 130. Prince Henry's tenure as chief of the active fleet ended in a big fight with Tirpitz over the direction of naval policy.

31. Hohenlohe-Schillingfürst, *Denkwürdigkeiten,* 462–463; Görlitz, *Kaiser,* 63, 64.

32. Görlitz, *Kaiser,* 26, relaying remarks by the Emperor from March 1906, BA-MA, N 159/3. On Müller's views of Tirpitz, see his diary, 4 February and 20 September 1912, 6 and 17 January 1913, BA-MA, N 159/4.

33. E.g., Tirpitz, Notes for a speech before senior officers on 20 October 1899, BA-MA, RM 3/1; idem, "Über die Entwicklung und Bedeutung des Flottengesetzes," Speech before high-ranking officers in Kiel on 4 April, 1910, BA-MA, RM 3/11680. Campaigning for office in the winter of 1895–96, Tirpitz had demanded the "working together of the top agencies of the navy in the same direction, shoulder to shoulder." Tirpitz, memorandum, 3 January 1896, and his notes for the imperial audience on 28 January 1896; BA-MA, N 253/3.

34. Tirpitz to Arnim, 30 November 1899, and the memorandum, written by an officer of the Imperial Naval Office in preparation for an upcoming imperial audience, 26 September 1899, BA-MA, RM 3/2. Compare Tirpitz's notes for an imperial audience on 15 June 1897 and his drafts for two letters to the command of the maneuver fleet, June and July 1895, BA-MA, N 253/4 and N 253/164.

35. For Tirpitz's reasoning in 1899, see the material in BA-MA, RM 3/2; Tirpitz to Büchsel, 27 and 29 July 1899, BA-MA, N 168/10; and Heeringen to Tirpitz, 11 August 1899, BA-MA, N 253/407. On this entire episode, compare Deist, *Flottenpolitik,* 88–94; Lambi, *Navy,* 164–66. In 1895, when he served with the High Naval Command, Tirpitz had already expressed an interest in the repression of dissenting voices. See his drafts for two letters to the command of the maneuver fleet, June and July 1895; BA-MA, N 253/164. On this, see also Deist, *Flottenpolitik,* 45–47.

36. Galster, *Seekriegsrüstung*; idem, *Küstenverteidigung*. On Bülow, see his letter to the chief of his press office, 19 September 1908, in Hammann, *Bilder,* 59–60; and his correspondence with Tirpitz between November 1908 and December 1909 in *GP* 28.

37. Tirpitz to Müller, 15 May 1907, Müller to Tirpitz, 22 May 1907, Müller to Galster, 9 and 19 October 1907, Müller to Koester, 8 December 1909, and Koester to Müller, 9 December

1909, in BA-MA, RM 2/924; Müller to Tirpitz, 16 October 1907, BA-MA, N 253/16; and the materials in BA-MA, RM 3/9757. On this entire episode, see Deist, *Flottenpolitik,* 251–53.
38. Scheerer, *Marineoffiziere,* 202–15.
39. Scheer, *Segelschiff;* Epkenhans, "Scheer"; Trotha, *Tirpitz;* idem, *Volkstum.*
40. See chapter 10.
41. Tirpitz, *Erinnerungen,* 43–44; Hallmann, *Weg,* 104–6. On the torpedo-gang, see also Kelly, *Tirpitz,* 66–67, 467–68 (list of members).
42. Tirpitz to Senden, 15 February 1896; BA-MA, N 160/5. Compare Görlitz, *Kaiser,* 11.
43. Tirpitz, *Erinnerungen,* 84. Compare Steinberg, *Deterrent,* 129–30; Epkenhans, *Tirpitz,* 25–30.
44. E.g., entry for 5 June 1910, in Hill, *Papiere,* 123; Hopman, Diary, 20 May 1914, in Epkenhans, *Leben,* 369.
45. Senden, Notes about Tirpitz, Spring 1896, BA-MA, N 160/1. Senden "hated" Tirpitz, according to Bülow, *Denkwürdigkeiten,* I: 68. On Senden and Tirpitz's early career, see Kelly, *Tirpitz,* 78–80, 103–28.
46. Entries for 5 February 1910, 5 June 1910, 30 September 1910, and 5 February 1911, in Hill, *Papiere;* Hopman, Diary, 2 January 1910, 28 June 1912, and 30 January 1913, in Epkenhans, *Leben.*
47. By contrast, Kelly, *Tirpitz,* and Gottschall, *Order,* present Tirpitz's ambition as a bureaucratic empire builder, his *Ressorteifer,* as the primary source of all conflict.
48. On the army, see Förster, *Militarismus.*
49. Tirpitz, Notes for imperial audience on 28 November 1898; and idem, Notes for a memorandum concerning the upcoming imperial audience on 28 November 1898, BA-MA, N 253/4 and RM 3/2.
50. Tirpitz, Comments on "Schlussvotum des Vorsitzenden der R-Kommission," 14 December 1904, BA-MA, RM 3/4.
51. Tirpitz to Holtzendorff, 20 April 1909, BA-MA, RM 3/8.
52. E.g., Capelle to Tirpitz, 11 September 1911; Tirpitz to Capelle, 13 September 1911; and Tirpitz, Notes for an imperial audience on 26 September 1911; in BA-MA, N 253/25.
53. Tirpitz to Müller, 30 April 1914, BA-MA, 3/10; Capelle, Notes for an Imperial presentation, 17 May 1914, including Tirpitz's comments, Tirpitz, Notes for an imperial audience on 23 May, 1914, BA-MA, N 253/29; Hopman, Diary, 15 June 1914, in Epkenhans, *Leben.*
54. Lambi, *Navy,* 164–70, 269–84; Berghahn, *Tirpitz-Plan,* esp. 331–41, 359–72, 448–65.
55. Bendemann, "Gedanken über die augenblickliche kritische Lage," 3 December 1904, BA-MA, RM 3/4. On the war scare, see chapter 2.
56. "Schlussvotum des Vorsitzenden der R-Kommission," 14 December 1904, BA-MA, RM 3/4.
57. Heeringen to Tirpitz, 15 September 1905; BA-MA, RM 3/3704.
58. Lambi, *Navy,* 280.
59. Büchsel, Notes for an imperial presentation on 7 January 1908, BA-MA, RM 5/893; Büchsel to Wilhelm II, 26 January 1908, RM 2/1553.
60. Prince Henry of Prussia to Wilhelm II, 21 December 1908, and Wilhelm II to Prince Henry, 9 January 1909, BA-MA, RM 2/1703; All-Highest Imperial Decree, 9 January 1909, BA-MA, RM 3/8.
61. Müller, Diary, 5, 9, and 12 January, 1909, BA-MA, N 159/3. See also Görlitz, *Kaiser,* 73–74.
62. On Admiral Baudissin's support of Bülow, see Tirpitz's comments on a letter by Bülow, which dated from 25 December 1908, in "Auszug aus den Akten über die Agreement-Frage," BA-MA, N 253/24. See Epkenhans, *Flottenrüstung,* 40–41.

63. Tirpitz to Holtzendorff, 20 April 1909, BA-MA, RM 3/8.

64. Holtzendorff to Tirpitz, 16 September 1911, BA-MA, RM 2/1703; Holtzendorff, Memorandum, 25 October 1911, BA-MA, N 253/25. Compare Capelle to Tirpitz, 11 and 14 September 1911, BA-MA, N 253/25; and entry for 5 June 1910 and 13 November 1911, in Hill, *Papiere*. Weizäcker served as Holtzendorff's flag lieutenant at that time.

65. Entries for 19 September 1910, 30 September 1910, 19 March 1911, in Hill, *Papiere*.

66. Müller, Notes, 12 September 1911, covering the events in early September, BA-MA, N 159/4; Entry for 2 November 1911, in Hill, *Papiere*; Hopman, Diary, 2 October 1911, in Epkenhans, *Leben*. For Holtzendorff's attempt to reach out to Secretary of State Kiderlen-Wächter, see multiple entries between September 1910 and July 1912, in Hill, *Papiere*.

67. See the correspondence between Heeringen and Tirpitz in June 1911, BA-MA, N 253/24; Heeringen to Bethmann-Hollweg, 7 October 1911, Tirpitz, *Aufbau*, 220–21; and Heeringen to Tirpitz, 24 November 1911 and 6 December 1911, BA-MA, RM 3/6678.

68. Müller, Diary, 27 October 1911, BA-MA, N 159/4, and Görlitz, *Kaiser*, 93; see also Tirpitz, Addendum to his notes for the imperial audience on 26 September 1911, BA-MA, N 253/25. Müller shared many of the concerns of Holtzendorff and Heeringen; see his diary entries from September 1911 through January 1912 in BA-MA, N 159/4, and Görlitz, *Kaiser*, 89–112. On Müller, compare Röhl, "Admiral," 653–59.

69. Capelle to Tirpitz, 11 September 1911, BA-MA, N 253/25.

70. Hopman, Diary, 16 November 1911, in Epkenhans, *Leben*; Trotha to Tirpitz, 31 March 1915, in Trotha, *Volkstum*, 29–31.

71. On the Bill, see Epkenhans, *Flottenrüstung*, 93–142; Lambi, *Navy*, 361–75.

72. Capelle, "Denkschrift zum Immediatvortrag," 22 May 1912, BA-MA, RM 3/6680.

73. Epkenhans, *Flottenrüstung*, 391–94.

74. Tirpitz to Pohl, 24 January 1914, Pohl to Tirpitz, 3 February 1914; BA-MA, RM 2/1648.

75. Lerchenfeld to Hertling, 9 May 1912, in Deuerlein, *Briefwechsel*, I: 159.

76. Entries for 29 July 1912 and 20 December 1912, in Hill, *Papiere*; Hopman, Diary, 18 May 1912, 8, 20, and 22 August 1912, 9 September 1912, 2 March and 28 March 1913, in Epkenhans, *Leben*; Holtzendorff to Levetzow, 26 October 1912, quoted in Gemzell, *Organization*, 123. On the navy secretary's fears that he was about to be toppled, see also the correspondence between Tirpitz and Capelle from August 1912, BA-MA, N 253/28.

77. Wilhelm II to Müller, 24 August 1912, and Müller to Wilhelm II, 28 August 1912, both alluding to Prince Henry's views, BA-MA, RM 2/1603.

78. On this suspicion, see Hopman, Diary, 9 September 1912 and 28 September 1913, in Epkenhans, *Leben*. On the emperor's disavowal of the plans for a bill in 1912–13, see Müller to Tirpitz, 4 and 6 January 1913, in Tirpitz, *Aufbau*, 370–71; on his halfhearted support in 1914, see Hopman, Diary, 22 May 1914, and Müller, Diary, 19 May 1914, BA-MA, N 159/4; on the Emperor's lack of interest, see the comments by Tirpitz and Müller about the Navy's Secretary imperial audience on 27 September 1913, in Hopman, Diary, 28 September 1913, and Müller, Diary, 27 September 1913.

79. E.g., Wilhelm II, Memorandum, 29 July 1912, enclosed in Müller to Tirpitz, 29 July 1912, Tirpitz to Müller, 2 and 5 August 1912, Wilhelm II, Comments on Tirpitz's letter from 5 August 1912, 12–15 August 1912, Müller to Tirpitz and Wilhelm, 20 August 1912, Trotha, Notes about an Imperial audience on 31 August, 1912, all in BA-MA, RM 2/1603, and Hopman, Diary, 31 August 1912, in Epkenhans *Leben*.

80. Berghahn, *Germany*, 138, has even argued that the "prestige" of Tirpitz had "evaporated." For assessments of Tirpitz's weakened position, see, for example, Capelle to Tirpitz, 20 August 1912, BA-MA, N 253/27; Hopman, Diary, 9 September 1912, 4 January 1913, 18 January 1913, in Epkenhans, *Leben*.

81. Tirpitz, *Ohnmachtspolitik,* 30–34, 128–280; Hopman, Diary, 10 November 1914, 13 and 28 December 1915, in Epkenhans.

82. Epkenhans, "Marine 1914/15."

83. Fischer, *Admiral,* 216–23. See also Pohl, *Aufzeichnungen.*

84. On this, see Deist, "Politik"; Herwig, *Corps,* 230–240; Gross, *Seekriegführung.*

85. *Hearings, General Board.*

86. Luce, "Navy."

87. Naval Policy Board, "Report."

88. Mahan, *Influence, 1660–1783;* idem, "Looking Outward" (1897).

89. Seager, *Mahan,* 219–307.

90. Spector, *Professors;* Hattendorf and others, *Sailors,* 11–68.

91. Dorwart, *Office,* 68–70.

92. This is a central theme in Costello, "Planning,"

93. GB to SN, 17 October 1903, 20 December 1905, 16 November 1906, 16 February 1907, and 28 January 1909; all in NA, RG 80, GB, SF 420-2, 446, and 401.

94. The recommendations of the BC are in NA, RG 80, BC, Letter Books and Minutes, covering the period from 1898 to 1907. The Board made its first recommendation on 14 November 1898.

95. Costello, "Planning," 65–90; McBride, *Change,* 38–88.

96. GB to BC, 26 January and 28 October 1904, 10 June, 11 July, 30 September, and 28 October 1905, NA, RG 80, Letter Book; BC to SN, 17 October 1904, NA, RG 80, Letter Books. On the idea of an all-big-gun battleship as it had been originally proposed in 1902–03, see Poundstone, "Size"; idem, "Armament," and the discussion in *PUSNI* 29 (1903): 435–43; Chambers, Memorandum, July 1903, enclosed on Sperry to GB, 1 February 1904, NA, RG 80, GB SF 420-6; Chadwick to Chambers, July 17, 1903, Chadwick, *Letters,* 301–2; W. Irving Chambers, "Memorandum," circa September 1904, NA, RG 80, GB, SF 420-2. Compare Stein, *Torpedoes.*

97. Friedman, *Battleships,* 51–74.

98. E.g., Fiske, "Policy": idem, "Ships"; Wainwright, "Battle"; Fiske, "Togo"; Gatewood, "Dimensions"; Wainwright, "Argument"; Sims, "Qualities." On Mahan, see his "Retrospect" (1902); idem, "Reflections" (1906); and his letters to Roosevelt in October 1906 and Henderson in January 1907; all in Seager and Maguire, *Letters,* III. Compare Mahan, "Lessons" (1899), and "Qualities" (1899), and Mahan to Long, 31 January 1900 and 15 February 1900, and to Roosevelt, 16 October 1902, in Seager and Maguire, *Letters,* II: 680–82; and III: 38–40.

99. GB to SN, 29 December 1905 and 28 January 1909; NA, RG 80, GB, SF 420 and 446.

100. Reuterdahl, "Needs"; *Hearings, Bill (S.3335);* Capps, *Report;* "Battleship Conference of 1908," 2 vols., NWCA, RG 8; Dewey to SN, 11 Nov 1908, forwarding a resume of Newport Conference, GB SF 420-2. For Hale's talk about abolishing the General Board, see *Army and Navy Journal* 45 (1908–9): 496 and 520 (issues from 11 and 18 January 1909). On Sims and Keys, see Morison, *Sims,* 176–215.

101. McBride, *Change,* 84.

102. Friedman, *Battleships,* 51–84; McBride, *Change,* 78–88. For consensus about the battleship design criticized by Fiske and Keys, see also SN to Hale, 9 March 1909, in *Hearings before the committee on Naval Affairs, United States Senate on the Bill (S.3335),* 253–57; and SN to Hale, 19 May 1909, NA RG 80, 1897–1915, File 26000–5.

103. Dewey to SN, 11 November 1908, forwarding a summary of the Newport Conference, NA, RG 80, GB, SF 420-2; "Battleship Conference of 1908," 2 vols., NWCA, RG 8.

104. Fiske, *Midshipman,* 475.

105. "Relations of the General Board to the Secretary of the Navy," 30 July 1914; NA, RG 80, GB, SF 401.

106. A biography is Spector, *Admiral*. See also V. Williams, "Dewey."
107. Fiske, *Midshipman*, 478.
108. Costello, "Planning," 30–32.
109. On Dewey as a public figure in 1898–1900, see Leeman, "Admiral."
110. Sargent to Dewey, 20 October 1905, LC, MD, Sargent Papers. On Dewey's war talk and its consequences, see Clifford, "Dewey."
111. Dewey to Taylor, 25 October 1900, LC, MD, Dewey Papers.
112. Washington Times, 25 December 1906; in LC, MD, Dewey Papers.
113. Barnette to Luce, 15 October 1905; LC, MD, Luce Papers; Keys to Sims, 27 November 1908, quoted in Spector, *Admiral*, 177–78.
114. Costello, "Planning," 19–20.
115. On the "war scare" of 1913, see chapter 3. On the following, compare my discussion in chapters 3 and 7.
116. Fiske, Diary, 18 and 26 October 1914; Fiske Papers, LC, MD.
117. Fiske, *Midshipman*, 546–71. For his official testimony in December 1914, see *Hearings, 1915*, 999–1047. Compare Coletta, *Fiske*, 131–78 For Fiske's views and behavior, see also his testimony before Congress in *Hearings, 1916*, 2887–976.
118. Fiske, Diary, 10 November 1914, LC, MD, Fiske Diary. On Blue and Winterhalter, see also the entries for 5, 6, 11, 12 November and 3 December 1914; GB, Proceedings, 24 September, 11, 12, 13, 27 November 1914, NA, RG 80; and their testimony before Congress in *Hearings, 1915*, 1–46, 571–838. Strikingly, Winterhalter accompanied Daniels before Congress and spoke at the secretary's official appearance.
119. Fiske, Diary, December 25, 1915, Fiske Papers, LC, MD; also: Fiske, *Midshipman*, 595–96.
120. Badger to Daniels, 26 January 1915; MD, LC, Daniels Papers; and GB, Proceedings, 19 January 1915; NA, RG 80, GB.
121. Dewey to SN, 5 March 1915, GB, NA, RG 80, SF 446
122. See the colorful episode relayed in Daniels, *Era*, 505–6.
123. Daniels, *Era*, chapter 53: "Friendship with Admiral Dewey," 501–12.
124. GB, Proceedings, 10 and 11 November 1914; NA, RG 80; Fiske, Diary, 11 November 1914, LC, MD, Fiske Papers.
125. E.g., Dewey to Padgett, 18 December 1914, LC, MD, Dewey Papers; Dewey to Daniels, 25 January 1915, LC, MD, Daniels Papers.
126. Fiske, "Dewey."
127. In his memoirs, Fiske wrote that "I had to carry on this fight alone, although the officers of the navy as a class supported me." *Midshipman*, 586.
128. Fiske, *Midshipman*, 572–84; Coletta, *Fiske*, 154–60.
129. As discussed in chapter 3.
130. Klachko, *Benson*; Trask, "Benson."

Conclusion

1. Beard, *Navy*, quotes: 68, 16, 88, 98, 193, 73, 74. For the chapter on Germany ("How von Tirpitz Played the Game," 14–38), Beard drew on Eckart Kehr's work on Wilhelmine battleship building, which had been brought to his attention by Alfred Vagts, his son-in-law.
2. A less scathing but still powerful critique of the American "naval expert" published only a few years later, in 1940, is G. Davis, *Navy*.
3. Conze et al., "Militarismus"; Berghahn, *Militarism*; Geyer, "Militarism"; Stargardt, *Idea*.

4. Chadwick, "Need," 643.

5. Vagts, *History*. I have taken the term "moral panic" from the discussion of Vagts's work in Geyer, "Militarism."

6. Repp, *Reformers*, 219–20.

7. Eley, "Empire."

8. Compare Geyer, "Crisis"; idem, "Strategy."

9. My understanding of older European notions of "power politics" and the "concert of powers" draws on Schroeder, *Transformation*.

10. On the German military as a "charismatic institution," see Hull, *Destruction*, 93–109, 327.

11. Ibid., esp. 1–4, 197–323.

12. Düllfer, *Weimar*; Schreiber, "Thesen."

13. Wagner, *Lagevorträge*, 20.

Bibliography

Archives

National Archives I and II, Washington, D.C., and College Park, Md.
Library of Congress, Manuscript Division, Washington, D.C.
U.S. Naval War College Archives, Newport, R.I.
Bundesarchiv-Militärarchiv, Freiburg
Bundesarchiv, Koblenz
Hauptstaatsarchiv, Dresden
Geheimes Staatsarchiv Preußischer Kulturbesitz, Berlin Dahlem
Politisches Archiv des Auswärbigen Amtes, Bonn

Published Primary Sources

Adams, Brooks. *America's Economic Supremacy* (New York, 1900).
———. *The New Empire* (New York, 1902).
———. "War as the Ultimate Form of Economic Competition." *PUSNI* 29 (1903): 829–81.
Allen, Gardner Weld, ed. *Papers of John Davis Long, 1897–1904* (Boston, 1939).
Annual Reports of the Navy Department (Washington, D.C., 1900–1920).
Bald, Detlef, ed. *Tradition und Reform im militärischen Bildungswesen: Von der preußischen Allgemeinen Kriegsakademie zur Führungsakademie der Bundeswehr. Eine Dokumentation 1810–1985* (Baden-Baden, 1985).

Bassermann, Ernst. *Tirpitz* (Berlin, 1916).
Beard, Charles A. *The Navy: Defense or Portent?* (New York, 1932).
Beehler, W. H. "Comment." *PUSNI* 31 (1905): 186–89.
Belknap, G. E. "Some Aspects of Naval Administration in War, with its Attendant Belongings of Peace." *PUSNI* 24 (1898): 263–300.
Benson, William Shepherd. *The Merchant Marine: "A Necessity in Time of War: A Source of Independence and Strength in Time of Peace"* (New York, 1923).
Berghahn, Volker R., and Wilhelm Deist. "Kaiserliche Marine und Kriegsausbruch 1914." *Militärgeschichtliche Mitteilungen* 7 (1970): 37–58.
———, eds. *Rüstung im Zeichen der wilhelminischen Weltpolitik Grundlegende Dokumente* (Düsseldorf, 1988).
Bernhardi, Friedrich von. *Denkwürdigkeiten aus meinem Leben* (Berlin, 1927).
Bernstorff, Hans. *Deutschlands Flotte im Kampf: Eine Phantasie* (Minden, 1908).
Borckenhagen, Ludwig. "Zum Studium der Seekriegsgeschichte." *Marine-Rundschau* 6 (1895): 49–69, 167–87.
———. "Der Krieg um Korea bis zur Einnahme von Port Arthur." *Marine-Rundschau* 6 (1895): 97–131.
———. "'Seeoffizierstypen' und andere Schriften von Mahan." *Marine-Rundschau* 13 (1902): 493–526.
Bradford, R. B. "Coaling Stations for the Navy." *Forum* 26 (1899): 732–47.
Bülow, Bernhard von. *Deutsche Politik* (Berlin, 1916).
———. *Denkwürdigkeiten,* 4 volumes (Berlin, 1930–31).
Calkins, C. G., et al. "Our Merchant Marine: The Causes of its Decline, and the Means to be taken for its Revival." *PUSNI* 8 (1882): 3–186.
Capps, Washington Lee. Report concerning Alleged Defects in Vessels of the United States Navy, Senate Document No. 297, 60th Congress, 1st session (Washington, D.C., 1908).
Chadwick, French Ensor. "Navy Department Organisation." *PUSNI* 20 (1894): 493–506.
———. "Explanation of Course at the Naval War College, June 4, 1901." *PUSNI* 27 (1901): 301–10.
———. "Opening Address Delivered by the President of the War College." *PUSNI* 28 (1902): 251–68.
———. "The Great Need of the United States Navy." *Munsey's Magazine* 33 (September 1905): 643–45.
———. *Selected Letters and Papers,* ed. Doris D. Maguire (Washington, D.C., 1981).
Colomb, Philipp. *Naval Warfare, Its Ruling Principles and Practice Historically Treated* (London, 1891).
Cooke, A. P. "Our Naval Reserve and the Necessity for its Organization." *PUSNI* 15 (1889): 170–97.
Cotton, Lyman A. "The Major Elements of War Efficiency." *PUSNI* 35 (1909): 667–73.
Corbett, Julian S. *Some Principles of Maritime Strategy,* ed. Eric Grove (Annapolis, 1988).
Cronan, W. P. "The Greatest Need of the U.S. Navy: Proper Organization for the Successful Conduct of War." *PUSNI* 42 (1916): 1137–69.
Cronon, David E., ed. *The Cabinet Diaries of Josephus Daniels, 1913–1921* (Lincoln, 1963).
Crosley, W. S. "The Naval War College, the General Board, and the Office of Naval Intelligence." *PUSNI* 39 (1913): 965–74.

Crowninshield, A. S. "The Dream of Navigators." *North American Review* 165 (1897): 695–700.
Daniels, Josephus. *The Wilson Era: Years of Peace, 1910–1917* (Chapel Hill, N.C., 1944).
Davis, Henry. "Some Thoughts on our Lack of a Naval Policy." *PUSNI* 41 (1915): 52–66.
Deist, Wilhelm, ed. *Militär und Innenpolitik im Weltkrieg 1914–1918* (Düsseldorf, 1970).
Deuerlein, Ernst, ed. *Briefwechsel Hertling-Lerchenfeld 1912–1917: Dienstliche Privatkorrespondenz zwischen dem bayerischen Ministerpräsidenten Georg Graf von Hertling und dem bayerischen Gesandten in Berlin Hugo Graf von und zu Lerchenfeld* (Boppard, 1973).
Dewey, George. "Naval Force for Summer Manoeuvres." *Navy League Journal* 1 (September 1903): 35–36.
———. *Autobiography of George Dewey, Admiral of the Navy* (New York, 1913).
Doenhoff, Richard A. von, ed. *The McCully Report: the Russo-Japanese War, 1904–05* (Annapolis, Md., 1977).
Driggs, W. H. "The Increase in Naval Strength." In *Notes on Naval Progress*, ed. Office of Naval Intelligence (Washington, D.C., January 1898), 65–80.
Eckardtstein, Herrmann von. *Lebenserinnerungen und Politische Denkwürdigkeiten*, 2nd edition (Leipzig, 1920).
Ellicott, John M. "The Composition of the Fleet." *PUSNI* 21 (1895): 537–48.
———. "Warship Design from a Tactical Standpoint." *PUSNI* 27 (1901): 51–66.
Ellsberg, Edward. "The Revival of the American Merchant Marine." *PUSNI* 37 (1911): 563–68.
Epkenhans, Michael, ed. *Das ereignisreiche Leben eines 'Wilhelminers': Tagebücher, Briefe, Aufzeichnungen von Albert Hopman, 1901 bis 1920* (Munich, 2004).
———. *Mein lieber Schatz! Briefe von Admiral Reinhard Scheer an seine Ehefrau August bis November 1918* (Bochum, 2006).
Firle, Rudolph "Die geschichtliche Entwicklung der japanischen Marine." *Marine-Rundschau* 17 (1906): 1227–30, 1368–77.
Fiske, Bradley A. "American Naval Policy." *PUSNI* 31 (1905): 1–80.
———. "Compromiseless Ships." *PUSNI* 31 (1905): 549–53.
———. "Why Togo Won." *PUSNI* 31 (1905): 807–9.
———. "The Civil and the Military Authority." *PUSNI* 32 (1906): 127–30.
———. "The Naval Profession." *PUSNI* 33 (1907): 475–578.
———. "Naval Power." *PUSNI* 37 (1911): 683–736.
———. "The Paramount Duty of the Army and Navy." *PUSNI* 40 (1914): 1073–74.
———. "Admiral Dewey: An Appreciation." *PUSNI* 43 (1917): 433–36.
———. *From Midshipman to Rear-Admiral* (New York, 1919).
———. *The Navy as a Fighting Machine*, ed. Wayne P. Hughes Jr. (Annapolis, Md., 1988).
Foster, F. F. "The War's Benefits." *PUSNI* 44 (1918): 1447–57.
Frost, H. H. "The Moral Factor in War." *PUSNI* 42 (1916): 349–85.
———. "The People's Role in War." *PUSNI* 43 (1917): 1113–50.
Fuchs, Walther Peter, ed. *Großherzog Friedrich I von Baden und die Reichspolitik 1871–1907*, 4 volumes (Stuttgart, 1968–80).
Fullinwider, S. P. "The Fleet and its Personnel." *PUSNI* 30 (1904): 1–29.
Galster, Karl. *Genügt unsere Küstenverteidigung?* (Kiel, 1907).
———. *Welche Seekriegsrüstung braucht Deutschland?* (Berlin, 1907).

Galster, M. "Besprechung der Aufsätze des Kapitäns A.T. Mahan in den 'Times,'" *Marine-Rundschau* 10 (1899): 217–32, 411–22, 601–07, 660–72.

Gatewood, Richard. "Approximate Dimensions for a 'Compromiseless Ship'." *PUSNI* 32 (1906): 571–83.

———. "Military Preparedness." *PUSNI* 40 (1914): 632–46.

Gibbons, John H. "Navy Leagues." *North American Review* 176 (1903): 758–64.

———. "The Need of a Building Program for Our Navy." *PUSNI* 29 (1903): 321–31.

Gleaves, Albert. "Some Foreign and Other Views of War and the Study and Conduct of War." *PUSNI* 40 (1914): 1301–21.

———. *The Admiral: The Memoirs of Albert Gleaves, USN* (Pasadena, C.A., 1985).

Goodrich, Caspar F. "Naval War College Closing Address, Session of 1897." *PUSNI* 23 (1897): 679–87.

———. "Esprit de Corps—A Tract for the Times." *PUSNI* 24 (1898): 1–24.

Görlitz, Walter, ed. *Regierte der Kaiser? Kriegstagebücher, Aufzeichnungen und Briefe des Chefs des Marinekabinetts Admiral Georg Alexander von Müller, 1914–1918* (Göttingen, 1959).

———. *Der Kaiser: Aufzeichnungen des Chefs des Marinekabinetts Admiral Georg Alexander v. Müller über die Ära Wilhelms II* (Göttingen, 1965).

Granier, Gerhard, ed. *Die deutsche Seekriegsleitung im Ersten Weltkrieg*, 4 volumes (Koblenz, 1999–2004).

Gröner, Wilhelm. *Lebenserinnerungen* (Göttingen, 1957).

Hall, Edward Hagaman. *The Hudson Fulton Celebration 1909. The Fourth Annual Report of the Hudson-Fulton Celebration Commission to the Legislature of the State of New York* (New York, 1910).

Halle, Ernst von. "Deutschland am Ende des XIX. Jahrhunderts." In idem, *See- und Volkswirtschaft: Reden und* Aufsätze (Berlin, 1902), volume 1, 13–135.

———. *Volks- und Seewirthschaft: Reden und Aufsätze,* 2 volumes (Berlin, 1902).

———. "Die Seeinteressen Deutschlands." In idem *Volks- und Seewirthschaft: Reden und Aufsätze* (Berlin, 1902), volume 1, 136–71.

———. "Die volks- und seewirtschaftlichen Beziehungen zwischen Deutschland und Holland 1898–1901." In idem, *Volks- und Seewirthschaft: Reden und Aufsätze* (Berlin, 1902), volume 2, 1–60.

———. "Die Bedeutung des nordamerikanischen Imperialismus." In idem, *Volks- und Seewirthschaft: Reden und Aufsätze* (Berlin, 1902), volume 2, 158–84.

———. "Weltmachtpolitik und Sozialreform" In idem, *Volks- und Seewirthschaft: Reden und Aufsätze* (Berlin, 1902), volume 2, 203–41.

———. "Die neueste Phase der Chamberlainschen Handels- und Schiffahrtpolitik." *Marine-Rundschau* 15 (1904): 145–68.

———. "Die drei Hauptbeweber auf dem Weltmarkt." *Marine-Rundschau* 16 (1905): 537–52, 726–44.

———. "Das Problem der Reichsfinanzreform." *Preußische Jahrbücher* 119 (1905): 495–507.

———. *Handelsmarine und Kriegsmarine* (Dresden, 1907).

———. "Die englische Seemachtpolitik und die Versorgung Großbritanniens in Kriegszeiten." *Marine-Rundschau* 17 (1906): 911–27, and 19 (1908): 804–15.

———. *Die Seemacht in der deutschen Geschichte* (Leipzig, 1907).

Hammann, Otto. *Bilder aus der letzten Kaiserzeit* (Berlin, 1922).

Hancock, J. Irving. *The Invasion of the United States* (Philadelphia, 1916).
Hayes, John D., and John B. Hattendorf, eds. *Writings of Stephen B. Luce* (Newport, 1975).
Hearings before the Committee on Naval Affairs, House of Representatives, on HR 15403, for a General Board. Statements of Secretary W.H. Moody et al. April 1904, 58th Congress, 2nd session.
Hearings before the Committee on Naval Affairs, United States Senate on the Bill (S.3335) to Increase the Efficiency of the Personnel of the Navy and Marine Corps of the United States, 60th Congress, 1st session.
Hearing on Council of National Defense, 24 January 1911, House Naval Affairs Committee, 61st Congress, 3rd session.
Hearing on Council of National Defense, 19 May 1911, House Naval Affairs Committee, 62nd Congress, 1st session.
Hearings on Estimates submitted by the Secretary of the Navy, 1915, House of Representatives (Washington, D.C., 1915).
Hearings Before the Committee on Naval Affairs, House of Representatives, 64th Congress, First Session on Estimates Submitted by the Secretary of the Navy, 1916, (Washington, D.C., 1916).
Hebbinghaus, Georg. "Biographisches über Mahan." *Marine-Rundschau* 19 (1908): 1130–46.
Heyking, Elisabeth von. *Tagebücher aus vier Weltteilen 1886/1904*, 4th edition (Leipzig, 1926).
Hill, Frank K. "Coordination Before and During the War." *PUSNI* 38 (1912): 563–93.
Hill, Leonidas E., ed. *Ernst von Weizäcker Papiere 1900–1933* (Berlin, 1982).
Hinds, A. W. "Peace, or War." *PUSNI* 41 (1915): 1409–20.
Hintze, Otto. "Staatsverfassung und Heeresverfassung." In idem, *Staat und Verfassung: Gesammelte Abhandlungen zur allgemeinen Verfassungsgeschichte,* ed. Gerhard Oestreich (Göttingen, 1962), 52–83.
Hohenlohe-Schillingfürst, Chlodwig zu. *Denkwürdigkeiten der Reichskanzlerzeit,* ed. Karl Alexander von Müller (Stuttgart, 1931).
Hollweg, Karl. "Admiralstabseinrichtungen der Hauptseemächte." *Marine Rundschau* 19 (1908): 1–29.
———. *Die Aufgaben der deutschen Flotte im Weltkriege* (Berlin, 1917).
Hood, John. "The Pacific Submarine Cable: Some Remarks on the Military Necessity and the Advantages of a National Cable." *PUSNI* 26 (1900): 477–88.
———. "Naval Administration and Organization." *PUSNI* 27 (1901): 1–27.
———. "The Monroe Doctrine: Its Meaning and Application at the Present Day." *PUSNI* 35 (1909): 657–66.
———. "Some Remarks Called Forth by the Able Essay of Pay Inspector Mudd—and a Plea." *PUSNI* 35 (1909): 385–91.
Hopman, Albert. *Das Logbuch eines deutschen Seeoffiziers* (Berlin, 1924).
Howard, W. L. "Increase in Naval Strength as Shown by Naval Budgets." In *Notes on Naval Progress,* ed. Office of Naval Intelligence (Washington, D.C., July 1900), 9–30.
Hulbert, Harold S. "Compulsory Citizenship Training." *PUSNI* 43 (1917): 985–87.
Hunt, Ridgely. "Naval Might." *PUSNI* 38 (1912): 7–68.
Hürter, Johannes, ed. *Paul von Hintze: Marineoffizier, Diplomat, Staatssekretär. Dokumente einer Karriere zwischen Militär und Politik, 1903–1918* (Munich, 1998).

Jackson, John P. "Preparedness: A Vital Necessity." *PUSNI* 42 (1916): 1559–89.
——. "A Plea for Universal Peace." *PUSNI* 43 (1917): 295–312.
Jefferson, Charles E. *Three Men behind the Guns* (New York, 1914).
Jones, N. L. "Details of Navy Department Administration; Navy Department Policies." *PUSNI* 40 (1914): 377–88.
Keim, August. *Erlebtes und Erstrebtes* (Hanover, 1925).
Kelly, J. P. Jerold. *Our Navy: Its Growth and Achievement*, 2nd edition (Hartford, 1897).
Kirchhoff, Herrmann. *Seekriegsgeschichte in ihren wichtigsten Abschnitten mit Berücksichtigung der Seetaktik*, 5 volumes (Hanover, 1909–21).
Knapp, Harry S. "The Navy and the Panama Canal." *PUSNI* 38 (1913): 931–48.
Knepper, Orlo S. "Some Navy Leagues." *Notes on Naval Progress, July 1901*, ed. Office of Naval Intelligence (Washington, D.C., 1901), 347–62.
Knight, Austin. "The Estimate of the Situation." *PUSNI* 41 (1915): 765–84.
Knox, Dudley. "The Role of Doctrine in Naval Warfare." *PUSNI* 41 (1915): 367–82.
——. "The General Problem of Naval Warfare." *PUSNI* 42 (1916): 23–45.
Kühlmann, Richard von. *Erinnerungen* (Heidelberg, 1948).
Lambert, Andrew, ed. *Letters and Papers of Professor Sir John Knox Laughton, 1830–1915* (Aldershot, 2002).
Laughton, John. "The Scientific Study of Naval History." *Journal of the Royal United Services Institution* 29 (1875): 217–41.
Lepsius, Johannes, Albrecht Mendelssohn Bartholdy, and Friedrich Thimme, eds. *Die Große Politik der Europäischen Kabinette, 1871–1914*, 40 volumes (Berlin 1922–27).
Liebknecht, Karl. "Militarismus und Antimilitarismus unter besonderer Berücksichtigung der internationalen Jugendbewegung." In idem, *Gesammelte Reden und Schriften* (Berlin, 1958), volume 1, 247–456.
Long, John D. *The New American Navy* (New York, 1903).
Luce, Stephen B. "War Schools." *PUSNI* 9 (1883): 633–57.
——. "United States Naval War College." *United Service* 12 (January 1885): 79–90.
——. "Our Future Navy." *North American Review* 149 (1889): 54–65.
——. "The Benefits of War." *North American Review* 153 (1891): 672–83.
——. "Naval Warfare under Modern Conditions." *North American Review* 162 (1896): 70–77.
——. "Naval Administration." *PUSNI* 28 (1902): 839–49.
——. "An Address Delivered at the United States Naval War College, Narragansett Bay, Rhode Island, June Second, Nineteen Hundred and Three." *PUSNI* 29 (1903): 537–45.
——. "War and its Prevention." *PUSNI* 30 (1904): 611–22.
——. "The Navy Department." *PUSNI* 31 (1905): 83–96.
——. "The U.S. Naval War College." *PUSNI* 36 (1910): 559–86, 683–96.
——. "On the True Relations between the Department of the Navy and the Naval War College." *PUSNI* 37 (1911): 83–86.
——. "On the Study of Naval History (Grand Tactics)." In *The Writings of Stephen B Luce*, ed. John D. Hayes and John B. Hattendorf (Newport, R.I., 1975), 71–97.
——. "On the Study of Naval Warfare As a Science." In *The Writings of Stephen B Luce*, ed. John D. Hayes and John B. Hattendorf (Newport, R.I., 1975), 47–68.
Mahan, Alfred Thayer. "Naval Education for Officers and Men." *PUSNI* 5 (1879): 345–76.

———. *The Navy in the Civil War: Gulf and Inland Waters* (New York, 1883).
———. "Address at the opening of the fourth annual session of the College, 6 August 1888." *PUSNI* 14 (1888): 621–38.
———. *The Influence of Sea Power Upon History, 1660–1783* (Boston, 1890).
———. *Admiral Farragut* (New York, 1892).
———. *The Influence of Sea Power Upon the French Revolution and Empire 1793–1812* (Boston, 1892).
———. "'The Practical Character of the Naval War College,' Delivered at the Opening of the Annual Session, 6 September 1892." *PUSNI* 19 (1893): 153–66.
———. "Blockade in Relation to Naval Strategy." *PUSNI* 21 (1895): 851–66.
———. *Der Einfluss der Seemacht auf die Geschichte 1660–1783* (Berlin, 1896).
———. "Hawaii and Our Future Sea Power." In idem, *The Interest of America in Sea Power, Present and Future* (Boston, 1897), 31–55.
———. "The Isthmus and Sea Power." In idem, *The Interest of America in Sea Power, Present and Future* (Boston, 1897), 59–104.
———. "Letter to the editor of the New York Times, 31 Jan 1893." In idem, *Interest of America in Sea Power, Present and Future* (Boston, 1897), 31–32.
———. "Possibilities of an Anglo-American Reunion." In idem, *The Interest of America in Sea Power, Present and Future* (Boston, 1897), 107–36.
———. "Preparedness for Naval War." In idem, *The Interest of America in Sea Power, Present and Future* (Boston, 1897), 175–214.
———. "Twentieth Century Outlook." In idem, *The Interest of America in Sea Power, Present and Future* (Boston, 1897), 217–68.
———. "The United States Looking Outward." In idem, *The Interest of America in Sea Power, Present and Future* (Boston, 1897), 3–27.
———. "Current Fallacies Upon Naval Subjects." In idem, *Lessons of the War with Spain and Other Articles* (Boston, 1899), 277–320.
———. "Distinguishing Qualities of Ships of War." In idem, *Lessons of the War with Spain and Other Articles* (Boston, 1899), 257–73.
———. *Der Einfluss der Seemacht auf die Geschichte: Zweiter Band 1783–1812: Die Zeit der französischen Revolution und des Kaiserreiches* (Berlin, 1899).
———. "Lessons of the War With Spain." In idem, *Lessons of the War with Spain and Other Articles* (Boston, 1899), 3–204.
———. "The Peace Conference and the Moral Aspect of War." *North American Review* 169 (1899): 433–47.
———. *The Problem of Asia and its Effects upon International Politics* (Boston, 1900).
———. "Considerations Governing the Disposition of Navies." In idem, *Retrospect and Prospect: Studies in International Relations Naval and Political* (Boston, 1902) 39–53.
———. "The Persian Gulf and International Relations." In idem, *Retrospect and Prospect: Studies in International Relations Naval and Political* (Boston, 1902), 209–51.
———. "Retrospect and Prospect." In idem, *Retrospect and Prospect: Studies in International Relations Naval and Political* (Boston, 1902), 3–35.
———. *Sea Power in Its Relations to the War of 1812*, 2 volumes (Boston, 1905).
———. "Reflections, Historic and Other, Suggested by the Battle of the Sea of Japan." *PUSNI* 32 (1906): 447–71.
———. *From Sail to Steam: Recollections of Naval Life* (New York, 1907).

———. "The Hague Conference and the Practical Aspect of War." In idem, *Some Neglected Aspects of War* (Boston, 1907), 157–93.
———. "The Hague Conference: The Question of Immunity of Belligerent Merchant Shipping." In idem, *Some Neglected Aspects of War* (Boston, 1907), 57–93.
———. "The Monroe Doctrine." In idem, *Naval Administration and Warfare: Some General Principles, with Other Essays* (London, 1908), 355–409.
———. "Principles Involved in the War Between Japan and Russia." In idem, *Naval Administration and Warfare: Some General Principles, with Other Essays* (London, 1908), 87–129.
———. "The Principles of Naval Administration." In idem, *Naval Administration and Warfare: Some General Principles, with Other Essays* (London, 1908), 1–48.
———. "Retrospect Upon the War between Japan and Russia." In idem, *Naval Administration and Warfare: Some General Principles, with Other Essays* (London, 1908), 133–73.
———. "Subordination in Historical Treatment." In idem, *Naval Administration and Warfare: Some General Principles, with Other Essays* (London, 1908), 243–72.
———. "The United States Navy Department." In idem, *Naval Administration and Warfare: Some General Principles, with Other Essays* (London, 1908), 49–85.
———. "The Value of the Pacific Cruise of the United States Fleet, 1908." In idem, *Naval Administration and Warfare: Some General Principles, with Other Essays* (London, 1908), 310–53.
———. *Armaments and Arbitration, Or: The Place of Force in the International Relations of States* (New York, 1911).
———. *Naval Strategy: Compared and Contrasted with the Principles and Practice of Military Operations on Land* (Boston, 1911).
———. *The Interest of America in International Conditions* (Boston, 1915).
———. "The Open Door." In idem, *The Interest of America in International Conditions* (Boston, 1915), 185–212.
———. "The Origin and Character of Present International Groupings in Europe." In idem, *The Interest of America in International Conditions* (Boston, 1915), 1–68.
———. "The Present Predominance of Germany in Europe—Its Foundations and Tendencies." In idem, *The Interest of America in International Conditions* (Boston, 1915), 69–124.
———. "Relations between East and West." In idem, *The Interest of America in International Conditions* (Boston, 1915), 125–84.
Maltzahn, Curt von. "Seeherschaft." *Neue Militärische Blätter* 46 (1895): 481–86.
———. *Der Kampf gegen die Seeherrschaft. Vortrag gehalten am 8 Januar in der Aula der Marine-Akademie* (Kiel, 1898).
———. "Das Meer als Operationsfeld und als Kampffeld." *Marine-Rundschau* (1904): 273–90, 412–26.
———. "Friedrich Ratzel. Ein Gedenkwort." *Marine-Rundschau* 16 (1905): 217–20.
———. "Was lehrt das Buch des Generals von Clausewitz 'Vom Kriege' dem Seeoffizier?" *Marine-Rundschau* 16 (1905): 683–702.
———. *Der Seekrieg: Seine geschichtliche Entwickelung vom Zeitalter der Entdeckungen bis zur Gegenwart* (Leipzig, 1906).
———. *Geschichte unserer taktischen Entwicklung*, 2 volumes (Berlin, 1910).

———. "Über die Entstehung und Verwertung seekriegsgeschichtlicher Schilderungen." *Marine-Rundschau* 21 (1910): 167–80.

———. *Der Seekrieg zwischen Russland und Japan 1904 bis 1905* (Berlin, 1912–14).

———. "Seestrategie in ihren Beziehungen zur Landstrategie nach englisch-amerikanischem Urteil." *Marine-Rundschau* (1912): 869–86.

Marble, Frank. "Battle of Yalu." *PUSNI* 21 (1895): 479–521.

Matthews, Franklin. *Back to Hampton Roads: Cruise of the U.S. Atlantic fleet from San Francisco to Hampton Roads, July 7, 1908–February 22, 1909* (New York, 1909).

———. *With the Battle-Fleet: Cruise of the sixteen battleships of the United States Atlantic fleet from Hampton Roads to the Golden Gate, December, 1907–May, 1908* (New York, 1909).

McKean, J. S. "War and Policy." *PUSNI* 40 (1914): 1–15.

Melville, George W. *Our Future on the Pacific* (Washington, D.C., 1898).

———. "Our Actual Naval Strength." *NAR* 176 (1903): 376–90.

———. "The Important Elements in Naval Conflicts." *Annals of the American Academy of Political and Social Science* 26, no 1 (1905): 123–36.

Michaelis, William. "Die Verwendung des internationalen Kabelnetzes im Seekriege." *Marine-Rundschau* 14 (1903): 807–35.

———. "Tirpitz' strategisches Wirken vor und während des Weltkrieges." In *Deutsche Marinen im Wandel: Vom Symbol nationaler Einheit zum Instrument internationaler Sicherheit,* ed. Werner Rahn (Munich, 2005), 397–426.

Miller, Roman J. *Around the World with the Battleships,* 3rd edition (Chicago, 1910).

Mitchell, Richard. "Our Trade with South America, with Special Reference to Brazil and the River Plate Republics." *Harper's Monthly Magazine* 94 (1896–97): 796–802.

Morison, Elting. *The Letters of Theodore Roosevelt,* 8 volumes (Cambridge, 1951–54).

Murdock, J. B. "Our Need of Fighting Ships." *PUSNI* 27 (1901): 247–67.

Nauticus. *Altes und Neues zur Flottenfrage: Erläuterungen zum Flottengesetz* (Berlin, 1898).

———. *Neue Beiträge zur Flottenfrage* (Berlin, 1898).

———. "Politische Machtstellung und Kriegsmarine." In Nauticus, *Beiträge zur Flottenfrage* (Berlin, 1898), 158–74.

———. "Arbeiterinteressen und die Marine." *Nauticus* 1 (1899): 20–29.

———. "Auswanderung." *Nauticus* 1 (1899): 59–65.

———. *Jahrbuch für deutsche Seeinteressen 1–16* (Berlin, 1899–1914).

———. *Beiträge zur Flotten-Novelle 1900* (Berlin, 1900).

———. "Die Blockade der nordamerikanischen Südstaaten." *Nauticus* 2 (1900): 89–123.

———. "Die deutschen Arbeiterinteressen, der Weltmarkt und die Flotte." *Nauticus* 2 (1900): 211–25.

———. "Die Entwicklung der englischen See- und Weltmacht." *Nauticus* 2 (1900): 124–47.

———. "Flotte und Kolonien." *Nauticus* 2 (1900): 65–73.

———. "Die modernen Weltreiche." *Nauticus* 2 (1900): 51–64.

———. "Die wirtschaftlichen Interessen Deutschlands in China." *Nauticus* 2 (1900): 249–73.

———. "Die Chinesische Frage." *Nauticus* 3 (1901): 137–52.

———. "Das Erstarken der Völker zur See." *Nauticus* 3 (1901): 114–36.

———. "Die Fortschritte fremder Kriegsmarinen." *Nauticus* 3 (1901): 39–70.

———. "Deutsche Auswanderung im 20. Jahrhundert." *Nauticus* 4 (1902): 264–80.
———. "Die Erschliessung Chinas." *Nauticus* 4 (1902): 110–28.
———. "Ein Jahr des Fortschrittes in China," *Nauticus* 5 (1903): 148–78.
———. "Weltpolitik und Seemacht." *Nauticus* 5 (1903): 128–47.
———. "Fragen des Seekriegsrechts." *Nauticus* 7 (1905): 232–45.
———. "Die Fortschritte der Funkentelegraphie, ihre wirtschaftliche und militärische Bedeutung." *Nauticus* 8 (1906): 477–96.
———. "Politische Rückblicke und Ausblicke." *Nauticus* 10 (1908): 1–19.
———. "Die befruchtende Wirkung der Flottengesetze auf die deutsche Industrie." *Nauticus* 14 (1912): 294–325.
———. "Die Technischen Hilfsmittel der Seestrategie." *Nauticus* 14 (1912): 228–69.
———. "Die militärische und rechtliche Bedeutung der Blockade." *Nauticus* 16 (1914): 279–308.
Naval Investigation. Hearings before the Subcommittee of the Committee on Naval Affairs, United States Senate, 66th Congress, 2nd session (Washington, D.C., 1920).
"Naval Manoeuvres, 1888." *Naval Annual* 2 (1888–89): 413–49.
Naval Policy Board. "Report of the Naval Policy Board, 20 January 1890." *PUSNI* 16 (1890): 201–77.
Naval War College Staff. "Notes on the Applicatory System of Solving War Problems, with Examples Showing the Adaptation of the System to Naval Problems." *PUSNI* 37 (1911): 1011–36.
Niblack, A. P. "Letters of a Retired Rear Admiral to His Son in the Navy." *PUSNI* 41 (1915): 367–82.
Noske, Gustav. *Erlebtes aus Aufstieg und Niedergang einer Demokratie* (Offenbach, 1947).
Nowak, Kurt von, and Friedrich Thimme, eds. *Erinnerungen und Gedanken des Botschafters Anton Graf Monts* (Berlin, 1922).
Nulton, Louis M. "Notes on Naval Budgets of 1902–03." In *Notes on Naval Progress,* ed. Office of Naval Intelligence (Washington, D.C., 1902), 449–70.
Office of Naval Intelligence, ed. *International Columbian Naval Rendez-vous and Review of 1893 and Naval Maneuvers of 1892* (Washington, D.C., 1893).
———, ed. *Notes on Naval Progress* (Washington, D.C., 1898–1903).
———. ed. *The American Naval Planning Section London* (Washington, D.C., 1923).
The Official Blue Book of the Jamestown Ter-Centennial Commission (Washington, D.C., 1909).
Palmer, Frederick. *With My Own Eyes* (New York, 1934).
Paullin, Charles Oscar. *Paullin's History of Naval Administration, 1775–1911* (Annapolis, 1968).
Peez, Alexander. *Zur neuesten Handelspolitik. Sieben Abhandlungen* (Vienna, 1895).
Persius, Lothar. *Menschen und Schiffe in der Kaiserlichen Flotte* (Berlin, 1925).
Peters, George H. "Recent Tendencies of Foreign Naval Development and the Effect Thereon of the Recent War with Spain." In *Notes on Naval Progress,* ed. Office of Naval Intelligence (Washington, D.C., 1899), 7–16.
Phelps, W. W. "Naval Industrialism, Naval Commercialism and Naval Discipline." *PUSNI* 39 (1913): 509–50.
Pohl, Heinrich. *Deutsches Seekriegsrecht: Quellensammlung* (Berlin, 1915).
Pohl, Hugo von. *Aus Aufzeichnungen und Briefen während der Kriegszeit* (Berlin, 1920).
Poundstone, Homer C. "Proposed Armament of Type Battleship of U.S. Navy, with some suggestions relating to armor protection." *PUSNI* 29 (1903): 377–411.

———. "Size of Battleships for U.S. Navy." *PUSNI* 29 (1903): 161–74.
Radford, G. S. "Organization: An Essay on Fundamental Principles, with Special Reference to the Navy." *PUSNI* 39 (1913): 1683–1718.
Raeder, Erich. *Mein Leben. Bis zum Flottenabkommen mit England 1935* (Tübingen, 1956).
Rahne, Werner. "Wilhelm II. und seine Marine. Kritische Beobachtungen während des Kaisermanövers in der Nordsee Herbst 1912. Aus den Erinnerungen von Vizeadmiral William Michaelis." *Marine-Rundschau* 73 (1976): 285–91.
Ratzel, Friedrich. *Politische Geographie* (Munich, 1897).
———. *Das Meer als Quelle der Völkergröße. Eine politisch-geographische Studie* (Munich, 1900).
———. *Politische Geographie oder die Geographie der Staaten, des Verkehrs und des Krieges*, 2nd revised edition (Munich, 1903).
———. "Die nordatlantischen Mächte." *Marine-Rundschau* 14 (1903): 911–39, 1047–62.
Reichsarchiv, ed. *Kriegsrüstung und Kriegswirtschaft. Anlagen zum ersten Band* (Berlin, 1930).
Reichsmarineamt. *Die Seeinteressen des Deutschen Reiches* (Berlin, 1898).
———. *Die Steigerung der Deutschen Seeinteressen von 1896 bis 1898* (Berlin, 1900).
———. *Die Entwicklung der deutschen Seeinteressen im letzten Jahrzehnt* (Berlin, 1906).
Report of the Merchant Marine Commission. Together with the Testimony at the Hearings, 3 volumes (Washington, D.C., 1905).
"Report of the three Admirals." In *British Naval Documents*, ed. John Hattendorf (Aldershot, 1993), 614–17.
Reuterdahl, Henry C. "The Need of a Continuous Building Programme for the Navy." *Outlook* 87 (25 February 1905): 185–88.
———. "The Needs of Our Navy." *McClure's Magazine* 30 (January 1908): 251–56.
———. "President Roosevelt and the Navy's Renaissance." *Pearson's Magazine* 30 (January 1908): 566–86.
———. "A Plea for a Better Understanding of the Navy." *Outlook* 91 (20 March 1909): 631–36.
Rich, Norman, and M. H. Fisher, eds. *Die Geheimen Papiere Friedrich von Holsteins*, 4 volumes (Göttingen, 1956–63).
Riggs, R. R. "The Question of Speed in Battleships." *PUSNI* 34 (1908): 235–46.
Rittenhouse, H. O. "The Preparedness of the Future." *PUSNI* 44 (1918): 733–85.
Rittmeyer, Rudolph. *Seekriege und Seekriegswesen in ihrer weltgeschichtlichen Entwicklung. Mit besonderer Berücksichtigung der großen Seekriege des XVII und XVIII Jahrhunderts*, 2 volumes (Berlin, 1907–11).
Roberts, T. G. "The Merchant Marine and the Navy." *PUSNI* 36 (1910): 1–40.
Rodgers, Frederick. "The Extent to Which the Navy of the United States Should Be Increased." *Annals of the American Academy of Political and Social Science* 26:1 (1905): 139–45.
Rodgers, William. "The Field of Work to be Filled by a Naval War College." *PUSNI* 37 (1911): 353–77.
———. "The Naval War College Course." *PUSNI* 38 (1912): 1235–40.
———. "The Relation of the War College to the Navy Department." *PUSNI* 38 (1912): 835–50.
Röhl, John C. G., ed. *Philipp Eulenburgs Politische Korrespondenz*, 3 volumes (Boppard, 1976–83).

Rohrbach, Paul. *Deutschland unter den Weltvölkern: Materialien zur auwärtigen Politik* (Berlin, 1903).
Roosevelt, Theodore. "Third Annual Message, 7 December 1903." In *A Compilation of the Messages and Papers of the Presidents,* ed. J. D. Richardson (New York, n.d.), volume 14, 6784–6814.
Roscher, Max. "Seekabelpolitik und –Organisation." *Marine-Rundschau* 23 (1913): 1071–91.
Rust, F. *Marinesorgen: Revision des Flottenprogrammes* (Berlin, 1904).
Sargent, Nathan. *Admiral Dewey and the Manila Campaign* (Washington, D.C., 1947).
Scheer, Reinhard. *Vom Segelschiff zum U-Boot* (Leipzig, 1925).
Scherer, André, and Jacques Grunewald, eds. *L'Allemagne et les problèmes de la paix pendant la Première Guerre mondiale: Documents extraits des archives de l'Office allemand des Affaires étrangères,* 4 volumes (Paris, 1962–78).
Schleinitz, Freiherr von. "Der Außen- und Kleinkrieg zur See und seine Bedeutung für Deutschland." *Deutsche Revue* 33:3 (1908): 132–49.
Schmitt, Carl. *Positionen und Begriffe im Kampf mit Weimar-Genf-Versailles 1923–1939* (Berlin, 1940).
———. *Der Nomos der Erde im Völkerrecht des Ius Publicum Europaeum* (Cologne, 1950).
———. *Land und Meer. Eine weltgeschichtliche Betrachtung* (Hohenheim, 1981).
Schroeder, Seaton. "Gleanings from the Sea of Japan." *PUSNI* 32 (1906): 47–93.
———. *A Half Century of Naval Service* (New York, 1922).
Schumpeter, Joseph A. "Zur Soziologie der Imperialismen." *Archiv für Sozialwissenschaft und Sozialpolitik* 46 (1919): 1–39, 275–310.
Seager, Robert, II, and Doris D. Maguire, eds. *Letters and Papers of Alfred Thayer Mahan.* 3 volumes (Annapolis, 1975).
Seligmann, Matthew, ed. *Naval Intelligence from Germany: The Reports of the British Naval Attachés in Berlin, 1906–1914* (Aldershot, 2007).
Sims, William S. "The Inherent Tactical Qualities of All-Big-Gun, One-Caliber Battleships of High Speed, Large Displacement and Gun-Power." *PUSNI* 32 (1906): 1337–66.
———. "Naval War College Principles and Methods Applied Afloat." *PUSNI* 41 (1915): 383–403.
———. "Cheer Up! There is no Naval War College." *PUSNI* 42 (1916): 857–60.
———. "Military Character." *PUSNI* 43 (1917): 437–62.
Soley, James R. *The Navy in the Civil War: The Blockade and the Cruisers* (New York, 1883).
Squier, George Owen. "The Influence of Submarine Cables Upon Military and Naval Supremacy." *PUSNI* 26 (1900): 599–622.
Staunton, Sidney A. "Naval Reserves and the Recruiting and Training of Men." *PUSNI* 15 (1889): 1–20.
Stein, Lorenz von. *Die Lehre vom Heerwesen als Theil der Staatswissenschaft* (Osnabrück, 1967).
Stenzel, Alfred. *Seekriegsgeschichte in ihren wichtigsten Abschnitten mit Berücksichtigung der Seetaktik* (Hanover, 1907).
———. *Kriegführung zur See. Lehre vom Seekriege,* ed. Hermann Kirchhoff (Hanover, 1913).
Still, William N., Jr. *The Queenstown Patrol, 1917: The Diary of Commander Joseph Knefler Taussig, U.S. Navy* (Newport, R.I., 1996).
Stirling, Yates. "Comment." *PUSNI* 30 (1904): 623–26.

———. "Organization for Navy Department Administration: A Study of Principles." *PUSNI* 39 (1913): 435–500.

Stockton, Herbert C. "Comment." *PUSNI* 24 (1898): 127–28.

———. "Submarine Cables in Time of War." *PUSNI* 14 (1898): 451–56.

———. "The American Interoceanic Canal: A Study of the Commercial, Naval and Political Conditions." *PUSNI* 25 (1899): 753–97.

———. *Preparation for War: A Discussion of Some of the Various Elements to be Considered in the Formation of Plans of Operations and in the Study of Campaigns, delivered May 31, 1899* (Washington, D.C., 1899).

———. "Would Immunity from Capture, During War, of Non-Offending Private Property Upon the High Seas Be in the Interest of Civilization?" *American Journal of International Law* 1 (October 1907): 930–43.

———. "Address, April 23." *American Society of International Law Proceedings* 61 (1909): 61–84.

———. "The International Naval Conference of London, 1908–1909." *American Journal of International Law* 3 (July 1909): 596–618.

———. "Address on the Codification of the Laws of Naval Warfare." *American Society of International Law Proceedings* 64 (1912): 115–23.

Strong, Josiah. *Expansion under New World Conditions* (New York, 1900).

Tampke, Jürgen, ed. *"Ruthless Warfare": German Military Planning and Surveillance in the Australia-New Zealand Region before the Great War* (Canberra, 1998).

Taylor, Henry C. "The Control of the Pacific." *Forum* 3 (1887): 407–16.

———. "Address Delivered to the Class at the Naval War College, Upon the Closing of the Session of 1894." *PUSNI* 20 (1894): 796–802.

———. "Naval War College. Closing Address, Session of 1895." *PUSNI* 22 (1896): 199–208.

———. "The Study of War." *North American Review* 162 (1896): 181–89.

———. "The Future of Our Navy." *Forum* 26 (March 1899): 1–20.

———. "Memorandum on General Staff for the U.S. Navy." *PUSNI* 26 (1900): 441–48.

———. "The Fleet." *PUSNI* 29 (1903): 803–7.

Thurn-Coblenz, H. "Drahtlose Telephonie bei der Kriegsmarine." *Marine-Rundschau* 22 (1911): 970–84.

Tirpitz, Alfred von. *Erinnerungen* (Leipzig, 1919).

———. *Der Aufbau der deutschen Weltmacht* (Stuttgart, 1924).

———. "Warum kam eine Flottenverständigung mit England nicht zustande?" *Süddeutsche Monatshefte* 23 (November 1925): 95–126.

———. *Deutsche Ohnmachtspolitik im Weltkriege* (Hamburg, 1926).

Trotha, Adolf von. *Volkstum und Staatsführung. Briefe und Aufzeichnungen aus den Jahren 1915–1920* (Berlin, 1920).

———. *Grossdeutsches Wollen: Aus den Lebenserfahrungen eines Seeoffiziers* (Berlin, 1924).

———. *Großadmiral von Tirpitz: Flottenbau und Reichsgedanke* (Breslau, 1933).

Trützschler, Robert Zedlitz. *Zwölf Jahre am deutschen Kaiserhof* (Berlin, 1924).

Turk, Richard W. *The Ambiguous Relationship: Theodore Roosevelt and Alfred Thayer Mahan* (New York, 1987).

Upton, Emory. *The Armies of Asia and Europe Embracing Official Reports on the Armies of Japan, China, India, Persia, Italy, Russia, Austria, Germany, France, and England* (New York, 1878).

Wagner, Gerhard, ed. *Lagevorträge des Oberbefehlshabers der Kriegsmarine vor Hitler 1939–1945* (Munich, 1972).
Wainwright, Richard. "Tactical Problems in Naval Warfare." *PUSNI* 21 (1895): 217–62.
———. "Our Naval Power." *PUSNI* 24 (1898): 39–87.
———. "The Battle of the Sea of Japan." *PUSNI* 31 (1905): 779–805.
———. "A Further Argument for the Big Ship." *PUSNI* 32 (1906): 1057–63.
Washburn, H. C. "The American Blind Spot." *PUSNI* 43 (1917): 1–41.
Weber, Max. "Parlament und Regierung im neugeordneten Deutschland." In idem, *Zur Politik im Weltkrieg: Schriften und Reden 1914–1918,* ed. Wolfgang J. Mommsen and Gangolf Hübinger (Tübingen, 1988), 212–26.
Wegener, Wolfgang. *The Naval Strategy of the World War,* ed. Holger H. Herwig (Annapolis, 1989).
Widenmann, Wilhelm. *Marine-Attaché an der kaiserlich-deutschen Botschaft in London 1907–1912* (Göttingen, 1952).
Wilkinson, Spenser. *The Brain of an Army: A Popular Account of the German General Staff* (London, 1890).
Williams, Dion. "The Nation's Greatest Need." *PUSNI* 43 (1917): 897–916.
Woodward, C. H. "The Navy's Participation at the Panama-Pacific Exposition." *PUSNI* 41 (1915): 167–72.
Yarnell, Harry. "The Greatest Need of the Atlantic Fleet." *PUSNI* 39 (1913): 1–38.

Secondary Sources

Abrahamson, James L. *America Arms for a New Century: The Making of a Great Power* (New York, 1981).
Albion, Robert Greenhalgh. *Makers of Naval Policy, 1798–1947.* Ed. Rowena Reed (Annapolis, 1980).
Allin, Lawrence C. *The United States Naval Institute: Intellectual Forum of the New Navy, 1873–1889* (Manhattan, Kans., 1978).
Anderson, Margaret Lavinia. "A German Way of War?" *German History* 22 (2004): 254–58.
Anderson, Stuart. *Race and Rapprochement: Anglo-Saxonism and Anglo-American Relations, 1895–1904* (Rutherford, N.J., 1981).
Angevine, Robert G. "The Rise and Fall of the Office of Naval Intelligence, 1882–1892: A Technological Perspective." *Journal of Military History* 62 (April 1998): 291–312.
Arnold, Peri E. "Policy Leadership in the Progressive Presidency: The Case of Theodore Roosevelt's Naval Policy and His Search for Strategic Resources." *Studies in American Political Development* 10 (Fall 1996): 333–59.
Bade, Klaus J. *Friedrich Fabri und der Imperialismus in der Bismarckzeit: Revolution-Depression-Expansion* (Freiburg, 1975).
Baecker, Thomas. "Das deutsche Feindbild in der amerikanischen Marine 1900–1914." *Marine-Rundschau* 70 (1973): 65–84.
———. "Mahan über Deutschland." *Marine-Rundschau* 73 (1976): 10–19, 86–102.
Baer, George W. *One Hundred Years of Sea Power: The U.S. Navy 1890–1990* (Stanford, Calif., 1993).

Bald, Detlef. *Der deutsche Offizier: Sozial- und Bildungsgeschichte des deutschen Offizierskorps* (Munich, 1982).

Balogh, Brian. "Reorganizing the Organizational Synthesis: Federal-Professional Relations in Modern America." *Studies in American Political Development* 5 (Spring 1991): 119–72.

Becker, Frank. *Bilder von Krieg und Nation: Die Einigungskriege in der bürgerlichen Öffentlichkeit Deutschlands 1864–1913* (Munich, 2001).

———. "Synthetischer Militarismus: Die Einigungskriege und der Stellenwert des Militärischen in der deutschen Gesellschaft." In *Das Militär und der Aufbruch in die Moderne 1860–1890,* ed. Michael Epkenhans and Gerhard P. Groß (Munich, 2003), 125–42.

Bederman, Gail. *Manliness and Civilization: A Cultural History of Gender and Race in the United States, 1880–1917* (Chicago, 1995).

Beeler, John. "A One Power Standard? Great Britain and the Balance of Naval Power, 1860–1880." *Journal of Strategic Studies* 15 (December 1992): 547–75.

———. "Steam, Strategy and Schurman: Imperial Defence in the Post-Crimean Era, 1856–1905." In *Far-Flung Lines: Essays on Imperial Defence in Honour of Donald Mackenzie Schurman,* ed. Greg Kennedy and Keith Neilson (London, 1997), 27–54.

Beers, Henry P. "The Development of the Office of the Chief of Naval Operations, Parts I and II." *Military Affairs* 10 (Spring 1946): 40–68, and (Fall 1946): 11–38.

Beisner, Robert. *From the Old Diplomacy to the New, 1865–1900.* 2nd edition (Arlington Heights, Ill., 1986).

Bender, Thomas. *A Nation Among Nations: America's Place in World History* (New York, 2006).

———, ed. *Rethinking American History in a Global Age* (Berkeley, 2002).

Berghahn, Volker R. "Zu den Zielen des deutschen Flottenbaus unter Wilhelm II." *Historische Zeitschrift* 210 (1970): 34–100.

———. *Der Tirpitz-Plan: Genesis und Verfall einer innenpolitischen Krisenstrategie unter Wilhelm II* (Düsseldorf, 1971).

———. *Germany and the Approach of War in 1914* (New York, 1973).

———. *Rüstung und Machtpolitik. Zur Anatomie des "Kalten Krieges" vor 1914* (Düsseldorf, 1973).

———. *Militarism: History of an International Debate* (Leamington Spa, U.K., 1979).

———. "Des Kaiser's Flotte und die Revolutionierung des Mächtesystems vor 1914." In *Der Ort Kaiser Wilhelms II in der deutschen Geschichte,* ed. John C.G. Röhl (Munich, 1991), 173–88.

———. "War Preparations and National Identity in Imperial Germany." In *Anticipating Total War: The German and American Experiences 1871–1914,* ed. Manfed Boemeke, Roger Chickering, and Stig Förster (Cambridge, 1999), 307–26.

Besteck, Eva. *Die trügerische "First Line of Defence": Zum deutsch-britischen Wettrüsten vor dem Ersten Weltkrieg* (Freiburg, 2006).

Bigelow, Donald Nevius. *William Conant Church and "The Army and Navy Journal"* (New York, 1952).

Bird, Keith W. *German Naval History: A Guide to the Literature* (New York, 1985).

Bleyberg, Derek M. "Government and Legislative Process in Wilhelmine Germany: The Reorganisation of the Tariffs Laws under Reich Chancellor von Bülow 1897 to 1902." PhD dissertation, University of East Anglia, 1979.

Blight, David W. *Race and Reunion: The Civil War in American Memory* (Cambridge, 2001).

Boemeke, Manfred, Roger Chickering, and Stig Förster, eds. *Anticipating Total War: The German and American Experiences, 1871–1914* (Cambridge, 1999).

Bogle, Lori Lyn. "TR's Use of PR to Strengthen the Navy." *Naval History* 21 (December 2007): 26–31.

Böhm, Ekkehart. *Überseehandel und Flottenbau: Hanseatische Kaufmannschaft und deutsche Seerüstung 1879–1902* (Düsseldorf, 1972).

Bönker, Dirk. "Maritime Aufrüstung zwischen Partei- und Weltpolitik. Schlachtflottenbau in Deutschland und den USA um die Jahrhundertwende." In *Zwei Wege in die Moderne Aspekte der deutsch-amerikanischen Beziehungen vor und im Ersten Weltkrieg,* ed. Jürgen Heideking and Ragnhild Fiebig-von Hase (Trier, 1998), 231–59.

——. "Naval Professionalism and the State in Turn-of-the-Century Germany and America." In *New Interpretations in Naval History: Selected Papers from the Thirteenth Naval History Symposium,* ed. William M. McBride and Eric P. Reed (Annapolis, 1998), 111–38.

——. "Admiration, Enmity, and Cooperation: US Navalism and the British and German Empires before the Great War." *Journal of Colonialism and Colonial History* 2 (2001).

——. "Zwischen Bürgerkrieg und Navalismus: Marinepolitik und Handelsimperialismus in den USA, 1865–1890." In *Das Militär und der Aufbruch in die Moderne 1860–1890,* ed. Michael Epkenhans and Gerhard P. Groß (Munich, 2003), 93–115.

——. "Military History, Militarization, and the 'American Century.'" *Zeithistorische Forschungen* 2 (2005): 105–9.

——. "Ein *German Way of War?* Deutscher Militarismus und maritime Kriegfuehrung im Ersten Weltkrieg." In *Das Deutsche Kaiserreich in der Kontroverse,* ed. Cornelius Torp and Sven-Oliver Müller (Göttingen, 2009), 308–22.

Bräckow, Werner. *Die Geschichte des deutschen Marine-Ingenieuroffizierskorps* (Oldenburg, 1974).

Braisted, William Reynolds. *The United States Navy in the Pacific, 1897–1909* (Austin, 1958).

——. *The United States Navy in the Pacific, 1909–1922* (Austin, 1971).

Bright, Charles. "The State in the United States during the Nineteenth Century." In *Statemaking and Social Movements: Essays in History and Theory,* ed. Charles Bright and Susan Harding (Ann Arbor, 1984), 121–58.

Bright, Charles, and Michael Geyer. "Where in the World Is America? The History of the United States in the Global Age." In *Rethinking American History in a Global Age,* ed. Thomas Bender (Berkeley, 2002), 63–99.

——. "Regimes of Global Order: Global Integration and the Production of Difference in Twentieth-Century World History." In *Interactions: Transregional Perspectives on World History,* ed. Jerry H. Bentley, Renate Bridenthal, and Anand A. Yang (Honolulu, 2005), 202–38.

Bristow, Nancy K. *Making Men Moral: Social Engineering during the Great War* (New York, 1996).

Browning, Robert S., III. *Two if by Sea: The Development of American Coastal Policy* (Westport, Conn., 1983).

Bruch, Rüdiger vom. *Wissenschaft, Politik und öffentliche Meinung: Gelehrtenpolitik im wilhelminischen Deutschland (1890–1914)* (Husum, 1980).

Bucholz, Arden. *Moltke, Schlieffen, and Prussian War Planning* (New York, 1991).

Bueb, Volkmar. *Die "Junge Schule" der französischen Marine: Strategie und Politik, 1875–1900* (Boppard, 1971).

Buhl, Lance C. "Maintaining an American Navy, 1865–1889." In *In Peace and War: Interpretations of American Naval History, 1775–1978*, ed. Kenneth J. Hagan (Westport, Conn., 1978), 145–73.

Burchardt, Lothar. *Friedenswirtschaft und Kriegsvorsorge: Deutschlands wirtschaftliche Rüstungsbestrebungen vor 1914* (Boppard, 1968).

Canis, Konrad. *Von Bismarck zur Weltpolitik: Deutsche Außenpolitik 1890–1902* (Berlin, 1997).

Capozzola, Christopher. *Uncle Sam Wants You: World War I and the Making of the Modern American Citizen* (Oxford, 2008).

Carpenter, Daniel P. "Centralization and the Corporate Metaphor in Executive Departments, 1880–1928." *Studies in American Political Development* 12:1 (1998): 106–47.

———. *The Forging of Bureaucratic Autonomy: Networks, Reputations, and Policy Innovation in Executive Agencies, 1862–1928* (Princeton, 2001).

Cecil, Lamar. *Wilhelm II: Prince and Emperor, 1859–1900* (Chapel Hill, 1989).

Challener, Richard L. *Admirals, Generals, and American Foreign Policy, 1898–1914* (Princeton, 1974).

Chambers, John Whiteclaw, III. *To Raise an Army: The Draft Comes to Modern America* (New York, 1987).

Chang, Gordon. "Whose 'Barbarism'? Whose 'Treachery'? Race and Civilization in the Unknown United States–Korea War of 1871." *Journal of American History* 89 (March 2003), 1331–65.

Chickering, Roger. *We Men Who Feel Most German: A Cultural Study of the Pan-German League, 1886–1914* (Boston, 1984).

———. "Review of Isabel Hull, *Absolute Destruction*." *German History* 24 (2006): 138–39.

———. "Militarism and Radical Nationalism." In *Imperial Germany 1871–1918*, ed. James Retallack (New York, 2008), 196–218.

Chisholm, Donald. *Waiting for Dead Men's Shoes: Origins and Development of the U.S. Navy's Officer Personnel System, 1793–1941* (Stanford, 2001).

Clarke, I. F. *Voices Prophesying War, 1763–1984* (London, 1966).

Clifford, John Garry. "Admiral Dewey and the Germans, 1903." *Mid-America* 49 (1967): 214–26.

Cohen, Deborah, and Maura O'Connor, eds. *Comparison and History: Europe in Cross-National Perspective* (New York, 2004).

Coletta, Paolo E. *Admiral Bradley A. Fiske and the American Navy* (Lawrence, Kans., 1979).

———. *Bowman Hendry McCalla: A Fighting Sailor* (Washington, D.C., 1979).

———. *French Ensor Chadwick: Scholarly Warrior* (Lanham, Md., 1980).

Conrad, Sebastian. *Globalisierung und Nation im deutschen Kaiserreich* (Munich, 2006).
Conrad, Sebastian, and Jürgen Osterhammel, eds. *Das Kaiserreich Transnational: Deutschland in der Welt 1871–1914* (Göttingen, 2004).
Conze, Werner, Reinhard Stumpf, and Michael Geyer. "Militarismus." In *Geschichtliche Grundbegriffe*, ed. Otto Brunner, Werner Conze, and Reinhart Koselleck (Stuttgart, 1978), volume 4, 1–47.
Coogan, John W. *The End of Neutrality: The United States, Britain, and Maritime Rights, 1899–1915* (Ithaca, 1981).
Cooling, Benjamin Franklin. *Benjamin Franklin Tracy: Father of the Modern American Fighting Navy* (Hamden, Conn., 1973).
———. *Gray Steel and Blue Water Navy: The Formative Years of America's Military-Industrial Complex, 1881–1917* (Hamden, Conn., 1979).
Costello, Daniel J. "Planning for War: A History of the General Board of the Navy, 1900–1914." PhD dissertation, Fletcher School of Law and Diplomacy, 1968.
Cramer, Kevin. "A World Of Enemies: New Perspectives on German Military Culture and the Origins of the First World War." *Central European History* 39 (2006): 270–98.
Crapol, Edward P. "From Anglophobia to Fragile Rapprochement: Anglo-American Relations in the Early Twentieth Century." In *Confrontation and Cooperation: Germany and the United States in the Era of World War I, 1900–1924*, ed. Hans-Jürgen Schröder (Providence, R.I., 1993), 13–32.
———. "Coming to Terms with Empire: The Historiography of Late Nineteenth-Century American Foreign Relations." In *Paths to Powers: The Historiography of American Foreign Relations to 1941*, ed. Michael J. Hogan (Cambridge, 2000), 79–116.
Crowl, Philip A. "Alfred Thayer Mahan: The Naval Historian." In *Makers of Modern Strategy from Machiavelli to the Nuclear Age*, ed. Peter Paret (Princeton, 1986), 444–77.
Crumley, Brian Tyrone. "The Naval Attaché System in the United States, 1882–1914." PhD dissertation, Texas A&M University, 2002.
Cummings, Damon E. *Admiral Richard Wainwright and the United States Fleet* (Washington, D.C., 1962).
Davis, Calvin DeArmond. *The United States and the First Hague Conference* (Ithaca, 1962).
———. *The United States and the Second Hague Peace Conference: American Diplomacy and International Organization* (Durham, N.C., 1975).
Davis, George T. *A Navy Second to None: The Development of Modern American Naval Policy* (New York, 1940).
Davis, Vincent. *The Admirals Lobby* (Chapel Hill, 1967).
Dehio, Ludwig. "Ranke und der deutsche Imperialismus." In idem, *Deutschland und die Weltpolitik im 20. Jahrhundert* (Frankfurt, 1961), 33–62.
———. "Gedanken zur deutschen Sendung." In idem, *Deutschland und die Weltpolitik im 20. Jahrhundert* (Frankfurt, 1961), 63–96.
Deist, Wilhelm. *Flottenpolitik und Flottenpropaganda: Das Nachrichtenbureau des Reichsmarineamtes 1897–1914* (Stuttgart, 1976).
———. "Die Politik der Seekriegsleitung und die Rebellion der Flotte Ende Oktober 1918." In idem, *Militär, Staat und Gesellschaft: Studien zur preußisch-deutschen Militärgeschichte* (Munich, 1991), 185–210.
Dickinson, Edward Ross. "Biopolitics, Fascism, Democracy: Some Reflections on our Discourse about 'Modernity.'" *Central European History* 37 (2004): 1–48.

Dorsey, Leroy G. "Sailing into the 'Wondrous Now': The Myth of the American Navy's World Cruise." *Quarterly Journal of Speech* 83 (1997): 447–65.

Dorwart, Jeffery M. *The Office of Naval Intelligence: The Birth of America's First Intelligence Agency 1865–1918* (Annapolis, 1979).

———. *Conflict of Duty: The U.S. Navy's Intelligence Dilemma, 1919–1945* (Annapolis, 1983).

Douglas, Susan J. "The Navy Adopts the Radio, 1899–1919." In *Military Enterprise and Technological Change: Perspectives on the American Experience*, ed. Merritt Roe Smith (Cambridge, Mass., 1985), 117–74.

Drake, Frederick C. *The Empire of the Seas: A Biography of Rear Admiral Robert Wilson Shufeldt, USN* (Honolulu, 1984).

Dülffer, Jost. *Weimar, Hitler und die Marine: Reichspolitik und Flottenbau, 1920–1939* (Düsseldorf, 1973).

———. *Regeln gegen den Krieg: Die Haager Friedenskonferenzen von 1899 und 1907 in der internationalen Politik* (Frankfurt, 1981).

———. "Limitations on Naval Warfare and Germany's Future as a World Power: A German Debate, 1904–1906." *War and Society* 3 (September 1985): 23–43.

———. "The German Reich and the Jeune Ecole." In *Marine et Technique au XIXe Siècle Acte du Colloque International, Paris, Ecole Militaire, les 20, 11, 12 Juin 1987* (Vincennes, 1988), 499–516.

———. "Vom europäischen Mächtesystem zum Weltstaatensystem der Jahrhundertwende." In idem, *Im Zeichen der Gewalt: Frieden und Krieg im 19. und 20. Jahrhundert* (Cologne, 2003), 49–65.

Ekirch, Arthur A., Jr. *The Civilian and the Military* (New York, 1956).

Eley, Geoff. "The German Navy League in German Politics, 1898–1914." PhD dissertation, Sussex University, 1975.

———. "Army, State, and Civil Society: Revisiting the Problem of German Militarism." In idem, *From Unification to Nazism: Reinterpreting the German Past* (Boston, 1986), 85–107.

———. "Sammlungspolitik, Social Imperialism, and the Navy Law of 1898." In idem, *From Unification to Nazism: Reinterpreting the German Past* (Boston, 1986), 110–53.

———. "Social Imperialism in Germany: Reformist Synthesis or Reactionary Sleight of Hand?" In idem, *From Unification to Nazism: Reinterpreting the German Past* (Boston, 1986), 154–67.

———. *Reshaping the German Right: Radical Nationalism and Political Change after Bismarck*, 2nd edition (Ann Arbor, 1991).

———. "The Social Construction of Democracy in Germany, 1871–1933." In *The Social Construction of Democracy of Democracy, 1870–1990*, ed. George Reid and Andrews Herrick (New York, 1995), 95–117.

———. "Introduction 1: Is there a History of the *Kaiserreich?*" In *State, Society and Culture in Germany, 1870–1930*, ed. Geoff Eley (Ann Arbor, 1997), 1–42.

———. "Empire by Land or Sea? Germany's Imperial Imaginary, 1871–1945." Lecture, German Historical Institute, 28 March 2007.

———, ed. *State, Society, and Culture in Germany, 1870–1930* (Michigan, 1997).

Ellis, Richard J. ed. *Speaking to the People: The Rhetorical Presidency in Historical Perspective* (Amherst, 1998).

Epkenhans, Michael. "Großindustrie und Schlachtflottenbau 1897–1914." *Militärgeschichtliche Mitteilungen* 43 (1988): 65–140.
———. "Zwischen Patriotismus und Geschäftsinteresse: F.A. Krupp und die Anfänge des deutschen Schlachtflottenbaus 1897–1902." *Geschichte und Gesellschaft* 18 (1989): 196–226.
———. *Die wilhelminische Flottenrüstung 1908–1914: Weltmachtstreben, industrieller Fortschritt, soziale Integration* (Munich, 1991).
———. "Die kaiserliche Marine im Ersten Weltkrieg." In *Der Erste Weltkrieg: Wirkung, Wahrnehmung, Analyse,* ed. Wolfgang Michalka (Munich, 1994), 319–40.
———. "Kriegswaffen—Strategie, Einsatz, Wirkung." In *Der Tod als Maschinist: Der industrialisierte Krieg 1914–1918,* ed. Rolf Spilker and Bernd Ulrich (Bramsche, 1998), 68–83.
———. "Admiral Reinhard Scheer—'Der Sieger vom Skagerrak': Eine biographische Skizze." In *Mein lieber Schatz! Briefe von Admiral Reinhard Scheer an seine Ehefrau August bis November 1918,* ed. Michael Epkenhans (Bochum, 2006), 17–71.
———. "Was a Peaceful Outcome Thinkable? The Naval Race before 1914." In *An Improbable War? The Outbreak of World War I and European Political Culture before 1914,* ed. Holger Afflerbach and David Stevenson (New York, 2007), 113–29.
———. "'Mund halten und Schiffe bauen'? Stapelläufe: Monarchische Repräsentation, politische Legitimation und öffentliches Fest." In *Das politische Zeremoniell im Deutschen Kaiserreich 1871–1918,* ed. Andres Biefang, Michael Epkenhans, and Klaus Tenfelde (Düsseldorf, 2008), 189–203.
———. *Tirpitz: Architect of the German High Seas Fleet* (Washington, D.C., 2008).
———. "Die Kaiserliche Marine 1914/15: Der Versuch der Quadratur des Kreises." In *Skagerrakschlacht: Vorgeschicht–Ereignis–Verarbeitung,* ed. Michael Epkenhans, Jörg Hillmann, and Frank Nägler (Munich, 2009), 113–38.
Fairbairn, Brett. *Democracy in the Undemocratic State: The German Reichstag Elections of 1898 and 1903* (Toronto, 1997).
Felker, Craig. *Testing American Sea Power: U.S. Navy Strategic Exercises, 1923–1940* (College Station, Tex., 2007).
Fiebig-von Hase, Ragnhild. *Lateinamerika als Konfliktherd der deutsch-amerikanischen Beziehungen 1890–1903: Vom Beginn der Panamerikapolitik bis zur Venezuela-Krise von 1902/03* (Göttingen, 1986).
———. "The United States and Germany in the World Arena, 1900–1917." In *Confrontation and Cooperation: Germany and the United States in the Era of World War I, 1900–1924,* ed. Hans-Jürgen Schröder (Providence, R.I., 1993), 33–68.
———. "Die USA und Europa vor dem Ersten Weltkrieg." *Amerikastudien* 39 (1994): 7–41.
Fiebig-von Hase, Ragnhild, and Jürgen Heideking, eds. *Zwei Wege in die Moderne: Aspekte der deutsch-amerikanischen Beziehungen 1900–1918* (Trier, 1998).
Filler, Louis. *The Muckrakers: Crusaders for American Liberalism* (University Park, Penn., 1976).
Finnegan, John Patrick. *Against the Spectre of a Dragon: The Campaign for American Military Preparedness, 1914–1917* (Westport, Conn., 1974).
Fischer, Jörg-Uwe. *Admiral des Kaisers: Georg Alexander von Müller als Chef des Marinekabinetts* (Frankfurt, 1992).

———. "Die Faszination des Technischen: Die Parlamentarischen Studienreisen zur kaiserlichen Flotte vor 1914." *Zeitschrift für Geschichtswissenschaft* 40 (1992): 1150–56.
Fitzpatrick, Matthew P. "A Fall from Grace? National Unity and the Search for Naval Power and Colonial Possessions, 1848–1884." *German History* 25:2 (2007): 135–61.
———. *Liberal Imperialism in Germany: Expansionism and Nationalism, 1848–1884* (New York, 2008).
Förster, Stig. *Der doppelte Militarismus. Die deutsche Heeresrüstungspolitik zwischen Status-Quo-Sicherung und Aggression* (Stuttgart, 1985).
———. "The Armed Forces and Military Planning." In *Imperial Germany: A Historiographical Companion*, ed. Roger Chickering (Westport, Conn., 1996), 409–29.
Förster, Stig, and Jörg Nagler, eds. *On the Road to Total War: The American Civil War and the German Wars of Unification, 1861–1871* (Cambridge, 1997).
Forstmeier, Friedrich. "Aus der Geschichte des Deutschen Flottenkommandos." In *Die Entwicklung des Deutschen Flottenkommandos* (Darmstadt, 1964), 9–29.
Frank, Elizabeth S. "Advocating War Preparedness: H. Irving Hancock's Conquest of the United States Series." *Primary Sources & Original Works* 4 (February 1997): 215–31.
Frankel, Richard E. *Bismarck's Shadow: The Cult of Leadership and the Transformation of the German Right, 1898–1945* (Oxford, 2005).
Friedewald, Michael. "The Beginnings of Radio Communications in Germany." *Journal of Radio Studies* 7 (2000): 441–63.
———. "Funkentelegraphie und deutschen Kolonien: Technik als Mittel imperialistischer Politik." *Von der Telegraphie zum Internet—Kommunikation in Geschichte und Gegenwart*, ed. Kai Handel (Freiberg, 2002), 51–63.
Friedman, Norman. *U.S. Battleships: An Illustrated Design History* (Annapolis, 1985).
———. *U.S. Submarines through 1945: An Illustrated Design History* (Annapolis, 1995).
Fry, Joseph A. "Imperialism: American Style, 1890–1916." In *American Foreign Relations Reconsidered, 1890–1993*, ed. Gordon Martel (London, 1994), 52–70.
Funck, Marcus. "Militär, Krieg und Gesellschaft. Soldaten und militärische Eliten in der Sozialgeschichte." In *Was ist Militärgeschichte?* ed. Thomas Kühne and Benjamin Ziemann (Paderborn, 2000), 157–74.
Galambos, Louis. "The Emerging Organizational Synthesis in Modern American History." *Business History Review* 44 (Autumn 1970): 279–90.
———. "Technology, Political Economy, and Professionalization: Central Themes of the Organizational Synthesis." *Business History Review* 57 (Winter 1983): 471–93.
Ganz, A. Harding. "Colonial Policy and the Imperial German Navy." *Militärgeschichtliche Mitteilungen* 21 (1977): 35–52.
Gat, Azar. *The Development of Military Thought: The Nineteenth Century* (Oxford, 1992).
Gemzell, Carl-Axel. *Conflict, Organization, and Innovation: A Study of German Naval Strategic Planning, 1888–1940* (Lund, 1973).
Geppert, Dominik. *Pressekriege: Öffentlichkeit und Diplomatie in den deutsch-britischen Beziehungen (1896–1912)* (Munich, 2007).
Geyer, Michael. "Die Geschichte des deutschen Militärs von 1860–1945 Ein Bericht über die Forschungslage (1945–1975)." In *Die moderne deutsche Geschichte in der internationalen Forschung, 1945–1975*, ed. Hans-Ulrich Wehler (Göttingen, 1978), 256–86.

———. *Aufrüstung oder Sicherheit: Die Reichswehr in der Krise der Machtpolitik* (Wiesbaden, 1980)
———. *Deutsche Rüstungspolitik 1860–1980* (Frankfurt, 1984).
———. "German Strategy in the Age of Machine Warfare, 1914–1945." In *Makers of Modern Strategy from Machiavelli to the Nuclear Age,* ed. Peter Paret (Princeton, 1986), 527–97.
———. "Historical Fictions of Autonomy and the Europeanization of National History." *Central European History* 22 (1989): 316–42.
———. "The Militarization of Europe, 1914–1945." In *The Militarization of the Western World,* ed. John R. Gillis (New Brunswick, N.J., 1989), 65–102.
———. "The Past as Future: The German Officer Corps as Profession." In *German Professions 1800–1950,* ed. Geoffrey Cocks and Konrad Jarausch (New York, 1990), 182–213.
———. "Militarism and Capitalism in the 20th Century." In *Arms Races: Technological and Political Dynamics,* ed. Nils Peter Gleditsch and Olav Njolstadt (London, 1990), 247–75.
———. "The Crisis of Military Leadership in the 1930s." *Journal of Strategic Studies* 14 (1991): 448–62.
———. "Review of David Herrmann, *The Arming of Europe.*" *American Historical Review* 102 (1997): 1150.
———. "Gewalt und Gewalterfahrung im 20 Jahrhundert. Der Erste Weltkrieg." In *Der Tod als Maschinist: Der industrialisierte Krieg 1914–1918,* ed. Rolf Spilker and Bernd Ulrich (Bramsche, 1998), 241–57.
———. "Urkatastrophe, Europäischer Bürgerkrieg, Menschenschlachthaus—Wie Historiker dem Epochenbruch des Ersten Weltkrieges Sinn geben." In *Der Weltkrieg 1914–1918: Ereignis und Erinnerung,* ed. Rainer Rothaus (Berlin, 2004), 23–34.
———. "The Space of the Nation: An Essay on the German Century." In *Strukturmerkmale der deutschen Geschichte des 20. Jahrhunderts,* ed. Anselm Doering-Manteuffel (Munich, 2006), 21–42.
———. "Where Germans Dwell: Transnationalism in Theory and Practice." *German Studies Association Newsletter* 31:2 (Winter 2006): 29–37.
Geyer, Michael, and Charles Bright. "World History in a Global Age." *American Historical Review* 100 (1995): 1034–60.
———. "Global Violence and Nationalizing Wars in Eurasia and America: The Geopolitics of War in the Mid-Nineteenth Century." *Comparative Studies in Society and History* 38 (1996): 619–57.
Giessler, Klaus-Volker. *Die Institution des Marineattachés im Kaiserreich* (Boppard, 1976).
Gillis, John R., ed. *The Militarization of the Western World* (New Brunswick, N.J., 1989).
Gleaves, Albert. *Life and Letters of Rear Admiral Luce, US Navy Founder of the Naval War College* (New York, 1925).
Goldschmidt, Hans. *Das Reich und Preußen im Kampf um die Führung: Von Bismarck bis 1918* (Leipzig, 1931).
Gollwitzer, Heinz. *Die Gelbe Gefahr: Geschichte eines Schlagwortes* (Göttingen, 1962).
Gosewinkel, Dieter. *Einbürgern und Ausschließen: Die Nationalisierung der Staatsangehörigkeit vom Deutschen Bund bis zur Bundesrepublik Deutschland* (Göttingen, 2001).

Gottschall, Terrell D. *By Order of the Kaiser: Otto von Diederichs and the Rise of the Imperial German Navy 1865–1902* (Annapolis, 2003).

Gottwald, Herbert. "Der Umfall des Zentrums Die Stellung der Zentrumspartei zur Flottenvorlage von 1897." In *Studien zum deutschen Imperialismus vor 1914,* ed. Fritz Klein (Berlin, 1976), 181–223.

Granier, Gerhard. *Magnus von Levetzow: Seeoffizier, Monarchist und Wegbereiter Hitlers. Lebensweg und ausgewählte Dokumente* (Boppard, 1982).

Grießmer, Axel. *Große Kreuzer der Kaiserlichen Marine 1906–1918: Konstruktionen und Entwürfe im Zeichen des Tirpitz-Planes* (Bonn, 1996).

———. *Linienschiffe der Kaiserlichen Marine 1906–1918: Konstruktionen zwischen Rüstungskonkurrenz und Flottengesetz* (Bonn, 1999).

———. *Massenverbände und Massenparteien im wilhelminischen Reich: Zum Wandel der Wahlkultur 1903–1912* (Düsseldorf, 2000).

Grimmer-Solem, Erik. "Imperialist Socialism of the Chair: Gustav Schmoller and German Weltpolitik, 1897–1905." In *Wilhelminism and its Legacies: German Modernities, Imperialism, and the Meanings of Reform, 1890–1933,* ed. Geoff Eley and James Retallack (New York, 2003), 107–22.

Gröner, Erich. *Die deutschen Kriegsschiffe 1815–1945,* volume 1 (Munich, 1965).

Gross, Gerhard P. *Die Seekriegführung der Kaiserlichen Marine im Jahre 1918* (Frankfurt, 1989).

Gunzenhäuser, Max. "Die Marine-Rundschau 1890–1914. Bericht und Bibliographie." In *Jahresbibliographie 1977: Weltkriegsbücherei Stuttgart* (Munich, 1978), 417–61.

Güth, Rolf. *Admiralstabsausbildung in der deutschen Marine* (Herford, 1979).

Hagan, Kenneth J. *American Gunboat Diplomacy and the Old Navy 1877–1889* (Westport, Conn., 1973).

———. "Alfred Thayer Mahan." In *Makers of American Diplomacy,* ed. Frank J. Merli and Theodore A. Wilson (New York, 1974), 279–304.

———. *This People's Navy: The Making of American Sea Power* (New York, 1991).

Hagenlücke, Heinz. *Die Vaterlandspartei: Die nationale Rechte am Ende des Kaiserreichs* (Düsseldorf, 1997).

Hallmann, Hans. *Der Weg zum deutschen Schlachtflottenbau* (Stuttgart, 1933).

Hamilton, Allen Lee. "Military Strategists and the Annexation of Hawaii." *Journal of the West* 15 (1976): 81–91.

Hankel, Gerd. *Die Leipziger Prozesse: Deutsche Kriegsverbrechen und ihre strafrechtliche Verfolgung nach dem Ersten Weltkrieg* (Hamburg, 2003).

Harrod, Frederick S. *Manning the New Navy: The Development of a Modern Naval Enlisted Force, 1899–1940* (Westport, 1978).

———. "Jim Crow in the Navy (1798–1841)." *PUSNI* 105 (1979): 46–53.

———. "Managing the Medium: The Navy and Motion Pictures before World War I." *Velvet Light Trap* 31 (Spring 1993): 48–58.

Hart, Robert A. *The Great White Fleet: Its Voyage Around the World, 1907–1909* (Boston, 1965).

Hassel, Ulrich von. *Tirpitz: Sein Leben und Wirken mit Berücksichtigung seiner Beziehungen zu Albrecht von Stosch* (Stuttgart, 1920).

Hattendorf, John B., and Lynn Hattendorf. *A Bibliography of the Works of Alfred Thayer Mahan* (Newport, R.I., 1986).

———. "History and Technological Change: The Study of History in the U.S. Navy, 1873–1890." In idem, *Naval History and Maritime Strategy: Collected Essays* (Malabar, Fla., 2001), 1–16.

———. "The Anglo-French Naval Wars (1689–1815) in Twentieth-Century Naval Thought." *Journal of Maritime Research* 3 (June 2001).

Hattendorf, John B., Mitchell Simpson III, and John R. Wadleigh, *Sailors and Scholars: The Centennial History of the U.S. Naval War College* (Newport, R.I., 1984).

Hays, Samuel P. "The Politics of Reform in Municipal Government in the Progressive Era." *Pacific Northwest Quarterly* 55 (October 1964): 157–69.

Headrick, Daniel R. *The Invisible Weapon: Telecommunications and International Politics 1851–1945* (New York, 1991).

Heffron, Paul T. "Secretary Moody and Naval Administrative Reform, 1902–1904." *American Neptune* 29 (January 1969): 30–53.

Hendrix, Henry J. *Theodore Roosevelt's Naval Diplomacy: The U.S. Navy and the Birth of the American Century* (Annapolis, 2009).

Herrick, Walter R., Jr. *The American Naval Revolution* (Baton Rouge, 1967).

Herrmann, David G. *The Arming of Europe and the Making of the First World War* (Princeton, 1996).

Herwig, Holger H. "Admirals versus Generals: The War Aims of the Imperial German Navy, 1914–1918." *Central European History* 5 (1972): 208–33.

———. *The German Naval Officer Corps: A Social and Political History, 1888–1918* (Oxford, 1973).

———. *Politics of Frustration: The United States in German Naval Planning, 1889–1941* (Boston, 1976).

———. "From Tirpitz Plan to Schlieffen Plan: Some Observations on German Military Planning." *Journal of Strategic Studies* 9 (1986): 53–63.

———. *Germany's Vision of Empire in Venezuela 1871–1914* (Princeton, 1986).

———. *"Luxury" Fleet: The Imperial German Navy 1888–1918*, 2nd edition (London, 1987).

———. "The Influence of A. T. Mahan upon German Sea Power." In *The Influence of History on Mahan*, ed. John B. Hattendorf (Newport, R.I., 1991), 67–80.

———. "Review of Rolf Hobson, *Imperialism at Sea*," *American Historical Review* 108 (2003): 593–94.

Herwig, Holger H., and David F. Trask. "Naval Operations Plans between Germany and the USA, 1898–1913: A Study of Strategic Planning in the Age of Imperialism." In *The War Plans of the Great Powers 1880–1914*, ed. Paul M. Kennedy (Boston, 1979), 39–74.

Hewitson, Mark. "Germany and France before the First World War: A Reassessment of Wilhelmine Foreign Policy." *English Historical Review* 115 (2000): 570–606.

———. *Germany and the Approach of the First World War* (Oxford, 2004).

Higham, Robin, ed. *A Guide to the Sources of United States Military History* (Hamden, Conn., 1975–98).

Hildebrand, Klaus. *Das vergangene Reich: Deutsche Außenpolitik von Bismarck bis Hitler 1871–1945* (Stuttgart, 1995).

Hilderbrand, Robert C. *Power and the People: Executive Management of Public Opinion in Foreign Affairs, 1897–1921* (Chapel Hill, 1981).

Hobson, Rolf. *Imperialism at Sea: Naval Strategic Thought, the Ideology of Sea Power, and the Tirpitz Plan* (Boston, 2002).

———. "Prussia, Germany and Maritime Law from Armed Neutrality to Unlimited Submarine Warfare, 1780–1917." In *Navies in Northern Waters 1721–2000,* ed. Rolf Hobson and Tom Kristiansen (London, 2004), 97–116.
Hoganson, Kristin L. *Fighting for American Manhood: How Gender Politics Provoked the Spanish-American and Philippine-American Wars* (New Haven, 1998).
Holzner, Burkart, and John Marx. *Knowledge/Application: The Knowledge System in Society* (Boston, 1979).
Horne, John, and Alan Kramer. *German Atrocities, 1914: A History of Denial* (New Haven, 2001).
Howeth, L. S. *History of Communications-Electronics in the United States Navy* (Washington, D.C., 1963).
Hubatsch, Walther. *Der Admiralstab und die obersten Marinebehörden in Deutschland 1848–1945* (Frankfurt, 1958).
Hull, Isabel V. *The Entourage of Kaiser Wilhelm II, 1888–1918* (Cambridge, 1982).
———. "Persönliches Regiment." In *Der Ort Kaiser Wilhelms II in der deutschen Geschichte,* ed. John C. G. Röhl (Munich, 1991), 3–24.
———. *Absolute Destruction: Military Culture and the Practices of War in Imperial Germany* (Ithaca, 2005).
Hussey, Michael Joseph. "'Do you know what it means when a man uses another man as a woman?' Sodomy, Gender, Class, and Power in the United States Navy, 1890–1925." PhD dissertation, University of Maryland, College Park, 2002.
Jefferies, Matthew Jefferies. *Contesting the German Empire, 1871–1918* (Oxford, 2008).
John, Richard. "Governmental Institutions as Agents of Change: Rethinking American Political Development in the Early Republic, 1787–1835." *Studies in American Political Development* 11:2 (1997): 347–80.
———. "Farewell to the 'Party Period': Political Economy in Nineteenth-Century America." *Journal of Policy History* 16 (2004): 117–25.
Kamberger, Klaus. "Flottenpropaganda unter Tirpitz. Öffentliche Meinung und Schlachtflottenbau (1897–1900)." PhD dissertation, University of Vienna, 1966.
Karsten, Peter. *The Naval Aristocracy: The Golden Age of Annapolis and the Emergence of Modern American Navalism* (New York, 1972).
———. "Armed Progressives: The Military Reorganizes for the American Century." In *The Military in America from the Colonial Era to the Present,* ed. Peter Karsten, 2nd edition (New York, 1986), 239–74.
———. "Militarization and Rationalization in the United States, 1870–1930." In *Militarization of the Western World,* ed. John R. Gillis (New Brunswick, N.J., 1989), 30–44.
Katznelson, Ira. "Flexible Capacity: The Military and Early American Statebuilding." In *Shaped by War and Trade: International Influences on American Political Development,* ed. Ira Katznelson and Martin Shefter (Princeton, 2002), 82–110.
Kaulisch, Baldur. "Zur überseeischen Stützpunktpolitik der kaiserlichen deutschen Marineführung am Ende des 19 Jahrhunderts und im ersten Weltkrieg." *Militärgeschichte* 19 (1980): 585–98.
———. "Zur Klärung der Einsatzmöglichkeiten der U-Boote in der deutschen Marine am Vorabend des Ersten Weltkrieges." *Militärgeschichte* 24 (1985): 369–76.
Keene, Jennifer D. *Doughboys, the Great War, and the Remaking of America* (Baltimore, 2001).

Kehr, Eckart. *Schlachtflottenbau und Parteipolitik 1894–1901: Versuch eines Querschnittes durch die innenpolitischen und ideologischen Voraussetzungen des deutschen Imperialismus* (Berlin, 1930).
———. *Der Primat der Innenpolitik: Gesammelte Aufsätze zur preußisch-deutschen Sozialgeschichte im 19. und 20. Jahrhundert,* ed. Hans-Ulrich Wehler (Berlin, 1965).
Keller, Morton. *Affairs of State: Public Life in Late Nineteenth-Century America* (Cambridge, 1977).
Kelly, Patrick J. *Tirpitz and the Imperial German Navy* (Bloomington, 2011).
Kennedy, Paul M. "The Development of German Naval Operation Plans against England, 1896–1914." In *The War Plans of the Great Powers 1880–1914,* ed. Paul M. Kennedy (Boston, 1979), 171–98.
———. *The Rise of the Anglo-German Antagonism 1860–1914* (London, 1980).
———. "Maritime Strategieprobleme der deutsch-englischen Flottenrivalität." In *Marine und Marinepolitik im kaiserlichen Deutschland 1871–1914,* ed. Herbert Schottelius and Wilhelm Deist, 2nd edition (Düsseldorf, 1981), 178–210.
———. *The Rise and Fall of British Naval Mastery,* 2nd edition (London, 1983).
———. *The Rise and Fall of the Great Powers: Economic Change and Military Conflict from 1500 to 2000* (London, 1988).
———. "Levels of Approach and Contexts in Naval History: Admiral Tirpitz and the Origins of Fascism." In *Doing Naval History: Essays towards Improvement,* ed. John B. Hattendorf (Newport, R.I., 1997), 143–49.
Kirschbaum, Joseph W. "The 1916 Naval Expansion Act: Planning for a Navy Second to None." PhD dissertation, George Washington University, 2008.
Klachko, Mary, with David Trask. *Admiral William Shepherd Benson: First Chief of Naval Operations* (Annapolis, 1987).
Kloosterhuis, Jürgen. *Friedliche Imperialisten: Deutsche Auslandsvereine und auswärtige Kulturpolitik 1906–1918* (Frankfurt, 1993).
Kocka, Jürgen. "Nach dem Ende des Sonderweges. Zur Tragfähigkeit eines Konzeptes." In *Doppelte Zeitgeschichte: Deutsch-deutsche Beziehungen 1945–1990,* ed. Arndt Bauernkämper, Martin Sabrow, and Bernd Stöver (Bonn, 1998), 364–375.
Kohn, Richard. "The Danger of War in an Endless 'War' on Terrorism." *Journal of Military History* 73 (January 2009): 177–208.
Koistinen, Paul A. C. *Mobilizing for Modern War: The Political Economy of American Warfare, 1865–1919* (Lawrence, Kans., 1997).
———. "The Political Economy of Warfare in America, 1865–1914." In *Anticipating Total War: The German and American Experiences, 1871–1914,* ed. Manfred F. Boemeke, Roger Chickering, and Stig Forster (Cambridge, 1999), 57–76.
Kolko, Gabriel. *The Triumph of Conservatism: A Reinterpretation of American History, 1900–1916* (New York, 1963).
König, Wolfgang. *Wilhelm II und die Moderne* (Paderborn, 2007).
Kramer, Paul A. "Empires, Exceptions, and Anglo-Saxons: Race and Rule between the British and U.S. Empires, 1880–1910." *Journal of American History* 88 (March 2002): 1315–53.
———. "Reflex Actions: Social Imperialism between the United States and the Philippines, 1898–1929." Paper presented to the Annual Meeting of the American Historical Association Chicago, January 2003.

———. *The Blood of Government: Race, Empire, the United States, and the Philippines* (Chapel Hill, N.C., 2006).
Kühne, Thomas, and Benjamin Ziemann. "Militärgeschichte in der Erweiterung: Konjunkturen, Interpretationen, Konzepte." In *Was ist Militärgeschichte?* ed. Thomas Kühne and Benjamin Ziemann (Paderborn, 2000), 9–46.
LaFeber, Walter. "A Note on the 'Mercantilist Imperialism' of Alfred Thayer Mahan." *Mississippi Valley Historical Review* 48 (1962): 674–85.
———. *The New Empire: An Interpretation of American Expansion 1860–1898* (Ithaca, 1963).
Lakowski, Richard. *U-Boote: Zur Geschichte einer Waffengattung der Seestreitkräfte* (Berlin, 1985).
Lambert, Andrew. *The Foundations of Naval History: John Knox Laughton, the Royal Navy, and the Historical Profession* (London, 1998).
———. "History as Process and Record: The Royal Navy and Officer Education." In *Military Education: Past, Present and Future*, ed. Greg Kennedy and Keith Neilson (Westport, Conn., 2002), 83–104.
———. "Wirtschaftliche Macht, technologischer Vorsprung und imperiale Stärke: Großbritannien als einzigartige globale Macht 1860 bis 1890." In *Das Militär und der Aufbruch in die Moderne 1860–1890*, ed. Michael Epkenhans und Gerhard P. Groß (Munich, 2003), 243–68.
———. "Great Britain and Maritime Law from the Declaration of Paris to the Era of Total War." In *Navies in Northern Waters 1721–2000*, ed. Rolf Hobson and Tom Kristiansen (London, 2004), 11–38.
Lambert, Nicholas A. "Admiral Sir John Fisher and the Concept of Flotilla Defence." *Journal of Military History* (October 1995): 639–60.
———. *Sir John Fisher's Naval Revolution* (Columbia, S.C., 1999).
———. "Transformation and Technology in the Fisher Era: The Impact of the Communications Revolution." *Journal of Strategic Studies* 27 (June 2004): 272–97.
Lambi, Ivo Nikolai. *The Navy and German Power Politics, 1862–1914* (Boston, 1984).
Lang, Michael. "Globalization and Its History." *Journal of Modern History* 78 (December 2006): 899–931.
Langer, William L. *The Diplomacy of Imperialism 1890–1902*, 2nd edition (New York, 1968).
Langley, Harold. "Winfield Scott Schley and Santiago: A New Look at an Old Controversy." In *Crucible of Empire: The Spanish-American War and Its Aftermath*, ed. James Bradford (Annapolis, 1993), 69–101.
Lasswell, Harold. *Essays on the Garrison State* (New Brunswick, N.J., 1997).
Lears, Jackson. *No Place of Grace: Antimodernism and the Transformation of American Culture, 1880–1920* (Chicago, 1981).
———. *Rebirth of a Nation: The Making of Modern America, 1877–1920* (New York, 2009).
Leeman, William P. "America's Admiral." *Historian* 65 (2000): 587–614.
———. *The Long Road to Annapolis: The Founding of the Naval Academy and the Emerging American Republic* (Chapel Hill, N.C., 2010).
Lehment, Joachim. *Kriegsmarine und politische Führung* (Berlin, 1937).
Lerman, Katherine. *The Chancellor as Courtier: Bernhard von Bülow and the Governance of Germany 1900–1909* (Cambridge, 1990).

Lingelbach, Gabriele. "Erträge und Grenzen zweier Ansätze: Kulturtransfer und Vergleich am Beispiel der französischen und amerikanischen Geschichtswissenschaft während des 19. Jahrhunderts." In *Die Nation Schreiben: Geschichtswissenschaft im internationalen Vergleich*, ed. Christoph Conrad and Sebastian Conrad (Göttingen, 2002), 333–59.

Link, Arthur S., and Richard L. McCormick. *Progressivism* (Arlington Heights, Ill., 1983).

Livezey, William E. *Mahan on Sea Power*, 2nd edition (Norman, Okla., 1981).

Loiperdinger, Martin. "The Beginnings of German Film Propaganda: The Navy League as Traveling Exhibitor, 1901–1907." *Historical Journal of Film, Radio and Television* 22 (August 2002): 305–13.

Maier, Charles S. "German War, German Peace." In *German History since 1800*, ed. Mary Fulbrook (London, 1997), 539–55.

Marder, Arthur J. *The Anatomy of British Sea Power: 1880–1905* (London, 1940).

Marienfeld, Wolfgang. *Wissenschaft und Schlachtflottenbau in Deutschland 1897–1906* (Frankfurt, 1957).

Martin, Christoper. "The 1907 Naval War Plan and the Second Hague Peace Conference: A Case of Propaganda." *Journal of Strategic Studies* 28 (October 2005): 833–56.

Marwedel, Ulrich. *Carl von Clausewitz: Persönlichkeit und Wirkungsgeschichte seines Werkes bis 1918* (Munich, 1978).

Mauch, Christof, and Kiran Klaus Patel, eds. *Wettlauf um die Moderne: Die USA und Deutschland 1890 bis heute* (Munich, 2008).

Maurer, John H. "Fuel and the Battle Fleet: Coal, Oil, and American Naval Strategy, 1898–1925." *Naval War College Review* 34 (November–December 1981): 60–77.

———. "American Naval Concentration and the German Battle Fleet, 1900–1918." *Journal of Strategic Studies* 6 (June 1983): 147–81.

———. "Mahan, World Politics, and Naval Rivalries, 1904–1914." In *The Influence of History on Mahan*, ed. John B Hattendorf (Newport, R.I., 1991), 157–66.

McBride, William. *Technological Change and the United States Navy, 1865–1945* (Baltimore, 2000).

McConnell, Stuart. *Glorious Contentment: The Grand Army of the Republic, 1865–1900* (Chapel Hill, N.C., 1992).

McCormick, Thomas J. *China Market: America's Quest for Informal Empire, 1893–1901* (Chicago, 1967).

McGerr, Michael E. *The Decline of Popular Politics: The American North, 1865–1928* (New York, 1986).

McNeill, William. *The Pursuit of Power* (Chicago, 1982).

Mehnert, Ute. *Deutschland, Amerika und die "Gelbe Gefahr." Zur Karriere eines Schlagworts in der Großen Politik, 1905–1917* (Stuttgart, 1995).

Messerschmidt, Manfred. "Völkerrecht und 'Kriegsnotwendigkeiten' in der deutschen militärischen Tradition seit den Einigungskriegen." *German Studies Review* 6 (1983): 237–70.

Meyer, Jürg. *Die Propaganda der deutschen Flottenbewegung 1897–1900* (Bern, 1967).

Miller, Edward S. *War Plan Orange: The US Strategy to Defeat Japan, 1897–1945* (Annapolis, 1991).

Millet, Allan R. "Military Professionalism and Officership in America." In *In Defense of the Republic: Readings in American Military History,* ed. David Curtis Skaggs and Robert Browning III (Belmont, Calif., 1991), 157–67.
Millis, Walter. *Arms and Men: America's Military History and Military Policy from the Revolution to the Present* (New York, 1956).
Mitchell, Nancy. *The Danger of Dreams: German and American Imperialism in Latin America* (Chapel Hill, N.C., 1999).
Mogk, Walter. *Rohrbach und das "Grössere Deutschland." Ethischer Imperialismus im Wilhelminischen Zeitalter* (Munich, 1972).
Mollin, Gerhard T. "Das deutsche Militär und die europäische Politik vor 1914: Vorrang der Außenpolitik oder Primat des internationalen Systems?" *Internationale Geschichte Themen—Ergebnisse—Aussichten,* ed. Wilfried Loth and Jürgen Osterhammel (Munich, 2000), 209–45.
Mombauer, Annika. *Helmuth von Moltke and the Origins of the First World War* (Cambridge, 2001).
Mommsen, Wolfgang J. *Grossmachtstellung und Weltpolitik 1870–1914: Die Außenpolitik des Deutschen Reiches* (Berlin, 1993).
Morgan, William Michael. *Pacific Gibraltar: U.S.-Japanese Rivalry over the Annexation of Hawai'i, 1885–1898* (Annapolis, Md., 2011).
Morison, Elting E. *Admiral Sims and the Modern American Navy* (New York, 1942).
Mühlhahn, Klaus. *Herrschaft und Widerstand in der "Musterkolonie" Kiautschou: Interaktionen, 1897–1914* (Munich, 2000).
Nägler, Frank. "Operative und strategische Vorstellungen der Kaiserlichen Marine vor dem Ersten Weltkrieg." In *Skagerrakschlacht: Vorgeschichte—Ereignis—Verarbeitung,* ed. Michael Epkenhans, Jörg Hillmann, and Frank Nägler (Munich, 2009), 19–56.
Neitzel, Sönke. *Weltmacht oder Untergang: Die Weltreichslehre im Zeitalter des Imperialismus* (Paderborn, 2000).
Nipperdey, Thomas. *Deutsche Geschichte 1866–1918,* 2 volumes (Munich, 1990–92).
O'Brien, Philipps Payson. *British and American Naval Power: Politics and Policies, 1900–1936* (Westport, Conn., 1998).
O'Connor, Raymond G. "Origins of the Navy 'General Staff'". In idem, *War, Diplomacy, and History: Papers and Reviews* (Lanham, Md., 1979), 77–88.
Offer, Avner. *The First World War: An Agrarian Interpretation* (Oxford, 1989).
O'Leary, Cecilia Elizabeth. *To Die For: The Paradox of American Patriotism* (Princeton, 1999).
Olivier, David H. *German Naval Strategy 1856–1888: Forerunners to Tirpitz* (London, 2004).
Osterhammel, Jürgen, and Niels P. Petersson. *Globalization: A Short History* (Princeton, 2005).
Overlack, Peter. "The Function of Commerce Warfare in an Anglo-German Conflict to 1914." *Journal of Strategic Studies* 20 (December 1997): 94–114.
———. "German War Plans in the Pacific, 1900–1914." *Historian* (Spring 1998): 578–93.
Owens, Richard Henry. "Peaceful Warrior: Horace Porter (1837–1921) and United States Foreign Relations." PhD dissertation, University of Maryland, 1988.
Oyos, Matthew M. "Theodore Roosevelt: Commander in Chief." PhD dissertation, Ohio State University, 1993.
Partridge, M. S. "The Royal Navy and the End of the Close Blockade, 1885–1905: A Revolution in Naval Strategy?" *Mariner's Mirror* 75 (1989): 119–132.

Paulmann, Johannes. "Internationaler Vergleich und interkultureller Transfer: Zwei Forschungsansätze zur europäischen Geschichte des 18. bis 20. Jahrhunderts." *Historische Zeitschrift* 267 (1998): 649–85.

Pearlman, Michael. *To Make Democracy Safe for America: Patricians and Preparedness in the Progressive Era* (Urbana, Ill., 1984).

Petersen, Peter B. "Fighting for a Better Navy: An Attempt at Scientific Management (1905–1912)." *Journal of Management* 16:1 (1990): 151–66.

Petter, Wolfgang. "Deutsche Flottenrüstung von Wallenstein bis Tirpitz." In *Deutsche Militärgeschichte in sechs Bänden 1648–1939*, ed. Militärgeschichtliche Forschungsamt (Herrsching, 1983), volume 5, 3–262.

———. "Die deutsche Marine auf dem Weg nach China: Demonstration deutscher Weltgeltung." In *Das Deutsche Reich und der Boxeraufstand*, ed. Susanne Kuß and Bernd Martin (Munich, 2002), 145–64.

Philbin, Tobias R. *Admiral von Hipper: The Inconvenient Hero* (Amsterdam, 1982).

Posen, Barry R. *The Sources of Military Doctrine: France, Britain, and Germany between the World Wars* (Ithaca, 1984).

Puleston, W. D. *The Life and Work of Captain Alfred Thayer Mahan, USN* (New Haven, 1939).

Rahn, Werner. "Strategische Optionen und Erfahrungen der deutschen Marineführung 1914 bis 1944: Zu den Chancen und Grenzen einer mitteleuropaeischen Kontinentalmacht gegen Seemächte." In *Deutsche Marinen im Wandel: Vom Symbol nationaler Einheit zum Instrument internationaler Sicherheit*, ed. Werner Rahn (Munich, 2005), 197–233.

Rappaport, Armin. *The Navy League of the United States* (Detroit, 1962).

Rauh, Manfred. *Föderalismus und Parlamentarismus im Wilhelminischen Reich* (Düsseldorf, 1973).

Reckner, James R. *Teddy Roosevelt's Great White Fleet* (Annapolis, 1988).

———. "Teddy's 'Ollie' and the Teflon Admiral: William S. Sims vs. Robley D. Evans in Theodore Roosevelt's Navy." In *New Interpretations in Naval History*, ed. Robert W. Love Jr., Laurie Bogle, Brian VanDerMark, and Maochun Yu (Annapolis, 2001), 169–218.

Reinhardt, Horst D. "Tirpitz und der deutsche Flottengedanke in den Jahren 1892–1898." PhD dissertation, University of Marburg, 1964.

Repp, Kevin. *Reformers, Critics, and the Paths of German Modernity: Anti-Politics and the Search for Alternatives, 1890–1914* (Cambridge, 2000).

Ritter, Gerhard. *Der Schlieffen-Plan* (Munich, 1956).

———. *Staatskunst und Kriegshandwerk: Das Problem des "Militarismus" in Deutschland, Volume II: Die Hauptmächte Europas und das wilhelminische Reich (1890–1914)* (Munich, 1960).

Rivera, Carlos R. "Big Stick and Short Sword: The American and Japanese Navies as Hypothetical Enemies." PhD dissertation, Ohio State University, 1995.

Rödel, Christian. *Krieger, Denker, Amateure: Alfred von Tirpitz und das Seekriegsbild vor dem Ersten Weltkrieg* (Suttgart, 2003).

Rodgers, Daniel T. "In Search of Progressivism." *Reviews in American History* 10 (1982): 113–32.

———. *Atlantic Crossings: Social Politics in a Progressive Age* (Cambridge, 1998).

———. "Exceptionalism." In *Imagined Histories: American Historians Interpret the Past*, ed. Anthony Molho and Gordon S. Wood (Princeton, 1998), 21–40.

———. "An Age of Social Politics." In *Rethinking American History in a Global Age,* ed. Thomas Bender (Berkeley, 2002), 250–73.
Röhl, John C. G. "Admiral von Müller and the Approach of War, 1911–1912." *Historical Journal* 12 (1969): 651–73.
———. *Wilhelm II: Der Aufbau der Persönlichen Monarchie 1888–1900* (Munich, 2001).
Røksund, Arne. *The Jeune École: The Strategy of the Weak* (Leiden, 2007).
Rosenberg, Emily S. *Spreading the American Dream: American Economic and Cultural Expansion, 1890–1945* (New York, 1982).
———. *Financial Missionaries to the World: The Politics and Culture of Dollar Diplomacy, 1900–1930* (Cambridge, 1999).
Rössler, Eberhard. *Geschichte des deutschen U-Bootbaues,* 2 volumes (Augusburg, 1996).
Rüger, Jan. *The Great Naval Game: Britain and Germany in the Age of Empire* (Cambridge, 2007).
Rydell, Robert W. *All the World's a Fair: Visions of Empire at American International Expositions, 1876–1916* (Chicago, 1984).
Safford, Jeffrey J. *Wilsonian Maritime Diplomacy, 1913–1921* (New Brunswick, N.J., 1978).
Savage, Carlton. *Policy of the United States toward Maritime Commerce in War* (Washington, D.C., 1934).
Schaffer, Ronald. *America in the Great War: The Rise of the War Welfare State* (New York, 1991).
Scheck, Raffael. "Der Kampf des Tirpitz-Kreises für den uneingeschränkten U-Boot-Krieg und einen politischen Kurswechsel im deutschen Kaiserreich 1916–1917." *Militärgeschichtliche Mitteilungen* 55:1 (1996): 69–92.
———. *Alfred von Tirpitz and German Right-Wing Politics, 1914–1930* (Atlantic Highlands, N.J., 1998).
Scheerer, Thomas. *Die Marineoffiziere der Kaiserlichen Marine: Sozialisation und Konflikte* (Bochum, 2002).
Schreiber, Gerhard. "Thesen zur ideologischen Kontinuität in den machtpolitischen Zielsetzungen der deutschen Marineführung 1897 bis 1945—Rückblick und Bilanz." In *Deutsche Marinen im Wandel: Vom Symbol nationaler Einheit zum Instrument internationaler Sicherheit,* ed. Werner Rahn (Munich, 2005), 427–49.
Schilling, Warner R. "Admirals and Foreign Policy, 1913–1919." PhD dissertation, Yale University, 1954.
Schluter, Randall Craig. "Looking Outward for America: An Ideological Criticism of the Rhetoric of Captain Alfred Thayer Mahan, USN, in American Magazines of the 1890s." PhD dissertation, University of Iowa, 1995.
Schneirow, Matthew. *The Dream of a New Social Order: Popular Magazines in America 1893–1914* (New York, 1994).
Scholl, Lars U. "Ernst von Halle und die wissenschaftliche Propaganda für den 'Tirpitz-Plan'." In Tjard Schwarz and Ernst von Halle, *Die Schiffbauindustrie in Deutschland und im Ausland,* ed. Lars U. Scholl (Düsseldorf, 1987), v–xxxi.
Schöllgen, Gregor. *Die Macht in der Mitte Europas: Stationen deutscher Außenpolitik von Friedrich dem Großen bis zur Gegenwart* (Munich, 1992).
Schröder, Hans-Jürgen, ed. *Confrontation and Cooperation: Germany and the United States in the Era of World War I, 1900–1924* (Providence, R.I., 1993).
Schröder, Joachim. *Die U-Boote des Kaisers: Die Geschichte des deutschen U-Boot-Krieges gegen Großbritannien im Ersten Weltkrieg* (Bonn, 2003).

Schroeder, Paul W. *The Transformation of European Politics, 1763–1848* (Oxford, 1994).
——— "International Politics, Peace, and War, 1815–1914." In *The Nineteenth Century*, ed. T. C. W. Blanning (Oxford, 2000), 185–209.
Schurman, Donald M. *Julian S. Corbett: Historian of British Maritime Policy from Drake to Jellicoe* (London, 1981).
Seager, Robert, II. *Alfred Thayer Mahan: The Man and His Letters* (Annapolis, 1977).
Seligmann, Matthew. "Intelligence Information and the 1909 Naval Scare: The Secret Foundations of a Public Panic." *War in History* 17 (2010): 37–59.
Semmel, Bernard. *Liberalism and Naval Strategy: Ideology, Interest, and Sea Power during the Pax Britannica* (Boston, 1986).
Sherry, Michael. *In the Shadow of War: The United States since the 1930s* (New Haven, 1995).
Shulman, Mark R. "The Rise and Fall of American Naval Intelligence, 1882–1917." *Intelligence and National Security* 8 (April 1993): 214–26.
———. *Navalism and the Emergence of American Sea Power 1882–1893* (Annapolis, 1995).
Shulman, Peter Adam. "Empire of Energy: Environment, Geopolitics, and American Technology before the Age of Oil." PhD dissertation, Massachusetts Institute of Technology, 2007.
Shy, John. "Jomini." In *Makers of Modern Strategy from Machiavelli to the Nuclear Age*, ed. Peter Paret (Princeton, 1986), 143–85.
Sieg, Dirk. *Die Ära Stosch: Die Marine im Spannungsfeld der deutschen Politik 1872 bis 1883* (Bochum, 2005).
Skocpol, Theda. *Protecting Soldiers and Mothers: The Political Origins of Social Policy in the United States* (Cambridge, 1992).
Skowronek, Stephen. *Building a New American State: The Expansion of National Administrative Capacities 1877–1920* (Cambridge, 1982).
Smith, Helmut Walser. *German Nationalism and Religious Conflict: Culture, Ideology, Politics, 1870–1914* (Princeton, 1995).
———. *The Continuities of German History: Nation, Race, and Religion across the Long Nineteenth Century* (Cambridge, 2008).
———. "When the Sonderweg Debate Left Us." *German Studies Review* 31:2 (2008): 225–40.
Smith, Woodruff D. *The Ideological Origins of Nazi Imperialism* (New York, 1986).
Snyder, David Allan. "Petroleum and Power: Naval Fuel Technology and the Anglo-American Struggle for Core Hegemony, 1889–1922." PhD dissertation, Texas A&M University, 2001.
Snyder, Jack. *The Ideology of the Offensive* (Ithaca, 1984).
Sondhaus, Lawrence. "The Imperial German Navy and Social Democracy." *German Studies Review* 19 (February 1995): 51–64.
———. "'The Spirit of the Army' at Sea: The Prussian-German Naval Officer Corps, 1847–1897." *International History Review* 17 (August 1995): 459–84.
———. *Preparing for Weltpolitik: German Sea Power before the Tirpitz Era* (Annapolis, 1997).
———. *Naval Warfare, 1815–1914* (London, 2001).
Spector, Ronald. "Roosevelt, the Navy, and the Venezuela Controversy: 1902–1903." *American Neptune* 32 (October 1972): 257–63.
———. *Admiral of the New Empire: The Life and Career of George Dewey* (Baton Rouge, 1974).

———. *Professors of War: The Naval War College and the Development of the Naval Profession* (Newport, R.I., 1977).
Spindler, Arno. "*Der Handelskrieg mit U-Booten.*" In *Der Krieg zur See 1914–1918*, ed. Marinearchiv, 5 volumes (Berlin, 1932–66).
Sprout, Harold, and Margaret Sprout. *The Rise of American Naval Power, 1776–1918* (Princeton, 1939).
Stadelmann, Rudolf. "Die Epoche der deutsch-englischen Flottenrivalität." In idem, *Deutschland und Westeuropa* (Schloß Laupheim, 1948), 85–146.
Stargardt, Nicholas. *The German Idea of Militarism: Radical and Socialist Critics 1866–1914* (Cambridge, 1994).
Stegemann, Bernd. *Die deutsche Marinepolitik 1916–1918* (Berlin, 1970).
Stein, Stephen K. *From Torpedoes to Aviation: Washington Irving Chambers and Technological Innovation in the New Navy, 1876–1913* (Tuscaloosa, Ala., 2007).
Steinberg, Jonathan. *Yesterday's Deterrent: Tirpitz and the Birth of the German Battle Fleet* (New York, 1965).
———. "The Copenhagen Complex." *Journal of Contemporary History* 1 (1966): 23–46.
———. "A German Plan for the Invasion of Holland and Belgium." In *The War Plans of the Great Powers 1880–1914*, ed. Paul M. Kennedy (Boston, 1979), 155–70.
Steinisch, Irmgard. "Different Path to War: A Comparative Study of Militarism and Imperialism in the United States and Imperial Germany, 1871–1914." In *Anticipating Total War: The German and American Experiences 1871–1914*, ed. Manfred F. Boemeke, Roger Chickering, and Stig Förster (Washington, D.C., 1999) 29–53.
Stephanson, Anders. *Manifest Destiny: American Expansion and the Empire of Right* (New York, 1995).
Stevenson, David. *Armaments and the Coming of War: Europe, 1904–1914* (Oxford, 1996).
Stewart, Daniel Wayne. "'The Greatest Gift to Modern Civilization': Naval Power and Moral Order in the United States and Great Britain, 1880–1918." PhD dissertation, Temple University, 1999.
Still, William N., Jr. *Crisis at Sea: The U.S. Navy in European Waters in World War I* (Gainesville, Fla., 2006).
Stingl, Werner. *Der Ferne Osten in der deutschen Politik vor dem Ersten Weltkrieg (1902–1914)* (Frankfurt, 1978).
Stöber, Gunda. *Pressepolitik als Notwendigkeit: Zum Verhältnis von Staat und Öffentlichkeit im Wilhelminischen Deutschland 1890–1914* (Stuttgart, 2000).
Strandmann, Hartmut Pogge von. "Staatstreichpläne, Alldeutsche und Bethmann Holweg." In idem and Immanuel Geiss, *Die Erforderlichkeit des Unmöglichen: Deutschland am Vorabend des Ersten Weltkriegs* (Frankfurt, 1965), 7–45.
Stürmer, Michael. "Deutscher Flottenbau und europäische Weltpolitik an der Jahrhundertwende." In idem, *Dissonanzen des Fortschrittes* (Munich, 1986), 151–65.
Sumida, Jon T. *In Defense of Naval Supremacy: Finance, Technology and Naval Policy, 1889–1914* (London, 1989).
———. *Inventing Grand Strategy and Teaching Command: The Classical Works of Alfred Thayer Mahan* (Washington, D.C., 1997).
Thiesen, William H. "Professionalization and American Naval Modernization in the 1880s." *Naval War College Studies Review* 49 (Spring 1996): 33–49.

Thoss, Bruno. "Nationale Rechte, militärische Führung und Diktaturfrage in Deutschland 1913–1923." *Militärgeschichtliche Mitteilungen* 42 (1987): 27–76.
Torp, Cornelius. *Die Herausforderung der Globalisierung: Wirtschaft und Politik in Deutschland 1860–1914* (Göttingen, 2005).
Trask, David F. *Captains and Cabinets: Anglo-American Naval Relations, 1917–1918* (Columbia, 1972).
———. "William Shepherd Benson. 11 May 1915–25 September 1919." In *The Chief of Naval Operations,* ed. Robert William Love (Annapolis, 1980), 3–22.
———. *The War with Spain in 1898* (New York, 1981).
Trubowitz, Peter. *Defining the National Interest: Conflict and Change in American Foreign Policy* (Chicago, 1998).
———. "Geography and Strategy: The Politics of American Naval Expansion." In *The Politics of Strategic Adjustment Ideas, Institutions, and Interests,* ed. Peter Trubowitz, Emily O. Goldman, and Edward Rhodes (New York, 1999), 105–38.
Tulis, Jeffrey K. *The Rhetorical Presidency* (Princeton, 1987).
Tyrell, Ian. *Transnational Nation: United States History in Global Perspective since 1789* (Houndsmill, 2007).
Vagts, Alfred, *Deutschland und die Vereinigten Staaten in der Weltpolitik* (New York, 1935).
———. *A History of Militarism: Romance and Realities of a Profession* (New York, 1937).
———. "Hopes and Fears of an American-German War, 1870–1915." *Political Science Quarterly* 54 (1939): 514–35.
Vlahos, Michael. "The Naval War College and the Origins of War Planning against Japan." *Naval War College Review* 33 (July–August 1980): 23–41.
Vogel, Jakob. *Nationen im Gleichschritt: Der Kult der "Nation in Waffen" in Deutschland und Frankreich, 1871–1914* (Göttingen, 1997).
Walle, Heinrich. "Das deutsche Kreuzergeschwader in Ostasien 1897 bis 1914: Politische Absichten und militärische Wirkung." In *Der Einsatz von Seestreitkräften im Dienst der auswärtigen Politik,* ed. Deutsche Marine-Institut (Herford, 1983), 32–50.
Ward, Robert D. "The Origin and Activities of the National Security League, 1914–1919." *Mississippi Valley Historical Review* 47 (June 1960): 51–65.
Wehler, Hans-Ulrich. *Bismarck und der Imperialismus* (Cologne, 1969).
———. *Das Deutsche Kaiserreich 1871 bis 1918* (Göttingen, 1973).
———. *Der Aufstieg des amerikanischen Imperialismus: Studien zur Entwicklung des Imperium Americanum 1865–1900* (Göttingen, 1974).
———. *Deutsche Gesellschaftsgeschichte III: Von der "Deutschen Doppelrevolution" bis zum Beginn des Ersten Weltkrieges 1849–1914* (Munich, 1995).
———. "The German 'Double Revolution' and the *Sonderweg,* 1848–79." In *The Problem of Revolution in Germany, 1789–1989,* ed. Reinhard Rürup (Oxford, 2000), 55–66.
Weigley, Russel F. *The American Way of War: A History of United States Military Strategy and Policy* (Bloomington, 1973).
Weinstein, James. *The Corporate Ideal in the Liberal State 1900–1918* (Boston, 1968).
Weir, Gary E. "Tirpitz, Technology, and Building U-boats, 1897–1916." *International History Review* 6 (May 1984): 174–90.
———. *Building the Kaiser's Navy: The Imperial Naval Office and German Industry in the von Tirpitz Era, 1890–1919* (Annapolis, 1992).

Welskopp,Thomas. "Identität ex negativo. Der 'deutsche Sonderweg' als Metaerzählung in der bundesdeutschen Geschichtswissenschaft der siebziger und achtziger Jahre." In *Die historische Meisterzählung: Deutungslinien der deutschen Nationalgeschichte nach 1945,* ed. Konrad H. Jarausch and Martin Sabrow (Göttingen, 2002), 109–39.

Wette, Wolfram. "Der Militarismus und die deutschen Kriege." In *Schule der Gewalt: Militarismus in Deutschland 1871 bis 1945,* ed. Wolfram Wette (Berlin, 2005), 9–30.

Wheeler, Gerald E. *Admiral William Veazie Pratt, U.S. Navy: A Sailor's Life* (Washington, D.C., 1974).

White, Leonard D. *The Republican Era, 1869–1901: A Study in Administrative History* (New York, 1958).

White, Morton. *Social Thought in America: The Revolt against Formalism* (New York, 1949).

Wiegand, Wayne A. *Patrician in the Progressive Era: A Biography of George von Lengerke-Meyer* (New York, 1988).

Williams, Vernon L. "George Dewey: Admiral of the Navy." In *Admirals of the New Steel Navy: Makers of the American Naval Tradition, 1880–1930,* ed. James C. Bradford (Annapolis, 1990), 222–49.

Williams, William A. *The Tragedy of American Diplomacy,* 2nd edition (New York, 1962).

Wilson, Mark. *The Business of Civil War: Military Mobilization and the State, 1861–1865* (Baltimore, 2006).

———. "Politics of Procurement: Military Origins of Bureaucratic Autonomy." *Journal of Policy History* 18 (2006): 44–73.

Winzen, Peter. *Bülows Weltmachtkonzept: Untersuchungen zur Frühphase seiner Außenpolitik, 1897–1901* (Boppard, 1977).

———. "Treitschke's Influence on the Rise of Imperialist and Anti-British Nationalism in Germany." In *Nationalist and Racialist Movements in Britain and Germany before 1914,* ed. Paul Kennedy and Anthony Nicholls (Oxford, 1981), 154–70.

———. "Zur Genesis von Weltmachtkonzept und Weltpolitik." In *Der Ort Kaiser Wilhelms II in der deutschen Geschichte,* ed. John C.G. Röhl (Munich, 1991), 195–222.

Witt, Peter-Christian. "Reichsfinanzen und Rüstungspolitik." In *Marine und Marinepolitik 1871–1914,* 2nd edition, ed. Herbert Schottelius and Wilhelm Deist (Düsseldorf, 1981), 146–77.

Wolz, Nicolas. *Das lange Warten. Kriegserfahrungen deutscher und britischer Seeoffiziere 1914 bis 1918* (Paderborn, 2008).

Yarsinske, Amy Waters. *Jamestown Exhibition: American Imperialism on Parade* (Charleston, S.C., 1999).

Yerxa, Donald A. *Admirals and Empire: The U.S. Navy and the Caribbean, 1898–1945* (Columbia, S.C., 1991).

Zeender, John K. *The German Center Party, 1890–1906* (Philadelphia, 1976).

Index

Abrahamson, James, 14
absolutism, of Kaiser, 10, 181–83, 226
Adams, Brooks, 44
Africa, 25, 31–32, 37, 58, 158
African Americans, in navy, 243. *See also* race
Alaska, 132, 136
"armed peace," 73
arms race, 2–3, 8–9, 73–74; naval force ratios in, 65–66, 75–79, 81, 85–89, 137–39, 340n53. *See also* German Naval Bill(s)
Army and Navy Journal (U.S.), 214
army tactics. *See* land warfare
Auslandsdeutsche. *See* migrants, German
Australia, 153, 157

Bachmann, Gustav, 282
Badger, Charles, 84, 192
Baer, George W., 95
battlecruisers, 80, 86, 111, 113–16, 121–22, 169, 285. *See also* cruiser warfare
battle fleet warfare, 102–24, 168–71, 303–4; alternatives to, 107–16, 150; Dreadnoughts in, 76–77, 81, 86, 122, 285, 292; German strategies for, 102–7, 114–16, 121–24, 138–39, 144–48, 259, 261–64; limitations on, 150–54; logistic support for, 128, 133–35; U.S. strategies for, 102–6, 112–13, 116–20, 127–37, 259–61, 290
Baudissin, Friedrich von, 66, 286, 287
Beard, Charles, 301–02, 309
Becker, Frank, 8
Belgium, 68, 155
Bendemann, Felix, 285; on Anglo-U.S. cooperation, 62; on German-Russian alliance, 34, 35
Benson, William Shepherd, 51–52, 192, 237; and Dewey, 298; on fleet's war readiness, 95, 96, 299; on naval expansion, 94
Berghahn, Volker R., 9–10, 178, 360n33; on Anglo-German naval force ratios, 75, 77
Bethmann-Hollweg, Theobald von, 76, 186; brinkmanship of, 87; public relations by, 203; and Tirpitz, 88–89, 228, 245
Bismarck, Otto von, 228, 244, 281, 359n25
"Black War Plan," 128–30, 338n12
blockade, 156; during Boer War, 158; contraband laws of, 150, 159–64, 166, 169–70; German plans against, 77, 86,

blockade *(continued)*
    105–11, 141–45, 164–65; "hunger," 149–50, 170; "observational," 142, 144; Tirpitz on, 152, 155–57; U.S. view of, 152–53, 157–58, 160–61; during U.S. Civil War, 154; of Venezuela, 91. *See also* commercial warfare
Blue, Victor von, 297
Boer War, 158
Borckenhagen, Ludwig, 256
Boxer Rebellion, 117, 121, 147
Boy-Ed, Karl, 273
Bradford, Royal B., 121
Bronsart von Schellendorf, Paul, 269
Bryan, William Jenings, 239
Büchsel, Wilhelm, 182, 265–66, 268; on German-U.S. cooperation, 62; on invasion of France, 141; on war readiness, 286
Buckle, Thomas, 261
Bülow, Berhard von, 66, 76, 183, 228; naval lobbying by, 204, 286; and Tirpitz, 186, 280, 281
Bureau for Information and General Parliamentary Affairs. *See* Information Bureau

cables, transoceanic, 104, 121, 123–24
Canada, 153, 166
Capelle, Eduard von, 58, 78, 287; on Anglo-German arms race, 66, 67; on battlecruisers, 114; on "Iron Budget," 180; lobbying by, 202, 205; on Navy League, 356n74; as Tirpitz's successor, 202
Capps, William, 290
Caprivi, Leo von, 156, 167
Caribbean Sea. *See* West Indies
censorship, 220, 281
Center Party (Germany), 179, 183, 231–32; and anti-Catholicism, 229; Naval League's attacks on, 212–13; naval lobbying of, 204–5, 223; and *Sammlungspolitik,* 231
Chadwick, French Ensor, 25, 43, 193; on naval experts, 302; at Naval War College, 270; public relations by, 215
Chamberlain, Joseph, 64
China, 25, 45; Boxer Rebellion in, 117, 121, 147; emigrants from, 242–43; German emigrants in, 31, 123, 153, 185; Japanese conflicts with, 37, 52, 131, 166, 270; and Russia, 37, 52, 131, 132; and United Kingdom, 28, 59; and United States, 36–42, 52–54, 70, 91, 153, 166, 195, 197

Churchill, Winston, 65, 76
"civilizing mission," 35–36, 44–45, 53, 240–41
Civil War (U.S.), 12, 13, 103, 108, 154, 166
Clausewitz, Karl von, 259, 271; Maltzahn on, 263; Tirpitz on, 103, 105, 262
coal, as naval fuel, 119, 128, 136
Coerper, Karl von, 63–64
Colomb, Philip, 365n53
colonialism. *See* imperialism
commercial warfare, 25, 108–11, 149–66, 304; British view of, 70, 150, 153, 168; cruisers for, 113–15, 152–54, 156–57, 161, 165; German view of, 151–54, 162–65, 167–71; submarines for, 111–13; unrestricted, 150, 168–71, 246; U.S. view of, 152–54, 157–58, 160–62, 165–71, 254; zone of, 161, 169–70. *See also* blockade; maritime law
continuous voyage doctrine, 161–62, 164–66
contraband laws, 150, 159–64, 166, 169–70
Coontz, R. E., 192
Copenhagen complex, 60
Corbett, Julian, 107
cruiser warfare, 107–10, 119, 122, 286; against commercial shipping, 113–15, 152–57, 161, 165, 169; Tirpitz on, 109, 153–54, 181. *See also* battlecruisers
Cuba, 120
Culebra island, 91, 120, 129, 146

Dähnhardt, Harald, 75
Daniels, Josephus, 84, 94, 175, 192; on fleet's war readiness, 296–99; public relations by, 203, 207
Darling, Charles H., 175
Davis, George T., 374n2
Debs, Eugene V., 239
Deist, Wilhelm, 208, 212
Denmark, 59–60; colonies of, 32, 119, 123; German threat to, 140–41
Dewey, George, 16–17, 134, 192, 276; on General Board, 17, 189, 190, 290, 293–96, 298, 351n82; on German threat, 48–50, 92, 295; on Japanese threat, 53, 56, 93; on Joint Army and Navy Board, 272, 294; lobbying by, 204–5; in Spanish-American War, 40, 294, 296; and Tirpitz, 17, 289, 294; during Venezuelan Crisis, 91–92, 295
Diederichs, Otto von, 265, 280–81; on American navy, 47; on Anglo-German

rivalry, 59–60; on German-Russian alliance, 34, 35; on U.S. invasion, 147
draft, military, 77, 247–48
Dreadnoughts, 122, 285, 292; Anglo-German naval force ratios in, 76–77, 86; German-U.S. naval force ratios in, 81. *See also* battle fleet warfare
Dülffer, Jost, 347n79

Eley, Geoff, 7–8, 312n44; on German Navy League, 212; on globalization, 303
Ellicott, John, 55
emigrants. *See* migrants
Entente Cordiale, 64
Epkenhans, Michael, 88, 327n81
experts, naval. *See* professionalism

Fatherland Party, 246–47
Fisher, John, 65; on battlecruisers, 110–11, 113; on preemptive strikes, 64
Fiske, Bradley A., 17, 191–92, 293–94; on commercial blockades, 157–58; on German power, 51–52, 268, 269; on Japanese character, 57; on Japanese threat, 54, 55, 83, 93, 135; lobbying by, 207, 293–94, 296–99; and Luce, 195; and Mahan, 254, 292; on militarism, 194, 237, 247, 248; on naval strategies, 260–61, 273, 297; on professionalism, 239; public relations by, 222, 297, 298
Fletcher, Frank, 84, 299
flotilla warfare, 111
Flottengesetz ("fleet law"), 179–80, 222–23, 284
"flying squadron," 122
Folger, William M., 52
France, 70, 72, 165; commerce-raiding strategy of, 108; and Indochina, 131; Naval Ministry of, 193; and Russia, 37, 53, 64, 68, 141, 156; as world power, 28
Franco-Prussian War, 108, 268
Free Association for German Fleet Lectures, 210–11

Galster, Curt von, 208; criticisms of, 281–82; on submarine warfare, 111
gender issues, and militarism, 240, 242, 248
General Board. *See* U.S. Navy General Board
geopolitics, 8, 41, 240, 302; Anglo-German naval force ratios in, 33, 77–79; Bethmann-Hollweg's view of, 228; Berghahn's view of, 9; British alliances in, 64; economic, 24–27, 58, 305; Mahan's views of, 238–41
German Army Bill: of 1893, 201; of 1912, 186; of 1913, 88, 186
German Colonial Society, 211
German General Staff, 264, 305; German navy and, 264–67, 304–305; as U.S. model, 193, 264, 268–69, 304–305
German Naval Bill(s), 80, 88, 178–80, 230; of 1898, 74, 181, 183, 196, 204, 211, 278, 279; of 1899, 31; of 1900, 74–76, 85, 181, 183, 196, 204, 211, 222, 231; of 1906, 76, 179, 181, 285; of 1908, 63, 285; of 1912, 76, 111, 213, 221, 284, 286, 288
German Naval War College. *See* Marineakademie
German Navy League, 211–13, 219, 231; anti-Catholicism of, 229; Capelle on, 356n74; Chickering on, 356n76; founding of, 212; Tirpitz on, 211; U.S. reaction to, 214, 218
Germany, 3–5, 48–52, 70; and Boer War, 158; British threat to, 59–60, 63–64, 66, 69–70, 88–90, 143, 150, 153, 168; British war plans of, 137–46, 164–65; Citizenship Law of, 185; commercial warfare views of, 151–54, 162–65, 167–68; emigrants from, 30–31, 35–36, 123, 153, 185, 235; industrialization of, 229–32; intraservice conflicts of, 275–89; Nazi, 7, 8, 309–10; Open Door policy of, 64; and Russian alliances, 33–35; *Sonderweg* ideology of, 7–11, 312n33; U.S. threat to, 48–51, 61–63, 91–92, 238, 295; U.S. view of, 5, 238, 263–65, 273–74; U.S. war plans of, 127–30, 146–48, 152–53, 166; as world power, 24, 27–36, 61–63, 74, 224–29, 232–35, 244–48, 258–59, 304
Geyer, Michael, 2, 4, 8, 252
Gibbons, John, 218–19
globalization, 23–28, 151; competitive, 303; and nationalism, 60, 64, 304; and naval expansion, 234–35, 258
Goodrich, Caspar F., 271
Great Britain. *See* United Kingdom
"Great White Fleet" (U.S.), 130, 216–17, 243
Gripenkerl, Otto von, 269
Guam, 120; Japanese threat to, 54, 132, 136; U.S. war plans for, 133–34, 136
Guantánamo Bay naval base, 120
gunboat diplomacy, 110, 121, 303

Hague Peace Conferences, 158–60, 163, 167
Haldane, Lord, 67
Hale, Eugene, 293
Halle, Ernst von, 27, 32, 259; on agricultural tariffs, 232; on commercial blockades, 156; as propagandist, 209; on social reform and Weltmachtpolitik, 361n62
Hancock, J. Irving, 125–26
Handelskrieg. *See* commercial warfare
Hanseatic shipping community, 211, 257
Hawaii, 131; Japanese threat to, 54–55, 132–36; Pearl Harbor naval base in, 120, 134, 136; U.S. annexation of, 40, 41, 54, 242
Heeringen, August von, 26, 143, 258, 268; on British blockade, 145; career of, 202, 282; at Information Bureau, 210–12, 232; on naval expansion, 232, 233; on public relations, 208, 221; on war readiness, 285, 287
Heligoland, 86, 121, 141, 285
Henry, prince of Prussia, 181, 182, 281, 286, 288
Herbert, Hilary A., 189
Hill, F. K., 197
Hinds, A. W., 248
Hintze, Paul von, 246
Hipper, Franz, 246
Hobson, Rolf, 10–11, 169, 327n23, 340n53
Hollmann, Friedrich von, 277
Holtzendorff, Henning von, 267, 268, 286–88; on battlecruisers, 113; as chancellor candidate, 244
Hopman, Albert, 28, 29; on Anglo-German affinity, 33; and Tirpitz, 32, 58, 227, 244–46; on Wilhelm II, 227
Hull, Isabel, 308, 347n7
Huse, Henry, 69–70

immigrants. *See* migrants
imperialism, 2, 9–11, 23–24, 40, 54; big-power conflicts over, 25, 42, 47–72; "civilizing mission" of, 35–36, 44–45, 53, 240–41; German social, 224–25, 234–39, 306; "mercantilist" rationale for, 253; U.S. social, 39, 224–25, 240–43, 306
Imperialism at Sea (Hobson), 169, 327n23, 340n53
Imperial Naval Office, 16, 229–31; censorship by, 281; intraservice conflicts of, 277–83; and National Defense Commission, 182; and Navy League, 211–13; propaganda of, 201–3, 208–13, 221–23, 234–35; Wilhelm II's relations with, 226–27. *See also* Tirpitz, Alfred von
India, 34, 37, 45
Indochina, 131
industrialism, 8, 23–24; corporate, 6, 235, 237, 306; German, 229–32, 312n44; United States, 235–37, 306
Influence of Sea Power Upon History (Mahan), 39–40, 154, 171, 253–58, 290–91
Information Bureau (Germany), 202, 208–11, 213, 221; on naval expansion, 232, 233
Interest of America in Sea Power (Mahan), 255–56, 317n91
International Prize Court, 158–59
intraservice conflict, 275–300; German, 275–89; United States, 276, 289–300
"Iron Budget," 178–80, 211. *See also* German Naval Bill(s)
Italy, 154, 165

Jackson, John P., 248
Japan, 43, 45; as Anglo-American ally, 62, 131; and China, 37, 52, 131, 166, 270; emigrants to U.S. from, 55–56, 92–93, 242–43; empire of, 28–29, 52–58; and Mexico, 55; naval expansion by, 81–83; U.S. war plans for, 127, 131–37, 152–53, 158; as U.S. threat, 29, 53–58, 82–84, 92–94, 117–18, 130–36, 296, 302; as world power, 28–29, 238, 270. *See also* Russo-Japanese War
Jefferson, Charles E., 1
Jeune École, 108
John, Richard, 11
Joint Board. *See* U.S. Joint Army and Navy Board
Jomini, Henri-Antoine de, 103–4, 152, 259, 261
Junkers, 229–31
Jutland, battle of (1916), 116, 247

Kaiser Wilhelm Canal, 86, 143
Karsten, Peter, 12–14, 218
Kehr, Eckart, 9, 225, 232, 374n1
Keim, August von, 212
Kennedy, Paul M., 78, 313n44
Keynesianism, military, 233, 302
Keys, Albert, 292–93
Kiaochow, China, 123, 153, 185
Kiderlen-Wächter, Alfred von, 87

Knight, Austin, 69, 192
Knorr, Eduard von, 277
Koester, Hans von, 141, 277, 280–82
Korea, 52, 56, 166
Kriegsgebiet ("war zone"), 161, 169–70
Krosigk, Günther von, 156–57
Krupp, Friedrich von, 231
Kulturkampf, 229

LaFeber, Walter, 13–14
Lambi, Ivo, 285
land warfare, naval strategies based on, 103–7, 259, 263–68, 271, 303–4
Langer, William L., 2
Lasswell, Harold, 176
Laughton, John Knox, 261
League of Nations, 42
Lengerke Meyer, George von, 191, 207, 271–72
Lieber, Ernst Maria, 205
Liebknecht, Karl, 1
Lincoln, Abraham, 166
List, Friedrich, 33, 258
lobbying, 13, 201–8; British, 202, 211, 214; German, 201–2, 204–6, 211–13, 220–23; United States, 203, 206–7, 221–23, 292–99. *See also* public relations
London, Declaration of (1909), 160, 161, 164, 168, 169
Long, John D., 175, 189, 190, 296
Luce, Stephen B., 38, 44; and Fiske, 195; on German threat, 50; lobbying by, 206; and Mahan, 103, 190, 193, 215, 259–61; nationalism of, 241; on naval strategies, 259–61, 290; on Pacific Fleet, 117; public relations by, 215

Machtstaat, 236, 244
Mahan, Alfred Thayer, 14, 17, 276, 289, 305; on Asian emigrants, 242–43; on British sea power, 71, 238–39; on "civilizing mission," 44–46; on commercial warfare, 152, 165; on Council of National Defense, 198; on diplomacy, 25; and Fiske, 254, 292; on German threat, 50, 51, 238; on global markets, 26; on Hawaii, 40, 41; and Jomini, 103–4, 152, 259, 261; and Luce, 103, 190, 193, 215, 259–61; on maritime law, 160; on military draft, 247; on Monroe Doctrine, 91; on Pacific Fleet, 117, 118; on Panama Canal, 120; on party politics, 236; on Philippines, 40; public relations by, 202, 215; and Roosevelt, 207; on Russian threat, 53; on social imperialism, 238, 240–43; as strategist, 102–7, 109, 151, 152, 259–61; Tirpitz on, 256; on U.S. global interests, 37–38, 40, 45
Mahan, Alfred Thayer, works of: *Influence of Sea Power Upon History,* 39–40, 154, 171, 253–58, 290–91; *Interest of America in Sea Power,* 255–56, 317n91; "The Prospects of an Anglo-American Reunion," 224; "The United States Looking Outward," 290
Mahan, Dennis Hart, 103
Maier, Charles, 10
Maltzahn, Curt von, 73; on commercial warfare, 109–10; on naval expansion, 233; on naval strategy, 262–63
Manchuria, 37, 52, 131, 166
Marble, Frank, 270
Margarita Islands, 129, 338n12
Marineakademie, 73, 256; curriculum at, 262, 264–66; as U.S. model, 271, 273
Marine-Rundschau (magazine), 107, 209, 256
maritime law, 60, 150, 158–71; continuous voyage doctrine of, 161–62, 164–66; and *Flottengesetz,* 179–80, 222–23, 284; Roosevelt on, 160, 166; Tirpitz on, 159–60, 163. *See also* commercial warfare
Mauch, Christof, 4
McAdoo, William, 189
McBride, William, 293
McCalla, Hendry, 352n97
McDonald, J. D., 242
McKinley, William, 166
Melville, George W., 23, 237
"mercantilism," 253
merchant marine (U.S.), 165, 236–37, 254, 255
Mexico, 55, 93, 95
Michaelis, Wilhelm, 263
Middle East, 37
Midway Islands, 132, 136
migrants: Asian, 54–56, 92–93, 242–43; German, 30–31, 35–36, 123, 153, 185, 235
military necessity *(Kriegsnotwendigkeit),* 168
mines, for coastal defense, 144, 162, 285
Miquel, Johannes von, 231
Moltke, Helmuth von, 265, 271
Mommsen, Theodor, 254
Monroe Doctrine, 36, 39–42; British support of, 70; German threat to, 48–51, 61–62,

Monroe Doctrine *(continued)*
  91–92, 295; Japanese threat to, 56; naval commitment for, 195, 197; suspension of, 91
Moody, William, 190
Morocco Crisis: First, 87, 155, 285; Second, 64, 87, 286. *See also* war scares
muckraking, 215, 356n96
Müller, Friedrich Max, 261
Müller, Georg Alexander von, 16, 25, 246, 266; on Anglo-German relations, 33, 87, 145; and Tirpitz, 280–82, 288; and Wilhelm II, 226–27

Nachrichtenbureau. *See* Information Bureau (Germany)
Napoleonic Wars, 103, 105, 260; commercial shipping during, 154
nationalism, 8, 304, 309; German, 224–35, 244–48, 306; and globalization, 60, 64, 304; and identity politics, 224, 235; United States, 224–25, 235–43, 306
National Security League (U.S.), 220
nativist policies, 55, 92–93, 242–43. *See also* race
Nauticus (yearbook), 36, 209
naval force ratios: Anglo-German, 65–66, 75–79, 85–89, 137–39, 340n53; U.S.-German, 80–81
navy leagues, 200; British, 211, 214; United States, 218–20. *See also* German Navy League
Nazism, 7, 8, 309–10
Netherlands, 70, 71, 257; colonies of, 32, 123; German occupation threat of, 140
Nipperdey, Thomas, 8

Office of Naval Intelligence (U.S.), 16, 56, 80, 216, 220–21, 291; and Naval War College, 191, 271–72; publications of, 357n98; public relations by, 203, 216, 220
oil, as naval fuel, 112, 119
O'Laughlin, John Callan, 204
Open Door policy: German, 64; United States, 36–42, 52–54, 70, 91, 195, 197
Operations Plan III, 137, 146–47
"Orange War Plan," 54, 127, 132–37, 339n33
"organizational ideology," 276, 368n4
Ottley, Charles, 171

Panama Canal, 36–42, 57, 136; opening of, 93, 96, 118; strategic impact of, 82–83, 120–21, 132, 134, 317n91

Panama-Pacific International Exposition, 122
Pan-Americanism, 27–28
Pan-German League, 211, 231
Paris, Declaration of (1856), 159
Patel, Kiran Klaus, 4
Pearl Harbor naval base, 120, 134, 136
Peez, Alexander von, 258
Philippines, 40, 121; German interest in, 123, 129, 317n102; Japanese threat to, 54, 55, 132, 135; U.S. naval base in, 120, 131, 135, 136. *See also* Spanish-American War
Pohl, Hugo von, 287
Populism. *See* Progressivism
Pratt, William, 70
press, freedom of, 220, 281
Proceedings of the United States Naval Institute, 44, 196, 215, 247–48, 255
professionalism, 3–8, 12–14, 200–207; criticism of, 301–10; German, 176–86, 220–23, 225–31, 266–67; and strategic plans, 127, 251–74; technocratic, 227–28, 234, 252, 259–63, 303; United States, 175–76, 187–99, 221–23
Progressivism (U.S.), 11–14, 235–37, 302, 306
propaganda. *See* public relations
public relations, 13, 200, 304; British, 211, 214; and censorship, 220, 281; and film industry, 217–18; German, 201–3, 208–13, 221–23, 234–35; United States, 202–4, 213–23, 295–98. *See also* lobbying
Puerto Rico, 129, 146; and Culebra island, 91, 120, 129, 146

race, 28–29, 33, 56–57, 242; Anglo-American ties based on, 44, 53, 62–63, 71, 242; and "civilizing mission," 35–36, 44–45, 53, 240–41; and class, 248; exclusionary laws based on, 55, 92–93, 242–43; and Nazi genocide, 8, 309; and Progressivism, 235–36
Raeder, Erich, 309
Ramsay, Francis, 291
Ratzel, Friedrich, 263
Reichstag, 176–81, 275; naval lobbying of, 201–2, 205–6, 209, 220–23; Social Democrats in, 234. *See also* German Naval Bill(s)
Richter, Eugen, 209
Rodgers, Daniel, 14
Rodgers, John, 242

Rohrbach, Paul, 36
Roman Empire, 45, 241, 254, 260
Roosevelt, Theodore, 118; lobbying of, 206, 207; on maritime law, 160, 166; as Navy secretary, 189, 318n6; public relations by, 215–17; and Sims, 190, 292
Rüger, Jan, 8, 210
Russia, 70; and China, 37, 52, 131, 132; and France, 37, 53, 64, 68, 141, 156; and German alliances, 33–35, 308; as world power, 27, 28, 37–38, 61
Russo-Japanese War, 29, 35, 52–53, 270; and Anglo-German rivalry, 59; German concerns about, 117; Mahan on, 260; Maltzahn on, 262–63; Sperry on, 56; Tirpitz on, 28, 315n51; U.S. concerns about, 90–91, 117, 127, 292

Salisbury, Lord, 27
Sammlungspolitik, 231, 235, 312n44
Samoa, 34, 59, 133
Scheer, Reinhard, 267, 282
Schlieffen, Alfred von, 140–41, 147
Schmitt, Carl, 149–50, 171
Schmoller, Gustav, 258–59
Schumpeter, Joseph, 11, 315n50
Scott, Percy, 113
Senden-Bibran, Gustav von, 16, 181; coup d'état plan of, 223; on Tirpitz, 280
Service Memorandum IX, 15–16, 256–57, 262; on "command of the sea," 151; on commercial warfare, 109; on strategic offensive, 105, 106, 138, 139, 143, 340n53. *See also* Tirpitz, Alfred von
Sherry, Michael, 11
Siegel, Rudolf, 163
Sigsbee, Charles D., 80
Sims, William S., 70, 270, 273; on battle-cruisers, 115; lobbying by, 292–93, 296; and Roosevelt, 190, 292
Sino-Japanese War, 270
Skowronek, Stephen, 239
Social Darwinism, 27, 305, 313n44
Social Democratic Party (SPD), 205, 208, 221, 223; and social reforms, 233, 234; Tirpitz on, 224, 229, 232–33, 245–46
social imperialism, 9–10, 224–25; German, 234–39; United States, 240–43
Sonderweg, 7–11, 312n33
South Africa, 58, 158
Spain, 25, 28, 70, 72

Spanish-American War, 38, 49, 70, 119; Dewey in, 40, 294, 296; German view of, 123; Mahan on, 260
Spector, Ronald, 14
Spencer, Herbert, 27. *See also* Social Darwinism
Sperry, Charles S., 134; on commercial warfare, 160–62, 165–66; on General Board's role, 351n82; on Japanese threat, 56
Stadelmann, Rudolf, 105
Stein, Lorenz von, 251, 252
Stenzel, Alfred, 105, 167, 262
Stockton, Charles H., 40, 151, 160, 162, 165
Stosch, Albrecht von, 185
Strong, Josiah, 44
submarine warfare, 78, 111–13, 144–46, 286, 308; consequences of, 150, 168–71; unrestricted, 150, 168–70, 246, 289; and U.S. neutrality, 95, 150, 170
Suez Canal, 133
Sumida, Jon, 254
Swift Board, 191, 351n82

Taft, Howard, 118, 207
tariffs, 60, 61, 64, 160, 230–32
Taylor, Frederick, 237
Taylor, Henry C., 17, 70, 188–91, 276; on Caribbean Sea, 39; on General Board, 294, 295; on Germany, 92, 130, 193, 194; on Japan, 55; lobbying by, 206–7, 290; on Monroe Doctrine, 48; nationalism of, 241; public relations by, 215, 218; on U.S. as world power, 43–44, 83; on Venezuelan Crisis, 91–92
technocrats, 227–28, 234, 252, 259–63, 303. *See also* professionalism
Thielmann, Max Freiherr von, 231
Three Admirals Report, 139
Tirpitz, Alfred von, 9, 10, 177–80, 275–89; on Anglo-German rivalry, 58–59, 63–67, 75–79, 85–89, 137–39; on battlecruisers, 114; on battle fleet warfare, 102–7, 264; and Bethmann-Hollweg, 88–89, 228, 245; on big-power war, 25, 89–90; and Bülow, 186, 280, 281; as chancellor candidate, 244–45, 281, 363n123; and Churchill, 65; and Clausewitz, 103, 105, 262; on commercial blockades, 152, 155, 156, 163, 167; on cruiser warfare, 109, 153–54, 181; on decisive battle, 104–6, 151, 152; and Dewey, 289, 294; on "flying squadron,"

Tirpitz, Alfred von *(continued)*
122; on German emigrants, 30–31, 35, 235; on German-U.S. rivalry, 61–63, 101; on Germany as world power, 27–29, 33, 61–63, 74, 306; on industrialization, 230–31, 312n44; lobbying by, 201–3, 205, 210–11, 220–23; on Mahan, 256; on maritime law, 159–60, 163, 179–80; on Navy League, 211–12; retirement of, 246; on Russian alliances, 34–35; on Russo-Japanese War, 28, 315n51; and Schmoller, 258–59; Social Darwinism of, 313n44; on Social Democrats, 224, 229, 232–33, 246; on submarine warfare, 111; on Triple Entente, 64; Wilhelm II's relationship with, 226–28, 246, 278–81, 288. *See also* Imperial Naval Office; *Service Memorandum IX*
torpedo boats, British, 139, 144
torpedo boats, German, 107, 111–12, 139, 264, 285, 286; public relations display of, 210; range of, 122; Tirpitz's protégés from, 282
"total war," 149–50, 171, 302, 308
trade blockade. *See* blockade
trade tariffs, 60, 61, 64, 160, 230–32
Treitschke, Heinrich von, 258
Triple Entente, 35, 64; and Anglo-German naval force ratios, 65, 78, 87
Trotha, Adolph von, 180, 227, 282

United Kingdom, 9, 32–35, 58–72, 261; Admiralty Board of, 193; commercial warfare against, 150, 156, 168–71, 246, 289; commercial warfare by, 70, 150, 153, 168; as German threat, 59–60, 63–64, 66, 69–70, 88–90, 143, 150, 153, 168; navy leagues of, 211, 214; as U.S. threat, 62, 70, 84; as world power, 27–28, 58–61
United States, 3–5; and Boer War, 158; British threat to, 62, 70, 84; Civil War of, 12, 13, 103, 108, 154, 166; commercial warfare by, 152–54, 157–58, 160–62, 165–68; Council of National Defense of, 197–98; exceptionalism of, 7; fictionalized attacks on, 125–28, 166, 221–22; and German-Japanese conflict, 82–83, 90–91; German threat to, 48–51, 61–63, 91–92, 238, 295; German war plans of, 5, 48–52, 127–30, 146–48, 152–53; "Great White Fleet" of, 130, 216–17, 243; intraservice politics of, 276, 289–300; Japanese threat to, 29, 53–58, 82–84, 92–94, 117–18, 130–36, 296, 302; merchant marine of, 165, 236–37, 255; naval expansion by, 79–84, 90–97, 195, 224–25; Open Door policy of, 36–42, 52–54, 70, 91, 195, 197; Russian threat to, 90–91, 117, 127, 292; as world power, 24–28, 36–46, 93, 306; during World War I, 93–97, 149–50, 169–70
Upton, Emory, 251–52
U.S. Joint Army and Navy Board, 117–18, 198–99, 272, 294
U.S. Naval Acts, 80, 96. *See also* German Naval Bill(s)
U.S. Naval Institute, 214
U.S. Naval War College, 16, 41, 289; on battlecruisers, 115; critics of, 291; curriculum at, 270–71; Daniels's influence on, 272; and General Staff, 193; Mahan's influence at, 260; and Office of Naval Intelligence, 191, 271–72; on Pacific fleet, 82–83, 117–18; public relations of, 203–4
U.S. Navy General Board, 90–97, 198; on battlecruisers, 115–16; on battle fleet warfare, 102–4; on commercial warfare, 161–62, 165–66; creation of, 189, 193–94, 296; Dewey on, 17, 189, 190, 290, 293–96, 298, 351n82; expansion plans of, 79–84, 92–94; on merchant shipping, 119; on Pacific fleet, 117–18; public relations of, 203–4, 206–7, 295; role of, 16, 290–94; on submarine warfare, 112–13
U.S. Office of Naval Intelligence. *See* Office of Naval Intelligence

Vagts, Alfred, 11, 200, 302, 374n1
Venezuelan crisis (1902–03), 5, 62, 91–92, 295
Vogel, Jakob, 8

Wainwright, Richard, 26, 197
war: and "armed peace," 73; "Black Plan" for, 128–30, 338n12; definitions of, 25, 171; limitation of, 149–71; "Orange Plan" for, 54, 127, 132–37, 339n33; science of, 6, 259–74, 305; "total," 149–50, 171, 302, 308. *See also* specific types, *e.g.*, commercial warfare
war scares: British, 58–60, 62–65, 202; German, 58–60, 62, 85–87, 143, 155, 286; U.S., 55–56, 92–94, 198, 295, 296. *See also* Morocco Crisis
war zone *(Kriegsgebiet)*, 161, 169–70
Washington Naval Conference (1921–22), 309

Wehler, Hans-Ulrich, 9
Weltreichslehre, 27–30, 33
Weltvolk, 36
West Indies: Danish, 119, 123; German interests in, 61, 123, 128–30; U.S. interests in, 38, 41, 119–20, 128–30
"White Fleet" (U.S.), 130, 216–17, 243
Widenmann, Gerhard, 33, 346n73
Wilhelm I, Kaiser, 226
Wilhelm II, Kaiser, 9–10; absolutism of, 10, 181–83, 226; as commander-in-chief, 267–68, 277, 278; coup d'état scenario by, 223, 226; Tirpitz's relationship with, 226–28, 246, 278–81, 288

Wilhelmshaven, 86
Wilkinson, Spenser, 269
Williams, William A., 13–14
Wilson, Mark, 13
Wilson, Woodrow, 299; on German blockade, 169; on Joint Army and Navy Board, 198–99; on naval expansion, 96
Winslow, Cameron, 192
Winterhalter, Albert, 297
World War I, 31–32, 42–43, 78, 274, 307–10; meanings of, 68–72; Russia during, 35; United States during, 93–97, 149–50, 169–70
World War II, 7, 8, 309–10